LAND-USE PLANNING

Other Books in the *Essentials of Canadian Law* Series

International Trade Law

Family Law

Copyright Law

The Law of Sentencing

Administrative Law

Securities Law

Computer Law 2/e

International Human Rights Law

Franchise Law

Legal Ethics and Professional Responsibility 2/e

Refugee Law

National Security Law: Canadian Practice in International Perspective

Public International Law 2/e

Individual Employment Law 2/e

The Law of Partnerships and Corporations 3/e

Civil Litigation

Religious Institutions and the Law in Canada 3/e

Detention and Arrest

Canadian Telecommunications Law

Intellectual Property Law 2/e

Animals and the Law

Income Tax Law 2/e

Fundamental Justice

Mergers, Acquisitions, and Other Changes of Corporate Control 2/e

Personal Property Security Law 2/e

The Law of Contracts 2/e

Youth Criminal Justice Law 3/e

Bank and Customer Law in Canada 2/e

The Law of Equitable Remedies 2/e

Environmental Law 4/e

Pension Law 2/e

International and Transnational Criminal Law 2/e

Remedies: The Law of Damages 3/e

Freedom of Conscience and Religion

The Law of Trusts 3/e

The Law of Evidence 7/e

Ethics and Criminal Law 2/e

Insurance Law 2/e

Immigration Law 2/e

Criminal Law 6/e

The Law of Torts 5/e

Bankruptcy and Insolvency Law 2/e

Legal Research and Writing 4/e

Criminal Procedure 3/e

Canadian Maritime Law 2/e

Public Lands and Resources in Canada

Conflict of Laws 2/e

Statutory Interpretation 3/e

The Charter of Rights and Freedoms 6/e

Constitutional Law 5/e

ESSENTIALS OF CANADIAN LAW

LAND-USE PLANNING

HOWARD EPSTEIN

IRWIN LAW

Published in 2017 by

Irwin Law Inc.
14 Duncan Street
Suite 206
Toronto, ON
M5H 3G8

www.irwinlaw.com

ISBN: 978-1-55221-434-3
e-book ISBN: 978-1-55221-435-0

Library and Archives Canada Cataloguing in Publication

Epstein, Howard, 1949–, author
Land-use planning / Howard Epstein.

(Essentials of Canadian law)
Includes bibliographical references and index.
Issued also in print and electronic formats.
ISBN 978-1-55221-434-3 (softcover).—ISBN 978-1-55221-435-0 (PDF)

1. Land use—Planning—Law and legislation--Canada. 2. Land use—Law and legislation—Canada. I. Title. II. Series: Essentials of Canadian law

KE5258 E67 2017 346.7104'5 C2016-908086-2
KF5692 E67 2017 C2016-908087-0

Printed and bound by CPI Group (UK) Ltd, Croydon, CR0 4YY

1 2 3 4 5 21 20 19 18 17

SUMMARY TABLE OF CONTENTS

DETAILED TABLE OF CONTENTS

ACKNOWLEDGEMENTS

My thanks to various people for various forms of support leading to the writing of this book. For early legal inspiration, thanks to Stan M Makuch of Cassels Brock, and formerly of both Dalhousie University and the University of Toronto law schools; the late Robert HN Blois QC, sometime-chair of the Nova Scotia Planning Appeal Board (predecessor to the NSUARB); Ed Tollefson, formerly of the Federal Department of Justice; and to Martin Loughlin, now professor of public law at LSE with whom I briefly taught at Osgoode Hall Law School when we were both young. Later, John Mascarin of Aird Berlis and editor of the *Municipal and Planning Law Reports* published a number of my articles. My thanks to planners Julio Maffini, a stellar witness; and Professors Jill Grant and Frank Palermo of the School of Planning at Dalhousie University. My thanks to architect Professor J Grant Wanzel of the Faculty of Architecture at Dalhousie University. My thanks to readers Professor Philip Girard of Osgoode Hall Law School; planner Jennifer Powley; Ontario Government planner Linda Tam; the late Professor Philip Pacey of Dalhousie University Department of Chemistry, and dedicated advocate for protection of built heritage; and Professor (retired) Dianne Pothier of Dalhousie University Law School. Finally, especial appreciation to Alan Ruffman, marine geologist, polymath, and quintessential citizen. Several of those thanked have offered me good advice, some of which I have ignored, making all shortcomings entirely my own.

INTRODUCTION AND THE LEGAL CONTEXT FOR LAND-USE PLANNING

Where do we live our lives? For everyone there is some sense of place. There is a network of contacts, a community. That community might well be online. Indeed, the interconnectedness of people through electronic means is an amazing, powerful phenomenon that is likely to intensify its influence on our lives and world events. Yet no matter how much this evolves or grows in influence, we do all live in a local, physical world as well. This too is a place of interconnectedness. Land use and land-use planning law has as its core preoccupation this interconnectedness.

Land use is a topic tightly related to property law where, however, it tends to attract only peripheral attention. In property law texts it has been termed "social control." Thus in Megarry and Wade, it is said that the rise of social control has been due to the view that "it is against the interests of the public at large for landowners to have an unfettered power to develop their land as they wish."[1] This is not a new phenomenon. However much traditional ideas of the law of property[2] may emphasize bundles of rights of owners that seem to be strongly associated with

1 Sir Robert Edward Megarry & William Wade, *The Law of Real Property*, 6th ed by Charles Harpum (London: Sweet & Maxwell, 2000) at 1336; see also Alan M Sinclair & Margaret E McCallum, *An Introduction to Real Property Law*, 6th ed (Markham, ON: LexisNexis Butterworths, 2012) at 47–48; Bruce Ziff, *Principles of Property Law*, 4th ed (Toronto: Carswell, 2006); and, generally, Mary Jane Mossman & Philip Girard, *Property Law*, 3d ed (Toronto: Emond Montgomery, 2014).

2 Our focus is on real property rather than personal property; that is, land rather than "moveables" or intangibles such as intellectual property or copyright.

immunity, privacy, independence, and perhaps even a notion of personhood[3] (a right to exclude others, a right to build, a right to grow and harvest crops, a right to hunt, a right to dig and extract from the earth, a right to use water if present, a right to manufacture or set up shop, a right to devise or sell in whole or in part, etc.), it is an integral part of the law of property that there are limits on such rights. Those limits flow from common law recognition that everyone has a neighbour, that their rights in the enjoyment and use of their property ought not to be unreasonably interfered with by someone else's exercise of rights, and that there is always some sort of physical interconnectedness. Hence the communal enterprise of planning.[4]

It is perhaps, though, too hasty at this point to assert "hence the communal enterprise of planning" without some additional history. In this case, the history is of limitations on unfettered property rights. Occupation of land appears to be an individual matter—a question of land as a commodity—but quickly proves to be a collective matter, and land becomes understood as a social resource. Indeed, even to speak of property rights at all implies a focus on the ownership of land—control of land by private persons—that does not accord with all cultures or periods of history. Often that focus excludes non-owner residents such as tenants. But for many cultures, land is not seen as something fungible. It is seen as a setting for human life, as a life-support system, as a resource held in trust for future generations, as sacred. Nor are these views limited to non-European First Nations or peoples occupying large and wild continents. In Europe, land known as "the common" or equivalent term existed along with private enclosures. Such places were for grazing, hunting, and recreation. Their waters were for fishing and were a common source of water for crops, animals, and milling. Land being used in common already implies a sense of communal interconnectedness.[5]

Modern property law sees itself as being concerned with "legal relations among people regarding control and disposition of valued resources."[6] The point Joseph Singer, a Harvard University professor of law,

---

3 For a discussion of some theories of property, see Margaret Jane Radin, *Reinterpreting Property* (Chicago: University of Chicago Press, 1993); Charles Geisler & Gail Daneker, eds, *Property and Values* (Washington, DC: Island Press, 2000).

4 This text is written for non-legal readers as much as for lawyers, but terms used frequently in law will appear. For example, the terms "nuisance" and "tort" are used in this chapter. Elsewhere, Latin maxims or other phrases typical of the law are used. There is a glossary at the end of the book.

5 At the same time, there may be questions regarding the nature of communal rights. See Ziff, above note 1 at 6–8.

6 Joseph William Singer, *Introduction to Property* (New York: Aspen Law & Business, 2001) at 2.

makes is that the law of property is not so much about the control exercisable by owners over their property as it is about the social context in which those rights interact with the rights of others. "Property is a system, as well as individual entitlement. Individuals do not live alone and the allocation and exercise of property rights affects others. Because this is so, property law rules have been developed to ensure that the system of property rights functions fairly and efficiently."[7]

While unfettered property rights is a myth, planning is a reality, inherent in even the earliest human endeavours from hunting to agriculture to the first forms of governance. In a major series of volumes collecting leading articles on planning, the series editor notes that "if one looks at education programmes and at much of the academic and political debate that takes place regarding planning, the question of the validity of planning *per se* is very much secondary to interest in its nature and extent."[8] Any debate over the validity of planning tends to be associated with the difficulty of developing robust plans for an unknown future, a difficulty widely acknowledged.[9] Planning theorists offer a variety of explanations for the struggle to agree on what planning is, including, for example, "the impossibility of talking about planning disconnected from actual institutional and political contexts; the several modes of doing planning theory and the dilemma of choosing among them; and the difficulty of incorporating power relations into planning discourse."[10] Difficult or not, planning is a major part of modern life. And as with all endeavours, there is a legal dimension. This text sets out to explore the various aspects of the law's interaction with land use and land-use planning.

The perspective I have come to may be set out in a few propositions, ideas that recur in this text: that land use is just as important as ownership; that it is more of a convention than anything else that land is treated as a separate topic, since modern science continues to show how connected are the elements of our life-support systems; that the planning of communities is preferable to resorting to litigation after the fact to sort out different claims; and that good planning is better than bad planning, and bad planning often arises from treating the undertaking as something better suited for the experts than as a public activity.

7 *Ibid* at 3.

8 Kenneth Button & Peter Nijkamp, "Series Preface" in Tüzin Baycan Levent et al, eds, *Urban Planning* (Northampton, MA: Edward Elgar, 2008) vol 9 at xi.

9 See, for example, Peter Hall, *Great Planning Disasters* (Berkeley, CA: University of California Press, 1980) ch 13.

10 John Friedmann, "Planning Theory Revisited" (1998) 6:3 *European Planning Studies* 245, reprinted in *Urban Planning*, above note 8 at 33.

This area of the law is of importance not only to planners and architects, and to those lawyers specializing in large-scale land-use development. There is a tendency for the legal profession to regard land-use planning (LUP) issues as relevant primarily to professional developers (or those opposing their development proposals), and not to the bulk of the population. For most general practice lawyers and for real estate lawyers, LUP law should be of greater significance than it is. One of the most common uses of lawyers made by the majority of Canadians is for the purchase of a home.[11] The involvement of a solicitor is an essential step in the process of buying land. Yet all too often, the role of the solicitor is to look only at the validity of title to land and does not extend to an exploration of the restrictions on use, a matter that is equally as vital to any prospective purchaser as whether there is clear title. Indeed, use restrictions on land in the general area of one's home is almost always of serious interest to purchasers, and yet this is not a standard part of the information offered by lawyers to their clients as part of the typical residential real estate transaction. (At the same time, zoning or other aspects of control over use of land are often of the essence in commercial or industrial real estate transactions, for which a "zoning confirmation letter" may well be sought from the municipality.[12]) It is not unusual in any standard residential real estate transaction for the mortgage lender to ask, rather *pro forma*, about zoning, and title insurance often includes provisions about zoning. But, as this text hopes to make clear, land-use restrictions can be various and complex. The mortgage holder may not be getting a full picture by inquiring in a cursory way, and the new owner may not be informed at all about land-use issues. It is my hope that this text will bring to the attention of the legal profession some of these issues, lead to discussion, and perhaps result in new modes of reporting in land transactions. There appears to be an opportunity for a value-added component to some real estate transactions.[13] Such a step would be in line with the Canadian Bar As-

---

11 See Michael Trebilcock et al, *Middle Income Access to Justice* (Toronto: University of Toronto Press, 2012).

12 Depending on the circumstances, a municipality issuing such a letter may well be estopped from later raising any objections to the owner's proposed use of the land; see *Polycorp Properties Inc v Halifax (Regional Municipality)*, 2011 NSSC 241.

13 There is some level of awareness amongst lawyers of this aspect of the quotidian real estate transaction—witness the usual inclusion in the real property volumes of the *Special Lectures of the Law Society of Upper Canada* of an essay on planning law, for example, Mary L Flynn-Guglietti, "A Municipal and Planning Law Primer" in Law Society of Upper Canada, *Special Lectures of the Law Society of Upper Canada 2002* (Toronto: Irwin Law, 2003) 271. The author discusses the land-use aspects of a real estate transaction, noting at 291 that "[d]ue to the

sociation's current thinking about transformation of legal services, a part of which is to "work . . . in conjunction with other professionals."[14]

To that effect, I have set out in Appendix A suggested land-use clauses to be included in a reporting letter for a residential real estate transaction.

Land-use disputes arise with no little regularity. Here are four examples, illustrating some central points:

Example 1: *Nuisance at Common Law*

In the 1985 New Brunswick case of *Desrosiers v Sullivan*,[15] a pig farm operation was in compliance with agriculture department rules, but as a residential community grew up nearby, odours from the lagoon for liquid manure became problematic for the other residents. The owner was sued; he was found to have committed a nuisance and was ordered to pay $30,000 in damages. Justice Stevenson's decision follows.

> The twenty-five plaintiffs brought this action claiming an injunction and damages in respect of an alleged nuisance created by the defendants' operation of a piggery on a farm on the Mountain Brook Road in the Village of Charlo . . . .
>
> Of the remaining twenty-two plaintiffs, fifteen live in homes and two in mobile homes that have been built or placed in the area since 1974. Five plaintiffs live in older homes. Several of those who own the newer homes are nevertheless natives of the area.
>
> The area was at one time strictly rural and mixed farming was the principal activity. In recent years mixed farming has declined, many building lots have been sold and bought, and homes have been built. The area has become more or less a bedroom community for people who work in and near the Town of Dalhousie.
>
> In 1974 the defendant, Terrance Sullivan, bought a farm property. He began farming in 1975. At first he had a few head of beef cattle and a small number of pigs. By 1977 he had decided to concentrate on swine and erected a new barn. In 1978 he increased the number of sows to 40. In 1980 he incorporated the defendant Sullivan Farms Ltd. and built a larger barn to accommodate 140 sows and 1,000 feeder

---

complexities of many municipalities' zoning by-laws and the limited information at your disposal, it may be necessary to limit the extent of your zoning enquiry, unless the client is prepared to hire the necessary experts to allow a more thorough enquiry concerning zoning compliance."

14 Canadian Bar Association, *Futures: Transforming the Delivery of Legal Services in Canada* (Ottawa: Canadian Bar Association, 2014) at 6.

15 (1985), 66 NBR (2d) 243 (QB) [*Desrosiers*].

hogs. He established a lagoon to handle the increased quantity of liquid manure from the larger operation. Although residents of the area had before 1981 noticed odours from the farm that were offensive but tolerable, in that year the odours from the farm, and specifically from the manure lagoon, became a serious matter . . . .

Not everyone has the same sensitivity to odours and several witnesses called by the defendants were not offended by the odours from the defendant's farm. The long parade of witnesses called by the plaintiffs however voiced a long litany of complaints which I will summarize.

Children refused to play outdoors because, they said, "it stinks out there". Older children would not stay at home. Residents could not dry and air their laundry on clothes lines. If laundry was exposed to the odour it had to be washed over again. Residents had to buy electric clothes dryers. They could not have outdoor barbeques, eat outdoors, use their verandahs or pursue normal outdoor recreational activities. Friends would cut their visits short or refuse to visit at all. Social activities had to be moved to other locations. Windows could not be opened and air-conditioners were no help. The pervasive odour interfered with sleep and with the relaxation and relief from stress of the work-place that people seek in their homes. Some suffered from nausea. The odour itself caused mental stress. The community was in such a state of siege by smell that one plaintiff who has now moved elsewhere said "All the people talked about was the smell". Individual dispositions and intra-family relationships were affected. Another witness said "It's no way to live at all".

The offensive odour was not continuous. It was worse in summer than in winter, when the wind blew from the farm toward particular plaintiffs than when it did not, and when certain climatic conditions existed than when they did not.

The plaintiffs have established by an overwhelming preponderance of evidence that the odours were so offensive as to constitute intolerable nuisance in the sense that it interfered with the plaintiffs' reasonable enjoyment of their properties . . . .

Residents of the community complained to the Village Council and to the Provincial Departments of Agriculture, Environment and Health. All recognized that a problem existed and sought ways to alleviate it . . . .

The defendants plead that they have complied with all building and zoning requirements and that they hold certificates of compliance issued by the Department of Agriculture and have met all requirements of the Department of the Environment.

> There are, it seems, no building or zoning regulations in the area . . . . But the character of a neighbourhood is not solely dependent on formal laws or regulations. It also depends on geography, actual land use, and environmental factors. While the Mountain Brook area may once have been strictly rural it has taken on a definite suburban character during the last twelve years. There can be no argument in this case about the plaintiffs having "come to the nuisance". The area had taken on its new character when the defendants began enlarging their operations.
>
> The defendants were issued so-called certificates of compliance by the Department of Agriculture in 1977 and in 1980 . . . .
>
> I have found, however, that s. 284 of Regulation 84-283 under the *Health Act*, R.S.N.B. 1973, c. H-2, now says that no pigsty, hog-raising establishment, abattoir, poultry house or other livestock operation shall be built within 90 m of any inhabited house or occupied dwelling, other than that of the owner . . . . The strikingly unrealistic feature of the regulation is that it prescribes a uniform minimum distance of 90 m whether the farmer is keeping one animal or a herd of several hundred.
>
> In any event compliance with rules and regulations contained in or authorized by legislation does not relieve one from the common law rule that he must conduct his activities in such a way as not to create a nuisance in the sense I have earlier mentioned.

Following the court decision in *Desrosiers*, the farmer Terrance Sullivan shot himself.[16] In a quick response, the New Brunswick legislature adopted the *Agricultural Operations Practices Act* "to provide security to farmers by eliminating some of the risks of damage or closure by a court because their operations are creating odours, noise, or dust, even though they are in compliance with the law," in the words of the MLA introducing the bill.[17] Legislative responses to court decisions are common; suicide dramatizes situations and commands attention.[18] Agricultural operations protection acts have been adopted

---

16 See Sue Calhoun, "Death on the Farm" *New Maritimes* (November/December 1990) at 10–19.

17 New Brunswick, Legislature, *Debates*, 50th Leg, 4th Sess (6 June 1986) at 3455.

18 A UK precedent is the 1954 suicide of Edward Pilgrim. Pilgrim agreed to pay the vendor of land he purchased the amount of the UK tax imposed for windfall profits, under the incorrect impression he was obliged to do so. Subsequently he had to pay the same sum to the Central Land Board. His suicide resulted in repeal of the law. See Malcolm Grant, *Urban Planning Law* (London: Sweet & Maxwell, 1982) at 24.

across Canada.[19] They offer immunity from lawsuits and in some instances exemption from municipal by-laws,[20] though not from general environmental laws. Farmers may apply to a board for a determination that they are engaged in a "normal farm practice," and complaints may be taken to the board. There is no power for the board to exempt a farm from a provincial rule.[21] Normal farm practice does not mean "those practices actually adopted by industry"[22] but requires an appropriate evaluative approach to "take into account a broad range of factors, including the nature and the extent of harm suffered by third parties."[23] Nor does the board have exclusive jurisdiction: nuisance actions may still be taken to the courts.[24]

Example 2: *Municipal Official Plans and Zoning*

Here is a CBC account of a land-use dispute that arose in an Ottawa neighbourhood.

> Some residents in Sandy Hill are angry about plans to build an eight-storey condominium complex in their neighborhood, despite existing zoning that caps building height at six storeys in their area. The proposed condo building would go up in the Robinson Village area, which is bordered by the Rideau River, the Queensway and the Lees Avenue transitway station.
>
> Homeowners say the eight-storey development will cause traffic congestion and infringe on the privacy of their backyards, as well as fail to fit in with its neighboring homes.
>
> Residents met with city representatives Wednesday to voice their concerns.
>
> Wendy Duschenes is one of them. She said the building would go up on the lot right next door to hers on Robinson Avenue and extend across three other adjacent lots.
>
> It comes after she and her neighbors spent more than a year ironing out a deal with the city in 2014 to raise the height limit from 4.5 to six storeys, she said.

---

19 See Jonathan J Kalmakoff, "'The Right to Farm': A Survey of Farm Practices Protection Legislation in Canada" (1999) 62 *Saskatchewan Law Review* 225; John Swaigen, "The 'Right-to-Farm' Movement and Environmental Protection" (1990) 4 *Canadian Environmental Law Reports (New Series)* 121.

20 See, for example, Ontario's *Farm Practices Protection Act*, RSO 1990, c F.6 and *Farming and Food Production Protection Act, 1998*, SO 1998, c 1; *Windset Greenhouses (Ladner) Ltd v Delta (Corp)*, 2003 BCSC 570.

21 *Hill and Hill Farms Ltd v Bluewater (Municipality)*, 2006 CanLII 31802 (Ont CA).

22 *Pyke v Tri Grow Enterprises Ltd* (2001), 55 OR (3d) 257 at para 74 (CA).

23 *Ibid.*

24 *Ibid.*

"We did think that was the end of it because it was a long process and we had been assured by our councillor, Mathieu Fleury, that that would be the end of it, that we would be capped at six storeys and the city would have sufficient means to counteract any appeal by a developer to the Ontario Municipal Board. That was in January 2015," Duschenes said.

But on Aug. 14, she and other residents received a letter from the city informing them that the limit was now eight storeys for the proposed development only.

The developer had appealed the six-storey zoning cap to the Ontario Municipal Board, arguing that the city should not have changed the "long-standing intent of the Official Plan to permit 10 to 30-storey development," the OMB said in its final proceeding note.

The city and the developer later "resolved their differences" on their own, the OMB said. The city's official plan was amended to allow the eight-storey development on the developer's property only, "subject to a step-back above the sixth floor as well as a holding provision." The OMB said it's satisfied the amendment represents "good land use planning."

Duschenes disagrees. "We're not pleased. Mostly we are really concerned about the lack of due process here. We were not informed that there was a hearing in January of 2015, we were not even informed that the OMB had made a decision in March, and it was only after rumours started surfacing on the street that we began to ask our councilor what was going on," she said. "We're perplexed, frankly. We're not pleased."

City Councilor Mathieu Fleury said the city wants denser development around transit stations but realized a six-storey limit was appropriate in Robinson Village. He said that when the developer appealed the decision to the OMB, a compromise was reached.

"I think they wanted 15 storeys [but] we settled on eight storeys, which is above the six-storey cap but it's specific to that property and doesn't change the ceiling maximum of the rest of Robinson Village," he said. He also said six storeys will remain the permanent limit in the village because the period to appeal the transit development plan has ended.

Duschenes said she's unconvinced, arguing that she has heard that guarantee before. "If one developer has been successful before the OMB, would [another developer] not use that as ammunition to have the same treatment?"[25]

---

25 Laurie Fagan, "Robinson Village Residents Upset by 8-Storey Zoning Exemption for Proposed Condo" *CBC News* (26 August 2015), online: www.cbc.ca/1.3205020.

These events involve the essentially political aspect of land-use planning, the illusory stability that the existence of an official plan offers to landowners, the fragility of notice provisions that might allow wide public participation in decision-making, a tendency of municipal governments to work more closely with professional developers than with the public, issues of what is compatible as between different land uses, the supervisory role of the provincial appellate body, and the existence of a complex legal system governing land use.[26]

The Ottawa neighbourhood example is also something of a middle class, urban land-use concern. Much of Canada is middle class and urban, so it is not surprising that a great deal of the legal conflicts arises in this context. But the land-use interests of other classes and those living in other locales are crucial to equity in land-use matters. Housing; the protection of agricultural lands; the sustainability of eco-systems; the economic base of the nation; energy production and use; First Nations interests; health and safety; and the social dimension of how communities are developed—all of these are a part of the law of land use and land-use planning.

Example 3: *Lawsuit over "Takings"*

Disputes over land use are often disputes among owners of adjacent or nearby property, but can also be disputes between owners and some level of government. The core issue then is often whether there exists regulation at all. The existence of extensive land use regulatory regimes represents a major contemporary reality for private owners of land. Yet many owners resent such restrictions or experience them as diminutions of value. Owners are not necessarily incorrect about this. Regulatory schemes may well change the marketplace value of land, up or down, and it is always a relevant consideration for lawmakers creating such schemes to decide whether any compensation ought to be available if the economic effect is a negative one. For the most part, compensation is not offered except in cases of outright expropriation, though the details of arrangements can be complicated. Thus, when buildings

---

26 For something of a parallel account of a dispute over land use, see A Wayne MacKay, "Case Comment: *Friends of the Public Gardens v Halifax*: The Anatomy of a Development Fight or You Can't Fight City Hall" (1985) 13 *Administrative Law Reports* 288. Professor MacKay offers a vivid narrative of the history of an attempt by a public-interest NGO to resist a development proposal for a condominium high-rise on a site adjacent to a major public amenity and involving demolition of buildings of historic interest. Often in land-use disputes, the details are important to grasp. And, as MacKay says at 313, in what often proves true, "I fear . . . that when the dispute is over it will be a reaffirmation of the old cliché that 'you can't fight city hall.'"

are designated as heritage places, it may be that no such designation will be undertaken without the consent of the owner, or grants may be available to assist in upkeep.[27] Still, the usual public policy choice is not to offer monetary compensation when land-use restrictions are adopted. Certainly that is universal in Canada regarding basic zoning.[28]

There are many circumstances in which conflicts between private owners and some level of government can arise. The 1984 decision of the Supreme Court of Canada in *Hartel Holdings Co v Calgary (City)*[29] raises at least some of the associated issues.

In *Hartel*, the company owned some 134 acres of land in Calgary that it planned to develop for residential purposes, but in a location where the city planned to establish a park.[30] Discussions about sale to the city were not successful. The lands, from the time of Hartel's purchase in 1971, had been zoned agricultural, which permitted a variety of very limited uses; these uses were expanded around the time the city adopted its first official plan in 1979, though any residential development had to be on lots no smaller than 20 acres. The General Municipal Plan contemplated a park in the area. New negotiations for purchase were still unsuccessful, but the city chose not to expropriate; it chose to wait. Hartel took the view that expropriation had taken place by reason of the city having "designated" its lands for a public purpose in the Plan. But the governing statute required expropriation (within six months) where the designation was "under a land-use by-law." Hartel called for a liberal interpretation of the statute, alleging that the combined Plan designation with the agricultural zoning in effect froze development of the land for all practical commercial purposes. The company was not successful. The Court said that bad faith or use of zoning powers for an improper purpose could attract negative consequences for a municipality, but "[t]here is nothing inherently wrong with a development freeze"; the lands had not been downzoned, and that a freeze "pursuant to a legitimate and valid planning purpose . . . seems to be exactly what the statute contemplates . . . . [T]he resulting detriment to the appellant [Hartel] is one that must be endured in the public interest. To force the City to acquire the land at the point when long-range planning decisions

27 See, for example, *Heritage Resources Act*, CCSM c H39.1, s 15. It is questionable whether owner consent is required: see *Tremblay v Lakeshore (Town)* (2003), 232 DLR (4th) 356 (Ont Div Ct).

28 See, for example, *Municipal Government Act*, RSA 2000, c M-26, s 621.

29 [1984] 1 SCR 337 [*Hartel*].

30 The park, Nose Hill, was ultimately established and is one of the outstanding attractions in the city. It is 1,129 hectares (2,790 acres). The Hartel lands were ultimately acquired. For an outline of the major steps in the process of establishing the park, see: Friends of Nose Hill Society, online: www.fonhs.org/history.html.

are initially made would thwart rather than promote the planning process . . . . Is there a point of time at which that tactic [waiting] is no longer acceptable? Should there be a cut-off point? If so, it seems to me that, having regard to the competing interests of the owner and the municipality, the proper forum for imposing such a cut-off is the legislature."[31]

Hartel is a case that suggests strongly that the general Canadian approach, including the approach of the courts, is to favour what is often referred to as the privilege theory of land-use law, rather than the private property theory. The private property theory, in the words of a leading UK academic, "holds that planning control is an interference with established proprietary rights, and that applicants are entitled to planning permission in the absence of cogent reasons to the contrary."[32] In contrast, the prevailing approach, privilege, "holds that planning permission for development is a privilege rather than an entitlement, and that developers may be called upon to bear all the social costs occasioned by the development."[33] *Hartel* is a case in which the plaintiffs tried to import into Canada the equivalent of the USA's *Bill of Rights* Fifth Amendment protection against "takings" of land, a concept broadly applied in the USA and extending there to protection against highly restrictive regulatory decisions by government, not only to actual expropriation. Canadian cases have plumped for the privilege theory of private property as early as the Toronto Separate Schools case,[34] where Viscount Cave stated:

> . . . it is true that, unless and until a by-law restricting the building upon any land is passed, the owner of the land has a right . . . to erect upon it such buildings as he may think proper. But the whole object and purpose of [the *Municipal Act*] is to empower the city authority, acting in good faith, to put restraints upon that right with a view to the protection of neighbouring owners . . . .[35]

---

31 *Hartel*, above note 29 at 354–55.

32 Grant, above note 18 at 334. "Planning permission" is the UK term for a grant of a right to use land in a particular way; in the UK, as-of-right zoning is not the main legal control tool, although there are qualified "automatic permissions" and certain "use classes" that do not require planning permission.

33 *Ibid*.

34 *Toronto (City) v Toronto Roman Catholic Separate School Board (Trustees of)*, [1926] AC 81 (JCPC) [*Toronto Separate Schools*].

35 *Ibid* at 87. See also *Canadian Petrofina Ltd v Martin*, [1959] SCR 453; *Halifax (City) v Wonnacott*, [1951] 2 DLR 488 (NSSC); and *Regina Auto Court v Regina (City)* (1958), 25 WWR 167 (Sask QB). In *Mariner Real Estate Ltd v Nova Scotia (Attorney General)* (1999), 177 DLR (4th) 696 at para 1 (NSCA), Cromwell JA, as he then was, explores, in an especially clear judgment, "the policy issue of how minutely government may control land without buying it."

Example 4: *Environmental Racism*

Land-use discrimination based on race[36] is typically manifested in three ways: the failure to provide a usual set of services such as paved roads, piped drinking water, sewers, and street lighting; the placement in a community of undesirable and possibly unsafe facilities such as garbage dumps, incinerators, and hazardous waste processing plants; or in placing people (through construction of low-income housing) in areas that are beset by pre-existing problems. It is also now understood to extend to excessive burden of development.

The term *environmental racism* comes from the research of American sociologist Robert Bullard. On behalf of a church organization, he simply created a map of the nation by county with overlays of concentration of population by race and then by location of hazardous waste facilities.[37] This graphically showed an overwhelming association of racialized counties to have hazardous waste plants. Since this work in 1987, the literature using the term has become extensive.[38] For a number of years, the Environmental Protection Agency of the US federal government included a branch dedicated to issues of environmental racism.

The awareness of race issues as manifested in land-use matters appears to be low in Canada. Thus, a 1990 article in *Plan Canada* titled "Equity in Siting Solid Waste Management Facilities" manages to explore its topic without once mentioning race (or class).[39] One text on

---

36 This differs from race-based or ethnicity-based discrimination in sale or renting of land, the history of which may be found in texts such as Walter Tarnopolsky, *Discrimination and the Law* (Toronto: Richard de Boo, 1982) and Constance Backhouse, *Colour-Coded, A Legal History of Racism in Canada 1900–1950* (Toronto: University of Toronto Press, 1999).

37 United Church of Christ Commission for Racial Justice, *Toxic Wastes and Race in the United States: A National Study of the Racial and Socioeconomic Characteristics of Communities with Hazardous Waste Sites* (New York: United Church of Christ, 1987). The United Church of Christ, with approximately two million adherents, has a long history of anti-racism activism in the United States. Public protests over the placement of hazardous facilities in black communities in the United States arose decades earlier.

38 See, for example, Robert Bullard, *Dumping in Dixie: Race, Class, and Environmental Quality* (Boulder, CO: Westview Press, 1990); Robert Bullard, *Confronting Environmental Racism* (Boston: South End Press, 1993); Bunyan Bryant & Paul Mohai, eds, *Race and the Incidence of Environmental Hazards* (Boulder, CO: Westview Press, 1992); Vicki Been, "What's Fairness Got to Do with It? Environmental Justice and the Siting of Locally Undesirable Land Uses" (1993) 78 *Cornell Law Review* 1001; Diane Schwartz, "Environmental Racism: Using Legal and Social Means to Achieve Environmental Justice" (1997) 12(2) *Journal of Environmental Law and Litigation* 409.

39 Reg Lang, "Equity in Siting Solid Waste Management Facilities" (1990) 30(2) *Plan Canada* 5.

environmental law asks, "What is the Canadian context for environmental justice? Is there evidence that people of colour, immigrants, or the poor bear a greater burden of environmental risk than the white middle class?"[40] Unfortunately, the answers are all too clear. Aboriginal communities and black communities have experienced enormous problems, in some instances ongoing, and, in all instances, from which they have not recovered.[41]

While it existed, Africville experienced both the absence of usual services plus the presence of undesirable facilities such as the city dump. Africville was a black community located on the Halifax peninsula on the shore of Bedford Basin and existed for over a century, from at least the 1850s through to its breakup and relocation in 1964–66 as a result of the city's desire to use the land for industrial purposes.[42] Many of the families moved from Africville into public housing in central-north Halifax and remain there several generations later, still largely marginalized from mainstream economic life in the city.

Although the experience of blacks, notably in Nova Scotia, has been particularly difficult and parallels that in the United States, more generally throughout Canada racial discrimination has manifested itself against First Nations peoples.[43] One of the main disputes has been over the move to establish dams for the generation of electricity in northern Quebec.[44] There have been similar land-use clashes with the Cree of Chemawawin in Manitoba, the Chipewyan of northern Saskatchewan,

---

40 Elaine Hughes et al, eds, *Environmental Law and Policy*, 3d ed (Toronto: Emond Montgomery, 2003) at 686.

41 See, for example, John Borrows, "Living Between Water and Rocks: First Nations, Environmental Planning and Democracy" (1997) 47 *University of Toronto Law Journal* 417; "Crown and Aboriginal Occupations of Land: A History & Comparison" (15 October 2005), online: www.attorneygeneral.jus.gov.on.ca; Stuart Gilby, *Variations on a Theme: Environmental Racism and the Adverse Effects of Natural Resource Extraction on the Aboriginal Peoples of Canada* (LLM Thesis, Dalhousie University, 1996) [unpublished]; Sherene H Razack, ed, *Race, Space, and the Law: Unmapping a White Settler Society* (Toronto: Between the Lines, 2002); Kaitlyn Mitchell & Zachary D'Onofrio, "Environmental Injustice and Racism in Canada: The First Step Is Admitting You Have a Problem" (2016) 29 *Journal of Environmental Law and Practice* 305.

42 The history is set out in Donald H Clairmont & Dennis W Magill, *Africville: The Life and Death of a Canadian Black Community*, 3d ed (Toronto: Canadian Scholars' Press, 1999). See also Robin Winks, *The Blacks in Canada: A History*, 2d ed (Montreal: McGill-Queens University Press, 1997).

43 Royal Commission on Aboriginal Peoples, *Report of the Royal Commission on Aboriginal Peoples* (Ottawa: Royal Commission on Aboriginal Peoples, 1996) vol 3.

44 See, for example, Lawrence Suskind & Patrick Field, *Dealing with an Angry Public* (New York: Free Press, 1996) at 160–77.

the Ojibwa at Grassy Narrows,[45] and others such as those at Oka, Ipperwash, and in Haida Gwaii.

As a tool to grapple with such issues, the law has something of a limited utility. Environmental laws, especially environmental assessments, may be a forum. But *Human Rights Codes* and the *Charter of Rights and Freedoms*, let alone the "unruly horse" of public policy,[46] have so far shown themselves to be of dubious utility in dealing with such situations.

* * * * *

Planning is one of the law's mechanisms for dealing with disputes, or, better, attempting to avoid disputes, whether the points of tension arise between private owners and some level of government or between or among private owners. Professor Singer identifies some "core tensions within property law,"[47] all of them relevant to the LUP enterprise. One is the right to exclude versus a right of access. Ownership implies a right to exclude non-owners, but it is not unlimited. Human rights laws forbid those offering services to the public from excluding members of the public on certain prohibited discriminatory grounds.[48] There are hunting and fishing laws that in some circumstances allow access to private land.[49] Inspection and search may be allowed through some specified mechanisms.[50] A second core tension is between privilege to use versus security from harm. We have already noted nuisance laws, now often expressed as zoning and/or environmental laws and how they serve to limit unreasonable uses of land. A third core tension is the power to transfer versus limits on disaggregation. An owner may sell, devise, or give away land, but public policy will disallow certain conditions attempted to be imposed on future owners,[51] and subdivision laws can control the size and shape of how land is parcelled in a sale.[52] The fourth core tension identified by Singer is immunity from loss versus power to acquire. Ownership is thought of as permanent,

45 See, for example, Geoffrey York, *The Dispossessed: Life and Death in Native Canada* (Toronto: Lester & Orpen Dennys, 1989).

46 See, for example, comments by Lord Denning MR in *Enderby Town Football Club Ltd v Football Association*, [1971] 1 All ER 215 (CA).

47 Above note 6 at 6.

48 See, for example, *Human Rights Code*, RSO 1990, c H.19, ss 1 & 2.

49 See, for example, *Protection of Property Act*, RSNS 1989, c 363, s 15(2).

50 See, for example, *Urban and Rural Planning Act, 2000*, SNL 2000, c U-8, s 105.

51 See, for example, *Re Peach Estate*, 2009 NSSC 383, where a testator sought to limit the sale of his property to "an Anglican or a Presbyterian."

52 See, for example, *Subdivision Regulations*, BC Reg 262/70, and *Land Title Act*, RSBC 1996, c 250.

but ownership may be lost through adverse possession by another[53] or by way of expropriation (also referred to as eminent domain),[54] and as seen in *Hartel*, use restrictions may be extensive to the point of freezing all practical commercial purposes even though not amounting to expropriation.

In all of these circumstances, unfettered rights of land ownership are seen to be illusory. Thinking together as a community about present and future circumstances allows for some measure of rational policies to be adopted. This is the subject matter of the law of LUP.[55]

The Ottawa neighbourhood dispute, and even the *Hartel* case, suggest that LUP law is mostly about small, local matters, perhaps even trivial ones. It is not. We can recognize that in many parts of the world what is a land-use issue can be of enormous importance. In Brazil there is massive, often illegal, logging that has both local and global implications. In Bangladesh there is regular devastation from flooding. China has just had a series of explosions in plants located in residential areas. Many nations are struggling with drought. Oil spills have polluted areas in Nigeria. Land-use issues arise in an overall context of the contemporary economic and political dynamics of the nation.[56] They can manifest in both small and large matters: disputes between neighbours over whether a shed is too close to the property line; issues of where commercial development should be allowed in a city; what is the extent of Aboriginal rights when major industrial infrastructure such as oil and gas pipelines are proposed; what to do with one-industry communities when the main employer goes out of business; the dangers of rail carriage of explosive cargoes through the centres of towns; how to reconcile competing interests in the use of Crown lands; how much and what land ought to be preserved; our ecological footprint,

53 See, for example, *Moore v McIndoe*, 2015 ABQB 353.

54 See, for example, *Expropriations Act*, RSO 1990, c E.26.

55 Law has been critiqued as operating "under the assumption that society was characterized by independencies and not interdependencies in its social and economic relations. Nuisance law was an exception . . .": Daniel R Mandelker, "The Role of Law in Social Change" (1970) 8 *Osgoode Hall Law Journal* 355 at 357.

56 Such thoughts may imply our topic is a "first world problem." This is not what I believe or intend. One commentator said: "The phrase 'first world problem' is these days used as a comical apology for moaning about trivia . . . . It's arguable that the phrase is condescending and dehumanising to literally everyone on the planet. For a start, it patronises those outside the 'first world' by implying that hunger, disease and war are not only prevalent among the global poor but in some way the sole condition of their lives.": Steven Poole, "Why the Phrase 'First World Problem' Is Condescending to Everyone" *The Guardian* (2 October 2015), online: http://gu.com/p/4cqgz/stw.

as Canadian researchers Wackernagel and Rees put it[57]—these are all LUP matters. Canada possesses a number of features that set a context for our topic. We are an enormous land mass[58] with a small population: the second-largest nation for hectares but with a population of only 36 million.[59] We have become significantly urban: 80 percent of us now live in cities or towns. The economy remains highly resource-based: from the time of the fur trade we have moved to resource activity in mining, forestry, fishing, agriculture, and energy, much of it exported unprocessed. We have one main trading partner, the United States, with which we share a border.[60] We are enormous users of energy. Global climate change is affecting us. Some of these facts may seem remote from land-use law, but context always matters. No-one dealing, as a lawyer or a planner or a political official, with land-use issues in Saskatchewan, for example, can properly do so without an understanding of agriculture; similarly, for forestry in British Columbia and energy in Alberta. LUP and its law involves thinking about the future, yet plans are always anchored in the past and the facts of the present. It is an evolving process.

Although *Hartel* involved municipal land-use regulation, the law of land use and of land-use planning is not co-extensive with municipal law. LUP is often thought of as a municipal power. And it is certainly the case that the exercise of land-use regulatory powers by municipalities does form much of the focus of this book.[61] But the two senior levels of government also have extensive land-use regulatory powers. For example, the federal government has regulatory control over its own lands, over national parks, over the territories, and over airports. The provincial governments have direct regulatory control over mining, forestry, and some energy undertakings, all of which are not or only

57 Mathis Wackernagel & William Rees, *Our Ecological Footprint* (Gabriola Island, BC: New Society, 1996).

58 After Russia, Canada is the second-largest nation: see www.worldatlas.com. See Roger Hooke et al, "Land Transformation by Humans: A Review" (2012) 22 *GSA Today* 4.

59 Canada is the thirty-seventh largest nation by population, similar to Morocco, Uganda, Iraq, Sudan, Poland, and Algeria: see online: www.nationsonline.org.

60 Two-thirds of the Canadian GDP is trade-related; trade with the United States is 71 percent of total trade.

61 For a short overview of the municipal land-use system in the United States, see Joseph William Singer, *Introduction to Property* (New York: Aspen Law, 2001) ch 13. The Canadian system is very similar to that of the United States, but there are important differences in the constitutional law context, the statutes, and the caselaw. No concise overview of Canadian land-use land exists, but the review article by Jane M Glenn, "Community and Municipal Planning Law" (1983) 15 *Ottawa Law Review* 131 is very useful, though dated.

in some limited way shared with municipalities. Both senior levels of government have environmental powers. The powers of the two senior levels of government flow from the division of powers specified in the *Constitution Act*. In addition, the common law of nuisance influences what owners and occupiers may do with their property. Nuisance extends to a variety of polluting activities, the ruling maxim being *sic utere tuo alienum non laedas* (use your own property in such a manner as not to injure that of another), which in the end means a recognition that everyone has a neighbour and all land forms part of a community.

Thus, there is a complex array of rules potentially affecting land use. It is certainly the case that municipal regulatory powers over land use are often first thought of when the topic of land-use is focused on. But because both the senior levels of government do have considerable powers over land use, and do implement them, quite independent of municipal rules, it is important to keep this point in mind. Indeed, the reconciliation of the respective jurisdictions of the three levels of government, as a matter of constitutional law, of statute interpretation, and as a matter of appropriate political choice, is an important aspect of land-use law. In addition to regulation by government, the common law continues to exist in full vigour, thus making the land-use choices of owners subject to a complex system of analysis. This appreciation of the layered system of applicable land-use laws is one of the main basic points to be made about the overall topic. How this interaction works may be illustrated by considering a proposed land use, say a bar selling alcohol. Such a proposed use would first have to meet the local zoning rules, likely that it be in a commercial area; there might be additional zoning restrictions. But at the same time, each province requires establishments selling alcohol to obtain a licence from an agency acting on behalf of the province. And even after these two levels of government have been satisfied, operation of a bar is subject to the common law of nuisance, so in the event of excessive noise, neighbours might bring a lawsuit to limit the noise or restrain the activity.[62] Thus, this is an activity that has to comply with three of the four land-use control regimes (federal, provincial, municipal, common law). The regimes exist in parallel. Many other types of activities must meet similar restrictions (e.g., pulp and paper mills, operating a quarry, building a home adjacent to a public beach), and no land use will be likely to be obliged to meet fewer than two of the rule regimes.

---

62 See, for example, *Balmain Hotel Group LP v 1547648 Ontario Ltd (cob Ménage)* (2009), 60 MPLR (4th) 262 (Ont SCJ), where a downtown Toronto hotel successfully brought action against a nearby nightclub to restrain late-night noise.

Another main point is that land-use law is highly political. Such a statement may be made about all areas of law, but when it comes to land use, the policy matters often seem to be quite at the surface, unavoidable both in analysis and in practice. Decisions made by elected officials in other policy areas are often at a more general level, that is, they tend to be more likely to be broad policy decisions; land-use decisions are sometimes at a general level but are also often very specifically focused on particular lots, blocks, or neighbourhoods. By "political" we should understand that often the specific relevant decisions are made by elected officials, that in many instances those decisions are mostly unconstrained, that in choosing one course over another the interests of one party or group may be preferred over another, that the rules may change, and that all of this is carried on in the midst of public scrutiny and debate.[63]

A third point is that to the extent that municipalities do exercise regulatory powers over land use, the central scheme required of them by provincial governments is the development of a formal plan (an official plan or OP) that envisions the objectives of the local community, combined with a set of zoning or land-use by-laws (LUBs), that implement and must be consistent with the official plan.

As a final starting point, the policy context for land-use law is often mainly the concern with sustainability as the most important general public interest matter. This consideration now supplements to the point of supplanting the policy context of protecting private property rights. Identification of sustainability as the main contemporary context for land-use law calls into question whether a branch of law that calls itself something to do exclusively with "land" should exist at all. For if the research and thoughts of those concerned with sustainability have taught us anything, it is that all natural systems are related. Land is not separate from the water or from the air, or from the biotic activities that have to do with air, water, and land. Thus the law of LUP should be associated with environmental law as much as it is usually associated with the law of property and with administrative law. We will inevitably deal with all of these areas of law to some extent.

---

63 There are many excellent works describing the politics of land use in Canada at the local level. Among them are James Lorimer & Evelyn Ross, eds, *The City Book: The Planning and Politics of Canadian Cities* (Toronto: Lorimer, 1976); John Sewell, *Up Against City Hall* (Toronto: J Lewis & Samuel, 1972); James Lorimer, *The Developers* (Toronto: Lorimer, 1978); Dimitri Roussopoulos, ed, *The City and Radical Social Change* (Montreal: Black Rose, 1982); Warren Magnusson & Andrew Sancton, eds, *City Politics in Canada* (Toronto: University of Toronto Press, 1983); James Lightbody, *City Politics, Canada* (Peterborough, ON: Broadview, 2006); and Philip Slayton, *Mayors Gone Bad* (Toronto: Viking, 2015).

This identification of sustainability as crucial is not a unique personal perspective. Some of the university schools of planning are part of or associated with programmes of environmental studies.

Indeed, one of the major debates within the LUP community, including the LUP law community, is the extent to which there will be an outright merger of environmental and LUP issues. Traditional LUP law is focused on the regulation of land uses by some level of government. Because the issues are usually seen as interdisciplinary, how broad the approach ought to be, especially in a law text, is a matter of judgment. This text sets out to explore the policy as well as the pure legal aspect of LUP law in Canada. The materials are selected to examine the nature of the problems that have been considered within the legal system in one form or another—whether by statute or litigation or both. Recognition of the nature of the underlying issues is important because laws are never static. It is only a starting point to ask what the law is on any given topic; laws are manifestations of policy, and policies can change. What the changes ought to be and how to accomplish them are the stuff of politics, and land-use questions are nothing if not highly political.

The text is directed to planners and lawyers both, as well as to anyone—municipal councillors and those who become active in residents' associations or who are concerned about environmental or sustainability issues—following issues in land use. The objective is to explore both the law and the policy aspects of various issues. We look at typical provisions in the law, not so much to attempt to state the exact current state of the law in a particular jurisdiction, but to attempt to understand how the law grapples with various issues, and to think about how the matters might be addressed differently.

Planners are particularly in need of some guidance on legal matters, but a word of warning: mastery of the contents of this text will certainly not make a planner able to act as her own lawyer. There is no substitute for proper professional advice. The best I hope for is that planners will come away able to identify when a legal issue is present, and to identify those occasions on which they need the professional advice of lawyers. And of course, as is the case in a consultation with any professional, it is always useful to have some rudimentary familiarity with the professional's discipline in order to help identify when a problem has a legal dimension, know better what information to offer a lawyer, and know what questions to ask.

Planners should also be aware that there is a well-established jurisprudence that can lead either to a finding of invalidity of planning decisions made by municipal councils if certain defects (procedural or substantive) taint the decisions, or to a finding of liability for the offering of negligent planning advice or for the consequences of improper planning.[64] There is potential for serious professional difficulties for planners, and it is important that the profession consider such precedents. Indeed, it is useful for professional planners to imagine judges peering over their shoulders as they help draft OPs and LUBs, and as they draft staff reports outlining options for decision-makers with supporting rationales. Cases such as *Rocky Point Metalcraft Ltd v Cowichan Valley (Regional District)*[65] illustrate this all too well. In *Rocky Point*, the judge examined in detail the staff report, which grappled with complex circumstances, including a difference between the OP designation of lands and their actual zoning, what it means to be in a "development permit area," and how OP guidelines were to be interpreted and applied. The result was an overturning of the municipality's decisions.

There are a number of topics that are not touched on directly in this text. The full range of municipal law is not examined, for example, elections, methods of governance, the corporate activities of municipalities, tort liability, the regulation of trades, the powers of associated bodies such as police commissions or school boards, and certain property matters such as the procedural formalities of expropriation, are not generally addressed. As noted above, the text concerns land use and not municipal law. In part this is because the broad range of municipal law matters would dwarf the topic of concern; in part because much of municipal law is not particularly relevant to land-use regulation; and in part because land use is governed by federal and provincial law, and also by private law remedies, just as much as it is by municipal regulation.[66]

At the same time, the main focus is on regulation of land use at the municipal level for several reasons. The first is that most Canadians do live not only in municipalities but in urban municipalities, where

---

64 On such matters as improper conduct of a public hearing, see, for example, *Pitt Polder Preservation Society v Pitt Meadows (District)*, 2000 BCCA 415; on negligent advice and improper issuance of permits, see, for example, *Bell v Sarnia (City)* (1987), 37 DLR (4th) 438 (Ont HCJ); *Gadutsis v Milne*, [1973] 2 OR 503 (HCJ); *Prince George (City) v Rahn Bros. Logging Ltd*, 2003 BCCA 31; *Build-A-Vest Structures Inc v Red Deer (City)*, 2006 ABQB 869; *Crawford v Torbay (Town)*, 2008 NLTD 161. On the consequences of improper planning, see *Kerlenmar Holdings Ltd v Matsqui (District)* (1991), 81 DLR (4th) 334 (BCCA) and *Medomist Farms Ltd v Surrey (District)*, [1992] 2 WWR 303 (BCCA).

65 2012 BCSC 756 [*Rocky Point*].

66 In the main encyclopedias of Canadian law, land-use planning is classified differently. In *Halsbury's Laws of Canada* and the *Canadian Encyclopedic Digest* there are volumes on "Planning and Zoning"; in *The Canadian Abridgment* there are volumes on "Municipal" law that include the land-use aspects of municipal law.

formal land-use planning regimes are now well-established and where it is municipal regulation that is most prevalent. A second reason is that much of the litigation over land-use matters has taken place in that context, that is, in attempts to have municipal planning decisions overturned. A third reason is that although there are many important provincial-level land-use regimes, such as for natural resources, many provinces have not fully asserted their undoubted powers to govern land uses centrally and have left much of this to local governments.

Another area of law not dealt with in the text to any great extent is property law (or landlord/tenant), at least on the technical side. Issues involving acquiring ownership, transfer of title, and land titles registration systems are omitted in their entirety, even though land use is generally closely related to ownership or occupancy. Easements, covenants, and expropriation are discussed because they are the land-use mechanisms of the common law. So, too, are subdivision regulations, which are a prime tool of control of land use, yet at the same time, due to the type of remedy available (invalidity of conveyance), are a matter of property law. It is entirely possible to understand the law of LUP without an exploration of traditional property law. At the same time, it must be remembered that property, tort, and LUP laws exist concurrently. Each area of law must be complied with and their various remedies are available when disputes arise. Further, respect for property rights is so engrained in the common law system that this factor is never far from the minds of lawmakers and judges in LUP matters. Also, some aspects of LUP emanate from the common law of nuisance; that is to say, the limitations, in the interests of neighbours, on what would otherwise be the free reign of land use that ownership is sometimes thought to imply. This legal doctrine is quite important, as LUP law can be seen as a system of restricting owners' rights in the interests of protecting the property rights of others. Finally, the law of real property is considered in Chapters 3 and 10 in the discussion of the concept of property and regulation as a form of "taking," to use the American constitutional law term.

Although property law is not directly addressed, the scope of LUP law—crucially —includes matters relating to buildings. In traditional property law terms, "land" includes any building on the land. Thus, ownership of the land includes ownership of buildings on the land. Certainly, this is a context reflected in the very concept of zoning. That is, the zoning of the land, typically defined as regulations about use, will often primarily address what can or cannot be built on the land. This text does cover buildings under such topics as non-conforming use, remedies, some building code matters, and zoning for aesthetics.

Also generally omitted from the text is natural resources law (energy, agriculture, mining, and forestry). These are all activities that have their own special laws. There is a small amount of discussion on these topics, but any land-use planning that is to be effective in parts of the country where these activities are conducted should be carried out with a more detailed examination of both the activity and the law that governs it. Texts and articles do exist on these topics.[67]

Also briefly outlined are the rudiments of Aboriginal law. It is not possible to overstate the importance of Aboriginal law to land-use matters. In many parts of Canada, major economic activities such as mining, forestry, energy, and fishing are subject to statutes, treaties, and land claims by First Nations peoples. The topic is complex and evolving.

Along with the rudiments of property law, administrative law is also essential to understanding the nature of the disputes that are frequently litigated. Many of the cases arise in this context and are discussed in the text.

Lawyers bring to this study the advantage of having a general framework of reference. They have experience reading statutes and cases and have a better understanding of how to determine whether a statute is applicable and whether a case has precedent value. They know how to spot and classify issues. For non-lawyers, the text includes notes referring them to sources that should be helpful in reading and interpreting legal material.

---

67 On agriculture, relatively few focused texts are to be found. The topic is not in *The Canadian Abridgment*; its "Key and Research Guide" volume refers readers to "Bankruptcy," "Chattel Mortgages," "Constitutional Law," "Creditors and Debtors," "Grain Laws," "Sale of Goods," and "Trade and Commerce." The *Canadian Encyclopedic Digest* (*CED*) in both its Western and its Ontario editions does have a section on "Agriculture." Various books or monographs deal with "law and the farmer" but tend to be summaries of property law (buying or selling a farm), contracts, tax, and family law. Two interesting exceptions are Marjorie L Benson, *Agricultural Law in Canada 1867–1995, with Particular Reference to Saskatchewan* (Calgary: Canadian Institute of Resources Law, 1996) and Donald E Buckingham & Ken Norman, eds, *Law, Agriculture and the Farm Crisis* (Saskatoon: Purich, 1992). On energy, the Canadian Institute of Resources Law at the University of Calgary publishes the *Canada Energy Law Service* (Toronto: Carswell, 1981) (loose-leaf). For an overview of mining law, see Chris Baldwin & Johanna Fipke, "Canadian Mining Law" (27 January 2010), online: www.lawsonlundell.com/media/news/135_CanadianMiningLaw.pdf. See also Barry J Barton, *Canadian Law of Mining* (Calgary: Canadian Institute of Resources Law, 1993) and Sierra Legal Defence Fund, *Digging Up Trouble* (Vancouver: Sierra Legal Defence Fund, 1998). On forestry, there is no comprehensive text; the law of forestry emerges in various articles and in texts on environmental law.

In addition, non-lawyers must remember that there may be significant variations in the law from province to province, even though the general approaches are quite similar. These variations may well be in the statutes that are adopted by the respective legislatures and also in the way the courts have interpreted those statutes. This book gives a general overview of Canadian LUP law, with examples drawn from all provinces to illustrate the various points. And, of course, laws change over time. Thus, while I have of course made efforts to be accurate and current, this book cannot be relied upon to state the law in any given jurisdiction at any given point in time.

Non-lawyers should also note that, although reference is sometimes made to UK and American cases and articles, great caution must be taken in considering how they apply in the Canadian context. A very important provision of the US Constitution, its Fifth Amendment, specifying that there shall be no "taking" of private property unless with compensation, has been interpreted by US courts to apply in some circumstances of regulation rather than just in instances of expropriation. Likewise, the "due process and equal protection of the law" provisions of the Fourteenth Amendment have tremendous reach, extending to such matters as exclusionary zoning, and subjecting many government decisions to scrutiny by the courts. There is no corresponding provision in Canadian constitutional law to the "takings" clause, and the *Canadian Charter of Rights and Freedoms* (the *Charter*) jurisprudence similar to the Fourteenth Amendment is still evolving. We refer to US cases because there are so many of them and because of the clarity of analysis that appears in the decisions of the higher courts. In a litigious nation, with eight times the Canadian population, many issues about which we can only speculate will already have been litigated, often repeatedly. Planning matters in the United Kingdom, likewise, are referred to where their courts have dealt with points that arise in Canada, though only where their laws are similar to ours.

In LUP law, a number of issues have been raised regularly and have been dealt with by the courts in ways that have led to considerable confusion. Among these issues are, who can enforce zoning by-laws?[68] May uses of land be virtually frozen?[69] What is a use of land?[70] How is LUP affected by economic considerations?[71] What steps are required for

---

68 *Orpen v Roberts*, [1925] SCR 364.

69 *Soo Mill & Lumber Co v Sault Ste-Marie (City)*, [1975] 2 SCR 78; *Hartel*, above note 29.

70 *Pickering (Township) v Godfrey*, [1958] OR 429 (CA).

71 *Friends of Lansdowne Inc v Ottawa (City)*, 2012 ONCA 273.

a municipality to head off an owner's intended uses?[72] To what extent may municipalities include environmental considerations in planning matters?[73] May official plan policies, apart from bylaws, be used to justify a court challenge to some proposed land use?[74] What is the appropriate ambit of municipal land use powers as compared with federal or provincial regulation?[75] Is there a diminution of governmental land-use regulation in light of certain international agreements?[76]

This last question is a particularly intriguing and potentially important one. Under NAFTA, Canada has assigned to trade dispute panels the power to determine when measures like zoning or environmental assessment amount to a form of expropriation or unfairness, requiring compensation to foreign owners. Cases like *United Mexican States v Metalclad Corp*[77] and *Re William Ralph Clayton and Bilcon of Delaware Inc and Government of Canada*,[78] discussed in Chapter 2, raise the question of just what set of rules respecting the obligation to pay compensation for land-use restrictions applies in Canada. The implications of what has already been agreed to by the federal government, through *NAFTA* and the World Trade Organization, are only now becoming clearer. Pending international agreements such as the *Trans-Pacific Partnership*, *Multilateral Agreement on Investment*, *General Agreement on Trade in Services*, and the *Free Trade Area of the Americas* may consolidate and expand the restrictions on what the Supreme Court of Canada has lauded as ". . . the principle of subsidiarity. This is the proposition that law-making and implementation are often best achieved at a level of government that is not only effective, but also closest to the citizens affected and thus most responsive to their needs, to local distinctiveness, and to population diversity."[79] Subsidiarity may in effect have been negotiated away. This is something more than a mere matter of confusion that can be sorted out with further court rulings. The potential implications here could be

---

72 *Toronto Separate Schools*, above note 34.

73 *Kynock v Bennett* (1994), 20 MPLR (2d) 257 (NSSCAD).

74 *Old St Boniface Residents Association Inc v Winnipeg (City)*, [1990] 3 SCR 1170.

75 *United Taxi Drivers' Fellowship of Southern Alberta v Calgary (City)*, 2004 SCC 19.

76 *United Mexican States v Metalclad Corp*, 2001 BCSC 664.

77 *Ibid.*

78 *Re William Ralph Clayton and Bilcon of Delaware Inc and Government of Canada, Award on Jurisdiction and Liability* (17 March 2015), online: italaw.com/sites/default/files/case-documents/italaw4212.pdf. See The Council of Canadians, "Bilcon Wins NAFTA Challenge against Canada over Gravel Quarry Expansion" (20 March 2015), online: http://canadians.org/blog/bilcon-wins-nafta-challenge-against-canada-over-gravel-quarry-expansion.

79 *114957 Canada Ltée (Spraytech, Société d'arrosage) v Hudson (Town)*, 2001 SCC 40 at para 3, L'Heureux-Dubé J; see also *R v Guignard*, 2002 SCC 14.

devastating for any effective local ambit of LUP law, indeed for any of the levels of government.

The law is often described as a system of binding rules applicable to a wide range of human activities, coupled with a mechanism for resolving disputes. Such a description may also be applied to planning, though LUP has a tie to land. In the words of Lord Scarman in *Westminster City Council v Great Portland Estates plc*,[80] "The test . . . of what is a material consideration in the preparation of plans or in the control of development in respect of planning permission and in local plans, is whether it serves a planning purpose, and a planning purpose is one which relates to the character of the use of the land." Willem Salet, professor of planning at the Universiteit van Amsterdam, has written:

> Planning theory pays relatively little attention to the relationship between planning and law. When it does, it usually does so in an instrumental way, with law being seen more as a means to implement a plan. The fact that intrinsic normative meanings underlie the evolution of law is often ignored. Planning practice, on the other hand, has a quite intensive relationship with law. In practice, planning agencies continually experience the true meaning of legal rules and are well aware that individual judges can send planning processes in completely new directions. In turn, legislative experts and judges are also aware of the role planning agencies fill. They realize all too well that planners' strategic acumen and ability to mobilize forces are factors to be reckoned with. In short, planning and law are two normative disciplines that are grounded in practice and more interconnected in practice than theory . . . . Planning and law find themselves in a real world in which solutions must be sought for social problems and social conflicts must be resolved in a peaceful manner."[81]

While Professor Salet describes the policy and practical aspects of law as something of a high calling, virtually any non-lawyer who has had contact with the legal system is likely to have become profoundly cynical, perhaps to the point of joining with Ambrose Bierce in his *Devil's Dictionary* definition of a lawyer as "one skilled in circumventing the law." Other legal commentators have been more positive: "Law at its best is expressive of a culture in which ancient doctrine is often skillfully applied to solution of contemporary problems."[82] But many

80 [1985] AC 661 at 670 (HL).

81 Willem GM Salet, "Evolving Institutions—An International Exploration into Planning and Law" (2002) 22 *Journal of Planning Education and Research* 26 at 26–28.

82 Julian Levi, "Urban Legal Studies Symposium" (1970) 8 *Osgoode Hall Law Journal* 345 at 387.

lawyers have a core of cynicism about their profession, and though not formally taught at law schools, it does seem to emerge. Rather than being a normative undertaking, as Professor Salet says, law, and perhaps also planning, often appear to be about technique rather than about something substantive. This is a problem for both disciplines. For if there is no or minimal transmission to generations of students of a set of values, there is every risk that the graduates as professionals will be no more than the servants of their nominal clients.

What is taught at law school? For whatever reason, little is usually made explicit about what law schools set out to achieve.[83] Broadly, there are four matters that characterize a typical curriculum. The first is blackletter law. This is the actual state of the law on some given subject, the combination of statutes and jurisprudence (decided cases) that together make up the basic body of knowledge necessary to begin to pronounce on how the law will deal with some new set of circumstances. The second is a set of legal skills. Various formulations of these skills exist. One is the DRAIN acronym: drafting, research, advocacy, interviewing, and negotiation; some add counselling.[84] The third matter taught is legal theory (jurisprudence or philosophy of law). Unfortunately, not much legal theory is taught, and it is not mandatory. Fourth is what is often termed "thinking like a lawyer." This amorphous concept can mean something no more innocuous than being able to identify the pertinent legal issue buried in a mass of facts, or could amount to socialization to become a member of the nation's elite.[85]

---

83 Some texts, not usually a part of law school curriculums, do exist. They range from the formalistic to the mildly critical to the journalistic to the highly critical. See, for example, Stephen M Waddams, *Introduction to the Study of Law*, 8th ed (Toronto: Carswell, 2016); Allan C Hutchinson, *The Law School Book*, 3d ed (Toronto: Irwin Law, 2009); Richard F Devlin, *Canadian Perspectives on Legal Theory* (Toronto: Emond Montgomery, 1991); David Stager, *Lawyers in Canada* (Toronto: University of Toronto Press, 1990); Allen M Linden, ed, *The Canadian Judiciary* (Toronto: Osgoode Hall Law School, 1976); Paul Weiler, *In the Last Resort* (Toronto: Carswell, 1974); Martin L Friedland, ed, *Courts and Trials* (Toronto: University of Toronto Press, 1975); Jack Batten, *Lawyers* (Toronto: Macmillan, 1980); Philip Slayton, *Lawyers Gone Bad* (Toronto: Penguin Canada, 2008).

84 See, for example, Stefan H Krieger & Richard K Neumann, *Essential Lawyering Skills*, 5th ed (New York: Aspen, 2015).

85 See Duncan Kennedy, "Legal Education as Training for Hierarchy" in David Kairys, ed, *The Politics of Law*, 3d ed (New York: Basic Books, 1998). Malcolm Gladwell, "Getting In" *The New Yorker* (10 October 2005), online: www.newyorker.com/magazine/2005/10/10/getting-in, reports on the importance of skills or characteristics such as "practical judgment, passion and engagement, . . . stress management . . ." for effective living as a lawyer, rather than effective studying of the law.

Most of the materials in this work deal with the rights of owners of land. Certainly the basics of LUP law have been worked out based on traditional concepts of ownership interests. This does not, however, reflect the reality of the citizenry in Canada. Many persons are not owners of land but are, rather, tenants. Overall, in Canada, tenants account for 38 percent occupancy of living space. To the extent that this is recognized in statutes, the language used is typically that of "residents," and no distinctions are usually made between owners and tenants, for example, in the opportunity to be a member of committees, to make representations to a municipal council, or to vote. In legal hearings, a resident's status is primarily relevant to the issue of standing, where a requirement to be "aggrieved," unless specially defined, will usually relate to ownership of land. Tenants' rights are relevant, however, to most LUP decisions, because all residents of a municipality are affected by these decisions, and of course all residents now have the chance to vote regardless of whether they own land. One of the very few cases to comment on the rights of tenants in the land-use context is the Supreme Court of Canada decision in *Saltfleet (Township) Board of Health v Knapman*,[86] in which the Court affirmed a duty to act judicially (and therefore afford affected persons such as tenants an opportunity to make representations at a hearing) on the part of a committee with power to condemn buildings and order occupants to vacate. However, tenants were not parties in the *Saltfleet* case, and comments regarding notice to tenants were *obiter*. The case may be read as limiting the legislated mechanism designed for the tenants' own safety, or as recognizing their adult ability to decide for themselves how to engage with the situation in which they found themselves. As with many LUP law matters, there is a real dilemma in sorting out the policy considerations at work. In a 1986 case in which an owner wished to demolish an apartment building, tenants were granted standing as intervenors, but *Saltfleet* was not cited, nor was the matter of entitlement to notice.[87] Despite the *Saltfleet* decision, the legal position of tenants is somewhat ambiguous, and likely depends on specific statutory provisions affecting particular situations. In British Columbia, for example, the *Local Government Act*[88] recognizes tenants as being on an equal footing with landowners when it comes to a municipality's obligation to give notice of some pending decisions. *Saltfleet* probably indicates that when a court is faced with a choice of how to interpret or apply laws, it will tend to do so in a way to put landowners and tenants on an equal footing. This is not, however,

86 (1956), 6 DLR (2d) 81 (SCC).

87 *Re Trivest Developments Ltd and City of Toronto*, 1986 CanLII 2754 (Ont HCJ).

88 RSBC 2015, c 1, s 499.

entirely clear. So, for example, in the 2006 demolition case of *Markwart v Prince Albert (City)*, where the building was described in subsequent litigation as "a dilapidated apartment complex that provides substandard accommodation to the troubled and the underprivileged,"[89] there was no reference at all to the tenants or the effects of the demolition order on them. To similar effect is the 2008 Alberta case of *New Vintage Homes Ltd v Vegreville*.[90] On the other hand, in *Neighbourhood of Windfields Ltd Partnership v Death*,[91] in which a restraining order was issued against various illegal rental uses by students, it was not to be enforced until the end of the school year so as not to inconvenience the tenants.

What is most intriguing about LUP law is that the issues are often of general importance to the daily life of significant numbers of people. Disputes over land use, in many parts of the world, often result less in recourse to the legal system and more in a show of raw reaction, including regular incidents of violence. The razing of hutongs in China, logging in Brazil, and access to water in Bangladesh are all examples of situations that have occasioned violence. Life in Canada is, for the most part, lived differently.

Although we recognize the issues as significant, framing those issues is a difficult matter; perhaps it is more accurate to say that the true issues are not always directly specified or entirely clear. One of the leading American scholars of LUP law, Charles Haar, has observed that

> the nature of the typical land use case differs very little from *Euclid* [*v Ambler*, a 1926 US Supreme Court decision]. Disgruntled property owners (sometimes developers, at other times their neighbors) seek access to the courts to redress the negative economic and social consequences of local decision-makers' acts or omissions. Litigants . . . call on the courts to draw useful lines between the valid exercise of the police power and confiscatory or arbitrary regulations that amount to due process violations . . . . Members of the judiciary still wrestle with the appropriate level of deference to state and local legislators and administrators.[92]

While the stuff of land-use litigation may not change, Haar has also written of "the underside of traditional height, area, and use zoning"; by this Haar means "its anti-competitiveness, socioeconomic exclusionary potential, rejection of a regional approach to land-use decision-making,

89 2010 SKQB 312 at para 2.

90 2008 ABQB 730.

91 (2009), 54 MPLR (4th) 247 (Ont SCJ).

92 Charles M Haar & Michael Allan Wolf, *Land-Use Planning*, 3d ed (Boston: Little Brown, 1989) at 190.

and emphasis on subjective (particularly aesthetic) considerations."[93] We look at some of these matters in the text. Take one Canadian example, that of postering. It is not unusual for by-laws to deal with public notices of a variety of kinds, either notices put on buildings deliberately by way of advertising what goods or services may be available there, or notices put on private or public places by others to take advantage of a prominent space. The matter is typically dealt with, if it reaches the courts, through the law of the *Charter of Rights*, and even though some analysis does look at the extent to which advertising influences thought (see *Peterborough (City) v Ramsden*[94]), the extent to which public discourse through formal news media is in the hands of a limited number of economic actors is not a focus; nor do these matters usually inform the debate about sign-control by-laws in front of municipal councils. Yet these are very significant issues, and they or their variants are on the agendas of municipal councils every day.

Various works on land use or land-use planning law in Canada have been an enormous help to me. The subject has an intriguing history as a matter for organized study. In the United Kingdom, the great legal scholar FW Maitland published *Township and Borough* (1898). J Redlich and FW Hirst followed with *Local Government* (1903), and Sidney and Beatrice Webb wrote on *English Local Government* (1922). Early compendiums of US law such as John F Dillon's *The Law of Municipal Corporations* (1873) were often referred to in Canadian cases.[95] Early Canadian texts took municipal corporations as their field of study, thus Meredith and Wilkinson's *Canadian Municipal Manual* (1917) and Robson and Hugg's work of the same title (1920). Ian McFee Rogers' first edition of *The Law of Canadian Municipal Corporations* appeared in 1959. The first basic text with a general law and planning ambit combined was JB Milner's 1963 *Community Planning*. It is the product of a professor of law, and the title and content indicate its broad intention. Milner's work is quite clearly out of date because of advances in the law, and is in any event out of print, but it set the tone for looking at the subject as one of law and of policy. This was followed by the next edition of Rogers' *The Law of Canadian Municipal Corporations* (1971)[96] and *Canadian Law of Planning and Zoning* (1973).[97] The latter is a standard ref-

---

93 *Ibid* at xxxii.

94 [1993] 2 SCR 1084 at 1097.

95 Dillon also wrote *Treatise on the Law of Municipal Corporations* (1872) and *Commentaries on the Law of Municipal Corporations* (1881).

96 Ian McFee Rogers, *The Law of Canadian Municipal Corporations* (Toronto: Carswell, 1971) (loose-leaf).

97 Ian McFee Rogers, *Canadian Law of Planning and Zoning* (Toronto: Carswell, 1973).

erence work to this day, regularly updated. It is somewhat difficult for non-lawyers to access, but it is comprehensive. In 1979, Lorne Giroux published *Aspects juridique du règlement de zonage au Québec*,[98] and in 1983, Professor Stan Makuch wrote *Canadian Municipal and Planning Law*,[99] continuing the tradition of informing the legal aspects of the subject by an appreciation of the realities on the ground; a second edition appeared in 2004. A recent book with a series of searching examinations of law and policy is *Public Interest, Private Property*, edited by Anneke Smit and Marcia Valiante.[100] Over the last decades, a plethora of specialized works has appeared, often geographically focused. Professor Frederick A Laux wrote *Planning Law and Practice in Alberta* in 1990.[101] William Buholzer published *British Columbia Planning Law and Practice* in 2001.[102] John G Chipman's *The Planning Act in Transition*,[103] published in 1996, is an Ontario example, setting out the changes to the statutory framework made in 1994 by the New Democratic Party government and then modified by the subsequent Progressive Conservative government. He also wrote *A Law Unto Itself* [104] in 2002, a study of the OMB. Revisions to the approach to municipal powers by the Ontario legislature has prompted two useful works, John Mascarin's *Ontario Municipal Act and Commentary*, [105] initially published in 2004 and then annually, and George Rust-D'Eye's *The Ontario Municipal Act: A User's Manual*.[106] Robert W Macaulay and Robert G Doumani's *Ontario Land Development: Legislation and Practice*[107] from 1991 is a solid Ontario text. An earlier British Columbia example is John Ince's

---

98 Lorne Giroux, *Aspects juridique du règlement de zonage au Québec* (Québec: Presses de l'Université Laval, 1979).

99 Stan Makuch, *Canadian Municipal and Planning Law* (Toronto: Carswell, 1983).

100 Anneke Smit & Marcia Valiante, eds, *Public Interest, Private Property* (Vancouver: UBC Press, 2016).

101 Frederick A Laux, *Planning Law and Practice in Alberta* (Toronto: Carswell, 1990). Athabasca University offers an online course on Local Government Law in Alberta (Legal Studies 479). The materials are posted at its site and are quite useful: see online: http://ocw.lms.athabascau.ca.

102 William Buholzer, *British Columbia Planning Law and Practice* (Markham, ON: LexisNexis, 2001).

103 John G Chipman, *The Planning Act in Transition* (Aurora, ON: Canada Law Book, 1996).

104 John G Chipman, *A Law Unto Itself* (Toronto: University of Toronto Press, 2002).

105 John Mascarin, *Ontario Municipal Act and Commentary* (Markham, ON: LexisNexis Canada, annual editions).

106 George Rust-D'Eye, *The Ontario Municipal Act: A User's Manual* (Toronto: Carswell, annual editions).

107 Robert W Macaulay & Robert G Doumani, *Ontario Land Development: Legislation and Practice* (Scarborough, ON: Carswell, 1991) (loose-leaf).

1977 *Land Use Law: A Study of Legislation Governing Land Use in British Columbia.*[108] Felix Hoehn surveyed the topic in his 1996 book *Municipalities and Canadian Law.*[109] The *Special Lectures of the Law Society of Upper Canada* series has featured LUP matters in various of its volumes, either as the main topic or as an aspect of some other topic, such as real estate: 1953, 1956, 1960, 1966, 1970, 1974, and 2002.

Quite apart from legal texts, there has been an organized study of municipalities in their various dimensions, including municipal governance, by political scientists, historians, sociologists, and geographers for some time. Kenneth Grant Crawford's 1954 *Canadian Municipal Government*[110] starts with a clear history of municipal government in Canada; its discussion of provincial-municipal relations is a firm reminder that there are few new problems being grappled with. A more modern text, Trudi Bunting and Pierre Filion's *Canadian Cities in Transition*[111] confirms this.[112] Jacob Spelt's 1955 *Urban Development in South-Central Ontario,*[113] looks at the historical factors leading to the emergence of Toronto as the leading urban area. Kent Gerecke's *The Canadian City*[114] helps in thinking about history, change, and the future, as does *The Changing Canadian Metropolis: A Public Policy Perspective,* Frances Frisken, editor.[115] Probably the best short account of the dynamics of land development in Canada is by political scientist Christopher Leo in a 2002 essay that takes a hard look at the interaction of theory, law, and reality.[116] In terms of library reference collections, universities that offer degrees in LUP tend to have decent collections, and the Toronto Public Library system has established a special collection known as the Urban Affairs Library, formerly located at the offices of the new municipality, Metro Hall, but now reincorporated into the library sys-

---

108 John Ince, *Land Use Law: A Study of Legislation Governing Land Use in British Columbia* (Vancouver: Continuing Legal Education Society of British Columbia, 1977).

109 Felix Hoehn, *Municipalities and Canadian Law* (Saskatoon: Purich, 1996).

110 Kenneth Grant Crawford, *Canadian Municipal Government* (Toronto: University of Toronto Press, 1954).

111 Trudi Bunting & Pierre Filion, eds, *Canadian Cities in Transition*, 2d ed (Don Mills, ON: Oxford University Press, 2000).

112 See also Pierre Filion et al, eds, *Canadian Cities in Transition*, 5th ed (Don Mills, ON: Oxford University Press, 2015).

113 Jacob Spelt, *Urban Development in South-Central Ontario* (Assen: Van Gorcum, 1955).

114 Kent Gerecke, *The Canadian City* (Montreal, Black Rose Books, 1991).

115 Frances Frisken, ed, *The Changing Canadian Metropolis: A Public Policy Perspective* (Toronto: Canadian Urban Institute, 1994).

116 Christopher Leo, "Urban Development: Planning Aspirations and Political Realities" in Edmund P Fowler & David Siegel, eds, *Urban Policy Issues: Canadian Perspectives*, 2d ed (Don Mills, ON: Oxford University Press, 2002) at 215.

tem's general collection; its resources are very impressive and are not limited to Ontario planning.

I mention these various texts because I hope to encourage participants to immerse themselves in the subject. The more, the better. At the same time, I do recognize that speed in finding relevant information is often important. After acquiring some basic grasp of the taxonomy and vocabulary of the subject, researchers should consult CanLII as a reliable online source for Canadian statutes, regulations, and cases. (Their materials do not include municipal official plans or by-laws.) This should be supplemented by consulting the *Municipal and Planning Law Reports* (MPLRs). The MPLRs are a collection of cases focused on our overall subject and include from time to time articles of commentary or analysis. There is no Canadian specialized journal dealing with land-use planning law.

There exists a tendency in the courts to recognize the limits of what can actually be accomplished towards promotion of a general sense of community or even of good relations between a couple of neighbours, through the mechanism of a lawsuit. Several cases include statements by judges hoping the parties will be able to settle matters better than they had to date, and, by implication, better than the courts have found themselves able to do.[117] In most lawsuits there are only two parties, but the implications of lawsuits involving land uses may well be of general interest. The civil procedure mechanism of intervenors gives some opportunity for other interests to be heard by the courts, but does nothing to turn a focused dispute into anything like an open, general, consultative or negotiating process, which might have a reasonable chance to produce acceptable community results.

The issues dealt with through LUP are important. Planning is a process of thinking about the future. Many of the problems that will have to be grappled with by the generation of planners now being educated are already upon us. They will become worse. The success of this grappling is what will save our life support systems, if that is indeed managed.

A theme of this book is transformation. As will become apparent to the reader in the final chapter, I am not very optimistic about the likelihood of useful change being accomplished before terrible disasters befall us.[118] Such a gloomy perspective calls into question whether the

117 See, for example, *Toronto Roman Catholic Separate Schools v Toronto (City)*, [1924] SCR 368 at 375.

118 For readable overview accounts of how human activities are changing the planet, see Curt Stager, *Deep Future* (New York: Thomas Dunne Books, 2011) and Elizabeth Kolbert, *The Sixth Extinction* (New York: Picador, 2014).

effort involved in the quotidian decisions that are generally the stuff of most local government agendas are worth it. I suppose we will find out. But in the meantime, I live in some significant hope that the connection of even the most ordinary of planning matters to the larger issues suggested, will be made, considered, and acted upon. For if we cannot change, then what are we doing here?

CHAPTER 1

THE PLANNING ENTERPRISE

A. PRELIMINARY

Organized land-use planning (LUP) emerged only within the last 100 to 125 years.[1] The modern landmarks often noted are the adoption by New York City of a comprehensive zoning code in 1916,[2] the drafting in 1928 of model statutes (the Standard City Planning Enabling Act and the Standard State Zoning Enabling Act developed by the US federal government) to establish a framework for municipal regulation of land use involving the adoption of an official plan to accompany and guide zoning by-laws, and the regime put in place in the United Kingdom through the *Housing, Town Planning etc. Act* of 1909 (followed by the *Town and Country Planning Act*s of 1947 and 1990). In Canada, organized LUP emerged at the end of the nineteenth century, with the earliest planning statutes being adopted in 1912 in New Brunswick, Nova Scotia, and Ontario.[3]

1 Attempts at planning in some limited ways are ancient. To some extent they characterized all cities from their very start. See Peter Hall, *Cities in Civilization* (London: Phoenix Giant, 1998).

2 It is also the case that in Germany, "zoning combining both use and height restrictions" had emerged in the 1880s; see Peter Moore, "Zoning and Planning: The Toronto Experience, 1904–1970" in Alan FJ Artibise & Gilbert A Stelter, *The Usable Urban Past* (Toronto: Macmillan, 1979) 316.

3 David H Sherwood, "Canadian Institute of Planners" *Plan Canada* (July 1994) at 20; Jeanne M Wolfe, "Our Common Past: An Interpretation of Canadian Planning

At the same time, it should be recognized that nuisances had been addressed by various statutes for centuries prior to that. Activities that produced objectionable odours, such as slaughterhouses, tanneries, and sewers, were regulated in limited ways. Early statutes required landowners to cut down high hedges along roadways where highwaymen might hide to rob passersby. Fires in seventeeth-century London and the spread of disease in compact communities led to versions of building codes. Nineteenth-century public health acts required minimum street widths to help control typhoid and cholera epidemics and to allow access by municipal service vehicles. In the United States, rules going back to colonial times regulated the location of gunpowder manufacture and storage, and slaughterhouses. Early special statutes addressed the concerns of public health, safety, and welfare. What has been a feature of this past century has been organized LUP as a common statute-based context for determining what is or is not permitted by way of land use, its evolution into a sophisticated system, a serious emphasis on planning being in the hands of municipal governments, and the emergence of a designated profession to lead the activity.

The existence of a regulated planning profession has not meant that there is clarity about the parameters of the undertaking. While, as a matter of process, planning is inherently a public exercise, and as a matter of objectives, it has regularly addressed sustainability, the nature of what ought to be studied is not completely clear. Certainly, there is abundant criticism of the results of planning. Still, it is a profession for which statements of values and standards of conduct exist. Indeed, violation of standards or other errors may lead to some form of legal liability. Even more than some other professions, planners are expected to be able to analyze, write about, and speak to their concerns and to be a part of formal legal processes.

B. NATURE OF THE PLANNING ENTERPRISE[4]

In order to survey land-use planning as an enterprise, we will look at some of the comments of leading Canadian and international planners, academics, and the professional bodies representing planners.

History" *Plan Canada* (July 1994); Harold D Kalman, *A History of Canadian Architecture* (Toronto: Oxford University Press, 1994) ch 12.

4 For a good selection of articles on various aspects of planning, see Edward Elgar's *Classics in Planning* multi-volume series, especially Hugo Priemus, Kenneth Button, & Peter Nijkamp, eds, *Land Use Planning* (Northampton, MA: Edward Elgar, 2007), and Tüzin Baycan et al, eds, *Urban Planning* (Northampton, MA:

Planning is typically referred to as an attempt, based on studies and on public consultation, to achieve a rational agenda for a community. On the other hand, those hostile to the enterprise suggest that planning "defined broadly [is] government intervention."[5] The Canadian Institute of Planners (CIP) defines planning as "the scientific, aesthetic, and orderly disposition of land, resources, facilities and services with a view to securing the physical, economic and social efficiency, health and well-being of urban and rural communities."[6] This offering is in line with the struggle to define the planning enterprise that is common in planning texts. Two texts that are commonly used in Canadian university LUP programmes are Hodge and Gordon, *Planning Canadian Communities,* and Hok-Lin Leung, *Land Use Planning Made Plain.*[7] Hodge says that the two principal reasons a community "is stimulated to undertake community planning [are a] . . . wish to solve some problems associated with its development; and/or to achieve some preferred form of development."[8] In either case, he says, planning involves both the built and natural environment. A community plan should promote economic growth and efficiency, environmental protection, and social justice and equity, all linked.[9] Leung emphasizes the public interest. "Typically, land use decisions are about the type, amount and location of uses of land. That is, 'What?', 'How much?' and 'Where?'"[10] He then lists a variety of "public interest elements" in planning: health and safety, convenience, efficiency, equity, environment and energy, visual amenity, economic matters, heritage conservation, transportation, physical infrastructure, and affordable housing. Hodge says "Over the course of Canadian planning, a number of issues have been transformed and become more complex, but none more so than environmental protection. The longstanding planning traditions of conservation, park planning, and open-space preservation began to give way . . . to concerns over ecosystems and biodiversity."[11]

Edward Elgar, 2008). See also Charles Hoch, *What Planners Do: Power, Politics and Persuasion* (Chicago: Planners Press, 1994).

5 Bishwapriya Sanyal, "Planning's Three Challenges" in Lloyd Rodwin & Bishwapriya Sanyal, eds, *The Profession of City Planning* (New Brunswick, NJ: Centre for Urban Policy Research, Rutgers University Press, 2000) 312 at 327.

6 "What Is Planning," online: www.cip-icu.ca/Becoming-a-Planner.

7 Gerald Hodge & David LA Gordon, *Planning Canadian Communities*, 5th ed (Toronto: Thomson Nelson, 2008); Hok-Lin Leung, *Land Use Planning Made Plain*, 2d ed (Toronto: University of Toronto Press, 2003).

8 Hodge & Gordon, above note 7 at 5.

9 *Ibid* at 385.

10 Leung, above note 7 at 2.

11 *Ibid* at 384.

All such statements seem relatively anodyne and unsatisfactory. This is so especially in the face of day-to-day reality of the issues that determine how we live our lives, how we interact with each other, and how we carry out the obligations we have to each other and to future generations. What they fail to do is tell us what planning is, in the sense of being able to predict how planners will approach any given problem, or what solutions might be offered. One has to wonder if planning is a discipline at all, and if so, what sort of subject it is. The literature of planning, even that which focuses on planning theory, leaves such points unanswered. The enterprise includes some practical skills, such as understanding geographic information systems (GIS) and understanding issues associated with transportation, but beyond these, it appears to be somewhat amorphous. Two Ontario lawyers, struggling in the 1970s to understand the planning process in Toronto, wrote,

> Many citizens watching formula-spouting experts wrangling about such apparent certainties as gross floor space indices, landscaped open space ratios and the like, conclude that planning is professional, legal and technical by nature. This conclusion, although understandable, is incorrect and dangerous. It confuses the *means* by which planning is carried on with the *essence* of planning. Fundamentally, planning is both political and a process: a process in that there can never be an end result that represents a permanent community consensus; political in that every planning decision benefits some interests and harms other interests. The treasure (in the form of property values) and amenities of some people are increased while those of other people are decreased.[12]

To the extent that planning is "scientific" and "orderly," the studies planners might rely on could derive from various disciplines. Leading among them are statistics, economics, geography, and sociology. Thus, sociologist RE Pahl,[13] though he says that "planning is a political exercise in determining who gets the 'urban goodies,'"[14] also sees a role for sociology in generating data that amounts to a programme of activities that a sociologist, working with planners at a regional or national level, might pursue. Such activities include:

---

12 David B Greenspan & Michael B Vaughan, "How the Zoning Game is Played: A Look at Land Use Procedures" (1972) 6 *Law Society Gazette* 50 at 51 [emphasis in original].

13 RE Pahl, *Whose City? And Further Essays on Urban Society*, 2d ed (Baltimore: Penguin, 1975). See also Richard E Foglesong, *Planning the Capitalist City* (Princeton, NJ: Princeton University Press, 1986); Leo Driedger, *Sociology of Canadian Cities* (Toronto: Oxford University Press, 1991).

14 Pahl, above note 13 at 2.

1. Appraisal of the "social health" of the region based on broad societal values, by analysing the distribution of appropriate social indicators in the light of the social goals they are designed to measure.
2. Reconsideration of existing goals and the reformation or designation of new goals in the light of this . . . .
3. A review of social "problems" and social goals in the light of the existing social and economic situation: social problems are the opposite of social goals.
4. The formulation of appropriate policies to achieve the social goals: these policies need not necessarily have a physical component.[15]

The American geographer Rutherford Platt, in a practical approach to thinking about land use, suggests starting with five questions: "What is a tract of land like? Where is it located with respect to other places or land uses? Why is it used in a particular way? How can it be better utilized to avoid harmful externalities and promote favourable ones? Who has the authority to cause beneficial changes in land use practices?"[16] Platt's questions proceed from the same perspective as the common law of property, that it is the setting of land, its relationship to its surroundings, that is always crucial.

What emerges from modern planning literature and its practice is that, as a matter of process, planning requires public participation, and as a matter of content, it strives for sustainability.[17] In a classic statement, Trent University geographer George Nader has said,

> City planning is concerned with anticipating and regulating the change in the physical environment in order to promote the orderly development of the city and to increase the social and economic benefits of urbanization. Cities exist essentially because of the advantages which spatial concentration affords to economic activities . . . and to social interaction . . . . These social and economic forces are in turn manifested in the physical organization of cities. The planner's concern with the physical elements of the city is therefore subordinate to the ultimate goal, which is the socio-economic well-being of the urban community. The aim of land use planning is to promote public welfare, and considerations of beauty, safety and health are therefore

15 *Ibid.*

16 Rutherford Platt, *Land Use and Society: Geography, Law, and Public Policy*, 2d ed (Washington, DC: Island Press, 2004) at 31–32.

17 There is a long history of a kind of planning for cities, not always identified as formal land-use planning. For a short listing, see architectural historian Spiro Kostof, *The City Shaped* (Boston: Little Brown, 1991) at 11–12.

> inseparable from the economic question of efficiency. Ultimately, the planner is concerned with people's happiness (. . . "quality of life"), and it is his job to translate this intangible goal into physical form for the spiritual enrichment of the urban community.[18]

Historian Peter Hall of University College London, in his massive work, *Cities in Civilization*, lauds the city as a "cultural crucible" and "innovative milieu," and the place of "the marriage of art, technology and organization."[19] But whether planning is for urban or for rural areas, it is ultimately a process of thinking about the future. And most current thinking about the future identifies sustainability as a central and pressing framework.

UK Planning Professor Patsy Healey has said,

> These notes are about the theory of planning as an activity and as a profession . . . . Two special points need to be made about the theory of any profession.
>
> There are always additional or auxiliary theories which need to be invoked. These are the theories of the object of professional attention and of its contexts, and similarly of the client and the client's context . . . . The urban planner . . . needs a theory of cities and urban development, and of human behaviour in urban systems, partly as depicted in economics, sociology and other social sciences. Also needed is an understanding of the social, political, and institutional milieu in which planning proceeds, and of the views and needs of his other clients.
>
> Moreover, the theory of a profession is of necessity a normative theory, which is capable of generating new norms of professional behaviour and new protocols of acceptable practice. A positive theory, which describes and explains the behaviour of the profession as it changes over time, is an instance of sociological or political theory applied to planning, but it is not a theory of planning. A most fundamental consequence of this observation is that *a theory of planning cannot be based solely on a study of the practice of planning.* We must replace the tautology "Planning is what planners do" with a precept "Planning is what planners ought to do . . . ."
>
> The professional's responsibility to serve the client is not unqualified. This becomes evident when we consider that the planner's client is not thought to be only an employer, like the planning commission, or an ultimate decision maker, like the city council, but equally the public (somehow defined) as well as subordinate or superordinate

---

18 George A Nader, *Cities of Canada*, vol 1 (Toronto: MacMillan, 1975) at 263.

19 See Hall, above note 1. Hall's views on the city as cultural crucible find resonance in the later writings of Richard Florida.

> bodies to whom the proximate client has responsibilities and duties . . . . We start from the widely accepted idea that the public planner's ultimate responsibility is to the public. The planner is in principle bound by the diverse goals of the many segments of this public; the planner does not impose his or her own goals, but seeks to evoke a plan by building a consensus through public discourse and interaction as a part of the planning process. In this context, however, the planner does not abandon professional responsibilities . . . .
>
> There is a professional duty to call to public attention the effect of conflicting goals on plan development, and the existence of laws, customs, or conditions which may militate against some public proposals . . . .
>
> The planner may also have to abandon neutrality in another case: when important parties at interest are not represented and where the planners may feel compelled to put forward views on their behalf. This may be the case for disenfranchised or alienated groups, and is especially true in respect of unborn generations, who will inherit much of the built environment now being planned, the natural environment about to be impacted by that building, and the consequences of public health and education policies currently being adopted.[20]

Planning has an extensive literature. Respected writers, not all of them planners,[21] although by training or experience seen as thoughtful and instructive, are widely cited, including Stuart Chapin, Jane Jacobs, Christopher Alexander, Lewis Mumford, Richard Babcock, Mike Davis, David Harvey, Peter Hall, Witold Rybczynski, JH Kunstler, and Richard Florida. There are lists of "the 100 best planning books." The American Planning Association (APA) published such a list in 2009 as a centennial marker.[22] Thinking about land use leads inevitably to a consideration of values. It is possible to place the profession of planning inside philosophical, economic, or political traditions. One of the strongest of these claims over the activity comes from those who see land use as a struggle between private and collective rights. David Harvey, for example, characterizes

---

20 Patsy Healey, "Commentaries" (1997) 24 *Environment and Planning B: Planning and Design* 483 [emphasis in original].

21 For example, Mark Kingwell, University of Toronto professor of Philosophy, has written intriguingly, and in the tradition of Walter Benjamin's observations on ruins, about cities and consciousness; see *Concrete Reveries: Consciousness and the City* (Toronto: Penguin Canada, 2008).

22 American Planning Association, "100 Essential Books of Planning," online: www.planning.org/library/greatbooks. Another list is by Brent Toderian, "The 100 'Best' Books on City-Making Ever Written?" (13 December 2013), online: www.planetizen.com/node/66462.

modern planning in Paris as having "etched relations of class privilege and domination into the very physical landscape of the city."[23]

Planning is an international enterprise. We may learn from the experience anywhere. What is striking about the best of the planning literature is that it is markedly gloomy about what has been accomplished. Peter Hall, while he is an admirer of cities, or at least of their potential (see his book *Cities in Civilization*),[24] is the author of *Great Planning Disasters*,[25] something of a counterweight to the former. The work is an analysis of large-scale planning undertakings, including a proposal for a new airport for London, England; proposals for new motorways also for London; and the process for establishing the Bay Area Rapid Transit (BART) system for San Francisco. His central point is just how extremely hard it is to assemble and take into account the appropriate information about long-term needs and behaviour.[26] Likewise, Charles Landry's (in what is perhaps the modern echo of Raymond Unwin's *Town Planning in Practice*[27]) *The Art of City Making*[28] details where our joint efforts at building places to live have gone wrong, from blandness to assaults on the senses to the dominance of the automobile to an unsustainable ecological footprint to the outright creation of misery.

Lewis Mumford in *The City in History*[29] has pointed out that from the time human settlements became anything larger than small villages, planning came into play:

> their [i.e. river] sudden floods or periodic inundations made it necessary for the village cultivators to band together to repair the storm damage, to guide the water around their fields to fend off drought, to create finally a whole network of embankments and canals and irrigation works. The construction of these utilities demanded a degree of social intercourse, co-operation, and long-range planning that the old self-contained village culture, complacently accepting its limitations, did not need or encourage. The very conditions that made large urban settlements a physical possibility also made them a social necessity.[30]

---

23 David Harvey, *Rebel Cities* (New York: Verso, 2012) at xiv.

24 Above note 1.

25 Peter Hall, *Great Planning Disasters* (Berkeley: University of California Press, 1980).

26 *Ibid* at 249ff.

27 Raymond Unwin, *Town Planning in Practice, An Introduction to the Art of Designing Cities and Suburbs*, 2d ed (London: TF Unwin, 1911).

28 Charles Landry, *The Art of City Making* (Sterling, VA: Earthscan, 2006). Some of Landry's other works are *The Creative City* (London: Earthscan, 2000) and *Riding the Rapids* (London: Building Futures, 2004).

29 Lewis Mumford, *The City in History, Its Origins, Its Transformations, and Its Prospects* (New York: Harcourt Brace, 1961).

30 *Ibid* at 56–57.

Mumford also points to the drive to create utopian conditions in cities.

Mumford admired Raymond Unwin, one of the early tutors of the planning profession.[31] One of Unwin's lead messages, writing at the time the United Kingdom first adopted "town planning" legislation, follows.

> The community can now exercise over what is virtually its estate the same oversight, the same regard for economic and efficient development that the owners of great industrial concerns have found so necessary. No longer need the community helplessly watch the banks of canals and the land bordering on its railway sidings being covered with endless rows of cottages, while, for want of access to these very canals and sidings the materials of those industries on which the economic life of the inhabitants depends have to be carted long distances . . . . Not only has industrial efficiency been seriously hampered for want of such organisation in the past, but too often the people's dwellings have spread over the least healthy areas because there the land happened to be cheapest, while large tracts of the most desirable sites for this purpose have been held up for one reason or another, or occupied by less important buildings. Further . . . houses have been crowded upon the land to the maximum extent, regardless of the fact that such crowding is uneconomical from every point of view, except that of sweating the maximum return of rent out of each acre of ground.[32]

Unwin favoured rational economic development and also homes with gardens at a density of approximately twelve houses per acre. He also emphasized the desirability of harmony of architecture in communities, noting that cheap transportation allowed the movement of building materials from place to place easily:

> Because we have cheap railway carriage, must we necessarily spend our time and energy in shuffling the materials characteristic of each district over the whole of the country? Surely it should be possible to check this process, and the first thing required is that both architects and the public should consider their buildings more from the point of view of their effect on the whole town. So long as each architect and each client thinks only of his own building, how individual and how noticeable he can make it, little progress in the total effect can be expected. Architects should be trained to think first of how their building will take its place in the picture already existing. The harmony, the unity which binds the buildings together and welds the

---

31 Above note 27.

32 *Ibid* at ix.

> whole into a picture, is so much the most important consideration that it should take precedence.[33]

This comment links architecture with planning, a connection that remains entirely pertinent.

Architect Christopher Alexander, in his brilliant work *A Pattern Language*,[34] identifies a series of features that make for classic cities, towns, neighbourhoods, and buildings: "It is shown there, that towns and buildings will not be able to become alive, unless they are made by all the people in society, and unless these people share a common pattern language, within which to make these buildings, and unless this common pattern language is alive itself."[35] The features, from large to small, are all connected: "In short, no pattern is an isolated entity. Each pattern can exist in the world, only to the extent that it is supported by other patterns: the larger patterns in which it is embedded, the patterns of the same size that surround it, and the smaller patterns which are embedded in it."[36] Alexander and his colleagues offer their features as a contrast to contemporary planning and building: "We believe . . . that the languages which people have today are so brutal, and so fragmented, that most people no longer have any language to speak of at all—and what they do have is not based on human, or natural considerations."[37] At the community level, Alexander lists and explains features such as "identifiable neighbourhoods," "neighbourhood boundaries," a "web of public transportation," a "four-story limit" of height, no more than "nine percent parking," and "access to water." The work is replete with photographs and drawings to make the case. The four-storey limit stands out, in comparison with many prevailing development proposals. Here is what Alexander says:

> There is abundant evidence to show that high buildings make people crazy. High buildings have no genuine advantages, except in speculative gains for banks and land owners. They are not cheaper, they do not help create open space, they destroy the townscape, they destroy social life, they promote crime, they make life difficult for children, they are expensive to maintain, they wreck the open spaces near them, and they damage light and air and view. But quite apart

33 *Ibid* at 363.

34 Christopher Alexander et al, *A Pattern Language* (New York: Oxford University Press, 1977); see also its companion book, Christopher Alexander, *The Timeless Way of Building* (New York: Oxford University Press, 1977).

35 *Ibid* at x.

36 *Ibid* at xiii.

37 *Ibid* at xvi.

> from all of this, which shows that they aren't very sensible, empirical evidence shows that they can actually damage people's minds and feelings. There are two separate bodies of evidence for this. One shows the effect of high-rise housing on the mental and social well being of families. The other shows the effect of large buildings, and high buildings, on the human relations in offices and workplaces."[38]
>
> Medical and other studies are then cited. The section concludes:
>
> We believe, therefore, that the "four-story limit" is an appropriate way to express the proper connection between building height and the health of a people. Of course, it is the spirit of the pattern which is most essential. Certainly a building five stories high, perhaps even six, might work if it were carefully handled. But it is difficult. On the whole, we advocate a four-story limit, with only occasional departures, throughout the town.[39]

The late professor of architecture history at the University of California, Berkeley, Spiro Kostof, wrote two influential books, *The City Assembled*[40] and *The City Shaped*.[41] Both are lavishly illustrated and are good companions to the Christopher Alexander books in that they show what our cities could be.

Well-documented has been the evolution of the legal framework and the actual experience in New York. For decades, the lead New York planner was Robert Moses. In his biography, *The Power Broker*,[42] historian Robert A Caro details the major roads and bridges, clusters of tall apartment houses both public and private, numerous parks and playgrounds, reclaimed shoreline, and cultural places such as Lincoln Center, all built during Robert Moses's time as lead planner. He shaped New York as it is today. "But," Caro asks,

> what did he build? What was the shape into which he pounded the city? To build his highways, Moses threw out of their homes 250,000 persons . . . . By building his highways, Moses flooded the city with cars . . . . By making sure that the vast suburbs, rural and empty when he came to power, were filled on a sprawling, low-density development pattern relying primarily on roads instead of mass transportation, he

38 *Ibid* at 115–16.

39 *Ibid* at 118.

40 Spiro Kostof, *The City Assembled: The Elements of Urban Form Through History* (London: Thames and Hudson, 1992).

41 Kostof, *The City Shaped*, above note 17.

42 Robert A Caro, *The Power Broker, Robert Moses and the Fall of New York* (New York: Vintage Books, 1974).

> insured that that flood would continue for generations . . . . More significant even than the number of the dispossessed were their characteristics: a disproportionate share of them were black, Puerto Rican—and poor . . . . When he built housing for poor people, he built housing bleak, sterile, cheap—expressive of patronizing condescension in every line. And he built it in locations that contributed to the ghettoization of the city, dividing up the city by color and income.[43]

Kostof places Robert Moses in the history of Haussmannization: large-scale expropriation to achieve a grand scheme, especially to build roads.[44] He quotes Moses as saying "When you operate in an overbuilt metropolis, you have to hack your way with a meat axe."[45] Caro's commentary brings out some of the main aspects of land use: the extent to which professionals make the most of the decisions or whether open democratic processes will prevail, the question of who benefits as against who is negatively impacted, and sustainability as a major concern.

In *After the Planners*, architecture professor Robert Goodman[46] says that planning shows mistaken results that

> . . . flow from their [planners'] adherence to the conventions of a repressive social structure which is biased against the people their plans are supposed to serve. Many of those committed to this structure probably don't see it in nearly as ideological terms as I have described. That people don't view themselves working within so explicit an ideology, however, doesn't contradict the fact that they do promote it through their actions. In fact, it is in that very ability of a social organization to promote a repressive ideology while masking its effects in the mannerisms and rhetoric of "freedom", "democracy" and "opportunity" that we find one of the unique forms of repression . . . . The planners' own form of ostensible "value free", "scientific" methods have contributed to this repression. Through this posturing, the real bias behind their plans, whether the bias is intended or not, has been obscured from the people they have affected.[47]

Journalist James Howard Kunstler in *The Geography of Nowhere* says:

---

43 *Ibid* at 19–20.

44 For the historical context within which George-Etienne Haussman (1809–92) worked, see Harvey, *Rebel Cities*, above note 23 at 7–8.

45 Spiro Kostof, *The City Assembled*, above note 40 at 269.

46 Robert Goodman, *After the Planners* (New York: Simon & Schuster, 1971).

47 *Ibid* at 12.

> Eighty percent of everything ever built in America has been built in the last fifty years, and most of it is depressing, brutal, ugly, unhealthy, and spiritually degrading—the jive-plastic commuter tract home wastelands, the Potemkin village shopping plazas with their vast parking lagoons, the Lego-block hotel complexes, the "gourmet mansardic" junk-food joints, the Orwellian office "parks" featuring buildings sheathed in the same reflective glass as the sunglasses worn by chain-gang guards, the particle-board garden apartments rising up in every meadow and cornfield, the freeway loops around every big and little city with their clusters of discount merchandise marts, the whole destructive, wasteful, toxic, agoraphobia-inducing spectacle that politicians proudly call "growth."
>
> The newspaper headlines may shout about global warming, extinctions of living species, the devastation of rain forests, and other world-wide catastrophes, but Americans evince a striking complacency when it comes to their everyday environment and the growing calamity that it represents.[48]

He continues:

> The process of destruction that is the subject of this book is so poorly understood that there are few words to even describe it. Suburbia. Sprawl. Overdevelopment. Conurbation (Mumford's term). Megalopolis . . . . Much of it occupies what was until recently rural land—destroying, incidentally, such age-old social arrangements as the distinction between city life and country life. To me, it is a landscape of scary places, the geography of nowhere, that has simply ceased to be a credible human habitat. This book is an attempt to discover how and why it happened, and what we might do about it.[49]

The emergence of schools of planning at Canadian universities coincided with the establishment of environmental science as a discipline and urban studies as a focus in other departments, including law.[50] With a focus on recent history in the United States, one academic noted "The urban riots in the mid-1960s kindled the belated discovery of poverty and racial tensions in North American cities. The concern of law teachers to introduce courses in the area of urban studies can be

---

48 James Howard Kunstler, *The Geography of Nowhere: The Rise and Decline of America's Man-Made Landscape* (New York: Simon & Schuster, 1993) at 10.

49 *Ibid* at 15. Kunstler's views have been elaborated in *Home from Nowhere* (New York: Simon & Schuster, 1996) and *The City in Mind* (New York: The Free Press, 2001).

50 See "Urban Legal Studies Symposium" (1970) 8 *Osgoode Hall Law Journal* 345.

traced to that time."[51] Law and planning have had a formal link in academic disciplines ever since. This link extends to departments of geography, where a subject of "legal geography" has become established[52] with studies ranging from neighbours' interactions over boundary trees[53] to homelessness.[54]

Some of the university programmes offer descriptions of their subject. At UBC, Calgary, Dalhousie, Guelph, Laval, Manitoba, Montreal, UNBC, UQAM, Queen's, Ryerson, Saskatchewan, Simon Fraser, Toronto, Waterloo, and York, there are both undergraduate and graduate planning programmes. The proliferation is some indicator of the interest in and utility of the subject. At the University of Toronto's website, the following has appeared:

> *What is Planning?*
> At the heart of planning lies a commitment to better cities, healthy environments and social and economic well-being for everyone. Planners pursue their ideals and objectives in the name of the public good as policy makers, public servants, builders, community organizers and political activists, working at all levels of government, with the non-profit sector or in private practice. Their specializations include land use, housing, transportation, urban design, social policy, public health, economic development, international development, and the environment—among others. Although the built environment of the city has been their traditional terrain of action, planners also work on social, economic and cultural issues and at various spatial scales. Their work, accordingly, ranges in territorial scope from the design of small towns to policy planning at the national level to international development. Indeed, the practice of planning today spans the entire local-global spectrum, taking into consideration the challenges and opportunities presented to cities, regions and nations by the forces of globalization . . . .
>
> In reality, of course, the operative definition of planning is keenly contested by a variety of traditions and their political values. The practice of planning, likewise, is the negotiated—or comprom-

---

51 Jeffrey Jowell, "Introduction," *ibid* at 345.

52 The leading Canadian scholar is Simon Fraser University's Nicholas Blomley. See Nicholas Blomley et al, eds, *The Legal Geographies Reader* (Oxford: Blackwell, 2001) and Irus Braverman et al, eds, *The Expanding Spaces of Law* (Stanford, CA: Stanford University Press, 2014).

53 Nicholas Blomley, "Learning from Larry: Pragmatism and the Habits of Legal Space" in Braverman et al, eds, *ibid* at 77.

54 Don Mitchell, "The Annihilation of Space by Law: The Roots and Implications of Anti-Homeless Laws in the United States" in Blomley et al, eds, above note 52 at 6.

> ised—outcome of a struggle between divergent perspectives held by different social groups on how the world works and what to do about it .... Of one thing we can, therefore, be certain: the meaning of planning in the twenty-first century will depend on how planners intervene with other political actors and work with communities in the emerging social and political struggles of our time.[55]

Some leading Canadian planners from the recent past, such as Humphrey Carver, Hans Blumenfeld, and Len Gertler, have written memoirs or have collections of essays that give accounts not only of their general activities but of what they believed and tried to accomplish as planners. Gertler edited a good collection of essays by Canadian planners that gives a useful account of these points.[56] In his introduction, he lists some of the

> [p]lusses in Canadian planning experience ... the establishment of a legal framework for planning in the provinces ... ; making metropolitan planning operational in a large urbanized complex ... ; establishing within one provincial jurisdiction a system of regional planning on a multi-municipal base, with executive and not just advisory powers ... ; building citizen participation into the planning process of a metropolis ... ; designing in a comprehensive and integrated fashion an entire new section of a city, with innovations in the forms of multiple housing and in the ways of coping with the automobile ... ; applying and elaborating the technique of new town building both for a resource-based town on the frontier ... and for an industrial satellite in a dynamic western park belt region ... ; and undertaking a national evaluation of the use and abuse of renewable resources, opening the way to an inter-disciplinary and regional approach to the study and solution of resource problems.[57]

Gertler's account has been brought up to date by Professor Jill Grant, who likewise examined the Canadian Institute of Planners's publication *Plan Canada*.[58]

Humphrey Carver (1902–95) trained in England as an architect, moved to Canada in 1930, and spent a long time as a senior functionary

---

55 Previously online: www.geog.utoronto.ca/programs/planning/planning%20new/planning.htm (accessed 29 March 2008). This is no longer available on the current U of T website.

56 Leonard O Gertler, *Planning the Canadian Environment* (Montreal: Harvest House, 1968).

57 *Ibid* at 11.

58 Jill Grant, ed, *A Reader in Canadian Planning: Linking Theory and Practice* (Toronto: Thomson Nelson, 2008).

in the Canadian Mortgage and Housing Corporation (CMHC) as well as teaching at the University of Toronto. His career focused on planning more than architecture, and his accounts vividly detail the history of community change as well as change in the profession over several decades.[59] Carver's memoir, *Compassionate Landscape*, is an autobiography that details his family history along with the story of the development of the planning enterprise in Canada, much of which he participated in. Intertwined with the account of the building of a career are the origins of the Community Planning Association of Canada (CPAC); the early government studies of land use and of housing issues; the first attempts at generating plans for cities such as Toronto; the evolution of provincial laws setting out how municipalities were to plan; and the important role of the federal government, through CMHC, in establishing a housing industry along with factual studies of the social issues planning grapples with. Housing was Carver's focus. This passage indicates his thoughts:

> Of course, doing urban research doesn't in itself, solve any problems at all or make cities any better to live in. The purpose of research is to find out the whole spectrum of choices that we have in organizing the environment around our chosen way of life. How an urban society makes these choices and acts upon them depends upon its capacity to take action within the unwieldy machinery of democratic government. And the choices ultimately depend upon society's philosophy of life and its sense of social justice.
>
> I have a continuing concern that there ought to be much more public discussion of housing so that policies really would develop out of a philosophy of life and out of a sense of social justice, rather than out of political opportunism and out of the pressures of the mortgage market. What makes the subject of housing so sensitive is that, in spite of all the technological advances and all the manipulation of financing it is still not possible to satisfy the housing needs of about one-third of the population without some fairly large redistribution of the public's money; to satisfy reasonable expectations for a good way of life, either incomes or housing costs have to be subsidized. How best to do this is what discussions of "housing policy" are all about.[60]

Social justice and public participation emerge in Carver's summing up as central to what he believed about the work he was doing. As

---

59 Carver's books are *Houses For Canadians* (Toronto: University of Toronto Press, 1948); *Cities in the Suburbs* (Toronto: University of Toronto Press, 1962); and *Compassionate Landscape* (Toronto: University of Toronto Press, 1975).

60 Carver, *Compassionate Landscape*, *ibid* at 160.

in any autobiography, there emerges a story that is implied. In Carver's, one of the things we see is how important professionals can be, through their work as bureaucrats or teachers as well as practitioners. Important, that is, in putting ideas into the overall political mix and seeking, long-term, to advance them.

Hans Blumenfeld (1892–1988), originally from Germany, worked in Europe, the Union of Soviet Socialist Republics, and the United States prior to coming to Canada in 1955. Like Carver, he also taught at the University of Toronto and worked as a leading planner in both Toronto and Montreal.[61] Blumenfeld was the lead drafter of the first official plan (OP) for Metropolitan Toronto, the original amalgamated Toronto-area entity created by the province from the core city plus twelve suburbs in 1954. He has written extensively about planning issues. The challenge of summing up was met head-on by Blumenfeld in a 1979 collection of his essays, *Metropolis . . . and Beyond*.[62]

One point that does emerge is his strong support for effective citizen participation. In his 1976 review of Harry Lash's book, *Planning in a Human Way*,[63] he commends the Greater Vancouver Regional District staff for their work to foster such participation:

> I completely agree with Harry Lash's stance "That effective citizens' participation was itself an objective." At the very least it raises the participants' self-esteem. Beyond that it may widen their contacts with other citizens and broaden their views of public affairs. At its highest level it can mean participation in all phases of the work of the planner or politician: assemble and analyze data, predict probable developments beyond the community's control, identify and foresee problems, develop alternatives for their solution, evaluate these and decide which one is likely to produce the most favorable ratio of desirable to undesirable results. Such participation, of course, requires more time and effort than most people are able and willing to devote.[64]

The sweep of his understanding of how land-use planning is to be approached is evident in his comments on "The Spirit of our Rural Past":

---

61 Blumenfeld's main books are *The Modern Metropolis* (Cambridge, MA: MIT Press, 1967); *Canadian Planning Issues* (Ottawa: Canadian Institute of Planners, 1976); *Metropolis . . . and Beyond* (New York: Wiley, 1979); and *Life Begins at 65* (Montreal: Harvest House, 1987).

62 Blumenfeld, *Metropolis . . . and Beyond*, above note 61 at v.

63 Harry Lash, *Planning in a Human Way* (Toronto: Macmillan, 1976). Lash was director of planning in the Greater Vancouver Regional District from 1969 to 1975.

64 Blumenfeld, *Metropolis . . . and Beyond*, above note 61 at 111.

> The United States and Canada developed during the first two centuries of white settlement as predominantly rural societies . . . . The bulk of the rural population lived not in compact villages or hamlets, but in scattered settlements. And, although only a minority of the present rural population consists of farmers, the isolated and independent farmstead set the pattern. For the European peasant, escaping from feudal fetters, North America was "the land of the free" because the land was free. The immigrant was free to do on and with his land whatever he pleased—to improve or destroy it, to buy and sell and mortgage it. This "fee simple" form of landed property has been enshrined in North American ideology as a "natural" right, as the basis of human freedom and dignity . . . . The city developed with "mining camp" mentality concentrated on immediate gain, with a ruthless disregard for ultimate consequences. As such, as a place for making a living, the North American city has been, and still is, highly attractive. But as a place for living, the city, with its increased noise and pollution, has become increasingly unattractive . . . .
>
> In both the United States and Canada the main source of revenue available to municipalities is the real property tax. Thus, while their obligations are proportional to people, their revenues are proportional to property. This has driven them to use their regulatory powers, in particular zoning, to prevent housing for low-income families. Zoning has been the main North American response to the problems created by the impact of the landowner's right to develop his property as he pleases on the value of the properties of his neighbors. It has been, and is, a measure of property protection more than one of planning. The provision of public works, the other major contribution of public authorities to the shaping of settlements, has largely followed private development rather than leading it. In the main, North American cities have been designed by the invisible hand of the market . . . .
>
> In Canada there has been no exodus of the upper-income groups from the central city. To the contrary, the center is becoming the preserve of the wealthy; working-class housing is disappearing not only from displacement by multistory apartment houses, but even more from rehabilitation to luxury standards. The net result has been the same on both sides of the border: a shrinking of the housing supply available to low- and moderate-income groups, with the dream of owning a single-family house farther from reality now than it was 20 years ago.[65]

Likewise, in a report for the United Nations Conference on Human Settlements of 1976, Blumenfeld surveyed "Canadian Planning Issues":

---

65 *Ibid* at 3–6.

> Whatever the reasons for disruption, citizens' participation has forcefully brought home the fact that people's main problems are not physical, but social, and call for "social planning." It is here, in the field of the "software" rather than of the "hardware" of physical planning, that there is the greatest scope for neighborhood participation and self-determination.[66]

Leonard Gertler (1923–2005) trained as a planner at McGill University, working in both the private sector and for the municipal governments of Edmonton and Toronto, later heading the University of Waterloo's School of Urban and Regional Planning.[67] Gertler, in his 2005 summing-up, *Radical Rumblings*, does make one observation about planning that is more than technical or the grumblings of a teacher: "I believe that writing is a skill that is particularly important for a planner—both to capture and express the complexities of an inherently interdisciplinary field, and to fulfill the essential role of communicator, laying out the consequences and options to decision-makers with the greatest possible clarity."[68] Much is said here: planners analyze and propose but do not decide; the profession should be a scholarly one rooted in knowledge; and there should be ongoing written explanation of what is being attempted and why. In terms of his practice, he had an eye for the necessity of hard infrastructure and was always mindful of the need for "balanced rural-urban development"[69] and "public discourse."[70] One "lesson from my rather intense involvement in the Toronto planning of the late 1950s and early 1960s is that the 'city is the people.' The goal of city planning must be human well-being. All the rest: official plans, zoning by-laws, housing and redevelopment schemes, are merely means to that end."[71]

Gertler's awareness of the rural-urban connection is akin to the contemporary idea of an ecological footprint[72]:

> From my Edmonton and Toronto experience I became much aware of the centrality in Canada of the *urban-centered* region: the area

66 *Ibid* at 88.

67 Gertler's main books are *Planning the Canadian Environment*, above note 56; *Regional Planning in Canada: A Planner's Testament* (Montreal: Harvest House, 1972); *Changing Canadian Cities: The Next 25 Years* (with Ron Crowley) (Toronto: McClelland & Stewart, 1979); and *Radical Rumblings: Confessions of a Peripatetic Planner* (Waterloo, ON: University of Waterloo, 2005).

68 *Ibid* at 284.

69 *Ibid* at 25.

70 *Ibid* at 76.

71 *Ibid* at 96.

72 Mathis Wackernagle & William Rees, *Our Ecological Footprint* (Philadelphia: New Society, 1996).

> encompassed by the city and its immediate environs: its habitat of land, water and air; and the "urban field", the area of intense activity between centralized functions and dispersed features extending into the countryside as far as 100 kms or more. A basic understanding of the geography of Canada . . . would lead to an appreciation of the *river valley* as a "natural unit" for the management of the use and development of natural resources in Canada.[73]

Memoirs of retired planners, or the thoughts of planners based in universities, occupied the field of Canadian planning literature for decades. Now, however, planners still in active practice have not been shy about putting their views on the record. Jennifer Keesmaat in Toronto and Larry Beasley in Vancouver are two who have stirred some controversy in recent years. Beasley was seen as an important leader in developing a dense, high-rise central city.[74] Keesmaat, who is an active blogger, went on record in favour of demolition of a section of the Gardner Expressway at a time when the mayor was advocating a different plan and the matter was before city council.[75]

Despite the general amorphousness of the discipline, planning, carried out in a professional manner, is widely endorsed as a crucial undertaking in the building of a community. Thus, in an Ontario Municipal Board (OMB) decision dealing with a rushed zoning decision, the OMB set aside the council's decision: "the actions of council represent a complete disregard for and an abuse of the planning process as it is intended to be implemented and followed. As a result, the board is satisfied that the interests of good planning and the public interest have not been properly served."[76] The Canadian courts have tended in recent years to take a somewhat benevolent, if undefined, view of planning. For example, in *Roman Catholic Episcopal Corp for the Diocese of Toronto, in Canada v Barrie (City)*, MacKinnon J of the Ontario Court General Division said that "[a] municipal council has no obligation to absolutely accept the professional advice of its planners. It has the right to reject that advice if it wishes so long as it, through its councillors, acts in good

---

73 Gertler, *Radical Rumblings*, above note 67 at 106 [emphasis in original].

74 For some comments from Beasley, see Jill Grant, "Experiential Planning, A Practitioner's Account of Vancouver's Success" (2009) 75:3 *Journal of the American Planning Association* 358.

75 See Emily Landau, "Troublemaker: Why Jennifer Keesmaat May Be Exactly What Toronto Needs Right Now" *Toronto Life* (5 August 2015) at 46, online: torontolife.com/city/toronto-chief-planner-jennifer-keesmaat. She was supported by Mayor John Tory, who said "I've set out my position and she's set out hers. She's perfectly entitled to do that as the city's chief planner."

76 *Re Village of Port Stanley Zoning By-law 2139* (1986), 18 OMBR 13 at 21.

faith," adding that planning is "an art, not a science."[77] In *507089 Alberta Ltd v Calgary (City)*, Alberta Queen's Bench Justice Rooke said, in discussing bad faith and the impropriety of a council taking irrelevant considerations into account: "considerations relevant to planning apply and to resort to considerations not related to planning is illegal. Moreover, Council can consider public policy, in these circumstances, only in accordance with sound planning principles."[78] What courts consider those principles to be is not entirely clear. Stray comments do appear. For example, in *Action Council of Reasonable Neighbours v Edmonton (City)*, Hembroff J rejected an assertion that where a non-profit organization was gifted land by the city for building a hospital but later proposed to sell the land, the city should take the fact of the windfall into consideration: "There were no strings attached to that gift . . . and in all events, I do not see it as any legal significance and certainly it had no bearing on proper planning considerations."[79] This would imply that a court may understand what is proper planning and what is not. Several decades earlier, the Alberta Court of Appeal, in *Actus Management Ltd v Calgary (City)* said, in comments on the scheme of the *Planning Act*,

> The concepts of a general plan require professional and technical skill and research for their proper formulation [and a land-use by-law] is related to them. But they are directed to the development of communities of people and are not to be viewed as an exercise in abstract planning. The underlying public interest of the people themselves in the nature and direction of the development of their community is recognized . . . .[80]

The implication is that the court will in part assess proper planning in terms of overall public good.

Planning is a communal activity. It involves the essential proposition that what would otherwise be the mostly unfettered use of land by its owners "not only . . . be restricted for the public good, but also that the use to which land is put should be determined by the long-term interests of the community as a whole . . . ."[81] This illustrates a difference between the effect of the common law of nuisance and modern LUP. While LUP certainly has some of its origin in the law of nuisance, which served and still serves to restrain objectionable activities, LUP

---

77 (1997), 39 MPLR (2d) 257 at para 22 (Ont Ct Gen Div).

78 (1996), 33 MPLR (2d) 247 at para 37 (Alta QB).

79 2003 ABQB 895 at para 38.

80 (1975), 62 DLR (3d) 421 (Alta SCAD).

81 Victor Moore, *A Practical Approach to Planning Law*, 10th ed (New York: Oxford University Press, 2007) at 1.

goes further in that it can in effect direct what activities are allowable entirely apart from prohibiting nuisances. The test becomes what is in the general public interest. The theoretical basis for planning is that the public interest can emerge from a democratic planning process. Certainly provincial planning statutes seem to be designed around this premise. Critics have, however, emphasized the difficulty in reconciling competing interests. In the end, they suggest, the best that can be accomplished is to choose one set of interests over another. Others have simply questioned whether planning tends towards the sterile and uninteresting. Dalhousie University planning professor Jill Grant says, "Planning is most effective when it supports community values."[82] At the same time, she points out how difficult it is to ascertain those community values. Certainly public participation is one very important way for professional planners and elected officials to assess this. And while any elitist model of LUP in which only the planners and politicians make decisions is hard to defend, it is also the case that the nature of public participation is itself hard to pin down.[83] According to Grant,

> The factors that motivate people to attend meetings, prepare briefs, or organize protests are complex and varied. Some people undoubtedly operate out of self-interest, while others may have the sense that they want to safeguard community interests . . . . We know that most people take no active role in planning activities. The best efforts to promote citizen participation usually result in low rates of involvement . . . . Planners continue to face uncertainty about what "the silent majority" thinks, expects, and wants.[84]

We return to this issue in Chapter 8.

It is obvious that the interaction of individual or private interests with those of the community at large makes for complex inquiry and calls for exploration of every element of what constitutes legitimate communal interests. An analysis of planning and zoning in Toronto from its early days up to 1970 states, "Although the police power was ostensibly used to promote order, safety, health, morals and the general welfare of society, there can be little doubt that in these early forms of zoning it was used to protect property values by controlling the effects of negative externalities."[85] Kunstler is also skeptical: "Zoning is not an art, but a limited set of crude classification techniques . . . . Zoning began as a pol-

---

82 Jill Grant, *The Drama of Democracy* (University of Toronto Press, 1994) at 215.

83 For important judicial comments on public consultation, see *Gardner v Williams Lake (City)*, 2006 BCCA 307.

84 Grant, *The Drama of Democracy*, above note 82 at 214.

85 Moore, "Zoning and Planning," above note 2 at 317.

itical response to the obnoxious effects of industry on human settlements. Originally, its intent was to keep factories away from houses, to create separate zones for industry to carry on its noisy and dirty activities."[86]

Indeed, one of the most famous of American cases, *Village of Euclid v Ambler Realty Co*,[87] involved the question whether zoning is a permitted government function at all. The village had created various use-classes, along with height restrictions and required minimum lot sizes. The owner of some raw land objected that the zoning had the effect of destroying most of its potential value. In upholding the zoning scheme, the US Supreme Court said:

> Building zone laws are of modern origin. They began in this country about twenty-five years ago. Until recent years, urban life was comparatively simple; but with the great increase and concentration of population, problems have developed, and constantly are developing, which require, and will continue to require, additional restrictions in respect of the use and occupation of private lands in urban communities. Regulations, the wisdom, necessity and validity of which, as applied to existing conditions, are so apparent that they are now uniformly sustained, a century ago, or even half a century ago, probably would have been rejected as arbitrary and oppressive. Such regulations are sustained, under the complex conditions of our day, for reasons analogous to those which justify traffic regulations, which, before the advent of automobiles and rapid transit street railways, would have been condemned as fatally arbitrary and unreasonable. And in this there is no inconsistency, for while the meaning of constitutional guaranties never varies, the scope of their application must expand or contract to meet the new and different conditions which are constantly coming within the field of their operation. In a changing world, it is impossible that it should be otherwise. But although a degree of elasticity is thus imparted, not to the *meaning*, but to the *application* of constitutional principles, statutes and ordinances, which, after giving due weight to the new conditions, are found clearly not to conform to the Constitution, of course, must fall.
>
> The ordinance now under review and all similar laws and regulations must find their justification in some aspect of the police power, asserted for the public welfare. The line which in this field separates the legitimate from the illegitimate assumption of power is not capable of precise delimitation. It varies with circumstances and conditions. A regulatory zoning ordinance, which would be clearly valid as

---

86 JH Kunstler, *Home From Nowhere*, above note 49 at 123.
87 272 US 365 (1926).

> applied to the great cities, might be clearly invalid as applied to rural communities . . . .[88]
>
> We find no difficulty in sustaining restrictions of the kind thus far reviewed. The serious question in the case arises over the provisions of the ordinance excluding from residential districts, apartment houses, business houses, retail stores and shops, and other like establishments. This question involves the validity of what is really the crux of the more recent zoning legislation, namely, the creation and maintenance of residential districts, from which business and trade of every sort, including hotels and apartment houses, are excluded. Upon that question this court has not thus far spoken . . . .[89] The matter of zoning has received much attention at the hands of commissions and experts, and the results of their investigations have been set forth in comprehensive reports. These reports, which bear every evidence of painstaking consideration, concur in the view that the segregation of residential, business and industrial buildings will make it easier to provide fire apparatus suitable for the character and intensity of the development in each section; that it will increase the safety and security of home life . . . .[90]

The Court did not dispute that the zoning had adversely affected the value of Ambler's land, value of land being strongly associated with permitted usage. But it took the view that before such ordinances could be said to be unconstitutional, they would have to be "clearly arbitrary and unreasonable, having no substantial relation to the public health, safety, morals, or general welfare." In validating zoning schemes as a usual exercise of the governmental "police power," the Court not only set a general precedent for the United States, but created a term now widely used to describe zoning—"Euclidean zoning"— or the separation of incompatible uses.

There is much that is objectionable in *Euclid.* What it suggests is that separation of uses is desirable, whereas a mixture of uses is often what creates vibrant and liveable communities according to many planners. For example, Jane Jacobs has written:

> For reasons I have analyzed at length in *The Death and Life of Great American Cities*, enterprises serving city consumers flourish most prolifically where the following four conditions are simultaneously met: (1) different primary uses, such as residences and working places, must be mingled together, insuring the presence of people

88 *Ibid* at 386–87 [emphasis in original].

89 *Ibid* at 390.

90 *Ibid* at 394.

> using the streets on different schedules but drawing on consumer goods and services in common; (2) small, short blocks; (3) buildings of differing ages, types, sizes and conditions of upkeep, intimately mingled; and (4) high concentrations of people.[91]

She also suggests that protection of single-family or detached housing is an important value. This point raises the function of zoning as a sociological phenomenon that tends to recognize and legitimize pre-existing land-use patterns, making evolution in communities difficult and sometimes keeping races and classes separate, something that has come under scrutiny in American courts as "exclusionary zoning."[92]

Although I have emphasized the public or communal aspects of land use, there are limitations on those. Private decisions by landowners tend to drive the nature of development as much as does the public process. Respect for private property rights means that governments are most clearly able to control new proposed developments, especially on raw land, more than they can on land that is already developed or where proposals fit the as-of-right designations that characterize a great deal of property. That is, planning is "primarily a regulatory function."[93] Indeed, unless a government is itself prepared to develop land, the initiative for building is entirely private. Planning may guide but it cannot always direct. It is often responsive. If positive planning is carried out, it may be through land assembly, decisions about placement of infrastructure, use of zoning flexibility tools such as development agreements, enforcement of building codes (to achieve slum clearance or building upgrades), private-public partnerships, creation of business parks, and other economic steps.

Importantly, planning's manifestation in legal tools shows an "uneasy balance between rules and discretion, and between flexibility and certainty."[94] Canadian political scientist Christopher Leo has written, "Involvement in the process of city planning often induces a feeling akin to our experience when we watch a film with excellent special effects. It all seems so real, and yet we know it is not. The words spoken in planning hearings and written in planning documents represent aspirations, often laudable ones, that have legal status and that are backed

---

91 See Jane Jacobs, *The Death and Life of Great American Cities* (New York: Vintage Books, 1963) and *The Economy of Cities* (New York: Random House, 1969) at 100.

92 See, for example, Robert B Wright & Morton Gitelman, *Cases and Materials on Land Use*, 5th ed (St Paul, MN: West, 1997) ch VIII.

93 Malcolm Grant, *Urban Planning Law* (London: Sweet & Maxwell, 1982) at 499. For comment on the property owner as the primary planner of land use, see Rutherford H Platt, *Land Use and Society: Geography, Law and Public Policy*, 3d ed (Washington, DC: Island Press, 2014) at 637.

94 Grant, above note 93 at 5.

by administrative and political processes. But if we look around, we frequently find that there is a disconnect between the bureaucratic and legal theory of planning and the reality on the street."[95] Professor Leo identifies the disconnect with an overwhelming power of developers to drive the whole process. The core interaction between private ambitions and public preferences is never far from any aspect of land-use planning.

From the beginning, the courts have had to struggle with serious public policy issues in the context of LUP litigation. So, too, have all parties to the planning exercise. The basic trade-offs or reconciliation of interests take place often in public forums. The main decision-makers are usually elected officials. In an intriguing article, "Acting for a Developer," lawyer Robert E Jarvis offered this comment at a Law Society of Upper Canada seminar in 1974: "What suggestions would I make to assist the lawyer in remaining relevant in this field of law? In my opinion the most important tool for a lawyer acting for any party involved in land use law would be a thorough working knowledge of our political system. This would include a knowledge of the nomination and campaign procedures followed by most political candidates . . . ."[96] I think this comes within an ace of saying that a money contribution to candidates would not go amiss. Electoral politics of course runs on money. Contributions are not illegal, though are usually regulated in a variety of ways. Land developers are usually solid contributors to municipal politicians. So long as specified amounts are not exceeded, and disclosure made as required, none of this is illegal. At the same time, corruption in government, often at the municipal level, is not unknown.[97] Canada has seen scandals in Montreal,[98] Toronto,[99] Winnipeg,[100] Edmon-

95 Christopher Leo, "Urban Development: Planning Aspirations and Political Realities" in Edmond P Fowler & David Siegel, eds, *Urban Policy Issues: Canadian Perspectives* (Toronto: Oxford University Press, 2002) 215.

96 Robert Jarvis, "Acting For a Developer" *Special Lectures of the Law Society of Upper Canada* (Toronto: Richard De Boo, 1974) 225 at 227.

97 A recent book by Philip Slayton, *Mayors Gone Bad* (Toronto: Viking, 2015) offers a lively account of some local government scandals.

98 Robert Poirier, mayor of Boisbriand, Quebec, from 1998–2005, was convicted of fraud, conspiracy, and breach of trust in connection with municipal contracts: "Ex-Montreal Area Mayor Found Guilty of Fraud, Conspiracy" *The Globe and Mail* (16 September 2015).

99 Denise E Bellamy, *Toronto Computer Leasing Inquiry, Toronto External Contracts Inquiry* (Toronto: City of Toronto, 2005).

100 Phil Sheegl, Chief Administrative Officer of Winnipeg, resigned his position in 2013 over allegations of improprieties in the sale of city land to a company with close ties to the mayor.

ton,[101] Laval,[102] London,[103] Peterborough,[104] and Sarnia.[105] The *Criminal Code* includes prohibitions against corrupt practices such as fraud and bribery;[106] other mechanisms ranging from conflict-of-interest laws to lobbyist registries to audits exist to restrain improper behaviour and promote transparency and accountability.[107] While much of the focus is on elected officials, many of the rules also apply to staff.

For many observers, the problem with the planning enterprise as it is carried out at the municipal level is not so much one of corruption in the sense of outright illegality as it is one of regulatory capture. This term describes a situation in which an entity whose main function is oversight of some undertaking becomes, over time and through the nature of the work, so drawn into contact with the representatives of that undertaking that it takes on or internalizes the important but narrow views of what should instead be regulated in the public interest.[108]

---

101 See *Edmonton (City) v Hawrelak* (1972), 24 DLR (3d) 321 (Alta SCTD).

102 Gilles Vaillancourt, mayor of Laval, was forced to resign in 2012 (having been mayor since 1989) following a police raid on his office and home; he was charged with gangsterism, a case still proceeding through the courts.

103 Joe Fontana, formerly a federal cabinet minister, was elected mayor of London, Ontario, in 2010. In 2012 he was charged with fraud relating to an invoice submitted for part of the cost of a family wedding when he was an MP. He was convicted and resigned as mayor.

104 Peterborough mayor Daryl Bennett was removed from the police board after an investigation found he had engaged in unbecoming conduct, including breaches of confidentiality and making threats to other members; the ruling is being challenged in court. See Joelle Kovach, "OCPC Panel Finds Mayor Daryl Bennett Guilty of Misconduct on Police Board" *The Peterborough Examiner* (31 December 2014).

105 *Royal Commission to Investigate Charges relating to the Purchase of Lands in the City of Sarnia by the Hydro Electric Power Commission of Ontario* (Toronto: The Commission, 1960); the validity of a municipality's authority to establish a public inquiry, if the terms of reference are carefully framed, was established in *Consortium Developments (Clearwater) Ltd v Sarnia (City)*, [1998] 3 SCR 3.

106 *Criminal Code*, RSC 1985, c C-46, ss 121, 122, &123. See Jack Shenker, "Which Are the Most Corrupt Cities in the World?" *The Guardian* (21 June 2016), online: http://gu.com/p/4ydk7/stw.

107 See John Mascarin, "The Conduct of Elected Municipal Officials—Can Their Behaviour Be Regulated?" (Paper delivered at the LSUC Six-Minute Municipal Lawyer, 13 May 2014). This paper offers an overview of various accountability mechanisms. Indeed, the law report series *Municipal and Planning Law Reports* regularly reports on cases raising conflict of interest issues: see under the key "Municipal Law—Council members—Conflict of interest."

108 In a case in point, the chief administrative officer of Halifax Regional Municipality was recruited in 2015 to become president of the largest local land development company: see Remo Zaccagna, "Butts Quits as Halifax CAO after 4 Years" *The Chronicle-Herald* (10 December 2015) A1; Roger Taylor, "CAO's Shift to Private Job Raises Questions" *The Chronicle-Herald* (16 December 2015) B1.

C. THE PLANNING PROFESSION: VALUES AND ETHICS

Planning is a profession. In some provinces it is regulated.[109] Possession of an appropriate university degree (usually at the Master's level) and membership in the Canadian Institute of Planners (CIP) are the usual requirements for designation as a planner and for qualification for employment. As with all professions, there is a core body of knowledge and skills, and a code of ethics. And, as with all professions, there is evolving debate over the nature of the appropriate core knowledge and skills. To some extent, planning is an amorphous undertaking. At its broadest, nothing relating to the possible future development of human communities should be excluded. Planners could be thought of as futurists. And though there is some emphasis in university programmes on such technical matters as geographic information systems (GIS), transportation, and the problems in layout of small housing developments, it is equally the case that an overall body of planning thought now relates to environmental or sustainability ideas and goals. Texts on environmental law now acknowledge the environmental dimension of LUP, usually as expressed at the municipal level of government. Thus, Doelle and Tollefson note that standard provincial laws creating and empowering local governments tend

> to give municipalities power and responsibility over a range of local matters, many of which have environmental implications and connections . . . . Examples of . . . powers often delegated by provinces to municipalities include: the power to pass by-laws dealing with noise and odour; the control of cosmetic pesticide use; the collection and disposal of solid waste . . . .[110]

The environmental or sustainability content of modern LUP is extensive.[111] The Supreme Court of Canada has recognized environmental matters as a legitimate municipal concern.[112] And courts in both the

---

109 See, for example, *The Community Planning Profession Act, 2013*, SS 2013, c C-21.1. Similar statutes exist in Alberta, Manitoba, Ontario, and Nova Scotia.

110 Meinhard Doelle & Chris Tollefson, *Environmental Law: Cases and Materials* (Toronto: Carswell, 2009) at 164–65.

111 See Howard M Epstein, "Subsidiarity at Work—The Legal Context for Sustainability Initiatives at the Local Government Level: How an Environmental Agenda Could Be Advanced by Canadian Municipalities" (2009) 63 *Municipal and Planning Law Reports* (4th) 56.

112 *Enterprises Sibeca inc v Frelighsburg (Municipality)*, 2004 SCC 61 at para 38; *114957 Canada Ltée (Spraytech, Société d'arrosage) v Hudson (Town)*, 2001 SCC 40 at para 3, citing *R v Hydro-Québec*, [1997] 3 SCR 213.

United States and the United Kingdom have commented on how much the activities are bound up together. US Supreme Court Justice O'Connor, in *California Coastal Commission v Granite Rock Co* said,

> The line between environmental regulation and land use planning will not always be bright . . . . However, the core activity described by each phrase is undoubtedly different. Land use planning in essence chooses particular uses for the land; environmental regulation, at its core, does not mandate particular uses of the land but requires only that, however the land is used, damage to the environment is kept within prescribed limits.[113]

The CIP has adopted both a Statement of Values[114] and a Code of Professional Conduct.[115] The leading US associations, the American Planning Association and the American Institute of Community Planning, also have codes of ethics.[116] Here are some extracts from the CIP:

> **Canadian Institute of Planners: Statement of Values**[117]
>
> *To respect and integrate the needs of future generations.*
> CIP members recognize that their work has cumulative and long-term implications. When addressing short-term needs, CIP members acknowledge the future needs of people, other species and their environments, and avoid committing resources that are irretrievable or irreplaceable.
>
> *To overcome or compensate for jurisdictional limitations.*
> CIP members understand that their work has a potential impact on many jurisdictions and interests. They must therefore practise in a holistic manner, recognizing the needs to overcome the limitations of administrative boundaries.
>
> *To value the natural and cultural environment.*
> CIP members believe that both natural and cultural environments must be valued. They assume roles as stewards of these environments, balancing preservation with sustainable development.

---

113 480 US 575 at 587 (1987).

114 Contained in Ontario Professional Planners Institute Professional Code of Practice, online: www.cip-icu.ca/Files/Provincial-Codes-of-Conduct/OPPI-Professional-Code-of-Practice.aspx.

115 See online: www.cip-icu.ca/Becoming-a-Planner/Codes-of-Professional-Conduct/CIP-Code-of-Professional-Conduct. The Code includes examples of conduct that would be a violation of the standard.

116 See online: www.planning.org/ethics/ethicscode.htm.

117 Above note 115.

To recognize and react positively to uncertainty.
CIP members believe that the long-term future is unpredictable and that adaptable and flexible responses to deal positively with this uncertainty must be developed.

To respect diversity.
CIP members respect and protect diversity in values, cultures, economies, ecosystems, built environments and distinct places.

To balance the needs of communities and individuals.
CIP members seek to balance the interests of communities with the interests of individuals, and recognize that communities include both geographic communities and communities of interest.

To foster public participation.
CIP members believe in meaningful public participation by all individuals and groups and seek to articulate the needs of those whose interests have not been represented.

To articulate and communicate values.
CIP members believe in applying these values explicitly to their work and communicating their importance to clients, employers, colleagues and the public.

CIP Code of Professional Conduct[118]

Minimum Standards for Codes of Professional Conduct: . . .

1. The Planner's Responsibility to the Public Interest

Members shall:
1.1 practice in a manner that respects the diversity, needs, values and aspirations of the public and encourages discussion on these matters;
1.2 provide full, clear and accurate information on planning matters to decision-makers and members of the public, while recognizing the employer or client's right to confidentiality and the importance of timely reporting;
1.3 acknowledge the inter-related nature of planning decisions and the consequences for natural and human environments;
1.4 provide opportunities for meaningful participation and education in the planning process to all interested parties.

---

118 Above note 116. [Examples of possible non-compliance ommitted.]

2. The Planner's Responsibility to Clients and Employers

Members shall:

2.1 provide independent professional opinion to clients, employers, the public, and tribunals; perform work only within their areas of professional competence;

2.2 undertake planning services with diligence and render services with appropriate preparation;

2.3 acknowledge the values held by the client or employer in work performed, unless such values conflict with other aspects of this Code;

2.4 respect the client or employer right to confidentiality of information gathered through a professional relationship, unless such right conflicts with other aspects of this Code;

2.5 inform the client or employer in the event of a conflict between the values or actions of the client or employer and those of this Code in a timely manner;

2.6 ensure timely and full disclosure to a client or employer of a possible conflict of interest arising from the Member's private or professional activities;

2.7 not offer or accept any financial or other inducements, including prospective employment, that could, or appear to, influence or affect professional opportunities or planning advice;

2.8 not, as an employee of a public agency, give professional planning advice for compensation to a private client or employer within the jurisdiction of the public agency without disclosure to the agency and written consent;

2.9 not, as a consultant to a public agency during the period of contract with the agency, give professional planning advice for compensation to others within the jurisdiction of the agency without disclosure to the agency and written consent in situations where there is the possibility of a conflict of interest arising.

3. The Planner's Responsibility to the Profession and Other Members

Members shall:

3.1 maintain an appropriate awareness of contemporary planning philosophy, planning theory and practice by obtaining professional education throughout their planning career, including complying with the Institute's continuing professional learning requirements;

3.2 not in professional practice, extra-professional activities or private life, engage in dishonourable or questionable conduct that may cast doubt on their professional competence or integrity or that may reflect adversely on the integrity of the profession;

3.3 ensure that advertising or promotional activities fairly and accurately communicate the expertise and skills offered, including professional qualifications and affiliations, education and experience;
3.4 act toward other Members and colleagues in a spirit of fairness and consideration and not falsely or maliciously injure the professional reputation, prospects or practice of another Member or other colleagues;
3.5 respect colleagues in their professional capacity and when evaluating the work of another Member, show objectivity and fairness and avoid ill-considered or uninformed criticism of the competence, conduct or advice of the Member; . . . .

Some municipalities have adopted their own principles to govern behaviour. Vancouver has a City Code of Conduct that provides, "City officials, staff, and advisory board members are keepers of the public trust and must uphold the highest standards of ethical behaviour. [They] are expected to . . . make decisions that benefit the community, act lawfully and within the authority of the Vancouver Charter."[119]

D. BURDEN OF PROFESSIONAL EXPERTISE

There are certain legal consequences to the status of professional. One is that it is possible to be held to a standard of performance, and a failure to meet that standard could, in some circumstances, lead to a finding of responsibility for consequent harms to others if the standard is breached. Cases such as *Bell v Sarnia (City)*[120] illustrate this. In the *Bell* case, a prospective purchaser of a convenience store attended at city hall and made inquiries at the zoning department as to what would be permitted uses in a C-1 zone. On two occasions, planners told him that a variety store with a takeout facility serving food was permitted: the variety store as a listed C-1 use and the takeout as an accessory use. Based on these assurances, Bell purchased the property, began operating the variety store, and obtained permits to make renovations, installing a kitchen and a takeout window. Later he applied to build an outdoor patio, eating area, and washrooms. At this point, the municipality took the view that the entire takeout operation was not an accessory use to a variety store and ordered removal of the deep fryer and grill, allowing only use of a microwave. Bell sued for damages on the basis of the tort

119 City of Vancouver, "Code of Conduct," online: http://vancouver.ca/files/cov/boards-committees-code-of-conduct.pdf.
120 (1987), 37 DLR (4th) 438 (Ont HCJ).

of negligent misrepresentation and was successful. The court found that there existed a duty of care on the part of the planners, that their special skills were being relied upon by Bell in circumstances where they knew that in giving advice they accepted some responsibility. The court also found that the advice was incorrect and negligent, and that Bell had relied upon the advice to his detriment. An intriguing point is that the court found negligence because of the relatively subtle issue of what amounts to an accessory use, something cases have defined as "customarily incidental, subordinate and exclusively devoted to the principal use." Analysis of the takeout function by the court concluded that it was unrelated to the variety store use in that it would not generate higher profits for the principal use. Indeed, this was the position ultimately taken by the municipality when it decided that the takeout function was not a proper accessory use.

The tort liability of planners (more typically, the municipality for which a planner acts) is dealt with here only in passing, but this part of the legal framework for the planning activity is something that illustrates the need for planners' familiarity with the subjects we do deal with in this text.[121] *Bell v Sarnia* is not a unique case. In *9182-6222 Québec Inc c Pointe-Claire (Ville de)*,[122] the town planner advised a potential purchaser that a variance needed to allow construction of a dwelling was a routine matter. The council turned down the variance several times, and the owner obtained an award of damages (based as much on bad faith as on the advice). In *Gadutsis v Milne*[123] a prospective lessee of premises asked Toronto officials whether a restaurant was a permitted use at the locale. The information given was that it was, and a permit was issued, but later cancelled when the city realized its error. The plaintiff recovered damages for rent paid and renovation work. In *Prince George (City) v Rahn Bros Logging Ltd*,[124] the city issued building permits in 1985 and 1993 to allow construction of a building and facilities for the company's lumber business. The land was not zoned for the use, and in 2000 the city obtained an injunction to end the use. Damages of $475,000 were awarded to enable the company to rebuild elsewhere. Tort cases are not at all invariably successful, even if the statements made by planners to members of the public are inaccurate

121 For a recent exploration of the tort question, see Peter Hogg & Patrick Monahan, *Liability of the Crown*, 3d ed (Scarborough, ON: Carswell, 2000) at 184–85; Stanley M Makuch et al, *Canadian Municipal and Planning Law*, 2d ed (Toronto: Thomson Carswell, 2004) at 113–30.

122 2012 QCCS 2422.

123 [1973] 2 OR 503 (HCJ).

124 2003 BCCA 31.

in some way. All aspects of a tort must be shown: negligent misstatement, circumstances in which the statement would be relied upon, and reliance to the detriment of the plaintiff. In *PSD Enterprises v New Westminster (City)*,[125] planners gave a "comfort letter" to a commercial property owner to encourage sale of its land, suggesting municipal support for any necessary rezoning of new premises, and also encouraged the owner to speak to council when the rezoning matter was before it, but at a stage of the proceedings when that was not allowed, resulting in cancellation of the hearing; a subsequent hearing turned down the rezoning. The owner's case was dismissed, the court finding that it was not reasonable for them to have relied on the advice.

Tort liability of governments is a complex area of law of its own, and although the principle of municipal liability for such planning-related matters as negligent misstatement by staff is well established, it is also the case that statutes often set a standard that exempts municipalities from liability completely, or save for gross negligence.[126] The cases also make a distinction between liability for decisions of policy (even where found to have been illegal or invalid for reasons of procedural errors) where there is usually no liability, and decisions that are administrative or executory where tort liability might arise.[127]

Liability of a sort also may arise if legal challenges are taken over matters that do not amount to a tort, and therefore potential liability to pay money damages. That is, matters may be taken to court for review on the basis of either alleged illegality or alleged unfairness in the hand-

125 2012 BCCA 319.

126 For some cases involving the liability of those other than planning staff, and of elected officials, see Basile Chiasson, "Municipal Liability for Negligent Subdivision Approval" (2009) 55 *Municipal and Planning Law Reports* (4th) 22; *Jung v Burnaby (District)* (1978), 91 DLR (3d) 592 (BCSC); *HL & M Shoppers Ltd v Berwick (Town)* (1977), 82 DLR (3d) 23 (NSSCTD); *Belleville v Moxam*, [1953] 4 DLR 151 (Ont HCJ); *Windsor Motors Ltd v Powell River (District)* (1969), 4 DLR (3d) 155 (BCCA); *The Pas (Town) v Porky Packers Ltd*, [1977] 1 SCR 51; *Sharadan Builders Inc v Mahler* (1978), 22 OR (2d) 122 (CA); *Kamloops (City) v Nielsen*, [1984] 2 SCR 2; *Wozniak v Erin (Town)* (2001), 20 MPLR (3d) 59 (Ont SCJ); *R v East Sussex County Council Ex p Reprotech (Pebsham) Ltd*, [2002] UKHL 8. In *Biskey v Chatham-Kent (Municipality)*, 2011 ONSC 413, the land was unsuitable for building without a special foundation. The municipality had supplied a previous owner with an environmental site assessment, but did not do this for a new purchaser, instead issuing a building permit. The municipality was found to have breached its duty of care and the owner was awarded some $400,000 in damages.

127 Thus in *Wiswell v Winnipeg (Greater)*, [1965] SCR 512, the municipality was found to have violated a required process, invalidating a rezoning by-law, but the company involved was not able to recover damages. See *Welbridge Holdings Ltd v Winnipeg (Greater)*, [1971] SCR 957.

ling of a file. To illustrate this latter point, the case of *Community Assn of New Yaletown v Vancouver (City)*[128] addressed issues around the adequacy of disclosure of information to the public and possible fettering of discretion by the way the municipality dealt with business arrangements with a developer. The residents challenging the decision were not successful, but the decision certainly shows how complex the circumstances associated with land-use planning may be, and how important it is for careful planning and legal advice to be combined.

A second legal consequence of planning being regarded as a profession is that professionals, as the recognized holders of specialized knowledge, may be looked to for opinions; these opinions may be sought during public processes designed to make policy choices, or during formal hearings. The opinions may extend to advice about what is a good planning decision in the public interest or what is the meaning of various provisions in bylaws or official plans. Most planners in the employ of a municipality will be called upon to write "staff reports" advising the municipal council or a committee about some development proposal. Such documents will have to present and interpret the applicable legal rules, will have to engage with issues around good planning in the public interest, will have to report on public comment received, will set out options, and will usually offer an opinion as to what choice is the appropriate one. In the event of appeals or legal action, the author may be subject to the testing of their opinion through questioning in cross-examination. It is the purview of experts, duly qualified as such, to be able to offer opinions to courts or tribunals. Lay persons may testify only to matters known or observed.[129] Opinion evidence is different, and in offering it experts may call upon their formal education, knowledge of authoritative works, experience, and judgment. Not all tribunals rely upon expert evidence to resolve LUP issues, but many do. Courts, however, will not normally hear expert planning evidence about the meaning of OPs and LUBs, seeing such questions as matters of the interpretation of laws and thus not calling for extraneous evidence.[130] The test for a court to accept expert evidence is whether it is necessary and reliable.[131]

In a formal hearing, the admissibility of expert evidence is measured as to its relevance, its necessity in assisting the decision-maker, the absence of any exclusionary rule, and the proper qualifications

---

128 2015 BCCA 227.

129 For an overview, see Glenn R Anderson, *Expert Evidence*, 3d ed (Markham, ON: LexisNexis, 2014).

130 See *Gain v Ideal Milk Haulage Ltd* (2003), 186 OAC 371 (CA).

131 See, for example, *Ottawa (City) v TKS Holdings Inc*, 2011 ONSC 7633.

of the witness. For planners, their ability to be of assistance depends upon the extent to which they may interpret sets of policies as set out in an OP and LUB. Such issues will be relevant according to the test being applied by the decision-maker. In Ontario, before the Ontario Municipal Board (OMB), the test in most instances will be whether the proposed measures or decision amounts to good planning in the public interest or meets the intent of the OP. In Nova Scotia, the appellate body, the Nova Scotia Utility and Review Board (NSUARB), is obliged to uphold the original municipal decision unless it cannot reasonably be said to be in accord with the intent of the OP. Planners giving evidence in such cases are often asked to give an opinion on the "ultimate issue," that is, to state, in effect, what they believe the result of the case ought to be. At one time, this sort of evidence was seen as inappropriate in that it usurped the function of the decision-maker. Since the decision of the Supreme Court of Canada in *R v Graat*,[132] that is no longer seen as a limit on the expert opinion evidence. What is a limit is the need for objectivity, meaning impartiality.

Certain formalities attach to the offering of expert advice and evidence.[133] Basic is the demonstration of appropriate qualifications and experience. Equally important is impartiality and independence. The loyalty of expert witnesses should be to their profession, not to their employer. The Supreme Court of Canada, in *White Burgess Langille Inman v Abbott and Haliburton Co*,[134] has explored the guidelines for assessing whether specific persons should be allowed to testify as experts, or whether any problems should just be taken into account as a matter of the weight of the evidence. The Court decided that the factors come into play both as regards admissibility and weight. The Court said,

> Underlying the various formulations of the duty are three related concepts: impartiality, independence and absence of bias. The expert's opinion must be impartial in the sense that it reflects an objective assessment of the questions at hand. It must be independent in the sense that it is the product of the expert's independent judgment, uninfluenced by who has retained him or her or the outcome of the litigation. It must be unbiased in the sense that it does not unfairly favour one party's position over another. The acid test is whether the expert's opinion would not change regardless of which party retained him or her . . . .[135]

---

132 [1982] 2 SCR 819.

133 Anderson, *Expert Evidence*, above note 129, ch 16.

134 2015 SCC 23.

135 *Ibid* at para 32.

Tribunals such as the OMB may be able to set their own rules for admissibility of evidence, and may be more flexible than the courts, though they will still look for a significant measure of independence.[136]

Because planning is something of an amorphous area of knowledge, there may be issues as to the parameters of what a planner may attest to, even when qualified as an expert. This will not be an issue in the writing of staff reports, where competence should be demonstrated in research and analysis, and where the limits of what may be considered will probably be quite flexible. At the same time, it is usual for other fields of expertise to be invoked, as, for example, for wind effects studies. But areas of knowledge such as demographics may be seen as something planners may speak to, if they are making reference to recognized, reliable, and standard sources of information, such as Statistics Canada data. Even in a formal hearing before a panel adhering to court-like rules of evidence, experts may consider sources of information they and others in their profession consider to be reliable, even though the information is not proven independently (though not if the evidence is obtained from a party to the case touching a matter directly in issue).[137]

Preparation for testimony will involve meeting with legal counsel. It is useful to have become familiar with the main decisions of the land-use appellate tribunal before which testimony will be given. There is no substitute for having read decisions in previous cases; this will give a feel for what types of evidence are valued, and what language might be persuasive.

In *Giafill Construction v Town of Oakville*,[138] the OMB was faced with a situation in which the town's planner had changed their opinion on a proposal to subdivide a property so as to create several lots, which would be undersize for the R-1 zoned area. The initial view had been favourable, but after meeting with disaffected neighbours, the opinion changed. The relevant OP policies had to do with "conformity," "negative effects," and "compatibility," all of which were somewhat flexible terms. The OMB decided that once a planner had considered these terms and arrived at an opinion, it was hard to see the rationale for a change; the new opinion was discounted.

---

136 See, for example, *Allarco Developments Ltd et al v Town of Ancaster* (1980), 10 OMBR 353; *Re Miller*, 2015 NSUARB 218; *Palm Place Developments Inc v Oakville (Town)* (2006), 52 OMBR 385.

137 *See Saint John (City) v Irving Oil Co Ltd*, [1966] SCR 581 and *R v Lavallee*, [1990] 1 SCR 852.

138 (1986), 18 OMBR 332.

E. HEARING TRANSCRIPT EXTRACTS

Planners need to be prepared for examination in formal hearings. Here are short extracts from some hearing transcripts. The full evidence of the various witnesses is not presented here. The extracts are to illustrate points:

1) Direct Evidence

This is an extract from the direct examination by a municipal lawyer, Ms Roxanne MacLaurin, of Halifax's city planner, Mitch Dickey, in support of a council decision to enter into two development agreements, the decision having been appealed to the NSUARB. The case is *Re Miller*.[139] It illustrates a logical, structured approach to placing opinion evidence on the record, including some leading of the witness. Important in the case was the interpretation of OP (Municipal Planning Strategy (MPS)) policies having to do with compatibility with buildings in a neighbourhood of mainly two to four storeys.

DIRECT EXAMINATION BY MS. MacLAURIN

MS. MacLAURIN: Mr. Dickey, can you please advise the Board with respect to your role in the planning matters concerning 2183 and 2215 Gottingen Street?

MR. DICKEY: Yes. It would be about two years ago, June of 2013, when I took on both files. The Housing Trust had previously been in discussion with a number of other staff members and managers, including Kelly Denty, Austin French, Richard Harvey, and during that time, the Housing Trust was seeking advice and refining its proposal. When they felt that they were ready to actually come in for development applications, I agreed to take on the files and I would be project manager for those files and shepherd them through the entire process, from application to conclusion.

MS. MacLAURIN: All right. And what was involved in that process?

MR. DICKEY: The process for the applications was to ensure The Housing Trust was providing all the appropriate materials; site plans, building plans, elevation drawings, detailed description of their project, what was required, make sure they were providing the required traffic study, considering infrastructure needs. The

139 Above note 136.

role—at that stage, when the application is complete, is to circulate the application to various departments. And while that is going on, I also circulated the project to the Peninsula Planning Advisory Committee and made a presentation to them. I also took the applications out to a public information meeting held in the community to allow public input on those applications. I worked on final evaluation of the projects with other staff, negotiated the detailed terms of the Development Agreements for each case, and prepared staff reports which I took forward to Halifax and West Community Council for their consideration. They agreed to hold public hearings, which were held, at which time I presented to Council. And following Council's decision, that decision was appealed, which had the result of the first trip here to the Board on the proposals. And since then with Council being in the position to approve the Development Agreements with the Schedule Q matter, I prepared the supplementary staff reports and presented those to Council and provided some advice relative to how to improve the Development Agreements, what was required. With the filing of another appeal, I prepared my expert evidence which has been submitted as part of HRM's materials.

MS. MacLAURIN: And, Mr. Dickey, did you also prepare a report in conjunction with this appeal?

MR. DICKEY: Yes, I did.

MS. MacLAURIN: And is that the report which has been filed with the Board contained at Exhibit M-29 at Tab 1?

MR. DICKEY: Yes, it is.

MS. MacLAURIN: And I'm just going to ask that you turn to last page of the report.

MR. DICKEY: Yes.

MS. MacLAURIN: And is the signature at that page your signature?

MR. DICKEY: Yes, it is.

MS. MacLAURIN: Are the opinions expressed in the report your opinions, Mr. Dickey?

MR. DICKEY: Yes, they are.

MS. MacLAURIN: And do you at this time adopt the contents of the report?

MR. DICKEY: Yes, I do.

MS. MacLAURIN: Is there anything that you're aware of since the preparation of your report that would result in you changing or modifying anything in the report, including any opinion that was expressed by you in the report?

MR. DICKEY: Yes, there would be one clarification I could offer. On page 22 of my report within that same exhibit, the first full paragraph, I stated:

> "This policy does not contain a specific height limit; however, Community Council approved the Development Agreement for a 12-storey building." (As read)

My information was incorrect and it was actually a 15-storey building that was approved in that instance.

MS. MacLAURIN: All right. And are there any other errors or corrections you seek to make at this time?

MR. DICKEY: There's a clarification in the—my staff report for each of the cases that [I] would like to raise [as] well.

MS. MacLAURIN: All right. And where is that located in the report?

MR. DICKEY: If I could get referred to the right exhibit. M-5; M-5, Tab 4, page 8, which is a page of the document.

MS. MacLAURIN: Okay.

MR. DICKEY: Down near the bottom of the page, under the heading, "Parking" I wrote—in each staff report the language is the same:

> "The parking requirements for as-of-right development are one parking space per residential unit, and one space per 1,000 square feet of commercial floor space." (As read)

That's not—within Area 8 that's actually incorrect. Not just myself but a number of others missed that within Area 8 there's an exemption for residential parking so within the Land Use By-law as it exists today, there is no parking requirement for as-of-right residential developments, and I wish to note that clarification.

MS. MacLAURIN: And I believe, Mr. Dickey, we dealt earlier with a change with respect to a schedule reference from Schedule D to Schedule E; and would you agree that that was a proper change to make to the contents of your report?

MR. DICKEY: Yes. Yes, that's correct. It was a typographic error where I referred to Schedule D and it should have been E.

MS. MacLAURIN: And is the opinion contained in your report at M-29 consistent with the opinions contained in your recommendation reports to Council?

MR. DICKEY: Sorry; which exhibit?

MS. MacLAURIN: My question was is the opinion contained in your report here in Exhibit M-9 that you filed in relation to this appeal, this report, are the opinions in this report consistent with the opinions contained in your recommendation reports to Council?

MR. DICKEY: Yes, they are.

THE CHAIR: Sorry; just to confirm for the record; did I hear you say Exhibit 9 or Exhibit 29?

MS. MacLAURIN: Exhibit M-29.

THE CHAIR: Yes, thank you.

MS. MacLAURIN: And, Mr. Dickey, what is your professional opinion with respect to the decisions of Council to approve a Development Agreement for each of the properties in question?

MR. DICKEY: It's my opinion as a professional Planner that Council gave due consideration to all relevant policies; and in approving each application made a decision that is reasonably consistent with the intent of the MPS.

MS. MacLAURIN: Mr. Dickey, what planning documents did you deem to be applicable to the two Development Agreement applications?

MR. DICKEY: The Halifax Municipal Planning Strategy is one, contained within that is the Peninsula North Secondary Planning Strategy. And there's also somewhat related the Regional Municipal Planning Strategy which has already been discussed.

MS. MacLAURIN: And, I'm sorry, did you mention the Land Use By-law as well?

MR. DICKEY: I'm sorry, I did not. The Halifax Land Use By-law for the—for peninsula Halifax.

MS. MacLAURIN: I wasn't sure if you missed mentioning it or I missed listening.

MR. DICKEY: Sorry.

MS. MacLAURIN: And are the properties located within a particular area within the Peninsula North Secondary Planning Strategy?

MR. DICKEY: Yes, they're within the final area, Area 8 of the Secondary Planning Area.

MS. MacLAURIN: What zoning applies to the two properties?

MR. DICKEY: Each property is designated major commercial under the MPS, and falling out of that through the Land Use By-law the C-2, general business zone, is applied to each property.

MS. MacLAURIN: And what uses are permitted within a C-2 zone?

MR. DICKEY: A C-2 zone is perhaps the broadest and most permissive zone in Halifax in that it permits low-density residential, medium density, and high-density residential uses. As-of-right, it also permits a very wide range of commercial uses ranging from a very—well, home occupations but minor commercial uses that might serve a very small area up to very large regional facilities that just might not serve surrounding neighbourhoods but the entire city or municipality.

2) Challenge to Objectivity

This is an extract from the cross-examination of a witness put forward as an expert in heritage matters during a hearing before a provincial land-use appellate body. The cross-examination is by Mr David Farrar of Dr Philip Pacey in the *Re Heritage Trust of Nova Scotia* case.[140] The issue was a proposal for two twenty-six storey buildings in the central business district of Halifax. Important in the case was the interpretation of OP (MPS) policies relating to the preservation of views from Citadel Hill to the harbour.

CROSS-EXAMINATION BY MR. FARRAR

Q. Dr. Pacey, when you started off your testimony, you indicated that one of the things that your group does is advocate on behalf of heritage properties, is that correct?
A. That is correct.
Q. And that is, in fact, what you are doing here today.
A. No, that is not what I'm doing here today. I spoke for the first few minutes as the President of the Heritage Trust which is one

140 *Re Heritage Trust of Nova Scotia*, 2007 NSUARB 122 [*United Gulf*].

of the appellants in this case, but I'm here today to give expert opinion evidence, and if that evidence happens to conflict with the objectives of the Heritage Trust, then I will give that opinion honestly and forthrightly.
Q. I see. So that in preparation for giving your evidence here today you've looked through all of the photographs that have been put before the—put in evidence here.
A. I can't be sure of that. I believe that a number of the photographs submitted by your client were not in readily visible format. In other words, they were on a CD and I can't be sure whether I've seen all of those or not.
Q. Okay. And you had an opportunity, certainly, to go throughout the area and take whatever photographs you needed in order for you to come here to give your expert opinion.
A. Yes.
Q. Yes. And that in doing that you could have taken photographs of heritage properties that were up against or adjacent to modern buildings, could you not?
A. I could have taken photographs of heritage properties that were up against modern buildings. I could have done so.
Q. Yes. You did not do so, sir.
A. I did not do so.
Q. No. And all of the photographs which you took, sir, of the heritage properties were taken from an angle where it would not show a modern building behind it.
A. That was certainly not done deliberately.
Q. Well, the St. Paul's Church, for example, the photograph you took of that, on three sides of that church there are modern buildings that would be shown from other photographic angles, would it not?
A. I would have—I guess the photograph is here and we could look at it. Well, as you can see, there is one modern building certainly showing in that, and that would be the Maritime Centre.
Q. Right.
A. You can see the Joseph Howe Building and you can see the Centennial Building . . . .

. . .

Q. Right. And when you're presenting images and photographs to this panel, you know that they are open to the public and the public may see them.
A. That is correct.
Q. And that in doing so you have to be accurate in the depictions that you have in those photographs.

A. That is correct. Yes.
Q. And you would not want to obscure some portion of the photograph in order to give an impression that this building may have an appearance different than what it actually does. You would not want to do that, would you, sir?
A. No.
Q. No. Because that could be misleading.
A. That is correct.
Q. Let's go to the photographs that are at—it's in H-3, I believe, and it's Tab No. 9—I'm sorry, Tab No. 8. And the pages are not numbered at Tab No. 8 but it's near the back of Tab No. 8 about three pages of photographs in. It is the one where you've cut and pasted the view, the side view of this building going down Sackville Street. Do you have that?
A. Yes, I do.
Q. And you gave evidence with respect to this photograph yesterday.
A. That is correct.
Q. And that was prepared by you after a lot of effort, I take it.
A. That is correct.
Q. And that photograph is not an accurate depiction of what is located at that site, is it?
A. This photograph was taken by me and I have not subtracted anything from the photographic portion of the picture. The image of the building is taken by xerography from the staff report.
Q. Right.
A. So if—this does not show the site as it looks at the moment, this shows the site as best I could with the building, the proposed building, superimposed.
Q. You did this to show the scale of the building as compared to buildings next to it, did you not, sir?
A. That is correct. To show the scale of the building as compared to the Zellers building in particular.
Q. And I take it that when you were doing that, because you were coming here to give expert unbiased evidence, that you wanted it to be as accurate as possible.
A. Yes, I did.
Q. So you would take it from an angle which would give you the most accurate depiction of the scale of this building compared to the buildings around it.
A. That is correct, particularly the Zellers building which could be used.

THE CHAIR

Mr. Farrar, would you like this marked as an exhibit?

MR. FARRAR

Yes, please.

THE CHAIR

It will be H-25.

EXHIBIT NO. H-25 (ENTERED)—GROUP OF 3 PHOTOS MARKED A, B AND C, SHOWING DOWNTOWN HALIFAX

BY MR. FARRAR

Q. You have a photograph that's been marked as H-25, Dr. Pacey?

A. If it is the top photograph that you've just passed me, that would be—

Q. Yes. And that's taken from a similar location as your photograph was taken.

A. This is taken from farther up the street. It appears to be about at the corner of Sackville and Argyle.

Q. And would you agree with me that this is a more accurate depiction than what your photograph shows?

A. No, I would not. I have no idea whether it is more accurate or less accurate. I would have to get a ruler and do some measurements to be able to determine that. If you want me to comment on the difference between the two photographs, I can do so. My photo—would you like me to do so?

Q. No, the beauty of this system is I get to ask the questions, Dr. Pacey.

A. Okay.

Q. Your photograph has cut off the top of the Canada Trust Building has it not?

A. My photograph does not cut that off. My photograph was taken with a camera held horizontally.

Q. Right.

A. The photograph which you have showed was taken with a camera held vertically, and it would appear also with a camera with a wider-angle lens than my camera, because you can see that even the width of my camera does not take in the Tramway Building or as much of the building with the Tim Hortons in it as your photograph.

Q. Yes.

A. So your photograph has been taken possibly with a digital camera, I don't know, or else with a wide-angle lens on a regular camera.

My photograph was taken with a regular camera, held horizontally, and nothing was subtracted from this photograph . . . .

Q. So I take it, doctor, that you did not feel it necessary to include the complete height of the building, the Canada Trust Building, in order to show the scale of this building compared to the other buildings.

A. I did not feel it necessary, and it wouldn't have been possible for me with the camera that I had.

Q. I take it, Dr. Pacey, that you could have access to whatever camera you needed to have in order to accurately put forward your evidence in this proceeding, could you not?

A. Yes, I could, and I have put forward my evidence accurately.

3) Cross-Examination — Preliminary

This is an extract from the cross-examination of the municipality's planner, Mr Paul Sampson, by Mr Ronald Pink, the lawyer representing the appellants at a hearing before the NSUARB. The case, *United Gulf*,[141] is the same as in the second example regarding objectivity of an expert witness. The extract is of the first questions asked, focused on a planner's ethical obligations, setting the stage for more detailed questions on the content of staff reports; it also sets a tone for the lawyer to be the dominant presence in the exchange.

THE CHAIR

Mr. Pink

MR. PINK

Yes, I'll have a few questions.

CROSS EXAMINATION BY MR. PINK

Q. Mr. Sampson, in preparation for this cross-examination it would be handy if you had available to you to begin with a copy of your staff reports, okay? If you'd keep them handy there, please, sir.

A. Okay.

Q. Mr. Sampson, let's begin, if we can, by talking about the role of the planner, and I understand in Nova Scotia there is a new Professional Planners Act. Are you familiar with that?

141 *Ibid.*

A. I don't believe it's actually in place at the moment. I could be wrong but—
Q. Yeah, I think it was in place just this past summer.
A. Okay.
Q. But you're familiar with the Act itself.
A. Yes.
Q. And would you agree with me that the role of the planner is to be neutral with respect to development proposals?
A. Yes.
Q. To be independent?
A. Yes.
Q. To be fully transparent to all interested parties?
A. Yes.
Q. And would you agree with me that the planner has a duty not only to his or her employer, i.e. HRM, but also to the public who come to rely upon your views and opinions?
A. Yes.
Q. Thank you. And, sir, I understand that you're a provisional member of the Canadian Institute of Planners.
A. That's correct.
Q. And that means that you, like Mr. Bray, have applied for and are being, I guess it is, reviewed over a period of time for membership, full membership?
A. Not necessarily, no.
Q. I thought you had to submit—had to—after you applied for membership, got a provisional membership, then there were some things you had to submit for a full membership. Is that—did I understand that incorrectly?
A. To obtain full membership, yes, there are some things that you have to submit, a logbook—
Q. Yes.
A. —and in my case, where I have a fair bit of work experience—
Q. Yes, indeed.
A. —and a degree in planning that—there will be a requirement for an oral interview.
Q. Okay. And you applied for membership when, sir?
A. I believe I have received provisional membership when I—while I was working with HRM and a student in the Dal planning program, so it was probably—provisional membership was probably in the mid–late '90s, mid to late '90s.
Q. Okay, and you have not completed it to this date?
A. No, I haven't.

Q. No. And are you familiar that the Canadian Institute of Planners has a statement of values and code of professional practices?
A. Yes.
Q. Yes. Let me show it to you, if I can, please.

THE CHAIR

Would you like this marked as an exhibit, Mr. Pink?

MR. PINK

Please, Mr. Chairmen

THE CHAIR

This will be H-33

MR. PINK

Thank you.

EXHIBIT NO. H-33 (ENTERED)—EXCERPT FROM CANADIAN INSTITUTE OF PLANNERS WEBSITE (6 PAGES), DATED FEBRUARY 10, 2007.

BY MR. PINK

Q. And I took this off the website, Mr. Sampson, and I presume that you've seen this before in your travels?
A. Yes.
Q. Yes. And just as you have said, in the second paragraph in the preamble it says:

> "Planners work for the public good, taking health, aesthetics, equity and efficiency into consideration. Planning respects the land as a community resource, contributing to the conservation of natural and cultural heritage and promoting healthy communities and improving the quality of life."

Right?
A. Correct.
Q. And then it goes on to talk about a statement of values, the first one:

> "To respect and integrate the needs of future generations. CIP members recognize that their work has cumulative and long-term implications."

Right?
A. Yes.

Q. And then in No. 3:

> "To value the natural and cultural environment. CIP members believes that both the natural and cultural environments must be valued. They assume roles as stewards of these environments balancing preservation with sustainable development."

Do you see that?

A. Yes.

Q. Yes. And No. 5:

> "To respect diversity. CIP members respect and protect diversity in values, cultures, economies, ecosystems, built environments and distinct places."

Right?

A. Correct.

Q. And then look at 7:

> "To foster public participation. CIP members believe in meaningful public participation by all individuals and groups and seek to articulate the needs of those whose interests have not been represented."

Right? So that's all part of the overall values of the Institute, right?

A. Right. Correct.

Q. And look at the primary responsibility of planners.
No. 1 below "Code of Practice":

> "The planner is responsible for the public interest. Members have a primary responsibility to define and serve the interests of the public. This requires the use of theories and techniques of planning that inform and structure debate, facilitate communication and foster understanding."

And then it goes on to talk about:

> "Accordingly, members shall practice in a manner that respects the diversity, needs, values and aspirations of the public and encourage discussion of these matters."

Right?

A. Um-hmm.

Q. That's one of your objectives, is to have a full discussion and debate on all planning issues, right?

A. That's correct.

Q. And that's why you have to be fully transparent and bring all issues to the table, right?
A. Sure.
Q. Right.

> "... to provide full, clear and accurate information on planning matters to decision-makers and members of the public while recognizing both their client's right to confidentiality and the importance of timely recommendations."

Well, in this sense you're in a little different position because your client—you don't represent a client per se, except for the HRM who is your employer, but your principal obligation is to the decision-makers and members of the public, right?
A. That's correct, yes.
Q. Right. And then:

> "... acknowledge the interrelated nature of planning decisions and their consequences for individuals, the natural and built environment and the broader public interest."

And you've seen that before?
A. Yes, I have.
Q. So, your role as a planner is to keep pretty much an open mind on lots of different issues for the natural and built environment as well as the broader public interest?
A. Yes.
Q. Right. And then:

> "... identify and promote opportunities for meaningful participation in the planning process."

Now, sir, would you agree with me that in your study of the MPS that you came to recognize that the MPS was a document which was prepared by the citizens of Halifax with the assistance of planning staff to guide future generations—future Councils with respect to development in the City?
A. Yes, I agree.
Q. And in that respect the public has a very great interest in the role and operation of the MPS?
A. Certainly.
Q. And that the MPS is a guiding document with respect to planning matters?
A. Yes.

Q. And that it's your duty, with respect, to uphold and defend the principles of the MPS?
A. Yes, that's correct.
Q. And it's your duty to report honestly and openly with respect to the operations of the MPS?
A. Certainly, yes.
Q. And it's your duty to be complete in your analysis?
A. Um-hmm.
Q. Right?
A. Yes.
Q. To be thorough?
A. Yes.
Q. To be exact?
A. When you can be exact, yes.
Q. When you can be, yes, indeed. And certainly not to mislead.
A. That's correct.
Q. Right. Now, sir, with respect to your staff report . . . .

CHAPTER 2

SOME LEADING CASES

All of the cases discussed in this chapter are decisions of the Supreme Court of Canada, save for the 1926 decision of the Judicial Committee of the Privy Council in the Ontario *Toronto Roman Catholic Separate Schools v Toronto (City)* case;[1] at the time such further appeals were possible. Thus the decisions are authoritative and the recent ones are frequently cited. In some instances, the cases have been superseded by statute or subsequent decisions, but they remain part of the fabric of LUP law. Together they offer a good introduction to some recurring themes and problems in LUP law. Most of the issues that were litigated in these cases are further considered in subsequent chapters. Notes below each case identify the main points emerging from the case or indicate controversies.

Not all of the Supreme Court of Canada decisions on LUP matters are summarized here. Even important cases such as *Old St Boniface Residents Association Inc v Winnipeg (City)*[2] (the meaning of bias in local government), *Nanaimo (City) v Rascal Trucking Ltd*[3] (the standard of judicial review for municipal decisions), and *British Columbia (Attorney General) v Lafarge Canada Inc*[4] (division of powers under the *Constitution Act*) are dealt with in other chapters. The reason for the placement is one of relative focus on land use. The cases placed elsewhere tend

1 [1924] SCR 368, rev'd [1926] AC 81 (JCPC).

2 [1990] 3 SCR 1170.

3 2000 SCC 13.

4 2007 SCC 23.

to be those where the legal aspects are more related to constitutional law, administrative law, or some other topic, and although the consequences for questions of how to process land-use matters are quite important, they are not so directly related to the main lines of legal thought about LUP law.

Several important themes are illustrated by the cases in this chapter, including:

- how to interpret statutes that grant powers to municipalities;
- whether compensation is or ought to be payable for restrictions on land use;
- the environmental regulatory powers of the three levels of government;
- remedies in instances of by-law breaches, including the standing of citizens to seek remedies; and
- judicial review of municipal dealings with land-use matters, including "reasonableness/discrimination" issues and the duty of fairness.

The cases follow chronological order.

MacIlreith v Hart Estate[5]

In *MacIlreith v Hart Estate*, the mayor of Halifax had attended a national meeting of mayors and councillors held by the predecessor organization of what is now the Federation of Canadian Municipalities (FCM). He was reimbursed expenses by the municipality. The lawsuit, brought by a taxpayer, sought recovery of the amount paid to the mayor on the basis that the incorporating statute made no provision for such payments. The taxpayer was successful. The Court held that the municipality was a "trustee" of taxes paid, and thus an individual taxpayer should have standing. In addition, the Court applied Dillon's Rule to reading the *Municipal Act*. A well-established principle of interpretation of municipal statutes, Dillon's Rule states that municipalities, as is the case with corporations, possess only those powers expressly conferred by statute, those powers necessarily or fairly implied by the express powers conferred by statute, and those powers essential to and not merely convenient for effecting the purposes of the municipality.

NOTES

1) Two points flow from this case. One is the precedent for recognition of standing for a ratepayer to challenge an expenditure. The other is its influence in the style of drafting of statutes granting powers to local governments. That is, there is a tendency to list powers in detail,

---

5 (1908), 39 SCR 657 [*MacIlreith*].

although this has been abandoned in some provinces, and the Supreme Court of Canada has recognized as valid the wide ambit of listed general categories of powers intended by those legislatures to be exercised by local governments.[6]

2) To this day, Nova Scotia's *Municipal Government Act* includes in its list of authorized spending powers that it is allowable to pay "the reasonable expenses incurred by the mayor or warden or a councillor for attendance at meetings and conferences . . . ."[7]
3) Dillon's Rule, while not entirely seen as a "rule," has not been abandoned either, though there is now a more marked tendency for courts to approach municipal statutes as they would any other statute, and follow the usual admonition of a province's *Interpretation Act* to give a "fair, large, and liberal" reading of what the legislature intended as its objects. This is in line with what is known as "the modern principle" of statute interpretation: "the words of a legislative text must be read in their ordinary sense *harmoniously* with the scheme and objects of the Act and the intention of the legislature" and also the words are "to be read in their *entire* context in *every* case, not just in cases where the words seem ambiguous."[8]
4) Municipal by-laws are also to be read according to the same rules of interpretation as apply to statutes.[9]
5) Notable cases applying the Dillon's Rule approach are *R v Greenbaum*,[10] *Sun Oil Co v Verdun (City)*,[11] *British Columbia v Pride Cleaners & Dyers Ltd*,[12] and *Ottawa Electric Light Co v Ottawa (City)*.[13]
6) *MacIlreith* was approved by the Supreme Court of Canada in the 1975 case of *Thorson v Canada (Attorney General)*,[14] which canvassed principles regarding the discretionary granting of standing. Standing remains a complex problem in land-use matters. *MacIlreith* establishes the right of a ratepayer to challenge illegal expenditures, but issues remain as to who is entitled to notice of pending decisions, who may make formal appeals, who may challenge the legality of decisions, and who may enforce rules.

---

6 See *United Taxi Drivers' Fellowship of Southern Alberta v Calgary (City)*, 2004 SCC 19.

7 *Municipal Government Act*, SNS 1998, c 18, s 65(s).

8 Ruth Sullivan, *Driedger and Sullivan on the Construction of Statutes*, 4th ed (Markham, ON: Butterworths, 2002) at 10 [emphasis in original].

9 See *Rexlington Heights Ltd v Ontario* (2005), 15 MPLR (4th) 117 (Ont SCJ).

10 [1993] 1 SCR 674.

11 [1952] 1 SCR 222.

12 (1964), 49 DLR (2d) 752 (BCSC).

13 (1906), 12 OLR 290 (CA).

14 (1975), 43 DLR (3d) 1 (SCC).

Montreal (City) v Morgan[15]

The respondent had constructed a public garage on a street (rue Jeanne-Mance) in violation of a city by-law that had declared: "the following streets are reserved exclusively for residential purposes . . . ." and then listed them. The city sought an order to have the building demolished or brought into compliance with the by-law. The owner raised three issues: (1) whether the *Montreal City Charter* authorized the by-law; (2) whether the by-law was sufficiently clear, precise, and definite; and (3) what consequences flow from any breach of the by-law. The *Charter* authorized the city "to regulate the kind of buildings [le genre des constructions] that may be erected on certain streets . . . ." The Court held that the section authorized regulation of "classes of buildings," which it understood to refer to type of uses. It cited "residential," "business," and "industrial" as examples of kinds of uses that could be regulated. Whether the garage was commercial or industrial, it was not residential. It rejected the contention that what was authorized was for the city to regulate construction materials, standards, and aesthetics only. It rejected the contention that power to "regulate" cannot in effect amount to a power to "prohibit" (but see Note 1 below). It also said that even though the by-law was not completely clear and thus required some construction, it was not characterized by such vagueness as to render it invalid. On the matter of enforcement, it rejected the contention that since a fine had been prescribed as a penalty for violation of the by-law, the city was limited to that remedy and could not seek demolition. The Court said, "But a person prepared to do so [i.e., pay a fine] cannot thus purchase the right to disobey the law."[16] The Court cited a provision in the Quebec *Code Civil* authorizing demolition or undoing of anything done in breach of an obligation.

NOTES

1) The 1896 case of *Toronto (City) v Virgo*[17] had established that a zoning power to "regulate" does not extend to a power to "prohibit" unless so defined in the governing statute. This remains good law. *Morgan* does not dispute that point, but does say that the principle applies at the regulation-making stage, not at the point of enforcement: thus

---

15 (1920), 60 SCR 393 [*Morgan*]. *Morgan* is an early example of a case from Quebec that involves its system of civil law. The *Code Civil* principles do not differ significantly from those of the common law as it prevails in the other provinces. Still, there are differences, and anticipating how cases from Quebec might apply elsewhere, and vice versa, sometimes requires care.

16 *Ibid* at 406.

17 [1896] AC 88 (JCPC).

a power to restrain what is not authorized may in effect prohibit a particular use.

2) One judge said that in a residential area both churches and schools would be allowable. Other judges found it unnecessary to pronounce on the point. Certainly, the governing zoning did not specify churches and schools as allowable uses in a residential area, though probably "acquired rights," that is, a legal pre-existing use, would protect any established churches and schools. *Morgan* was decided decades prior to the *Charter*-protected right of freedom of religion; how that right interacts with land-use regulation is an evolving question: see Chapter 4.
3) This is an early example of a court ordering demolition of a building that was built in violation of municipal rules. It is usual to allow some opportunity for the owner to bring its building into conformity with the rules rather than moving immediately to the remedy of demolition.
4) The Court considered the omnibus powers section of the *Montreal Charter* but noted that given the existence of a specific power of regulation, the general power to pass by-laws for the good government of the city could not be invoked. This point resurfaces in *114957 Canada Ltée (Spraytech, Société d'arrosage) v Hudson (Town)*,[18] discussed below in this chapter.
5) *Morgan* is most often cited as authority for the proposition that by-laws are not necessarily invalid if their terms call for construction, and also for its approval of the general principles of scrutiny of municipal by-laws on the basis of reasonableness set out in the 1898 United Kingdom case of *Kruse v Johnson*,[19] principles of judicial review that seem to remain in full vigour despite extensive evolution of the language of administrative law in Canada: see Chapter 9, Section C(2)(a).

Toronto Roman Catholic Separate Schools v Toronto (City)[20]

The Roman Catholic Separate School Board had purchased lots on a residential street to build a school. It had submitted its construction plans to city staff for review. Before a building permit was issued, neighbours raised objections, and the city considered adopting a zoning by-law that would have limited uses to residential. City staff were instructed not to issue a building permit pending consideration of the new by-law, which was subsequently adopted. The School Board sued for issuance

18 2001 SCC 40 [*Spraytech*].
19 [1898] 2 QB 91.
20 Above note 1.

of the building permit. The Court ordered the permit to be issued: "The right of the owner of land . . . to make use of it, subject to the existing by-laws, in the erection of such buildings upon it as he thinks proper to erect, is preserved inviolate down to the time when the restrictive by-law is actually passed . . . . That right . . . includes the right to receive the necessary permit for the erection of a building proposed to be erected in conformity with the law in force for the time being."[21]

NOTES

1) This decision was reversed by the Judicial Committee of the Privy Council upon further appeal. The Privy Council stated: "The whole purpose of [the statute granting authority to zone] is to empower the city authority, acting in good faith, to put restrictions upon that right [to a permit] with a view to the protection of neighbouring owners . . . and the . . . proprietary right . . . is limited by the powers of the city to be exercised for the protection of his neighbours . . . ."[22]
2) The core issue of whether a municipality can defeat an owner's access to a building permit when it becomes aware of a proposed use that it has reason to doubt the wisdom of, remains a serious matter. Here there was no protected non-conforming use that might have been expanded: the proposal was for construction of a new building, hence it was crucial for the owner to obtain a permit in order to crystallize its rights.
3) Such cases are relatively common. For example, in *Dalhousie University v Halifax (City)*,[23] the university secured a court order for issuance of a building permit to construct a sports complex even though its paperwork was incomplete. Neighbours objected to the proposed use of the land, and the city council was in the process of considering a change in the by-law. In *Al-Musawi c Westmount (Ville de)*,[24] the plans submitted in support of an application for a building permit were found not to be substantially complete and thus the owner was not entitled to a permit.
4) The circumstances might have allowed for allegations of bad faith, but the case did not proceed on that basis.
5) Statutes now generally specify routes for a municipality to delay issuance of a building permit in these circumstances. Thus, Ontario's *Planning Act*[25] allows for establishing an interim control by-law to

---

21 *Ibid* at 374 (SCC).
22 Above note 1 at 86 (JCPC).
23 (1974), 9 NSR (2d) 643 (SCAD).
24 2012 QCCS 606.
25 *Planning Act*, RSO 1990, c P.13, s 38.

allow for study of appropriate land-use policies, and to do so quickly without public notice in advance.

6) The Supreme Court of Canada offered a suggestion:

> The appellants having succeeded in establishing their legal rights, we cannot refrain from expressing a hope that even now with the co-operation so far as necessary or useful of all parties concerned, it may be possible to make other arrangements which will relieve the residents of the street of the very grave detriment and hardship arising from the presence of the school . . . .[26]

The Court does not specify exactly what "grave detriment and hardship" arises from the presence of a school in a predominantly residential street. Probably it had in mind noise and/or traffic. This opinion of the Court is similar to the views of the US Supreme Court in *Village of Euclid v Ambler Realty Co*,[27] where it noted, commenting on apartment houses in residential areas: "the privilege of quiet and open spaces . . . enjoyed by those in more favored localities"[28] being taken advantage of by new construction of a different type.

Orpen v Roberts[29]

City of Toronto by-laws prohibited erecting buildings any closer to the street than 25 feet, on the north side of Carlton Street between Sherbourne Street and Homewood Avenue. Despite this setback requirement, a building permit was issued to allow construction of an apartment building to be located in part on that setback strip. Orpen, the owner of a nearby home, objected and sought an injunction both to restrain issuance of the building permit and the construction itself. Orpen's lawsuit was unsuccessful. The Court assumed that the by-law had been breached and also that the homeowner was "prejudicially affect[ed] . . . in respect of the amenities and the value of her property."[30] The question became whether the by-law could in effect be enforced by a member of the public. The Court asked whether the by-law was "passed for the benefit of the person asserting the right to reparation or other relief" or "whether the remedies provided by the statute are intended to be the sole remedies available by way of guarantees to the public for the observance of the statutory duty."[31] The Court noted that

26 Above note 1 at 375 (SCC).
27 272 US 365 (1926).
28 *Ibid* at 394.
29 [1925] SCR 364 [*Orpen*].
30 *Ibid* at 369.
31 *Ibid* at 370.

the *Municipal Act* in its "Penalties and Enforcement of By-laws" sections had been amended between 1904 and 1913, so the provision that either the municipal corporation or any ratepayer could bring an action now omitted the reference to ratepayers. The Court concluded that the legislature had intended "that in respect of such contraventions there could be no remedy except such as is given or authorized by the Act."[32] Apart from the history of the statute, the Court on general principles appeared to favour limiting the opportunity for members of the public to take legal action to enforce by-laws. "In effect, if this contention be sound, such a by-law creates in favour of any proprietor who may be prejudicially affected in his property by an infringement of any of the prohibitions of such a by-law, a negative easement (enforceable in the same manner as a restrictive covenant) over the property within the area where the by-law operates."[33]

NOTES

1) Ontario has amended its *Municipal Act* so as to allow a taxpayer to take action to restrain a violation of a by-law. This is not the case in all provinces. *Orpen*'s limitation on the standing of a member of the public to take legal action to enforce a by-law remains good law, but has to be understood to have a modern context as to discretion to grant standing. Contemporary cases that follow *Orpen* include *Scholton v Chemainus Health Care Centre*[34] and *Caldwell v Saskatoon (City)*.[35]
2) The rationale in *Orpen*, as in the precedent it cites, *Tompkins v Brockville Rink Co*,[36] where rules against wood construction contained in "a fire limits by-law" were not seen as being for the benefit of neighbours, is not entirely convincing. It is quite easy to see such by-laws as having been "passed for the benefit of the person asserting the right to reparation or other relief."
3) If the action complained of amounts to a nuisance, a plaintiff may seek to enforce the by-law: *Gosse v Farkvam*[37] and *Palmer v Burnaby (City)*.[38]
4) In some circumstances, by-laws may be understood to create an actionable statutory duty, though more usually their function in

32 *Ibid* at 373.
33 *Ibid* at 370.
34 1995 CanLII 319 (BCSC).
35 1969 CanLII 557 (Sask QB).
36 (1899), 31 OR 124 (HCJ).
37 2008 BCCA 210.
38 2006 BCSC 165.

a tort action will be to crystallize a standard of care or to assist in recognizing a new common law duty of care: *Johnston v Canada (Attorney General)*.[39]

5) There may be a duty on the part of a municipality to enforce its by-laws, though for the most part enforcement is discretionary and an order of mandamus will not issue. Nonetheless, non-enforcement, including issuance of permits that allow construction not in conformity with the law, will always raise the question of why the rules are not being enforced, especially where complaints have been made. This is bound to lead to suspicions of corruption or at least of some special relationship or unexplained arbitrariness. This undermines democratic institutions.
6) Standing to enforce a by-law is not the same as "public-interest standing" as first articulated by the Supreme Court in the trilogy of cases *Thorson v Canada (Attorney General)*,[40] *Nova Scotia (Board of Censors) v McNeil*,[41] and *Canada (Minister of Justice) v Borowski*,[42] where it recognized a discretion to allow standing in instances of alleged excess of jurisdiction.
7) At the same time, many courts do approach standing as a matter of discretion, with analysis based on principles similar to those for public interest standing: Is the matter justiciable? Is there a serious issue to be raised as to the validity of the legislation or the administrative acts? Is the applicant directly affected or does the applicant have a genuine interest? Is there another reasonable and effective way to bring the issue before the courts? See *Dartmouth (City) v Mountain Ash Court Property Owners Association*.[43]
8) The plaintiff, Isabella Orpen, was the spouse of Abraham Orpen (1854–1937), a well-known and wealthy member of the Toronto criminal class, a saloon owner, and a bookmaker.[44] There is no reason to see the Court's decision as affected by this.

Kuchma v Taché (Rural Municipality)[45]

The municipality's by-law closed a part of a road allowance. The plaintiff sought to quash the by-law, alleging various aspects of illegality.

---

39 (1981), 128 DLR (3d) 459 (Ont HCJ).
40 [1975] 1 SCR 138.
41 [1976] 2 SCR 265.
42 [1981] 2 SCR 575.
43 1994 CanLII 3996 (NSCA).
44 Suzanne Morton, *At Odds: Gambling and Canadians 1919–1969* (Toronto: U of T Press, 2003).
45 [1945] SCR 234 [*Kuchma*].

The Court stated as a test of by-laws that they are nullities if they have "not been passed . . . in good faith and in the public interest."[46] The onus of demonstrating bad faith and the absence of public interest is on the plaintiff. Here, the road allowance was not generally maintained by the municipality, it served some farms but there were other roads available to those farms, and some portions of the road had been taken over by some farms for their private use. There had long been disputes before the municipal council as to whether the road should be closed or kept open. "The parties affected had taken sides . . . . Any compromise or adjustment suggested by the council had proved to be of no avail, and therefore the council quite properly concluded that in the public interest it should now determine the question. In so doing, it has effected a compromise; it retained Mr. Kuchma's way of ingress and egress to the west and closed the one and a half mile to the east."[47]

NOTES

1) The *Municipal Act* provided that an application to quash a by-law shall not be entertained "unless it is made within one year from the passing of the by-law." The action had been commenced out of time, but the Court took the position that the time limit only applied in instances where the enactments "are made within the limits of its jurisdiction, in good faith and in the public interest . . . . A by-law which has not been passed by a municipal corporation in good faith and in the public interest, when passed is a nullity, and cannot be changed or made otherwise by lapse of time, approval, registration or promulgation."[48]
2) The Court said: "Upon the question of public interest, courts have recognized that the municipal council, familiar with local conditions, is in the best position of all parties to determine what is or is not in the public interest and have refused to interfere with its decision unless good and sufficient reason be established."[49] The Court linked this point with a council acting in bad faith and through fraud and partiality, that is, in haste or without affording a fair hearing.
3) A contemporary court might use the language of deference to the municipal council, but *Kuchma* appears to remain a good guide for how to test the validity of a by-law in similar circumstances. It is routinely cited in contemporary cases.

---

46 *Ibid* at 239.
47 *Ibid* at 242–43.
48 *Ibid* at 235.
49 *Ibid* at 243.

Central Jewish Institute v Toronto (City)[50]

The Institute proposed to purchase a building that was in use as a residence and rooming house, with the intention of turning it into a school. There were no zoning restrictions in place. Neighbours became aware of the intention and persuaded the city to adopt zoning that limited the area to single-family residential uses. The Institute, in anticipation of a possible change in the zoning, started to use a portion of the building as a summer school; the rest of the building remained occupied by the tenants while a sale was pending. At issue was whether a non-conforming use (NCU) had been established at the time of the adoption of zoning and whether the NCU may be expanded throughout the building. The Court said,

> The extent of the user of premises as a school would vary from time to time and in the months of July and August it is well-known that the pupils in the ordinary classes are on vacation. It is true that the appellant had not conducted a summer school [at its previous location] but there was nothing to prevent it commencing such a school as part of its curriculum. According to the evidence, a nursery school is part of the course provided by the appellant, and the mere fact that no grade classes were held [at the new location] prior to the date of the passing of the by-law does not prevent [a non-conforming use]. It is not necessary that the entire premises, that is every room in the building, be used. While a *bona fide* intention to use is not sufficient . . . it is an important element in considering the evidence as to actual user. There is no doubt, in the present case, as to the purpose of the appellant in purchasing the premises . . . .[51]

One of the other judges said,

> It will be seen that the [statutory] exemption is not to the existing use but to the building; and there is no implication that it is the whole of the building that must be so used or that the use must be the sole use. The language would be satisfied by a partial use as if, for instance, an owner was carrying on a grocery store on the ground floor . . . . If that same business were extended to the upper storey, could it be said that the exemption did not continue or was lost?[52]

---

50 [1948] SCR 101 [*Central Jewish Institute*].

51 *Ibid* at 105, Kerwin J.

52 *Ibid* at 109, Rand J.

NOTES

1) Until the 2001 decision of the Supreme Court in *Saint-Romuald (City) v Olivier*,[53] discussed in Chapter 7, Section B, which established a new framework for analysis of the topic, *Central Jewish Institute* was the leading case regarding non-conforming uses or as termed in Quebec, "acquired rights."
2) The particular problem that was the focus of *Central Jewish Institute*, whether an NCU may be expanded within the building, is now often addressed by local by-laws authorized by provincial legislation. It is also possible to view this point as one of defining the extent of the NCU in the first place, rather than as one of expansion of a use.

Verdun (City) v Sun Oil Co[54]

At issue in this case was the location of a gas station. The company met the specified requirements of the by-law. Nonetheless, the council refused a permit to build, apparently motivated by the presence nearby of three other gas stations. The municipality had been conferred authority to regulate zoning ("the location . . . of industrial and commercial establishments . . . to divide the municipality into districts or zones . . ."). However, the by-laws adopted in effect treated the power conferred on it by legislation to regulate land usage as a discretionary process for the council. This was not the power conferred by the legislature.

NOTES

1) Attempts at converting a power to regulate into a discretionary power are not uncommon. The Toronto case of *Canadian Institute of Public Real Estate Cos v Toronto (City)*,[55] discussed in Chapter 6, Section H(2), is virtually identical to *Sun Oil*. When the legislature grants a local government a power to adopt regulatory rules, such as zoning, a council may not treat this as a power to consider instances individually and as a matter of discretion.
2) The Court was very clear: "[The by-law] effectively transforms an authority to regulate by legislation into a mere administrative and discretionary power to cancel by resolution a right which, untrammeled in the absence of any by-law, could only . . . be regulated. This is not what [the *Cities and Towns Act*] authorizes."[56]

---

53 2001 SCC 57.

54 [1952] 1 SCR 222 [*Sun Oil*].

55 (1979), 25 NR 108 (SCC). See also *MacArthur v Charlottetown (City)*, 2005 PESCTD 37.

56 Above note 54 at 229.

Saumur v Québec (City)[57]

The city adopted a by-law that prohibited the distribution in the streets of pamphlets, books, circulars, or tracts without the permission of the chief of police. Jehovah's Witnesses were engaged in passing out such literature. They challenged the by-law as *ultra vires* and as an interference with freedom of religion. A majority of the Court sided with the objectors, though for different reasons. Four of the majority found the by-law to be *ultra vires* since in its essence it dealt not with regulation of the streets but with the content of the material, a matter for the federal Parliament. One judge saw the by-law as *intra vires* but not applicable to the Jehovah's Witnesses since it interfered with their freedom of religion. Since the adoption of the *Charter of Rights* in 1982, such issues would involve its provisions.[58]

Vic Restaurant Inc v Montréal (City)[59]

The city adopted a licensing by-law applicable to restaurants and bars. A licence was required to allow the conduct of business. A part of the process involved approval from the director of the city police department. The Court set aside the by-law on the basis of unauthorized delegation of powers. That is, the municipal council was the entity vested by statute with the power to issue licences and had not been granted the authority to delegate that function to any other entity, nor had it been granted the authority to delegate the setting of criteria for the issuance of licences. In the absence of such statutory authority, the result could be arbitrary administration of the by-law.

NOTES

1) Improper or unauthorized delegation of a power remains a valid basis for challenge of the legality of a by-law. Examples are *Strathcona (County) v Allan*,[60] *Lamoureux v Beaconsfield (City)*,[61] and *Glenella Mangement v Winnipeg (City)*.[62]
2) Licensing is a form of land-use control, commonly used. It differs from zoning in that zoning focuses on location and licensing focuses on the nature of the business, although some provincial statutes granting licensing powers do include a power over location as an adjunct.

57 [1953] 2 SCR 299.
58 See Chapter 4, Section E.
59 [1959] SCR 58 [*Vic Restaurant*].
60 2006 ABCA 129.
61 (1976), [1978] 1 SCR 134.
62 (1985), 40 Man R (2d) 53 at para 23 (QB).

3) *Vic Restaurant* should be read in conjunction with the 1960 Supreme Court decision in *Toronto (City) v Outdoor Neon Displays Ltd.*[63]

Scarborough (Township) v Bondi[64]

In 1938, the municipality adopted a by-law regulating the street frontage required for the erection of a dwelling in a residential neighbourhood. The requirement was for a minimum of 100 feet. The neighbourhood was one where the average size of lots was 45,000 square feet (i.e., an acre). Subsequently, on three occasions the by-law was amended so as to allow homes to be built on lots having less street frontage than 100 feet but where the overall size of the lots was large. Bondi owned a portion of what had been a triangular lot, fronting on two streets. On one street, the frontage was 221 feet and on the other, 333 feet (36,797 square feet total). Under the 1938 by-law, four dwellings could have been built on the original lot. However, a portion of the lot had been sold and only one dwelling had been constructed on it. Bondi proposed to subdivide the remaining portion of the original lot and construct two dwellings since they would both have road frontages of over 100 feet. In response to neighbours' concerns, the municipality amended the by-law so as to allow only one dwelling on Bondi's lot. Bondi challenged the by-law on the substantive grounds that it was discriminatory (in the municipal, not in the human rights sense), and also on the procedural grounds that Scarborough had not complied with provincial requirements that the permission of the Ontario Municipal Board be secured in advance. The Court rejected the allegation that the by-law was discriminatory, but did strike down the by-law because of the process flaw. The Court said that spot-zoning was not necessarily discriminatory. It saw the by-law as designed to achieve an overall legitimate planning purpose, the preservation of neighbourhood character. It was inherent in the idea of zoning that on one side of an arbitrary line something was allowed that would not be allowed on the other side.

NOTES

1) While planners often profess not to approve of spot-zoning, it is a tool commonly used by municipalities. *Bondi* illustrates that it is very difficult to attack spot zoning on legal grounds, unless bad faith or some other legal flaw can be shown. The main potential basis for challenge of spot zoning is the absence of public purpose, that is, that the zone was changed solely for the benefit of the owner.

---

63 [1960] SCR 307.

64 [1959] SCR 444 [*Bondi*].

In *Bondi*, the Court saw the spot zoning as benefitting the overall neighbourhood.

2) *Bondi* is often cited for its comments on discrimination in establishing zones: "The mere delimitation of the boundaries of the area affected by such a by-law involves an element of discrimination. On one side of an arbitrary line an owner may be prevented from doing something with his property which another owner, on the other side of the line, with a property which corresponds in all respects except location, is free to do."[65] Thus, in the 1985 Supreme Court of Canada decision in *Montréal (City) v Arcade Amusements Inc*,[66] discussed below in this chapter, the Court referred to *Bondi* and said, "The power to discriminate is generally implicit in zoning matters."[67]
3) The issue of discrimination arose because of some earlier jurisprudence regarding a permitting system in Toronto for lumber yards. In *Toronto v Mandelbaum*,[68] instead of zoning land, the by-law required a permit to be issued by the council. In disallowing the system, the Court said that in exercising a power to regulate, a municipality may only pass general regulations and not discriminate by granting permission to one owner but not another. In fact, *Mandelbaum* should have been understood not as being about discrimination but as in line with the principle later enunciated in *Verdun v Sun Oil* and *Canadian Institute of Public Real Estate Companies v Toronto*,[69] in which the Court pointed out that where a municipality is granted a regulatory power, it cannot enact a regulation that repeats the words of the statute and, in effect, turn a regulatory power into an administrative one.
4) The "discrimination" issue raised in *Bondi* focused on discrimination against one landowner, or that owner's property. Discrimination also arises in cases where the issue is that of unauthorized discrimination against a class or group. In *Arcade Amusements*,[70] by-laws made a distinction based on the age of persons so far as access to amusement arcades. The Court regarded this as unauthorized discrimination.[71]
5) It is difficult to agree with the Court that the municipality was not showing bad faith. Most of the indicia were present: a rezoning in

65 *Ibid* at 451.
66 [1985] 1 SCR 368 [*Arcade Amusements*].
67 *Ibid* at para 130.
68 [1932] 3 DLR 604 (Ont HCJ) [*Mandelbaum*].
69 Above note 55.
70 Above note 66.
71 *Ibid* at para 102ff.

reaction to public pressure rather than arising from a planning exercise, a focus on only one property, a dubious planning rationale, speed, unusual procedures.[72]

6) The Court did not think that the planning rationale was dubious. What it said was that the undesirability of a home built on an 11,000-square-foot lot in a neighbourhood of 45,000-square-foot lots "required no further comment." In saying so, the Court was apparently speaking for the principle of maintaining land value, although there was no specific evidence of diminished land value in the neighbourhood if the smaller lot were to be allowed, nor was the municipality's rationale for its by-law articulated. If not land value, the principle may have been uniformity of class, although 11,000-square-foot lots are about two to three times the size of most urban residential lots, and it is not clear that there would be much in the way of class differential in the result. In the United States, numerous cases have attacked lot size rules as exclusionary, though with mixed results. The attacks have been based on allegations of improper motive (acting for private and not the public interest) and unreasonableness, though also in some instances on the basis of racial discrimination.[73]
7) Apparently wanting to suggest awareness of fairness in the situation, the Court said "There was at that time [i.e., when the original by-law was adopted] no indication that [the lot] would be divided into two parcels" and "If the municipality had foreseen this subdivision at the time . . . can it be doubted that it could have provided that the 100 ft. frontage should be taken to refer to the frontage on Hill Crescent and not to . . . Annis Road?" and "It was at that time impossible to foresee how lot 98 with its peculiar shape . . . would eventually be subdivided."[74] But this is highly speculative. Indeed, is there some obligation on a municipality to investigate the impact of zoning decisions on all properties in an affected area? To do so is not difficult, since the municipality possesses ownership information inclusive of lot shapes and sizes.
8) The Court characterized zoning as involving "arbitrary" lines. This is unfortunate wording. Frequently the courts will look for some planning rationale in assessing whether to interfere in land-use decisions. Planning recommendations and policies should not be "arbitrary." If a zoning line truly is arbitrary, then there is no reason for it

72 For another bad faith case, see *HG Winton Ltd v North York (Borough)* (1978), 6 MPLR 1 (Ont Div Ct) [*Winton*].

73 See, for example, *Aronson v Town of Sharon*, 346 Mass 598, 195 NE2d 341 (1964).

74 Above note 64 at 452.

and no reason it cannot be altered. If there is a planning rationale, then although circumstances may change over time, thus leading to other possible planning considerations and results, in terms of demarcation, it is best if the rationale be stated; hence the utility of official plans. In *HG Winton Ltd v North York*,[75] *Bondi* is cited for the proposition that, "It is, of course, well recognized that every zoning by-law is discriminatory, in the sense that the municipality chooses the types of uses it will permit in certain or all parts of the land under its jurisdiction, and is not invalid on that account . . . ."[76] The court omits the reference to "arbitrary" lines and adds, instead, "But there must be proper planning grounds or standards to warrant discriminatory distinctions between property owners in the same position, classification or zoning category."[77]

Toronto (City) v Outdoor Neon Displays Ltd[78]

A detailed by-law regulated the erection of signage on private property. The company proposed to erect a neon sign on the roof of a building in downtown Toronto. The building inspector refused a permit. The by-law was challenged as amounting to an illegal delegation of power to the official. The by-law was upheld, but the city was ordered to issue the permit, since it was agreed that the standards had been complied with. The Court of Appeal saw the by-law as amounting to unauthorized delegation to the official, but the Supreme Court saw the building inspector's function as merely that of ascertaining whether the prescribed standards, set by the municipal council, had been complied with; that the inspector had to be satisfied as to the "location" of the sign did not add a standardless discretion or establish a new criterion: the inspector was limited to ensuring the sign was erected in accordance with the plans submitted and that no other by-law forbade signage at the location.

NOTES

1) Signage is a matter almost always regulated by municipalities. Cases arise with some regularity, advertising and other forms of public communication being integral to commerce and free speech. See *Peterborough (City) v Ramsden*,[79] discussed in Chapter 4.
2) Unauthorized delegation of decision-making remains a potential basis for challenge of a by-law or of the decisions made under it. *Vic*

75 Above note 72.
76 *Ibid* at para 22.
77 *Ibid.*
78 Above note 63.
79 [1993] 2 SCR 1084.

Restaurant, above in this chapter, illustrates how a discretionary power of a municipal council may not be delegated, unless so authorized by provincial legislation. Where there is a power granted to allow delegation, sufficiently clear standards to be enforced should be specified.[80]

Ottawa (City) v Boyd Builders Ltd[81]

The core issue in *Boyd Builders* was how, if at all, a municipality may frustrate the opportunity of a landowner to secure a permit to construct a building. The particulars of the case are now primarily of historical interest since statutes have for the most part clarified the specifics of how municipalities may respond to information regarding proposed developments that raise planning concerns. The most efficacious of these is adoption of an interim control area by-law, which may be done expeditiously. In *Boyd Builders*, land had been left unzoned, apparently in error. The owners applied for a building permit for a nine-storey apartment building in an area generally zoned R-1. The city refused the building permit and moved to clarify the zoning. Boyd applied to court for an order of mandamus to have the building permit issued. The court adjourned the proceedings until the city's zoning by-law could be reviewed by the OMB (at that time, a necessary procedural step in adoption of a by-law). The Court of Appeal and subsequently the Supreme Court of Canada saw Boyd as entitled to a mandamus on a test of the state of the law at the date the building permit was applied for; there should have been no adjournment of the court hearing. The *prima facie* right of owners to use their property as they see fit (and to obtain a permit to do so) could be controlled by zoning or rezoning if the municipality can show three things: a clear intent to restrict or zone usage (usually shown by the passage of a by-law) before the hearing of the mandamus application, that the council has proceeded in good faith, and that the council has acted with dispatch.

Oriole Lumber Ltd v Markham (Township)[82]

Oriole Lumber is a case about accessory use in commercial/industrial property. We examine the case as an aspect of accessory use in Chapter

---

80 See, for example, *Sampson v Kingston (City)* (1981), 33 OR (2d) 105 at para 36 (HCJ): "The key requirement is that the municipality state, with sufficient clarity and concreteness, the contents of the standards to be enforced. In that way, the secondary bodies will only be carrying out administrative functions instead of legislative ones."

81 [1965] SCR 408 [*Boyd Builders*].

82 [1968] SCR 549 [*Oriole Lumber*].

7, which focuses on ways in which basic zoning becomes flexible. Here, the importance of the case is in the Court's remarks about how it approached the by-laws: "It was the basis of the official plan that there should be a series of categories of use of premises and to those categories the municipal council assigned various designations. It is these designations which are the vocabulary of the legislative scheme for use of lands within the township and which should govern the primary determination of whether a proposed building is in accordance with the various subsidiary land use by-laws . . . ."[83] The observation that an official plan (OP) creates a "vocabulary" is one that remains a part of the general understanding that courts bring to reading an overall regulatory scheme in matters of land use: OPs, Land-Use By-laws (LUBs), and sometimes the empowering statutes.

NOTES

1) The Ontario Court of Appeal had previously enunciated the same approach in *Cambridge Leaseholds Ltd v Thomas C Watkins Ltd*,[84] where the court read "retail store" and "department store" as necessarily meaning something different in an LUB:

> It is reasonable to believe that by making these two items separate and distinct in the by-law they are to bear a different connotation and that the term "retail store" is not sufficiently comprehensive to include department store . . . . If the by-law is to be read so that no portion of it becomes ineffectual or superfluous the term "department store" . . . must bear a different meaning to "retail store" appearing in the same section.[85]

2) A similar point was made in *McCauley Community League v Edmonton (City)*,[86] where the court focused on whether a building was to be classified as "apartment housing" or "extended medical treatment services" under the language of the by-law, when the intended use was for persons with chronic substance abuse problems. To a similar effect is *1121472 Ontario Inc v Toronto (City)*,[87] where the distinction made in the by-laws was between a restaurant and an entertainment

83 *Ibid* at 552.

84 [1966] OJ No 65 (CA), appeal allowed with costs, [1966] SCR v [*Cambridge Leaseholds*]. The decision is cited in *Burns Lake (Village) v Krause*, 2007 BCSC 730, to the effect that words in by-laws are to be read so no portion of it becomes ineffectual or superfluous.

85 *Cambridge Leaseholds*, above note 84 at para 20.

86 2011 ABCA 327.

87 (1998), 47 MPLR (2d) 23 (CA).

facility, and *Militky v Drummond/North Elmsley (Township)*,[88] where a paintball facility was seen as better classified as a place of recreation rather than a private park.

Association des Propriétaires des Jardins Taché Inc v Entreprises Dasken Inc[89]

A developer built two ten-storey apartment buildings in Hull. The permits were issued by the city in error since the zoning in the area was low-density residential. When the projects were first announced, residents in the area objected and notified the city and the developer of the error. The city disputed that an error had been made, and the construction went ahead while the matter proceeded to court. The plaintiffs were ultimately successful and the buildings were ordered to be demolished within a six-month period. On the matter of standing, the Association, not being an owner of land, was held not to have standing, but the individual landowner, Mme Brossard, was held to have an interest sufficient to maintain the action. A provincial statute, the *Cities and Towns Act*, required a vote by a majority "in number and in value" of owners to change residential zoning and this had not occurred. The city's engineering department had issued an incorrect map. In challenging an illegal action, the owner need not show pecuniary loss. The injunction was sought promptly, and in proceeding to build, the developer took a risk. Demolition was an available remedy.

NOTES

1) On standing, this case considers but does not overrule *Orpen*, though it is hard to disentangle its focus on an illegal act from the facts in *Orpen*. Commenting on the standing issue in *Dasken*, Professor (as he then was) Thomas Cromwell said, "The precise basis of the decision . . . is unclear."[90] The result "is not clear about the interest necessary to give the plaintiff standing . . . ."[91]
2) One of the judges, Abbott J (dissenting), noted that zoning may constitute a form of expropriation without compensation and it is essential that the area affected be described in clear and precise terms. Although he would have ruled against the plaintiffs and was in the minority, and although zoning is not now usually seen as the equivalent of expropriation, this observation as to what is desirable in drafting amounts to sound advice.

---

88 2015 ONCA 408.
89 (1971), 26 DLR (3d) 79 (SCC) [*Dasken*].
90 Thomas A Cromwell, *Locus Standi* (Toronto: Carswell, 1986) at 60.
91 *Ibid* at 65.

3) It is unusual for statutes to require a vote by owners or residents to validate zoning. It is more usual to see this sort of provision in cases of proposed borrowing. Should a council, on its own and apart from authorization by a provincial statute, propose to be bound by a referendum on a matter of policy, this would amount to illegal delegation. See, for example, *Davies v Forest Hill (Village)*.[92]
4) The governing Quebec statute empowered the Superior Court, at the request of a municipality "or any other interested person" to order cessation of an illegal use "or, if there is no other useful remedy, the demolition of the structure or the restoration of the land to its former condition." For an American case with similar facts and result, see *Parkview Associates v City of New York*,[93] where a thirty-one-storey apartment building was required to have its top twelve floors removed.
5) For a discussion of the case, see Carole Barriere's article, "Justice et Politique ou l'Affaire Dasken,"[94] which includes plans of the site, showing the zoning.
6) The buildings were actually demolished. See Cameron Harvey's article, "Municipal Law," where the author reports watching the demolition on television.[95]

Soo Mill & Lumber Co v Sault Ste-Marie (City)[96] and *Sanbay Developments Ltd v London (City)*[97]

This pair of cases involves the same point: whether a municipality may, even in the absence of some specific statutory power, freeze the use of land pending future planning. In *Soo Mill*, the OP identified a "holding category" overlay on top of the assigned zoning "in order to delay . . . development for their designated use until they appear to be ready for such development and until the standards appropriate to the designated use can be satisfied." The land in question was zoned for apartment buildings but under the "H" designation could only be used for agricultural purposes until the city deemed the time to be appropriate for their development. In *Sanbay*, much the same situation arose. The by-law linked its hold to adopting amendments "to provide details concerning permitted building areas, parking areas, open space, external design

92 [1965] 1 OR 240 (HCJ).
93 519 NE2d 1372 (NYCA 1988).
94 (1972) 7 *Revue juridique Thémis ns* 519.
95 (1974) 6 *Ottawa Law Review* 485 at 497.
96 [1975] 2 SCR 78 [*Soo Mill*].
97 [1975] 1 SCR 485 [*Sanbay*].

and regulations governing the size, floor area, and character and use" of the buildings. The Court declined to strike down the zoning.

NOTES

1) Some earlier cases had ruled that, unless authorization was clear, zoning adopted by a municipality could not be expressed to be temporary, nor had the idea of prematurity found much favour with the courts: see *Etobicoke (Township) Board of Education v Highbury Developments Ltd.*[98] *Soo Mill* and *Sanbay* in effect find a way around such restrictions.
2) In an article by Pamela Bagg, "Case Comment: The Implications of *Soo Mill* and *Sanbay* on Development Control by Municipalities"[99] the author raises the issue of how a municipality is to achieve control over the tempo of development. She says that "the ability to put a temporary hold on an area, to permit the completion of planning studies leading to the development of new planning standards or devices, is a legitimate objective. It is the manner of attaining these objectives which is of concern."[100] Bagg notes that the Court sees an "H" designation as legitimate in two situations: as an interim stopgap measure pending development of more elaborate zoning regulations, and to prevent premature development as measured by the municipality's preparedness to provide the area with proper services. Her concern is over the question of how a decision is to be made to lift the "H" designation. She advocates for criteria to be set out in the OP as a matter of fairness and reasonable certainty of outcome and suggests that otherwise the matter becomes discretionary for the council without any stated criteria.
3) Holding zones are quite common. Ontario's *Planning Act* now specifically allows for "H" zones.[101] Municipalities often desire to control the tempo of development not only for reasons of the need to develop more detailed land-use controls or to prepare for services and infrastructure, but as a part of their overall assessment of the needs of the community for particular types of land uses, including an estimate of whether the projects proposed will succeed. This last may be seen as a matter exclusively for the developer of land, but there is a negative consequence for a municipality to have buildings that are eyesores or shuttered; in addition, oversupply of

98 [1958] SCR 196.
99 (1976) 14 *Osgoode Hall Law Journal* 217.
100 *Ibid* at 226.
101 Ontario *Planning Act*, above note 25, s 36.

some particular form of building will not generate the hoped-for tax revenues.

4) An alternative to an "H" overlay is to zone land in an inappropriate manner, creating what Bagg calls "an indirect holding zone." This device is also known as a "placeholder" by-law, that is, a use that is not anticipated to actually materialize, thus allowing council to consider individual proposals as they come forward. Developers are thus encouraged to make a particular proposal to the municipality, which, if interested, engages in spot zoning, perhaps in conjunction with an OP amendment. Both this alternative and the "H" zone itself, to the extent that the new zoning might include detailed specifications for the proposed development, amount to something like a development agreement.
5) It is also the case that some provinces have a particular mechanism for controlling the tempo of development, usually known as "development control" or "interim control." Thus, Ontario's *Planning Act* has, in section 38, since 1973, allowed for immediate freezing of activity pending completion of planning studies. No advance notice or a hearing is necessary.
6) The basic power to adopt an OP implies that provisions for a pause in development might be included, but a five-year pause is "highly debatable" as a valid exercise of that power.[102]
7) Not all courts have been persuaded by the *Soo Mill* and *Sanbay* cases. In 1978, the British Columbia Court of Appeal refused to read that province's legislation as authorizing a holding zone, and distinguished the Supreme Court of Canada decisions as particular to Ontario, where the laws "differ substantially" from BC's.[103] That decision is somewhat dubious.
8) Chief Justice Laskin, who wrote the decisions, was particularly interested in LUP law. His LLM thesis was on the Ontario Municipal Board.[104]

Harrison v Carswell[105]

The employees of a business were on a legal strike. The business was located, as a tenant, in a shopping centre, and there was peaceful picketing on the sidewalk in front of the business. A picketer faced multiple charges of trespass under the *Petty Trespass Act* of Manitoba. Convictions

---

102 *Re Ottawa (City)*, 2012 ONSC 3851 (Div Ct).

103 *Karamanolis v Port Coquitlam (City)* (1978), 97 DLR (3d) 289 (BCCA).

104 See Philip Girard, *Bora Laskin: Bringing Law to Life* (Toronto: University of Toronto Press, 2005) at 94–95.

105 [1976] 2 SCR 200.

were upheld by the Court. The view of the majority was that, although there is an unrestricted invitation to the public to enter the premises of the shopping centre, the owner has sufficient control or possession of the common areas to allow it to invoke remedies in trespass. The majority declined to enter into an assessment of the relative values of rights in private property as compared with rights of labour organizations. Trespass was illegal and it was for the legislature to make changes if it chose.

NOTES

1) The minority saw picketing as sanctioned by law, and no incompatibility between the assertion of those rights with private property rights. Thus, picketing could not be carried on at places and times not available to the public, but could be otherwise.
2) This is a pre-*Charter* case. The Supreme Court has recognized picketing as containing an element of expression to be protected under section 2(b) of the *Canadian Charter of Rights and Freedoms*;[106] see *British Columbia Government Employees' Union v British Columbia (Attorney General)*.[107] At the same time, *Charter* rights apply so as to offer freedoms as against government, not as against private persons.

Lamoureux v Beaconsfield (Ville)[108]

At issue was an application to the municipality for permits to operate a service station. The by-law specified two conditions: that the location not be within 250 feet of another service station, nor within 750 feet of a house of worship, college, convent, school, orphanage, or hospital, and that there not be significant objection from surrounding owners. The latter condition was in these terms: "If two-thirds (in number) of the owners . . . object . . . no such permit shall be granted." More than two-thirds of the owners did object, and the applicant sought to have the by-law quashed as an improper delegation of power. The court upheld the by-law, characterizing the vote by nearby owners as an acceptable "condition precedent":

> Instead the by-law takes into account, in each particular case, the wishes of adjacent landowners, who are the very people affected by the proposed use, as one of the conditions precedent to the obtaining of a specific permit. In my opinion this is in accord with the principle

106 Part I of the *Constitution Act, 1982*, being Schedule B to the *Canada Act 1982* (UK), 1982, c 11 [*Charter*].

107 [1988] 2 SCR 214.

108 Above note 61.

of zoning legislation and the provision was not *ultra vires* of the respondent municipality.[109]

NOTES

1) It is hard to justify the decision in this case. It seems manifest that this is an instance of unauthorized delegation of a decision-making power by the municipal council. By the terms of the by-law, the council agrees to be bound by the results of a vote, the very thing that is objectionable according to the idea of unauthorized delegation.
2) At the same time, the case does acknowledge the validity of the grounds put forward as the basis for the challenge to the by-law, that is, that unauthorized delegation may invalidate by-laws.

Prince George (City) v Payne[110]

A leading case on the limits of municipal regulatory authority is *Prince George (City) v Payne*, in which the Court was dealing with a refusal to issue a business licence to a sex shop. The Court saw the power to regulate in that way as not amounting to a power to prohibit the activity:

> The discretion contained [in the statute] wide as it is, must be exercised judicially. It is not a judicial exercise of discretion to rest decision upon an extraneous ground. The common law right of the individual freely to carry on his business and use his property can be taken away only by statute in plain language or by necessary implication . . . . It has long been decided . . . that a statutory power conferred upon a municipal council to make by-laws for regulating and governing a trade does not, in the absence of an express power of prohibition, authorize the making it unlawful to carry on a lawful trade in a lawful manner.[111]

NOTES

1) The earlier authority cited by the Court is *Toronto (Municipality) v Virgo*.[112]
2) Thus, the Court decided that the refusal of the licence was an *ultra vires* decision: simply not authorized by the statute.
3) The Court also decided that the decision had been taken upon an improper ground, that is, one of protecting public morality, manifested in this case by the council's distaste for a shop offering for

109 *Ibid* at 142.
110 [1978] 1 SCR 458.
111 *Ibid* at 463 and 468.
112 Above note 17.

sale "so-called 'marital aids' . . . encompassing 'a wide range of masturbatory and erotic devices and substances not entirely consistent with heterosexual activity let alone conducive to or in furtherance of connubial bliss' . . . ."[113] The words quoted by the Supreme Court come from the trial-level decision. This was the extraneous ground. The court's description of the council meeting is,

> At that later meeting a representative of the Prince George Ministerial Association addressed Council and likened the products of the adult boutique to heroin and other cultural poisons. In the debate which followed one of the aldermen declined to peruse the catalogues depicting the items to be sold in the boutique, concluding "from what I see on the streets, this town doesn't need any instruction in this matter." Another alderman observed "I guess you'd have to say I carry my narrow-mindedness to Council with me" while a third, who also opposed the granting of the licence, stated that a community "has to take a stand on the matter," and went on to observe that "some of this sex is better left in the barnyard."[114]

Issues of extraneous considerations have become complicated in subsequent cases. Courts are sometimes prepared to give deference to municipal councils and see such comments as not fully determinative of how the decision was made, or look at the number of councillors citing extraneous considerations and then calculate if the result would be different if some votes are discounted. The issue remains somewhat unclear.

4) The Court also flagged fair process issues:

> The facts are capable of raising an issue over the application of natural justice rules. Before giving the applicant a hearing Council decided against the application. The applicant was then called upon to show reasons why the licence should not be withheld. One of the aldermen decided to refuse the application without perusing the catalogues depicting the items to be sold. The applicant was denied an opportunity to speak in reply to the representative of the Prince George Ministerial Association. Interesting questions arise as to burden and *audi alterem partem* but I do not deem it necessary to consider them in view of the conclusion which I have reached on other aspects of the case.[115]

---

113 Above note 110 at 462.

114 *Ibid* at 460–61.

115 *Ibid* at 469.

There is at least some suggestion in this comment that unfairness, if exhibited by only one member of a council, may be sufficient to taint a decision; some subsequent cases have suggested that a larger number of councillors behaving in an inappropriate manner may be required for a court to set aside a decision.

Edmonton (City) v Tegon Developments Ltd[116]

In *Tegon*, the Supreme Court upheld, with very short reasons, the decision of the Alberta Court of Appeal,[117] which had invalidated a municipal freeze on all development in an area of the city so as to allow time for the provincial government to designate historic buildings under the *Heritage Act*. The area at issue was Old Strathcona. The Court of Appeal saw the designation as *ultra vires*. The reasons offered were both that the *Planning Act* could not extend to heritage matters in the face of a specific different statutory scheme, and that a power to regulate a "use" of land could not authorize a freeze.

NOTES

1) The latter basis for the decision tends to contradict the *Soo Mill* and *Sanbay* cases.
2) Depending on the stated purposes of a province's *Planning Act*, it may be that other courts would reach a different conclusion as to whether heritage matters are legitimately a part of land-use planning, though another case, *Valley View Heritage Association Inc v Estevan (City)*,[118] reached the same conclusion as the Alberta courts in *Tegon*.
3) It has been suggested that *Tegon* may also imply "that the enactment of by-laws which attempt, for whatever reason, to preserve existing buildings and structures cannot be justified by reference to powers to regulate land use."[119] A prudent measure would be for the power to regulate demolition to be specified as a municipal power in provincial legislation.

R v Bell[120]

North York had adopted a by-law regulating the use of certain residential areas, expressed in terms that said each permitted "dwelling unit"

116 (1978), 121 DLR (3d) 760 (SCC) [*Tegon*].
117 (1978), 81 DLR (3d) 543.
118 (1989), 47 MPLR 24 (Sask QB).
119 See Robert Ward, "Heritage Conservation in British Columbia" (1988) 22 *University of British Columbia Law Review* 61 at 99.
120 [1979] 2 SCR 212 [*Bell*].

was to be a "separate set of living quarters designed or intended for use . . . by an individual or one family alone." "Family" was then defined to be two or more persons "living together and interrelated by bonds of consanguinity, marriage, or legal adoption" and included non-paying guests, domestic servants, and foster children. A tenant who shared a dwelling unit with two other unrelated persons was charged with violating the by-law. In entering an acquittal, the Court said the by-law was invalid. Personal characteristics were not a proper basis for control of density or any issue related to land use or zoning. "People zoning" is not within the scope of the *Planning Act*. The by-law was unreasonable in the sense set out in *Kruse v Johnson*, that is, an "oppressive or gratuitous interference with the rights of those subject to them as could find no justification in the minds of reasonable men"[121] and therefore the legislature was not to be seen as having intended to confer such authority; the by-law was *ultra vires*.

NOTES

1) Despite this clear decision, it remains relatively common for municipal by-laws to be drafted in terms of "family" occupancy. Such by-laws are vulnerable to legal challenge. Possible alternatives are "residential detached," "residential semi-detached," or "single housekeeping establishment." In *Smith v Tiny (Township)*,[122] the court said that by-laws may be written so as to use the word "family" flexibly, which may appear from the overall context, and not run afoul of *Bell*.
2) In "We Are (Not) Family—Zoning By-laws and Reasonableness—a Comment on *R v Bell*,"[123] Susan G Himel says,

> The reluctance of the courts to intervene in reviewing the reasonableness of municipal by-laws has grown increasingly over the last century. However, [*Bell*] is an example of how our highest Court is not prepared to allow municipalities to enact legislation which affects human rights without having clear legislative authority.

3) What amounts to "people zoning" can be quite contentious. In *Re Regional Municipality of Waterloo OP Amendment No 58*[124] an issue was raised about the effect of an interim control by-law adopted due to an "over-concentration" of "single-person, low-income households." This was challenged as a violation of the principles in *Bell*,

---

121 *Ibid* at 222.
122 (1980), 27 OR (2d) 690 (HCJ).
123 (1980) 1 *Supreme Court Law Review* 367 at 367.
124 (2010), 64 OMBR 283.

as well as on *Charter* grounds. In *Rosen v Blue Mountains (Town)*,[125] the OMB took the view that the adoption of an interim control by-law that put a hold on seasonal temporary accommodation for six months while considering appropriate land use did not amount to making a distinction on the basis of the user rather than the nature of the use of land.

4) Although it is sometimes difficult to distinguish between "user" and "use," *Bell* has been applied in other cases: see, for example, *Alcoholism Foundation of Manitoba v Winnipeg (City)*,[126] *Greater Victoria School District No 61 v Oak Bay (District)*,[127] and *Rosen v Blue Mountains (Town)*.[128]
5) At the same time, there have been cases that distinguished *Bell*. In *Faminow v North Vancouver (District)*,[129] the court was dealing with by-laws that allowed secondary suites in homes if the occupants were related to the occupants of the principal dwelling. The court said that *Bell* prohibited only unreasonable or inequitable zoning distinctions based on family. *Faminow* was itself distinguished in a subsequent British Columbia case, *Tenants' Rights Coalition v Delta (Corporation)*,[130] on various grounds.[131]
6) *Bell* has been critiqued by Professor Stan Makuch, who says:

> the result reached by the Supreme Court of Canada appears sound enough, but the reasoning behind the result is obscure because the court adoption of the invalidity of "land zoning by people zoning" is not sufficiently elaborated on . . . . No attempt is made to assess the purpose of restricting the allowable use to families or a minimum of unrelated persons. A better approach in all cases, it would seem, would be to consider the purpose of the *Planning Act* and zoning, and to interpret the by-law and the scope of the zoning power in the context of that purpose. The zoning power is intended to prevent nuisance and physical interference with land and ensure that uses are physically compatible.[132]

---

125 (2011), 69 OMBR 243.
126 (1990), 65 Man R (2d) 81 (CA).
127 2006 BCCA 28.
128 2012 ONSC 4215 (Div Ct).
129 (1988), 61 DLR (4th) 747 (BCCA).
130 (1997), 42 MPLR (2d) 165 (BCSC).
131 See John Mascarin, "Annotation" (1998) 42 *Municipal and Planning Law Reports* (2d) 166.
132 Stan Makuch et al, *Canadian Municipal and Planning Law*, 2d ed (Toronto: Thomson Carswell, 2004) at 198–99.

7) The Ontario *Planning Act* now provides that "The authority to pass a [zoning] by-law does not include the authority to pass a by-law that has the effect of distinguishing between persons who are related and persons who are unrelated in respect of the occupancy or use of a building . . . ."[133]
8) In the United Kingdom, a form of "people zoning" has been upheld in several cases, under their overall system of granting of planning permission with conditions. Thus, in *Fawcett Properties Ltd v Buckingham County Council*,[134] a condition limiting occupancy of a dwelling to be constructed in a green belt area to natural resources workers (forestry, agriculture, or the like) was upheld. The condition had been challenged as unreasonable since personal characteristics could not be a valid planning concern.

Homex Realty & Development v Wyoming (Village)[135]

The owner and subdivider of a parcel of land entered into an agreement with the village for the installation of physical services in the subdivision. Various lots were sold to Homex before the services were installed. The village passed by-laws that deemed the lots purchased by Homex not to be a registered plan of subdivision and providing that the village would not assume responsibility for a water pipeline constructed by Homex or permit its connection to the municipal water supply system. Homex had not been notified of the pending motions before the council.

NOTES

1) It is a feature of control of subdivisions that the subdivider is financially responsible for the installation of hard services such as sewage, water, and roads. The dispute in Homex had to do with responsibility for those costs. The Court concluded that Homex had assumed the obligation to construct the services, but intended not to fulfil them.
2) The case is noted, however, for its comments on notice and the opportunity to participate in municipal decision-making. Homex was not notified of the council's consideration of deregistering its subdivision. The decision is thus very similar to the case of *Wiswell v Winnipeg (Greater)*;[136] in both, the Court viewed the decision being

---

133 Ontario *Planning Act*, above note 25, s 35(2).
134 [1961] AC 636 (HL).
135 [1980] 2 SCR 1011.
136 [1965] SCR 512.

made as akin to a *lis*, and therefore quasi-judicial rather than purely legislative.

3) Because of the failure to afford an opportunity to Homex to be heard, the decision of the council could be set aside. However, *certiorari* is a discretionary remedy, and here the Court was not prepared to quash the council decision because Homex's behaviour disentitled it to the relief it sought.
4) The judges in dissent agreed with the majority on the obligation of affording an opportunity to be heard, but were prepared to adopt a different framework of analysis for judging what fairness obligations applied.

St Peter's Evangelical Lutheran Church (Ottawa) v Ottawa (City)[137]

The church purchased a building of heritage interest with the intention of demolishing it so as to expand its parking lot. It applied to the city for a demolition permit; the city responded by designating the building under the *Heritage Act*. The church then applied to the city for permission to demolish a designated heritage building. The city council denied the application. However, under the *Heritage Act*, the city was obliged to notify an owner of its decision within ninety days, failing which the application was deemed to have been granted. Although representatives of the church were present at the city council meeting at which the decision was made, and therefore knew of the decision, the requisite formal notice was not given to the church. The church commenced demolition. The matter was litigated, with the city seeking an injunction to prevent the demolition and the church seeking to have its right to demolish recognized. The Court read the statute in a purposive manner, as designed to protect heritage buildings, but also as manifesting limits on the extent to which private property rights were to be interfered with. It was held that a breach of the notice provisions for the refusal of permission to demolish invalidated the city's actions.

NOTES

1) The decision is taken as emphasizing the importance of proper notice to landowners when decisions are taken that affect their rights. The full ambit of this obligation is now to be assessed in light of the factors subsequently established by the Supreme Court of Canada in the case of *Baker v Canada (Minister of Citizenship and Immigration)*,[138] though there is no reason to believe that the *St Peter's*

---

137 [1982] 2 SCR 616 [*St Peter's*].
138 [1999] 2 SCR 817 [*Baker*].

decision would now be any different. Regarding the *Baker* factors, see Chapter 8, Section C.

2) The Court said,

> The Ontario *Heritage Act* was enacted to provide for the conservation, protection and preservation of the heritage of Ontario. There is no doubt that the *Act* provides for and the Legislature intended that municipalities, acting under the provisions of the Act, should have wide powers to interfere with individual property rights. It is equally evident, however, that the Legislature recognized that the preservation of Ontario's heritage should be accomplished at the cost of the community at large, not at the cost of the individual property owner, and certainly not in total disregard of the property owner's rights. It provided a procedure to govern the exercise of the municipal powers, but at the same time to protect the property owner . . . .[139]

Hartel Holdings Ltd v Calgary (City)[140]

In *Hartel*, discussed in the Introduction, a hotel had been designated as a heritage building; the owner claimed this so negatively affected its ability to operate the business that it amounted to constructive expropriation and claimed compensation.

NOTES

1) What is usually in issue in such cases is not an outright "taking," which would be expropriation and would involve transfer of title to the expropriating authority, thus triggering an obligation to pay compensation at common law and by statute. What is at issue is a "partial taking" or "regulatory taking," where rules governing use are seen as being so restrictive that all effective economic use has been lost.
2) Many landowners resent land-use regulation to the point of seeming to believe that the US's Fifth Amendment to its Constitution is a part of Canadian law. It is not. Nonetheless, comment and litigation based on language of a "taking" of land through regulation appears in Canada with some regularity as if there were a constitutional entitlement.
3) Entitlement to compensation in the case of any particular government restriction on a right to use land depends entirely on whether it is specified in the governing statute. Some regulatory schemes do so provide. See also *British Columbia v Tener*, immediately below in this chapter.

139 Above note 137 at 623–24.

140 [1984] 1 SCR 337 [*Hartel*].

British Columbia v Tener[141]

The British Columbia government decided to establish a park on Crown land for which some individuals had a resource use contract. The mineral claims dated from 1934; the Wells Gray Provincial Park was established around it in 1939. The present owners and their predecessors had staked some sixteen claims. In the 1970s, the status of the park was upgraded, and from 1975 on the claim holders were denied access, finally being told in 1977 that no new exploration or development work would be allowed. The claims were held subject to regulatory laws that might be in place from time to time. The company claimed its property right had been expropriated and claimed compensation. The claim was upheld on the basis that the company had a property right, an interest in land in the nature of a *profit-à-prendre*, which had been taken by the government.

NOTES

1) Regarding mining on public lands, the essence of the matter as to an entitlement to compensation appears to be whether a right has crystallized. In most provinces, modern mining laws adopt a scheme of discretionary licensing so as to try to avoid the result in *Tener*.
2) Establishing new public parks on land where there has been prospecting and therefore some hope of future profits from establishing a mine or on which there had been a forestry tenure agreement, can lead to extensive public debate over whether compensation should be available. This has been particularly contentious in British Columbia.[142]
3) The situation may be complicated for governments dealing with companies based in NAFTA nations, or others for which investor rights are established by treaty, in light of the arbitration decisions in *United Mexican States v Metalclad Corp*[143] and *Re William Ralph Clayton and Bilcon of Delaware Inc and Government of Canada*.[144] As things now stand, it is the federal government and not the provinces or municipalities that is responsible for payment of any dam-

---

141 [1985] 1 SCR 533 [*Tener*].

142 See *Report of the Commission of Inquiry into Compensation for the Taking of Resource Interests* (Schwindt Commission) (Vancouver: The Commission, 1993) and the response of Gregory J McDade, "Report on Compensation Issues Concerning Protected Areas" (Vancouver: Sierra Legal Defence Fund, 1993).

143 See Howard Epstein, "*NAFTA*, Other International Agreements and Local Government Jurisdiction—Comments on *United Mexican States v Metalclad Corp*" (2003) 34 *Municipal and Planning Law Reports* (3d) 44.

144 See The Council of Canadians, "Bilcon Wins *NAFTA* Challenge against Canada over Gravel Quarry Expansion" (20 March 2015), online: http://bit.ly/29PTckC via @CouncilofCDNS.

ages awards even if the objectionable actions are those of a province or a municipality.

Montréal (City) v Arcade Amusements Inc[145]

Montreal adopted a by-law to regulate arcades where "amusement machines" (slot machines, video games, etc.) were available. The restrictions limited the number of machines, restricted food offerings to a snack bar and non-alcoholic beverages, forbade arcades in the city's historical district, banned arcades from any building used for housing, adopted a separation distance (200 metres) from schools and parks, and banned admittance to any person under eighteen. Four objections were raised: (1) that the by-laws were essentially criminal law and therefore beyond the power of the municipality to enact since criminal law is reserved under the Constitution to the federal government, (2) that the *Montréal City Charter* did not authorize this set of by-laws, (3) that the rules were impermissively vague, and (4) that the by-laws were unreasonable and discriminatory. On the constitutional law point, the Court found that the purpose of the by-law was "to protect children and adolescents against commercial exploitation by the owners of amusement machines" and also "to prevent crime." It saw these as valid municipal purposes, and not in their essence criminal law. The by-law did not seek to prohibit the activity, but to regulate it as to use and location. As for the *Montréal City Charter*, the Court saw the by-law in part as one of zoning, not of prohibition, even though the limitation was very wide; and it saw it in part as regulation of commerce—both being matters authorized by the *City Charter*. As to vagueness, the Court discussed the term "young children" (an apparatus designed to amuse young children was exempted from the by-law); it found the term to be in need of construction but not so imprecise as to be void.[146] As to unreasonableness, the Court agreed that the distinction made as to a particular age was not authorized by the *City Charter*. "The rule that the power to make by-laws does not include that of enacting discriminatory provisions unless the enabling legislation provides the contrary has been observed from time immemorial in British and Canadian public law."[147] The Court cited *Kruse v Johnson*.[148] This part of the by-law was severable.

---

145 [1985] 1 SCR 368.

146 An older UK text on administrative law, SA deSmith, *Judicial Review of Administrative Action*, 2d ed (London: Stevens & Sons, 1968) at 339, says "The test of uncertainty is uncertain . . ." and so it remains.

147 Above note 145 at para 102.

148 Above note 19.

NOTES

1) The result of the various restrictions as to location was that arcades could be located in only about 1 percent of the commercial or industrial areas of the city. The Court saw this limitation, though very wide, as not amounting to prohibition.[149]
2) The Court said that in characterizing the by-law for constitutional purposes, it did not matter whether the method chosen to deter crime was "really effective," so long as the municipality showed good faith and there was some factual basis for the choice.[150]
3) There was extensive discussion of unauthorized discrimination, focused on the issue of age. The Court reviewed previous cases, concluding,

> I hasten to say that I do not necessarily agree with all the reasons contained in these precedents. Thus, I do not feel that a distinction between minors and adults should be compared . . . with a discrimination affecting women, married or unmarried, soldiers, the elderly, labourers and certain tradesmen. The latter distinctions are prima facie arbitrary and irrational, whereas a distinction based on youth is in general prompted by considerations which are completely reasonable in the narrow sense, as many of these judgments have noted. However, it is not in the narrow sense of the word "reasonable" which we must consider, but its legal sense. Moreover, and most importantly, there is a relevant analogy between the class of children and adolescents on the one hand and that for example of women and the elderly. Both are significant groups of the population and both are equally powerless to alter their physical or psychological condition. It must be held that, in the absence of express provisions to the contrary or implicit delegation by necessary inference, the sovereign legislator has reserved to itself the important power of limiting the rights and freedoms of individuals in accordance with such fine distinctions. The principle transcends the limits of administrative and municipal law. It is a principle of fundamental freedom.[151]

The problem of unauthorized discrimination, or unauthorized distinctions, has potential to clash with a liberal approach to reading statutes granting powers to municipalities; it is more in line with the Dillon's Rule approach (e.g., in *MacIlreith v Hart Estate*) than the

149 Above note 145 at para 47.
150 *Ibid* at para 25.
151 *Ibid* at para 118.

approach in cases such as *Spraytech*, below in this chapter. It is to be expected that this problem will be raised in future cases.

4) The Court approved the device of separation distances from schools and parks.[152] This is in line with the leading US decision from its Supreme Court in *Young v American Mini Theatres, Inc*,[153] which allowed separation distances to be imposed so as to keep adult motion picture theatres from locating within 500 feet of residential areas or within 1,000 feet of any two other "regulated uses" (e.g., adult bookstores, pool halls).
5) The Court was not prepared to second-guess the city as to its choice of concentration or dispersal of particular land uses.[154]
6) The Court mentioned various municipal purposes that it saw as legitimate: protection of the environment, safeguarding of the national heritage, aesthetics, noise and traffic control, and concentrating commerce or industry in one part of the city so as better to provide services. The test was whether the city "acts reasonably and in good faith in the public interest."[155]
7) In discussing vagueness, the Court said that by-law language should leave "as little room as possible for the arbitrary and subjective."[156] DeSmith says that the way to approach vagueness of a by-law is to consider whether it is "so uncertain as to have no ascertainable meaning or was so unclear in its effect as to be incapable of certain application."[157]
8) Owners of arcades in existence prior to the by-law remain protected through "acquired rights," that is, non-conforming use rights.[158]
9) The *Montréal City Charter* contained a provision that the listing of specific powers does not derogate from the general powers conferred. This is a statutory reversal of a normal principle of interpretation and is a point returned to in *Spraytech* and similar cases.

St Pierre v Ontario (Minister of Transportation and Communication)[159]

In 1961, the St Pierre family purchased 125 acres outside of London in a quiet rural area, intending it as a place for retirement, and built their home. In the mid-1970s, the provincial government purchased some

152 *Ibid* at para 73.
153 427 US 50 (1976).
154 Above note 145 at paras 62–63.
155 *Ibid* at para 72.
156 *Ibid* at para 91.
157 Lord Woolf et al, *DeSmith's Judicial Review*, 6th ed (London: Sweet & Maxwell, 2007) ss 11–40.
158 Above note 145 at para 37.
159 [1987] 1 SCR 906 [*St Pierre*].

land immediately adjoining the St Pierre property and by 1977 had opened a highway. The St Pierres filed a claim for compensation under the *Expropriation Act*. The Court ruled that no compensation was payable. The *Act* made payment available if land was taken, but no land had been taken. The *Act* also made payment available in cases of injurious affection even where no land has been taken. Jurisprudence had established that four conditions must be met to establish such a claim: (1) the damage must result from an act rendered lawful by statutory powers, (2) the damage must be such as would have been actionable under common law, (3) the damage must be an injury to the land itself and not a personal injury or an injury to business or trade, and (4) the damage must be occasioned by the construction of the public work, not by its user. The Court found that what was being asserted was one of a change in neighbourhood, loss of privacy, and loss of a view, none of which was actionable at common law. There was no nuisance. Nuisance involved striking a balance between conflicting claims of landowners, and the government was not making an unreasonable use of its land.

NOTES

1) Nuisance remains a potent category of claim to adjudicate reasonableness of use of land and is discussed in Chapter 3. It is possible in circumstances similar to that of the St Pierres to attempt to take the government to court on the basis of nuisance rather than injurious affection. However, there is a defence of statutory authority, which is almost always successful.[160] But see *Antrim Truck Centre Ltd v Ontario (Transportation)* for a change in focus in such cases.[161]
2) Claims of injurious affection may be advanced if "the action of the public authority substantially altered the nature of the claimant's property itself or at least interfered to a significant extent with the actual use being made of the property, with a resultant loss of value of the property."[162]
3) The Court said

> The Minister is authorized—indeed he is charged with the duty—to construct highways. All highway construction will cause disruption. Sometimes it will damage property, sometimes

---

160 See *Susan Heyes Inc (cob Hazel & Co) v Vancouver (City)*, 2011 BCCA 77. The claim was advanced because the business had been disrupted for three years while a transit line was being constructed. The court found that the city had created a nuisance, but was absolved from paying damages due to having statutory authority to do the work.

161 2013 SCC 13 [*Antrim Truck Centre*].

162 Above note 159 at para 11.

> it will enhance its value. To fix the Minister with liability for damages to every landowner whose property interest is damaged, by reason only of the construction of a highway on neighbouring lands, would place an intolerable burden on the public purse. Highways are necessary; they cause disruption. In the balancing process inherent in the law of nuisance, their utility for the public good far outweighs the disruption and injury which is visited upon some adjoining lands. The law of nuisance will not extend to allow for compensation in this case.[163]

4) Subsequently, in the 2013 *Antrim Truck Centre* case, the Court considered the position of the owner of a truck stop that included a restaurant and gas bar servicing drivers of a highway, which became a secondary route after the opening of a major highway parallel to it. The result was that the owner was virtually put out of business. The Court upheld an award for business loss and loss in value of land as decided by the OMB. In considering the matter of the law of nuisance, the Court focused on the need for the interference with occupation of land to be both substantial and unreasonable. Weak claims could be eliminated on the former point. So far as unreasonableness, in the context of interference caused by projects carried out by a public authority that further the public good, the Court noted that *St Pierre* should not be read to mean that "great public good out-balances even very significant interference"[164] or there would be no point in a statutory provision providing a right of compensation for injurious affection. Also, *St Pierre* involved injury which "was a simple loss of amenities." The focus should be on whether the interference suffered by the claimant is unreasonable, not on whether the nature of the defendant's conduct is unreasonable. The exercise involves a balancing of the gravity of the harm against the utility of the defendant's conduct in all of the circumstances. There is no specific list of factors. "Generally speaking, the acts of a public authority will be of significant utility . . . . [The] purpose [of injurious affection] is to ensure that individual members of the public do not have to bear a disproportionate share of the cost of procuring the public benefit."[165] "The distinction is thus between, on the one hand, interferences that constitute the 'give and take' expected of everyone and, on the other, interferences that

163 *Ibid* at para 13.
164 Above note 161 at para 37.
165 *Ibid* at para 38.

impose a disproportionate burden on individuals. That . . . is at the heart of the balancing exercise involved . . . ."[166]

R v Greenbaum[167]

Greenbaum was selling T-shirts on the sidewalk at the corner of Yonge and Bloor streets in Toronto. He was charged under a prohibitory by-law since he held no licence and was not working out of any nearby store. He was acquitted. The Court found no statutory authorization for the city's by-law. Authorization to regulate sidewalk obstructions did not extend to regulating sale of merchandise. Authorization to regulate public nuisances did not apply since the activity was not always a nuisance. Authorization to regulate or prohibit activity that encumbered sidewalks did not apply since the by-law was overbroad. The omnibus power did not apply since the municipality was attempting to use other, specific powers in its statute. The Court also found the by-laws to be discriminatory in the sense that the statute did not authorize the municipality to make a "distinction between free-standing street vendors and owners/occupants of abutting property."

NOTES

1) *R v Sharma*[168] was a companion case to the same effect.
2) As in *Arcade Amusements*, the issue of what distinctions between classes of activity may lawfully be made, was an important issue. The courts are prepared to view with vigilance by-laws that impinge upon civil or common law rights of citizens.

Shell Canada Products Ltd v Vancouver (City)[169]

Shell was in the business of selling petroleum products and had tendered from time to time for supply to the city. Vancouver city council passed a resolution declaring that it would not do business with companies also doing business in South Africa, at that time an Apartheid nation. Shell was doing business in South Africa. It challenged the resolution as beyond the powers of the city, that is, it does not relate to a municipal purpose; it also challenged it as unauthorized discrimination. The Court (split 5:4) ruled that the resolution should be quashed. The essentially extraterritorial nature of the resolution, with no explicit statutory authority conferred, put it beyond the usual range of municipal purposes, and any doubt should be resolved in favour of the citizen. On the matter

---

166 *Ibid* at para 39.
167 [1993] 1 SCR 674.
168 [1993] 1 SCR 650.
169 [1994] 1 SCR 231.

of unauthorized discrimination, the Court said the discrimination between companies doing business in South Africa and those that do not was not a matter of choice for commercial or business reasons that could reasonably be implied as permissible for the municipality to make.

NOTES

1) This is not a land-use case. Its relevance for our purposes is in its examination of what is a valid municipal purpose. This case needs to be read in conjunction with *Spraytech*, where a broad view was taken of the omnibus powers granted to municipalities.
2) The majority said, "No doubt Council can have regard for matters beyond its boundaries in exercising its powers, but in so doing, any action taken must have as its purpose benefit to the citizens of the City."[170] This statement may be seen as an endorsement of the environmental movement's maxim "think globally, act locally" but with the caveat that some local benefit must be involved. It is not clear what link might be necessary to show in order to justify a by-law that looks outside the local geographic area. Thus, in *Eng v Toronto (City)*,[171] a by-law that dealt with sale and use of shark fins was struck down as beyond the municipality's jurisdiction. There are many explicit and undoubted municipal powers that may be used to advance an environmental agenda. But the full ambit is yet to emerge.
3) The minority judges took a more expansive view of municipal purposes, something beyond the provision of basic services. Good government, they thought, allowed the municipalities themselves to decide what is in the best interests of their citizenry.[172]
4) The approach of the majority was that what is not clearly allowed to be done by the city is to be disallowed, and the opposite view is that what is not clearly disallowed should be seen as permissible.[173] This is an ongoing point of tension in LUP law.
5) For a current analysis of how courts should read statutes granting powers to municipalities, see *Northern Construction Enterprises Inc v Halifax (Regional Municipality)*.[174] At issue was the extent of municipal authority over "developments adjacent to quarries" in light of provincially retained jurisdiction over quarries themselves. The court, while acknowledging the general benevolent approach to reading statutes such as the *Halifax Regional Municipality Charter*,

170 *Ibid* at para 100.
171 2012 ONSC 6818.
172 Above note 169 at para 93.
173 *Ibid* at para 40.
174 2015 NSCA 44.

so as to achieve their purpose, saw crushing facilities, wash stations, and stockpiling areas as essential components of a quarry and not as developments "adjacent" to quarries.

6) Similarly, in *Eng v Toronto (City)*,[175] the city had adopted a by-law prohibiting sale of shark fins for their use in food. The by-law was struck down as not having a valid municipal purpose. Attempts by the city to classify the by-law as relating to animals, or justified as a measure relating to "health and safety," the "social well-being of the city," or the environment, were all rejected by the court. The court focused on the overall purpose of the powers conferred by statute as being to enable the city "to respond to municipal issues."

114957 Canada Ltée (Spraytech, Société d'arrosage) v Hudson (Town)[176]

The Quebec town of Hudson adopted a by-law limiting the cosmetic domestic use of chemical pesticides. The by-law was challenged by commercial appliers of pesticides. The by-law prohibited their use, with numerous exceptions: swimming pools, inside a building, agriculture (though registration of intended usage was required), to protect drinking water, to control pests that "constitute a danger to human beings." Golf courses were given a five-year phase-out period. Biological pesticides were allowed. Two challenges were made to the by-law: (1) that it was not authorized by the *Cities and Towns Act* and (2) that it conflicted with legislation of the provincial and the federal governments. The Court found legitimate authorization in the omnibus powers section of the *Act*, the power granted to make by-laws for the "peace, order, good government, health, and general welfare" of the town. Regarding conflict with the laws of the senior levels of government, the Court said that an actual operative conflict would be necessary to invalidate a municipal by-law otherwise validly enacted.

NOTES

1) *Spraytech* is seen as an endorsement of municipal engagement with environmental issues. The Court applied the observation of La Forest J in *R v Hydro-Québec*[177] that "the protection of the environment is a major challenge of our time. It is an international problem, one that requires action by governments at all levels" to support its approval of the by-law.
2) *Spraytech* is also an endorsement of use by municipalities of the omnibus powers clauses of provincial statutes. Some leading prior

---

175 Above note 171.
176 Above note 18.
177 [1997] 3 SCR 213.

cases such as *Morrison v Kingston*[178] had severely limited the use of omnibus powers. At the same time, the Court said that where a specific power is granted, the omnibus powers clause could not be used to expand the specific power.

3) Very broadly, and with variations by province, the distribution of regulating authority regarding pesticides in Canada is that the federal government regulates what pesticides may be licensed for use; the provincial governments tend to regulate licensing of commercial applicators, and climate or weather conditions for use; and municipalities may choose whether to further restrict pesticide use.
4) The Court says both that the approach to the use of omnibus powers is one of "caution" since "such open-ended provisions do not confer an unlimited power"[179] and that municipal powers are to benefit from "generosity of interpretation."[180] Overall, it is the latter statement that appears to emerge from *Spraytech*.
5) The principle of "operative conflict" was not new in *Spraytech*. The leading prior case was *Superior Propane Inc v York (City)*.[181] A municipal by-law may be invalid if the provincial legislation indicates, by enacting a comprehensive scheme, an intent to occupy the field, or also if obeying one set of rules means disobedience of the other. Conflict is a point now usually addressed by statute; thus Ontario's *Municipal Act, 2001* states, "A by-law is without effect to the extent of any conflict with . . . a provincial or federal Act or a regulation made under such an Act . . . ."[182]
6) Delineation of municipal jurisdiction vis-à-vis provincial jurisdiction is a complex matter. Where there is no invalidity of municipal jurisdiction by reason of operative conflict, there is room for both levels to exercise regulatory powers, and indeed, municipal regulation may be more stringent than provincial rules: see, for example, *Greater Vancouver (Regional District) v Darvonda Nurseries Ltd*[183] and other cases cited in Chapter 11. In some instances, municipal jurisdiction is seen to exist where provincial jurisdiction does not.[184]

---

178 [1937] 4 DLR 740 (Ont CA).

179 Above note 18 at para 20.

180 *Ibid* at para 26.

181 (1995), 27 MPLR (2d) 1 (Ont CA).

182 SO 2001, c 25, s 14.

183 2008 BCSC 1251.

184 See the unusual case of *Stevens v Capital (Regional District)*, 2010 BCSC 445, in which a local government rule prohibiting construction of a residence on private managed forest land prevailed over a provincial regulation that would have allowed one residence to be constructed.

6) Crucially, *Spraytech* states that where there is valid municipal jurisdiction, rules adopted may require higher standards than provincial laws.[185]

Pacific National Investments Ltd v Victoria (City)[186]

In the 1980s, Victoria conceived a plan to develop former industrial lands around its inner harbour, for residential uses along with public parks and paths. A Crown corporation was created to carry out the scheme. A "master agreement" set out the plan in the form of a contract, which was registered as a restrictive covenant against the land. Pacific National Investments (PNI), a private company, purchased some of the lands, intending to develop them according to the master agreement. The city subdivided the land and adopted zoning to facilitate the development. PNI moved in phases. After completing some of the parks and residential buildings, it wanted to move on to complete its planned construction. However, residents opposed the rest of the construction, and the city rezoned the remaining land to limit buildings there to one storey. PNI had not obtained development permits for the next phase of its planned construction. PNI took the view that the downzoning was a violation of the master agreement and sued for breach of contract or in the alternative for compensation for unjust enrichment to the city due to the construction of the parks. The company's lawsuit was unsuccessful. The Court refused to find that there was an implied term in the master agreement that the zoning would remain in place for a reasonable period of time; indeed, it said that "Zoning is a legislative power. On its face, the statute [the *Municipal Act*] provides for no power to constrain the future use of this legislative power."[187] Indeed, the Court said that, absent specific authorization by provincial law, for a council to be able to fetter future councils on a matter of zoning would be contrary to public policy.[188]

NOTES

1) If PNI had obtained development permits, its rights to construct would have crystallized and the subsequent change in zoning

---

185 For an exploration of the issues in *Spraytech*, see Howard Epstein "Case Comment: *Spraytech v Town of Hudson*" (2001) 19 *Municipal and Planning Law Reports* (3d) 56.

186 2000 SCC 64.

187 *Ibid* at para 38.

188 For a similar situation (a contract to purchase a former fire station subject to rezoning prior to closing), when the municipality refused to rezone there was no basis for a suit based on breach of contract: *Doherty v Southgate (Township)* (2006), 23 MPLR (4th) 12 (Ont SCJ).

would not have affected it, save that its development would have become a non-conforming use.

2) The circumstance of first-phase residents opposing the development of subsequent phases is something developers of large projects encounter from time to time. It can also occur in neighbourhoods that are in the process of change, and independent of proposals from one developer. In part, this just illustrates the inherently political nature of land-use planning; in part it suggests that spot zoning or partial planning has its drawbacks.
3) The facts raise the issue of how a municipality may legitimately stall or defeat a proposed development if it thinks it is undesirable, and the corresponding issue of how a developer may secure a right to proceed if it thinks opposition may arise to what it has in mind.
4) However desirable it might be as a matter of zoning flexibility, and certainty for developers, to have a mechanism that allows for "contract development," that mechanism was not available at the time under British Columbia legislation. A clear statutory authorization is needed for a council to bind future councils on matters of land use. British Columbia had a system to allow and regulate development agreements between 1971 and 1978, but it was repealed. A new system was adopted in 1993 to permit bargaining for amenities in exchange for higher density than the zoning would allow and to bind future councils.[189]
5) The decision opens with a statement by LeBel J often mentioned: "Land law may look like a dry, forbidding, and not very fashionable subject. Sometimes, however, it involves broad issues of policy and the principles of municipal governance."[190] There is very strong language in the decision about the obligation of municipal councils to "govern based on the best interests of their residents and based on conceptions of the public good"[191] and not to attempt to fetter the discretion of future councils.[192]
6) The British Columbia legislation included what is a standard provision in municipal laws, that "Compensation is not payable to any person for any reduction in the value of that person's interest in land, or for any loss or damages that result from the adoption of an official community plan . . . or a bylaw . . . ."

189 Above note 186 at paras 45–50.
190 *Ibid* at para 1.
191 *Ibid* at para 71.
192 *Ibid* at paras 18 and 62–64.

7) The Court did leave open a claim for PNI to compensation for the construction of walkways, a seawall, roads, and some parkland, on the basis of unjust enrichment.[193]

Congrégation des témoins de Jéhovah de St-Jérôme-Lafontaine v Lafontaine (Village)[194]

A Jehovah's Witness congregation sought to build or locate a church in the village. Not being successful in finding an appropriately zoned lot (P-3), it sought to have a lot rezoned so as to accommodate their church. The municipality responded to the first request by referring the matter to a committee for study, having staff meet with the congregation, and providing a map of P-3 areas. Still unable to find a suitably zoned lot, the congregation requested on two subsequent occasions to have property rezoned. The village sent a letter of refusal, repeating that P-3 lots were available. The congregation sued to have the municipality be required to rezone. The Court set out the principles for how the village should have considered the matter and remitted it to the village for reconsideration. It said the municipality must "exercise the powers conferred upon it fairly, in good faith and with a view to the public interest."[195] There was a duty of procedural fairness. The issue was the content of that duty. In the circumstances, the duty "required the municipality to carefully evaluate the applications for [rezoning] and to give reasons for refusing."[196]

NOTES

1) The congregation alleged infringement of freedom of religion guaranteed by the *Charter of Rights and Freedoms* and the *Quebec Charter of Human Rights*. The case was not decided on that basis. The case is, nonetheless, highly suggestive of the applicability of the federal *Charter's* section 2(a) freedom of religion provision to land uses. Still, in *Montréal (Ville de) c Église de Dieu Mont de Sion*,[197] a congregation sought to establish a church in a zone where the use was not permitted and its *Charter* challenge was not successful. The court said it had not established that other locations were not available.
2) It is impossible to read this case without some awareness of a very difficult history in Quebec between governmental authorities and Jehovah's Witnesses. See, for example, the case of *Roncarelli v Duplessis*.[198]

---

193 *Ibid* at para 75.
194 2004 SCC 48.
195 *Ibid* at para 2.
196 *Ibid* at para 12.
197 2011 QCCS 4281.
198 [1959] SCR 121.

3) All judges, including those in dissent, agreed that in these circumstances the municipality was obliged to give reasons, also referred to as "sufficient reasons," "valid reasons," and "more detailed reasons."[199] This is not the prevailing practice at municipal councils. The possibility of discerning a coherent set of reasons from freewheeling political debate has been doubted by some courts: see, for example, *Kirkfield Park & Arthur Oliver Residents Association Inc v Winnipeg (City)*.[200]

Canadian Pacific Railway Co v Vancouver (City)[201]

CPR owned a six-mile-long rail corridor from downtown Vancouver to the Fraser River, known as the Arbutus Corridor.[202] Rail traffic had tapered off, and in 1999, CPR had applied to federal authorities for permission to abandon the line. The city had been aware of the likelihood of abandonment since 1986 and had from time to time considered its future. The city adopted a plan amendment and by-law designating the corridor "only as a public thoroughfare, for the purposes of" transportation (rail, transit, cyclist path) or as a greenway (pedestrian or cyclist path). CPR was willing to sell the corridor, but the city had made no offer. The lands had been rendered uneconomic. The company challenged the city's by-law as designation for a public purpose as a street, entailing an obligation to purchase, and also alleged procedural unfairness in the process. The Court found there had been no violation of the *Vancouver Charter*, which allowed official plan designation and land-use controls, and declared there was no injurious affection through use of these powers. There had been no designation for use as a street, and thus no obligation to purchase. So far as process, the Court saw no fundamental defects in the hearing notice, saw CPR as having sufficient materials to allow it to participate effectively in the process, and did not see the amendment of the draft by-law after the hearing as prejudicial. On the content of the notice, the Court said ". . . what is required is fairness, not perfection."[203]

---

199 Above note 194 at paras 12–13 and 89–92.

200 (1996), 132 DLR (4th) 448 (Man CA).

201 2006 SCC 5.

202 See Ryan Goldvine, "In Good Faith to Whom? An Analysis of Judicial Deference to Municipal Authority and the Dispute over the Arbutus Corridor" (2006) 11 *Appeal* 40.

203 Above note 201 at para 46.

NOTES

1) Claims that some government regulatory action is tantamount to expropriation and should therefore attract compensation are frequently made, but are difficult to sustain in court.
2) The statement that what is required is "fairness not perfection" has become an important observation in cases challenging land-use decisions on the basis of defects in process. See, for example, *Heritage Trust of Nova Scotia v Halifax (Regional Municipality).*[204]
3) There has been subsequent litigation between the parties. CPR has abandoned its application to be allowed to discontinue the rail line. It has declared an intention to use the line for rail car storage and training of drivers. Over the years, the public had planted gardens on portions of the corridor, used it as a path, and for some parking of vehicles. CPR wanted to clear the area prior to resumption of its use, including spraying with herbicides to clear vegetation. The city sought an injunction to halt any of this. It asserted that the line was no longer subject to federal jurisdiction because of its long abandonment. CPR agreed not to pursue vegetation control immediately. In a preliminary ruling, the city's injunction application was refused: *Vancouver (City) v Canadian Pacific Railway Co.*[205] In 2016, the city purchased the corridor, with the intention of creating a transportation greenway.
4) Changes in economic activity, demographics, and social attitudes lead to new land development opportunities. The CPR case illustrates this for a rail line. Other lands that have commonly become available for different purposes include former service stations, manufacturing plants, schools, and places of worship including associated buildings such as former convents. It is not unusual for such places to have considerable land and to be conveniently placed for repurposing. As these transitions occur, disputes have arisen over appropriate new use, extending, in the case of former schools, to appropriate disposition of a publicly owned asset.[206]

204 2007 NSSC 28.

205 2015 BCSC 76.

206 See, for example, *Jono Developments Ltd v North End Community Health Association*, 2014 NSCA 92; *Halifax (Regional Municipality) v Anglican Diocesan Centre Corp*, 2010 NSCA 38; *Losani Homes Ltd v Hamilton (City)* (2010), 66 OMBR 179; *Friends of Lansdowne Inc v Ottawa (City)*, 2012 ONCA 273.

CHAPTER 3

SOURCES OF AUTHORITY: COMMON LAW

A. PRELIMINARY

Our focus in this chapter is primarily on the use of the common law by private individuals or corporations in regards to the control of the use of land, rather than by action of some level of government. Government action could be regulatory, or could involve a municipality invoking common law remedies in an attempt to abate some nuisance, or could extend to use of a combination of a by-law plus the remedy of an injunction.[1]

The common law is of significance in land-use matters first, because it continues to be a possible source of remedies in many instances of disputes, and second, because formalized legislative regimes that deal with land-use matters evolved from the principles of the common law and reflect its main concerns, such as respect for private property, separation of incompatible uses, and reconciliation of competing values.

Prior to the development of detailed statutory control regimes, the common law constituted the only available remedy. Professors Mossman and Girard note that "[e]asements and covenants have been

---

1 Thus, in *Ramara (Township) v Mullen*, 2012 ONSC 2220, the municipality, empowered by provincial legislation to control nuisances, had adopted such a by-law and successfully sought an injunction against a landowner operating an outdoor furnace that was producing problematic dark smoke. The basis of the power to seek a remedy was a statutory one conferred on the local government, not the common law.

characterized as mechanisms of 'private' land-use planning."[2] These formal agreements, or implied restrictions, have historically worked, and continue to work, along with actions based in nuisance or trespass so as to offer essentially individual and private land-use regulatory restrictions.

> Before there existed any public control over the use and development of land, landowners were free to use land in any way they wished, subject only to any limitations in the grant under which they held the land and to obligations placed upon them at common law. In essence, therefore, provided an owner acted within the limitation of his estate or interest, and committed no nuisance or trespass against his neighbour's property, he was free to use his land for the purpose for which it was economically best suited.[3]

Essentially, any notion that ownership of land implies unfettered rights of use has never been the case; the law has always placed limits on unreasonable use of land. It has always been possible to seek a remedy (money as compensation or an injunction) from the courts for actions that amount to nuisance. In environmental law, common law remedies for pollution have been a traditional approach and continue to be available. They are often referred to as "toxic torts." Tort law and property law are relevant also through the law relating to such matters as trespass and easements.

The common law is not generally replaced by statutory regulation, but issues of their interaction do arise. One important example of a modern statute replacing common law is for the creation of new lots; it was an entitlement of ownership at common law to be able to sell a part of one's property, but this is now entirely controlled by subdivision rules. As to the common law of nuisance, it remains in full vigour as a system of land-use control that parallels the largely statutory regimes of the federal, provincial, and municipal governments. Nuisance claims will, however, take into account other regulatory schemes such as zoning. The 1985 case of *Desrosiers v Sullivan*[4] case illustrates the interaction of the systems. Faced with a claim by residential neighbours about a legal pig farm due to odour, the New Brunswick court had to decide what standard of reasonable use applied in the community. The courts were available to the neighbours, who found the odour objectionable, even though the farm was not in violation of any zoning or agricultural laws.

---

2 Mary Jane Mossman & Philip Girard, *Property Law: Cases and Commentary*, 3d ed (Toronto: Emond Montgomery, 2014) at 637.

3 Victor Moore, *A Practical Approach to Planning Law*, 10th ed (New York: Oxford University Press, 2007) at 1.

4 (1985), 66 NBR (2d) 243 (QB) [*Desrosiers*].

The case also illustrates the interaction of the courts and legislatures, for after the decision awarding damages to the complaining neighbours, the New Brunswick legislature adopted a statute designed to protect agricultural operations from nuisance lawsuits (a "right-to-farm" law). The political nature of land-use regulation appears quite clearly in this dispute's subsequent history.

For many aspects of the common law of property and tort, statutory regimes have been adopted that either codify the common law, or modify it, or supplement it. Statutory frameworks for creating conservation easements are an example.

It is of the essence of many common law actions over land that, even if framed as issues over ownership, they are focused on use. This is almost always the core issue in right-of-way cases, as illustrated in something of a specialized case over a right-of-way involving a public beach in *Lanty v Ontario (Minister of Natural Resources)*,[5] in which a cottager unsuccessfully attempted to show that she had a legal right to drive over a public beach located in a provincial park so as to access her property.

Contemplating common law instruments and remedies such as restrictive covenants and nuisance lawsuits invites comparison with statutory regulation, as to efficacy. What are the advantages of the systems? Statutory regulation, especially the various forms of land-use planning, involves a public process with input from all comers; the rules are known in advance of the investment of resources, thus reducing uncertainty. Does this mean that zoning or some other land-use regulation should be preferred to the common law? In the face of extensive statutory regulation, has the common law or parts of it become superfluous?

B. PROPERTY

1) Land

A key aspect of property law is its definition of what "land" is. Use, by definition, flows from our understanding of land. Ownership normally entails a right to harvest crops, to fell trees, to excavate, to extract gravel, and to dig for minerals. Mineral rights, however, are quite restricted. Flowing from the theory that all property is the property of the Crown, the Crown has always withheld ownership of valued minerals. At common law, gold and silver were property of the Crown, and not the landowner. Statutory regulation is now the relevant set of controls, however.

---

5 2006 CanLII 1452 (Ont SCJ).

Thus, extraction of minerals, oil and gas, and coal becomes a matter for licensing and the payment of royalties. These regulatory regimes are examined in Chapter 5.

Although a maxim related to ownership (*cuius est solum eius est usque ad coelum et ad inferos*) implies ownership of a wedge that extends to the centre of the earth and out into space, not only does property law recognize limitations in subsurface rights, but there are limits on ownership and control of air space. Condominiums are a form of ownership, which, if in the sky, is created by statute and not easily recognized at common law. At common law, it was not possible to sell a piece of property located in the sky.[6] We deal very little with condominiums, for which internal rules are often important as to allowable uses.

Ownership boundaries where land is adjacent to water is an issue on which the law varies from province to province. An old maxim is that the boundary extends to the middle of the river, but in some provinces river beds are deemed Crown land,[7] and the results may vary according to whether the waterway is navigable. Further, just as erosion may reduce the size of a portion of land, so may accretion add to it. This branch of the law is not clear; some cases have distinguished between gradual change and sudden change.[8] With global climate change, drought conditions, if extreme, may lead to increased attention to such issues.

2) Servitudes

The law of servitudes (easements and covenants) allows for certain restrictions on use of property to be created, as a matter affecting the title to land. They are not akin to personal contracts affecting only the original parties, but run with the land: future owners are bound. Easements and covenants are "rights of use over property that belongs to another."[9] Servitudes are still very much a vigorous part of Canadian law bearing on land use. Technical rules apply.[10] Ziff notes,

> The easement is a versatile tool . . . [but] four doctrinal limits circumscribe [their] scope . . . . First, there must be a dominant tenement (which

---

6 But see *Iredale v Loudon* (1908), 40 SCR 313 and the discussion in Bruce Ziff, *Principles of Property Law*, 6th ed (Toronto: Thomson Carswell, 2014) at 365.

7 See, for example, *Public Lands Act*, RSA 2000, c P-40; *Beds of Navigable Waters Act*, RSO 1990, c B.4.

8 See, for example, *Southern Centre for Theosophy Inc v State of South Australia*, [1982] AC 706; *Brainard v Texas*, 12 SW3d 6 (Texas 1999); *Re Darrach* (1995), 135 Nfld & PEIR 153 (PEISCTD).

9 See Ziff, above note 6 at 379.

10 See Ziff, *ibid* at 385ff.

> enjoys the benefit of the easement) and a servient tenement (which is burdened) . . . . Second, the easement must accommodate the dominant land . . . . The right must be reasonably necessary for the enjoyment of the dominant tenement . . . there must be reasonable proximity . . . [though] the properties do not have to be contiguous . . . . Third, the . . . tenements cannot both be in the hands of the same person . . . . Fourth, the easement must be capable of forming the subject matter of a grant . . . rights under an easement must not be too vague . . . .[11]

Easements may be express or implied, or may arise through estoppel or prescription. They may be positive, that is, allowing the holder "to engage in some activity on the servient tenement,"[12] or negative, that is, restricting some specified activities on the servient land. Negative easements are not often recognized, being seen as an excessive burden on land; thus, rights to light or to a view are not recognized. They cannot require the expenditure of money by the owner of the servient tenement, except for maintenance of fences. Easements may terminate through abandonment, through a change in circumstances that makes the easement irrelevant to the dominant tenement, or through merging of ownership of the dominant and servient lands.

Covenants, the other main form of servitude, evolved for the greater certainty of the parties, and are formal. When used, they may be of greater significance than local zoning. They may address type of land use and the quality of construction, and extend to heritage preservation and protection of green space. They may be only negative in nature; they are often termed "restrictive covenants" for that reason. However, the line between positive and negative covenants is not clear.[13] The technical requirements for restrictive covenants are similar to those for easements (that they be for the benefit of the dominant tenement and be intended to run with the land). Frequently they are made part of building schemes.

The classic example of a servitude is a right-of-way. The right of passage over another's land is readily seen as a benefit to the dominant land and a burden to the servient land. It may restrict building rights, impact upon privacy, and affect market value. But if created properly and is clear in its terms, such servitudes are valid. There are other uses that may arise as servitudes, for example, to establish a sewer line so

---

11 *Ibid* at 381–83. For a policy discussion of restrictive covenants, see Bruce Ziff, "Bumble Bees Cannot Fly, and Restrictive Covenants Cannot Run" in Anneke Smit & Marcia Valiante, eds, *Public Interest, Private Property* (Vancouver: UBC Press, 2016) 59.

12 Ziff, above note 6 at 384.

13 Ziff, *ibid* at 425, refers to the difference as "superficial."

as to connect to municipal facilities;[14] the courts have even recognized the use of another's chimney to direct smoke as a form of servitude.[15] It is not unusual for subdivisions to be created with various restrictive covenants, such as a prohibition on keeping horses or livestock,[16] or on style of construction of buildings, or on front yard clotheslines. It is possible for the covenants to deal with as many types of matter as a zoning by-law.[17] Because formal government rules to control uses represent a system of its own, private covenants may supplement those rules and add burdens to the land.[18]

Apart from express easements, the law recognizes some implied ones. Thus, no property is to be landlocked; an easement of necessity is implied.

And an easement may arise through use over time. This arises from the provisions of *Limitations Acts,* which disallow challenges to uses that are "open, continuous, notorious, and adverse" after some set period of years. Such claims may prevail over public (Crown) land as well as over private land.[19] Such easements are not easy to establish. Because they arise not through consensual grant, but in circumstances of long use, such claims are scrutinized carefully by the courts.[20]

Easements may arise over public lands and create a public right-of-way. In essence, this amounts to creation of a highway. The rules that apply to establishment of a public right-of-way are quite restrictive. Two recent cases explore this: *Re Witherall*[21] and *Bassett v Mitton.*[22] Both cite English common law.

The courts have power to cancel, or in some cases to modify, restrictive covenants. For example, British Columbia's *Property Law Act* allows a court to do so if satisfied that "by reason of changes in the character of the land, the neighbourhood or other circumstances . . . the registered charge or interest is obsolete."[23] The idea of "change in

---

14 *Burke v Kroeker*, 2005 BCCA 242.

15 *Garfinkel v Kleinberg*, [1955] 2 DLR 844 (Ont CA).

16 See, for example, *Rice v Condran*, 2012 NSSC 95.

17 See Pierre Filion & Michelle Alexander, "Restrictive Covenants: Hidden Obstacles" (1995) 35:1 *Plan Canada* 33.

18 See, for example, *Tanti v Gruden*, 1999 ABCA 150, where a restrictive covenant prohibiting any commercial activity in a residential area in Edmonton was deemed effective regardless of municipal rules.

19 See, for example, *Meaford (Municipality) v Grist*, 2011 ONSC 5195.

20 See, for example, *Temma Realty Co v Ress Enterprises Ltd*, [1968] 2 OR 293 (CA).

21 2014 NLTD(G) 57.

22 2012 PECA 13.

23 *Property Law Act*, RSBC 1996, c 377, s 31; see *Parker v Kamloops (City)*, 2012 BCSC 61. In the USA, restrictive covenants may be cancelled as a matter of com-

the neighbourhood" may bring zoning into play. Thus in *Laurence v Century Holdings Ltd*,[24] the previous owner of land imposed a covenant restricting use to a single-family dwelling. Most of the nearby area was zoned C-3 (commercial) and had restaurants and motels, though the lot in question was zoned residential. The previous owner refused to lift the covenant. The court determined that the covenant no longer served any useful purpose, and noted that if there were to be any commercial development, a rezoning would be necessary and the previous owner would be able to make representations during the public process. The example of *Laurence* suggests that in British Columbia, in areas where there is a system of zoning, covenants as to type of use might always be cancelled. *Odyssey Tower Properties Ltd v Surrey (City)*[25] is an example of a court refusing to cancel a restrictive covenant that established a pedestrian right-of-way. Much depends on the wording of the applicable statute. In *Galloway v Coldstream (District) (Approving Officer)*,[26] a restrictive covenant in favour of the municipality was modified by the court. The complex circumstances illustrate how careful purchasers must be in assessing the potential for development on adjacent land if such development would seriously negatively affect them. In Alberta, the *Land Titles Act* allows for cancellation if the "covenant conflicts with the provisions of a land-use bylaw or statutory plan . . . and the modification or discharge is in the public interest."[27] It is often difficult to show conflict with by-laws since, typically, they "are merely permissive."[28]

Utilities are often empowered to use the land of others for purposes of placing their infrastructure, and to do so without expropriation or purchase. Generally, in urban areas, basic utility infrastructure such as water pipes, gas lines, and Internet wiring will be on public land.[29] But elsewhere, major infrastructure such as oil and gas pipes will frequently cross private land. Thus under Ontario's *Ministry of Government*

---

mon law; see Joseph William Singer, *Introduction to Property* (New York: Aspen, 2005).

24 (1985), 64 BCLR 33 (SC).

25 2006 BCSC 1842.

26 2007 BCSC 33 [*Galloway*].

27 RSA 2000, c L-4, s 48(4).

28 *Ukranian Senior Citizens Home of St John v Torres*, 2009 ABQB 725 at para 20; *Seifeddine v Hudson's Bay Traders* (1980), 108 DLR (3d) 671 (Alta CA).

29 For a discussion of some aspects of the interaction of the federal regulatory agency, the CRTC, with municipal powers, see *Federation of Canadian Municipalities v AT&T Canada Corp*, 2002 FCA 500; see also A Neil Craik & Carol Anne O'Brien, "CRTC Decision re Exclusive Access to Subdivision Trenches" (1999) 4 *Municipal and Planning Law Reports* (3d) 225. The Federation of Canadian Municipalities has an advisory note, "Dealing with Telecom Companies" (Ottawa: Federation of Canadian Municipalities, 2009).

Services Act,[30] "government public utility easements" may be created, a public utility meaning a waterworks, water supply system, sewage works, steam or hot water distribution system, electrical power or energy generating system, transmission or distribution system, street lighting system, natural gas works or supply system, or transportation system.

Some legislation nullifies certain restrictive covenants. For example, Nova Scotia's *Clothesline Act* eliminates restrictive covenants that had served to prohibit clotheslines. The *Act* was adopted as a measure to advance the use of solar power, a value seen as more important than any aesthetic concern about clotheslines. To the same effect is O Reg 97/08 under the *Green Energy Act, 2009*,[31] which provides that an occupant is "permitted to use [a clothesline] . . . despite any restraint imposed at law that would otherwise prevent or restrain their use, including . . . a municipal by-law, a condominium by-law, an encumbrance on real property or an agreement."

A new form of easement is the conservation easement. Most provinces have adopted legislation to allow for creation of conservation easements, for example, Ontario's *Conservation Land Act*,[32] Saskatchewan's *The Conservation Easements Act*,[33] and the *Alberta Land Stewardship Act*.[34] Conservation easements might be entered into between private persons, but the common law regarding easements has limitations that hamper their efficacy. In *Willman v Ducks Unlimited (Canada)*,[35] the purported easement was found not to exist because no dominant tenement existed; the agreement was one between the original contracting parties, and a subsequent owner was not bound. Having a statutory framework assists the process and can finesse common law problems.[36] In *Nature Conservancy of Canada v Waterton Land Trust Ltd*,[37] the court said, describing the new regime, "A conservation easement is typically arranged between a private entity, such as a landowner, and a conservation organization or government agency and then embodied in a written agreement. In Alberta these are then registered on the title to the land. These agreements

30 RSO 1990, c M.25, ss 8 and 11. See also the *Ministry of Infrastructure Act, 2011*, SO 2011, c 9, Schedule 27.

31 SO 2009, c 12, Schedule A; the regulation was originally enacted under the predecessor statute, *Energy Conservation Leadership Act, 2006*, now repealed.

32 RSO 1990, c C.28.

33 SS 1996, c C-27.01.

34 SA 2009, c A-26.8, as amended.

35 2004 MBCA 153.

36 See, generally, Arlene Kwasniak, "Conservation Easements: Plusses and Pitfalls, Generally and for Municipalities" (2009) 46 *Alberta Law Review* 651.

37 2014 ABQB 303 [*Waterton Land Trust*].

contain perpetual restrictions to the use of the land."[38] The statutes eliminate the restrictions of the common law as to dominant tenements, against positive easements, in the case of lapse through non-enforcement, or in the case of a change in use of the surrounding land. In the *Waterton Land Trust* case, the plaintiff had sold the land to the defendant subject to a conservation easement that was intended to allow wildlife migration across the land. The purchaser intended to raise bison on the land, which required fencing. Fencing had been on parts of the land, and the easement allowed this to remain, and be repaired, but restricted the height of the fencing. Issues arose over the repair and height of the replacement fencing, leading to an application to the court to interpret the conservation easement. It is also possible to apply to a court to terminate a statutory conservation easement if continuance "would produce a severe hardship for the applicant."[39] In *Nature Conservancy of Canada v Mattus*,[40] the owner sought to terminate the easement because it wished to place wind turbines on the undeveloped land.

An important limitation on the efficacy of conservation easements is that, in most provinces, they are treated as all other private land so far as being available for prospecting and mining. That is, expropriation may take place, as through a minister's vesting order or order of a surface rights board, if there is thought to be commercial mineral potential. Manitoba[41] and Quebec[42] have provisions that allow the minister to withdraw from prospecting, exploration, or mining lands that it would be in the public interest to protect; in Manitoba, there has been co-operation between the government and the main land trust organizations to identify lands that are to be closed to exploration and staking.

3) Support

There is an obligation at common law not to remove support for neighbouring land. This is another instance of the law's recognition that ownership is not a matter of isolated occupation and enjoyment with blithe indifference to circumstances. The deliberate change in contours of land through such undertakings as excavation may result in subsidence or erosion of adjacent land; this is actionable as nuisance. The right is both lateral and vertical; that is, it applies at the borders of land and underneath. The obligation is to the land itself, not directly to buildings

---

38 *Ibid* at para 19.
39 Above note 33, s 10.
40 2011 SKCA 135.
41 *Mines and Minerals Act*, CCSM c M162, s 14.
42 *Mining Act*, CQLR c M-13.1, s 304.

on it, though if injury to buildings flows from the damage to the land it is actionable.[43] Uneven levels of adjacent properties is a common feature.[44] In *Bamlett v Osterling*,[45] the owner of a lot that sloped towards the adjacent lot had constructed a retaining wall and placed some fill on the neighbouring lot to help support the wall. A subsequent purchaser proposed to excavate to build a driveway. The court granted an injunction to restrain the excavation and refused to treat the fill as a trespass.

4) Waste

Someone with less than a fee simple interest in land is usually constrained at common law from committing waste. The law of waste may be thought of as the common law's form of taking into account intergenerational equity. That is, the point is to require someone in temporary possession of land not to harm the land such as to impair the rights of future owners. "The principles of waste possess certain characteristics that are all too typical of English land law—they are elaborately embroidered and archaic."[46] Nonetheless, the principles have been applied in Canadian cases, such as *Stewart v Sherstobitoff*,[47] where unauthorized cutting of timber was at issue, and *Weist v Smith*,[48] where the issue was appropriate husbandry of crops. Modern cases involving waste tend to focus on "permissive" waste, in which property is neglected and becomes run down, rather than "voluntary" or "equitable" waste, in which the value is diminished through deliberate actions.

5) *Private Ways Act*[49]

Nova Scotia has a *Private Ways Act*, which allows both the provincial cabinet and a municipal council to settle land-use and ownership issues between parties. The legislation appears to be unique in the country and dates to 1765. For cabinet, the power is tied to economic development. Thus the triggering circumstance is stated: "Every owner or occupier of any mine, mill, quarry, farm or factory who is desirous of transporting the[ir] produce . . . to a railway or public way, or to

43 *Delorme v Metcalfe Realty Co Ltd*, [1968] 1 OR 124 (HCJ). Justice Haines had no hesitation in applying the right of support to a building, without stumbling over issues of land as distinct from its buildings or whether the right applies only to land in its raw state as in *LeBlanc v Poirier* (1992), 129 NBR (2d) 262 (QB).

44 *Ardavicius v Kairys* (2009), 251 OAC 114 (Div Ct).

45 (1964), 47 DLR (2d) 61 (Alta SCTD).

46 Ziff, above note 6 at 164.

47 [1938] 1 DLR 578 (Sask CA).

48 [1927] 1 DLR 448 (Sask KB).

49 *Private Ways Act*, RSNS 1989, c 358.

tidal or other waters or elsewhere, and every owner or occupier of any timber lands who desires to enter upon such lands and cut the timber or wood thereon and remove the same . . . and who is unable to agree for a right of way with the owner or owners of any lands which it is necessary to cross in order to effect such entry or transportation, may present a petition to the Governor in Council."[50] At the discretion of cabinet, the petition may trigger a commission of inquiry to report and recommend; a right of way may be created by order of cabinet, subject to arbitration regarding compensation to be paid, and disallowing any right of way "through a house, building, orchard or garden."[51] Municipal councils have similar powers to establish a commission to respond to a petition "for the obtaining and laying out of a private way or road" if such is "the most practicable and reasonable means of access for the person or persons petitioning for the way or road to his or their lands or property or rights."[52] The municipal power is not specifically tied to economic development and is more associated in practice with the problem of landlocked, or inconveniently situated, residential lots.

It is not unusual for land titles to be quieted through application to court for determination of various rights in the land.[53] The special feature of the *Private Ways Act* is that it sorts out a land-use issue through a remedy affecting title to the land.[54] That is, with a view to sorting out appropriate uses of the land in question, a level of government may transfer title from one private owner to another, a process distinct from expropriation for public purposes.[55]

C. TORT

1) Trespass

Since the 1765 case of *Entick v Carrington*,[56] it has been established that "By the laws of England every invasion of property, be it ever so minute, is a trespass. No man can set his foot upon my ground without any licence but he is liable to an action, though the damage be nothing." The

---

50 *Ibid*, s 2.

51 *Ibid*, s.5.

52 *Ibid*, s.17.

53 See, for example, British Columbia's *Land Title Inquiry Act*, RSBC 1996, c 251, or Nova Scotia's *Quieting Titles Act*, RSNS 1989, c. 382. *Goulden v Nova Scotia (Attorney General)*, 2013 NSSC 253, discusses the interaction of the statutory schemes.

54 For a contemporary application of the statute, see *Cron v Halifax (Regional Municipality)*, 2010 NSSC 460.

55 *Ibid*.

56 (1765), 19 Howell's State Trials 1029.

contemporary relevance of this form of action for land use arises primarily for access to property to use it for purposes of disseminating information or to allow or ease construction on an adjoining property.

Statutes such as the *Petty Trespass Act* (Nova Scotia) or *Trespass to Property Act* (Ontario) offer avenues for an owner to exclude those seen as undesirable. But the law has developed so as to accommodate competing interests to a certain extent. The Supreme Court of Canada has said that not only statutes, but the common law, should be interpreted to reflect the *Canadian Charter of Rights and Freedom* (*Charter*).[57] This seems to imply no absolute right to exclude others, at least for some locales, if they are engaging in free expression and regardless of whether the land in question is publicly owned, as was Dorval Airport in *Committee for the Commonwealth of Canada v Canada*[58] or privately owned, as in cases such as *Grosvenor Park Shopping Centre Ltd v Cave et al*[59] and *Harrison v Carswell*.[60] In *Grosvenor Park*, a shopping centre was the locale; the court declared there was no "quasi-public property," a view that has been severely critiqued[61] and seems now not to be the prevailing view.

During elections, enumerators, candidates, and canvassers are entitled to have access to apartment buildings,[62] thus removing certain election activity from the realm of trespass.

Access to private land for purposes of hunting and fishing are considered in Chapter 5, Section K. Should there be trespass for recreational purposes onto lands that might be regarded as possibly available, such as forested areas, pastures, utility corridors, trails, and private roads, there still exists a duty for the owner not to "create a danger with the deliberate intent of doing harm."[63]

Awards of damages have been made in instances of trespass to facilitate construction in, for example, *Carr-Harris v Schacter*[64] and *Epstein*

57 Part I of the *Constitution Act, 1982*, being Schedule B to the *Canada Act 1982* (UK), 1982, c 11. See, for example, *RWDSU, Local 558 v Pepsi-Cola Canada Beverages (West) Ltd*, 2002 SCC 8 at para 37.

58 [1991] 1 SCR 139.

59 1963 CanLII 432 (Sask QB) [*Grosvenor Park*].

60 [1976] 2 SCR 200.

61 See, for example, Raj Anand, *Report of theTask Force on the Law Governing Trespass to Publicly-Used Property as It Affects Youth and Minorities* (Toronto: Ministry of the Attorney General, 1987); Lisa Loader, "Trespass to Property: Shopping Centres" (1992) *8 Journal of Law and Social Policy* 254.

62 See, for example, *The Election Act, 1996*, SS 1996, c E-6.01, regarding enumeration and its *Residential Tenancies Act, 2006*, SS 2006, c R-22.0001, regarding candidates and canvassers.

63 *Occupier's Liability Act*, RSO 1990, c O.2, s 4.

64 [1956] OR 994 (HCJ) [*Schacter*].

v Cressey Development Corp.[65] In *Schacter*, the defendant, in constructing an apartment building, trespassed, including excavating under the plaintiff's property. The award of damages included $5,000 in exemplary damages. In *Cressey*, the builder placed temporary anchor rods on the plaintiff's property. No surface damage was done, and the rods were removed after; some debris remained buried about twenty-five feet below the plaintiff's property, but this was not likely to interfere with future development. The court saw actual injury since, as an alternative to building up to the lot line, the defendant could have set back part of its building, and the proximity diminished the value of the plaintiff's land. Compensatory damages were awarded of $25,000 plus exemplary damages of $45,000. In both of these cases, the plaintiff had declined to enter into an encroachment agreement.

In *Ghalioungui v Mississauga (City)*,[66] the city trespassed on the plaintiff's property during construction of a road and a bridge, including an element of the construction that constituted an ongoing trespass. Damages were awarded of $10,000 plus $15,000 in punitive damages. The court said, "It was highly presumptuous, arrogant and callous for the City [and the contractor] to presume they could proceed to use the property for construction of a road and a bridge and for the continuing trespasses of the gabion and supporting soil without Mr. Ghalioungui's consent."[67]

Actions based in trespass related to use of air space during construction have tended to be successful. A leading case is *Lewvest Ltd v Scotia Towers Ltd.*[68] An injunction was granted to halt the trespass. This is understandable since, for properties that are adjacent, the desire to use air space to effect construction on one property will usually reflect the potential to use air space to construct on the property next door. However, once the opportunity has been exercised, the developer that is second in time may never be able to use the air space of the first developer.

There is some statutory modification of this aspect of trespass. For example, in the *City of St John's Act*, the municipal council is empowered to allow use of a party wall for construction, or to allow access to neighbouring land to facilitate alteration, repair, or maintenance of an existing building (though not construction). The council may require security to be posted against damage and may require a money contribution to be made to the property affected.[69] Party wall agree-

65 (1992), 89 DLR (4th) 32 (BCCA) [*Cressey*].
66 2005 CanLII 9333 (Ont SCJ).
67 *Ibid* at para 109.
68 (1981), 126 DLR (3d) 239 (Nfld SCTD); see also *Woollerton & Wilson Ltd v Richard Costain Ltd*, [1970] 1 All ER 483.
69 *City of St John's Act*, RSNL 1990, c C-17, s 387.

ments may be entered into by adjacent owners and registered against title.[70]

Some courts have doubted that trespass is the appropriate form of action and have suggested that nuisance should be used to characterize the interference. Such analysis challenges the traditional maxim *cuius est solum ejus est usque ad coelum et ad infernos* (ownership goes from the centre of the earth to the heavens): see *Didow v Alberta Power Ltd*,[71] where the unqualified maxim characterizing the nature of land ownership was rejected in favour of a view that looks to actual use of air space or its effective possession (i.e., future potential use). In *Didow*, the electric utility erected power poles adjacent to the plaintiff's land, obtained permission from the Surface Rights Board[72] to place guy wires, then built the poles with arms thirty-five feet in the air, but over the plaintiff's land. Because of the permanence, the court regarded this as trespass, even though there was no interference with the agricultural activities being carried on and though zoning rules governing future construction on the plaintiff's land required a considerable setback from the lot lines.

Another manifestation of actions in trespass has to do with encroaching or border trees. As trenchantly said by the British Columbia Court of Appeal in *Anderson v Skender*,[73] the trees do not trespass, but people may commit trespass if they trim or remove trees. Ontario makes specific reference to "boundary trees" in the *Forestry Act*.[74] A clutch of cases shows the nature of disputes that may arise between neighbours over such trees, for example, *R v Vastis*,[75] a prosecution for unauthorized removal, and *Scheuermann v Gross*,[76] which concerns the interaction between provincial and municipal regulatory regimes. In *Perdue v Vanderham*,[77] a suit in trespass for cutting trees was successful. Damages of $20,000 was awarded for the unauthorized removal of forty-seven trees, about 100 years old, plus $12,500 for loss of amenities.

NOTES

1) The United Kingdom has an *Access to Neighbouring Land Act 1992*, which allows for an application to be made to court for an access order if permission cannot be obtained from the relevant owner.

---

70 See, for example, *The Real Property Act*, CCSM c R30, s 76.
71 [1988] 5 WWR 606 (Alta CA) [*Didow*].
72 *Surface Rights Act*, RSA 2000, c S-24.
73 [1994] 1 WWR 186 (BCCA).
74 RSO 1990, c F.26, s 10.
75 2006 ONCJ 347.
76 2015 ONCJ 254.
77 (2004), 4 MPLR (4th) 86 (Ont SCJ).

Access may be granted to facilitate maintenance, repair, or demolition of a building (though not for construction); for repair of drains, sewer pipes, or cables; and for vegetation removal. The courts must balance the applicant's request with the interference or hardships of the owner who would be affected by the order.

2) It is possible for drones, also referred to as "unmanned aerial vehicles," "remotely piloted air vehicles," or "autonomous programmable vehicles," to trespass. If they crash, they might cause inconvenience, damage, or injury. If carrying cameras, they will invade privacy.[78] There has been speculation that they might be used for purposes of violence. They do not appear to be regulated, unless viewed as a type of helicopter,[79] although there are restrictions under the *Defence Production Act*.[80]
3) A leading case in Texas dealing with fracking as a trespass decided that under the oil and gas extraction regime that prevails there, fracking carried out under land adjacent to the land where the drilling originates does not amount to trespass: see *Coastal Oil & Gas Corp v Garza Energy Trust*.[81]

2) Rule in *Rylands v Fletcher*[82]

Unlike nuisance, for which the test of reasonableness is key, there are circumstances of strict liability for certain actions. This has come to be known as "the rule in *Rylands v Fletcher*," a reference to an 1868 House of Lords decision. In *Rylands v Fletcher*, a mill operator had constructed a water reservoir over old coal mines; due to the weight, a shaft gave way and flooded adjacent mines, causing damage. Unfortunately, there is little agreement as to what principle the case actually stands for, and there has been some evolution in its characterization. A good contemporary understanding is that it imposes strict liability for abnormally dangerous uses of land.[83] What that amounts to is not always clear. It has been successfully pleaded in *Mihalchuk v Ratke*[84] regarding the drift of

---

78 The article by Graham Mayeda, "My Neighbour's Kid Just Bought a Drone . . . New Paradigms for Privacy Law in Canada" (2015) 35 *National Journal of Constitutional Law* 59, despite its title, does not deal with drones, but does review privacy law.

79 See *Canadian Aviation Regulations*, SOR/96-433 pursuant to the *Aeronautics Act*, for a definition of "helicopter."

80 RSC 1985, c D-1.

81 268 SW3d 1 (Texas 2008).

82 (1868), LR 3 HL 330 [*Rylands*].

83 *Restatement of the Law Second: Torts 2d* (St Paul, MN: American Law Institute, 1977).

84 (1966), 57 DLR (2d) 269 (Sask QB).

herbicide,[85] *Curtis v Lutes*[86] regarding the spread of set fire,[87] *Gertsen v Toronto (Metro)*[88] regarding the explosion of gas originating in the use of organic material as landfill, and *MacDonald v Désourdy Construction Ltée*[89] regarding damage to a house occasioned by nearby blasting.

As with nuisance, the rule in *Rylands v Fletcher* is often raised in environmental cases if they invoke the common law. A leading Canadian case is *Palmer v Nova Scotia Forest Industries.*[90] The plaintiffs sought to prevent the aerial spraying of herbicides by a forestry company in Cape Breton. The action was based in nuisance, trespass, riparian rights, and on the rule in *Rylands v Fletcher.* The plaintiffs were unsuccessful on all grounds.[91] In considering *Rylands*, the judge said,

> The complete burden of proof, of course, rests upon the plaintiffs throughout for all issues asserted by them . . . . I am satisfied that a serious risk to health, if proved, would constitute irreparable harm and that damages would not be an adequate remedy. Further, recognizing the great width and elasticity of equitable principles, I would have no hesitation in deciding that such a situation would be one of the strongest which would warrant the exercise of the Court's discretion to restrain the activity which would create the risk. This matter thus reduces itself now to the single question. Have the plaintiffs offered sufficient proof that there is a serious risk of health and that such serious risk of health will occur if the spraying of the substances here is permitted to take place? . . . . Similarly, there has been no basis established for the application of the rule in *Rylands v Fletcher*, as neither the danger of the substance nor the likelihood of its escape to the plaintiffs' lands has been proved.[92]

The case is often cited as illustrating the difficulty of resolving complex

---

85 See also *Morassutti v Lanoue*, [2000] OJ No 1586 (SCJ), as an example of a dispute between two farmers (herbicide spraying of soybeans damaging tomato plants). But see, contra, *Palmer v Nova Scotia Forest Industries* (1983), 60 NSR (2d) 271 (SCTD) [*Palmer*].

86 [1953] 4 DLR 188.

87 Ontario had protection from liability for the spread of accidental fires: *Accidental Fires Act*, RSO 1990, c A.4, a statute that has been repealed.

88 (1973), 2 OR (2d) 1 (HCJ).

89 (1972), 27 DLR (3d) 144 (NSSCTD).

90 Above note 85.

91 The case is well known not only because of its legal principles but for the involvement of Elizabeth May, later head of the Sierra Club of Canada and then the Green Party of Canada, who wrote a book about the case, *Budworm Battles* (Halifax: Four East, 1982). There is also a documentary film *Herbicide Trials* (1984), directed by Neal Livingston. The case was the focus of an article by Professor Bruce Wildsmith, "Of Herbicides and Humankind: Palmer's Common Law Lessons" (1986) 24 *Osgoode Hall Law Journal* 161.

92 Above note 85 at paras 538, 546–47, and 600.

public policy issues in the court, as well as calling into question the nature of burden of proof in circumstances of potential environmental harm. That is, should the nature of burden or standard of proof be altered in any way so as to take into consideration the precautionary principle?

Traditional rules regarding burden of proof (who asserts must prove) and standard of proof (the civil test is on the balance of probabilities) can imply that the scientific evidence needed to show risk must be very clear. Whether, and if so how, this might evolve is not obvious. The adoption of the "precautionary principle" in general environment statutes,[93] and as endorsed by the Supreme Court of Canada in *Spraytech*,[94] suggests that it might have potential application in some common law cases. One commentator has said

> The precautionary principle may be the creative normative wedge to rethink common law doctrines such as nuisance and injunctive requirements. Something less than a serious health risk, for example, reasonable medical or ecological concern, might be considered to amount to a nuisance. The burden of proof might be shifted regarding a reasonable concern from plaintiff to defendant, who would have to show the lack of a reasonable or ecological concern before being allowed to undertake industrial or development activities.[95]

In commenting on this point, Professor Wildsmith said,

> Scientific uncertainty results in the benefit of the doubt being given to the chemicals. In a court of law, chemicals are presumptively innocent. The classical analysis illustrated by the *Palmer* case values the right to produce and use chemicals over possible adverse human health effects. As Nunn J's view demonstrates, the court is normally only concerned with the probable and not the possible . . . . One response to the burden of proof problem would be to enact new legislation.[96]

This has yet to occur.

NOTES

1) The scientific understanding of the health effects of herbicides and pesticides has moved forward greatly since the *Palmer* decision.

---

93 See, for example, *Canadian Environmental Protection Act, 1999*, SC 1999, c 33, s 2(1)(a).

94 *114957 Canada Ltée (Spraytech, Société d'arrosage) v Hudson (Town)*, 2001 SCC 40 [*Spraytech*].

95 David VanderZwaag, "The Concept and Principles of Sustainable Development" (1993) 13 *Windsor Yearbook of Access to Justice* 39; for comment on Professor VanderZwaag's suggestion, see HM Epstein, "Case Comment: *Spraytech v Town of Hudson*" (2001) 19 *Municipal and Planning Law Reports* (3d) 56.

96 Wildsmith, above note 91 at 177.

There has been much written on these effects.[97] Professor Doelle says, "The case [*Palmer*] was brought at a time when there was an active debate about the health and environmental risks of some of the chemicals present in the herbicides to be sprayed; today, the harmful effects of these chemicals are well documented and undisputed."[98]

3) Nuisance

Lawsuits based in nuisance continue to have significant potential as a means to control undesirable uses of land. Such actions, however, are beset with difficulties.[99]

It is a tradition of the British common law that the courts will adjudicate on alleged unreasonable uses of land. The recorded cases go back to 1610 and *Aldred's Case*,[100] in which householder William Aldred brought action against his neighbour Thomas Benton on the basis that Benton had built a pigsty too close to his property, resulting in unbearable odour. Aldred was successful, the court noting that no-one has a "right to maintain a structure upon his own land, which, by reason of disgusting smells, loud or unusual noises, thick smoke, noxious vapors, the jarring of machinery, or the unwarrantable collection of flies, renders the occupancy of adjoining property dangerous, intolerable, or even uncomfortable to its tenants . . . ." Disputes have arisen over problems such as odour,[101] noise,[102] dust,[103] fumes,[104] and vibrations[105]—grouping

97 See, for example, John Largo, *Our Children's Toxic Legacy*, 2d ed (New Haven, CT: Yale University Press, 1998); William J Rea, "Pesticides" (1996) 6 *Journal of Nutritional and Environmental Medicine* 55; Kathleen Cooper et al, *Environmental Standard Setting and Children's Health*, Report of the Canadian Environmental Law Association and the Ontario College of Family Physicians, CELA Publications (May 2000); and House of Commons Standing Committee on Environment and Sustainable Development, *Pesticides: Making the Right Choice for the Protection of Health and the Environment* (May 2000).

98 Meinhard Doelle & Chris Tollefson, *Environmental Law: Cases and Materials* (Toronto: Carswell, 2009) at 49.

99 For a focused overview, see Gregory Pun et al, *The Law of Nuisance in Canada*, 2d ed (Markham, ON: LexisNexis Canada, 2015).

100 (1610), 77 ER 816, [1558–1774] All ER Rep 622.

101 See, for example, *Newmarket (Town) v Halton Recycling Ltd* (2006), 25 MPLR (4th) 249 (Ont SCJ), where a municipality was the plaintiff. For comment on the decision see Richard Haigh & Batya Nadler, "And No More Shall We Shout" (2006) 34 *Supreme Court Law Review* (2d) 83.

102 See, for example, *Montréal (City) v 2952-1366 Québec inc*, 2005 SCC 62, where a municipality was the plaintiff. For comment on the decision, see Haigh & Nadler, above note 101.

103 *Pwllbach Colliery Co Ltd v Woodman*, [1915] AC 634 (HL).

104 *Manchester Corp v Farnworth*, [1930] AC 171 (HL).

105 *Grosvenor Hotel Co v Hamilton*, [1894] 2 QB 836.

of factors later described by the courts as "emanations,"[106] although this is not a limiting characterization of the tort of nuisance. Nuisance is a flexible concept. The Supreme Court of Canada has said that nuisance "may take a variety of forms, ranging from actual physical damage to land to interference with the health, comfort or convenience of the owner or occupier of land."[107] And in *Nor-Video Services Ltd v Ontario Hydro*,[108] it was said that,

> The notion of nuisance is a broad and comprehensive one which has been held to encompass a wide variety of interferences considered harmful and actionable because of their infringement upon or diminution of an occupier's interest in the undisturbed enjoyment of his property . . . . The category of interests covered by the tort of nuisance ought not to be and need not be closed, in my opinion, to new or changing developments associated from time to time with normal usage and enjoyment of land.

In assessing nuisance claims, the courts will consider the severity of the interference, the character of the neighbourhood, whether the plaintiff is abnormally sensitive, and the utility of the defendant's conduct.[109] Common law nuisance claims require the courts to engage in policy-making through balancing interests.

Many of the land-use disputes taken to the courts as matters of nuisance were issues between two immediate neighbours, and involved therefore quite localized issues of the nature of reasonable use of land. Others involved multiple neighbours, such as challenges to brothels,[110] street prostitution,[111] pornography stores,[112] and infectious disease hospitals.[113] Still others involved larger communities and raised issues we now categorize as being environmental because they challenged large-scale industrial pollution.[114]

---

106 *Hunter v Canary Wharf Ltd*, [1997] 2 All ER 426 (HL), Goff LJ.

107 *Tock v St John's Metropolitan Area Board*, [1989] 2 SCR 1181 at 1190–91.

108 (1978), 84 DLR (3d) 221 at 231 (Ont HCJ).

109 See, for example, *Susan Heyes Inc (cob Hazel & Co) v Vancouver (City)*, 2011 BCCA 77.

110 *Thompson-Schwab v Costaki*, [1956] 1 All ER 652 (CA); *Poirier v Turkewich* (1964), 42 DLR (2d) 259 (Man QB).

111 *British Columbia (Attorney General) v Couillard* (1984), 11 DLR (4th) 567 (BCSC). See Jamie Cassels, "Prostitution and Public Nuisance: Desperate Measures and the Limits of Civil Adjudication" (1985) 63 *Canadian Bar Review* 764.

112 *Laws v Florinplace Ltd*, [1981] 1 All ER 659 (Ch D).

113 *Shuttleworth v Vancouver General Hospital*, [1927] 2 DLR 573 (BCSC). This action was not successful.

114 For an exploration of the use of common law in the context of environmental issues, see Mario D Faieta et al, *Environmental Harm: Civil Actions and Compensation* (Toronto: Butterworths, 1996).

Significantly, the Supreme Court of Canada has been on record since 1928 about the potential for nuisance actions to protect the environment. In the frequently cited words of Rinfret J in *Groat v Edmonton (City)*,[115] "Pollution is always unlawful and, in itself, constitutes a nuisance."[116] Lawsuits over noise or odour may appear quaint, and indeed they are sometimes reflective of a more pastoral era or of particularly salubrious settings. However, the principles that evolved through the common law have serious potential for application in circumstances where advances in scientific knowledge lead us to a better understanding of the health implications of so many aspects of contemporary life.[117]

There are two categories of nuisance: public and private. Private nuisance involves disputes over alleged unreasonable use of land by an immediate or nearby neighbour, where the effects are somewhat localized. Public nuisance involves generalized effects, where, although the general public is adversely affected, no-one is usually affected more than anyone else. Tort actions for public nuisance may be brought only by the attorney general, although if any individuals can show that they have been affected more than the general public, they may take action over public nuisances.

Examples of private nuisance cases are *Appleby v Erie Tobacco Co*[118] for odour emitted from a tobacco factory, and *Oakley v Webb*[119] and *Balmain Hotel Group LP v 1547648 Ontario Ltd*[120] for noise from industrial and commercial operations. In *Guinan v Ottawa (City)*,[121] the municipality was the defendant and was found liable in nuisance for damage done to the homeowner's foundation and lawn by the roots of a tree located on city land, this illustrating the variety of nuisances. In their analysis, courts have considered the nature of the community and whether the objected-to use is more than a mere inconvenience, but have not taken into consideration any special susceptibility of a plaintiff or that the plaintiff "came to the nuisance" (i.e., moved to the area after the nuisance existed).[122] Compliance with a regulatory regime will not automatically be a defence in a nuisance action. Even if a land use complies with applicable zoning, environmental, or agricultural rules, nuisance

115 [1928] SCR 522.

116 *Ibid* at 532. On this topic generally, see Jamie Benidickson, *Environmental Law*, 4th ed (Toronto: Irwin Law, 2013) ch 5.

117 See David Boyd, *Cleaner, Greener, Healthier* (Vancouver: UBC Press, 2015).

118 (1910), 22 OLR 533 (Div Ct).

119 (1916), 38 OLR 151 (SCAD).

120 (2009), 60 MPLR (4th) 262 (Ont SCJ) [*Balmain*].

121 2010 ONSC 807.

122 This last point was established as early as 1896 by the Supreme Court of Canada in *Drysdale v Dugas* (1896), 26 SCR 20.

actions could still be successful. Thus, in *St-Laurent Cement Inc v Barrette*,[123] a cement plant was held liable in nuisance for emissions of dust even though statutory standards were complied with, and in *Balmain*,[124] an action to restrain noise from a downtown Toronto bar late at night was successful even though the bar was licensed, its hours of operation complied with applicable laws, and the land was zoned appropriately. We saw the same point arising in the *Desrosiers* case.

A classic statement about neighbourhood and its relation to whether a nuisance has been committed is found in the 1879 United Kingdom case of *Sturges v Bridgman*:[125] "whether anything is a nuisance or not is a question to be determined, not merely by an abstract consideration of the thing itself, but in reference to its circumstances; what would be a nuisance in Belgrave Square would not necessarily be so in Bermondsey."[126] Or, in the words of an American case using a more homey turn of phrase, "a pig in the parlor instead of the barnyard."[127]

In assessing the nature of the community, the courts will take into account changes, as in *Desrosiers*, where residential construction altered the overall setting: "The area was at one time strictly rural and mixed farming was the principal activity. In recent years mixed farming has declined, many building lots have been sold and bought, and homes have been built. The area has become more or less a bedroom community for people who work in and near the Town of Dalhousie."[128] Conversely, this approach to considering the nature of the neighbourhood includes taking into account the legality of the use complained of if that use is new to the area. That is, the nature of the neighbourhood will be assessed according to the new, legal, state of affairs, not on the prevailing mode of life prior to authorized change. Thus, in the United Kingdom case *Gillingham Borough Council v Medway (Chatham) Dock Co Ltd*,[129] the court considered the noise complaints of residents of what had been a quiet neighbourhood in the context of the changes due to the establishment

---

123 2008 SCC 64.

124 Above note 120.

125 (1879), 11 Ch D 852 (CA).

126 The UK Court of Appeal characterizes Bermondsey, a district in London, as having tanneries and other "manufacture of a noisy or unsavoury character." In Toronto, a solid waste transfer station is located in an industrial park on Bermondsey Road; one might think that either the road was named, or the transfer station located, by someone with a sense of humour, but a guide to street names claims it was named for the home district in the United Kingdom of the first tenant in the park, a cookie manufacturer.

127 *Village of Euclid v Ambler Realty Co*, 272 US 365 at 388 (1926).

128 *Desrosiers*, above note 4 at para 5.

129 (1992), [1993] QB 343 [*Gillingham*].

of a major shipping container operation, and not as the neighbourhood had been previously.[130] In *Gillingham*, the court said: "It has been said, no doubt correctly, that planning permission is not a licence to commit nuisance and that a planning authority has no jurisdiction to authorise nuisance. However, a planning authority can, through its development plans and decisions, alter the character of a neighbourhood."[131]

Closely associated with public action that alters the nature of a neighbourhood is the question of whether statutory authorization affords a defence to an action brought in nuisance against some government actor. The leading case is *Tock v St John's Metropolitan Area Board*,[132] in which the plaintiff landowner's property was damaged by flooding following a heavy rain, due to a blockage in the city's storm sewer. The Supreme Court of Canada ruled that statutory authority could be a defence in either of two ways. First, where the statute imposed a duty to be performed and the inevitable result of so acting would be a nuisance, it was not actionable unless there was negligence; the nuisance was authorized. Second, if the statute conferred authority (but not a duty) to undertake a function and also specified the manner or location of the function, and the inevitable result of so acting on the conferred authority was a nuisance, it was not actionable unless there was negligence. Statutory authority is thus not an automatic defence:

> . . . if the legislation confers an authority on a public body and also gives it a discretion, not only whether or not to do the thing authorized but also how to do it and in what location, then if that public body decides to do the thing authorized, it must do it in a manner and at a location which will avoid the creation of a nuisance. If the public body implements the thing authorized in a way or at a location which gives rise to a nuisance, it will be liable therefore, whether there is negligence or not.[133]

Public nuisance has evolved as somewhat difficult for private individuals to establish their standing. In *Hickey v Electric Reduction Co of Canada*,[134] fish in Placentia Bay were poisoned by discharge from the defendant's phosphorous plant, making them of no commercial value. It has frequently been recognized that pollution of waterways and the

---

130 See also *Wheeler v Saunders Ltd*, [1995] 2 All ER 697 (CA).

131 *Gillingham*, above note 129 at 359.

132 Above note 107.

133 *Ibid*, headnote.

134 (1970), 21 DLR (3d) 368 (Nfld SC) [*Hickey*].

oceans amounts to a public nuisance.[135] The plaintiff fishers were not, however, allowed to proceed with their nuisance action because the nuisance "was committed against the public." Recognition of class action lawsuits,[136] as well as the altered standing rights of individuals under the Ontario *Environmental Bill of Rights, 1993* (*EBR*),[137] has allowed for greater potential use of public nuisance as a form of action. Ontario's Environmental Commissioner has noted that under the *EBR*, since it went into effect in 1994, there have been a series of cases pursued as public nuisance involving such situations as an industrial fire, problems with drinking water, and a propane facility explosion.[138]

Because matters of public nuisance involve activity that may well be criminal in nature, or a violation of other regulatory statutes, public nuisance tort actions have become rare. Related to this is the requirement to show some degree of fault, much akin to the standard for negligence.[139]

NOTES

1) Common law remedies continue in force even though the activity complained of might be regulated by statute or by-law. Thus, landowners need to be aware of the possibility of a common law action even where there is compliance with other law. The systems exist in parallel.
2) It is possible to seek an anticipatory injunction as part of a nuisance or other action. These are termed *quia timet* injunctions. *Palmer* was a case involving a request to the court for a *quia timet* injunction.
3) Makuch says that zoning "has democratized the nuisance doctrine"[140] and suggests the same regarding restrictive covenants, characterizing zoning as "a major improvement."[141] He means that zoning can deal with broad geographic areas, is public in nature, allows for participation by all interested parties, and invokes the state as enforcer.

---

135 See, for example, *Canada (National Harbours Board) v Hildon Hotel (1963) Ltd* (1967), 61 WWR 75 (BCSC); *Cormier v Blanchard* (1980), 30 NBR (2d) 198 (CA).

136 See, for example, *Class Proceedings Act*, RSBC 1996, c 50.

137 SO 1993, c 28.

138 See Environmental Commissioner of Ontario, "Small Things Matter, Annual Report 2014/2015" (November 2015), online: http://docs.assets.eco.on.ca/reports/environmental-protection/2014-2015/2014_2015-AR.pdf.

139 *Overseas Tankship (UK) Ltd v The Miller Steamship Co*, [1966] 2 All ER 709 (PC) [*Wagon Mound (No 2)*]; see also *Ross v Wall* (1980), 14 CCLT 243 (BCCA) and *Assie v Saskatchewan Telecommunications* (1978), 7 CCLT 39 (Sask CA).

140 Stan Makuch et al, *Canadian Municipal and Planning Law*, 2d ed (Toronto: Thomson Carswell, 2004) at 196.

141 *Ibid* at 195.

4) To Makuch's list, we might add that a wider set of factors may enter into the policy choices made in establishing laws; common law entails serious uncertainty of result, and in zoning an array of remedies broader than for nuisance is usually available, or easier to obtain: fines, stop-work orders, demolition, and near-automatic injunctions. Uncertainty is a hugely significant factor. The distinct advantage of statutory regulation is that the rules are known in advance of investment decisions. But this applies only where there are well-thought-out regulatory schemes that take into account both existing and possible future surrounding conditions. It is potentially devastating for landowners to find their businesses shut down due to nuisance claims, or for residents to have to deal with incompatible industrial or other uses. For a detailed critique of the utility of private law for environmental protection, see *Ball & Bell on Environmental Law*.[142]
5) Whether water rights are treated as a matter of property law or of tort, the rules amount to the same thing: ownership of land implies a right to reasonable use of adjacent flowing water (riparian water), surface water, and underground water. Rights associated with riparian water are usually seen as a matter of property law. As with other rights, there are limits at common law. The limits are based on recognition of a shared interest of others in likewise being able to make reasonable use of the water. Issues have to do with quantity and quality. Reasonable use means maintenance of overall quantity of the flowing water and no pollution. An injunction is the usual remedy. *Canada (National Capital Commission) v Pugliese*[143] illustrates a right to extract groundwater, but not to the point of causing subsidence on other land. Modern cases framed in nuisance seem to be rare. Water rights are now regulated by statute, including royalties to be paid for withdrawal for bottling. A typical earlier case is *KVP Co v McKie*[144] from 1949, in which an injunction was obtained against a polluting pulp and paper plant that was killing fish stocks through discharge of its effluent. The case illustrates not only the nature of nuisance law but also interaction with the legislature: after the plaintiff's court victory, the Ontario legislature dissolved the injunction.[145]
6) Harvard law professor Joseph Singer has written,

---

142 Stuart Bell & Donald McGillivray, *Ball & Bell on Environmental Law*, 5th ed (London: Blackstone, 2000) at 277–82.

143 (1979), 25 NR 498 (SCC).

144 [1949] SCR 698.

145 *The KVP Company Limited Act, 1950*, SO 1950, c 33.

> One major function of nuisance doctrine is to ensure that property use, as well as ownership, does not result in an unfair distribution of burdens associated with the development of land. Land uses that are perfectly legitimate in an isolated district become illegal if located in a built-up community. Each owner is entitled to some benefit from his or her land, and nuisance law ensures that the benefits and burdens of conflicting property uses are not distributed unfairly . . . . It has always suggested a limitation on property rights that cannot be fully comprehended by efficiency analysis . . . . Nuisance law allows for contextual consideration of the appropriate distribution of benefits and burdens of land ownership and use among neighbours.[146]

But the actual values at work in the process requires careful focus on the full grouping of relevant cases. An important statement frequently made is a repeat of the comment in the 1879 case *Sturges v Bridgman*,[147] that "What would be a nuisance in Belgrave Square would not necessarily be so in Bermondsey," a statement approved in some Canadian cases.[148] Locale is seen as a relevant factor in the balancing exercise. Does this mean, as one commentator has suggested, that "Those who suffer most from the ravages of pollution are the least worthy of protection"?[149] McLaren, former dean of law at the University of Windsor, wrote that *Sturges v Bridgman* means

> that the closer the plaintiff lives to an industrial environment the less freedom from the necessary by-products of that milieu he can claim . . . . The validity of this circumstantial factor as an important element in the weighting process presupposes that there is always some degree of real choice in terms of where a person lives and the life style he enjoys . . . . Today . . . with clear evidence that a sizable minority of the population exist in a social and economic environment in which choice is illusory and thus are compelled to live in areas in which a pollution blight exists with little hope of relocation, discrimination on this grounds of physical proximity to pollution sources is inequitable.[150]

146 Joseph Singer, "Property" in David Kairys, ed, *The Politics of Law*, 3d ed (New York: Basic Books, 1998) at 253–54.

147 Above note 125. A physician obtained an injunction against a confectioner in business in the area in which the physician established his surgery.

148 *Appleby v Erie Tobacco Co* (1910), 22 OLR 533 (Div Ct); *Walker v Pioneer Construction Co (1967) Ltd* (1975), 56 DLR (3d) 677 (Ont HCJ).

149 John PS McLaren, "The Common Law Nuisance Actions and the Environmental Battle" (1972) 10 *Osgoode Hall Law Journal* 505 at 534.

150 *Ibid* at 533–34.

If this acceptance of the status quo is inherent in nuisance law, are statutory rules on emissions an improvement?

7) One of the main types of farming leading to clashes with neighbours is hog operations.[151] This is due to odour from sewage lagoons. Cases such as *Desrosiers* should not be seen to imply that nuisance suits against hog operations may be won easily. The key fact in *Desrosiers* was the change in the nature of the neighbourhood away from purely agricultural uses. The decision should be contrasted with *MacGregor v Penner*,[152] where the area was agricultural and the plaintiff was not successful in advancing complaints over odour and flies. Regulation seems the preferable approach to such matters. Separation distances are often required, and, unlike the provincial rules mentioned in *Desrosiers*, are usually tied to size of the operation. In Ontario, the Ministry of Agriculture, Food and Rural Affairs has Minimum Distance Separation (MDS) Formulae that bind the Normal Farm Practices Protection Board and have also been adopted as a code by some municipalities.[153] Despite the picture in cases such as *Desrosiers*, that agriculture is typically a small, family operation, the trend in Canada has been towards agri-business. The trend away from small family farms has been identified as involving indicia such as decrease in number of farms, increase in acres per farm, increase in mechanization, increase in use of hired labour, and increased specialization.[154] "Confined," sometimes "concentrated," "animal feeding operations" (CAFOs) are particularly contentious.
8) Hog farms are not the only form of intensive livestock operation. In *Morton v Loon Lake No 561 (Rural Municipality)*,[155] the council was dealing with a proposal to change zoning so as to allow a set of lake-

151 See, for example, "Hog Factory Pollution in Canada" *The Gallon Environment Letter* (30 September 1999), online: https://listserv.brown.edu/?A2=ind9910A&L=ENVST-L&F=&S=&P=698. *Country Pork Ltd v Ashfield (Township)* (2002), 60 OR (3d) 529 (CA), illustrates the existence of a clash of values over use of land for hog farms, but involving interim control by-laws rather than the common law of nuisance. See also *Elite Swine v Moosomin (Rural Municipality No. 121)*, 2007 SKCA 38.

152 [1994] 2 WWR 251 (Man CA).

153 See the by-law put in issue in *Hill and Hill Farms Ltd v Bluewater (Municipality)*, 2006 CanLII 31802.

154 See, for example, Tom Murphy, "From Family Farming to Capitalist Agriculture: Food Production, Agribusiness and the State" in Bryant D Fairley et al, eds, *Restructuring and Resistance: Perspectives from Atlantic Canada* (Toronto: Garamond, 1990) at 190.

155 2011 SKQB 264.

side cottages to be built next door to a cattle ranch. The municipality's OP contained policies about intensive livestock operations (ILOs), though the term was undefined. However, the policies obliged the council to consider the proximity of neighbouring activities only when dealing with a proposal to establish an ILO, not to consider the presence of an ILO when considering a lakeside development.[156] Given the potential drinking water problems, as horribly illustrated in the Walkerton, Ontario, situation,[157] there is enormous potential for future incompatibility of uses between ILOs and residential uses, as the imbalance in the OP policies such as in this case shows.

9) An amenity that is not protected by the law of nuisance is a view; nor is an eyesore a nuisance.[158] In *Aldred's Case* of 1610,[159] it was said that ". . . for prospect which is a matter of delight and not of necessity, no action lies for stopping thereof, and yet it is a great commendation of a house that has a long and large prospect . . . . But the law does not give an action for such things of delight." This has been echoed by the Supreme Court of Canada in *St Pierre v Ontario (Minister of Transportation and Communications)*.[160] But see Notes 10 and 11 immediately below in this chapter.

10) Traditional nuisance claims are tied to our general main senses: hearing (noise), smell and taste (odour and fumes), and touch (dust and vibration). As just noted, the sense of sight, however, is not accounted for in common law nuisance. It is understandable that a view, a "prospect which is a matter of delight," may well not be protected if what is claimed is in essence that neighbours may not develop their land at all. But what of offences against aesthetic sensibility? May a neighbour build an appallingly ugly building or is the problem of aesthetics too subjective a matter? Subjectivity is not a problem for other instances of nuisance or for written regulations. Thus, in *Desrosiers*, the odour was characterized as "stink," though it was also tied to reactions such as nausea, disinclination of friends to visit, windows being kept shut, and clothes left on a laundry line

---

156 *Ibid* at para 36.

157 See Chapter 11, Section C(3)(a).

158 See, for example, *Morris v Dominion Foundries & Steel Ltd*, [1947] 2 DLR 840 (Ont HCJ).

159 Above note 100.

160 [1987] 1 SCR 906. See also *Becze v Edmonton (City)* (1993), 13 Alta LR (3d) 61 (QB); *Dube v La-Ko Enterprises Ltd* (1988), 92 NBR (2d) 117 (QB); and *Galloway*, above note 26. *Galloway* is problematic; although the court correctly states that protection of a view is not a legal right, it may well be a relevant land-use planning consideration, and the court may have conflated the two aspects.

needing to be re-washed. In *Kruse v Johnson*,[161] a case we encounter later because of its importance in defining unreasonableness as a test for municipal by-laws, the issue was noise; the by-law, which was upheld, provided, "No person shall sound or play upon any musical or noisy instrument or sing in any public place or highway within fifty yards of any dwelling-house after being required by any constable or by an inmate of such house personally, or by his or her servant, to desist." The test for "noise" in *Kruse* was quite subjective. Noise lends itself to somewhat objective measurement: in *Gillingham Borough*, for example, evidence was led as to decibels generated by the truck traffic as compared to the levels in a quiet bedroom, to when communication starts to become difficult, and to when the threshold of pain is reached. It is now quite common for by-laws to deal with noise.[162] The Supreme Court of Canada has said that aesthetics is a legitimate matter of municipal regulatory concern.[163] How should it be approached if the common law offers no guidance?

11) Wind turbines have been challenged as nuisances, though with very little success. Thus, in the US cases of *Rassier v Houim*,[164] *Rankin v FPL Energy, LLC*,[165] and *Burch v Nedpower Mount Storm LLC*[166] none of the claims were successful. *Burch* is particularly interesting in that the court suggested that loss of a view, if linked with other nuisance factors, could be a proper basis for a nuisance action. (The Kansas Supreme Court has also said that since aesthetics is a valid basis for municipal zoning, regardless of nuisance, municipalities may ban or regulate the location of wind turbines.[167])

12) Airport noise[168] has also led to some nuisance lawsuits. In the leading case, from British Columbia, the plaintiffs were not successful, the courts being of the view that there was a valid defence of statu-

---

161 [1898] 2 QB 91.

162 See Konstantine J Stavrakos, "Municipal Noise By-laws" (2011) 86 *Municipal and Planning Law Reports* (4th) 40.

163 *Peterborough (City) v Ramsden*, [1993] 2 SCR 1084 at paras 38 and 40. The point has been made in other cases, though the full ambit of what this implies has yet to be explored in Canadian cases; see however, Holly Susong & Kenneth Pearlman, "Regulating Beauty: A Review of Recent Law Journal Literature" (2000) 14:4 *Journal of Planning Literature* 637.

164 488 NW2d 635 (ND 1992).

165 266 SW3d 506 (Texas CA 2008).

166 647 SE2d 879 (W Va Ct App 2007) [*Burch*].

167 *Zimmerman v Board of County Commissioners of Wabaunsee County*, 218 P3d 400 (Kan 2009).

168 For older articles, see Hugh Silverman & John Evans, "Aeronautical Noise in Canada" (1972) 10 *Osgoode Hall Law Journal* 607 and Colin H McNairn, "Airport Noise Pollution: The Problem and the Regulatory Response" (1972) 50 *Cana-*

tory authorization under the principles set out in *Tock v St John's Metropolitan Area Board*.[169] In *Sutherland v Vancouver International Airport Authority*,[170] local residents were situated approximately four kilometres from one of the runways. Originally successful at trial, the decision was reversed by the Court of Appeal; one issue was the location of the runway: various options were available, but once selected, the runway had been authorized by a minister's certificate under the *Canadian Aviation Regulations*: "It is beyond question that the operation of the North Runway is authorized by statute . . . the *Canadian Aviation Regulations* directs the Minister to consider both 'aviation safety' and the broader 'public interest' in issuing an airport certificate."[171] Some objective information about noise levels may be found in the Noise Exposure Forecasts (NEFs) issued by Transport Canada.[172] Noise issues may be addressed in the environmental assessment (EA) process for an airport, although in instances of airports relatively close to urban areas, the solutions are limited.[173] Given the federal power to establish airports, and the limitations of the common law, land-use planning by municipalities so as to establish separation distances for incompatible uses, or warnings, may be the only response.[174] Some airports have voluntarily offered payments for sound insulation.[175]

13) Odour and noise, both common nuisances, differ in that the latter is more easily measured objectively. Odour may involve analysis by air sampling to determine the concentration of certain molecules such as hydrogen sulphide, but is usually a subjective matter. Ontario has adopted an *Air Pollution—Local Air Quality* regulation.[176]

---

dian Bar Review 248; for background, see TM McGrath, *History of Canadian Airports* (Toronto: Lugus, 1992).

169 Above note 107.

170 2002 BCCA 416.

171 *Ibid* at paras 98 & 99. For the *Canadian Aviation Regulations*, see SOR/96-433.

172 They are offered in the form of NEF contour maps.

173 See David Estrin, "Noise Impact Evaluation and Regulation in Canadian Transportation Planning" (2004); online: www.envirolawcan.com/Documents/final%20acoustica%20conference%20(portugal)%20paper(v1).doc.

174 See, for example, *Greater Toronto Airport Authority v Regional Municipality of Peel* (1998), 36 OMBR 447, where noise warning notices were required for residential development in the vicinity of Pearson Airport. In Ontario, provincial guidelines warn against municipalities allowing development that will interfere with airport operations: Ontario Ministry of the Environment, "Guideline D-1: Land Use Compatibility" (July 1995).

175 See *Spencer v Greater Fredericton Airport Authority*, 2004 NBQB 392.

176 O Reg 419/05 deals with various contaminants, setting standards at the point of impingement. Still, the nuisance aspect of odour is generally indicated by

14) Access to sunlight is also a limited matter at common law. In the United Kingdom, there existed a doctrine of "ancient lights" that did allow for protection of access to sunlight, if long established. It is a negative easement. Any such common law rights have not survived in Canada. *Limitation Acts* restrict any attempt to enforce right to light.[177] Sunlight means several things: natural light for illumination and for well-being, the absence of shadow and therefore reduced heating costs, and now, with advances in technology, access to light to power solar panels. Solar energy has prompted some American courts to recognize access to sunlight as a valid part of nuisance law[178] but this has not been the prevailing view, which is that some statutory framework is necessary. Many American jurisdictions have adopted laws that lead to limited protection for solar panels through nullification of covenants that disallow them or empowering municipalities to regulate access to light.[179]
15) Buildings or other installations in themselves can constitute a nuisance. Thus, in *TH Critelli v Lincoln Trusts and Savings Co*,[180] the complaint was that, by increasing the height of a building, snow would build up on the adjacent building; this required reinforcement of the roof. The plaintiff was successful in recovering damages. In *Nor-Video Services Ltd v Ontario Hydro*,[181] television reception was at issue. Ontario Hydro constructed a transformer station and high voltage lines situated so that a cable television service was interfered with. The court said that the problem was not in the construction or maintenance of the utility's facilities, but simply in their location with respect to another legitimate user of land. In so ruling, the Canadian courts differed from the approach of the UK courts as in *Hunter v Canary Wharf Ltd*,[182] where interference with

---

factors such as frequency, intensity, duration, offensiveness, and location. For a discussion, see Annik Forristal et al, "Land Use Compatibility—Noise & Odour" (November 2013), online: www.mcmillan.ca/Files/169078_Paper%20re%20Land%20Use%20Compatibility%20-%20Noise%20%20Odour%20-%20November%202013.pdf.

177 See *Earl Putnam Organization Ltd v Macdonald* (1978), 21 OR (2d) 815 (CA).

178 See *Prah v Maretti*, 321 NW2d 182 (Wis 1982).

179 See Colleen M Kettles, "A Comprehensive Review of Solar Access Law in the United States" (October 2008), online: Solar America Board for Codes and Standards www.solarabcs.org/about/publications/reports/solar-access/pdfs/Solaraccess-full.pdf.

180 (1978), 86 DLR (3d) 724 (Ont HCJ).

181 (1978), 19 OR (2d) 107 (HCJ).

182 [1997] AC 655 (HL).

television reception as a result of the construction of a large tower block was held not to be actionable nuisance.

16) Although rare, some polluters have obtained consents from potentially affected neighbours either in the form of a prospective release or an easement. This may operate as a defence in a nuisance action.[183] Smoke easements are allowed under an Ontario statute dating from 1918, designed to protect the Inco nickel smelter in Sudbury.[184] Faieta et al have suggested such easements might be "considered void as against public policy in respect of a subsequent purchaser,"[185] that is, they might be personal contracts rather than actual easements, which run with the land.
17) Some early US cases found funeral homes to be nuisances in residential areas.[186] These and similar cases also found funeral homes to be a business and not a profession, and thus not appropriate for home-based professional activities.
18) Motive is generally not relevant in a nuisance action. Courts have, however, taken differing views of this. In *Bradford Corp v Pickles*,[187] the House of Lords said that an "ill motive" does not enter into the assessment of whether there is a nuisance. The case involved drilling a well so as to reduce quantity of groundwater available to a neighbour. But in 1936, the UK Court of Appeal in *Hollywood Silver Fox Farm Ltd v Emmett*[188] said that in an action for nuisance by noise, the motive of the noise-maker must be considered. The case involved shooting guns to frighten foxes in a fur farm during breeding season. "Spite fences" are sometimes erected by neighbours to interfere with views or to shadow others, as a part of some dispute, although by-laws may restrict what may be built. Vegetation may act as a spite fence: see *Wilson v Handley*.[189]
19) Cases such as *Hickey*[190] demonstrated the inherent weakness of the common law as a tool to address serious environmental harms. They were part of the background against which many jurisdictions began to adopt statutory control regimes for harmful emissions or discharges in the 1970s.

---

183 See *British Columbia Forest Products Ltd v Nordal* (1954), 11 WWR (NS) 403 (BCSC).

184 *Industrial and Mining Lands Compensation Act*, RSO 1990, c I.5.

185 Above note 114 at 263.

186 See, for example, *Osborn v City of Shreveport*, 79 S 542 (La 1918) and *In Re Dawson*, 277 P 226 (Okla 1928).

187 [1895] AC 587 (HL).

188 [1936] 2 KB 408.

189 97 Cal App 4th 1301 (2002).

190 Above note 134.

20) Part of the evolution of the law of public nuisance has been allowance of class actions.[191] However, what is required is certification by the court that there is an identifiable class with common issues, and that a class action would be a preferable procedure. Cases such as *Pearson v Inco Ltd*[192] show how difficult it is to obtain effective certification. Health-related claims were not certified, on the basis that they were too individualized, though claims related to property values were certified.[193]
21) Nuisance actions should not be written off as a means for dealing with pollution. Several decades ago the US Supreme Court noted that "changed circumstances or new knowledge may make what was previously permissible no longer so." This appeared in *Lucas v South Carolina Coastal Council*,[194] primarily a "takings" case. The implication is that as scientific knowledge advances, there may be new applications of nuisance law. Since *Lucas*, in the United States, wetland destruction has been seen as a nuisance,[195] as has construction in a floodplain,[196] destruction of a saltmarsh,[197] and harm to a particular watershed.[198] However, an attempt to establish global climate change as a nuisance was not successful.[199] Most recently, an opposite result was reached in the Netherlands.[200] There has been some speculation that a similar lawsuit might be possible in Canada.[201]

---

191 See, for example, *Class Proceedings Act, 1992*, SO 1992, c 6. In the environmental context for public nuisance, see *Environmental Bill of Rights, 1993*, SO 1993, c 28, s 103.

192 (2006), 261 DLR (4th) 629 (Ont CA).

193 See also *Durling v Sunrise Propane Energy Group Inc*, 2012 ONSC 6570 and Meinhard Doelle, "The Sydney Tar Ponds Case: Shutting the Door on Environmental Class Action Suits in Nova Scotia?" (2015) 27 *Journal of Environmental Law and Practice* 279.

194 505 US 1003 at 1031 (1992) [*Lucas*].

195 *Commonwealth v Blair*, 805 NE2d 1011 (Mass App Ct 2004); *Cook v Sullivan*, 829 A2d 1059 (NH 2003).

196 *Gove v Zoning Board of Appeals of Chatham*, 831 NE2d 865 (Mass 2005).

197 *Palazzolo v Rhode Island*, 533 US 606 (2001).

198 *Machipongo Land & Coal Co Inc v Commonwealth*, 799 A2d 751 (Pa 2002).

199 *Connecticut v American Electric Power Co*, 406 F Supp 2d 265 (SDNY 2005).

200 See Arthur Neslen, "Dutch Government Ordered to Cut Carbon Emissions in Landmark Ruling" *The Guardian* (24 June 2015), online: http://gu.com/p/4a49a/stw.

201 Hugh Wilkins, "The Justiciability of Climate Change: A Comparison of US and Canadian Approaches" (2011) 34 *Dalhousie Law Journal* 529. Jeff Gray, "Canadian Courts Could Face Climate-Change Cases" *The Globe and Mail* (15 September 2015), online: http://fw.to/gEm3xIU.

CHAPTER 4

SOURCES OF AUTHORITY: FEDERAL-LEVEL POWERS AND THE CONSTITUTION ACTS

A. PRELIMINARY

The materials in this chapter set out the basics of how constitutional law affects understanding of land-use regulation.

The Constitution is always a starting point for understanding any area of law. There are two parts to this. One is that the *Constitution Act, 1867*[1] sets out the separation of powers between the federal and the provincial legislatures. While there is interaction and overlap, for the most part the separation of powers is important. So far as municipalities—mostly the creatures of the provinces—are concerned, separation of powers means that if a topic (a head of power) is a federal matter, then no province has authority to purport to grant jurisdiction over the topic to a municipality, and no municipality can exercise that power. An example is criminal matters. The *Constitution Act, 1867* assigns jurisdiction over criminal law exclusively to the federal Parliament. Although provinces have authority to attach penalties to breaches of their regulatory statutes (and may allow municipalities to do so as well), if a provincial statute or a municipal by-law were seen by the courts in

1 (UK), 30 & 31 Victoria, c 3, reprinted in RSC 1985, Appendix II, No 5. There are numerous Constitution Acts, including 1867, 1871, and 1982. Until 1982, they were Acts of the UK Parliament. With the 1982 enactment, the *Constitution Act, 1982*, being Schedule B to the *Canada Act 1982* (UK), 1982, c 11, constitutional arrangements were patriated. The 1982 Act includes the *Canadian Charter of Rights and Freedoms*.

their "pith and substance" to be criminal law, those laws would be constitutionally invalid.

The other part to the Constitution is the *Canadian Charter of Rights and Freedoms* (*Charter*). The *Charter* offers certain protections to people against their governments. As with the division of powers, violation of a *Charter*-protected right would result in the invalidity of a law unless it was seen as a justified infringement.[2]

The separation of powers aspect of the Constitution is not a simple issue. Although *The Constitution Act, 1867* lists federal and provincial powers, and although there is a controlling interpretive idea that all topics, even those not contemplated at the time the Constitution was first written (1867), are to be found in the Act, the results can be complicated. Cases such as the 2007 decision of the Supreme Court of Canada in *British Columbia (Attorney General) v Lafarge Canada Inc*[3] show how difficult it sometimes is to sort out which order of government has jurisdiction over some particular land use.

Some new topics, such as aeronautics, have been seen by the courts as exclusively assigned to the federal level. Some, such as the environment, have been seen as being divided between the two senior levels. And municipalities have no constitutional status at all, which is illustrated by the 1997 decision of the Ontario Court of Appeal in *East York (Borough) v Ontario (Attorney General)*[4] (though as levels of government, the *Charter*, or most of it, applies to them).

One important consequence of the division of powers is that the federal Parliament has hugely important land-use regulatory powers, a fact often not sufficiently appreciated. The topics range from national parks to some provisions of the *Criminal Code*. In any land-use issue, it is necessary first to consider the division of powers question under the *Constitution Act*.

Because of the assignment to the federal legislature of jurisdiction over "Indians, and Lands reserved for the Indians . . ." and because section 35 of the *Constitution Act, 1982* addresses treaty rights and unsurrendered rights, the topic of Aboriginal interests in land is dealt with here. The topic is complex and rapidly evolving. Since Aboriginal law is a distinct legal subject, we do no more than note its importance and consider the broad points associated with land-use law.

As for the *Charter*, some attempts at land-use regulation can be challenged as infringements of guaranteed rights. Is postering a right of free expression? What about billboards? Is gardening? Are limits

---

2 See Section E(2)(i), below in this chapter.

3 2007 SCC 23 [*Lafarge*].

4 (1997), 43 MPLR (2d) 155 (Ont CA).

on the height of fences an interference with liberty or security of the person? What about fortifications of a motorcycle club's building? Can zoning speak in terms of "family" occupancy? Where may demonstrations occur? If zoning separates residential land uses by socio-economic class, does this offend the *Charter*?

And, since the *Charter* allows for a government to justify an infringement of rights in some circumstances (section 1), what justifications must be made out, that is, how the *Oakes* test[5] plays out in land-use matters will frequently be the focus in litigation.

B. DIVISION OF POWERS: MAIN CONSEQUENCES

The central provisions of the *Constitution Act* setting out the division of powers between the two senior orders of government are sections 91, 92, and 92A:

> *Legislative Authority of Parliament of Canada*
> 91. It shall be lawful for the Queen, by and with the Advice and Consent of the Senate and House of Commons, to make Laws for the Peace, Order, and Good Government of Canada, in relation to all Matters not coming within the Classes of Subjects by this Act assigned exclusively to the Legislatures of the Provinces; and for greater Certainty, but not so as to restrict the Generality of the foregoing Terms of this Section, it is hereby declared that (notwithstanding anything in this Act) the exclusive Legislative Authority of the Parliament of Canada extends to all Matters coming within the Classes of Subjects next hereinafter enumerated; that is to say,
>
> 1A. The Public Debt and Property.
> 2. The Regulation of Trade and Commerce.
> . . .
> 5. Postal Service.
> . . .
> 7. Militia, Military and Naval Service, and Defence.
> . . .
> 9. Beacons, Buoys, Lighthouses, and Sable Island.
> 10. Navigation and Shipping.
> 11. Quarantine . . .

5 See the discussion of this test from the case *R v Oakes*, [1986] 1 SCR 103 [*Oakes*], in Section E(2)(i), below in this chapter.

. . .

12. Sea Coast and Inland Fisheries.

. . .

24. Indians, and Lands reserved for the Indians.

. . .

27. The Criminal Law.
28. The Establishment, Maintenance, and management of Penitentiaries.
29. Such Classes of Subjects as are expressly excepted in the Enumeration of the Classes of Subjects by this Act assigned exclusively to the Legislatures of the Provinces.

And any Matter coming within any of the Classes of Subjects enumerated in this Section shall not be deemed to come within the Class of Matters of a local or private Nature . . . assigned exclusively to the Legislatures of the Provinces.

Subjects of exclusive Provincial Legislation
92. In each Province the Legislature may exclusively make Laws in relation to Matters coming within the Classes of Subjects next hereinafter enumerated; that is to say,

. . .

5. The Management and Sale of the Public Lands belonging to the Province and of the Timber and Wood thereon.

. . .

7. The Establishment, Maintenance, and Management of Hospitals, Asylums . . . .
8. Municipal Institutions in the Province.

. . .

10. Local Works and Undertakings other than . . . :
    (a) Lines of Steam or other Ships, Railways, Canals, Telegraphs, and other Works and Undertakings connecting the Province with any other or others of the Provinces, or extending beyond the limits of the province:

    . . .

    (c) Such Works as, although wholly situate within the Province, are before or after their Execution declared by the Parliament of Canada to be for the general Advantage of Canada or for the Advantage of Two or more of the Provinces.

. . .

13. Property and Civil Rights in the Province.

. . .

16. Generally all matters of a merely local or private Nature in the Province.

92A. In each province, the legislature may exclusively make laws in relation to (a) exploration for non-renewable natural resources in the province; (b) development, conservation and management of non-renewable natural resources and forestry resources in the province, including laws in relation to the rate of primary production therefrom; and (c) development, conservation and management of sites and facilities in the province for the generation and production of electrical energy.

. . .

95. In each Province the Legislature my make Laws in relation to Agriculture in the Province . . .; and it is hereby declared that the Parliament of Canada may from Time to Time make Laws in relation to Agriculture in all or any of the Provinces; and any Law of the Legislature of a province relative to Agriculture . . . shall have effect in and for the Province as long and as far only as it is not repugnant to any Act of the Parliament of Canada.

96. The Governor General shall appoint the Judges of the Superior Courts in each Province . . .

. . .

108. The Public Works and Property of each Province enumerated in the Third Schedule to this Act, shall be the Property of Canada.

. . .

125. No Lands or Property belonging to Canada or any Province shall be liable to Taxation.

. . .

132. The Parliament and Government of Canada shall have all Powers necessary or proper for performing the Obligations of Canada or of any Province thereof, as Part of the British Empire towards Foreign Countries, arising under Treaties between the Empire and such Foreign Countries.

There are several main consequences of this federal/provincial division of powers.

1) Municipalities are not specifically enumerated as an order of government with any powers of their own. The scheme of the *Constitution Act* is to divide powers between the two senior orders of government. Any powers to be exercised by municipalities must, therefore, derive from one of the other orders of government and be granted by them.

In the years prior to the formation of Canada in 1867, various discontents led to the establishment of a commission to study issues. Lord Durham's Report of 1839 tended to favour constitutional recognition of local government.[6] This view was not adopted, though, and Canada was formed with a scheme for the division of powers between two orders of government. Subsequently, section 35 of the *Constitution Act, 1982* gave some constitutional recognition to Aboriginal self-government, the nature of which remains unclear.

Municipalities have made various proposals for recognition of their independence in the constitution.[7] And from time to time there are statements that suggest either a quasi-constitutional status for municipalities or some political convention that limits the ability of senior orders of government to make decisions on their behalf. For example, this appears in the 1993 *Report of the Ontario Fair Tax Commission*: "In practice, a quasi-constitutional relationship has evolved which effectively recognizes local government as a third order of government and provides for a significant degree of stability in the provincial-municipal relationship and in the roles played by local governments."[8] It is precisely this sort of statement that has been rejected by the courts.[9] Formal constitutional recognition of local government would require amendment of the *Constitution Act*, a difficult objective both practically and politically.[10] Other advocates of greater powers for municipalities

---

6 See Jacques L'Heureux, "Municipalities and the Division of Powers" in Richard Simeon, ed, *Intergovernmental Relations*, Royal Commission on the Economic Union and Development Prospects for Canada, No 63 (Toronto: University of Toronto Press, 1985).

7 See, for example, Editorial, "Constitutional Recognition of Local Government" (June 1999) *Municipal World* 26. The Federation of Canadian Municipalities adopted a resolution in favour in 1998. For a review of the history, see Michael Dewing & William R Young, "Municipalities, the Constitution, and the Canadian Federal System," Background Paper BP-276E (Ottawa: Library of Parliament, 1991). Also see Jack Masson, *Alberta's Local Governments: Politics and Democracy* (Edmonton: University of Alberta Press, 1994) at 61–66.

8 Ontario Fair Tax Commission, *Fair Taxation in a Changing World* (Toronto: University of Toronto Press, 1993) ch 11.

9 See Peter Hogg, *Constitutional Law of Canada*, 3d ed (Scarborough, ON: Carswell, 1992) vol 1, ch 16 and vol 2, ch 34. For an earlier account, see Dale Gibson, "The Constitutional Position of Local Government in Canada" (1980) 11 *Manitoba Law Journal* 1.

10 Another proposal that is sometimes made is that major cities such as Toronto should become new provinces; see, for example, Mary W Rowe, ed, *Toronto: Considering Self-Government* (Owen Sound, ON: Ginger Press, 2000).

suggest the powers could be included in the provincial statutes that establish municipalities, especially the major cities.[11]

2) Sections 91(8) "Municipal Institutions in the Province," (13) "Property," and (16) "Generally all matters of a merely local or private Nature in the Province" are generally taken as the source of provincial authority for control of local governments. So extensive are those powers that they extend to permitting unilateral amalgamation (which also implies dissolution) of local governments as well as the listing, expanding, or restricting of local government powers. See, for example, *East York (Borough) v Ontario (Attorney General)*[12] and *Baie d'Urfé (Ville) c Québec (Procureur général)*.[13] Municipalities simply have no inherent right to exist, let alone any entitlement to particular powers or functions.
3) Not all municipalities must be creatures of the provinces. It is possible for the federal government to create municipalities, though, because of the assignment of an exclusive power over municipal institutions to the provinces in section 92(8) of the *Constitution Act, 1867*, the federal power is indirect. That is, the territorial governments are created by Parliament and in turn create municipalities. The National Capital Commission, in existence since 1899, does not operate with an elected governing body, and so although as a major landowner in the Ottawa-Gatineau area, its long-range planning is of signal importance there, it is probably not appropriate to think of it as a local "government"; the source of the power to create the National Capital Commission is the POGG clause.[14] At the same time, it is amenable to administrative law remedies: see *Community Before Cars Coalition v National Capital Commission*.[15] In the territories, municipalities such as Yellowknife, Whitehorse, and Iqaluit are created by their territorial governments, which have been granted province-like powers akin to those set out in section 92 of the Act.[16] For towns such as Banff and Jasper, located in national parks, there

11 See, for example, Ron Levi & Mariana Valverde, "Freedom of the City: Canadian Cities and the Quest for Governmental Status" (2006) 44 *Osgoode Hall Law Journal* 409.

12 Above note 4.

13 (2001), 23 MPLR (3d) 163 (Que SC). Similarly, school boards have failed to establish any recognition of their autonomy. This reinforces the absence of status for municipalities. See *Public School Boards Assn of Alberta v Alberta (Attorney General)*, 2000 SCC 45, especially paras 33, 34, and 38.

14 *Munro v Canada (National Capital Commission)*, [1966] SCR 663.

15 1997 CanLII 6179 (FC).

16 See *Northwest Territories Act*, SC 2014, c 2, s 2, s 18; *Nunavut Act*, SC 1993, c 28, s 23; *Yukon Act*, SC 2002, c 7, s 18.

exist different but special arrangements. For Banff, an agreement exists between the provincial and federal governments pursuant to Alberta's *Park Towns Act*,[17] which recognizes it as an Alberta town. The anomaly of this has been commented on: Professor Frederick Laux notes the "apparent contradiction. How can Alberta create a municipal corporation to exercise Alberta-mandated local government functions in an area under federal jurisdiction by virtue of it being within a national park? Moreover, how can Alberta law exert control over lands owned by the Crown in right of Canada?"[18] This appears to be an example of inter-delegation of powers as recognized in the Prince Edward Island Potato Marketing Board case of *Prince Edward Island (Potato Marketing Board) v HB Willis Inc*[19] or overlapping authority. The propriety of the arrangement has been recognized.[20] For Jasper, no federal-provincial agreement has been entered into, and the town is governed by a set of federal regulations, the *Town of Jasper Zoning Regulations*.[21]

4) Although municipalities have no independent constitutional status, once they are established they are levels of government, and the restrictions of the *Charter of Rights* that limit governmental powers do apply to them.[22] For more detail, see Section E(1), below in this chapter. The one *Charter* provision that does not seem to apply is section 3, the right to vote. In *Haig v Canada (Chief Electoral Officer)*,[23] the Supreme Court of Canada noted that by its terms, the *Charter* applies only to federal and provincial elections and not to referendums or municipal elections.[24]
5) The absence of constitutional status is a part of what leads courts to invoke Dillon's Rule (strict and narrow interpretation). Courts read provincial statutes that are the source of local government powers according to principles that differ from the way they read the *Constitution Act*, the source of the powers for the senior orders of

17 *Parks Towns Act*, RSA 2000, c P-2.

18 Frederick Laux, "The Banff Incorporation: A Lesson in Co-operative Federalism" (1991) 29 *Alberta Law Review* 633.

19 [1952] 2 SCR 392.

20 *698114 Alberta Ltd v Banff (Town)*, 1999 ABQB 59.

21 CRC, c 1111, as amended.

22 See *McCutcheon v Toronto (City)* (1983), 41 OR (2d) 652 (HCJ).

23 1993 CanLII 58 (SCC).

24 The case did not concern municipalities and so the comment about the scope of section 3 is technically *obiter*, but it is clear. For discussion of fairness in voting at the municipal level, see Howard Epstein, "Electoral Boundaries and the Problem of Vote Dilution in Municipal Elections" (2004) 48 *Municipal and Planning Law Reports* (3d) 259.

government. The *Constitution Act* is seen as needing to be read as a "living tree," which implies preparedness to adapt its terms to new, unforeseen circumstances.

6) The absence of constitutional status leads to the applicability of the maxim *delegatus non potest delegare*—a delegate may not in turn delegate. Since municipalities are delegates of the powers of the province, they may not in turn delegate their powers to another entity, unless authorized to do so by provincial statute. Thus, staff may be restricted in what they can do, and a council may not bind itself to the results of a referendum (usually in the guise of a "neighbour-consent ordinance").[25]

   At the same time, there is widespread recognition that modern administrative governments require a bureaucracy to achieve efficiency. This was noted—though for the United Kingdom's national government—as early as 1915 in *Local Government Board v Arlidge*,[26] and noted again in *Carltona Ltd v Commissioners of Works*[27] in 1943. Municipal government is different than a central, unitary government. In general, specific statutory authority is needed for a council to grant decision-making authority to staff, and in any event, staff are to be given specific rules or criteria to apply, not a complete independent discretion.[28] When staff are granted a clear statutory power to make decisions, as is typical for building code matters, they are not unfettered and must still apply the applicable laws and are subject to appeal or judicial scrutiny on a reasonableness standard, and for some issues, on a correctness standard.[29]

7) Municipalities have no automatic powers of extraterritoriality. They are seen as more like special-purpose corporations and less like natural persons. To some extent, this appeared in *Shell Canada Products Ltd v Vancouver (City)*,[30] where making decisions based on influencing public policy elsewhere was disallowed. Municipalities are, however, frequently granted power to purchase land outside their territorial limits and to enter into co-operative arrangements, including for land-use planning, with other nearby municipalities.

---

25 See *Vic Restaurant Inc v Montreal (City)*, [1959] SCR 58 [*Vic Restaurant*] and *Lamoureux v Beaconsfield (City)*, [1978] 1 SCR 134.

26 [1915] AC 120.

27 [1943] 2 All ER 560 (CA).

28 See *Vic Restaurant*, above note 25; *Outdoor Neon Displays Ltd v Toronto (City)* (1960), 22 DLR (2d) 241 (SCC); *Kirkpatrick v Maple Ridge (District)* (1980), 14 MPLR 19 (BCSC); *R v Buena Vista Kennels 1979 Ltd*, 2010 SKQB 195.

29 See, for example, *Vanderheede Farms Ltd v Norfolk (County) Chief Building Official*, 2011 ONSC 1525.

30 [1994] 1 SCR 231.

Some provinces have granted municipalities legal personhood.[31] The implications of this remain unclear.

8) The federal power to enter into international agreements such as *NAFTA* is undoubted. The effect of such agreements, however, is problematic so far as subnational governments (provinces and municipalities) are concerned. Jurisprudence dating back to 1937 established that in entering into an international agreement, the federal government could not thereby bind the provinces to act if the subject matter of the agreement was within a topic area assigned exclusively to the provinces by the separation-of-powers provisions of the *Constitution Act*.[32] A consequence of investor-right provisions of treaties such as *NAFTA* is that an arbitration decision might award damages to a foreign company as a result of regulatory activities of a subnational government; this could extend to land-use regulation such as zoning or certain environmental processes such as environmental assessments. This occurred in *United Mexican States v Metalclad Corp*[33] and in *Re William Ralph Clayton and Bilcon of Delaware Inc and Government of Canada*.[34] Although it is the federal government that is obliged under an international treaty to pay any such awards, the dynamic has a chilling effect on subnational governments.[35]

   The federal government has launched a court challenge to the *Bilcon* arbitration decision, claiming that the award "contains decisions on matters beyond the scope of the submission to arbitration."[36]The first portion of the arbitration award in which it was determined that Canada was liable to pay damages was released 17 March 2015; the amount of damages claimed is $101 million, but the appropriate quantum has not yet been ruled on.

---

31 See, for example, Ontario's *Municipal Act, 2001*, SO 2001, c 25, s 9.

32 *Canada (Attorney General) v Ontario (Attorney General)*, [1937] AC 326 (JCPC) [*Labour Conventions Case*].

33 2001 BCSC 664 [*Metalclad*].

34 *Award on Jurisdiction and Liability* (17 March 2015) [*Bilcon*], online: italaw.com/sites/default/files/case-documents/italaw4212.pdf.

35 See Howard M Epstein, "*NAFTA*, Other International Agreements and Local Government Jurisdiction — Comments on *United Mexican States v Metalclad*" (2003) 34 *Municipal and Planning Law Reports* (3d) 44 [Epstein, "*NAFTA*"].

36 See Global Affairs Canada, NAFTA — Chapter 11 — Investment: Cases Filed against the Government of Canada, online: www.international.gc.ca/trade-agreements-accords-commerciaux/topics-domaines/disp-diff/gov.aspx?lang=eng.

C. DETERMINATION OF SOURCE OF AUTHORITY

In the process of analysis by the courts in deciding which of the senior levels of government may legitimately exercise authority over some topic, some principles of interpretation or guidelines have emerged. Issues around land use have arisen in the context of arguments over the scope of the federal authority in criminal law, trade and commerce, navigation and shipping, plus the peace, order, and good government (POGG) clause as weighed against provincial authority over Property and Civil rights, and matters of a merely local or private nature.

1) Pith and Substance: Property and Land-Use Planning

The assignment to provinces of regulatory power over land-use planning arises from its authority over property and civil rights. The approach to "classification of a law for purposes of federalism involves first identifying the 'matter' of the law, and then assigning it to one of the 'classes of subjects' in respect of which the federal and provincial governments have legislative authority under ss. 91 and 92 of the *Constitution Act* . . . ."[37] A law's "matter" is its leading feature or true character, its "pith and substance" as distinguished from incidental effects. In *Johnson v Alberta (Attorney General)*,[38] Hogg on *Constitutional Law*[39] is quoted to the effect that, "The creation of property rights, their transfer and their general characteristics are within property and civil rights in the province. Thus, the law of real and personal property and all its various derivatives, such as landlord and tenant, trusts and wills, succession on intestacy, conveyancing, and *land use planning*, are within provincial power." In *Johnston*, the provincial government adopted legislation to control the development of shopping centres, including any under development that had obtained permits, limiting overall size. The province owned shares in a company that proposed a development that would include a shopping centre. The plaintiffs were rival developers. The law was challenged as being in essence about commercial competition and therefore within federal jurisdiction. There was a presumption of constitutional legitimacy that had not been rebutted.

---

37 *Johnston v Prince Edward Island*, 1995 CanLII 3484 at para 105 (PEISCTD), DesRoches J [*Johnston*].

38 [1954] SCR 127 [*Johnson*].

39 Above note 9 at s 21.11(a) [emphasis added].

The law was primarily directed to regulation and control of land.[40] By way of contrast as to result, *Canada Post Corp v Hamilton (City)*[41] determined that, while the city possessed land-use planning powers, they did not extend to establishing a licensing and fee system to control the placement of community mailboxes by the federal agency. Federal law allows for the installation of mail receptacles "on any public place, including a public roadway . . . ."[42] The pith and substance of the by-law was directed at an activity assigned by section 91(5) to the federal government.[43]

2) Pith and Substance: Double Aspect — Criminal Law

Jurisdiction over criminal matters is an undoubted federal matter. It is specified in the *Constitution Act*. Furthermore, there is wide latitude for the federal government to decide what activities are to be considered as criminal. Problems have arisen over topics such as prostitution or gambling. Attempts by municipalities to control street prostitution, widely seen as a nuisance, have been struck down by the courts as essentially criminal law. See *R v Westendorp*,[44] where a Calgary by-law aimed at street prostitution and particularly focused on the communication and solicitation aspects was struck down. The Court saw nothing in the by-law that attempted to regulate the use of private property. The by-law in question was so clearly duplicative of *Criminal Code* provisions that the result was not surprising. The approach to the issue as one of legitimate double aspects did not arise, as it has in other cases associated with sex work or "adult entertainment." The same result applies to gambling, with an Alberta attempt to ban slot machines.[45] A recent case upheld a municipal by-law that prohibited street fighting. In *R v Keshane*,[46] the court saw a legitimate provincial purpose anchored in the "property and civil rights" provincial power as justifying the municipal by-law, which was designed to provide safe and enjoyable public places by deterring public fighting. It saw legitimate double aspects to the federal and provincial

---

40 The *Johnston* case also raises questions of bad faith and abuse of authority, whether doctrines about "reasonableness" apply, as well as a claim for compensation. None of these points was successful.

41 2015 ONSC 3615.

42 *Mail Receptacles Regulations*, SOR/83-743.

43 The by-laws were also invalidated as impermissibly vague: not allowed by the *Municipal Act*, s 14, which invalidates a by-law "to the extent of any conflict with a . . . Federal Act or regulation . . ."; and because of the doctrine of paramountcy.

44 [1983] 1 SCR 43.

45 *Johnson*, above note 38.

46 2012 ABCA 330.

laws. Provinces do have statutes that are aimed at nuisance uses of property, including uses that are criminal, such as the *Safer Communities and Neighbourhoods Acts*[47] and British Columbia's *Safe Streets Act*,[48] that may be invoked in cases of nuisance panhandling, drug use, or prostitution. These statutes have not been struck down as an unwarranted invasion of federal powers. Their justification as provincial matters is that there are adverse effects on the community or neighbourhood[49] and are akin to statutes or by-laws that are calculated to preserve peace or suppress conditions associated with crime.[50] With the Supreme Court of Canada decision in *R v Bedford*,[51] the question of local controls over street prostitution or the placement of bordellos may well arise again.[52] Provinces or municipalities do also already regulate many aspects of sex work, such as escort services, non-therapeutic massage, lap dancing, nude dancing, and some erotic displays, all of which laws have been justified under "double aspect" analysis.[53]

3) Exhaustiveness: POGG and Aeronautics

In 1867, when the *British North America Act* was written, air flight, apart from hot-air balloons, was unknown. Naturally enough it is not mentioned as a head of power in the Act. When air flight became a reality, the question of jurisdiction over airports, their location, and their activities became a matter for litigation. Approaching the constitution as a living tree and applying the idea of "exhaustiveness" means that all possible activities are to be seen as being assigned to one of the levels of government, unless shared. It was early determined that aeronautics generally was a federal matter. In 1931, in *Reference re: Regulations*

---

47 See, for example, *The Safer Communities and Neighbourhoods Act*, SS 2004, c S-0.1; *Safer Communities and Neighbourhoods Act*, SNS 2006, c 6; SY 2006, c 7.

48 SBC 2004, c 75.

49 See *Bedard v Dawson*, [1923] SCR 681.

50 See *Montreal (City) v Arcade Amusements Inc*, [1985] 1 SCR 368.

51 *Canada (Attorney General) v Bedford*, 2013 SCC 72 [*Bedford*].

52 For a discussion, see Howard M Epstein "Zoning Sex Work" (2011) 5 *Digest of Municipal & Planning Law* (2d) 1; Elaine Craig, "Sex Work By Law: *Bedford*'s Impact on Municipal Approaches to Regulation of the Sex Trade" (2011) 16 *Review of Constitutional Studies* 205.

53 See, for example, *International Escort Services Inc v Vancouver (City)* (1988), 42 MPLR 181 (BCSC); *Pimenova v Brampton (City)* (2004), 49 MPLR (3d) 1 (Ont SCJ); *Ontario Adult Entertainment Bar Association v Toronto (Metropolitan)* (1995), 29 MPLR (2d) 141 (Ont Div Ct); *R v Mara* (1996), 27 OR (3d) 643 (CA); *Rio Hotel v New Brunswick (Liquor Licensing Board)*, [1987] 2 SCR 59; *913719 Ontario Ltd (cob Adults Only Video) v Mississauga (City)* (1996), 33 MPLR (2d) 171 (Ont Ct Gen Div).

and Control of Aeronautics,[54] it was decided that section 132 of the *Constitution Act*, the treaty-making power, under which the federal government had signed an international treaty regarding aeronautics, was consistent with its assertion of control over the subject. Subsequently, in *Johannesson v West St Paul (Rural Municipality)*,[55] the basis for federal control was asserted to be the POGG clause since the matter "goes beyond local or provincial concern because it has attained such dimensions as to affect the body politic of Canada . . . ." In *Johannesson*, the municipality, acting upon a specific grant of power from the province to regulate "aerodromes," had banned them. Both the statute and the by-law were declared *ultra vires*. The POGG clause is a potent force in the view of most courts when dealing with matters not explicitly enumerated in *The Constitution Act, 1867*. The Court did not see aeronautics as a merely local or private matter, nor as one limited to property and civil rights in the province, even if some flights might be within the province only. The Court recognized that aeronautics has a land-use aspect, but said, "it is impossible to separate the flying in the air from the taking off and landing on the ground and it is, therefore, wholly impractical, particularly when considering the matter of jurisdiction, to treat them as independent one from the other."[56] This practicality tends to characterize decisions on questions of constitutional jurisdiction. In *Walker v Ontario (Minister of Housing)*,[57] the city of Chatham had established an airport, and as it expanded its runways, encountered resistance from farmers owning adjacent land. The federal government had not put in place height restrictions applying to adjacent lands so as to protect flight paths. The farmers erected silos that would interfere. The province adopted regulations to control the height, but these were found to be beyond provincial jurisdiction and therefore of no effect.[58] The court did say that some aspects of aerodromes might be within provincial legislative competence, and although that might be the case for some matters such as sales tax, the trend has been for courts to see provincial and municipal functions such as by-laws or building codes as excluded from airports.[59] To the same effect is *Quebec (Attorney General) v Lacombe*,[60] where a municipal by-law prohibiting aerodromes

---

54 [1932] AC 54 (JCPC).

55 [1952] 1 SCR 292 [*Johannesson*].

56 *Ibid* at 319.

57 (1983), 144 DLR (3d) 86 (Ont CA) [*Walker*].

58 To similar effect, regarding a municipal by-law is *Mullaney v Red Deer (County No 23)*, 1999 ABQB 434.

59 See, for example, *R v Executive Helicopter Services Inc* (1995), 30 MPLR (2d) 7 (Ont CA).

60 2010 SCC 38 [*Lacombe*].

in a vacation-home area was ruled ineffective to defeat a federally licensed commercial aerodrome. Likewise, in *Quebec (Attorney General) v Canadian Owners and Pilots Association*,[61] a dispute arose over use of land that had been designated by the province as protected agricultural land, for construction of an aerodrome under authorization from the federal government. This brought into conflict two communal values: a national system of aeronautics and provincial protection of land for agricultural purposes. The Court found in favour of the federal exercise of power. In *Lacombe*, the Supreme Court of Canada said there was no provincial or municipal power to attempt to regulate the location of aerodromes. In *Laferriere*, the Court said there was a provincial power to designate lands as agricultural use only, but that power did not apply where the federal government had decided when and where aerodromes could be built. Interjurisdictional immunity was invoked.

There are several land-use aspects to aeronautics. One is the location of airports. Another is their nuisance aspect as a source of noise. Another is the necessity for flight across nearby land. Another is safety. All of these appear to fall within exclusive federal jurisdiction. The *Aeronautics Act*[62] provides a regulatory code. This extends to the adoption of airport plans and associated zoning regulations, which are to be filed at local land title registries. Sets of regulations exist for the major airports. Where flight paths are established and height restrictions apply to buildings on the lands of adjacent owners, compensation is payable. No doubt this was the core issue in *Walker*.[63] The restrictions can apply over a wider area. For example, the following provision, a typical one, has relevance in the siting of landfills: "No owner or lessees of any land to which these Regulations apply shall permit any part of that land to be used for the disposal of any waste that is edible by or attractive to birds."[64] The underlying policy is presumably to minimize the chance of birds being drawn into jet engines and occasioning damage or disaster.

An attempt to shield a municipally improper land use behind federal jurisdiction over aeronautics failed in *2241960 Ontario Inc v Scugog (Township)*.[65] The landowner planned to build an aerodrome and brought in fill in preparation for construction of a runway. In the absence of any federal permit for an aerodrome, the court saw arguments of federal jurisdiction as irrelevant and the site alteration as violative of municipal rules; the operation of the fill by-law did not prohibit the construction of an aerodrome.

61 2010 SCC 39 [*Owners and Pilots*].

62 RSC 1985, c A-2.

63 Above note 57.

64 *Halifax International Airport Zoning Regulations*, SOR/94-241, s 7.

65 2011 ONSC 2337.

4) Interjurisdictional Immunity/Federal Paramountcy: Ports

Canada has always been a trading nation. The *Constitution Act* assigns jurisdiction over what in 1867 were seen as the major economic activities to the federal government. This includes navigation and shipping, and thus harbours and ports. The case of *BC v Lafarge Canada Inc*[66] focused on the interaction of federal and provincial jurisdiction over the lands surrounding harbours. At issue was a proposed "twin batch plant" the company wanted to build on land leased from the Vancouver Port Authority (VPA), a federal agency. Aggregate was to be shipped in and mixed with cement to produce concrete for use in local construction projects. Neighbours objected and raised the issue of whether the company had to obtain a permit from the municipality in addition to commercial consent from the VPA. The VPA argued that since the proposed project was to be on federal lands, it enjoyed immunity from provincial (and therefore municipal) jurisdiction, federal public property being listed in section 91(1A) as exclusively a federal matter. In the alternative, it raised federal paramountcy in light of operational conflict between the VPA rules for land development and those of the municipality (the point of difference being allowable height). The Court said it was not inclined to apply the idea of interjurisdictional immunity

> where, as here, the legislative subject matter (waterfront development) presents a double aspect. Both federal and provincial authorities have a compelling interest. Were there to be no valid federal land-use planning controls applicable to the site, federalism does not require (nor, in the circumstances, should it tolerate) a regulatory vacuum, which would be the consequence of interjurisdictional immunity.[67]

Instead, the Court applied principles of federal paramountcy, the result being that the VPA rules regarding height superseded the municipal ones, and no municipal permit was required. In a subsequent case, *Durham (Regional Municipality) v Todd*,[68] the validity of the federal government entering into an agreement with a municipality to control a harbour, pursuant to the *Fishing and Recreational Harbours Act*,[69] was recognized, the effect being that local regulations over moorage and display of lights became valid and were not ousted by any doctrine of paramountcy or interjurisdictional immunity.

---

66 Above note 3.

67 *Ibid* at para 4.

68 2010 ONCJ 122 [*Todd*].

69 RSC 1985, c F-24.

5) Double Aspect Doctrine: Trade and Commerce

For the most part, the federal government is seen as exercising a lead power over trade and commerce, as manifested, for example, in anti-combines legislation. There is potential, however, for interaction with the provincial power over property and civil rights.[70] Several cases have touched on this issue.[71] In *Re Actus Management Ltd and City of Calgary*,[72] the court, in dealing with municipal rules that disallowed an "overconcentration" of certain businesses in an area, was careful to try to use language that avoided any obvious intrusion into a federal head of power.

6) Double Aspect Doctrine: Environment

Although "natural resources" and their control was a preoccupation of the original *Constitution Act, 1867*, the implied approach was one of anthropomorphic use; concern over "environment" appeared later. It then fell to the courts to determine how jurisdiction over the topic ought to be viewed under the federal/provincial allocation of powers in the Constitution. A series of cases established that there should be shared jurisdiction. The federal government may exercise the POGG power, the fisheries power, the navigable waters power, the criminal law power, and others. The provinces may use their power over matters of a local nature. This dynamic played out in *114957 Canada Ltée (Spraytech, Société d'arrosage) v Hudson (Town)*[73] and various cases following it, in which provincial and thus municipal jurisdiction over aspects of the environment has been recognized as compatible with federal jurisdiction. In *Spraytech*, the issue was regulation of pesticides. The federal power had been used to determine what products could be sold in Canada; provincial laws regulated licensing and some conditions of use; and there was no operational conflict for a municipality to further regulate their use. In *Chalets St-Adolphe inc v St-Adolphe d'Howard (Municipalité de)*,[74] a municipality expressed concerns over pollution of a lake and adopted rules limiting use of their public boat ramp to residents. The court saw the measure as not justifiable as an environmental benefit, and an interference with the core of the federal power over navigation.

---

70 For an overview, see *General Motors of Canada Ltd v City National Leasing Ltd*, [1989] 1 SCR 641.

71 See, for example, *Shell Canada Products Ltd v Vancouver (City)*, [1994] 1 SCR 231; *Quebec (Attorney General) v Canada (National Energy Board)*, [1994] 1 SCR 159; *Canadian Transit Co v Windsor (City)*, 2015 FCA 88.

72 (1975), 62 DLR (3d) 421 (Alta SCAD).

73 2001 SCC 40 [*Spraytech*].

74 2011 QCCA 1491.

D. FEDERAL GOVERNMENT LAND-USE POWERS[75]

In 1974, PM Troop, a federal Department of Justice lawyer, gave a talk to the Law Society of Upper Canada on "Federal Land Use Control"[76] in which he offered a partial survey of the topic. He stated:

> The power of the Parliament of Canada to make laws in respect of land use is not well known. It may be a surprise to many lawyers that Parliament has such jurisdiction at all. The fact is that the Government of Canada, through appropriate legislation, has been controlling the use of lands within the provinces for a long time. The objectives may not be quite the same as those of the province but land use control it is and, in the appropriate circumstances, will have to be taken into account in the planning and execution of any land development scheme.

Troop surveyed a half-dozen topics of federal land-use jurisdiction. But the list is actually much more extensive. Here we shall look at some thirty-one topics of federal regulatory control or associated powers.[77]

- Land ownership
- Expropriation
- Declaratory power
- Northern Canada/territories
- Aboriginal peoples
- National Capital Commission
- National parks/Historic sites
- Public harbours
- Aeronautics
- Canada Post
- Navigable waters
- Archaeology
- Species at risk
- Pest control
- Atomic energy/Uranium mining
- Boundaries
- International treaties/*NAFTA*
- National defence
- Emergencies
- Parliament Hill
- Sable Island
- Ministry of Urban Affairs

---

75 For a fuller account of the topic, see Howard M Epstein, "The Living Rooms of the Nation—the *Criminal Code* and other Federal Land-Use Regulatory Powers: Comments on *R. v. Clark*" (2005) 8 *Municipal and Planning Law Reports* (4th) 234.

76 (1974) *Special Lectures of the Law Society of Upper Canada* 63.

77 It is certainly possible to classify the federal powers differently. Further, one aspect not examined is the federal spending power. While this is not a direct land-use power, it has been used so as to affect land uses, usually in conjunction with the exercise of power by the other levels of government. Thus, making a national bid for large-scale sporting events such as the Olympics is usually supported by the federal level and can have major land impacts. The federal government has offered municipalities funding to improve their environmental infrastructure.

- Interprovincial pipelines
- Communications
- Federally regulated corporations
- Fisheries
- Environment
- Transportation
- Housing
- Taxation
- *Criminal Code*

1) Land Ownership

Land ownership by the federal government implies the opportunity to adopt land-use regulations, but, as discussed in the SCC decision in *Lafarge*[78] (see Section C(4), above in this chapter), the mere fact of federal ownership of lands does not immunize them from potential regulation by the province as an incidental effect of its exercise of land-use planning authority. The courts are not inclined to apply the idea of interjurisdictional immunity. They will tend to look at compatibility of regulatory regimes, though in circumstances of conflict, the federal rules will be paramount. Nor will the fact of federal ownership in itself negate the opportunity for members of the public to exercise *Charter*-protected rights, such as those of assembly or free speech.[79]

2) Expropriation

Expropriation sets the stage for federal regulation, though this is not necessary if there is some head of power that allows the federal government to regulate, absent ownership. There is a power of expropriation that exists as an adjunct to the exercise of specific federal powers.[80] The *Expropriation Act*[81] sets out procedures. The Act contemplates the possibility of expropriation of provincially owned land.[82] Controversy attaches to expropriation where the original intended use does not proceed. There have been disputes over land expropriated by the National Capital Commission and for a possible airport at Pickering, Ontario, as examples.

---

78 Above note 3.

79 *Committee for the Commonwealth of Canada v Canada*, [1991] 1 SCR 139; *Montréal (City) v 2952-1366 Quebec Inc*, 2005 SCC 62.

80 See, generally, Andree Lajoie, *Expropriation et federalisme au Canada* (Montreal: University of Montreal Press, 1972).

81 *Expropriation Act*, RSC 1985, c E-21.

82 Section 6(4). One commentator has suggested some circumstances for the limitation of the power of expropriation: see John AH Clay, "Expropriation: A Federal Tool" (2002) 15 *Canadian Journal of Administrative Law and Practice* 1 at 7.

3) Declaratory Power

The *Constitution Act, 1867* allows the federal government to expand its jurisdiction by declaring a local work or undertaking to be "for the general advantage of Canada."[83] This triggers federal land-use regulation. This power has been used for nuclear energy and grain elevators;[84] of the almost 500 instances of such declarations, they have primarily been for local railways and other commercial/industrial infrastructure.[85]

4) Northern Canada/Territories

Almost 40 percent of Canada's land mass is outside the borders of the provinces, and hence under federal jurisdiction: "The Parliament of Canada may from time to time make provision for the administration, peace, order, and good government of any territory not for the time being included in any province."[86] Legislative assemblies have been established for each of the three territories, thus ceding a significant measure of self-government to residents of the north. Major resource undertakings there, such as pipelines and diamond mines, are subject to federal environmental assessment laws; some activities are subject to special legislation.[87] Aboriginal interests are a major factor in development proposals. Special legislation to implement land-claims settlements exist.[88] Special tribunals exist to deal with a variety of mining activities and rights.[89]

5) Aboriginal Peoples

The law relating to Aboriginal peoples and associated land-use rights is complex and in a rapid process of evolution.[90] Rights are anchored

---

83 *Constitution Act, 1867*, ss 92(10)(c) and 91(29).

84 See *R v Thumlert* (1959), 20 DLR (2d) 335 (Alta SCAD) and *Jorgenson v Canada (Attorney General)*, [1971] SCR 725. Canadian companies may also use the *NAFTA* arbitration mechanism; TransCanada Corp has filed a claim against the United States over its rejection of the Keystone XL pipeline project: See "TransCanada Files $15-billion *NAFTA* Claim over U.S. Rejection of Keystone Pipeline" *The Globe and Mail Report on Business* (27 June 2016) B3.

85 See Lajoie, above note 80 and Hogg, above note 9, ss 5.3(i) and 22.8.

86 *The Constitution Act, 1871* (UK), 34–35 Victoria, c 28, s 4.

87 *Yukon Environmental and Socio-economic Assessment Act*, SC 2003, c 7.

88 See *Gwich'in Land Claim Settlement Act*, SC 1992, c 53.

89 *Nunavut Waters and Nunavut Surface Rights Tribunal Act*, SC 2002, c 10; *Yukon Surface Rights Board Act*, SC 1994, c 43.

90 In *Daniels v Canada (Indian Affairs and Northern Development)*, 2016 SCC 12, the Supreme Court decided that rights associated with Indian status apply to Metis and non-status Indians. Although section 35 of the *Constitution Act, 1982* came

in treaties and also in unsurrendered rights, as recognized in section 35 of *The Constitution Act, 1982*. The federal government has assumed responsibility for Aboriginal peoples through *The Constitution Act, 1867*, section 91(24) ("Indians, and Lands reserved for the Indians . . ."), which has been manifested largely through the *Indian Act*.[91] It is a stated goal of many Aboriginal peoples to move themselves out of the legal context of the *Indian Act* and into a situation of self-government.[92] Thus, various modern comprehensive agreements have been negotiated and many others are in the process of being negotiated.

Some of what we know from decided cases is that:

- "The European Settlements of Canada did not terminate Aboriginal peoples' interest in the land. This interest and Aboriginal customary law are presumed to have survived the assertion of Crown sovereignty and were incorporated into the common law."[93]
- Rights may be voluntarily surrendered by way of treaties, or may have been unilaterally extinguished by the federal Crown prior to 1982.
- Aboriginal and treaty rights have constitutional status but "these rights are not absolute and remain subject to justifiable infringement by the Crown."[94]
- To justify infringement, governments should be able to demonstrate that it is in the broader public interest to do so.

> [T]he development of agriculture, forestry, mining, and hydroelectric power, the general economic development of the interior of British Columbia, protection of the environment or endangered species, the building of infrastructure and the settlement of foreign populations to support those aims, are the kinds of objectives that are consistent with this purpose and, in principle, can justify the infringement of aboriginal title.[95]

---

into effect at the same time as the *Charter*, section 35, regarding Aboriginal peoples, is not a part of the *Charter*; thus Aboriginal rights are not subject to the *Charter*'s section 1 "reasonable limits" provision nor to its section 33 "notwithstanding" provision.

91 *Indian Act*, RSC 1985, c I-5, as amended.

92 See Canada, Royal Commission on Aboriginal Peoples, *Report of the Royal Commission on Aboriginal Peoples* (Ottawa: The Commission, 1996), especially vol 1 at 679; vol 5 at 154–65. Aboriginal peoples includes First Nations under the *Indian Act*: Metis, status Indians, and non-status Indians.

93 Thomas Isaac, *Aboriginal Law*, 3d ed (Saskatoon: Purich, 2004) at 2; *Calder v British Columbia (Attorney General)*, [1973] SCR 313.

94 Isaac, above note 93 at 26; the *Constitution Act, 1982*, ss 35 and 25, being Schedule B to the *Canada Act 1982* (UK), 1982, c 11; *Mitchell v Canada (Minister of National Revenue)*, 2001 SCC 33.

95 *Delgamuukw v British Columbia*, [1997] 3 SCR 1010 at para 165 [*Delgamuukw*].

- Aboriginal title deals with claims of rights to land and is a sub-category of Aboriginal rights. As it is a right to the land itself, Aboriginal people are not limited to "traditional" uses of the land; they are only restrained by the rule that the land must remain usable by future generations. Rights can exist independent of title and may be site specific.[96]
- The extent of Aboriginal title is evolving.[97]
- Aboriginal lands are inalienable, save to the Crown, which has a fiduciary duty to deal with the land for the benefit of the surrendering peoples.[98]
- Legislation covers various aspects of land-use questions.[99]
- Aboriginal rights such as hunting and gathering or cutting timber cannot be exercised on private property that is occupied and visibly used for a purpose incompatible with Aboriginal rights, at least for lands covered by Treaty No 8.[100]
- Aboriginal rights on Crown land are as specified by treaty, or, in the absence of a treaty, depend on whether there is evidence as to historical circumstances that support an Aboriginal right or title.[101]
- In the absence of a settled claim, the Crown has a duty to consult with the claimants prior to authorizing any land use that might infringe Aboriginal rights on Crown land.[102]
- Aboriginal land is held communally.[103]
- Self-government agreements are being negotiated and some have been completed.[104]

---

96 *R v Van der Peet*, [1996] 2 SCR 507; *R v Adams*, [1996] 3 SCR 101.

97 *Delgamuukw*, above note 95.

98 *Guerin v Canada*, [1984] 2 SCR 335.

99 *Indian Act*, above note 91, especially ss 18, 20, 35, 81, 88, and 93; *First Nations Land Management Act*, SC 1999, c 24.

100 *R v Badger*, [1996] 4 WWR 457 (SCC) [*Badger*].

101 *R v Marshall*, [1999] 3 SCR 456 (SCC); *R v Marshall (reconsideration)*, [1999] 3 SCR 533.

102 *Tsilhqot'in Nation v British Columbia*, 2014 SCC 44; *Rio Tinto Alcan Inc v Carrier Sekani Tribal Council*, 2010 SCC 43; Thomas Isaac & Anthony Knox, "The Crown's Duty to Consult Aboriginal People" (2003) 41 *Alberta Law Review* 49; James I Reynolds, *A Breach of Duty* (Saskatoon: Purich, 2005); Kenneth Coates & Dwight Newman, "The End Is Not Nigh: Reason over Alarmism in Analysing the *Tsilhqot'in* Decision" (Ottawa: MacDonald Laurier Institute, S 2014), online: www.macdonaldlaurier.ca/files/pdf/MLITheEndIsNotNigh.pdf; *Enge v Mandeville et al*, 2013 NWTSC 33.

103 *Osoyoos Indian Band v Oliver (Town)*, 2001 SCC 85.

104 Canada, Indian and Northern Affairs Canada, *Federal Policy Guide: Aboriginal Self-government* (Ottawa: Indian and Northern Affairs Canada, 1995).

- Indian band councils can exercise powers akin to zoning.[105]
- Provincial laws of general application apply to Aboriginal peoples while off reserve unless they deal with matters that more than incidentally affect "Indianness" or the "core of Indianness"; on reserve such laws apply because they have been incorporated by reference through the *Indian Act.*[106]
- In the three Prairie provinces, hunting, trapping, and fishing "for food" are protected by the "Natural Resources Agreements" of the *Constitution Act, 1930.*[107]
- Municipal zoning is probably not applicable to reserves. The British Columbia Court of Appeal decision in *Surrey (District) v Peace Arch Enterprises Ltd*[108] ruled that reserve land is protected from municipal zoning.
- In all its dealings with Aboriginal peoples, the Crown must act with honour.[109]

Other forms of provincial land-use control that have been litigated include licensing the destruction of culturally significant trees,[110] timber harvesting on Crown land for personal use,[111] and hunting for food.[112]

It is not uncommon for reserve lands, or lands subject to claims, to be within or proximate to established municipal units. This has led to explorations of how the Aboriginal peoples and local governments could usefully interact.[113] Examples of communities in which formal agreements have been worked out are Brantford, Ontario, and Kelowna, British Columbia.[114]

---

105 *Indian Act*, above note 91, ss 81, 83, and 85.1; *Whitebear Band v Carpenters Provincial Council Saskatchewan*, [1982] 3 WWR 554 (Sask CA).

106 *Indian Act*, above note 91, s 88; *R v Dick*, [1985] 2 SCR 309; *Delgamuukw*, above note 95; *R v Francis*, [1988] 1 SCR 1025; *Four B Manufacturing Ltd v United Garment Workers of America*, [1980] 1 SCR 1031.

107 20–21 George V, c 26 (UK). See *R v Horseman*, [1990] 1 SCR 901.

108 (1970), 74 WWR 380 (BCCA) [*Peace Arch*]. *Peace Arch* was approved by the Supreme Court of Canada in *Cardinal v Alberta (Attorney General)*, [1974] SCR 695.

109 *Badger*, above note 100.

110 *Kitkatla Band v British Columbia (Minister of Small Business, Tourism and Culture)*, 2002 SCC 31 (law held applicable).

111 *R v Bernard*, 2003 NBCA 55; *R v Sappier*, 2004 NBCA 56.

112 *R v Powley*, 2003 SCC 43.

113 See Evelyn J Peters, ed, *Aboriginal Self-Government in Urban Areas*, Proceedings of Workshop held 25–26 May 1994 (Kingston, ON: Institute of Intergovernmental Relations, 1995).

114 The two agreements are Grand River Notification Agreement of 1996 and Gallagher Canyon Master Agreement of 2000; see Kasia Tota, "The Old/New Neighbours: Breaking Ground in Collaborative Land Use Planning between First Nations and Local Governments" in Jill Grant, ed, *A Reader in Canadian*

6) National Capital Commission

This topic was discussed in Section B, above in this chapter, in discussion of some of the main consequences of the basic constitutional law arrangements as affects land use.[115]

7) National Parks/Historic Sites

There are forty-six national parks established pursuant to the *Canada National Parks Act*.[116] Of the essence of a park is severely restricted activity.[117] The Act requires management plans to advance the ecological integrity of the park. Still, visitor services are permissible as are some utility corridors, water extraction for use by adjacent lands, some renewable resource harvesting, and some Aboriginal use. Some parks accommodate settlements and commercial activities (e.g., ski runs), much of which is controversial.[118] The particular position of Banff and Jasper has been noted. National historic sites involve designation only,[119] not any restriction in land use, except for designated heritage railway stations for which there are prohibitions against alteration or demolition without authorization.[120]

8) Public Harbours

Not a specified head of power, "public harbours" are listed as Property of Canada under Schedule III of the *Constitution Act*. There has been extensive litigation, chiefly about the geographic bounds of the harbours.[121] The issue of the interaction of federal and provincial land-use regimes for land around harbours has been settled in the *Lafarge* case,

---

Planning: Linking Theory and Practice (Toronto: Thomson Nelson, 2008) 328. See also Joanne Heritz, "Municipal-Aboriginal Advisory Committees in Four Canadian Cities: 1999–2014" (2016) 59(1) *Canadian Public Administration* 134.

115 For a short account by a planner who was a member of the NCC's Planning Committee for fourteen years, including comments on the green belt, see Hans Blumenfeld, *Life Begins at 65* (Montreal: Harvest House, 1987) at 269–70.

116 *National Parks Act*, SC 2002, c 32.

117 For a history of national parks in Canada, see Claire E Campbell, ed, *A Century of Parks Canada, 1911–2011* (Calgary: University of Calgary Press, 2011).

118 See, for example, *Canadian Parks and Wilderness Society v Superintendant of Banff National Park* (1994), 77 FTR 218 (TD); *Sunshine Village Corp v Canada (Parks)*, 2004 FCA 166.

119 *Historic Sites and Monuments Act*, RSC 1985, c H-4 as amended.

120 *Heritage Railway Stations Act*, RSC 1985, c 52 (4th Supp) as amended.

121 See Gerard V La Forest, *Natural Resources and Public Property under the Canadian Constitution*, 2d ed (Toronto: University of Toronto Press, 1969) at 49ff.

discussed in Section C(4), above in this chapter. It is permissible for the federal government to delegate its powers to another order of government. Thus in *Todd*,[122] there was a prosecution over a boat-owner's non-compliance with a municipal rule regarding placement of a mooring buoy and failure to use lights; the defence based on paramount federal powers failed due to the delegation, as well as absence of a conflict in the rules.

9) Aeronautics

This topic was discussed in Section C(3), above in this chapter. To that discussion it is useful to add that there is a record of federal-provincial cooperation in land use associated with airports. Thus, the federal government expropriated some 18,600 acres of land in 1972 for a possible airport at Pickering, Ontario. The provincial government placed a buffer around the federal lands at the same time.[123] Although the lands remain set aside, and the provincial buffer also exists, this initial co-operation evaporated when the province decided it was unwilling to build roads to service the site; studies show no immediate need for the airport.

10) Canada Post

The use of land for installation of community mailboxes was confirmed as a legitimate exercise of a federal power, leaving no room for local regulatory controls, in *Canada Post Corp v Hamilton (City)*.[124]

11) Navigable Waters

The federal government was clearly assigned this topic under the *Constitution Act* ("Navigation and Shipping"). The land-use implication arises from the practical analysis shown in such cases as *Lafarge*[125] (control over shipping implies control over land-based shipping facilities) or *Johannesson*[126] (control over aeronautics implies control over airports) as well as from the terms of the federal statute itself, which claims jurisdiction over the land approaches to undertakings that can interfere with navigation. The *Navigation Protection Act* requires a

---

122 Above note 68.

123 See *Canada (Attorney General) v Berrywood Farms Inc*, 2006 CanLII 6079 (Ont Div Ct).

124 Above note 41.

125 Above note 3.

126 Above note 55.

ministerial permit for any "work" that is to "be built or placed in, on, over, under, through or across any navigable water." "Work" is defined to include "any device or thing, whether temporary or permanent, that is made by humans."[127] The predecessor statute defined "work" to include "any bridge, boom, dam, wharf, dock, pier, tunnel or pipe and the *approaches* or other works necessary or appurtenant thereto," and there is no reason to see the new definition as excluding the "approaches" and, therefore, land. Ministerial permitting triggers the federal environmental assessment process.

12) Pipelines

Interprovincial or international pipelines for transportation of oil or natural gas are subject to federal jurisdiction, exercisable through the National Energy Board (NEB). A certificate of public convenience and necessity must be sought. Purely intraprovincial facilities and some parts of interconnected systems are subject to provincial control. Overall, the topic is an extensive one with a substantial literature.[128] Environmental assessment accompanies the application for an NEB certificate, often a joint federal-provincial process.[129] There is a special statute for any pipeline that would join Alaska to the rest of the continental United States.[130]

13) Communications

This topic was determined to be a federal matter by 1932.[131] The topic includes radio, television,[132] telephone systems,[133] cable, and satellites. The placing of communications towers is a controversial matter, with

127 RSC 1985, c N-22, s 2.

128 See, for example, Constance D Hunt & Alastair R Lucas, *Oil and Gas Law in Canada* (Toronto: Carswell, 1990).

129 See, for example, Sable Gas Projects, *The Joint Public Review Panel Report* (Ottawa: The Panel, 1997). The major pipelines currently under review are Trans Mountain, Northern Gateway, and Energy East. Keystone XL is a Canadian proposal for a pipeline mainly in the USA. The Federal Court of Appeal recently overturned approval of the Northern Gateway proposal on the basis of inadequate consultation with Aboriginal peoples; see *Gitxaala Nation v Canada*, 2016 FCA 187.

130 *Northern Pipeline Act*, RSC 1985, c N-26.

131 *Reference re Regulation and Control of Radio Communication*, [1932] AC 304 (JCPC).

132 *Quebec (Public Service Board) v Canada (Attorney General)*, [1978] 2 SCR 191.

133 *Alberta Government Telephones v Canadian Radio-television and Telecommunications Commission*, [1989] 2 SCR 225.

complaints focusing on aesthetics as well as allegations of potential health effects. The Canadian Radio and Telecommunications Commission has authority to set terms for access to municipal property for installation of cables.[134] There is no room for local regulation: *Rogers Communications Inc v Châteauguay (City)*.[135]

14) Federally Regulated Corporations

The federal government may incorporate companies with objects that extend beyond provincial ones. Banks and railroads are examples. Once incorporated, though, the lands of the companies are not necessarily regulated by the federal government; local land-use rules will be applicable save for operative conflict with any federal rules, and local laws may not go beyond having an incidental effect on the federal matter. Local laws may not impair the "status and essential powers" of a federally incorporated company.[136] A contemporary example is *R v Canadian Pacific Ltd*,[137] in which the railroad company was found to be obliged to follow provincial pollution laws (regarding smoke from a controlled burn to eliminate weeds); the rationale was that "undertakings within the exclusive jurisdiction of Parliament usually are subject to provincial statutes of general application. The only exception . . . applies when the provincial statute taken as a whole bears essentially upon the management and control of the [federal] undertakings . . . ."[138]

15) Environment

The environment is not a matter expressly assigned to either the federal or the provincial governments under *The Constitution Act, 1867*. The courts have recognized divided jurisdiction,[139] with the federal sources of authority being the POGG clause, criminal law, fisheries, and others. The two main federal statutes are the *Canadian Environmental Protection Act, 1999* (*CEPA*)[140] and the *Canadian Environmental Assessment Act,*

---

134 *Federation of Canadian Municipalities v AT & T Canada Corp*, 2002 FCA 500.
135 2016 SCC 23.
136 *John Deere Plow Co v Wharton*, [1915] AC 330 (JCPC).
137 [1995] 2 SCR 1028.
138 *Ibid* (appeal dismissed with very short reasons); the passage quoted is from the Ontario Court of Appeal decision: (1993), 103 DLR (4th) 255 at 263.
139 *R v Crown Zellerbach Canada Ltd*, [1988] 1 SCR 401; *Friends of the Oldman River Society v Canada (Minister of Transport)*, [1992] 1 SCR 3; *R v Hydro-Québec*, [1997] 3 SCR 213.
140 SC 1999, c 33.

2012 (*CEAA*).[141] The *Fisheries Act*, *Transportation of Dangerous Goods Act*, *Canada Wildlife Act*, *Canada National Parks Act*, and the *Migratory Birds Convention Act* are also relevant. *CEPA* sets standards to control polluting emissions. The *CEAA* triggers environmental assessments when the proponent of an undertaking is the federal government or a federal agency, when federal financing is present, or when a federal permit is required. The assessment process involves different levels of intensity of scrutiny, with most projects not involving public hearings.[142] Environmental law is akin to the planning process in that it sets standards but also requires consideration in advance of the costs and benefits of proposed developments.

16) Fisheries

Not stated in the *Constitution Act* as a land-oriented power, the *Fisheries Act*[143] nonetheless is an important statute for control of land-based activities. It prohibits harmful alteration, disruption, or destruction of fish habitat,[144] thereby influencing such activities as forestry.[145] The Act is also used to permit the use by mining works of some waters for mine waste effluent[146] and to set standards for pulp and paper plant effluent[147] and waste water.[148]

17) Archaeology

The *CEAA* and the *Cultural Property Export and Import Act*[149] require reporting and protection for a variety of archaeological finds.[150] Reportable finds can include artifacts on top of the soil, petroglyphs, fossils,

141 SC 2012, c 19, s 52.

142 For analysis and critique, see David Boyd, *Unnatural Law: Rethinking Canadian Environmental Law and Policy* (Vancouver: UBC Press, 2003) at 152–53; Andrew Nikiforuk, *The Nasty Game: The Failure of Environmental Assessment in Canada* (Toronto: Walter and Duncan Gordon Foundation, 1997).

143 RSC 1985, c F-14.

144 *Ibid*, s 34, with a change in wording.

145 *R v Northwest Falling Contractors Ltd*, [1980] 2 SCR 292, a prosecution of a logging business.

146 *Metal Mining Effluent Regulations*, SOR/2002-222; see Andrew Gage, "Fish Lakes and Tailings Ponds" (2011) 22 *Journal of Environmental Law and Practice* 1.

147 *Pulp and Paper Effluent Regulations*, SOR/92-269.

148 *Wastewater Systems Effluent Regulations*, SOR/2012-139.

149 RSC 1985, c C-51.

150 See, generally, Parks Canada, *Unearthing the Law: Archaeological Legislation on Lands in Canada*, by Marc Denhez (Halifax: Archaeological Services Branch, Parks Canada, 2000), online: www.pc.gc.ca/docs/r/pfa-fap/index.aspx.

paleontological findings, and human remains. Encountering archaeological items is common.[151]

18) Species at Risk[152]

The *Species at Risk Act*[153] creates a system for the designation of species needing protection, combined with "incentives to support voluntary stewardship actions," applicable to both Crown and private lands. The logic of the law is to recognize that species require spaces. The legislation has the potential to block otherwise allowable land development.[154]

19) Pest Control

A broad range of powers exists under the *Plant Protection Act* designed to deal with non-native "pests" that can harm agricultural crops or forestry. The statute is administered by the Canadian Food Inspection Agency (CFIA), which may issue orders for quarantine of places such as warehouses and farms, and for confiscation or destruction. Control measures such as aerial spraying may be undertaken.[155] Inspectors have a power of entry.

20) Atomic Energy/Uranium Mining

Atomic energy is a matter of federal jurisdiction through the exercise of the declaratory power.[156] As Hogg says,

> In 1946, after the atomic bombs had been dropped on Japan, the federal Parliament passed the *Atomic Energy Control Act*. The Act created

151 Lisa Seip, "Archaeology and Municipalities: The Missing Link" *Municipal World* (September 2004) at 21.

152 This is treated separately from "Environment" in Section D(15), above in this chapter, because it grapples with the issue of compensation, a significant preoccupation of land-use law.

153 SC 2002, c 29.

154 See Daniel Leblanc, "Quebec Hopping Mad over Federal Intervention to Protect Frog" *The Globe and Mail* (23 June 2016), reporting that an emergency order under the statute would block "part of a residential project south of Montreal." At issue was habitat for the western chorus frog. "The federal order will protect two square kilometers of land in the municipality of La Prairie, Que., that include the area where 171 housing units . . . were to be built."

155 As in Vancouver in 1992: see *Edwards v Canada (Minister of Agriculture)* (1992), 8 CELR (NS) 81 (FCTD).

156 *Constitution Act, 1867*, s 92(10)(c). See *Nuclear Safety and Control Act*, SC 1997, c 9, and *Nuclear Fuel Waste Act*, SC 2002, c 23.

> a category of "prescribed substances," which included uranium, and the Act declared that all works and undertakings "for the production, refining, or treatment of prescribed substances" were works for the general advantage of Canada.[157]

Land issues have to do with mining; placement of facilities (nuclear reactors, as used for scientific research, medical purposes, or for the generation of electricity); and the transportation and storage or disposal of mine tailings, spent fuel rods, or other radioactive waste. Exploration for and mining of uranium is a provincial matter. Nuclear power stations are located at Point Lepreau, New Brunswick; Gentilly, Quebec; and Kincardine, Pickering, and Clarington in Ontario. The main federal regulatory agency is the Atomic Energy Control Commission. The problem of waste management was studied in 1977[158] and in 1998,[159] resulting in creation of the Nuclear Waste Management Organization to continue consideration of deep geological disposal.[160] Location of candidate sites remains controversial.[161] Because electricity generation plants, owned and administered provincially, also produce radioactive waste, often referred to as "low-level" or "intermediate" waste, their disposal is also regulated federally. A proposal to bury such waste near Kincardine, Ontario, about 1.2 kilometres from Lake Huron is being resisted by area residents.[162]

21) Boundaries

Physical boundaries establish legal jurisdiction. The shoreline jurisdiction of provinces ends at the low-water mark. International boundary disputes are settled through the principles of international law, the results having potential to alter provincial boundaries or those of the territories.[163]

---

157 Hogg, above note 9 at 29-5.

158 F Kenneth Hare et al, *The Management of Canada's Nuclear Wastes*, Policy Report EP 77-6 (Ottawa: Energy, Mines and Resources Canada, Energy Policy Sector, 1977).

159 Blair Seaborn & Canadian Environmental Assessment Agency, *Nuclear Fuel Waste Management and Disposal Concept*, Report of the Nuclear Waste Management and Disposal Concept Environmental Assessment Panel, EN-106-30/1-1998E (Hull, QC: The Panel, 1998).

160 See Nuclear Waste Management Organization, online: www.nwmo.ca.

161 See Charles Wilkins, "The Deep" *Report on Business Magazine* (March 2015) at 54ff; Bertrand Marotte, "Uranium Still Unwelcome in Quebec" *The Globe and Mail* (27 July 2015) B3.

162 "Concern over Plan to Bury Nuclear Waste Sparks Petition to Feds" *The Canadian Press* (22 January 2016).

163 For an account of the establishment of the boundaries of the Prairie provinces, see Derek Hayes, "Drawing the Lines" *Canadian Geographic* (January/February 2005) at 48–49.

22) International Treaties/*NAFTA*

The *Metalclad*[164] case has brought out the potential for *NAFTA* or other international trade treaties that include investor-rights provisions to trigger claims for money damages when land-use regulation by any order of government is seen as "expropriation or equivalent to expropriation." The Canadian judge reviewing the *Metalclad* arbitration award said,

> The Tribunal gave an extremely broad definition of expropriation for the purposes of Article 1110. In addition to the more conventional notion of expropriation involving a taking of property, the Tribunal held that expropriation under NAFTA includes covert or incidental interference with the use of property which has the effect of depriving the owner, in whole or in significant part, of the use or reasonably-to-be-expected economic benefit of property. *This definition is sufficiently broad to include a legitimate re-zoning of property by a municipality or other zoning authority.*[165]

It is crucial to note that an international treaty entered into by the federal government cannot invalidate legitimate provincial or municipal land-use regulation, because of the division of powers and as recognized in the 1937 *Labour Conventions*[166] case. Nonetheless, there is real political pressure on provincial and municipal governments not to regulate land uses in ways that might expose the federal government to liability to pay *NAFTA* claims.[167] Similar to *Metalclad* is the arbitration decision in the *Bilcon* case, which called into question the environmental assessment process.[168] Some *NAFTA* articles deal with water extraction, and fears have been expressed that allowing commercial sales of groundwater could lead to an ongoing right of access by *NAFTA* partners for export of water.[169]

---

164 *Metalclad*, above note 33. The decision of the *NAFTA* arbitration panel can be found at (2001) 1 *Asper Review of International Business and Trade Law* 1.

165 *Metalclad*, above note 33 at para 99 [emphasis added].

166 *Labour Conventions Case*, above note 32.

167 For a fuller discussion, see Epstein, "*NAFTA*," above note 35.

168 *Bilcon*, above note 34. Another *NAFTA* claim has been filed, by Windstream Energy LLC, arising from Ontario's decision to cancel offshore placement of wind turbines in Lake Ontario: see Richard Blackwell, "Canada Faces $568-million *NAFTA* Claim" *The Globe and Mail Report on Business* (15 February 2016). Canadian companies may also use the *NAFTA* arbitration mechanism. TransCanada has filed a claim agains the United States over its rejection of the Keystone XL pipeline project: see "TransCanada Wants $15-billion for Rejection of Keystone XL" *The Globe and Mail Report on Business* (27 June 2016) B3.

169 See, for example, Boyd, above note 142 at 61–64.

23) National Defence

The *National Defence Act*[170] sets the framework for the military to carry on its training and exercises within the confines of bases, and there is authority in the Act to authorize military exercises ("manoeuvres") anywhere in the country.[171]

24) Emergencies

The *Emergencies Act*[172] (replacement of the *War Measures Act*) allows cabinet declaration of an emergency to trigger orders and regulations on an ascending basis of intensity tied to the class of the emergency and extending to "prohibition of travel to, from or within a specified area," "evacuation of persons," "requisition, use or disposition of property," "regulation or prohibition of any public assembly that may reasonably be expected to lead to a breach of the peace," and other measures. The Act incorporates various safeguards of liberties.

25) Parliament Hill

Control of activities in the parliament buildings rests with the Speaker of the Commons. This is so by virtue of federal ownership as well as the constitutional convention of parliamentary privilege.[173] As interpreted by the courts, the *Charter* is inapplicable to matters of parliamentary privilege[174] and is no basis for a right to demonstrate (assembly/speech) or other rights such as freedom of the press. The privilege is the right to "exclude strangers." This extends to the precincts of the buildings.[175]

26) Sable Island

The actual item as listed in section 91(9) of *The Constitution Act, 1867* is "Beacons, Buoys, Lighthouses, and Sable Island," words that are reflected in Part VII of the *Canada Shipping Act, 2001*.[176] Lighthouses and their survival have been the focus of no little controversy in recent years as

170 RSC 1985, c N-5.

171 *Ibid*, s 257.

172 *Emergencies Act*, RSC 1985, c 22 (4th Supp).

173 See *Parliament of Canada Act*, RSC 1985, c P-1.

174 *New Brunswick Broadcasting Co v Nova Scotia (Speaker of the House of Assembly)*, [1993] 1 SCR 319.

175 *R v Behrens*, 2004 ONCJ 327.

176 SC 2001, c 26. "Beacons, buoys, lighthouses" and so on are referred to as "aids to navigation" (s 125).

the federal government has been selling them or turning them over to community groups to care for. Sable Island has had a human presence for some 200 years, related primarily to lighthouse and research functions. The station serves as an emergency support for mariners, the military, and nearby ocean drilling rigs. In 2013 it was designated as a national park reserve, although the possibility of drilling for petroleum was explicitly allowed for within one nautical mile of the low-water mark.[177]

27) Ministry of Urban Affairs

At various times, starting in the 1970s, and despite absence of constitutional jurisdiction, the federal government has created cabinet positions responsible for "Urban Affairs." The main function is to direct funding to municipalities to influence infrastructure building or renewal, homelessness, immigration, early childhood education, and energy use.[178]

28) Transportation

Railroads are the main aspect of transportation of contemporary concern as a land-use matter, apart from airports (discussed in Sections C(3), above, and D(9), below in this chapter) and ports (discussed in Section C(4), above in this chapter). Concerns arise over matters of safety, given the nature of the cargoes that may be carried. The explosion of a train carrying combustible fuels in the town of Lac-Mégantic in 2013[179] vividly illustrates how important is safe regulation. Railroad safety is regulated federally.[180] Local jurisdiction tends to be quite limited, on the principles set out under the heading of "federally regulated corporations," although given this incident, there may be provincial or municipal attempts at dealing with the location of rail lines, design of crossings, and sounding of warning horns, and issues of jurisdiction to order remediation of pollution, or to prosecute, will arise.

177 *Expansion and Conservation of Canada's National Parks Act*, SC 2013, c 28, s 6.

178 See, for example, Harry Kitchen & Enid Slack, "Special Study: New Finance Options for Municipal Governments" (2003) 51 *Canadian Tax Journal* 2215 at 2265–266.

179 On 6 July 2013, a parked freight train carrying crude oil rolled downhill into the town and derailed, resulting in a fire and explosion. Forty-seven people died, and there was extensive property damage.

180 See, for example, *Railway Safety Act*, RSC 1985, c 32 (4th Supp); *Transportation Appeal Tribunal of Canada Act*, SC 2001, c 29; *Transportation of Dangerous Goods Act, 1992*, SC 1992, c 34.

29) Taxation

One American planner says that "the tax system is the most important land-use control we have."[181] It is not necessary to agree with this assertion to recognize that taxation is an important public policy instrument. The taxation of real estate is a complex matter. Development can be influenced by tax regimes, including the federal taxation instruments of corporate tax rates, sales tax, depreciation, and capital gains.[182]

30) Housing

Preceding creation of the federal Ministry of Urban Affairs, the presence of the federal government as a director of land use was focused on housing. It led by provision of plans and financing. The first national legislation was adopted in 1935 as the *Dominion Housing Act*,[183] a Depression-era measure. Initially designed to promote low-income rental housing, the post–World War II programmes expanded to facilitate reconstruction, and later to aid urban renewal. Through CMHC, the federal government remains a significant agency in housing policy,[184] including for co-op or non-profit housing.

31) *Criminal Code*

The *Criminal Code* regulates land-use activities in a variety of its sections. The ones appropriate to single out are those that should be regarded as flowing from private land ownership or right of occupancy, or from interferences with others' use or enjoyment of property. Examples are: common nuisance;[185] bawdy houses;[186] causing a disturbance;[187] disturbing religious worship;[188] nudity;[189] and indecent act in a public place.[190] In

181 Norman Williams Jr, "The Future of Land Use Controls" in Robert W Burchell & David Listokin, eds, *Future Land Use* (New Brunswick, NJ: Rutgers State University Center for Urban Policy Research, 1975) at 29.

182 See Canadian Home Builders Association, "CHBA Position on Federal Taxes on Housing" (August 2001); Israel Mida & Kathleen Stewart, "The Capital Cost Allowance System" (1995) 43 *Canadian Tax Journal* 1245. See also James Howard Kunstler, *Home From Nowhere* (New York: Simon & Schuster, 1996) ch 7.

183 SC 25–26 Geo V, c 58.

184 See "History of CMHC," online: www.cmhc-schl.gc.ca/en/corp/about/hi.

185 *Criminal Code*, RSC 1985, c C-46, as amended, s 180(1).

186 *Ibid*, s 210.

187 *Ibid*, s 175.

188 *Ibid*, s 176.

189 *Ibid*, s 174.

190 *Ibid*, s 173(1)(a).

support of investigation, warrants authorizing entry to search premises may be obtained.[191] No doubt, issue may be taken with the choice of any of these as land-use matters or with the omission of others. But taken as a whole, they do illustrate that the criminal law as an instrument for the declaration of social values does interact with property rights, privacy, and certain regulations of other levels of government.

E. *CHARTER OF RIGHTS* FACTORS[192]

The *Canadian Charter of Rights and Freedoms* was adopted as part of the 1981/82 patriation of the Constitution. All of the *Charter* came into effect 17 April 1982 except for section 15, which took effect three years later so as to allow governments an opportunity to bring statutes into conformity with it. The terms relevant to land-use planning follow:

> Whereas Canada is founded upon principles that recognize the supremacy of God and the rule of law:
>
> 1. The *Canadian Charter of Rights and Freedoms* guarantees the rights and freedoms set out in it subject only to such reasonable limits prescribed by law as can be demonstrably justified in a free and democratic society.
>
> *Fundamental Freedoms*
>
> 2. Everyone has the following fundamental freedoms:
> (*a*) freedom of conscience and religion;
> (*b*) freedom of thought, belief, opinion and expression, including freedom of the press and other media of communication;
> (*c*) freedom of peaceful assembly; and
> (*d*) freedom of association.
>
> *Democratic Rights*
> 3. Every citizen of Canada has the right to vote in an election of members of the House of Commons or of a legislative assembly and to be qualified for membership therein.
>
> . . .

---

191 *Ibid*, s 487.

192 For *Charter* issues generally, see Robert Sharpe & Kent Roach, *The Charter of Rights and Freedoms*, 5th ed (Irwin Law, 2013); Gérald A Beaudoin & Stéphane Beaulac, eds, *The Canadian Charter of Rights and Freedoms*, 5th ed (Markham, ON: LexisNexis Canada Inc, 2013).

Mobility Rights

6. (1) Every citizen of Canada has the right to enter, remain in and leave Canada.

(2) Every citizen and every person who has the status of a permanent resident of Canada has the right

(*a*) to move and to take up residence in any province; and

(*b*) to pursue the gaining of a livelihood in any province.

(3) The rights specified in subsection (2) are subject to

(*a*) any laws or practices of general application in force in a province other than those that discriminate among persons primarily on the basis of province of present or previous residence . . .

Legal Rights

7. Everyone has the right to life, liberty, and security of the person and the right not to be deprived thereof except in accordance with the principles of fundamental justice.

8. Everyone has the right to be secure against unreasonable search or seizure.

. . .

Equality Rights

15. (1) Every individual is equal before and under the law and has the right to the equal protection and equal benefit of the law without discrimination and, in particular, without discrimination based on race, national or ethnic origin, colour, religion, sex, age or mental or physical disability.

(2) Subsection (1) does not preclude any law, program or activity that has as its object the amelioration of conditions of disadvantaged individuals or groups including those that are disadvantaged because of race, national or ethnic origin, colour, religion, sex, age or mental or physical disability.

. . .

Enforcement

24. (1) Anyone whose rights or freedoms, as guaranteed by this *Charter*, have been infringed or denied may apply to a court of competent jurisdiction to obtain such remedy as the court considers appropriate and just in the circumstances.

General

25. The guarantee in this *Charter* of certain rights and freedoms shall not be construed so as to abrogate or derogate from any aboriginal, treaty or other rights or freedoms that pertain to the aboriginal peoples of Canada . . . .

. . .

Application of Charter

32. (1) This *Charter* applies

(*a*) to the Parliament and government of Canada in respect of all matters within the authority of Parliament . . . ; and

(*b*) to the legislature and government of each province in respect of all matters within the authority of the legislature of each province.

33. (1) Parliament or the legislature of a province may expressly declare in an Act of Parliament or of the legislature, as the case may be, that the Act or a provision thereof shall operate notwithstanding a provision included in section 2 or sections 7 to 15 of this *Charter*.[193]

. . .

Part II

35. (1) The existing aboriginal and treaty rights of the aboriginal peoples of Canada are hereby recognized and affirmed.

(2) In this Act, "aboriginal peoples of Canada" includes the Indian, Inuit and Metis peoples of Canada . . . .[194]

. . .

Part VII

General

52. (1) The Constitution of Canada is the supreme law of Canada, and any law that is inconsistent with the provisions of the Constitution is, to the extent of the inconsistency, of no force or effect.

1) Application of *Charter*

The *Charter* applies to all levels of government in Canada, including municipalities, though they are not specifically mentioned in the *Charter*. This was determined as early as 1983 in the traffic ticket case of *McCutcheon v Toronto (City)*.[195] Since then, there has been no doubt as to the *Charter*'s application to local government. This has been confirmed by the Supreme Court of Canada in *Peterborough (City) v Ramsden*,[196] which analyzed a municipal by-law dealing with postering in light of the *Charter* protection of freedom of expression, and *Godbout v*

---

193 Note that the override provision does not apply to all sections of the *Charter*.

194 This section, although a part of *The Constitution Act, 1982*, is not a part of the *Charter*.

195 (1983), 22 MPLR 139 (Ont HCJ).

196 [1993] 2 SCR 1084 [*Ramsden*].

Longueuil (City),[197] which dealt with a residency requirement as a condition of employment. The one part of the *Charter* that seems not to apply to local government is section 3, the right to vote. In *Haig v Canada (Chief Electoral Officer)*,[198] a 1993 Supreme Court of Canada decision having to do with the right to vote in a referendum, L'Heureux-Dube J said, "The wording of the section, as is immediately apparent, is quite narrow, guaranteeing only the right to vote in elections of representatives of the federal and the provincial legislative assemblies. As professor Peter Hogg notes in *Constitutional Law of Canada* . . . the right does not extend to municipal elections or referenda."[199] On the same principle, there is no reason to see municipalities as able to invoke the "notwithstanding" provision of section 33.

The decision in *Godbout* offers a good explanation of the rationale for the rest of the *Charter* applying to local governments, as well as comments on the general nature of local government:

> The possibility that the Canadian *Charter* might apply to entities other than Parliament, the provincial legislatures and the federal or provincial governments is, of course, explicitly contemplated by the language of s. 32(1) inasmuch as entities that are controlled by government or that perform truly governmental functions are themselves "matters within the authority" of the particular legislative body that created them . . . . Were the *Charter* to apply only to those bodies that are institutionally part of government but not to those that are—as a simple matter of fact—governmental in nature (or performing a governmental act), the federal government and the provinces could easily shirk their *Charter* obligations by conferring certain of their powers on other entities and having those entities carry out what are, in reality, governmental activities or policies . . . . Clearly, this course of action would indirectly narrow the ambit of protection afforded by the *Charter* in a manner that could hardly have been intended and with consequences that are, to say the least, undesirable. Indeed, in view of their fundamental importance, *Charter* rights must be safeguarded from possible attempts to narrow their scope unduly or to circumvent altogether the obligations they engender . . . .
>
> Having set out what I take to be the guiding principles, I turn now to examine directly the *Charter* application issues in this appeal. The main issue concerns whether the Canadian *Charter* applies to municipalities—like the appellant—at all. To my mind, the analysis

197 [1997] 3 SCR 844 [*Godbout*].

198 [1993] 2 SCR 995.

199 *Ibid* at 1031.

> I have undertaken thus far leads inexorably to the conclusion that it does. While this Court has never before expressly endorsed that proposition, we have done so inferentially, inasmuch as we have already applied the *Charter* to municipal by-laws without specifically engaging in an analysis of the application issue . . . . Indeed, municipalities—though institutionally distinct from the provincial governments that create them—cannot but be described as "governmental entities". I base this finding on a number of considerations.
>
> First, municipal councils are democratically elected by members of the general public and are accountable to their constituents in a manner analogous to that in which Parliament and the provincial legislatures are accountable to the electorates they represent. To my mind, this itself is a highly significant (although perhaps not a decisive) indicium of "government" in the requisite sense. Secondly, municipalities possess a general taxing power that, for the purposes of determining whether they can rightfully be described as "government", is indistinguishable from the taxing powers of Parliament or the provinces. Thirdly, and importantly, municipalities are empowered to make laws, to administer them and to enforce them within a defined territorial jurisdiction . . . .
>
> I would add one further thought at this point. This approach appears entirely consistent with the traditional legal status of municipalities as governmental bodies. Before the Canadian *Charter*, the courts had interpreted the powers conferred on municipalities by the provinces as being restricted to making by-laws that were "reasonable", the general effect of which was to limit municipalities from encroaching on individual rights . . . . While the by-laws at issue in the latter cases were upheld, the idea that the reasonableness doctrine serves to protect individual rights is apparent from the passages cited. In the *Charter* age, it seems wholly fitting that "reasonableness" should be read in light of what the *Charter* has to say about the rights of the individual. And an attempt by the legislature to so express a municipal statute as to permit a municipality to breach *Charter* rights would, it seems to me, itself be contrary to the *Charter* mandate . . . . For all these reasons, then, I am firmly of the opinion that the Canadian *Charter* applies to municipalities.[200]

It is also the obligation of all competent tribunals to apply the *Charter* to matters legitimately before them. While section 24 offers remedies for *Charter* violations to be available through the courts, this is not exclusive jurisdiction, in the sense that since section 52 declares

---

200 *Godbout*, above note 197 at paras 48–55.

the Constitution to be "the supreme law of Canada," all other laws must be interpreted in light of the *Charter* and laws that are inconsistent with the *Charter* are of no force or effect. Still, not all tribunals possess the power to interpret and apply the law as part of their jurisdiction. A series of Supreme Court of Canada decisions[201] has determined that for an administrative tribunal to be able to interpret and apply the *Charter*, it must have been assigned jurisdiction to interpret and apply the law, express or implied. At the same time, the tribunal must already have jurisdiction over the whole of the matter before it, namely the parties, subject matter, and remedies sought. Land-use appellate bodies are generally empowered to determine questions of law as they arise before them, and both the Ontario Municipal Board (OMB) and the Nova Scotia Utility and Review Board (NSUARB) have seen themselves to possess that power in a way that extends to *Charter* questions.[202] For the OMB, this jurisdiction has been, at least by implication, confirmed by the courts.[203] Nonetheless, the OMB has been cautious; in *Re Toronto (City) Zoning By-law No 138-2003*,[204] the board saw its power as being not to apply unconstitutional laws yet not extending to being able to disallow laws (zoning by-laws) on that basis alone.

Charter rights are conferred on "everyone," though section 15 rights are conferred on "individuals"; section 3 and section 6 rights are conferred on "citizens." It has been held that section 15 rights may not be invoked on behalf of another person, and thus an association cannot claim any violations, even if its members might qualify.[205]

Not all *prima facie* violations of *Charter*-protected rights lead to declarations of invalidity or other remedies. Section 1 offers a government the opportunity to justify a *Charter* violation on the basis that it

---

201 *Cuddy Chicks Ltd v Ontario (Labour Relations Board)*, [1991] 2 SCR 5; *Cooper v Canada (Canadian Human Rights Commission)*, [1996] 3 SCR 854 [*Cooper*]; *Nova Scotia (Workers' Compensation Board) v Martin*, 2003 SCC 54.

202 For a discussion of the overall topic, and citation of various cases, see Howard Epstein, "Land Use Appellate Bodies and the *Charter*" (2002) 29 *Municipal and Planning Law Reports* (3d) 29.

203 See *Toronto (City) v Goldlist Properties Inc* (2003), 44 MPLR (3d) 1 (Ont CA), referring at para 41 to *Bell Canada v Canadian Telephone Employees Assn*, 2003 SCC 36 and *Cooper*, above note 201. Predecessor cases go back to *Minto Construction Ltd v Ontario (Regional Assessment Commissioner, Region No 3)* (1989), 43 MPLR 121 (Ont HCJ).

204 (2004), 47 OMBR 168 [*Deveau*]. The case is also referred to as *Deveau*. At issue was the placement of emergency shelters for the homeless, to be allowed throughout the city but with a separation distance from other shelters and to be located on arterial roads.

205 *Thunder Bay Seaway Non-Profit Apartments v Thunder Bay* (1991), 5 OR (3d) 667 (Div Ct); see also *Peninsula South Community Association (Re)*, 2002 NSUARB 7.

is a reasonable limit. In the leading case of *R v Oakes*,[206] the Supreme Court of Canada set out a method of analysis for a section 1 argument, now commonly referred to as the *Oakes* test.

2) Sections and Their Effect

Various sections of the *Charter* have been suggested as applicable to land-use matters. Not all of the submissions made in cases have been successful. The *Charter* jurisprudence for land-use matters is to be regarded as evolving.

a) Section 2(a): Freedom of Conscience and Religion

Freedom of religion under the *Charter* has now been clearly delineated by the Supreme Court of Canada as state neutrality, a form of "separation of church and state." This emerged in *Mouvement laique québécois v Saguenay (City)*,[207] in which municipal councils were held to infringe freedom of religion by holding prayer sessions for councillors at the start of meetings. The politicization of faith has been more of a tumultuous debate in the United States than in Canada. There, such issues as the teaching of creationism or intelligent design, state funding for health services that include abortions, research into stem cells, state funding for faith-based organizations as deliverers of social services, and religious broadcasting are all matters for active debate.[208] Such debates are at a lower level of intensity in Canada. But along with state neutrality, the Supreme Court of Canada has suggested that some accommodation of religious practices must be shown by governments to make freedom of religion effective. Two land-use cases decided in 2004 engaged with this. In *Syndicat Northcrest v Amselem*,[209] the Court interpreted Quebec's *Charter of Human Rights and Freedoms* so as to require accommodation of the Jewish practice of building temporary outdoor shelters once per year on the balconies of an apartment building. This case did not involve the Canadian *Charter*, nor did it involve any government action; at the same time, the terms of the Quebec *Charter* are quite similar to the Canadian *Charter*. In *Congrégation des témoins de Jéhovah*

206 *Oakes*, above note 5. *Oakes* is a criminal law case about the presumption of innocence.

207 2015 SCC 16.

208 See, for example, Richard Moon, "Freedom of Religion under the *Canadian Charter of Rights*: The Limits of State Neutrality" (2012) 45 *University of British Columbia Law Review* 49; Chris Hedges, *American Fascists: The Christian Right and the War on America* (New York: Free Press, 2006).

209 2004 SCC 47.

de St-Jérôme-Lafontaine v Lafontaine (Village),[210] the freedom of religion rights of a congregation were violated by not properly considering its request for a change of zoning so as to allow establishment of a church. Three of the justices (in dissent) went further and wrote that if no land were to be available, the absence of appropriately zoned land would amount to infringement of freedom of religion, and that although normally positive steps are not required of governments, in these exceptional circumstances the municipality would have to amend its by-law. The decision in *Lafontaine* does not determine the full scope of freedom of religion in land-use matters.[211] In a case with similar facts to *Lafontaine*, *Jehovah's Witnesses v South Easthope (Township)*,[212] the board ruled that excluding houses of worship as a permitted use in areas zoned for agriculture, and refusing to rezone, does not violate the *Charter*'s freedom of religion guarantee. Citing the Supreme Court of Canada decision in *R v Big M Drug Mart Ltd*,[213] it said ". . . freedom is subject to limitations, including order, as well as the fundamental rights and freedoms of others. From this the board interprets that to include matters such as official plans, by-laws and provincial policy. It does not mean freedom from conformity to the law."[214] See also *Residents for Sustainable Development in Guelph v 6&7 Developments Ltd*,[215] where leave was granted—a question involved was the effect of a proposed development on an adjacent religious retreat centre that valued silence and contemplation. In a case that preceded *Lafontaine*, *Hutterian Brethren Church of Eagle Creek v Eagle Creek (Rural Municipality) No 376*,[216] the Saskatchewan Court of Appeal in 1984 interpreted municipal by-laws regarding housing so as to accommodate the communitarian living mandated by the Hutterite religion, citing the *Charter*.

In *Sarnia (City) v River City Vineyard Christian Fellowship of Sarnia*,[217] the church had renovated its basement to operate as a homeless men's shelter. The city tolerated this until an emergency shelter was built elsewhere, and then moved to halt the use. The by-law de-

210 2004 SCC 48 [*Lafontaine*], discussed in Chapter 2.

211 In *Grushman v Ottawa (City)* (2001), 20 MPLR (3d) 10 (Ont Div Ct), at issue was whether a zoning change to allow a funeral home in a residential area infringed the cultural and religious beliefs of Asian residents. Because the issue had not been raised in the preceding hearing before the OMB, the court did not allow the issue to be raised with the court.

212 (1995), 32 OMBR 143 [*South Easthope*].

213 [1985] 1 SCR 295.

214 *South Easthope*, above note 212 at 158.

215 2005 CanLII 8714 (Ont Div Ct).

216 [1983] 2 WWR 438; (1982), 21 Sask R 361 (CA).

217 2015 ONCA 494.

fined church use to mean "a building used by a religious organization for public worship and church-sponsored community activities and projects . . . but shall not include a soup kitchen or food bank . . . ." The church raised a freedom of religion issue, but the matter was resolved by the court reading the by-law to extend to the shelter as a "church-sponsored community activity and project." Though the Court of Appeal did not deal with the *Charter* issue, at first instance the judge, while recognizing that freedom of religion protects the "right to act" on beliefs "where that practice has a nexus with [the] religious beliefs,"[218] said "Thus the restriction is on the location of the shelter, not on the congregation's ability to operate one."[219]

> RCV or any religious organization is not prohibited from believing in their obligation to do good works as part of their religious belief. However, good works are hardly the exclusive domain of religious organizations. To allow any individual or organization to operate outside properly enacted zoning legislation and related by-laws in the name of doing "good works" would render such legislation virtually unenforceable and would involve an imposition of another's concept of their religious mandate on the community as a whole in violation of the clearly expressed wishes of the community in relation to planning order. Consideration must also be given to section 15 of the *Charter* that guarantees all individuals the right to "the equal protection and equal benefit of the law" without discrimination based on religion amongst other reasons. Individuals living near the shelter location have a right to expect that zoning by-laws will be enforced in respect of everyone.[220]

The trial judge concluded that if there had been any interference with freedom of religion, it had been trivial and insubstantial.

The Supreme Court of Canada decision in *Lafontaine*[221] suggests that there needs to be some accommodation of religious groups as to a physical location for the practice of their religion. But that is not unlimited. In *Montréal (Ville de) c Église de Dieu Mont de Sion*,[222] a church sought to establish itself in a zone where the use was not permitted, but as it was not able to show that other locations were not available, the *Charter* challenge was not successful. In *Congregation of the Followers of the Rabbis of Belz to Strengthen Torah c Val-Morin (Municipalité de)*,[223]

---

218 *Ibid*, rev'd 2014 ONSC 1572 at para 19.
219 *Ibid* at para 20.
220 *Ibid* at para 21.
221 Above note 210.
222 2011 QCCS 4281.
223 2008 QCCA 577.

two cottage properties had been converted to use as a house of worship and a school; an order of cessation of the uses was sought, successfully. Freedom of religion was not an absolute right, according to the court; other sites in the municipality were available for the uses. In *R v Harrold*,[224] a pre-*Charter* case, a conviction for violation of a noise by-law was upheld even though the noise came from religious worship. In the United States, there has long been a struggle with such issues as whether a municipality must have zoning that allows for houses of worship or whether the focus ought to be on some wider area than one municipal district; whether a wide range of accessory uses may shelter under freedom of religion, whether houses of worship require other uses to adapt to their presence so as not to interfere with their core functions, or whether houses of worship must restrict their practices so as not to interfere with other established uses.[225] There are US precedents that apply in virtually any fact situation.

The jurisprudence on land-use related *Charter* section 2(a) issues exists within a context set by other *Charter* cases dealing with the same section. Reference should be had to *Alberta v Hutterian Brotherhood of Wilson Colony*,[226] in which the Court examined whether the province could require photos to be a mandatory part of a driver's licence where the adherents found this in violation of their tenets. A majority of the Court found the requirement to be justified under section 1 of the *Charter*.

The series of cases involving the British Columbia community of Bountiful and prosecutions for polygamy under section 293 of the *Criminal Code* raise issues about freedom of religion and other sections of the *Charter*. The cases are useful to review less because of the nature of the *Charter* analysis but because they raise the issue of how society should approach isolated communities. Isolation facilitates the possibility of exploitation, whether of children or of women or of labourers in work camps, or of other vulnerable persons. The Bountiful cases set out facts that illustrate the nature of social harm in that particular community.[227]

---

224 [1971] 3 WWR 365 (BCCA).

225 See, for example, *Lakewood, Ohio Congregation of Jehovah's Witnesses v Lakewood*, 699 F2d 303 (6th Cir 1983) (zoning); *Grosz v City of Miami Beach*, 721 F2d 729 (11th Cir 1983) (religious service in a private home); *Islamic Centre v City of Starkville*, 840 F2d 293 (5th Cir 1988) (discrimination in granting permits); *Jesus Center v Farmington Hills Zoning Board of Appeals*, 544 NW2d 698 (Mich Ct App 1966) (homeless shelter in a church). For an early discussion, see James E Curry, *Public Regulation of the Religious Use of Land* (Charlottesville, VA: Michie, 1964).

226 2009 SCC 37.

227 See *Criminal Code of Canada (Re)*, 2009 BCSC 1668; 2010 BCSC 517; 2011 BCSC 1588; *Blackmore v British Columbia (Attorney General)* 2009 BCSC 1299; 2015 BCSC 1099.

While on their face, the cases are not oriented to land-use issues as legal matters, land-use as a form of social control is immediately brought to mind as the facts are considered. In the instance of Bountiful, the community was established as one for a particular religion, the Fundamentalist Church of Jesus Christ of Latter Day Saints; other communities based on religion or doctrine have been established. Communal living or communal ownership are not uncommon. None of this need be problematic. Doukhobors, Mennonites, Amish, and Hutterites are all examples of religion-based communities that have located in Canada.[228] In Alberta, attempts were made in the past to disallow communal ownership of land.[229] This history is important to know. But the theocratic basis of any particular community is not the land-use issue, but rather its isolation from interaction with others in society. At its core, interaction leads to the possibility of help when help is needed. There are laws that require the registration of births, provide for education of children, establish occupational health and safety standards, and make various forms of exploitation criminal offences. Are these sufficient if there is little or no practical opportunity for residents to invoke these laws or other forms of assistance? And if there are some mechanisms that might be put in place, such as forbidding private roads, would these be appropriate or practical if the isolated community is a large farm or a mining or energy or forestry operation?

b) Section 2(b): Freedom of Expression

The leading municipal-level case is the 2005 decision of the Supreme Court of Canada in *Montreal (Ville) v 2952-1366 Quebec Ltd.*[230] At issue was a municipal by-law prohibiting noise that emanated from inside commercial

---

228 For a history of some of these communities, see George Woodcock & Ivan Avakumovic, *The Doukhobors* (Toronto: McClelland and Stewart, 1977); William Janzen, *Limits on Liberty: The Experience of Mennonite, Hutterite and Doukhobor Communities in Canada* (Toronto: University of Toronto Press, 1990); Alvin J Esau, *The Courts and the Colonies* (Vancouver: UBC Press, 2004); Janet Epp Buckingham, *Fighting Over God* (Montreal: McGill-Queens University Press, 2014).

229 *The Land Sales Prohibition Act, 1944*, SA 1944, c 15, later *The Communal Property Act, 1947*, SA 1947, c 16, was in force from 1942 to 1973, restricting the size of communal land ownership, the proximity of Hutterite colonies to one another, and the amount of land that could be so owned in individual municipalities. The legislation was upheld in *Walter v Attorney General of Alberta*, [1969] SCR 383. It has been replaced by the more benevolent *Religious Societies' Land Act*, RSA 2000, c R-15. A Saskatchewan municipality attempted to put in place a by-law similar to the older Alberta legislation, but the by-law was struck down on the basis of bad faith: see *R v Vanguard Hutterian Brethren Inc*, [1979] 6 WWR 335 (Sask Dist Ct).

230 Above note 79.

establishments. The law was challenged on *Charter* grounds by a business that announced its activities through loudspeakers aimed out to the street. The Court saw the infringement of freedom of expression as minimal, and also justified under section 1, even though the by-law was not framed in terms of objective measures of sound such as decibels. Equally important is *Ramsden v Peterborough*,[231] in which the municipality enacted a by-law that prohibited all postering on public property. "The issue is whether the absolute ban on such postering infringes the *Charter* guarantee of freedom of expression, and if so whether that infringement is justified under s. 1 . . . ." Following section 2(b) jurisprudence as set out in *Irwin Toy Ltd v Quebec (Attorney General)*,[232] the Court posed three steps in analysis: Does postering constitute expression? Is postering on public property a protected activity under section 2(b)? Is the purpose or effect of the by-law to restrict freedom of expression? The Court found that "Postering has historically been an effective and relatively inexpensive means of communication. Posters have communicated political, cultural and social information for centuries."[233] It also found that although not all public property is always available for free expression, postering "fosters political and social decision-making and thereby furthers at least one of the values underlying s. 2(b)."[234] It also found that although the by-law was content-neutral and thus its purpose was not to restrict expression,[235] its effect was to limit expression.[236] In sum, section 2(b) was violated by the by-law. Analysis then shifted to any possible justification under section 1, *quod vide*.

Since *Ramsden*, other postering and signage cases have been litigated. See, for example, *R v Guignard*[237] and *Vann Niagara Ltd v Oakville (Town)*[238] (signs), *Vancouver (City) v Jaminer*[239] (rooftop signs), and *Vancouver (City) v Zhang*[240] (political signage and rudimentary shelter on a sidewalk). Many of these cases turn on section 1 analysis of proportionality. In *Guignard*, the Supreme Court of Canada invalidated a by-law that restricted "counter advertising" outside an industrial zone. The Court recognized the importance of communication that engaged commercial

231 Above note 196 at para 1.
232 1989 CanLII 87 (SCC).
233 Above note 196 at para 20.
234 *Ibid* at para 34.
235 *Ibid* at para 38.
236 *Ibid* at para 39.
237 2002 SCC 14 [*Guignard*].
238 2003 SCC 65.
239 2001 BCCA 240.
240 2010 BCCA 450 [*Zhang*].

advertising by criticizing practices, products, or services. Visual pollution was not a sufficient municipal concern to defeat this right.

The case of *Bell v Toronto (City)*, the decision of which is pleasant to read, involved the growing of a naturalistic garden in front of a Toronto house, consisting of tall grasses, trees, and bushes. The court found this activity to be a *Charter*-protected mode of expression such that a conviction under a by-law prohibiting "excessive growth of weeds and grass" could not be sustained.[241] The by-law was subsequently amended so as to withstand *Charter* scrutiny. This form of freedom of expression has been recognized by the Ontario Court of Appeal, though subject to limitations on the grounds of "public safety through visibility on roadways."[242]

Commercial expression has been held to be protected by the *Charter*.[243] As with all freedom of expression cases, the focus has been on whether there has been a more-than-trivial interference, and if so whether it can be justified under section 1. In *R v Pinehouse Plaza Pharmacy Ltd*,[244] the issue was a pharmacy's illuminated outdoor ad, placed in violation of a by-law that prohibited external advertising save for on windows and doors. This was seen as infringement of freedom of expression, but the tests of section 1 were seen to have been met.[245] The obverse of *Charter* protection for commercial speech is that those who picket and seek to boycott commercial enterprises are also protected: *Daishowa Inc v Friends of the Lubicon*.[246]

An attempt to attack a by-law that required bilingual exterior signage on commercial premises on section 2(b) *Charter* grounds was not successful.[247] The court found that any impairment of freedom of expression was minimal, and if it existed was justified under section 1. Nor was an amorphous attempt to challenge a municipality's subdivision terms at the OMB successful. The complainant said, "Our use we make in our homes is part of our expression . . . . Even if we have

241 (1996), 39 CRR (2d) 152 (Ont Prov Div).

242 *Counter v Toronto (City)* (2003), 39 MPLR (3d) 308; the words quoted appear in the lower court decision: (2000), 99 CRR (2d) 302 at para 33 (Ont SCJ).

243 For a discussion, see Christopher J Williams, "Municipal Regulation of Signs and Freedom of Expression" (1998) 4 *Digest of Municipal and Planning Law* 179 at 191–96.

244 (1991), 4 MPLR (2d) 1 (Sask CA) [*Pinehouse Plaza*].

245 The section 1 analysis in *Pinehouse Plaza* has been criticized: see John P McEvoy, "The *Charter* and Municipal Law in New Brunswick" (1992) 126 *New Brunswick Reports* (2d) 1 at 11.

246 (1998), 39 OR (3d) 620 (Gen Div).

247 *Galganov v Russell (Township)*, 2012 ONCA 409.

a slope on our property. It's the total prohibitive nature that calls for a *Charter* challenge. This is private homes." The board commented:

> There were two difficulties with that approach. First, it presupposed a definition of "expression" so open-ended as to be virtually meaningless. If, say, rules about soil erosion are construed as limiting "expression'" then is there *any* legislation which does *not* infringe the *Charter*? More importantly . . . . *Even if* one's own home were a form of "expression" protected by the *Charter* . . . subdivision is not about one's *own* home, but about conveying property to *others*, where there are no protected rights in play. There is no constitutional right to subdivide land.[248]

More serious issues regarding freedom of expression than postering and signage have arisen.[249] *Zhang* is one example, and so too is *Batty v Toronto (City)*,[250] the main case concerned with the political demonstrations known as "Occupy." The issues are associated with the interactions of those using public space for purposes of political expression and other users of the space. In *Batty*, the city asked for an injunction to dismantle tent camps established in public parks. The court accepted that freedom of expression was at issue, but took the view that the ouster was justified. It referred to "hogging" the park, "intimidation" of other users, the fact that demonstrations had gone on for some time, and the availability of other ways to communicate the message. The decision has been criticized. Professor Richard Moon has said, "The courts, though, may have been too willing to discount the significance of the Occupy message or too quick to see a conflict between that message and other uses of the property."[251] Moon's point is reinforced by such statements as the following from *Smiley v Ottawa (City)*,[252] where the justice of the peace presiding said, "Miss Smiley indicated to the Court that she felt the need to support the overall Oc-

---

248 *Re Humanics Universal Inc* (2012), 97 MPLR (4th) 285 at paras 51–53 (OMB) [emphasis in original].

249 See Richard Moon, *The Constitutional Protection of Freedom of Expression* (Toronto: University of Toronto Press, 2000).

250 2011 ONSC 6785; 2011 ONSC 6862 [*Batty*]. See Sarah E Hamill, "Private Rights to Public Property: The Evolution of Common Property in Canada" (2012) 58 *McGill Law Journal* 365, for a discussion of *Batty*. Hamill says that the idea of governments as owners of land has overwhelmed the idea of governments as holders of common property in trust for the public.

251 Richard Moon, "Demonstrations on Campus and the Case of Israeli Apartheid Week" in James L Turk, ed, *Academic Freedom in Conflict* (Toronto: Lorimer, 2014) 185 at 194.

252 2012 ONCJ 479.

cupy Movement and agreed with its mantra regarding the 1% versus 99%. The issue appears to be one of wealth and power distribution with 1% having and controlling more than their share. The *a priori* question regarding where this 1% calculation came from, and its validity, remains unanswered."[253] The snide tone of the comment just adds to the general ignorance displayed, since Nobel Prize–winning economist Joseph Stiglitz had, in 2011, written a widely remarked article "Of the 1%, by the 1%, for the 1%."[254] Other "Occupy" cases are *Victoria (City) v Thompson*,[255] *Vancouver (City) v O'Flynn-Magee*,[256] and *Calgary (City) v Bullock (cob Occupy Calgary)*.[257]

Associated with the circumstances in *Ramsden* and *Batty* are instances of expression in locales such as airports or shopping centres, or for purposes of secondary picketing during labour disputes.[258] The theories under which freedom of expression (and assembly) operate for state-owned property involve compatibility of function, whether there is a public arena entitlement, and balancing the furtherance of values with the needs of the state. In *R v Marcocchio*,[259] trespass charges were brought against a person who had been banned from attending meetings of the Joint Action Group (JAG), a federal-provincial public entity charged with finding solutions to the pollution of the Sydney Tar Ponds, former site of a steel mill. In assessing the defence based on section 2(b) of the *Charter*, the magistrate noted:

> The simplicity and ease with which a private landowner may prohibit another person from entering on property, merely by issuing or posting a notice under the PPA, with summary procedures available upon breach, are desirable features of the legislation from that point of view. That very ease, however, might open up potential abuses of individual rights where government property is being used as a public forum. The *Protection of Property Act* should not be available to government, or agencies or arms of the government, as a convenient tool to quell the voices of those who disagree with it or who might

253 *Ibid* at para 8.

254 *Vanity Fair* (31 March 2011), online: www.vanityfair.com/news/2011/05/top-one-percent-201105; see also his "The 1 Percent's Problem" *Vanity Fair* (31 May 2012), online: www.vanityfair.com/news/2012/05/joseph-stiglitz-the-price-on-inequality.

255 2011 BCSC 1810.

256 2011 BCSC 1647.

257 2011 ABQB 764.

258 See, for example, *Committee for the Commonwealth of Canada v Canada*, [1991] 1 SCR 139; *RWDSU, Local 558 v Pepsi-Cola Canada Beverages (West) Ltd*, 2002 SCC 8.

259 2002 NSPC 7.

> foment public opinion to such an extent that it would impede government from its preferred course of action.
>
> For example, one might imagine a hypothetical case where government was involved in a public consultation about the issuance of an aquaculture lease. The government department rents a community hall and invites the public to participate in a public forum. Prior to the meeting, one particular individual has caused an annoyance or proven to be an embarrassment to a government official, as a result of which the official in charge of organizing the meeting sends a notice under the PPA banning the particular individual from the Hall. A copy is sent to the local police force so that when the individual arrives he is arrested and removed. The potential nuisance is eliminated. I emphasize that there is no evidence in this case of any such instance of arbitrary and badly motivated behavior from a governmental official. I set it out merely to indicate a recognition that given the other civil and criminal law provisions potentially applicable . . . the Courts should not countenance the inappropriate use of a PPA notice to quell dissent where there is no indication of an interference with the use of property or with due process. Where a private landowner needs no reason whatsoever to ban someone from their property, government, as a property owner, where the property is used as a public forum, will most often be required to justify such a step. This brings us to the crux of the matter, the application of s. 1 of the *Charter*.[260]

In *Galganov v Russell (Township)*,[261] no *Charter* violation was found when the town adopted a by-law requiring commercial signs to be in both English and French. There was no restriction of activity (signage) that conveyed meaning.

Picketing has been held to be a form of expression attracting *Charter* protection, as in the case of *BCGEU v British Columbia (Attorney General)*,[262] but not so as to apply to private property, where picketing may amount to a trespass. Subsequent cases on picketing such as *UFCW Local 1518 v KMart Canada Ltd*,[263] in which the Court found that secondary-site peaceful leafleting was a protected activity, have not altered that.

It has been claimed that hunting is a form of *Charter*-protected expression. In 1999, Ontario cancelled a bear hunt. The court challenge

---

260 *Ibid* at paras 77 & 78.

261 2010 ONSC 4566.

262 [1988] 2 SCR 214.

263 [1999] 2 SCR 1083.

brought by the Ontario Federation of Hunters and Anglers invoked the *Charter* along with other issues. The litigation seems to have petered out, and the *Charter* issue remains unresolved.[264]

c) Section 2(b): Freedom of the Press

Vendors of newspapers have claimed a right not to be denied access to the public sidewalks as a place for placing boxes to distribute their publications. See, for example, *Canadian Newspaper Co v Quebec (City) Director of Public Road & Traffic Services*,[265] in which a total prohibition was seen not to be a justifiable infringement of freedom of the press, a decision akin to that in *Ramsden* regarding postering. To the same effect is *Canadian Newspapers v Victoria (City)*.[266]

d) Section 2(d): Freedom of Association

Although this section is usually raised in the context of labour relations, in *Unger v Onondaga (Township)*,[267] an unsuccessful attempt was made to raise it on the question whether a refusal to allow subdivision of agricultural property to create lots for family members violates section 2(d) (and also sections 6(2)(a) and 7).

e) Section 6: Mobility Rights

Sequence and tempo of development controls, manifesting in holding zones, can delay, perhaps for a very long time, the possibility of development of particular properties, often large tracts. Holding zones and certain other forms of land-use controls such as minimum size of lots may be a disguised form of discrimination. In the United States, issues of freedom of mobility have also been discussed as a factor relevant to challenges of by-laws that control growth.[268]

Mobility (along with section 7 "security of the person") was put in issue by non-resident owners of agricultural land in Prince Edward Island, especially by companies seeking to enlarge their holdings in support of sourcing potatoes. The issue was put to the courts in *Reference re Lands Protection Act (PEI)*.[269] The case determined that laws that

---

264 *Ontario Federation of Anglers and Hunters v Ontario (Ministry of Natural Resources)* (1999), 43 OR (3d) 760 (SCJ); (2001), 196 DLR (4th) 367 (Div Ct), rev'd [2002] OJ No 1445 (CA). See also *Xentel DM Inc v Windsor (City)*, [2004] OJ No 3656 (SCJ).

265 (1986), 33 MPLR 28 (Que SC).

266 (1989), 63 DLR (4th) 1 (BCCA).

267 (1997), 34 OMBR 439.

268 See cases such as *Golden v Planning Board of the Town of Ramapo*, 285 NE2d 291 (NY 1972); *Village of Belle Terre v Boraas*, 416 US 1 (1974).

269 (1987), 40 DLR (4th) 1 (PEISCAD).

limited non-ownership of land in Prince Edward Island did not offend section 6: the section was not directed towards the protection or preservation of property or economic rights within the province.

> Its entire *raison d'être* is to permit free, uninterrupted and unimpeded passage from one political subdivision to another . . . . This rite of passage . . . has naught to do with . . . the right of the province to manage its own environment, and its own resources, including land, provided that it does so on the basis of general application within the province.[270]

The one other "mobility" case in Canada involving an attack on land-use controls had to do with ice cream vending trucks. In *Corporation (City of Brampton) v Mister Twister Inc*,[271] a prosecution for operating the business without a licence led to a *Charter* challenge to the by-law. The court ruled that section 6 protects freedom of mobility from province to province rather than establishing a general right to work.

f) Section 7: Security of the Person

There are two major cases applying this section to land-use matters,[272] *Victoria (City) v Adams*[273] on homelessness and *Canada (AG) v Bedford*[274] on street prostitution.

In *Adams*, the British Columbia Court of Appeal dealt with the following issue:

> [W]hen homeless people are not prohibited from sleeping in public parks, and the number of homeless people exceeds the number of shelter beds, does a bylaw that prohibits homeless people from erecting any form of temporary overhead shelter at night—including tarps attached to trees, boxes or other structure—violate their constitutional rights to life, liberty and security of the person . . . ?[275]

The court found that in these circumstances, in the inevitable conflict between the need of homeless individuals to "perform essential, life-sustaining acts in public" and the responsibility of the government to maintain orderly, aesthetically pleasing parks and streets, the *Char-*

---

270 *Ibid* at 15.

271 2011 ONCJ 271.

272 *Godbout*, above note 197, was a case that raised section 7 of the *Charter* in the context of a municipal rule requiring employees to reside in the municipality, and while it offers useful analysis of how section 7 is to be approached, it does not deal with a land-use matter.

273 2009 BCCA 563 [*Adams*].

274 *Bedford*, above note 51.

275 *Adams*, above note 273 at para 1.

ter protected the homeless, and the by-law could not be justified under section 1.[276] In a subsequent case, *Johnston v Victoria (City)*,[277] the court interpreted its ruling in *Adams* as limited to overnight accommodation and not as having enunciated a public right to erect tents in parks during the daytime, and also as requiring the supporting facts as to necessity.

In *Bedford*, the Supreme Court of Canada, in 2013, invalidated several sections of the *Criminal Code* that dealt with prostitution. Prostitution itself is not illegal in Canada. What the *Criminal Code* did was control various activities associated with prostitution—solicitation, bawdy houses, and living off the avails of prostitution. The Court concluded that the effect of the laws was to make prostitution unsafe for the sex workers, since they could not work indoors in a location they could control, nor could they hire staff to protect them; they were forced to work the streets and to make quick judgments about clients. Solicitation, which is seen as a nuisance and which the courts had already ruled must be persistent to found a conviction, remains an offence. Parliament has responded to the *Bedford* case by amending the *Criminal Code* so as to make it a crime to be a client of a prostitute.[278]

NOTES

1) In light of the central rationale of *Bedford*, Professor Elaine Craig notes that "Municipal lawmakers will need to consider the impact that their bylaws have on the safety of sex workers. They will need to recognize that the community's interest in reducing public nuisance will not justify zoning and licensing bylaws that aggravate the already dangerous working conditions of many sex workers in Canada."[279]

---

276 *Ibid* at paras 3–5 and 10. For comment, see Sarah Buhler, "Cardboard Boxes and Invisible Fences: Homelessness and Public Space in *City of Victoria v Adams*" (2009) 27 *Windsor Yearbook of Access to Justice* 209 and Sarah Hamill, "Private Property Rights and Public Responsibility: Leaving Room for the Homeless" (2011) 30 *Windsor Review of Legal and Social Issues* 91.

277 2011 BCCA 400. In *British Columbia v Adamson*, 2016 BCSC 584, an interim injunction to remove an encampment of homeless persons from green space outside the Victoria law courts was refused; the case was approached not as a *Charter* matter but on the basis of principles applicable to interim injunctions.

278 As the *Bedford* case was going through the courts, several articles examined the land-use policy aspects. See, for example, Epstein, "Zoning Sex Work," above note 52; Elaine Craig, "Sex Work By Law: *Bedford*'s Impact on Municipal Approaches to Regulation of the Sex Trade" (2011) 16 *Review of Constitutional Studies* 205. As background to municipal regulation of other forms of sex work, see David Farley, "Erogenous Zones and Public Policy" (1990) 30:2 *Plan Canada* 19.

279 Craig, above note 278 at 206–7.

2) *The Globe and Mail* newspaper has urged legalization (i.e., decriminalization plus business-type regulation). The new provisions of the *Criminal Code* are under court challenge. If made legal, how should it be regulated? How should zoning regard it? Is it appropriate as a home-based business? Should it be isolated? Do the precedents in Nevada, Australia, or in Europe assist?
3) In *Dorval (Ville) c Provost*,[280] an attempt was made to challenge the municipal by-law regulating the height of fences, invoking section 7 of the *Charter*. The landowner had two children, ages one and three, and had erected a 6-foot fence to assure the security of the children, as well as to protect privacy; the by-law limited fences in the neighbourhood to 4 feet. The court gave little credence to the argument:

> With respect, I have great difficulty seeing how a municipal by-law providing for a height restriction on fencing in residential neighbourhoods could possibly threaten to deprive respondent or his family of "life, liberty, or security of the person" . . . . It is difficult to imagine how a municipality could regulate the height of fences in accordance with the ages or physical agility of children of property owners or other personal circumstances of that kind.[281]

4) Begging in the streets has become a common phenomenon in Canada. Some municipal by-laws[282] and provincial statutes such as *Safe Streets Acts*[283] have attempted to regulate or eliminate the activity. There has been speculation as to whether various provisions of the *Charter* might be applicable. In an article from 2000 reviewing the then state-of-play, the conclusion is:

> Beggars who contravene panhandling by-laws are not publicly whipped anymore; in our more polite, "civilized" society, they are simply moved out of the way, in the name of public order. Unless constructive efforts are made to better the beggar's lot—through social assistance, genuine employment counseling (as opposed to workfare), increased housing, and better access to social services—the panhandling by-laws become an exercise in large-scale social self-deception. Scapegoating beggars and removing them from sight does a great disservice to the concept of public order. True public order springs from a democratic community which

280 1994 CanLII 6067 (Que CA).

281 *Ibid*.

282 These are both anti-panhandling and anti-squeegeeing. Vancouver, Edmonton, Calgary, Saskatoon, Winnipeg, Sudbury, Kingston, Hamilton, Quebec City, and Saint John are all reported to have such by-laws.

283 See, for example, *Safe Streets Act*, SBC 2004, c 75.

> works openly to address its problems, and allows all citizens to see, hear and engage in a debate toward their solutions.[284]

Begging may be regarded as a matter of security of the person or as a form of speech or as involving poverty as a category of discrimination.

5) Hamill[285] points out that in *Adams*, the issue was not one of competing claims to property but one of survival:

> While reference to the temporary nature of the sleeping shelters is essential to the success of the homeless people's claim, it does ignore the fact that the homeless differ from other citizens in one key way: they have no private property of their own. The understanding that citizens only want *temporary* access to [public] property assumes that they have private property of their own to retreat to. For the vast majority of people, this assumption of a private property interest is correct. The homeless are, by contrast, excluded from all private property unless they secure the owner's permission to be there. Thus, they must spend their lives on publicly accessible property, but it is assumed that a person only wants or needs *temporary* access to such property. The homeless, therefore, are permanently on property to which they have only a temporary right to access and use.[286]

6) An attempt has been made to assert section 7 protection for the keeping of urban hens. In *Calgary (City) v Hughes*,[287] the defendant linked the keeping of hens to a section 15 issue, poverty, as well as section 2(a), freedom of conscience; the essence of the claim was that the keeping of hens as a source of food for an impoverished family was *Charter*-protected. The assertions of *Charter* rights in the circumstances were not successful, mainly on the basis of a lack of evidence to support them. In *Millership v Kamloops (City)*,[288] an attempt was made to challenge municipal fluoridation of the drinking water supply, but was unsuccessful.

---

284 Dina Graser, "Panhandling for Change in Canadian Law" (2000) 15 *Journal of Law and Social Policy* 45 at 90–91; see also Nicholas Blomley, "Begging to Differ: Panhandling, Public Space, and Municipal Property" in Eric Tucker et al, eds, *Property on Trial: Canadian Cases in Context* (Toronto: Irwin Law for The Osgoode Society for Canadian Legal History, 2012) at 393.

285 Above note 276.

286 *Ibid* at 95 [emphasis in original].

287 2012 ABPC 250.

288 2003 BCSC 82.

7) In *Manicom v Oxford (County)*,[289] an attempt was made to invoke section 7 as part of a tort claim based in nuisance and other common law forms of action. The core issue was the proposed siting of a landfill. A *quia timet* injunction was sought. Regarding the *Charter*, the majority viewed section 7 as having no application where the issues had essentially to do with assertion of property rights. The dissenting judge would have allowed the claim to proceed on the basis that section 7 could apply to personal health issues. In *Operation Dismantle Inc v Canada*,[290] the federal cabinet had approved allowing the United States to test unarmed cruise missiles over Canadian territory. A challenge invoked section 7, alleging the testing could produce a greater risk of nuclear attack. The Court regarded this as contingent on possible reactions to belligerence of a foreign nation, and thus an imponderable.
8) It has been suggested that section 7 might extend to offering environmental protections.[291] That is, "life, liberty and security of the person" might be seen as extending to healthy, or not unhealthy, life-support systems such as air and water.[292] An attempt to challenge the *Nuclear Liability Act* on this basis, alleging that the statutory limit of $75 million as damages in an accident was inadequate and its existence compromised safety, was unsuccessful: see *Energy Probe v Canada (Attorney General)*.[293] There has also been a challenge to the statutory standard under Ontario's *Environmental Protection Act*[294] requiring an objector to show "serious harm to human health" as being too onerous. The issue was raised before the Environmental Review Tribunal in reviews of permits issued to authorize various wind farms. In *Dixon v Ontario (Director, Ministry of Environment)*,[295] the court saw the Ontario statute requirement as conforming to the *Charter* protection of security of the person. In

289 (1985), 34 CCLT 148 (Ont Div Ct).

290 [1985] 1 SCR 441.

291 See, for example, Nathalie J Chalifour, "Environmental Justice and the *Charter*: Do Environmental Injustices Infringe Sections 7 and 15 of the *Charter*" (2015) 28 *Journal of Environmental Law and Practice* 89.

292 For a list of the few cases that have raised section 7 in an environmental context, and a discussion of the possibility of adopting constitutional environmental rights, see David Boyd, *The Right to a Healthy Environment* (Vancouver: UBC Press, 2012) at 212.

293 (1994), 17 OR (3d) 717 (Gen Div). Section 15 of the *Charter* was also invoked.

294 RSO 1990, c E.19, ss 142.1 and 145.2.1.

295 2014 ONSC 7404. The court considered a 2014 study by Health Canada of the effects of wind turbines, which had found no definitive link to ill effects.

Toronto (City) Official Plan Amendment No 358 (Re),[296] the OMB was asked to consider the CO_2 emissions and depletion of aggregates that would be a consequence of allowing demolition of an existing convalescent hospital and its replacement; section 7 was raised but then abandoned.[297] The issue of fracking has also led to an attempt to bring this issue to court. The New Brunswick Anti-Shale Gas Alliance has commenced a proceeding invoking section 7.[298] If successful, such a determination would offer a constitutional law context for measuring the adequacy of the environmental regulatory regimes of the federal, provincial, and municipal governments. The issues are complex and the result of the litigation is far from clear. In several cases, section 7 has been raised as applicable to environmental issues.[299] So far, the courts have tended to be unwilling to see the *Charter* as offering general freestanding guarantees on social matters that may be seen as more properly within the realm of political discourse. Thus, in *Tanudjaja v Canada (Attorney General)*,[300] an attempt to challenge overall national and provincial housing policies was seen as not justiciable. The applicants in that case were not challenging a particular statute.[301]

9) The section has been used to strike down a by-law on the basis of vagueness and overbreadth; see *R v Pawlowski*.[302] In *R v Heywood*,[303] a prohibition aimed at a convicted sex offender that banned the person's presence on or near playgrounds and many other places

---

296 (2007), 55 OMBR 129.

297 The board took the occasion to suggest that environmental matters raised as planning issues should be set out with "precision, vigour, and on a scientific and quantifiable basis": *ibid* at 136–38.

298 CBC News, "Anti-shale Gas Group Suing New Brunswick Government" (23 June 2014), online: cbc.ca www.cbc.ca/1.2684758.

299 For an overall review of the *Charter*'s potential, see Lynda Collins, "An Ecologically Literate Reading of the *Canadian Charter of Rights and Freedoms*" (2009) 26 *Windsor Review of Legal and Social Issues* 7.

300 2014 ONCA 852, leave to appeal to SCC refused, [2015] SCCA No 39.

301 There is an active debate within political science and philosophy, going back two centuries, as to whether political emancipation, manifested in the type of equality offered by the *Charter* "may actually entrench the very forms of inequality and relations of power from which we seek to be freed" (Patchen Markell, *Bound By Recognition* (Princeton, NJ: Princeton University Press, 2003) at 128); that is, by excluding wealth and its attributes such as social rank, education, and occupation, from the idea of what is needed to be equal, it "disguises their status as forms of power" (Markell, *ibid* at 129).

302 2011 ABCA 267 at para 7. See also *1022049 Alberta Ltd v Medicine Hat (City)*, 2007 ABCA 108.

303 [1994] 3 SCR 761.

was found to be overbroad under the section; this was the Supreme Court of Canada's first application of overbreadth. In *Osoyoos (Town) v Rattlesnake Canyon Family Entertainment Park Inc*,[304] the vexed question of how to regulate noise was examined. Although the by-laws used subjective terms such as "tend to disturb," "quiet," "peace," "rest," "enjoyment," and the like, the court was not prepared to find them so vague as to offend section 7; it did, however, find the by-law to be overbroad in the sense of being arbitrary or disproportionate. In *Suncor Energy Products Inc v Plympton-Wyoming (Town)*,[305] the court found a by-law definition of "property" to be unintelligible, a useless guide to owners as to how to locate wind turbines.

10) In the case *Canada (Attorney General) v PHS Community Services Society*,[306] a supervised drug-injection service that had been previously granted an exemption permit allowing it to operate under the *Controlled Drugs and Substances Act*[307] was denied a further permit. The Supreme Court of Canada found the refusal of the permit to interfere with the section 7 rights of the drug-addicted clients, the result being that the minister was ordered to grant the exemption, and the clinic was permitted to continue to operate.[308]

11) In *Allard v Canada*,[309] there was a finding that section 7 rights operated to mean persons in need of marijuana for medical reasons could not be prohibited from access under the single-source system adopted by the federal government pursuant to the *Marihuana for Medical Purposes Regulations*.[310] The case built on similar rulings with respect to other aspects of regulation of use of the substance in such cases as *R v Parker*[311] and *R v Smith*.[312] This will, as in *Bedford*, have implications for possible local land-use regulation as to places where the right may be exercised.

---

304 2005 BCSC 307.

305 2014 ONSC 2934.

306 2011 SCC 44 [*Insite*].

307 SC 1996, c 19.

308 The case is also relevant to issues of paramountcy, interjurisdictional immunity, and co-operative federalism because of the interaction of provincial health regimes and the criminal law.

309 2016 FC 236 [*Allard*].

310 SOR/2013-119.

311 (2000), 188 DLR (4th) 385 (Ont CA).

312 2015 SCC 34.

g) Section 8: Right to Be Secure against Unreasonable Search and Seizure

The *Charter* offers protections against unreasonable search and seizure. This provision has significant applicability generally in that it offers some security against intrusion in places where one would expect to be afforded privacy, such as a place of residence. As it applies to police forces, its ambit has regularly been tested in situations in which evidence has been gathered. Its application in land use relates to searches conducted by officials pursuant to non-criminal, regulatory statutes. In *Wangler v Fort Erie (Town)*,[313] secton 8 of the *Charter* was raised where a municipal by-law enforcement officer seized debris that the owner was collecting with a view to its ultimate use in construction. The applicant argued that entry on private property and seizure without judicial authorization violated the *Charter* provision. The court cited appellate court and Supreme Court of Canada decisions, saying that there are various activities usually involved in enforcement of regulatory by-laws, such as an inspection, for which reasonable and probable cause to believe an offence has been committed is not required.[314] Most authorizing by-laws include a requirement that the entry be "reasonable" or be carried out at a "reasonable time."

Even absent that, the *Charter* and common law principles would require the entry and seizure to be reasonable. The courts held that an inspection is a search which attracts *Charter* scrutiny

> but that a lower standard applies to a search conducted to enforce regulatory standards than to a search conducted to enforce the criminal law . . . . The wording of s. 8 of the *Charter* does not prohibit inspections without prior [judicial] authorization. It simply imposes a requirement of reasonableness . . . . The requirement of reasonableness is a flexible standard to be applied in the context of the particular case . . . . The standard of reasonableness required of the by-law depends largely on identifying the privacy interest which is at stake and the severity of intrusion on that privacy interest . . . . For the most part, there is no requirement that regulatory powers, like the power of inspection . . . . be exercised on belief or suspicion of non-compliance. Rather, they are based on the common sense assumption that the threat of unannounced inspection may be the most effective way

---

313 2010 ONSC 2404.

314 See *Belgoma Transportation Ltd v Ontario (Director of Employment Standards)* (1985), 51 OR (2d) 509 (CA); *Allen v Hamilton (City)* (1987), 59 OR (2d) 498 (CA); *Orillia (City) v Nicol*, [1997] OJ No 916 (CA) [*Nicol*]; *Comité paritaire de l'industrie de la chemise v Potash*, [1994] 2 SCR 406.

> to induce compliance . . . . The object of the search, garbage and refuse, has a low expectation of privacy.[315]

Expropriation has been held not to be a violation of the protection against seizure: *Quebec (Attorney General) v Laroche*.[316] Likewise, the OMB in *Brighton (Municipality) Official Plan Amendment No. 20 (Re)*[317] found that an official plan (OP) designation of agricultural land as "Environmental Protection and Rural" did not amount to expropriation without compensation or a violation of the *Charter*.

h) Section 15: Equality Rights

So far there have been relatively few cases in which section 15 equality issues have been raised in the context of land use. The cases that have been decided are not particularly interesting, except for *Alcoholism Foundation of Manitoba v Winnipeg (City)*.[318] What is more compelling is speculation about possible uses of the section, especially in light of some American jurisprudence.

In *Alcoholism Foundation*, the central facts are not set out with sufficient particularity so as to allow a full understanding of what the court was grappling with. The city adopted by-laws that established minimum separation distances for group homes,[319] apparently required them to apply for permission to be established ("they are discriminated against since they, and they alone, must apply to the various community and city committees for permission to form and live together as a group or 'family'"[320]), and definitions were used that focused on the term "family." All these provisions were challenged under section 15. The three judges gave different reasons for declaring the various definitions used in the by-laws to be of no force or effect. One statement was that "The disputed by-law's wording amounts to 'people' zoning and

---

315 *Nicol*, above note 314 at paras 7–10; see also *Meade v Armstrong (City)*, 2011 BCSC 1591.

316 2002 SCC 72.

317 (2003), 46 OMBR 78.

318 (1990), 65 Man R (2d) 81 (CA) [*Alcoholism Foundation*].

319 The issue of group homes presents some difficult land-use aspects. In the case *Berjawi v Ottawa (City)*, 2011 ONSC 236, not raising any *Charter* issues, the city permitted a group home for battered women, which was challenged by neighbours. The by-law definition of group home was "a supervised residential use building in which three to ten persons, exclusive of staff, live as a group . . . ." The issue was that with children, the building would be occupied by twenty to thirty persons. The court upheld a "practical context" approach to interpreting the by-law to exclude children from the total occupants.

320 *Alcoholism Foundation*, above note 318 at para 45.

that, under the *Charter* and its current interpretations, is objectionable and discriminatory."[321] Another was:

> It is simply not acceptable since the advent of the *Charter* to prohibit a use of land with reference to the attributes of those who may use it, at least where the attributes are those which distinguish members of a disadvantaged group and where there is no evidence to show that such a prohibition is one which can be demonstrably justified as reasonable in a free and democratic society. The city may be right . . . that it can outlaw institutional usage of land within residential areas . . . . But the city cannot define such institutions by reference to the attributes of those who live in them.[322]

One judge disapproved of the use of separation distances, but the two others did not specifically address the point.

In *Thunder Bay Seaway Non-Profit Apartments v Thunder Bay*,[323] the non-profit sought to purchase city-owned land to accommodate a residence for individuals who had completed rehabilitation for alcoholism and substance abuse. The sale was opposed by neighbours, and the motion to sell was defeated at city council. Mandamus was sought to compel the sale. It was alleged that the decision was made for irrelevant considerations, was discriminatory, in bad faith, and in violation of section 15 of the *Charter*. In short reasons, the court found that since no by-law had been passed, no *Charter* issue arose. This position now seems unlikely to be sustainable in light of the Supreme Court of Canada decisions in *Godbout* and *Lafontaine*. In another case, an assertion that land developers were treated differently by a municipality than were ordinary residents was held not to amount to a section 15 issue.[324] In *Goth v Oakville (Town)*,[325] opponents of the siting of a residential care facility for seniors attempted to raise a section 15 *Charter* issue. The board noted the terms of section 15(2) of the *Charter*, which allows discriminatory by-laws when their purpose is to ameliorate the conditions of disadvantaged individuals such as seniors.

What is worth speculating about is whether consideration of section 15 might lead to a view that residential zoning is itself inherently improperly discriminatory, or whether some forms of land-use regulation (such as minimum lot sizes) might be found to be improper in their

321 *Ibid* at para 48.
322 *Ibid* at paras 65 & 66.
323 Above note 205.
324 *Friends of Ragged Beach Inc v Witless Bay (Town) Town Council*, 2011 NLTD(G) 108.
325 (1995), 32 OMBR 388.

effect.[326] Section 15's enumerated prohibited grounds of discrimination do not extend to class, or as it is usually referred to, poverty. Still, in cases such as *Dartmouth/Halifax County Regional Housing Authority v Sparks*,[327] class-based discrimination when linked to one of the enumerated grounds, in this case race, led to a finding of invalidity of a part of a statute having to do with tenants' rights.[328] It may be that the courts will come to see other forms of discrimination than those specified in section 15 as being covered by it, as analogous grounds. So far only citizenship, Aboriginal off-reserve residence, marital status, and sexual orientation have been seen as analogous grounds. Attempts to see class as an analogous ground under the *Charter* have not been successful. In Nova Scotia, and despite *Sparks*, the Court of Appeal has rejected poverty as coming within the ambit of section 15.[329] A case involving panhandling took the same view.[330]

Traditional Euclidean or exclusionary zoning segregates activities, especially place of residence, on the basis of economic value. The effect, if not the stated purpose of zoning, is to exclude people from living in certain municipal districts by reason of their economic resources. Some commentators are quite explicit about this; see, for example, Rogers as quoted in *Service Corp International (Canada) Inc v Burnaby (City)*.[331] To the same effect is the well-known observation of Judson J in *Scarborough (Township) v Bondi*,[332] a case regarding minimum lot size (a proposal for a 10,000-square-foot lot in an area of 45,000-square-foot lots): "The objection to the proposed buildings on comparatively small lots in a neighbourhood such as this is apparent and needs no further comment." Even in the *Alcoholism Foundation* case, the Manitoba Chief Justice made identical comments to the same effect: "The city has had the right to protect the neighbourhood integrity of its various districts, be they commercial, manufacturing, retail or residential areas. Ratepayers building $150,000 or $200,000 single-family homes are entitled

326 In *Allard*, above note 309, a case about access to medical marijuana, there was some discussion of affordability as a *Charter* factor. See, for example, para 15. The court made no finding on the point, but its comments suggest that its relevance could be shown with appropriate evidence.

327 (1993), 101 DLR (4th) 224 (NSCA) [*Sparks*].

328 See also *Falkiner v Ontario (Ministry of Community and Social Services, Income Maintenance Branch)* (2002), 59 OR (3d) 481 (CA).

329 *Boulter v Nova Scotia Power Inc*, 2009 NSCA 17.

330 *Federated Anti-Poverty Groups of BC v Vancouver (City)*, 2002 BCSC 105.

331 (1999), 9 MPLR (3d) 242 (BCSC) discussed in Chapter 10, Section C; rev'd on other grounds 2001 BCCA 708. See also Chapter 6, Section J for a discussion of economic exclusion.

332 [1959] SCR 444 at 450.

to expect that only similar homes will be built in their vicinity, and that the integrity of that particular zoned area of the community will not be interfered with or reduced by allowing homes having one-third the value to be built next to them or near them, or occupied by more than one family. That was and should be an entirely legitimate concern of the city councillors. Likewise, they should be free to protect those of lesser means from infiltration in their areas by businesses, manufacturers and other commercial ventures not in conformity with their legitimate aspirations for a protected modest residential area."[333] This is the making of distinctions on the basis of economic class. Does this offend the *Charter*?

In the United States, this issue may be traced to *Village of Euclid v Ambler Realty Co*,[334] the origin of the term "Euclidian zoning." *Euclid* established the constitutionality of the basic device of exclusionary zoning. In the case, zoning was introduced for the first time in a municipality previously unzoned. The owner of land intended for industrial or commercial development or for apartment buildings, complained of the inherent diminution of value when its land became zoned for single-family residential purposes. The US Supreme Court upheld zoning and classified it not as akin to exercise of an eminent domain power and therefore involving a "taking" under sections 5 and 14 of the *Bill of Rights*, but as an exercise of the regulatory "police" power and not requiring any compensation. The Court considered first separation of industrial/commercial uses from residential. The Court then considered the exclusion of apartment buildings ("business and trade of every sort, including hotels and apartment houses")[335] from a single-family-use district. The Court endorsed this on the basis of making it "easier to provide fire apparatus suitable for the character and intensity of the development in each section; that it will increase the safety and security of home life; greatly tend to prevent street accidents, especially to children, by reducing the traffic . . . ; decrease noise . . . [; and] preserve a more favourable environment in which to rear children . . . ."[336] In doing so, it referred to apartment buildings in these terms: "the development of detached house sections is greatly retarded by the coming of apartment houses, which has sometimes resulted in destroying the entire section for private house purposes; . . . in such sections very often the apartment house is a mere parasite, constructed in order to take advantage of the open spaces and attractive surroundings created by the

333 *Alcoholism Foundation*, above note 318 at para 41.
334 272 US 265 (1926) [*Euclid*].
335 *Ibid* at 390.
336 *Ibid* at 394.

residential character of the district." There is more to this same effect in the judgement of the Court. The language seems to indicate approval of the by-law scheme on the undoubted class basis that apartments are "parasites" and "near nuisances" in private house areas. Indeed, in the lower court judgment appealed from in *Euclid*, the language identifying exclusion as the purpose of zoning is even more explicit: "In the last analysis, the result to be accomplished is to classify the population and segregate them according to their income or situation in life."[337]

When the effect of such segregation accomplished through zoning is to exclude the poor, or even persons of moderate income, from developing communities, the American courts may declare zoning to be invalid: see *Southern Burlington County NAACP v Town of Mount Laurel*,[338] and *Hills Development Co v Township of Barnards*.[339] These cases apply standards to a municipality as a whole and are generally taken to require that the municipality has a duty to provide a reasonable opportunity for the construction of low-income housing. At the same time, the American courts have clearly entered into detailed scrutiny of the actual effects of zoning over quite a wide territory. In *Mount Laurel II*, the court said,

> The provision of decent housing for the poor is not a function of this Court. Our only role is to see to it that zoning does not prevent it, but rather provides a realistic opportunity for its construction . . . . The actual construction of that housing will continue to depend . . . on the economy, on private enterprise, and on the actions of the other branches of government at the national, state and local level. We intend here only to make sure that if the poor remain locked into urban slums, it will not be because we failed to enforce the Constitution.[340]

American discrimination law has evolved since the 1970s and is now usually based on the *Fair Housing Act*; nonetheless, class-based discrimination claims do not evoke strict scrutiny in constitutional law terms, and poverty is not a suspect classification.[341] The Canadian jurisprudence so far is essentially to the same effect (though not relying on the concepts of strict scrutiny or suspect classification).

Constitutional scholars Beaudoin and Mendes say,

---

337 *Village of Euclid v Ambler Realty*, 297 F 307 at 316 (ND Ohio 1924).

338 336 A2d 713 (NJ 1975) [*Mount Laurel I*]; 456 A2d 390 (NJ 1983) [*Mount Laurel II*].

339 510 A2d 621 (NJ 1986) [*Mount Laurel III*].

340 Above note 338 at 352.

341 See *Arlington Heights v Metropolitan Housing Development Corp*, 429 US 252 (1977).

> Poverty would seem to meet most of the criteria for determining analogous grounds, and the additional factors incorporated within the ground of social condition strengthen this argument. By definition, poverty is associated with economic disadvantage, which in turn leads to social disadvantage. People living in poverty are subject to prejudice and stereotypes. For most, poverty is beyond the unilateral control of the individual and is at least as difficult to change as religion, citizenship or marital status. It is related statistically to enumerated grounds such as race and sex. While it almost never represents a fundamental choice in a person's life, it certainly is an important part of a person's life. In terms of residential and employment segregation and lack of educational opportunity, it has similarities to the conditions that give rise to the phrase "discrete and insular minority." It is "inherited" in the sense that one's economic status and education level are statistically related to those of one's parents. Persons living in poverty lack their fair share of political influence, and programs related to poverty may be undervalued in the political process as compared with universal programs such as health.[342]

The devices resulting in socio-economic segregation need not be zoning for single-family residential purposes; large lot size or value of building to be constructed or type of materials can also have this effect. The large lot size issue has been litigated in the United States: see, for example, *National Land and Investment Co v Kohn*;[343] *Guaclides*

---

342 Gérald A Beaudoin & Errol Mendes, eds, *The Canadian Charter of Rights and Freedoms*, 4th ed (Markham, ON: LexisNexis Butterworths, 2005) at 1010–011. In the 5th edition of the book, above note 192, this passage has been modified though only in that the authors say (at 998) that "[t]he interrelated grounds of poverty and social condition . . . have not been recognized as analogous grounds and thus fall outside the protection of section 15," though no Supreme Court of Canada case directly on point is cited. For a recent examination of the economic data, see John Miles et al, "Neighbourhood Inequality in Canadian Cities," Statistics Canada Research Paper Series No 160 (Ottawa: Statistics Canada, Analytical Studies Branch, 2000). See also Armine Yalnizyan, *The Growing Gap* (Toronto: Centre for Social Justice, 1998) and Robert A Murdie & Carlos Teixeira, "The City as Social Space" in Trudi Bunting & Pierre Fillion, eds, *Canadian Cities in Transition* (Don Mills, ON: Oxford University Press, 2000) 198 at 209–10 on the emergence of an underclass. A direct recognition of economic segregation as a fact of municipal land-use policies is found in Leslie A Stein, *Latent Abuses of Municipal Discretion: Interference with Freedom* (LLM Thesis, Osgoode Hall Law School, 1969) [unpublished]. Stein focuses especially on the effect of regulations specifying minimum floor areas. For the situation in the United States, see David Massey & Nancy Denton, *American Apartheid: Segregation and the Making of the Underclass* (Cambridge, MA: Harvard University Press, 2003).

343 215 A2d 597 (Pa 1965).

v Englewood Cliffs;[344]; *Fulling v Palumbo*;[345] and *Oakwood at Madison, Inc v Madison*.[346]

Quite clearly, the practical effect of zoning for single-family use or requiring large lot size is to exclude those who are not able to afford this standard of housing. Whether this set of circumstances will lead to any *Charter* challenge of the non-nuisance basis of zoning, or if such a challenge is taken whether it would be successful, remains an intriguing outstanding question. And if the issue is not justiciable as a *Charter* matter, it nonetheless remains a serious policy concern to be addressed by lawmakers and planners.

i) Section 1: Justification

Charter rights are not absolute. Not only are they open to interpretation as to the scope of the right[347] and to limitations such as findings of trivial impairment, but section 1 of the *Charter* itself provides that an order of government may attempt to show that any limitation on a *Charter* right imposed by law is justified. The Supreme Court of Canada has set out a framework for analysis of this issue in *Oakes*,[348] a guide often referred to as "the *Oakes* test." The postering case, *Ramsden v Peterborough*,[349] illustrates application of the test in a land-use context. The Court is to consider first whether the object of the law is pressing and substantial. If so, it is to consider whether the law is rationally connected to the objectives. Then it is to consider the overall proportionality of the law, that is, whether it is a minimum impairment of the *Charter* right, carefully designed to achieve the objectives of the law, and not arbitrary, unfair, or based on irrational considerations. In *Ramsden*, the Court noted that "The by-law seeks to avoid littering, aesthetic blight, traffic hazards, and hazards to persons engaged in the repair and maintenance of utility poles." It found that objective to be pressing and substantial. "Similarly, the total ban is rationally connected to these objectives. By prohibiting posters entirely, litter, aesthetic blight and associated hazards are avoided." "The question therefore becomes whether the by-law restricts expression as little as is reasonably possible." The Court identified alternatives such as a more limited sweep for the by-law or providing particular locations for posters. "These kinds of alternatives could control the concerns . . . in a manner which is far less restrictive

344 78 A2d 435 (NJ Super Ct App 1952).

345 283 NE2d 272 (NY 1967).

346 283 A2d 353 (NJ 1971).

347 See, for example, *Irwin Toy Ltd v Quebec (Attorney General)*, [1989] 1 SCR 927.

348 Above note 5.

349 Above note 196.

than the by-law . . . . Moreover, the benefits of the by-law are limited while the abrogation of the freedom is total, thus proportionality between the effects and the objective has not been achieved."[350]

In *R v Watson*,[351] the two accused demonstrated against abortion inside a designated "access zone" established under British Columbia's *Access to Abortion Services Act*.[352] The statute allowed cabinet to establish through regulations "access zones" in which various activities were not allowed, including protests, sidewalk interference, besetting, physical interference, or intimidation of service providers or patients. Spratt carried signs stating that "abortion is murder" and "unborn persons have the right to live"; he also handed out brochures about health effects of abortion. Watson carried a cross and held a sign saying "you shall not murder." The court found that the right to free expression was violated by the Act. The issue became whether the Act was justified. The court examined the history of access to abortion medical services and opposition to them, and concluded that the legislative objectives were important. The court found a rational connection between the establishing of access zones and the objectives of the Act. In terms of proportionality, it considered that although the size of the access zone could have been smaller or differently configured, there was minimal interference;[353] it considered that the effects of the measures were not out of proportion with the importance of the Act's objectives. The convictions of the accused were upheld.

3) *Charter* Summary

The *Charter* has been shown to be relevant to various land-use issues. As with all constitutional matters, it provides a context or a limitation that has to be screened for as rules are promulgated. The question is the effect and not only the surface content of any rule.

Because *Charter* law continues to evolve, it is possible and necessary to try to imagine circumstances in which *Charter* issues might be raised as relevant to land-use matters. The disadvantaged will no doubt

---

350 *Ibid* at paras 40, 41, 45, & 46.

351 2008 BCCA 340.

352 RSBC 1996, c 1.

353 It cited *Montreal (City) v 2952-1366 Quebec Inc*, above note 79 at para 94 to the effect that: ". . . elected officials must be accorded a measure of latitude. The Court will not interfere simply because it can think of a better, less intrusive way to manage the problem. What is required is that the City establish that it has tailored the limit to the exigencies of the problem in a reasonable way . . . ."

seek to use sections such as section 7 and section 15. Environmental matters may well find some resonance in the *Charter.*

In an early, speculative article about the *Charter,* it was suggested that "the *Charter,* as drafted, has only limited effect [upon a municipality's power to control the use of land] and that any specific entrenchment of property rights would not particularly change this result."[354] The authors first focus on expropriation and non-resident ownership rules. So far as land use, they see *Charter* procedural rights as not expanding those available under general administrative law principles, but do see some potential for use of section 15 on equality issues. Actual jurisprudence in the subsequent decades has shown greater potential than initially thought.

United States cases under their *Bill of Rights* suggest some circumstances in which *Charter* issues might arise. Some examples, among many thousands, are *Schad v Borough of Mount Ephraim*[355]—live nude dancing is a constitutionally protected activity, and if a municipality wishes to control it, it must justify its restrictions; *Marks v City of Roseberg*[356]—palmistry is a constitutionally protected form of communication; *Framingham Clinic Inc v Board of Selectmen of Southborough*[357]—an abortion clinic cannot be made a prohibited use; *Grosz v City of Miami Beach*[358]—converting a garage for religious services violates the zoning and is not a protected activity in the circumstances; and *National Land and Investment Co v Kohn*[359]—large lots may be discriminatory depending on overall circumstances. Many current US cases are based not on their *Bill of Rights* but on the *Religious Land Use and Institutionalized Persons Act* (RLUIPA)[360] and therefore will not usually have any precedential worth in Canadian *Charter* cases, although they may well as to policy when laws are being written.

Because of the nature of the *Oakes* test, the courts are inevitably drawn into policy analysis and weighting of social benefits.

---

354 Robert G Doumani & Jane M Glenn, "Property, Planning and the *Charter*" (1989) 34 *McGill Law Journal* 1036 at 1038.

355 452 US 61 (1981).

356 670 P2d 201 (Or 1983).

357 367 NE2d 606 (Mass 1977) and 415 NE2d 840 (Mass 1981).

358 721 F2d 729 (11th Cir 1983).

359 215 A2d 597 (Pa 1965).

360 42 USC 2000cc et seq. See Michael Giaimo & Lora Lucero, *RLUIPA Reader* (Chicago: American Planning Association, 2009).

CHAPTER 5

SOURCES OF AUTHORITY: PROVINCIAL-LEVEL LAND-USE PLANNING POWERS

A. PRELIMINARY

The materials in this chapter address the main provincial systems of land-use regulation, that is, those in which the provincial government itself is the exclusive regulator, or in which it takes the lead but shares its power with municipalities.

Always a preliminary question is the extent of provincial jurisdiction. Thus, it is necessary to consider the extent of provincial jurisdiction in conjunction with federal jurisdiction, as set out in Chapter 4.[1]

Among the main provincial land-use regulatory regimes, some are well known, such as those for natural resources (agriculture, forestry, mining, and energy) and heritage properties, but there are many more. As with federal-level regulation, the direct provincial regulatory schemes are abundant.

1 An adjunct issue is the boundaries of federal lands within a province, though questions of the boundaries between provinces do arise. This chapter is to be read in conjunction with constitutional law matters for purposes of determining which matters are subject to regulation by which of the senior levels of government. See, generally, Chapter 4. This is especially important regarding resources: see Gérard V La Forest, *Natural Resources and Public Property Under the Canadian Constitution* (Toronto: University of Toronto Press, 1969) at 44. For example, the Railway Belt lands, established to facilitate construction of the transcontinental railroad, involved various transfers between the two senior levels of government, with a long history involving some complications, including for Aboriginal law. See, for example, *Campbell v British Columbia (Attorney General)*, 1994 CanLII 2365 (BCSC) and cases cited therein.

Environmental assessments and other environmental laws are a leading example of provincial-level regulation of land-use.

To some extent, this chapter looks again at the interaction between municipal control and provincial laws, encountered earlier in Chapter 2. In general, unless there is actual functional conflict in the rules adopted, if both levels of government have authority over some topic, then not only may both sets of rules co-exist, but municipal rules may be more stringent than provincial ones.[2]

The topic also raises the policy question of what is the appropriate level of government at which particular activities ought to be regulated. That is, what makes for efficiency and accountability in the allocation of regulatory responsibilities? The answers are not always clear, and regimes of shared jurisdiction are common as are changes in the overall arrangements.

In most provinces, the provincial Crown is the owner of significant areas of land. As owner, it is able to determine what land uses will be permitted. Both for Crown lands and for private lands, some provinces have attempted direct, large-scale land-use planning exercises, mainly British Columbia, Quebec, and Ontario. In the 1990s, British Columbia undertook extensive public consultation about land use in the face of serious tension over forestry and mining uses. Since the provincial Crown owns some 90 percent of the land in British Columbia, a province with vast rural area, and given Aboriginal claims and the criticism by the environmental, hunting, fishing, and tourism interests, creating the Commission on Resources and the Environment (CORE) made sense. In Ontario, legislation such as the *Places to Grow Act* and the *Greenbelt Act* has focused on directing development, in broad terms, in the areas of greatest population density. In both provinces, sustainability has been a major factor in creating policy.

Because the provincial Crown is a major owner of land, its policies are important. To a certain extent, the applicable rules exist in statutory silos (for example, mining, forestry, water, endangered species, archaeology, parks) even though an overall ecosystem approach is warranted, and achievable, given the advances in the state of scientific and technical knowledge. "Public land law" is not a commonly cited term in Canada, unlike the United States, but has started to emerge as a topic with the recent text *Public Lands and Resources in Canada*.[3]

2 See, for example, *Prince George (City) v Payne*, [1978] 1 SCR 458; *Edmonton (City) v Tegon Developments Ltd* (1981), 121 DLR (3d) 760 (SCC); *Croplife Canada v Toronto (City)* (2005), 10 MPLR (4th) 1 (Ont CA); and especially *114957 Canada Ltée (Spraytech, Société d'arrosage) v Hudson (Town)*, 2001 SCC 40 [*Spraytech*].

3 Elaine L Hughes, Arlene J Kwasniak, & Alastair R Lucas, *Public Lands and Resources in Canada* (Toronto: Irwin Law, 2016).

B. OWNERSHIP OF LAND

There are four main aspects to provincial direct ownership of land for planning purposes. The first is the extent to which it chooses to subject itself to municipal or internal provincial-level jurisdiction. The second is its voluntary acceptance of environmental assessment processes. The third is the way in which it chooses to impose rules regarding use of its lands. The fourth is acquisition and sale restrictions.

1) Crown Not Bound

The Crown is not bound by rules, even its own rules, unless it specifies that it is. This flows from the general doctrine of Crown immunity and from statutory provisions such as Ontario's *Legislation Act*, where section 71 provides, "No Act or regulation binds Her Majesty or affects Her Majesty's rights or prerogatives unless it expressly states an intention to do so."[4] Likewise, the Crown is not bound by municipal land-use enactments in any province, because it has not chosen to place itself in that position. Those leasing Crown land do not share this immunity.[5] The most provincial governments have assented to is to take into account municipal policies; for example, in Nova Scotia, the *Municipal Government Act* says, "A department of the Province, before carrying out or authorizing any development in a municipality, shall consider the planning documents of the municipality."[6]

There are some exceptions. For example, in Alberta, under both the *Dangerous Goods Transportation and Handling Act*[7] and the *Drainage Districts Act*,[8] the Crown is specified as being bound, in the former as to the required safety standards and in the latter as to being obliged to make payments as a landowner towards the construction and maintenance of drainage works.

2) Environmental Assessment

An important example of the Crown choosing to bind itself regarding land use is for environmental assessments. Thus, Ontario's *Environmental*

---

4 *Legislation Act, 2006*, SO 2006, c 21, Sched F. See also the *Crown Agency Act*, RSO 1990, c C.48 for elaboration of what are Crown agencies.

5 *Squamish (District) v Great Pacific Pumice Inc*, 2000 BCCA 328.

6 SNS 1998, c 18, s 197; see also Ontario's *Municipal Act, 2001*, SO 2001, c 25, s 3 and *Planning Act*, RSO 1990, c P.13, ss 50(3) & (4).

7 RSA 2000, c D-4, as amended.

8 RSA 2000, c D-16.

Assessment Act[9] provides: "This Act applies to (a) enterprises or activities or proposals, plans or programs in respect of enterprises or activities by or on behalf of Her Majesty in Right of Ontario or by a public body or public bodies or by a municipality or municipalities"[10] and also: "This Act binds the Crown."[11] Such provisions raise environmental issues from the level of discretionary policy to a matter of public obligation.

3) Rules for Use of Crown Land

Private ownership of land in Canada is estimated at approximately 11 percent of the total mass. In all provinces, the provincial Crown is a major owner of land, though the extent of this varies enormously from approximately 9 percent in Prince Edward Island to approximately 90 percent in British Columbia. Most of these lands are rural or wilderness. And private industrial and commercial enterprises are not just interested in, but often encouraged to look at, Crown land for extractive purposes, chiefly forestry and mining. Some provinces have adopted a classification system akin to zoning as a way to pre-determine what areas will be available for what activities. Quebec, for example, has a "Plan Nord," first adopted in 2012 and updated in 2015, to guide development.[12] Ontario, after extensive public consultations in a process called "Lands for Life" (started in 1997), adopted, through its Ministry of Natural Resources, a guidance document, "Ontario's Living Legacy: Approved Land Use Strategy" for Crown lands, amounting to approximately 45 percent of the area of the province.[13] Subsequently, Ontario adopted a "Guide for Crown Land Use Planning" and a Crown Land Use Policy Atlas (CLUPA),[14] ultimately anchored in the authority of the *Public Lands Act*.[15] These systems do not automatically entitle the activities: logging and mining are still subject to formalities of advance review of the specific proposals and are subject to termination. The overall approach is to identify existing infrastructure and com-

9 RSO 1990, c.E.18.

10 *Ibid*, s 3(a).

11 *Ibid*, s 4.

12 Gouvernement du Québec, "The Plan Nord toward 2035, 2015–2020 Action Plan" (7 April 2015), online: www.plannord.gouv.qc.ca/wp-content/uploads/2015/04/Long_PN_EN.pdf.

13 For a detailed account of Ontario's system, see J F Castrilli, "Ontario's Forest, Land Use, and Mining Initiatives of 1999 and the Management of Public Land in Canada in the 21st Century: One Step Forward, Two Steps Back" (2002) 43 *Canadian Environmental Law Reports (New Series)* 11.

14 Online: www.ontario.ca/page/crown-land-use-policy-atlas.

15 *Public Lands Act*, RSO 1990, c P.43.

mitments (roads, parks, dams, electrical power lines, energy corridors, mines and claims, forestry licences) and then to establish framework policy based on principles such as sustainability, multiple use, and optimization of social and economic benefits.[16] In British Columbia, a process that evolved from the CORE exercise in the 1990s (see Section A, above in this chapter) led to various regional plans emanating from the Land Use Coordination Office (LUCO). Attempts were made to reconcile competing interests such as forestry, mining, energy, conservation, recreation, and Aboriginal claims.[17]

4) Purchase and Sale

We encounter this issue again in Chapter 10, Section I, as an aspect of the economics of land-use regulation. The issue is the circumstances in which the Crown may purchase or expropriate land, and what rules, if any, apply when the Crown disposes of land. Purchase and sale are tied to contemplated use. It is not unusual for provincial governments to acquire title to land necessary for construction of public works such as highways. If this becomes controversial, it usually relates to whether the public work is necessary or appropriately placed, and negative impacts on adjacent owners may well be a real issue.[18] When land has been identified for future use by a province, there is no obligation to notify owners (or potential purchasers) until an order for expropriation has issued. There is, however, pressure on a province to move expeditiously, which arises from the dynamic of avoiding a more expensive cost of expropriation if raw or underutilized land becomes developed. This is in contrast to designation by a municipality where notice may be given through a filing in a Land Titles office, and there are permitted delays in expropriation, often lengthy ones. As an example of speed when land is to be acquired by a province, Manitoba's *The Expropriation Act* provides for a declaration of expropriation which lapses after six months.[19] When it comes to disposition of public lands, there are relatively few limitations, though it is an open policy question whether there ought to be. In Nova Scotia, *Ministerial Land Transactions Regu-*

16 See, for example, British Columbia's Integrated Land and Resource Registry and Nova Scotia's Integrated Resource Management Plan.

17 See, for example, Tim Thielmann & Chris Tollefson, "Tears from an Onion: Layering, Exhaustion, and Conversion in British Columbia Land Use Planning Policy" (2009) 28 *Politics and Society* 111.

18 See, for example, *St Pierre v Ontario (Minister of Transportation and Communications)* (1987), 39 DLR (4th) 10 (SCC).

19 CCSM c E190, s 4.

lations[20] provide that dispositions of land may be to municipalities and non-profits, or to support economic activity, or to alleviate hardship. Expropriation to support third-party economic activity is allowable where the purchaser can show it has not been able to acquire land by purchase. In Manitoba, where land has been expropriated but is later offered for sale, the previous owner has a first chance to repurchase "on the terms of the best offer received," though only if still the owner of a residual portion of land not expropriated.[21]

C. ENVIRONMENTAL REGULATION AND ASSESSMENT[22]

Provincial governments have adopted standards to govern polluting emissions. They are limited in their ability to do so by the division of powers provisions of the *Constitution Act, 1867.* Provincial jurisdiction over the environment (which is not a head of power specified in the *Constitution Act, 1867*), derives from the same set of powers leading to general authority over land use: property and civil rights, matters of a merely local or private nature, mines and minerals, non-renewable natural resources, forestry and electrical energy, local works and undertakings, and the ownership of public lands. But, if acting within their proper realm of authority,[23] provinces may—and have—adopted regulatory regimes. Thus, provinces regulate SO_2, CO_2, NO_x, methane, and mercury emissions from industries such as those making concrete or generating electricity, control discharges from agricultural activities, control herbicide and pesticide use, regulate mining and forestry, have put in place endangered species rules, and make laws regulating energy

20 NS Reg 75/2005.

21 Above note 19, s 51.

22 Environmental law is a topic of its own, and though land-use law is tightly connected with it, those wanting to pursue environmental law issues in more detail should consult the various texts that focus on it as their exclusive topic, for example, Meinhard Doelle & Chris Tollefson, *Environmental Law*, 2d ed (Toronto: Carswell, 2013); Jamie Benidickson, *Environmental Law*, 4th ed (Toronto: Irwin Law, 2013); David Boyd, *Unnatural Law* (Vancouver: UBC Press, 2003); David Boyd, *Cleaner, Greener, Healthier* (Vancouver: UBC Press, 2015); Elaine Hughes et al, *Environmental Law and Policy*, 3d ed (Toronto: Emond Montgomery, 2003); Meinhard Doelle, *The Federal Environmental Assessment Process* (Markham, ON: LexisNexis Canada, 2008).

23 Leading cases exploring federal and provincial jurisdiction are *R v Crown Zellerbach Canada Ltd*, [1988] 1 SCR 401; *Friends of the Oldman River Society v Canada (Minister of Transport)*, [1992] 1 SCR 3; *R v Hydro-Québec*, [1997] 3 SCR 213.

from hydrocarbons. In British Columbia, legislation restricts development around bodies of water under the *Fish Protection Act*[24] and the *Riparian Areas Regulation*,[25] which require a professional's certification as to the suitability of land for development if it is within 30 metres of a natural water boundary.[26] Several provinces have regulations and/or policies with respect to remediation of polluted sites (brownfields), especially Ontario, Alberta, and British Columbia.[27] The Canadian Council of Ministers of the Environment (CCME) has emphasized that the "polluter pays" and "beneficiary pays" principles should apply,[28] although the policy choice of who ought to pay is not easy. No "Superfund" akin to those established in the United States exists.[29]

In some of these areas, the provinces share regulatory powers with the federal government. Arising out of the international negotiations over global climate change (that first led to the 1997 Kyoto Protocol as a framework, including what were intended as binding targets for greenhouse gas (GHG) reductions) current rounds of negotiations look in part to subnational governments for implementation. Thus, the provincial role on this important matter may increase.

For the most part, provinces have not chosen to share their environmental regulatory powers explicitly with municipal governments. That is, formal EAs and the discretion to grant environmental permits remain a provincial function. The situation is not clear-cut, however, given the range of generalized powers assigned to local governments (such as over nuisances or to deal with health, safety, and welfare) and the regulation of water and sewage and transportation. Indeed, the specified planning mandate of local governments often mentions sustainability as an objective. Quebec, in 2006 legislation, the *Municipal Powers Act*,[30] says that "Toute municipalité locale peut adopter des règlements en matière d'environnement." The extent of local government powers over the environment is the main focus of Chapter 11. However, the interaction of the powers of the two levels of government is a crucial point. Municipalities possessing no inherent powers, their

---

24 SBC 1997, c 21.

25 BC Reg 376/2004.

26 See *Yanke v Salmon Arm (City)*, 2011 BCCA 309.

27 See, for example, *Environmental Protection Act*, RSO 1990 c E.19, s 168.

28 Canadian Council of Ministers of the Environment, *Recommended Principles on Contaminated Site Liability* (Winnipeg: Canadian Council of Ministers of the Environment, 2006).

29 See various pieces of American legislation: *Oil Pollution Act*, 33 USC §§ 2701–2761; *Clean Water Act*, 33 USC §§ 1251–1387; *Comprehensive Environmental Response Compensation and Liability Act*, 42 USC §§ 9601–9657.

30 CQLR c C-47.1, ss 4 and 19.

authority derives from provincial statutes that create them and set out their authority. The attitude of the courts has been as enunciated by La Forest J in the 1997 case *R v Hydro-Québec*—that protection of the environment is a problem "that requires action by governments at all levels."[31] Flowing from this view, the Supreme Court of Canada in 2001, in *114957 Canada Ltée (Spraytech, Société d'arrosage) v Hudson (Town)*,[32] was prepared to interpret the omnibus powers clause in Quebec legislation governing municipalities so as to authorize regulation of domestic use of pesticides, even though both the federal and provincial governments also regulated aspects of pesticide use. The case has been widely seen as opening up possibilities for municipalities to take a variety of environmental measures. And in fact, in subsequent cases, courts have not only confirmed that, but have ruled that if some aspect of environmental regulation is properly a matter for local governments, shared jurisdiction with the province allows the local government to impose more stringent rules than exist at the provincial level, so long as there is no operative conflict.[33]

The rise in importance of environmental law has not been limited to the use of prescriptive rules. An important innovation has been environmental assessment (EA) (also known as environmental impact assessment (EIA)). As with land-use planning, the object is to think in advance of actual construction about the possible adverse consequences. EA can lead to a decision to prohibit a proposed undertaking or to the imposition of impact-control requirements specific to the undertaking. EAs, and what sort of EA will be required, are triggered by certain factors, including the type and size of the project. Thus, in Saskatchewan, *The Environmental Assessment Act*[34] allows the minister to determine the scope of the EA and the content of studies to be submitted, and to establish classes of developments. In Nova Scotia there are activities or undertakings that are Class I (rendering plants, those that create pressure-treated wood, storage facilities for chemicals, mines, small pits and quarries, short highways, etc.) and Class II (pulp mills, cement plants, petrochemical manufacture, solid waste incinerators, large oil refineries, etc.), the difference being that the latter require a review panel.[35] Such systems of classification limit opportun-

31 Above note 23 at para 127.

32 Above note 2.

33 See, for example, *Greater Vancouver (Regional District) v Darvonda Nurseries Ltd*, 2008 BCSC 1251 [*Darvonda*]; *Saint John (City) v Merzetti*, 2005 NBCA 16 [*Merzetti*].

34 SS 1979-80, c E-10.1, s 5(2)(e).

35 *Environmental Assessment Regulations*, NS Reg 26/95, as amended.

ities for public participation. British Columbia environmental lawyer David Boyd has written, "Many provincial laws governing EA suffer from the same flaws that plague the federal process: narrow application, limited scope, excessive discretion, provisions that are never used, limited opportunities for public participation, and a lack of independent decision-making."[36] For some undertakings, there may be a joint federal-provincial EA if the scope of what is proposed spans their constitutional jurisdictions. Thus, in 2014, a joint federal-provincial panel dealt with the proposal for a third dam on the Peace River in British Columbia ("Site C"). Another example is the 1997–98 process for the Sable Offshore Energy Project, which examined the establishment of facilities for sub-sea drilling for natural gas off the coast of Nova Scotia combined with an onshore processing plant and pipelines across Nova Scotia and New Brunswick, primarily for export to the United States.[37] Full panel EAs are rare.[38] The logic of different levels of intensity of environmental scrutiny is tied to whether applications are routine or highly complex and specialized. Although municipalities are often assigned "sustainability" as a part of their policy-adoption mandate, municipal official plans are not made subject to EA.[39]

In *Ottawa (City) v Sample*,[40] it was determined that the Ontario Municipal Board (OMB), as part of its consideration of what constituted good land-use planning, could consider environmental issues, and that the Ministry of Environment did not have exclusive jurisdiction over environmental matters. Issues that had been examined in the context of an environmental assessment could be reconsidered as aspects of *Planning Act* jurisdiction assigned to municipalities. Not all tribunals

---

36 Boyd, *Unnatural Law*, above note 22 at 155.

37 There have also been joint federal-provincial panels for a proposed sewage treatment plant to be located in Halifax Harbour (*Halifax Harbour Cleanup Project: Report of the Federal-Provincial Environmental Assessment Review Panel for the Halifax-Dartmouth Metropolitan Wastewater Management System* (FEARO) (Ottawa: The Review Panel, 1993)); for a proposed basalt quarry on Digby Neck, Nova Scotia; for the Joslyn North Oil Sands Mine Project in northeastern Alberta (2008); uranium mining developments in northern Saskatchewan (2013); Sydney Tar Ponds (2006); Marathon Platinum Group Metals and Copper Mine Project (2011); the Lower Churchill (2011); and others.

38 See Boyd, *Unnatural Law*, above note 22 at 148–63.

39 In Harry Poch, *Corporate and Municipal Environmental Law* (Toronto: Carswell, 1989) at 297–300, the suggestion is made that, depending on the definition of "undertaking" or equivalent term in the province's environmental laws, a province could subject an official plan to a formal EA. No instances are known, and a provincial government concerned over sustainability policies of a municipality could take other steps to deal with the situation.

40 (2001), 42 MPLR (3d) 165 (Ont SCJ) [*Sample*].

have taken so wide a view; *Sample* should be contrasted with the Nova Scotia decision in *Kynock v Bennett*[41] and the OMB itself in *Greenspace Alliance of Canada's Capital v Ottawa (City)*.[42]

In addition to direct environmental regulation and EAs, there are related statutes. Ontario has an *Environmental Bill of Rights, 1993*,[43] and Nova Scotia has an *Environmental Goals and Sustainable Prosperity Act*.[44] *EGSPA* is aspirational. It sets out principles such as the "health of the economy, the health of the environment, and the health of the people are interconnected,"[45] but also sets targets and target dates for the reduction of GHGs, NO_x, SO_2, and mercury, along with aims regarding drinking water standards. Ontario's *Environmental Bill of Rights* declares a "right to a healthful environment,"[46] sets minimum levels of public participation for determining environmental decisions, establishes an Environmental Commissioner with review and reporting powers, and confers a right to sue on "any person resident in Ontario"[47] for contraventions that have "caused or will imminently cause significant harm to a public resource." The *Bill* binds the Crown.[48] Although the *Bill* is an important piece of legislation, it is not seen as creating a generalized and enforceable right at large to a healthy environment;[49] some specific step in the adopted formalized process needs to be challenged, such as the granting of permits.[50]

D. CONTROL OF LOCAL GOVERNMENTS

One of the main exercises of land-use power by a province is the creation of local governments to take on the process of detailed decision-making. Municipalities themselves may be dissolved by the province, amalgamated, or renamed.[51] Among others, University of Victoria urban studies

41 (1994), 20 MPLR (2d) 257 (NSSCAD).
42 [2007] OMBD No 564 (OMB) distinguished *Sample*.
43 SO 1993, c 28, as amended [*Bill*].
44 SNS 2007, c 7, as amended [*EGSPA*].
45 *Ibid*, s 3(2).
46 Above note 43, Preamble.
47 *Ibid*, s 84.
48 *Ibid*, s 120.
49 *Clean Train Coalition Inc v Metrolinx*, 2012 ONSC 6593. For comment, see David Boyd, "Elements of an Effective Environmental Bill of Rights" (2015) 27:3 *Journal of Environmental Law and Practice* 201.
50 See, for example, *Dixon v Ontario (Director, Ministry of Environment)*, 2014 ONSC 7404 regarding permits for wind farms.
51 See, for example, *East York (Borough) v Ontario (Attorney General)* (1997), 43 MPLR (2d) 155 (Ont CA) [*East York*].

professor Warren Magnusson has argued strongly for legal recognition of rights to local self-government,[52] but it is exactly this point that has been rejected by the courts as not part of the present law. In *East York*, a challenge was brought to court over the creation by the province of the amalgamated entity the City of Toronto.[53] Amalgamation was a common feature of the restructuring of municipal governments in the 1990s. Major entities created were in Toronto, Montreal, Vancouver, Halifax, and Quebec City.[54] For some, the model chosen was of two-tier governance, though in others there was outright merger of the pre-existing municipalities.[55] The core idea was a mixture of the desire to achieve efficiencies in the delivery of services such as police and fire, the integration of transportation and other land-use planning over a wide region, and a shift of debt as well as revenue-generation capacity. Several lawsuits attempted to challenge amalgamations. In *East York*, an attempt was made to raise both *Charter* issues and distribution of powers issues under the *Constitution Act, 1867*. The *Charter* issues were freedom of expression (section 2(b)) and equality (section 15). The court's analysis left very little room for any possible challenge:

> The appellants' submission is that the *City of Toronto Act, 1997* is violative of the appellants' *Charter* rights. They do not suggest any curtailment of a right to vote. The basis of the *Charter* submissions appears to be that the ratio between numbers of voters and elected representatives under the new legislation is too high, and, in any event, higher than the ratios found in the neighbouring municipalities. The extent of the ratio, the appellants argue, necessarily diminishes access to

52 See, for example, Warren Magnusson, "Are Municipalities Creatures of the Provinces?" (2005) 39:2 *Journal of Canadian Studies* 5; Warren Magnusson, *Local Self-Government and the Right to the City* (Montreal: McGill-Queens University Press, 2015).

53 *City of Toronto Act, 1997*, SO 1997, c 2 [since repealed].

54 For discussion of some of these amalgamations, see Andrew Sancton, "Metropolitan and Regional Governance" in Edmund P Fowler & David Siegel, eds, *Urban Policy Issues: Canadian Perspectives*, 2d ed (Don Mills, ON: Oxford University Press, 2002); John Sewell, *Local Self Government Bulletin* [on file with original author; no longer available online]; Igor Vojnovic & Dale Poel, "Provincial and Municipal Restructuring in Canada: Assessing Expectations and Outcomes" (2000) 23 *Canadian Journal of Regional Science*, online: www.cjrs-rcsr.org/archives/23-1/INTRO-ENG.pdf; Harry H Hiller, *Urban Canada*, 2d ed (Don Mills, ON: Oxford University Press, 2009) at Introduction and 308–9; Harvey Schwartz, "Toronto Ten Years after Amalgamation" (2009) 32:3 *Canadian Journal of Regional Science* 483; Joseph Kushner & David Siegel, "Citizen Satisfaction with Municipal Amalgamations" (2005) 48:1 *Canadian Public Administration* 73.

55 See Gerald Hodge & David Gordon, *Planning Canadian Communities*, 5th ed (Toronto: Thomson Nelson, 2008) at 238–40.

> elected representatives . . . . There is neither jurisprudential nor evidentiary support for these arguments. While conceding that voter/representative ratios are theoretically relevant, and that the distribution of these ratios may in certain circumstances be found to be discriminatory, there is no reliable evidence that the particular ratios in this case fall below constitutional standards . . . . With respect specifically to s. 15 . . . the equality guarantee . . . has not been violated . . . . We have difficulty identifying what the threshold "distinction" is in this case, let alone concluding that it is discriminatory in intent or impact . . . . There is, in our view, no merit in the appellants' submission that the provincial government exceeded its jurisdiction under s. 92(8) of the Constitution when it promulgated the *City of Toronto Act, 1997*. The division of powers between federal and provincial governments found in ss. 91 and 92 of the Constitution allocated responsibility over "municipal institutions" to the provincial governments. The appellants argued alternatively that this authority was circumscribed by implicit constitutional conventions . . . or by implicit constitutional norms . . . not to effect change to a municipal institution without its consent. There is, with respect, no evidence of the existence either of a constitutional norm or of a constitutional convention so restricting the provinces. When altering municipal institutions, there are undoubtedly sound political reasons for a provincial government to exercise great care in the process . . . . However, courts can only provide remedies for the public's grievances if those grievances violate legal, as opposed to political proprieties. What is politically controversial is not necessarily constitutionally impermissible. In 1896, the Privy Council confirmed that s. 92(8) gave provincial legislatures the right to create legal bodies for the management of municipal affairs, a right which included the right to amalgamate such bodies and establish their geographic boundaries . . . . No case subsequently decided has ever diluted this fundamental authority.[56]

In 2001, the Quebec courts upheld the Montreal amalgamation in *Baie d'Urfé (Ville) c Québec (Procureur général)*.[57] Bill 170 was challenged on various grounds, similar to those in *East York*. The municipal points were:

> Elle est ultra vires des pouvoirs de l'Assemblée nationale du Québec aux termes du paragraphe 92(8) de la Loi constitutionnelle de 1867 . . . . Elle contrevient aux principes non écrits (ou structurels) de la Constitution . . . . Elle défavorise les arrondissements qui remplacent les villes fusionnées au profit d'un pouvoir exécutif central . . . . Elle

56 *East York*, above note 51 at paras 4, 5, and 9–13.

57 (2001), 23 MPLR (3d) 163 (Que CS).

> exproprie illégalement les biens et les actifs des Villes sans accorder une compensation juste et raisonnable . . . .[58]

The court rejected all of the claims, for example,

> Les institutions municipales ne possèdent pas un statut constitutionnel indépendant. Il n'existe aucune obligation pour une province de créer et maintenir des municipalités ou des institutions municipales. Et si de telles institutions n'existaient pas, l'ensemble de leurs pouvoirs seraient exercés par le gouvernement provincial.[59]

The nature of the planning function the provinces assign to municipalities is the subject of Chapter 6. Here, it is sufficient to note that where local governments do not adopt official plans or have not chosen to adopt land-use by-laws for either the whole or a part of their territory, there will still be control exercised through various provincial regulatory regimes. Thus, for a lot to be developed as a residence, provincial environmental or health rules will control sewage and drinking water installations, transportation rules will control the nature of road access, and the building code will control safe construction and some energy matters.

In Chapter 6 we examine the many ways in which the provincial level of government exerts influence on local governments even while establishing them as the instrument of control over detailed land-use decisions. One of the main ones is the Statement of Provincial Interest (SPI), Provincial Policy Statements (PPS), or equivalent, in which the province establishes a policy framework for municipalities as they craft their official plans and make their decisions. Thus in Ontario, the *Planning Act*, section 3 allows the minister to issue policy statements (subject to cabinet approval) "on matters relating to municipal planning that in the opinion of the Minister are of provincial interest"; where this occurs, all planning decisions, including those of the OMB, "shall be consistent with" the policy statements.[60]

E. RESETTLEMENT

Moving families or entire communities is a major undertaking. Governments have tried to do this in various circumstances. One is in order to

58 *Ibid* at para 12.

59 *Ibid* at para 96; the decision was upheld by the Quebec Court of Appeal: (2001), 27 MPLR (3d) 173.

60 Ontario *Planning Act*, above note 6, s 3.

promote economic development or to support otherwise unsustainable communities. The other is simply to make way for other uses such as dams.

"The largest government-sponsored relocation of people in Canadian history"[61] was the Newfoundland and Labrador "Centralization Programme" (also called the "Fisheries Household Resettlement Programme"), in place in different iterations from 1954 through 1975. It was aimed at small fishing outports, communities with links to the outside only through ferry service. Some 263 communities comprising approximately 27,500 people were moved. The programme was voluntary, though hard to resist; the government paid the cost of moving plus some cash. The motivation was to lessen dependence on the fishery as well as to make essential government services such as health care and education easier to deliver. New industries in "growth areas" (mining, pulp and paper mills, urbanization, air force bases) were in need of workers. *The Canadian Encyclopedia* says: "The resettlement program . . . is generally viewed as a failure. Despite the superior social services of growth centres, especially education, many new industries failed and resettled workers were displaced from their traditional livelihoods in the fishery. Social dislocation and alienation arose from poor social and economic integration within new communities."[62] A variant of the programme is still in effect today.[63] Substantial cash payments are on offer, though only if 90 percent of the full-time residents vote to accept. In some outports, this community discussion has become particularly complicated because significant numbers of summer residents have purchased homes and are dependent on the continued existence of the rest of the community, but are not eligible to vote on relocation.

One of the main lessons of the experience of relocation is that its effects can be ongoing, sometimes multi-generational.[64]

---

61 Tina Loo, "'The Government Game': Resettlement Then and Now" (6 June 2013), online: http://activehistory.ca/2013/06/the-government-game-resettlement-then-and-now.

62 Robert D Pitt, "Newfoundland Resettlement Program," online: Historica Canada www.thecanadianencyclopedia.ca/en/article/newfoundland-resettlement-program; see also Melanie Martin, "The Resettlement Program," online: Heritage Newfoundland & Labrador www.heritage.nf.ca/articles/politics/resettlement-program.php.

63 Loo, above note 61.

64 See comments on the Africville relocation in Truth and Reconciliation Commission of Canada, *The Final Report of the Truth and Reconciliation Commission of Canada*, vol 1, Summary (Toronto: James Lorimer & Co Ltd, 2015) ch 11, especially at 135ff; as well as the Royal Commission on Aboriginal Peoples account of the effects of the relocations it studied.

In addition to the Newfoundland outport relocations, there have been other instances undertaken in a declared attempt to benefit the particular community. In 1948, the Mushua Innu of Labrador were relocated from Davis Inlet to Nutak in northern Labrador, a unilateral decision. The community moved back on its own after two years. In 1967, the government encouraged another move to a nearby island. The community consisted of some 500 persons, living in conditions of abject poverty. Publicity about the living conditions led to another move, to Sango Pond (Natuashish), 15 kilometres away. The relocation was negotiated in an agreement reached in 1996, though the construction of the new homes delayed actual movement of residents until 2002–2003. In neither case was the move a social or an economic success, even though significant sums were invested.[65]

The main communities affected by government-led relocations have been Aboriginal. The details have been set out in *The Report of the Royal Commission on Aboriginal Peoples*.[66] In its chapter "Looking Forward, Looking Back" is an account of "Relocation of Aboriginal Communities." The scope of the account extends to displacement by European settlers, to land purchases, to treaties, and to the establishment of reserves. Confining a focus to "deliberate initiatives by governments to move particular Aboriginal communities for administrative or development purposes,"[67] examples are given of Inuit moved from Pond Inlet (Baffin Island) and Inukjuak (Quebec) to the High Arctic in the 1950s, to more recent moves in Burns Lake and Tsulquate (British Columbia), and Easterville and Tadoule Lake (Manitoba). The RCAP says "the practice of relocation was widespread. There are dozens of examples."[68] The examples involving making way for development go back to 1830 involving the Ojibwa of the Saugeen Peninsula (Ontario) to make way for agricultural development and the Songhees in Victoria in 1911 to allow for urbanization.[69]

---

65 See, for example, Timothy A Powers, *Conscious Choice of Convenience: The Relocation of the Mushua Innu of Davis Inlet, Labrador* (MA Thesis, Saint Mary's University, 1997) [unpublished]; Aušra Burns, "Moving and Moving Forward: Mushuau Innu Relocation from Davis Inlet to Natuashish" (2006) 35 *Acadiensis* 64.

66 Royal Commission on Aboriginal Peoples, *Report of the Royal Commission on Aboriginal Peoples*, vol 1 (Ottawa: The Commission, 1996) ch 11 [RCAP], online: www.lop.parl.gc.ca/content/lop/researchpublications/prb9924-e.htm.

67 *Ibid* at 395.

68 *Ibid* at 397.

69 In addition to RCAP, various studies exist. See, for example, Frank Tester & Peter Kulchyski, *Tammarniit (Mistakes): Inuit Relocation in the Eastern Arctic, 1939–63* (Vancouver: UBC Press, 1994); Alan R Marcus, *Relocating Eden, The Image and Politics of Inuit Exile in the Canadian Arctic* (Hanover, NH: University Press of New England, 1995); Melanie McGrath, *The Long Exile* (London: Fourth Estate, 2006).

Among the most controversial relocations have been those associated with grand projects such as dams. The RCAP cites two examples: "The Cheslatta Carrier Nation in northwestern British Columbia lost its communities when the Kemano dam was built on the Nechako River in the 1950s. The communities of the Chemawawin Cree were relocated because of construction of the Grand Rapids hydro dam in Manitoba a few years later."[70]

The James Bay Cree were not unilaterally relocated, but the Quebec government, starting in the 1970s, proposed to develop several phases of an enormous hydroelectric generation project and started to do so without advance consultation. Lands claimed by the Cree were to be flooded, which implied relocation. A settlement was negotiated in 1975, the first modern land claim agreement. It sets out the environmental and social protection regimes for the territorial regions of James Bay and Nunavik. A second phase of the project was started in 1986 and led to additional concerns.[71] A follow-up agreement, known as La Paix des Braves, was entered into in 2002. Several acts implement the results of the negotiations.[72] The multi-decade interaction has been written about extensively.[73]

Abandonment of communities that have become uneconomic happens just as often on its own, without any government direction. Ghost towns, places that are generally remote and were dependent on one main employer now out of business, are common. The Canadian economy remains heavily resource-based; thus fluctuations in the market for commodities such as minerals or lumber can easily lead to collapse of the viability of small communities. The re-routing of road or rail links can also lead to collapse or significant dwindling of such communities, though this is often associated with market changes.[74] Proposals for

---

70 Above note 67 at 399.

71 For a discussion of the importance of open and effective public consultation in this context, see Lawrence Susskind & Patrick Field, "Hydro-Québec and the Cree: Clashing Cultures" in *Dealing with an Angry Public* (New York: The Free Press, 1996) 160.

72 *An Act Approving the Agreement concerning James Bay and Northern Québec*, CQLR c C-67; *An Act respecting the Cree Nation Government*, CQLR c G-1.031; *An Act to Ensure the Implementation of the Agreement concerning a New Relationship between le Gouvernement du Québec and the Crees of Québec*, CQLR c M-35.1.2.

73 See, for example, several works by the former premier of Quebec, Robert Bourassa, *La Baie James* (Montreal: Editions du Jour, 1973); *Deux fois la Baie James* (Montreal: La Presse, 1981); *L'énergie du Nord* (Montreal: Libre Expression, 1985); and see James F Hornig, ed, *Social and Environmental Impacts of the James Bay Hydroelectric Project* (Montreal: McGill-Queens University Press, 1999).

74 Canada seems to have approximately 500 ghost towns: see Wikipedia lists by province, online: https://en.wikipedia.org/wiki/Lists_of_ghost_towns_in_Canada. Some works have attempted to document ghost towns, for example,

repopulation of such former communities are occasionally made; such initiatives are mainly private and little has occurred. One example of a government-led initiative is the British Columbia town of Ocean Falls. In 1975, faced with the imminent closure of the pulp mill, the main local employer, the provincial government, purchased the town and established a local economic development company, Ocean Falls Corporation, to extract water from the town's lake and sell the water.

F. REGIONAL PLANNING AND GREENBELTS

The essence of municipal government is that it is local, whereas land-use issues are often regional in scope. In light of a mismatch between political boundaries and need for regional co-ordination, provincial governments have resorted to a variety of instruments. Among them are allowing municipalities to plan jointly with others, setting policy direction through Statements of Provincial Interest, outright amalgamation so as to create larger municipalities, and also initiation of large-scale planning exercises led by the province, sometimes resulting in legislation. It is this latter instrument that is to be examined here.[75]

Two main examples are British Columbia's Commission on Resources and the Environment (CORE) process, and Ontario's *Places to Grow Act, 2005*, plus its *Greenbelt Act, 2005*. Both provinces have grappled with issues associated with large urban concentrations—Vancouver (the Greater Vancouver Regional District (GVRD)) in British Columbia, and Toronto (the Greater Golden Horseshoe (GGH)) in Ontario—including problems of sprawl, pressure on agricultural lands as well as other resources, and infrastructure needs and cost.[76]

CORE was at work between 1992 and 1996. It gained its credibility through the stature of the commissioner, Stephen Owen, who was known from having been the province's ombudsman.[77] Its mandate was to undertake multi-stakeholder discussions to try to work out plans for

---

Ron Brown, *Ontario's Ghost Town Heritage* (Erin, ON: Boston Mills Press, 2007); Bruce Ramsey, *Ghost Towns in British Columbia* (Vancouver: Mitchell Press, 1963). Some settlements were religion-based, others no more than mining or forestry camps with very small populations.

75 Statements of Provincial Interest, including the important Ontario PPS and Manitoba's PLUP, are examined in Chapter 6.

76 New Brunswick has long had an emphasis in its land-use planning on regional approaches. See *Regional Service Delivery Act*, SNB 2012, c 37, and the *Community Planning Act*, RSNB 1973, c C-12. The province takes the lead in planning for the seven regions established.

77 See Juergen Hansen, "Was CORE Outcome Win-Win?" (1997) 13 *ADR Forum* 1.

resource use in four regions: Vancouver Island, Cariboo-Chilcotin, and East and West Kootenay.[78]

Greenbelts are not a new phenomenon.[79] Martin Elson's UK study identifies the purpose of greenbelts as "to check the further growth of a large built up area; to prevent neighbouring towns from merging into one another; and to preserve the special character of a town."[80] Development boundaries had been a part of long-range planning for London in the 1940s and 1950s, but formalized greenbelts arose more commonly in the United Kingdom after 1970. British Columbia has a *Greenbelt Act*.[81] Ontario's greenbelt legislation has had an adverse effect on future development plans of owners in the area, especially owners of agricultural land. Cases such as *1057330 Ontario Inc v Melrose Properties Inc*[82] illustrate this. Even though development hopes and plans of landowners are inchoate rather than entitlements, the Ontario government treated land developers in a special manner, entering into some land-swap arrangements for Crown land outside the restricted area.[83]

An important point arises as to whether greenbelt issues may be taken to court following OMB hearings. Although some greenbelt area land-use issues may be appealed to the OMB, one court has said that further appeals to the Divisional Court are not available since issues of interpretation of the Greenbelt Plan are not questions of law; the *Greenbelt Act* authorizes a plan which is "a collection of policy statements" which it is within the jurisdiction of the OMB to interpret, not matters for the court.[84] To the contrary, regarding the Growth Plan, the Divisional Court said, "Interpretation of an official plan raises questions of law. Official plans must conform to provincial policy and plans. It follows that the interpretation of a provincial policy or plan is also a question of law."[85] The judge in *Niagara* also said, "Such questions of

---

78 The publications of CORE include *Finding Common Ground* (1994), *Planning for Sustainability* (1994), *Dispute Resolution* (1995), and *A Provincial Land Use Strategy for British Columbia* (1994).

79 See Martin J Elson, *Green Belts: Conflict Mediation in the Urban Fringe* (London: Heinemann, 1986).

80 *Ibid* at xxiii.

81 RSBC 1996, c 176.

82 2010 ONSC 483, especially at para 18.

83 Pierre Filion & Anna Kramer, "Transforming Toronto" in Anneke Smit & Marcia Valiante, eds, *Public Interest, Private Property* (Vancouver: UBC Press, 2016) 137 at 160.

84 *583753 Ontario Ltd v York (Regional Municipality)*, 2007 CanLII 40538 at paras 9 and 11 (Ont Div Ct).

85 *Niagara (Regional Municipality) v Ontario (Municipal Affairs and Housing)*, 2009 CanLII 66619 at para 7 (Ont Div Ct) [*Niagara*].

law engage the policy expertise of the Board and attract a standard of reasonableness."[86]

The federal government has used the provincial greenbelt legislation to stop consideration of changes in land use in the vicinity of its lands expropriated in 1972 for a possible airport in Pickering.[87]

The Ontario greenbelt is not the first large-scale planning exercise in the province. The Niagara Escarpment, for which the first plan was adopted in 1985, and the Oak Ridges Moraine (2002) are also areas that cross a number of municipalities and have had special legislation to govern them. The Niagara Escarpment Commission was first established in 1973 pursuant to special legislation.[88] The commission, appointed by the provincial government, was given a mandate to plan for the Escarpment, which extends some 724 kilometres through south and central Ontario, passing through eight counties.[89] All of these areas are a part of the "Greater Golden Horseshoe" area (though the Niagara Escarpment's northern portions are outside). A recent study of the planning needs of the area, "Planning for Health, Prosperity and Growth in the Greater Golden Horseshoe 2015–2041"[90] is predicting a growth in population from 9 million to 13.5 million by 2041.[91] It was established to evaluate the various plans, concluding that they "provide a strong foundation for the region" though also that "there is an urgent need to improve the plans and ensure effective actions to curb sprawl, grow the Greenbelt, support agriculture and address traffic congestion."[92]

G. AGRICULTURE

Agriculture has been a matter of public policy since the time of initial European contact and subsequent land grants. The main thrust of modern provincial-level land-use policies having to do with agriculture has been the preservation of productive land. At the same time, there has

86 *Ibid.*

87 See *Canada (Attorney General) v Berrywood Farms Inc*, 2006 CanLII 6079 (Ont Div Ct).

88 *Niagara Escarpment Planning and Development Act*, SO 1973, c 52.

89 A UK precedent for such a special planning body is the Broads Authority, created pursuant to the *Norfolk and Suffolk Broads Act 1988* (UK), c 4.

90 Ontario, *Report of the Advisory Panel on the Coordinated Review of the Growth Plan for the Greater Golden Horseshoe, the Greenbelt Plan, the Oak Ridges Moraine Conservation Plan and the Niagara Escarpment Plan* (December 2015), online: www.mah.gov.on.ca/Asset11110.aspx?method=1 [Crombie Report].

91 *Ibid* at 9.

92 *Ibid* at 4.

been recognition of the potential for some polluting activities to come from agriculture, and some policy is aimed at reducing those harms. The basic facts, as noted by University of Western Ontario geographer MJ Troughton are, "The primary purpose of agriculture is to provide an adequate, sustained food supply, and the primary setting for agricultural production is the rural area . . . . Both . . . occupy and incorporate extensive land areas, the quantity and quality of which is of particular significance in their evaluation and management."[93]

In terms of preservation of productive land, various policy tools have been used, primarily at the provincial level. Some land has been designated as available only for agricultural use subject to special permission for change. In Prince Edward Island, controls on non-resident ownership have been put in place.[94] A similar law has been in place in Saskatchewan since 1974 through a *Farm Ownership Act*.[95] All provinces have adopted "right to farm" laws to try to minimize lawsuits against farmers engaging in normal farm practices.

Canada has a national Land Inventory that identifies classes of land according to its potential for beneficial use. Land is classed according to its capability for agriculture, forestry, recreation, and wildlife. For agricultural land capability, classes range from 1 to 7, with 1 being the highest and 7 the lowest. Based on such information, British Columbia led the way in 1973 by establishing an Agricultural Land Reserve aimed at protecting the best agricultural land.[96] Because some of the best agricultural land is located in the Lower Mainland, there were competing interests from urbanization and associated land development proposals. It took several years to fully identify the boundaries, and the province put in place a freeze on development approvals until that process was finished in 1975. Both public and private land was designated. There was some purchase of land by the government. Various changes have been made to the boundaries and to the process since the 1970s, but the Reserve remains in place, administered by a commission. The system has always had a strong political aspect in that

93 Michael J Troughton, "Agriculture and Rural Resources" in Bruce Mitchell, ed, *Resource Management and Development, Addressing Conflict and Uncertainty* (Toronto: Oxford University Press, 1991) 54 at 54.

94 *Lands Protection Act*, RSPEI 1988, c L-5, although the first PEI restrictions were enacted in 1972 through amendments to the *Real Property Act* to limit non-residents to ownership of no more than ten acres of land or more than 330 feet of shore frontage.

95 *The Saskatchewan Farm Security Act*, SS 1988–89, c S-17.1.

96 *Agricultural Land Reserve Act*, RSBC 1996, c 10, repealed and replaced by *Agricultural Land Commission Act*, SBC 2002, c 36.

appeals to the cabinet have been available, and used, for example, to allow for golf courses.[97]

Quebec adopted a similar system not long after British Columbia, establishing its Commission de protection du territoire agricole du Québec in 1979.[98] Several cases at the Supreme Court of Canada have upheld the validity of the Quebec system.[99] It remains somewhat contentious.[100]

In Ontario, protection of agricultural lands was a function of local governments, supported by Provincial Policy Statements (PPSs) to influence OP policies, until the Greenbelt Plan of 2005 and the Growth Plan of 2006. The PPS on agriculture varied in its effectiveness according to the stricture of whether OPs must "have regard" to it or "be consistent" with it.[101] The 2015 Crombie Report on the interaction of the various Ontario provincial land plans in the GGH area noted that "The Greenbelt Plan provides a stronger level of protection for agriculture than the PPS and the Growth Plan. For example, it states that: Settlement area expansions can only be considered as part of a 10-year plan review; conversion of land in prime agricultural areas to [other] rural land uses . . . is not permitted."[102] The Growth Plan does permit expansion of residential uses into agricultural areas subject to various criteria as to the availability of reasonable alternatives.[103] The OMB has dealt with a number of cases involving issues around preservation of agricultural lands and has generally supported the overall policy.[104]

Regulation through a focus on non-resident ownership has been the main policy choice in Prince Edward Island.[105] A mix of objectives

---

97 For a history, see Emily Yearwood-Lee, *History of the Agricultural Land Reserve* (Victoria, BC: Legislative Library of British Columbia, 2008).

98 *An Act respecting the Preservation of Agricultural Land and Agricultural Activities*, CQLR c P-41.1.

99 *Veilleux v Québec (Commission de protection du territoire agricole)*, [1989] 1 SCR 839; *Gauthier v Québec (Commission de protection du territoire agricole)*, [1989] 1 SCR 859; *Venne v Québec (Commission de protection du territoire agricole)*, [1989] 1 SCR 880.

100 See Lorne Giroux, "Agricultural Land Protection in Quebec: A Victim of Its Own Success?" (1992) 38 *Resources* 1.

101 On this point, see Chapter 6, Section E.

102 Crombie Report, above note 90 at 91.

103 See, for a brief discussion, *Niagara (Regional Municipality) v Ontario (Municipal Affairs and Housing)*, 2009 CanLII 66619 (Ont Div Ct).

104 See, for example, *Mercier v Norfolk (County)* (2002), 44 OMBR 173, where a vehicle repair shop was seen as too large an operation to meet the designation of small-scale repairs in support of agriculture; *Wilkins v Havelock-Belmont-Methuen (Township)* (2001), 43 OMBR 159, where expansion of greenhouses in a rural area was approved.

105 The Supreme Court of Canada has upheld Prince Edward Island's right to so legislate: see *Morgan v Prince Edward Island (Attorney General)* (1975), 55 DLR (3d) 527 (SCC).

is involved, not only the protection of agricultural land.[106] The reasons articulated for wanting to control non-resident ownership vary from purely economic, to those focused on appropriate land use, to a general concern for stewardship of the environment, to the social. It is understandable that these concerns are mixed up together. Economic reasons include a concern about rise in prices thus potentially putting land beyond the reach of local purchasers; increased assessments and hence increased property taxes; and a change in the nature of the local economy away from the production of goods and towards seasonal tourism services. Land-use reasons include conversion of natural resource land (farms, woodlots) to cottage lots; the non-use of land if held for extended periods for speculative purposes; an implied or actual restriction in access to what may have been seen or used as community resources such as hiking trails, the seashore, or for berrying. Stewardship reasons include increased stress on the land, erosion of the shore, or risk of pollution of groundwater—all associated with increased density of population. Social reasons include fear of change in local community culture.[107]

In provinces with SPIs, one of the objectives always stated is preservation or protection of agricultural land. In offering guidance or in some cases outright limitations on municipal policy choices, the provinces have shown recognition of an important element of land-use planning. Manitoba's provincial land-use policies (PLUPs) are particularly detailed.[108]

Conservation easements have been facilitated by provincial governments and have been used to protect agricultural land. Thus, in Alberta, the Southern Alberta Land Trust Society is an example of an entity that uses conservation easements to protect land such as grassland and wetlands, particularly focused on the drainage area of the South Saskatchewan River.[109]

"Normal farm practices" are protected from lawsuits based in nuisance. The ambit of such legislation was examined in this book's Introduction in the discussion of the *Desrosiers v Sullivan* case.[110] Dumping fill is not a normal farm practice (and in this instance violated the Oak

---

106 PEI Royal Commission on the Land, *Everything Before Us*, by Douglas Boylan (Chair) (Charlottetown, PEI: Island Information Service, 1990).

107 For a discussion, see Heather Breeze, *Exploring the Implications of Non-Resident Land Ownership in Nova Scotia* (MA Thesis, Dalhousie University, 1998) [unpublished] at 43–51.

108 See *Provincial Planning Regulation*, Man Reg 81/2011.

109 See Southern Alberta Land Trust Society, online: www.salts-landtrust.org.

110 (1985), 66 NBR (2d) 243 (QB).

Ridges Moraine Conservation Plan, which prohibited site alteration): *Uxbridge (Township) v Corbar Holdings Inc.*[111] Nor does the OMB have jurisdiction to declare that assessment farming is a normal farm practice so as to exempt property from the taxes that would otherwise be payable. Its jurisdiction is limited to "agricultural lands in agricultural areas," which does not apply if the land is zoned commercial or light industrial: see *Oakville (Town) v Read (cob Read Farms)*,[112] where the landowner paid tenants to farm the land.

There is something of a tendency on the part of appeal bodies to regard the existence of *Agricultural Practices Protection Acts* as an answer to objections to rezoning of nearby lands to potentially incompatible uses. Thus in *Re Rovers*,[113] the Nova Scotia Utility and Review Board (NSUARB) refused to reverse municipal permission for a nine-unit condominium near to a farming operation, citing the Act as affording protections from potential nuisance actions. *Rovers* illustrates a dynamic in which one farmer chooses to develop the land for non-agricultural purposes, contributing to the transformation of an area or community and creating potential conflicts.

Professor Troughton notes the change to an agribusiness model, dating to the 1920s:

> The inevitable result is a minority of large farms, in specific locations, contributing the majority of output . . . . However, in pursuit of its goal of a lower unit-cost of production, industrial agriculture becomes more and more dependent on non-renewable inputs and, in the process, places severe pressures on natural environmental systems (e.g. soil erosion and degradation, soil and water pollution, waste accumulation).[114]

Ontario has chosen to regulate the agricultural use of pesticides. *Grain Farmers of Ontario v Ontario (Ministry of the Environment and Climate Change)*[115] attempted to challenge regulations under the *Pesticides Act*[116] that control the use of neonicotinoid-treated seeds, but were not successful. The assertion that property rights were affected was not accepted: "I am of the view that the application is concerned with the economic interests of the affected farmers rather than any property rights. Prior to [the regulation] the farmers did not have an unrestricted

111 2012 ONSC 3527.
112 2011 ONCA 22.
113 2014 NSUARB 59 [*Rovers*].
114 Above note 93 at 60.
115 2015 ONSC 6581, aff'd 2016 ONCA 283 [*Grain Farmers*].
116 RSO 1990, c P.11.

right to use their lands as they wished but were subject to a highly regulated pesticide regime."[117]

In Alberta, the establishment of concentrated feeding operations (CFOs) is under the supervision of the Natural Resources Conservation Board, which "must have regard to, but is not bound by a municipal development plan."[118] The flexibility of this requirement was explored in *Grow North Inc v Alberta (Natural Resources Conservation Board)*,[119] where it was treated much the same as the requirement that municipalities have regard for Statements of Provincial Interest, a topic examined in Chapter 6, Section E. The proposed CFO in question in *Grow North* was for "four feedlot barns that would collectively house a total of 5,000 beef finishers . . . part of a larger planned project that would include bio-digesters, electrical generation facilities, an abattoir, a packing plant and an ethanol plant."[120] The scale of the proposed operation illustrates the need for serious regulatory oversight.[121] The municipalities involved had in place an inter-municipal development plan with stringent policies, which, when compared with the rather weak policies of the Saskatchewan rural municipality of Loon Lake No 561,[122] are even more impressive:

> Applications to the NRCB for the establishment or expansion of CFOs shall not be supported by the County unless they are compatible with adjacent land uses, do not generate adverse health or environmental effects, follow the Agricultural Operations and Practices Act guidelines, and meet or exceed the following separation distances: (a) 3.2 kilometres from an adjacent municipality, Hamlet, Indian Reserve or a multi-lot country residential subdivision.[123]

In Ontario, the Ministry of Agriculture, Food and Rural Affairs has engaged with the problem of interaction of agricultural uses with residential uses by offering municipalities model by-laws that can address the issue through minimum distances of separation (MDS). The MDS formulae are based on both the type and intensity of the agricultural operation and the extent of the nearby residential uses. They have been

117 *Grain Farmers*, above note 115 at para 35 (ONSC).
118 *Agricultural Operation Protection Act*, RSA 2000, c A-7, s 25(4)(g).
119 2011 ABCA 236 [*Grow North*].
120 *Ibid* at para 15.
121 See Jim Schwab, *Planning and Zoning for Concentrated Animal Feeding Operations* (Washington, DC: American Planning Association, 1998).
122 See *Morton v Loon Lake No 561 (Rural Municipality)*, 2011 SKQB 264.
123 *Grow North*, above note 119 at para 5.

widely adopted. Their existence offers a standard that can guide development decisions, whether formally adopted in local rules or not.[124]

Fur farming is carried on primarily in Nova Scotia, Ontario, and Newfoundland and Labrador. According to the Fur Institute of Canada, there are some 289 licensed fur farms in Canada, which generate approximately $200 million per year in pelt sales.[125] The most commonly farmed animals are mink and fox. About two-thirds to three-quarters of Canada's pelts come from farming, rather than trapping.[126] The main environmental issues involve odour and waste management. Nova Scotia adopted a *Fur Industry Act* in 2010,[127] followed by *Fur Industry Regulations* in 2013.[128] Licensing requires a site approval plan and permit, and offers standards of handling in a "humane manner"[129] and "clean and sanitary conditions."[130] The Act supersedes the *Farm Practices Act*. The regulations provide for a feces storage system, limits means of disposal,[131] and requires surface and groundwater monitoring. Separation distances from property lines, off-farm dwellings, and wells and watercourses are specified.[132] News reports indicate issues regarding compliance.[133]

H. MINING

Ownership of land usually excludes ownership of minerals. Provincial *Mines Acts* regulate access to land, including private land, by prospectors.[134] Typically, there is a "free-entry" system, which means licensed prospectors may access land to explore and possibly stake a claim (although British Columbia, Ontario, Quebec, and Newfoundland and Labrador have adopted online staking as an alternative to physical

---

124 See various publications of the ministry, especially the 2006 *Minimum Distance Separation Implementation Guidelines*, Publication 707.

125 See online: http://fur.ca/fur-trade/canadas-fur-trade-fact-figures.

126 Trapping is dealt with under Section K, below in this chapter.

127 SNS 2010, c 4.

128 NS Reg 4/2013.

129 Above note 127, s 31.

130 *Ibid*, s 32.

131 Above note 128, s 25.

132 *Ibid*, s 41.

133 Geoff Bird, "Mink Breeders Failing to Meet New Rules" (5 February 2016), online: http://allNovaScotia.com.

134 For an overview, see Ramsay Hart et al, "Introduction to the Legal Framework for Mining in Canada" (July 2012), online: Mining Watch Canada http://miningwatch.ca/sites/default/files/Introduction%20to%20the%20Legal%20Framework%20for%20Mining%20in%20Canada.pdf.

staking). Urban areas are typically exempt, as are parks and other special protected areas, albeit sometimes subject to special permission.[135] Following staking, work must be done to maintain the claim's status.

Should a mine be proposed for development, environmental assessment is required in all provinces (with some triggers applicable as to size) except Ontario, where the EA process is only applicable to mines if specifically ordered by the minister. Most current Ontario mine proposals voluntarily submit to the EA process or are subject to a federal EA.[136] As a source of water pollution, mines can be major problems.[137] Tailings ponds have failed;[138] mines at Hemlo and Matachewan in Ontario and Mount Polley in BC are well-known examples. Acid drainage has harmed waterbodies.[139] The minerals themselves, especially heavy metals (lead, zinc, silver, cadmium, copper, iron, etc.), can be a source of serious environmental and health problems.[140]

When a mine is ready for closure, issues arise as to restoration. Restoration to the pre-disturbance state of the land is normally not required. Bonds, letters of credit, or self-assurance are looked to as a form of guarantee that the required closure work will be done.[141] Still, there

---

135 See, for example, New Brunswick's *Clean Water Act*, SNB 1989, c C-6.1, s 14; Nova Scotia's *Environment Act*, SNS 1994-95, c 1, s 105.

136 For a full account, see Mining Watch Canada, "The Big Hole: Environmental Assessment and Mining in Ontario" (December 2014), online: http://miningwatch.ca/sites/default/files/the_big_hole_report.pdf.

137 See Earle A Ripley & Robert E Redmann, *Environmental Effects of Mining*, 2d ed (Delray Beach, FL: St Lucie Press, 1996); Earle A Ripley et al, *Environmental Impact of Mining in Canada* (Kingston, ON: Centre for Resource Studies, Queen's University, 1978). The Mount Polley event prompted British Columbia to revise its Mine Health Safety and Reclamation Code; see "Report on Mount Polley Tailings Storage Facility Breach" Independent Expert Engineering Investigation and Review Panel (30 January 2015) and comments by the Centre for Science in Public Participation (27 July 2016), online: www.csp2.org.

138 *Ibid*.

139 The now-closed Britannia Mine (copper) in British Columbia, in operation from 1900–79, is an example.

140 See JO Duruibe et al, "Heavy Metal Pollution and Human Biotoxic Effects" (2007) 2(5) *International Journal of Physical Sciences* 112.

141 For an overview, see Joseph Castrilli, "Report on the Legislative, Regulatory, and Policy Framework Respecting Collaboration, Liability, and Funding Measures in relation to Orphaned/Abandoned, Contaminated, and Operating Mines in Canada" (2007), online: National Orphaned/Abandoned Mines Initiative www.abandoned-mines.org/wp/wp-content/uploads/2015/06/Jurisdictional LegislativeReview2007.pdf.

are numerous orphaned or abandoned mine sites.[142] And Ontario's Environmental Commissioner has critiqued the effectiveness of the restoration guarantees system.[143]

Overall, there is a marked tendency for governments to look to the mining sector to regulate itself voluntarily. Led by discussion at the national level under the auspices of Natural Resources Canada, accords such as the Whitehorse Mining Initiative Leadership Council Accord have brought together representatives of the mining industry, government, unions, Aboriginal peoples, and environmental organizations to work out principles for the industry.

Ontario has adopted a new Mineral Development Strategy.[144] It notes there are 70 million hectares of land available for staking in Ontario, and that gold is the most-sought mineral. There are forty operating mine sites. Although "an environmentally responsible industry" is a term used, the Strategy offers little on this. The Ontario Environmental Commissioner, in a November 2015 report, pointed to problems in mining:

> Some entire categories of proposal notices are chronically inadequate. For example, instrument proposal notices for exploration permits under the Mining Act consistently lack the basic information needed for a member of the public to provide any sort of meaningful comment . . . . The notice does not include an explanation in plain language of what the proposed activities entail or what their effects could be.[145]

Financial assurance against anticipated rehabilitation costs are in some instances uncollected or insufficient, implying a likely cost to the public of remediation of former mine sites,[146] and there has been inadequate recovery for the value of water extraction by the mining industry.[147]

In British Columbia, there are mines located inside of provincial parks, for historical reasons. Exploration in parks is also a feature of regulatory regimes in Saskatchewan, Nova Scotia, Newfoundland and

---

142 For a review of performance, see National Ophaned/Abandoned Mines Initiative, www.abandoned-mines.org.

143 Ontario Environmental Commissioner, "Small Things Matter: Annual Report 2014/2015" (November 2015) at 13, online: http://docs.assets.eco.on.ca/reports/environmental-protection/2014-2015/2014_2015-AR.pdf.

144 Ontario Ministry of Northern Development and Mines, "Ontario Mineral Development Strategy" (2015), online: www.mndm.gov.on.ca/en/mines-and-minerals/mineral-development-strategy.

145 Above note 143 at 13.

146 *Ibid* at 43–44.

147 *Ibid* at 85. The Commissioner's comment also applies to other industrial water-takers.

Labrador, and Ontario. Ontario's *Provincial Parks and Conservation Resources Act, 2006*[148] prohibits mining, with some government discretion to permit it.[149]

The mining of uranium is a controversial matter in some provinces. It is carried out only in Saskatchewan, though there has been some preliminary exploration in Labrador and Ontario. In Nova Scotia, there is a legislated prohibition.[150] In *Frontenac Ventures Corp v Ardoch Algonquin First Nation*,[151] sentences of incarceration and fines were imposed for contempt of court when First Nations objectors to exploratory drilling for uranium on land subject to an Aboriginal claim blocked the company; the punishments were set aside on appeal.

Pits and quarries are not treated as full mines. Pits are facilities for the extraction of aggregates; quarries are the same but involve blasting.[152] In Ontario, New Brunswick, Newfoundland and Labrador, and the Northwest Territories, there is separate legislation to deal with aggregate extraction.[153] In all cases, consideration of applications for licensing tends to be treated as something of a routine matter, although localized issues as to noise and potential disturbance of groundwater are frequently put in issue.[154] In Ontario, permission is made subject to municipal zoning. There are significant exceptions from the basic licensing system so as to allow for "aggregate permits" for Crown land, and "wayside permits" for temporary projects as part of highway construction.

There may be shared jurisdiction between provinces and the federal government for environmental assessment of some mines, if the ex-

148 SO 2006, c 12, s 31.

149 See *Ontario (Minister of Transportation) v 1520658 Ontario Ltd*, 2011 ONCA 373 at paras 53–56.

150 *Uranium Exploration and Mining Prohibition Act*, SNS 2009, c 6.

151 2008 ONCA 534.

152 Not all provincial regulation makes this distinction, usually referring to "pits and quarries" together. In *Adams v McDougall (Municipality)* (2008), 52 MPLR (4th) 289 (Ont SCJ), the distinction was made, but in a by-law, not a statute. There is no quarrying on Prince Edward Island, because the soil has no gravel.

153 *Aggregate Resources Act*, RSO 1990, c A.8; *Quarriable Substances Act*, SNB 1991, c Q-1.1; *Quarry Materials Act, 1998*, SNL 1998, c Q-1.1; *Commissioner's Land Act*, RSNWT 1988, c C-11. The New Brunswick and Northwest Territories Acts focus on Crown land. Ontario has recently proposed changes to its legislation, through Bill 39, the *Aggregate Resources and Mining Modernization Act, 2016*, 2nd Sess, 41st Leg, Ontario, 2016.

154 See, for example, *Citizens Against Melrose Quarry v Ontario (Environment and Climate Change)*, 2015 CanLII 59648 (Ont ERT); *Northern Construction Enterprises Inc v Halifax (Regional Municipality)*, 2015 NSCA 43.

tent of the proposed undertaking extends to the *Fisheries Act* or other federal regulatory topics.[155]

Whether there is sharing of jurisdiction with municipalities is dependent on what aspect is focused on. There is no direct municipal regulatory authority. The issue has been the extent to which the provincial level regulatory schemes ought to be regarded as exhaustive, thereby pre-empting local government regulation at all. The courts have tended to see provincial *Mining Acts* as complete codes; according to the Supreme Court of Canada in *Multiple Access Ltd v McCutcheon*,[156] the purpose of the provincial law could be frustrated by any municipal by-laws on the topic. Another way in which the question has been approached has been for the courts to consider whether municipal laws touching on mining or on aggregate extraction are laws about "the use of the land" at all; if they are not about the use of land, then there is no municipal jurisdiction, since the by-law-making power is generally set out in the governing legislation in terms referring to regulation of "the use of land." Thus, in *Annapolis (County) v Hankinson*,[157] a quarry was not seen as a use of land. Cases have, however, gone both ways on this point. In an important case, *Squamish (District) v Great Pacific Pumice Inc*,[158] the British Columbia Court of Appeal saw the province's mining laws as compatible with municipal zoning; it rejected claims that the mining laws were a complete code or that there was direct conflict. It said, "[to] begin with the view the mining regime must take precedence over the local government regime is to give precedence where the legislature stated none. To construe the phrase 'mines or minerals' to include all mining activities on the surface of land is to preclude any municipal control over mining activity within its boundaries, and to do indirectly that which the legislature chose not to do directly."[159]

> Simply put, the *Mineral Tenure Act* and the *Mines Act* . . . do not require the respondent to offend the appellant's by-law . . . . The by-law is one more regulation with which a miner must comply if he wishes to exercise surface rights derived from a mineral lease. Because there is no conflict between the surface right the appellant seeks to exercise and the appellant's by-law, of the sort that makes impossible

155 See, for example, Joint Review Panel, *Environmental Assessment of the White's Point Quarry and Marine Terminal Project: Joint Review Panel Report* (Ottawa: Joint Review Panel, 2007), online: www.novascotia.ca/nse/ea/whitespointquarry/WhitesPointQuarryFinalReport/pdf.

156 [1982] 2 SCR 161.

157 2002 NSSC 149.

158 2003 BCCA 404.

159 *Ibid* at para 47.

compliance with both enactments, the provincial legislation presents no impediment to the enforcement of the zoning by-law.[160]

To a similar effect is *Cowichan Valley (Regional District) v Cobble Hill Holdings Ltd*,[161] where the municipality was able to enforce land-use by-laws against operating a landfill or contaminated waste facility for a provincially licensed quarry site that had permits to bring in the disputed materials.

Even if a municipality has no direct jurisdiction over aggregate extraction, some of its rules of general application may still apply. The powers to control traffic, including designation of haulage routes, or noise, or to limit or license soil removal may all become relevant. As with the exercise of all municipal powers, there must be a proper purpose and no bad faith; thus new rules adopted after a quarry has been proposed or established that are clearly related to that enterprise and intended to frustrate it might well be set aside by the courts as improperly motivated. There is some indication that a general soil removal control by-law will be seen as capable of coexisting with provincial mining control laws;[162] the by-law defined "soils" as "clay, silt, sand, gravel, cobbles, boulders, peat or other substance of which land is naturally composed, down to and including bedrock." In British Columbia, municipal soil removal control laws must be approved by the Minister of Energy, Mines and Petroleum Resources.[163]

I. FORESTRY AND TREES

As with mining, forestry is a significant component of the Canadian economy. Forested land covers about half of the national landmass, upwards of 300 million hectares, almost all of which is Crown land. It is a basic component of the provincial economies of British Columbia, Ontario, Quebec, and New Brunswick.[164] Ontario's *Crown Forest Sustainability Act, 2004*[165] is the framework legislation for Crown land available for forest activities. Cases have examined such matters as its interaction

160 *Ibid* at paras 63–64.

161 2016 BCSC 489.

162 See *Loucks v Abbotsford (City)*, 2006 BCSC 1859.

163 See *Brouwer v British Columbia (Minister of Energy, Mines and Petroleum Resources)*, 2002 BCCA 511 (in chambers).

164 See Michel Charron, "Sustainable Forest Management in Canada," Library of Parliament PRB 05-13E (2005), online: Parliamentary Research Division www.lop.parl.gc.ca/content/lop/ResearchPublications/prb0513-e.pdf.

165 SO 1994, c 25.

with Aboriginal interests,[166] environmental assessment,[167] and endangered species.[168] In British Columbia, the *Forest Act*[169] and the *Forest Practices Code of British Columbia Act*[170] govern logging on Crown land. Given the enormous extent of provincial Crown land in British Columbia, these statutes are of the greatest importance.[171]

Forestry activities may be regulated by the province on private land,[172] but for the most part, the thrust of forestry regulation is to control licensed harvesting on Crown land. Localized regulation of tree cutting tends to be left to municipalities.[173]

A variety of factors interact: overall planning for use, protection of land as species habitat, respect for Aboriginal interests, long-term harvest sustainability, and the regulation of harvesting. To some extent the nature of the intended end uses influence all of the listed factors. Thus, pulp and paper, wood chips, lumber, and biomass for energy generation are all end uses that lead to decisions about where harvesting will be permitted (which implies road-building), annual allowable cut, methods of harvesting (e.g., clear-cutting, shelter harvest), and interaction with watercourses or wetlands. Overall, sustainability is a major aim of public policy,[174] motivated by support for an ongoing forestry industry and now bolstered by increased understanding of forests as ecosystems.[175] Additional concerns are fires and insect pests.

166 *Keewatin v Ontario (Minister of Natural Resources)*, 2006 CanLII 35625 (Ont SCJ).

167 *Guindon v Ontario (Minister of Natural Resources)*, 2006 CanLII 2051 (Ont Div Ct).

168 *Wildlands League and Federation of Ontario Naturalists v Lieutenant Governor in Council*, 2015 ONSC 2942.

169 RSBC 1996, c 157.

170 RSBC 1996, c 159.

171 See Monique Ross, *A History of Forest Legislation in Canada, 1867–1996*, Occasional Paper No 2 (Calgary: Canadian Institute of Resources Law, 1997), online: http://prism.ucalgary.ca/jspui/bitstream/1880/47210/1/OP02History.pdf.

172 See, for example, *Private Managed Forest Land Act*, SBC 2003, c 80, which establishes a property tax reduction as an inducement for private woodlot owners to adopt silviculture plans, and ousts local government jurisdiction "that would have the effect of restricting a forest management activity" (s 21).

173 For a review of municipal regulation of trees, see Eran Kaplinsky, "Private Tree Protection Bylaws: In the Public Interest?" in Smit & Valiante, eds, *Public Interest, Private Property*, above note 83 at 195. Violation of tree-cutting by-laws can lead to substantial fines: see *Mike Safronick Tree Care Ltd v Vancouver (City)*, 2011 BCSC 1599.

174 See, for example, Martin Luckert et al, *Policies for Sustainably Managing Canada's Forests: Tenure, Stumpage Fees, and Forest Practices* (Vancouver: UBC Press, 2011).

175 See, for example, M Patricia Marchak, *Logging the Globe* (Montreal: McGill-Queens University Press, 1995); Herb Hammond, *Seeing the Forest among the Trees: The Case for Ecosystem-based Conservation Planning* (Vancouver: Polestar, 1991); Jeremy Wilson, *Talk and Log: Wilderness Politics in British Columbia, 1965–96* (Vancouver: UBC Press, 1998).

The main instrument for control is private forest tenure on Crown land.[176] Tenure arrangements are contracts to allow harvesting subject to legislation and the contract's terms, including the obligation to pay stumpage fees.[177] Although the particulars vary from province to province, tenure arrangements tend to be classified as large, medium, and small, with the main differences having to do with size of area made available and duration, ranging from five years, to ten to fifteen years, to twenty-five years.[178]

Given the centrality of allowable annual cut (AAC) as a point of departure for overall activity, the term tends to be less well defined than it might be. Its components are specified (e.g., sustained yield, estimates of growth rates, silviculture activity, losses due to fire)[179] but such components necessarily imply estimates. The various aspects, and their application to particular tenures, have been litigated.[180]

David Boyd's article, "Seeing the Forest through the Trees,"[181] discusses interim injunctions in forestry disputes. In *Caddy Lake Cottagers Assn v Florence-Nora Access Road Inc*,[182] an injunction was granted to prohibit the construction of a road on the basis that "Damages will not compensate for a destroyed forest." The case is one of several in which the difficulty of obtaining an interim injunction in natural resources matters has somewhat moderated in recent years. The interim injunction granted regarding proposed logging in Clayoquot Sound[183] illustrates the issues:

> If an injunction prevents MacMillan Bloedel from logging pending the trial and it is decided that MacMillan Bloedel has the right to log, the timber will still be there. The position of the Indians is quite different .... The forest that the Indians know and use will be permanently destroyed .... If logging proceeds and it turns out that the Indians

---

176 For a review of British Columbia's elaborate system of regulation of forest uses, see M Haddock et al, "Guide to Forest Land Use Planning" (Vancouver: West Coast Environmental Law Research Foundation, 1999).

177 Ross, above note 171 at 4.

178 MK Luckert & FJ Salkie, "Forestry in Canada: Transitions and Emerging Policy Issues" (1998) 24 *Canadian Public Policy* S1.

179 See, for example, *The Forest Resources Management Act*, SS 1996, c F-19.1, ss 13–15; *Forest Resources Management Regulations*, RRS c F-19.1 Reg 1, ss 4 & 5.

180 See, for example, *British Columbia (Minister of Forests) v Canadian Forest Products Ltd*, 2000 BCCA 456 as to stumpage appraisal; *Sierra Club of Western Canada v British Columbia (Chief Forester)*, 1993 CanLII 1858 (BCSC) as to how sustainability is accounted for in the AAC; *Western Canada Wilderness Committee v British Columbia (Chief Forester)*, 1996 CanLII 3588 (BCSC) as to AAC and owl habitat.

181 (2001) 38 *Canadian Environmental Law Reports (New Series)* 61.

182 (1998), 126 Man R (2d) 230 (CA).

183 *MacMillan Bloedel Ltd v Mullin*, [1985] 3 WWR 577 (BCCA).

> have the right to the area with the trees standing, it will no longer be possible to give them that right. The area will have been logged. The courts will not be able to do justice in the circumstances.[184]

As with mining, when Crown land is reassigned a use that results in termination of a licensed forestry activity, for example when it is designated as park or wilderness, issues of compensation arise. Richard Schwindt, author of a report on this issue for the British Columbia government,[185] has said that "Through its allocation of private rights to public resources the Crown has created expectations backed by investments. As a result, the owners of mineral and timber interests should be compensated when these interests are taken for a public purpose."[186] This view has been seriously contested by an array of environmental organizations, which distinguish between those rights that have vested and those that are contingent on future government approval, with compensation to be paid only in the former case, and on a carefully calculated basis.[187] Compensation for infrastructure, as land is set aside for parks and protected areas, was provided for in the Ontario 1999 Forest Accord.[188] The West Coast Environmental Law Association has pointed out that the government's focus on compensation only for industrial interests is misplaced:

> . . . there are other resource compensation issues . . . that require immediate attention. Chief among these is the paucity of practicable, reasonable procedures for compensating holders of private interests, such as individuals, landowners, water licensees, trapline holders, guide-outfitter licensees and aboriginal interest-holders, who suffer damage as a result of the activities of the forestry or mining industries . . . .[189]

---

184 *Ibid* at 591–92.

185 British Columbia, Commission of Inquiry into Compensation for the Taking of Resource Interests, *Report of the Commission of Inquiry into Compensation for the Taking of Resource Interests*, by Richard Schwindt (Vancouver: The Commission, 1992), online: www.for.gov.bc.ca/hfd/library/documents/bib2241.pdf.

186 *Ibid* at 147. See also Richard Schwindt & Steven Globerman, "Taking of Private Rights to Public Natural Resources: a Policy Analysis" (1996) 22 *Canadian Public Policy* 205; Nigel Bankes, "Ethics and Resource Takings: The Schwindt Report" (1993) 41 *Resources* 1.

187 See Gregory J McDade on behalf of Sierra Legal Defence Fund et al, "Report on Compensation Issues Concerning Protected Areas" (March 1993), online: www.for.gov.bc.ca/hfd/library/documents/bib66565.pdf.

188 Ontario Ministry of Natural Resources (March 1999), online: www.ontla.on.ca/library/repository/mon/3000/10300145.pdf.

189 William J Andrews for West Coast Environmental Law Association, "Comments on the 'Schwindt Report'" (12 February 1993), online: www.wcel.org/sites/default/files/publications/Comments%20on%20the%20Schwindt%20Report.pdf.

In *Denman Island Local Trust Committee v 4064 Investments Ltd*,[190] at issue was whether the trust (essentially the municipal government for the island[191]) was empowered to regulate tree cutting or forest practices on private land in light of the existence of a provincial regulatory scheme set out in the *Forest Land Reserve Act*.[192] The court found that the trust's power to regulate land use, including environmental matters, could not extend to preventing the general removal of trees without a permit since the local government powers existed in a context of a provincial scheme of forest management; the local powers were limited to protecting sensitive areas (prone to flooding, soil erosion, avalanche). The case is useful as offering an overview of the forestry regulatory laws in British Columbia.

Urban forests were formerly specified as a jurisdictional power for Ontario municipalities. Now, under the spheres of jurisdiction approach, "environmental well-being" is identified as a power,[193] supplemented by a power for local municipalities to "prohibit or regulate the destruction or injuring of trees"[194] and for upper-tier municipalities to do the same for "woodlands" that are one hectare or more in area, and in so doing they "shall have regard to good forestry practices as defined in the *Forestry Act*."[195] The result is probably as set out in the *Denman* case.

J. ENERGY

Canada has added energy to its traditional production and export of natural resources such as minerals, timber, and food. Regulation of energy is a constitutionally entangled matter, with both federal and provincial jurisdiction. Basically, international and interprovincial energy matters are regulated federally, but intraprovincial energy infrastructure is regulated by each province, including ownership of underground coal, oil, and gas.[196] This has meant a provincial focus on fossil fuel generation facilities, dams, and other hydroelectric generation, along with transmission lines, and oil and gas extraction, although some of these

190 2001 BCCA 736 [*Denman*].

191 See *Islands Trust Act*, RSBC 1996, c 239.

192 RSBC 1996, c 158 (repealed).

193 *Municipal Act, 2001*, SO 2001, c 25, as amended, s 11(1)(5).

194 *Ibid*, s 135(1). For a discussion, see Kaplinsky, above note 173.

195 Above note 193, ss 135(2), (3), and (5).

196 Offshore rights are not addressed in these comments. For such cases, see *Reference Re: Ownership of Offshore Mineral Rights (British Columbia)*, [1967] SCR 792; *Reference re: Continental Shelf*, [1984] 1 SCR 86; *Reference re: Ownership of the Bed of the Strait of Georgia and Related Areas*, [1984] 1 SCR 388.

projects trigger both federal and provincial EA and permitting processes. The main policy issue is the interaction of energy supplies in support of modern life with their adverse health effects and negative environmental impacts. As a nation, we use large amounts of energy, much of it fossil-fuel based. We have also experienced coal-mining illnesses and deaths, oil spills, acid rain damage to watercourses and buildings, smog, and accidents that have involved explosions such as the Lac-Mégantic event. The main legal policy issues have to do with demarcation of lines of jurisdiction between the federal and provincial governments, and, for provincial matters, whether there are specific assigned powers for local governments or implied room for their exercise of power.

1) Electricity Infrastructure

The main utility regulated by the provinces is that which establishes its electricity system. Its generation, transmission, and distribution are the fundamental components. Because of electricity's central importance to the day-to-day functioning of our lives, this is a major public policy matter. So, too, as a source of government income, all aspects of the electricity enterprise is closely watched. As a land-user, electrical utilities are important: they require large corridors plus routes for delivery. Whether publicly or privately owned, they are usually granted expropriation powers and rights of placement of associated infrastructure.[197] In *Grey Highlands (Municipality) v Plateau Wind Inc*,[198] the Ontario Energy Board had made a determination that the company was an electricity "distributor." The consequence was that it was enabled to build its distribution system facilities on municipally owned road allowances. This is an example of a provincially regulated land-use scheme overriding local jurisdiction.

2) Dams

Canada has a significant number of dams associated with our major rivers—there are almost 1,000 large dams.[199] The Canadian Dam Association (CDA) says "Canada is now the world's biggest producer of hydro power." Not all dams are for generation of hydro power; some function

197 See, for example, *Power Corporation Act*, RSS 1978, c P-19, s 14 for a publicly owned utility, and *Nova Scotia Power Privatization Act*, SNS 1992, c 8, s 19 for a privately owned utility.

198 2012 ONSC 1001 (Div Ct).

199 See Canadian Dam Association, online: www.imis100ca1.ca/cda. The CDA publishes "Dam Safety Guidelines" and "Application of Dam Safety Guidelines to Mining Dams" as well as various technical bulletins.

to provide flood protection and/or irrigation and/or municipal water supply. A partial list, with the rivers or basins is: Alameda (Souris), Beauharnois (St Lawrence), WAC Bennett (Peace), Bersimis (Bersimis), Big Horn (North Saskatchewan), Caniapiscau (Caniapiscau), Churchill Falls (Churchill), Daniel Johnson (Manicouagan), Gardiner (South Saskatchewan), Keeyask (Nelson), Kemano (Nechako), Kettle Rapids (Nelson), La Grande (La Grande), Long Spruce (Nelson), Mactaquac (Saint John), Manicouagan (Manicouagan), Mica (Columbia), Old Man River (Old Man River), Qu'Appelle (Qu'Appelle), Revelstoke (Columbia), Robert Bourassa (La Grande), and Sir Adam Beck (Niagara). Regulation is generally under a *Water* or *Water Security Act* (British Columbia, Alberta, Saskatchewan, Manitoba, New Brunswick, and Newfoundland and Labrador) or under a *Mines Act* (British Columbia, Ontario, and Quebec). Dams are subject to environmental assessment.

Among the most serious problems associated with dams has been that of mercury in food fish, discovered after the Churchill River diversion was constructed. Flooding converted mercury to methylmercury, a toxic substance that bioaccumulates in fish. Aboriginal people were the most affected. Dams have been challenged as not effective in delivering some of their claimed benefits in controlling floods and providing water for irrigation, as well as being the source of environmental damage.[200] Still, formal environmental assessments have tended to offer approval of dam projects. Thus, the Report of the Joint Federal-Provincial Review Panel for Nalcor's Lower Churchill Generation Project in Newfoundland and Labrador[201] identified both adverse environmental effects as well as socio-economic benefits and made recommendations for mitigation changes.[202]

3) Oil and Gas

Carbon-based fuels remain central to energy and the economy. Most vehicles operate on them, and a significant portion of electricity is generated from them. A significant amount is exported, requiring pipelines. Thus, their extraction and transportation represent a major land use. Inter-

---

200 Edward Goldsmith & Nicholas Hildyard, *The Social and Environmental Effects of Large Dams* (San Francisco: Sierra Club Books, 1984).

201 This addressed the Muskrat Falls and Gull Island proposed dams and associated infrastructure, online: www.ceaa.gc.ca/050/documents/53120/53120E.pdf.

202 See "Government of Canada Response to the Report of the Joint Federal-Provincial Review Panel for Nalcor's Lower Churchill Generation project in Newfoundland and Labrador" online: www.ceaa-acee.gc.ca/050/documents/54772/54772E.pdf.

national and interprovincial pipelines are regulated federally. Provincial jurisdiction is focused on exploration and extraction, and intraprovincial infrastructure.[203] Fingarson and Shouldice are somewhat sanguine about the industry, saying "the oil and gas industry . . . is materially different from forestry in its effects on land use. Many oil and gas operations are compatible with ecosystem preservation goals."[204] This is a highly contested assertion, and leaves out of account the effects of fracking, release of methane, accidents, and the use of the products themselves.

The duty to consult Aboriginal peoples is an especially important factor, applying to all levels of government.[205]

In Ontario, natural gas storage and safety were matters formerly exclusively regulated by the province. In *Superior Propane Inc v York (City)*,[206] the core issue was the interaction of provincial and municipal regulatory rules affecting the storage of natural gas. Commercial gas storage sites often exist in populated areas. York had adopted by-laws to regulate the capacity, height, spacing, and buffering of such tanks. Their by-laws were challenged by the company because the topic was regulated by the province under the *Energy Act*. The Court of Appeal said: "the *Energy Act* and the regulation enacted under it, contain a comprehensive scheme to regulate propane dispensing, installation, handling, and storage, and . . . these matters are not subject to legislative authority by municipalities."[207] Nonetheless, the court still looked at details of "operative conflict" rather than relying only on the notion of a general provincial intent to occupy the field. Operative conflict was the test adopted by the Supreme Court of Canada in *Spraytech*.[208] Environmental lawyer, now Ontario's Environmental Commissioner, Dianne Saxe, has written that "*Superior Propane* may not still be the law. Now that municipalities have more powers and more respect from the courts, and now that propane facilities are self-regulated . . . instead of regulated by the province, could and should municipalities wade back into the business of regulating safety?"[209] Under the *Technical Standards*

203 For a useful overview, see John Fingarson & Robert Shouldice, "The Oil & Gas Industry and Land Use Issues in British Columbia" (1994) 32 *Alberta Law Review* 203.

204 *Ibid* at 204.

205 See Heather L Treacy et al, "The Current State of the Law in Canada on Crown Obligations to Consult and Accommodate Aboriginal Interests in Resource Development" (2007) 44 *Alberta Law Review* 571.

206 (1995), 27 MPLR (2d) 1 (Ont CA).

207 *Ibid* at 3.

208 Above note 2.

209 Dianne Saxe, "Sunrise Propane Explosion: What Should Municipalities Do?" (November 2008) *Municipal World* 65.

and Safety Act, 2000,[210] risk and safety management plans are to be prepared for the province, including hazard distances, although minor variances may be made by municipal committees, and municipal jurisdiction is also engaged for subdivisions and other approvals.[211]

4) Hydraulic Fracturing

Fracking[212] has emerged as a method to extract gas, especially from underground formations that do not lend themselves to traditional drilling methods. It has been in commercial use since 1949 and become common in recent decades. A major US case, which determined that fracking so as to extract gas from underneath another's property is not a trespass as the concept has developed in Texas in the context of energy law,[213] described fracking thus:

> This is done by pumping fluid down a well at high pressure so that it is forced out into the [rock or sandstone] formation. The pressure creates cracks in the rock that propagate along the azimuth of natural fault lines in an elongated elliptical pattern in opposite directions from the well. Behind the fluid comes a slurry containing small granules called proppants—sand, ceramic beads, or bauxite are used—that lodge themselves in the cracks, propping them open against the enormous subsurface pressure that would force them shut as soon as the fluid was gone. The fluid is then drained, leaving the cracks open for gas or oil to flow to the wellbore. Fracking in effect increases the well's exposure to the formation, allowing greater production.

Concerns over amount of water to be used, the possibility of inducing seismic events, the possibility of pollution of groundwater, and disposal of fracking wastes have led to controversy. Fracking is widely used in the United States, and also to some extent in Canada. It is being studied in various jurisdictions, including Nova Scotia, British Columbia, Quebec,

---

210 SO 2000, c 16.

211 *Ibid*, ss 6, 33, 34, 39, and 45. See *Propane Storage and Handling*, O Reg 211/01; *Minor Variance Applications*, O Reg 200/96; *Official Plans and Plan Amendments*, O Reg 543/06; *Plans of Subdivision*, O Reg 544/06; *Zoning By-laws, Holding By-laws and Interim Control By-laws*, O Reg 545/06.

212 See Donald N Zillman et al, eds, *The Law of Energy Underground* (Oxford: Oxford University Press, 2014); Kevin Luft et al, "Regulatory and Liability Issues in Horizontal Multistage Fracturing" (2012) 50 *Alberta Law Review* 403; Nigel Bankes, "Non-Conventional Oil and Gas Reserves and the Legal Issues Associated with Hydraulic Fracturing in Canada" (2013) 15 *International Environmental and Resource Law Committee Newsletter* 4.

213 *Coastal Oil & Gas Corp v Garza Energy Trust*, 268 SW3d 1 (Tex 2008).

Alberta, and Ontario.[214] There are de facto moratoriums in New Brunswick, Newfoundland and Labrador, and Quebec.[215] Nova Scotia has banned the importation of fracking wastewater.[216] Examples of earthquakes caused by fracking, as in British Columbia,[217] raise questions of possible lawsuits, perhaps based in the Rule in *Rylands v Fletcher.* (The United Kingdom has recently expanded fracking opportunities to allow it under national parks, that is, to angle in from outside at a depth of at least 1.2 kilometres, and also to allow it under private homes.[218]) It is reasonable to expect fracking cases to go before the courts. So far there have been few, and the one most directly dealing with alleged injury, *Ernst v EnCana Corp*,[219] has at this time dealt only with preliminary matters.[220] In *British Columbia (Oil and Gas Commission) v Western Canada Wilderness Committee*,[221] it was determined that the commission could issue recurrent short-term approvals for fracking under the *Water Act*.

5) Carbon Capture and Storage

Carbon capture and storage (CCS) is a technology often associated with what is called "clean coal," though it is also applicable to emissions of CO_2 from other carbon energy sources, especially natural gas. In a

214 See, for example, Alberta Energy Resources Conservation Board, "Discussion Paper: Unconventional Gas Regulatory Framework—Jurisdictional Review" Report 2011-A (28 January 2012); Nova Scotia Departments of Energy and Environment, "Jurisdictional Review of Hydraulic Fracturing Regulation" (Report for Nova Scotia Hydraulic Fracturing Review Committee) (2012).

215 The New Brunswick Commission on Hydraulic Fracturing has reported, and the activity is unlikely to proceed in that province; see "Supporters, Opponents Doubt Fracking Will Come to NB after Report" *CBC News* (26 February 2016), online: www.cbc.ca/1.3466309. Moratoriums also exist in Scotland and Wales. See Dr Ray Gosine (Chair), Newfoundland and Labrador Hydraulic Fracturing Review Panel Report, *Unconventional Opportunities & Challenges: Results of the Public Review of the Implications of Hydraulic Fracturing Operations in Western Newfoundland* by Dr Ray Gosine, Chair (31 May 2016), online: http://nlhfrp.ca/wp-content/uploads/2016/05/Executive-Summary.pdf.

216 *Importation of Hydraulic Fracturing Wastewater Prohibition Act*, SNS 2013, c 36.

217 Betsy Trumpener, "Earthquake in Northern BC Caused by Fracking, Says Regulator" *CBC News* (16 December 2015), online: www.cbc.ca/1.3367081.

218 Damian Carrington, "Fracking Will Be Allowed under National Parks, UK Decides" *The Guardian* (12 February 2015).

219 2014 ABQB 672.

220 For an exploration of the circumstances, see Andrew Nikiforuk, *Slick Water* (Vancouver: Greystone, 2016). For a review of fracking litigation, see Wally Braul et al, "Water Use Challenges to Oil and Gas Developments" (2015) 53 *Alberta Law Review* 323.

221 2014 BCSC 1919.

leader in *The Economist*, the process is described: "There does, however, seem to be a way of reconciling coal and climate. It is called carbon capture and storage (CCS) or carbon sequestration, and entails hoovering up carbon dioxide from the smokestacks of power plants and other big industrial facilities and storing it safely underground, where it will have no effect on the atmosphere."[222] It is far from clear that CCS is an economical or effective technology.[223] Pilot projects are underway.

6) Uranium

The use of nuclear material for any purpose is regulated federally, but its mining is regulated provincially. The provinces, as owners or regulators of electricity generation facilities, are also able to determine whether to use nuclear materials for that purpose. New Brunswick (Point Lepreau), Quebec (Gentilly), and Ontario (Bruce, Darlington, and Pickering) have nuclear-powered plants. Nuclear energy represents some 15 percent of Canada's electricity and some 60 percent of Ontario's.[224] Mining is carried out only in Saskatchewan. It is banned in Nova Scotia. Issues of nuclear waste and long-term disposal are managed federally.

7) Solar and Wind

There are serious reasons that are leading to a global shift towards renewables as a source of electrical energy, and a diminishing role for fossil-fuel use. Climate change has been the main driver, but so too has negative health effects of emissions. Energy from solar panels and wind turbines is relatively expensive, and is intermittent, but is becoming more widely used. How are they to be accommodated?[225]

Installations are subject to formal environmental assessment. Issues raised range from noise, to flicker, to blade throw, to electromagnetic interference, to avian mortalities. Aesthetics is a matter that has also been raised as a concern. Setback distances from surrounding uses, especially residences, are frequently raised as an issue. In *Huron-Kinloss (Township) Official Plan (Re)*,[226] the OMB refused to increase the set-

---

222 "The Illusion of Clean Coal" *The Economist* (5 March 2009) 20, online: http://econ.st/JwOJSV. See also "Trouble in Store," *ibid* at 74, online: http://econ.st/JwOVSh.

223 See James Meadowcroft & Oluf Langhelle, eds, *Catching the Carbon: The Politics and Policy of Carbon Capture and Storage* (Northampton, MA: Edward Elgar, 2009).

224 Canadian Nuclear Association, online: https://cna.ca/.

225 See Nickie Vlavianos, "The Regulation of Wind Power in Alberta: The Case of Municipalities" (2011) 22 *Journal of Environmental Law and Practice* 125.

226 (2004), 48 OMBR 439.

back distance from the prevailing 400 to 700 metres to a requested 1,200 metres, saying the increase was not supported by the evidence. In *Dixon v Ontario (Director, Ministry of Environment)*,[227] permits for three wind farms had been appealed unsuccessfully to the provincial Environment Review Tribunal (ERT); a further appeal to the courts found that the ERT had appropriately applied the tests as to "serious harm to human health" that controlled the situation.[228] In *Hanna v Ontario (Attorney General)*,[229] an attempt was made to challenge the minimum setback requirements established for wind turbines on the basis of the precautionary principle; the court found that the principle was one of a series of considerations applicable to the setting of setbacks and did not trump the other principles.

In addition to the EA process, land-use appeals may be available. In a 2006 Nova Scotia case, the concerns about a proposed development were rejected as part of a preliminary determination of standing: in *Re Milner*,[230] the appellant owned property 2.5 and 4 kilometres from the site proposed to be developed as a wind farm, distances the board saw as sufficiently removed from the site as not to amount to the appellant having a *bona fide* (i.e., objective) reason to believe the use and value of his land would be negatively affected. In *Canadian Hydro Developers, Inc v Amaranth (Township)*,[231] the town refused to adopt an amendment to its OP and LUB so as to accommodate a 23-unit wind farm, and was upheld by the board on the basis of reasonable concerns over noise, even in the face of the Provincial Policy Statement supporting development of renewables. In *Huron-Kinloss (Township) Official Plan (Re)*,[232] the board saw a 1,200-metre setback requirement as excessive.

Solar may be seen as having two possible formations: small-scale, individual building-based installations, and also larger-scale installations. Both are for the generation of electricity (called "solar thermal" or "photovoltaics"), while solar energy may also be used for the immediate generation of hot water and space heating ("solar hot water"); the technologies are similar but distinct: solar hot water is practical only for very local use. The main policy issue is whether a province should put in place laws that guarantee ongoing protection for solar installations, especially rooftop panels. The Saskatchewan Law Reform Commission

---

227 2014 ONSC 7404 [*Dixon*].

228 *Dixon* also examines the *Green Energy Act* and section 7 of the *Charter*.

229 2011 ONSC 609 (Div Ct).

230 2006 NSUARB 102.

231 (2008), 59 OMBR 229.

232 Above note 226.

has studied the matter, issuing a good report in 2007, "Background Paper: Solar Access Legislation":[233]

> Solar access legislation is intended to ensure that a property owner's access to sunlight for solar energy generation will not be jeopardized by development on a neighbouring property. Such legislation has been widely adopted in the United States . . . . The [Prebble] Report[234] suggests that "solar energy will be an important component of building construction in the future. Moreover, commercial and residential building owners are going to install solar technology in existing homes."
>
> Because of the high cost of photovoltaic panels to produce electrical power directly from sunlight, large-scale solar generation of electrical power is not currently as attractive as alternative energy sources such as wind farms. There is, however, potential for small-scale solar power generation for individual residences and commercial buildings. Residential solar power installations have a small footprint and can typically be installed on roofs of existing buildings. In the near future, the Report suggests that solar hot water and space heating systems will likely be more popular than electrical power generation. Water is heated by pumping it through a rooftop heat collector . . . .
>
> If homeowners and businesses invest in solar energy systems, they need assurance that future development on neighbouring properties will not block access to sunlight. Saskatchewan legislation does not explicitly deal with solar access. At present, the only practical way to ensure access to sunlight is by negotiation of agreements with neighbouring landowners. Such agreements could be registered in the Land Titles Office as easements, which would be binding on future owners of the neighbouring properties. However, under the existing law, even a long established solar installation has no protection in the absence of an easement.
>
> Advocates suggest that solar access legislation would protect the investment and effort of property owners who install solar energy systems. Because typical solar installations are placed on the roofs of residential or commercial buildings, problems of solar access as neighbouring properties are developed or re-developed can be expected to be frequent . . . .

---

233 Law Reform Commission of Saskatchewan, "Background Paper: Solar Access Legislation" (October 2007), online: http://lawreformcommission.sk.ca/LRCSolarAccess.pdf.

234 Saskatchewan, Legislative Secretary for Renewable Energy Development and Conservation, *Prebble Report on Renewable Energy and Conservation in Saskatchewan*, by Peter Prebble (Regina: Crown Investments Corporation, 2006) at 43–44.

However, protection of solar access has detriments as well as benefits. If the law protects a right to sunlight in the absence of an agreement with neighbouring property owners, it places limits on the rights of land owners to use and develop their property. Limitations on land use are of course a well established part of land use planning, particularly through municipal zoning bylaws. Limitations are deemed to be justified to protect both the interests of neighbours, and the wider public good. Trade-offs between the rights of a land owner and the rights of neighbours are inevitably required. The challenge for policymakers is to find the appropriate balance between the rights of owners of solar installations and their neighbours.

The balance point depends on the relative importance of the competing interests of property owners who install solar energy installations and their neighbours. Because solar energy installations are to be expected to become much more common, and because of the social value attached to alternative energy sources, advocates of solar access legislation argue that the equation is changing. From a strictly legal perspective, shifting the balance toward greater protection for access to sunlight would not represent a novel departure from the principles that govern relations between neighbouring property owners . . . .

Solar access legislation might include:

1. Clarification and extension of the law governing the grant of solar access easements . . . .
2. Creation of rights to solar access by operation of law when no easement has been negotiated and registered . . . .
3. Permits for solar access . . . .
4. Zoning for solar access . . . .

How far it is appropriate to shift the balance in favour of protecting solar access is a question of policy. This paper identifies, but does not resolve, the policy issues.[235]

8) Geothermal

Geothermal energy is regulated in some provinces. Primarily, the statutes designate geothermal as a form of clean or renewable energy. British Columbia has a *Geothermal Resources Act*[236] and also lists geothermal as a renewable under its *Clean Energy Act*.[237] Nova Scotia designates

235 *Ibid* at 2–5.
236 RSBC 1996, c 171.
237 SBC 2010, c 22.

certain areas as "geothermal resource areas"' under the *Mineral Resources Act*. Ontario includes geothermal as a form of renewable energy under its *Green Energy Act, 2009*.[238] Alberta, Manitoba, Quebec, and Newfoundland and Labrador also make some provisions for regulation.

Geothermal means a form of energy in which heat is extracted from the ground or from water, or both, and may be small-scale in that it serves only one residential building or site, or larger in that it serves commercial or industrial buildings or sites. Since 1988, Springhill, Nova Scotia, has extracted heat from flooded former coal mines and uses it to serve an industrial park. The basic mechanism is of a heat pump. The Nova Scotia legislation defines "geothermal resource" as "a substance, including steam, water and water vapor that is found anywhere below the surface of the earth and that derives an added value from the natural heat of the earth present in, resulting from or created by the earth."[239] British Columbia's *Geothermal Resources Act* has a similar definition.

There is no obvious intent to share jurisdiction with local governments. Thus, the British Columbia legislation states, "The right, title and interest in all geothermal resources in British Columbia are vested in and reserved to the government and the government may dispose of them only under this Act."[240] Such a provision may be read as establishing title vis-à-vis private owners of surface land, but may also be intended to have a wider ambit. Cases involving geothermal energy have had to do with disputes over construction and not whether local governments have any residual jurisdiction.[241] Indeed, municipalities have been licensees under the provincial laws.[242] There may be some local jurisdiction as administrators of building code standards, or an ability to require renewable energy as part of development agreements. Despite the point not being specifically addressed in provincial legislation, local governments may be able to set stricter standards, or require use of renewable energy such as geothermal, under the principles that were set out in *Spraytech*,[243] *Darvonda*,[244] and *Merzetti*.[245]

---

238 SO 2009, c 12, Sch A.

239 *Mineral Resources Act*, SNS 1990, c 18, s 2(ha).

240 Above note 236, s 2.

241 See, for example, *Water Shed Conditioning Ltd v Bird Construction Ltd*, 2015 NSSM 38, having to do with installation of a large geothermal field to service a new correctional facility.

242 See, for example, *Re Springhill (Town)*, 2015 NSUARB 12.

243 Above note 2.

244 Above note 33.

245 Above note 33.

K. HUNTING, FISHING, AND TRAPPING

The active search for food (and in the case of trapping, of pelts) is a tradition emanating from a regard of animals as a common resource, to be available for all-comers. It was a necessity for Indigenous peoples and was taken up by European settlers. It remains a valued activity. It is, however, now strictly regulated as to licensing and location, including through the laws of trespass. This is so although some of the largest provinces—Ontario, Quebec, and British Columbia—have adopted "right to hunt" laws. The right to hunt laws are more symbolic than executory; they declare "a person has the right to hunt and fish in accordance with the law."[246]

The existing laws require licensing, and prescribe training, age limits, place restrictions, times of day and of year, types of weapons, dress, and what animals may be hunted. In most provinces, hunting and fishing are subject to private property rights. However, in Nova Scotia, anglers are entitled to cross private property to access fishing places: under the *Angling Act*,

> Any resident of the Province shall have the right to go on foot along the banks of any river, stream or lake, upon and across any uncultivated lands and Crown lands for the purpose of lawfully fishing with rod and line in such rivers, streams or lakes . . . . The rights conferred . . . shall not in any way limit or restrict the right of any owner . . . to compensation for actual damages caused . . . and shall not be construed to give the right to build any fires upon such lands.[247]

It is not unusual for hunters and anglers to be permitted to enter private property unless posted with signs forbidding them.[248] In New Brunswick, salmon fishing is limited to those owning the land adjacent to the river, thus leading to litigation about ownership.[249]

Updated laws now usually invoke "conservation" as a value. Thus, in Quebec "conservation" is defined as "the pursuit of the optimum natural

---

246 See *Heritage Hunting and Fishing Act, 2002*, SO 2002, c 10; *An act to amend the Act respecting the conservation and development of wildlife*, SQ 2002, c 82; *The Hunting and Fishing Heritage Act*, SBC 2002, c 79. For analysis and commentary, see Vaughan Black, "Rights Gone Wild" (2005) 54 *University of New Brunswick Law Journal* 3.

247 *Angling Act*, SNS 1989, c 14 as amended, s 3.

248 See, for example, *Fish and Wildlife Act*, SNB 1980, c F-14.1, s 80(10).

249 See, for example, *Routh v Bowes* (1983), 47 NBR (2d) 425 (CA); *Quieting of Titles Act (Re)*, 2010 NBQB 428. See the New Brunswick Government's "Fish Book" for details regarding Crown Reserve Waters, private or leased waters, and other rules, online: www2.gnb.ca/content/dam/gnb/Departments/nr-rn/pdf/en/Fish/Fish.pdf.

productivity of all living resources and the protection of the ecological systems . . . ."[250] Trapping, usually also associated with the use of snares, is regulated.[251] Licences are required. For example, in Prince Edward Island, the *Fur Harvesting Regulations* under the *Wildlife Conservation Act*[252] defines a "body-gripping trap," a "box trap," a "foot-encapsulating trap," a "foot-hold trap," a "running pole set," and a "spring pole set," all variants of devices to capture animals. A course of education is required prior to qualification for a licence. Traps are to have identification tags. Seasons are established. Fur-bearing animals are listed. Toothed traps, deadfalls, and hooks are prohibited. According to the Fur Institute of Canada,[253] a fur industry advocacy organization, the most commonly trapped animals are muskrat, beaver, marten, squirrel, and raccoon. Sales of pelts are on the order of $100 million per year. There are about 50,000 active trappers, half of whom are Aboriginal. There exists an Agreement on International Humane Trapping Standards.[254]

L. WATER SYSTEMS, WETLANDS, AND BEACHES

Management of water has diverse aspects.[255] The main anthropomorphic focuses are on drinking water and agricultural purposes, as well as in support of forestry, and in prevention of flooding. Both surface and groundwater are matters of concern.

In the Prairie provinces there exists a Prairie Provinces Water Board, dating from the 1930s, which provides a forum for the governments to discuss equitable sharing of surface water that flows between or among the provinces. The board has no legislative or regulatory powers; it operates on consensus. The flow of water is from west to east. Under a "Master Agreement on Apportionment,"[256] in place since 1969, Al-

250 *An Act Respecting the Hunting and Fishing Rights in the James Bay and New Québec Territories*, CQLR c D-13.1, s 2.

251 This topic is treated apart from fur farming, which is discussed under the heading "Agriculture" in Section G, above in this chapter.

252 RSPEI 1988, c W-4.1; PEI Reg EC663/04.

253 See online: http://fur.ca. There also exists the Fur Council of Canada, which is more focused on the manufacture of fur garments.

254 Available online: www.face.eu/international-agreements/aihts.

255 The provincial jurisdiction is over fresh water, not oceans. For an overview, see, for example, Mark Sproule-Jones, ed, *Canadian Water Politics* (Montreal: McGill-Queens University Press, 2008); Marq De Villiers, *Water: The Fate of Our Most Precious Natural Resource* (Boston: Houghton Mifflin, 2001).

256 Available online: www.ppwb.ca/information/79/index.html.

berta is entitled to net depletion of one-half of the natural flow of water arising in or flowing through the province, Saskatchewan receives the remainder and is entitled to the same net depletion. A similar system exists in the United States, where it is highly contested, especially in current circumstances of water shortages.[257]

Provincial regulation of the safety of drinking water is examined in Chapter 11. National standards, expressed as "guidelines," exist for drinking water: Health Canada's Guidelines for Canadian Drinking Water Quality.[258] The guidelines deal with microbial, chemical, radiological, and aesthetic aspects of quality. Environment Canada also has guidelines as to deleterious substances in drinking water, with many specifics as to particular lakes, rivers, and estuaries. Municipalities are required to protect their water sources through Statements of Provincial Interest or equivalent. Three provinces have legislation governing water quality, and all have subdivision regulations that require testing to ensure there is potable water available as a preliminary to building if lots are not connected to a municipal water supply. Some provincial governments also have established separation distances for agricultural activities.

Most provinces now have legislation to regulate bulk water extraction. Normally, extraction would be a common law right (subject to reasonable limits, not adversely affecting other users). As with other aspects of the common law, regulation introduces some measure of certainty and tends to avoid lawsuits between neighbours. In British Columbia, for example, the *Water Act*[259] first set fees for bulk extraction, including limiting licensing to a term of fifteen years. Subsequently, the *Water Protection Act*[260] limited further issuance of licences, a policy that had been in place since 1991, but at that time implemented through Orders-in-Council.[261]

---

257 See, for example, David Owen, "Where the River Runs Dry" *The New Yorker* (25 May 2015), online:www.newyorker.com/magazine/2015/05/25/the-disappearing-river.

258 Available online: www.hc-sc.gc.ca/ewh-semt/pubs/water-eau/sum_guide-res_recom/index-eng.php.

259 RSBC 1979, c 479.

260 RSBC 1996, c 484.

261 For an account, see *Rain Coast Water Corp v British Columbia*, 2010 BCSC 54. British Columbia also regulates the licensing of water suppliers through its *Drinking Water Protection Act*, SBC 2001, c 9 and *Water Users' Communities Act*, RSBC 1996, c 483. Ontario has proposed a two-year moratorium on new or expanded water-takings from groundwater by bottling companies; see Ministry of the Environment and Climate Change, News Release, "Ontario Taking Action to Protect Clean Water" (17 October 2016).

Wetlands are valued as important ecosystems. All provinces have statutes or regulations to protect them.[262] As illustrated by the decision in *Leblanc v New Brunswick (Minister of Environment)*,[263] the rules are taken seriously. Leblanc owned land fronting on the ocean, which was subject to flooding from storm surge or high tide. He wanted to install a concrete retaining wall, but was refused permission by the Environment Department on the basis that the portion in question was wetland, though not formally designated as such. Two statutory regimes applied: the *Clean Environment* Act[264] and the *Clean Water Act*.[265] The court found that the department could invoke the *Clean Water Act* provision and that the decision was not unreasonable.

Beaches are valued for both private and public use. There is obvious potential for clashes over access as well as issues over removal of sand for commercial or industrial purposes. The more that is learned about the ecosystem of beaches, the more reason there is to protect them. Beaches may be associated with dunes, with marshland, and with habitat for birds and other animals.

There is public ownership of beach area between the high- and low-water marks. This does not always conveniently deal with the problem of access. Often beaches desired for use by the public are incorporated into parks,[266] or are designated as public beaches. Ontario's *Public Lands Act* allows the province to enter into agreements with municipalities for the control and management of beaches.[267] *Mossman v Nova Scotia (Attorney General)*[268] established that the provincial designation of a beach under the *Beaches Act* was a decision that attracted a fairness process for owners of land directly affected. Notification and an opportunity to be heard were seen as required, though the court was not prepared to specify the nature of the opportunity to be heard. Among the consequences of designation are prohibitions on removal of "sand, gravel, stone or other material" as well as limitations on development. Sand (quartz) is in demand for construction purposes such as concrete manufacture or roads and their bases, and for industrial purposes such as abrasives, glass manufacture, or in hydraulic fracturing.

262 See, for example, *Watercourse and Wetland Protection Regulations*, PEI Reg EC720/08; *Environmental Protection and Management Regulation*, BC Reg 200/2010.

263 2007 NBQB 390.

264 RSNB 1973, c C-6, s 6.1(2).

265 SNB 1989, c C-6.1, s 15(1).

266 Parks Acts, such as Ontario's, allow for regulation of activities on beaches.

267 *Public Lands Act*, RSO 1990, c P.43, s 44.

268 (1995), 140 NSR (2d) 321 (SC).

M. HERITAGE

Special heritage protection legislation exists in each province. The regimes have been seen as excluding the use of *Planning Act* or similar powers to designate buildings for heritage protection.[269] Saskatchewan's *The Heritage Property Act*[270] illustrates a typical regime for the protection of heritage property. It allows for both provincial (section 38) and municipal (section 11) designation, with essentially parallel definitions, procedures, and consequences. A notice of intention to consider designation prohibits any alteration, restoration, repair, disturbance, transportation, adding on, change, move, or demolition without written approval (section 23). Owners are to be given notice, and there is to be public notice. A decision to designate is to be recorded in the Land Titles registry (section 11). If advisory committees are created they must be consulted. Designations are subject to appeal (section 14). Grants, loans, tax relief, or other support may be made available (section 28). Both the minister (section 4) and a mayor (section 25) may issue temporary stop orders for up to sixty days if they become aware of anything "likely to result in damage or destruction to any heritage property." Owners may not allow the integrity or existence of designated property to be put in jeopardy through neglect or lack of maintenance; an owner may be ordered to effect repairs, or the government may take the necessary steps itself and recover the cost (section 71). The minister may exempt from designation any property if designation would preclude development that is of major significance and public benefit (section 71). A Heritage Foundation is established (section 5). Individual properties as well as Heritage Conservation Districts may be designated (section 11). Designation does not result in any injurious affection (section 75). Protections are extended to pictographs, petroglyphs, burial objects and mounds, and human skeletal remains pre-1700 (section 64).

The cases well illustrate aspects of heritage designation of buildings in Canada. The schemes vary as to the level of government possessing the power to designate buildings: it may be the province, it may be municipalities, it may be a shared power.[271] There may be designation

269 *Valley View Heritage Association Inc v Estevan (City)* (1989), 47 MPLR 24 (Sask QB); *Tegon Developments Ltd v Edmonton (City)* (1977), 81 DLR (3d) 543 (Alta CA).

270 SS 1979-80, c H-2.2.

271 See Marc Denhez, *Protecting the Built Environment* (Ottawa: Heritage Canada, 1978); Robert Ward, "Heritage Conservation in British Columbia" (1988) 22 *University of British Columbia Law Review* 61.

of the interior of buildings,[272] though more often it is limited to the exterior. There may be compensation schemes or grants available to assist with upkeep.[273] Although consent of the owner to the designation is not always required, notice is.[274] The main consequence of designation is some form of restriction on demolition. Heritage designation may extend beyond one building and include streetscapes or districts. There is a process for de-listing a property.[275]

Although the emphasis is often on individual structures, what can be treated as subject to heritage protection can be documents, objects, landscapes, sites, districts, and even intangibles such as skills, knowledge, and practices.[276]

What is missing from the legislation is a system for evaluation of the heritage value of buildings, as well as protection for the interior. Systems do exist.[277]

The systems of designation are designed to avoid demolition of heritage buildings while their status is being considered. Thus, no consent from an owner to consideration for designation is required, nor is notice of possible consideration required. Notice to the owner is given at the moment there is some intention to designate; this maintains the status quo.[278] Designated buildings are not immune from demolition. Under the Saskatchewan legislation, government consent to demolition is a prerequisite, but in most provinces usually an owner may demolish after some set period. An owner giving notice of intention to demolish can start a process of negotiation that may involve purchase or special development benefits if the building is preserved.

It is not unusual for municipalities and some provinces to adopt a practice of not considering property for heritage designation unless the owner

---

272 For an important case recognizing designation in part because of interior features, see *Re Toronto College Street Centre Ltd and City of Toronto* (1986), 31 DLR (4th) 402 (Ont CA), dealing with the Eaton's store building, at College and Yonge Streets.

273 Under Saskatchewan's *Regional Heritage Site Preservation Regulation*, Sask Reg 39/75, a municipality or non-profit organization must acquire title to a site if they have received a grant to assist in its preservation: s 8.

274 *Saint Peter's Evangelical Lutheran Church (Ottawa) v Ottawa (City)*, [1982] 2 SCR 616.

275 See, for example, *Lehn v Winnipeg (City)*, 2010 MBQB 175.

276 See, for example, Quebec's *Cultural Heritage Act*, CQLR c P-9.002.

277 Canada's Historic Places, "The Standards & Guidelines for the Conservation of Historic Places in Canada: A Federal, Provincial and Territorial Collaboration," 2d ed (2010), online: www.historicplaces.ca/media/18072/81468-parks-s+g-eng-web2.pdf. See, for example, Harold Kalman, *The Evaluation of Historic Buildings* (Ottawa: Parks Canada, 1980); Ontario, Ministry of Culture, *Heritage Property Evaluation* (Toronto: Ministry of Culture, 2006).

278 See, for example, *Ontario Heritage Act*, RSO 1990, c O.18, s 30.

has consented. This was challenged in *Tremblay v Lakeshore (Town)*.[279] The court ruled the practice to be unreasonable, and an impermissible fettering of the municipality's discretion as assigned to it by the legislation. Indeed, such a practice may well lead to immediate demolition of the building being considered if the owner has development plans.

In *Harvard Investments Ltd v Winnipeg (City)*,[280] the owner of the Fort Garry Hotel claimed compensation and damages against the city as a result of the listing of the building on its Building Conservation List. It had been listed over the objections of the owner, and the city had refused to de-list the hotel, thus frustrating the possibility of demolition. Neither the governing provincial legislation nor the civic by-law made provision for any compensation to be paid to an owner of a designated heritage building. The court rejected claims that the designation amounted to something like expropriation, and that there was a common law obligation to compensate.

> I am in agreement with the City's position that the listing and designation of the hotel as an historic building was merely an exercise of a regulatory power similar to the regulation of lands through a zoning bylaw. While it may have the effect of limiting and curtailing the use of the lands, it does not amount to a taking nor does it vest any rights in the property in the City. I therefore hold that Harvard is not entitled to any compensation from the City for the designation of the hotel as an historic building.[281]
>
> . . .
>
> Neither City of Winnipeg By-law 1474/77 nor the enabling legislation . . . makes provision for the payment of compensation to owners of buildings which are listed on the City's Buildings Conservation List. Harvard points out that the Heritage Acts of British Columbia, Alberta, Ontario and New Brunswick "recognize that a heritage designation may cause economic loss and when that occurs, compensation should be paid." I do not accept the argument that those statutory provisions reflect a codification of common law principles that are applicable in Manitoba. In my view, they are statutory provisions which the legislatures in particular provinces have enacted with the purpose of shifting at least part of the burden of preserving buildings of special architectural or historic interest, from the owners of those buildings to the community at large.[282]

---

279 (2003), 232 DLR (4th) 356 (Ont Div Ct).
280 (1995), 30 MPLR (2d) 149 (Man CA).
281 *Ibid* at para 11, quoting the trial judge.
282 *Ibid* at para 14.

The court distinguished US cases on "takings" and rejected the claim there had been an expropriation: "There was a 'taking away' . . . in that the effect of the listing was to preserve in perpetuity the exterior of the hotel and certain described interior elements. But . . . the City acquired nothing; nothing was added to the value of public property."[283] To the same effect is *Some Fine Investments Ltd v Nova Scotia (Attorney General)*,[284] where damages were sought for the provincial designation of a building. The court emphasized that compensation was a matter of discretion.

Although some owners resent the designation of their property as of heritage value, there may be advantages. Thus, some municipalities have adopted policies that offer development advantages for designated heritage sites if the owner agrees to added protections.[285]

The setting of designated heritage buildings is a problematic issue. An important aspect of appreciation of a heritage building may be the ability to see it without distractions. Thus, there may well be policies adopted that deal with compatibility of any nearby new construction. The particulars are often a matter for interpretation. In one instance, the Legislative Assembly of Ontario sought to limit construction of buildings about one kilometre away on the basis that policies of the City of Toronto as to the views of the Queen's Park location would be violated and the view negatively impacted. The OMB ruled as to the appropriate place for optimal "picture postcard" viewing of the Legislature, interpreting the OP policies, and this decision was upheld on appeal.[286]

In some instances, special legislation has been adopted for sites seen as aspects of provincial heritage. Nova Scotia has an act regarding Peggy's Cove.[287] Land-use planning in the Peggy's Cove Preservation Area is placed in the hands of a commission. Prince Edward Island has a *Lucy Maud Montgomery Foundation Act*,[288] which creates a board to own and manage the site of the author's birth. No special powers are granted. In Saskatchewan, the Wascana Centre and the Meewasin Valley Authority are examples.[289] The Wascana Authority is to create a master plan and adopt by-laws to implement it; likewise, the Meewasin Valley Authority is to adopt a development plan for its area.

283 *Ibid* at para 20.

284 (1990), 97 NSR (2d) 66 (SCTD).

285 See, for example, *Heritage Trust of Nova Scotia v Nova Scotia (Utility and Review Board)* (1994), 128 NSR (2d) 5 (CA).

286 See *Avenue-Yorkville Developments Ltd v Toronto (City)*, 2011 ONSC 258 (Div Ct).

287 *Peggy's Cove Commission Act*, RSNS 1989, c 339.

288 RSPEI 1988, c L-18.

289 *The Wascana Centre Act*, RSS 1978, c W-4; *Meewasin Valley Authority Act*, SS 1979, c M-11.1.

N. ARCHAEOLOGY/TREASURE TROVE

As an aspect of heritage, artifacts also attract some measure of protection. Often discovered artifacts are those of Indigenous peoples.[290] Usually a discovery prompts an obligation to report the find to provincial authorities for evaluation. To some extent there may be interaction with treasure trove legislation, which focuses on active hunters searching for treasure under licence, and may provide for the discoverer to retain finds after payment of a royalty.[291] Newfoundland and Labrador exempts from protection fossils and paleontological sites if disturbed during lawful activities under their *Mineral Act*, *Petroleum and Natural Gas Act*, and the *Quarry Materials Act, 1998*.[292]

O. PARKS AND PROTECTED AREAS

There is often a contemporary competition between a set of values that sees land as valuable primarily for its extractive potential, and other values manifested in such uses as recreation and tourism. This was not always the case. Early examples of land being designated as park frequently allowed for mining and some logging. Grazing on public land or leasing for other agricultural purposes is not unknown, but not usual in parks.

As owner of Crown land, provincial governments may designate some land as park land, or as a wilderness area. It may also purchase or expropriate land for the purpose. The restrictions on use are a continuum, ranging from no use to general public access for recreation, including overnight camping.

In British Columbia there is a mine in a provincial park (Strathcona Provincial Park on Vancouver Island, established 1911), though new mining uses are not allowed; the mine dates from 1939, when exploration and mining were a permitted use.[293]

Wilderness areas are often governed by separate legislation. They are the areas with the greatest restrictions on use. In 1987, the Brundtland

290 See Catherine Bell, *First Nations Cultural Heritage and Law* (Vancouver: UBC Press, 2008), and *Protection of First Nations Cultural Heritage* (Vancouver: UBC Press, 2009).

291 See, for example, *Oak Island Treasure Act*, SNS 2010, c 39.

292 *Historic Resources Act*, RSNL 1999, c H-4, s 36.

293 Nanaimo's Morden Colliery Historic Provincial Park is a small park that features the remains of a coal mine, not an active mine.

Commission[294] suggested that no less than 12 percent of the land mass of each jurisdiction be set aside as protected area. In part this had to do with carbon sequestration through forests, and in part with providing habitat for wildlife. Recently, the appropriate target percentage has been suggested by some commentators to be 17 percent, following the Convention on Biological Diversity, to which Canada is a party,[295] although a 2011 editorial in the journal *Conservation Biology* has suggested that 50 percent of the global land mass should be set aside from development.[296]

P. TRANSPORTATION

Making provision for vehicle traffic through the construction and maintenance of highways is seen as so fundamental a function of provincial governments that it is often the exclusive mandate of a department with its own minister and a sizeable budget. For example, under Saskatchewan's *Highway and Transportation Act* "The Minister is responsible for managing transportation systems with a view to supporting the economic growth and social well-being of Saskatchewan . . . ."[297]

Such statutes contain significant land-use provisions. Access rights to highways from adjacent lands are extinguished and made subject purely to regulation, thus eliminating a common law property right.[298] The common law right is to have access at any point to public roads for any kind of traffic necessary for the reasonable enjoyment of the adjacent land and which would not cause a substantial nuisance.[299] The government is empowered to expropriate lands as needed, and may enter upon private land without expropriation in support of public improvements.[300] Signage may not be placed (with some exceptions) within 400 metres of a highway unless by permit.[301] Further, no construction is permitted within the designated distance, nor alterations to existing buildings, nor planting of trees or shrubs, except by permit.[302] The

294 World Commission on Environment and Development, *Our Common Future* (New York: Oxford University Press, 1987) at 165–66.

295 See online: www.biodivcanada.ca.

296 Reed F Noss et al, eds, "Bolder Thinking for Conservation" (2011) 26(1) *Conservation Biology* 1.

297 *Highways and Transportation Act, 1997*, SS 1997, c H-3.01, s 3(2).

298 *Ibid*, s 12.

299 See *Toronto Transit Commission v Swansea (Village)*, [1935] SCR 455; *Chivers v British Columbia*, 2005 BCCA 305.

300 Above note 297, ss 14, 16, 18 & 19.

301 *Ibid*, s 29; also *Sign Control Regulations*, RSS c H-3.01, Reg 10.

302 Above note 297, s 32.

signage and construction controls offer an interesting environmental benefit in that land is set aside for what amounts to 200,000 square metres (or about 48 acres) for every kilometre of highway where the setback is 100 metres.

Outside of formal local government areas, it is the provincial government that is responsible for construction, maintenance, and administration of highways. The process raises issues of designation for future use, injurious affection, signage, and other restrictions. Highways are also subject to formal EA.

Q. CEMETERIES

Memorials of the dead have long been associated with both formal civic recollection and taboos.[303] Originally located in the midst of towns, cemeteries have tended to migrate to the outskirts or to remote areas, and to have become large-scale.[304] The functional utility of this is questioned by planners, who suggest it is "essential . . . to reinstate the connection between burial grounds and local communities."[305]

> Never build massive cemeteries. Instead, allocate pieces of land throughout the community as grave sites—corners of parks, sections of paths, gardens, beside gateways—where memorials . . . can be ritually placed . . . . Give each grave site . . . a quiet corner where people can sit . . . or a bench under a tree, where people can be alone with their memories.[306]

Rather than locating cemeteries centrally, they are now usually required to be some distance from highways (as well as from sources of drinking water). Under existing legal constraints, it is forbidden to

---

303 Nineteenth century French historian Fustel de Coulanges, in *The Ancient City, A Study on the Religion, Laws, and Institutions of Greece and Rome* (1864; repr, Baltimore: Johns Hopkins University Press, 1980), explores the importance of beliefs about the soul, death, and burial rites. See also Thomas Laqueur, *The Work of the Dead: A Cultural History of Mortal Remain* (Princeton, NJ: Princeton University Press, 2015).

304 Sensitivity about the fact of death as manifested in cemeteries has even led to their absence from one famous planned community, the town of Celebration, developed by the Disney companies; see Andrew Ross, *The Celebration Chronicles* (New York: Ballantine Books, 1999) at 211.

305 See, for example, Christopher Alexander et al, *A Pattern Language* (New York: Oxford University Press, 1977) at 356. See also Christopher Coutts et al, *Planning for the Deceased* (Chicago: American Planning Association, 2013).

306 Alexander et al, above note 305 at 356–57.

disturb human remains. This implies constraints on construction that involves excavation. Discovery of human remains must be reported to the police or government archaeologists or both. This can lead to clashes over uses. In British Columbia, there are some 44,000 identified archaeological sites.[307] But many are discovered during construction, or claims are asserted when activity affects sites. There is potential for conflict with First Nations claims.[308]

Provincial legislation provides a framework for land use associated with cemeteries[309] but many issues remain. Provinces usually have two main statutes, a *Cemeteries Act* and a *Funeral and Cremation Services Act* or equivalent. Ontario has a thorough, modern statute, the *Funeral, Burial and Cremation Services Act, 2002*.[310] Crematoriums may be required to register for a class environmental assessment due to the requirement for an air approval certificate.[311]

The provincial laws vary as to whether bodies must be buried in designated commercial cemeteries. New Brunswick's statute contemplates a family cemetery, though all rules apply as with commercial enterprises. Further, "unless human remains are cremated, the burial or storage of human remains shall be in a cemetery, crypt, mausoleum or vault."[312] Cremated remains may be buried, placed in a columbarium, or given to the next-of-kin.[313] Although bodies have in the past been buried in churches, Saskatchewan's *Cemeteries Act* prohibits burial under buildings.[314]

There are current suggestions that favour a return to localized family burial plots on home property. There are, of course, potential problems with such a practice; given the contemporary pattern of frequent moves, families would lose the opportunity to visit such gravesites, plus the presence of graves is likely to devalue property.[315]

---

307 A record is kept pursuant to the *Heritage Conservation Act*, RSBC 1996, c 187.

308 Justine Hunter, "The Problems That Arise When Cemeteries Are Not Cemeteries under the Law" *The Globe and Mail* (9 January 2015), online: http://fw.to/cGoimBd.

309 Including a provision that subdivision rules for the creation of lots do not apply to the sale of burial plots; see, for example, *Municipal Government Act*, SNS 1998, c 18, as amended, s 268(2)(d).

310 SO 2002, c 33.

311 See *South Etobicoke Residents & Ratepayers Association Inc v Ontario Realty Corp*, 2005 CanLII 19654 (Ont CA).

312 *General Regulation*, NB Reg 94-129 under the *Cemetery Companies Act*, s 19(1).

313 *Ibid*, s 19(2).

314 *The Cemeteries Regulations 2001*, RRS c C-4.01, Reg 1.

315 In the United Kingdom, there are cases that indicate home burial may be regarded as an accessory use. See Chapter 7, Section C.

Health rules have to do with avoidance of water pollution or the possible spread of disease. However, there is no serious reason to believe that dead bodies are a source of infection: "most viruses and bacteria, even those that could potentially cause disease, only live for a few additional hours in a dead body. The rare virus that survives longer (for example, HIV, up to sixteen days) poses no more harm in a dead body than in a living body."[316] Still, embalming fluids, if used, are a potential source of pollution.

There is no provision for open-air pyres, leaving bodies in the open for birds and other animals,[317] composting, or freezing as an adjunct to composting. Both old and new methods of dealing with bodies are currently being promoted and are in limited use.[318] Some religions, for example, Hindus and Sikhs, favour cremation, including open-air cremation. There are emerging forms of "green burial." Such demands will lead to pressure for changes to accommodate the preferences.

Rules are aimed at prevention of contamination of ground or surface water. Thus in regulations under New Brunswick's *Cemetery Companies Act*,[319] no portion of a cemetery may be established "on land that is subject to flooding, on land where ground water or bedrock is situated less than two metres below the land surface . . . within seventy-five metres of a watershed, aquifer or ground water recharge area that is used as a source of water for a public water supply system."[320] Although there is a duty to take precautions "to prevent the contamination of a body of water that is located within or near the boundaries of the cemetery,"[321] bodies need not have caskets or boxes, though the grave depth is then required to be increased from 0.9 metres to 1.3 metres.[322]

---

316 Caitlin Doughty, *Smoke Gets in Your Eyes* (New York: WW Norton & Co, 2014) at 173.

317 The *Criminal Code*, RSC 1985, c C-46, s 182, creates two offences: neglecting to perform any duty imposed by law with reference to the burial of a dead body, and indecent interference or offering any indignity to a dead body or human remains. The former offence seems to link to provincial legislation; if there is no obligation to bury bodies and other means of disposal are approved, there would be no offence. The latter has potential to be ambiguous, but it is unlikely that if provincial laws allow a variety of methods of dealing with a body, that there would be an offence.

318 See, for example, Doughty, above note 316; Mary Roach, *Stiff* (New York: WW Norton & Co, 2003); Christine Quigley, *The Corpse: A History* (Jefferson, NC: McFarland, 2005); Graeme Bayliss, "Dissolving the Dead" *The Walrus* (March 2016) at 30.

319 RSNB 1973, c C-1.

320 *General Regulation* under the *Cemetery Companies Act*, NB Reg 94-129, s 4.

321 *Ibid*, s 5.

322 *Ibid*, s 7.

Special rules apply to the disposition of bodies that have some specified communicable diseases.[323]

New Brunswick allows municipalities some jurisdiction, to the extent they may adopt by-laws requiring walls or fences for cemeteries.[324] In *Westside Cemeteries Ltd v City of Etobicoke*,[325] the OMB did not allow free-standing columbaria[326] to be added to an existing cemetery, seeing them as neither a minor variance nor a permitted expansion of a non-conforming use.

In *Gaudaur v Etobicoke (City)*,[327] a case in which leave to appeal a decision of the OMB was sought, the court found that persons who had contracts for burial were not owners of land in a cemetery and therefore not entitled to specific notice of an OP amendment to permit construction of a condominium building on a decertified and severed portion of the cemetery lands.

R. COASTS

As with energy, there is divided jurisdiction that comes into play for matters affecting coasts, though the main powers are provincial.[328] Still, the federal government exercises powers under the *Navigable Waters Protection Act* that extend to controlling some dams and bridges and their approaches, thus bringing land-use into play, and also under the *Fisheries Act* so far as land-based activities negatively affect fisheries. Overall, there is regulatory clutter, which arises from both split jurisdiction as well as a complex idea of what is involved in regulating the coast.

There are many ways in which we consider and interact with the coast. There are wharves for commercial fishing. There are homes for permanent habitation. There are beaches for recreation and for clamming. There are seasonal dwellings. There are launch points for pleasure craft. There are parks. Coasts are a major draw for tourism. There are associations with history. There are shipping harbours for the im-

---

323 See, for example, *Bodies of Deceased Persons Regulation*, Alta Reg 135/2008.

324 *Cemetery Companies Act*, above note 319, s 7.

325 (1986), 19 OMBR 366.

326 "Columbarium": a structure lined with recesses for urns containing ashes of those who have been cremated, in *The Penguin English Dictionary* (New York: Penguin Books, 2000).

327 (1997), 35 OR (3d) 551 (Div Ct).

328 The *Constitution Act, 1867*, s 91(12) gives the federal government jurisdiction over "Sea Coast and Inland Fisheries" but this has been interpreted not as direct jurisdiction over coasts, but over activities that affect fisheries: see *R v Fowler*, [1980] 2 SCR 213 and *R v Northwest Falling Contractors Ltd*, [1980] 2 SCR 292.

port and export of goods. In many communities, the waters receive effluent. If experiments in tidal energy go forward, the coastlands may be places involved in the generation and transmission of electricity. Coasts are the site for lighthouses, recently abandoned by the federal government. Of course the claims on the coast are not purely anthropocentric. There are wetlands that are homes to plants and animals. Birds nest. Shores accrete; more often they erode.

The province can and does regulate some coastal land-use activities, as through a focus on beaches, parks, and endangered species legislation. But it could create a generalized coastal zone management law. Coastal zone management has a number of possibilities for content. First, it could set minimum standards affecting landowners as to ways to use or refrain from using their land, so as to protect the coasts. This is not necessarily simple. It tends to imply that we have the scientific knowledge at a level sufficient to allow us to understand what coastlands are, their functions in the natural world. To some extent we do know about this, though there is more to learn. Following the precautionary principle, which is public policy set out in *Environment Acts*, we do not need to know everything before taking protective steps.

Key to such a statute would probably be setbacks for any proposed development. Because these setbacks would have to be tied to an appreciation of the particular parcel and its surrounding location, it is probably better to establish, and establish clearly, that they are minimums that could be increased by local municipalities. Setbacks are contentious, as indeed are any government-imposed controls on private landowners, but are quite legal. Indeed, the subdivision process and basic zoning tend to allow for such controls by municipalities already. What I am suggesting is that a more detailed provincial regime of setbacks could form the core of a new statute. In British Columbia, which is a coastal province, there have been a large number of cases litigating issues around setbacks; examples are *Moore v Saanich (District)*,[329] *Capital (Regional District) v Smith*,[330] and *579340 BC Ltd v Sunshine Coast (Regional District)*.[331] For owners, such restrictions are highly problematic, and any regime established by the province should be as clear as possible about its rules, and how they would apply in a variety of circumstances. Any coastal strategy should specify whether affected landowners are to be paid compensation, and if not, this should be explicit.

Other possible content for such a statute could come from consideration of American precedents, both federal and state. The US federal

329 (1995), 30 MPLR (2d) 132 (BCSC).
330 (1996), 33 MPLR (2d) 15 (BCSC).
331 2005 BCSC 1203.

government owns coastland, some administered through their National Parks Service, or the National Oceanographic and Atmospheric Administration. It also has a *Coastal Barrier Resources Act* (1982), which encourages state planning for the coasts, especially through financial incentives. At the state level, there are precedents in South Carolina, Washington, Rhode Island, and California. California's *Coastal Act*[332] provides that the following principles are to characterize rulings from the Coastal Commission and also local governments; in fact, the California law characterizes them as "standards":

- development shall not interfere with the public's right of access to the sea
- coastal areas suitable for water-oriented recreational activities that cannot readily be provided at inland water areas shall be protected for such use
- marine resources shall be maintained, enhanced, and where feasible, restored. Special protection shall be given to areas and species of special biological or economic significance. Uses of the marine environment shall be carried out in a manner that will sustain the biological productivity of coastal waters . . . .
- Environmentally sensitive habitat areas shall be protected against any significant disruption of habitat values, and only uses dependent on those resources shall be allowed within those areas. Development in areas adjacent to environmentally sensitive habitat areas and parks and recreation areas shall be sited and designed to prevent impacts which would significantly degrade those areas, and shall be compatible . . . .
- New . . . development . . . shall be located . . . where it will not have significant adverse effects, either individually or cumulatively, on coastal resources.

So these principles cover public access, recreation, protecting the marine environment, sensitive areas, and general development. Each has elaborations, and the overall statute reads rather like an OP.

The statute has been subject to judicial scrutiny, two of the most famous cases being the 1987 decision of the US Supreme Court in *Nollan v California Coastal Commission*,[333] which dealt with the public right of access across some private land, and a South Carolina case, *Lucas v South Carolina Coastal Council*,[334] dealing with whether tight regulatory rules call for monetary compensation to the landowner.

332 Public Resources Code, Division 20, California *Coastal Act*, 2010.
333 483 US 825 (1987).
334 505 US 1003 (1992).

S. SNOWMOBILES AND ALL-TERRAIN VEHICLES (OFF-HIGHWAY VEHICLES)

Several provinces have statutes dealing directly with all-terrain vehicles (ATVs), also termed off-highway vehicles (OHVs).[335] Saskatchewan and Ontario have statutes dealing specifically with snowmobiles. For the most part, the statutes deal with licensing and safety. Trespass is reinforced by such provisions as "No person shall operate an off-highway vehicle on private property without the written permission of the owner or occupier."[336] Regulations made under these and other acts, usually those dealing with Crown lands, address the place of use of such vehicles. They tend to be quite specific as to place. Thus, Newfoundland and Labrador's *Wilderness Reserve Regulations, 1997*[337] prohibit use of snowmobiles in some wilderness areas, though they allow their use in Bay du Nord Wilderness Reserve "except within the winter range of the caribou herd as identified in the management plan"; the electric utility may, with written permission, use snowmobiles and ATVs. A variety of issues are in play: the potential for harm to sensitive lands and to flora, noise, and compatibility of modes of use, often as to trails. Ontario's *Motorized Snow Vehicles Act*[338] provides for a system of trails permits.

T. *HUMAN RIGHTS CODES*

For the most part, when land-use matters engage issues of human rights, the matters are considered in the context of the *Charter*. There are exceptions, however. The crucial difference is that the *Charter* offers protections against government interference with the guaranteed rights, whereas provincial *Human Rights Codes* are directed at both governments and private individuals or corporations. Thus, there is some scope for operation of non-discrimination principles in a realm where the common law would have allowed for the individual choice of the landowner. The ambit of *Human Rights Codes* is limited to the specified instances set out. We noted earlier that certain common law aspects of the bundle of rights seen as constituting what is involved in private ownership have been altered by statute. *Human Rights Codes* typically

---

335 Off-highway Vehicles Acts: Nova Scotia (RSNS 1989, c 323), PEI (RSPEI 1988, c O-3), Quebec (CQLR c V-1.2).

336 Nova Scotia *Off-highway Vehicles Act*, above note 335, s 14(1).

337 NLR 65/97.

338 RSO 1990, c M.44.

limit the power of exclusion of others as well as the power of alienation, on specified grounds. Thus, Ontario's *Human Rights Code*[339] declares that "every person has a right to equal treatment with respect to services, goods and facilities without discrimination" and also to "the occupancy of accommodation." The prohibited grounds of discrimination are "race, ancestry, place of origin, colour, ethnic origin, citizenship, creed, sex, sexual orientation, gender identity, gender expression, age, marital status, family status or disability."[340] That *Code* is supplemented by the *Ontarians with Disabilities Act, 2001*.[341] Manitoba's *The Human Rights Code*[342] prohibits discrimination regarding sale of real property. Invocation of *Human Rights Codes* occurs through filing a complaint. Provinces have bound themselves under their *Human Rights Codes*. Where the *Codes* are silent, some discriminatory provisions may not be enforced on the ground of vagueness, not relating to use of the land in question, or as contrary to public policy.[343]

Various aspects of housing have been considered in terms of human rights.[344] In *Syndicat Northcrest v Amselem*,[345] the Quebec *Charter* was used to establish a right for Jewish residents of a co-op building to build temporary shelters on their balconies as part of a religious celebration. More pressing are issues associated with affordable housing and discrimination manifested through decisions as to location of particular forms of housing, such as group homes or supportive housing.[346] In cases such as *Advocacy Centre for Tenants Ontario v Kitchener (City)*,[347]

---

339 RSO 1990, c H.19.

340 *Ibid*, ss 1 & 2.

341 SO 2001, c 32.

342 CCSM c H 175, s 17.

343 On this, Canadian courts have an undistinguished history. See Walter S Tarnopolsky, *Discrimination and the Law in Canada* (Toronto: R de Boo, 1982), especially his discussion at 23–24 of *Noble v Alley*, [1951] SCR 64, and *Re Wren*, [1945] OR 778 (HCJ).

344 Apart from housing as a human right, the involvement of the provincial governments in housing varies, though the needs remain unmet; see comments of Professor J David Hulchanski, "Rethinking Canada's Housing Affordability Challenge," a discussion paper prepared for the Government of Canada's Canadian Housing Framework Initiative (January 2005).

345 2004 SCC 47.

346 See Lilith Finkler, "Zoned OUT: Restrictive Municipal By-laws and Psychiatric Survivor Housing" in Ontario, Psychiatric Patient Advocate Office, *Honouring the Past, Shaping the Future: 25 Years of Progress in Mental Health Advocacy and Rights Protection*, Psychiatric Patient Advocate Office, 25th Anniversary Report (Toronto: Queen's Printer, 2008). The anti-poverty organization ACORN Canada promotes inclusionary zoning and offers a model by-law; see online: www.acorncanada.org.

347 (2010), 64 OMBR 283 [*ACTO*].

issues of separation distances between such facilities, offered on the basis of avoiding over-concentration of social services and so as to encourage integration of residents in the community, have come under scrutiny. In *ACTO,* the city had identified a neighbourhood as having a significant concentration of persons with disabilities, on social assistance, and/or living in group homes or rent-to-income housing, and saw the concentration as creating "'an unhealthy social environment' which put the neighbourhood on a 'downward trajectory.'" The city adopted OP and zoning changes to effect "a neighbourhood ban on all new facilities for the target population, and on all new dwellings other than single detached, except where approved on a 'site-by-site' basis . . . ." In an interim ruling, the board accepted the principle of decentralization as an appropriate objective but also found that the municipality had not gone through an acceptable planning analysis and process, taking into account Provincial Policy Statements regarding accessibility for persons with disabilities, or its own OP policies that address housing based on low income. In an earlier case, *Re Toronto (City) Zoning By-law No 138-2003,*[348] the board examined a by-law dealing with the establishment of public emergency shelters for the indigent and homeless, the rules involving separation by a set distance from other such facilities. The rule was challenged as a *Charter* matter, and the board accepted the device of separation distances as legitimate.

Although the main thrust of *Human Rights Codes* is at private parties, some government actions or policies may become a focus of scrutiny. This could extend to mobility rights and thus the need for curb-cuts or accessible public transportation. Because housing is a fundamental need, and has been decreed internationally to be a human right,[349] housing policies in particular have been examined. The Ontario Human Rights Commission has issued commentary on the housing policies of the City of Toronto:

Comment of the Ontario Human Rights Commission on the City of Toronto's Proposed Zoning By-law

September 25, 2009

> The Ontario Human Rights Commission (the "Commission") thanks the City of Toronto ("City") for the opportunity to comment on its proposed zoning by-law. The Commission will focus its comments on sections of the zoning by-law that have human rights implications,

---

348 (2004), 47 OMBR 168.

349 *International Covenant on Economic, Social, and Cultural Rights*, GA res 2200A (XXI), 21 UNGAOR Supp (No16) at 49, UN Doc A/6316 (1966), 993 UNTS 3, entered into force 3 January 1976, online: www2.ohchr.org/english/law/cescr.htm.

and in particular on elements that have implications for the inclusion or exclusion of people from Ontario Human Rights Code-protected groups . . . .

Housing as a Human Right

The international community has long recognized that housing is a fundamental and universal human right that must be protected in law. Canada has ratified several international human rights instruments that recognize the right to housing. In doing so, Canada has endorsed the view that housing is a human right. The challenge for Canada is to make these high-level principles a lived reality for Canadians. Human rights bodies, federal, provincial and municipal governments play critical roles in making this happen. Municipalities, including municipal councils, policy makers, planners and program designers, have unique opportunities to ensure people's human rights are respected in the design and delivery of housing and housing legislation.

The Commission is providing comment on the City's proposed zoning by-law because the by-law has the potential to affect the housing rights of many people across the City, particularly with respect to those living in affordable housing (group homes, seniors' residences, shelters, lodging houses, etc.). The right to be free from discrimination in housing under the Code could extend to the development of affordable housing projects for people and groups identified by the Code. In addition, the Commission believes it is important to highlight the City's progressive vision of housing and human rights through its newly developed Housing Charter.

The Toronto Housing Charter

The Commission commends the City for its development of the Housing Charter, which is a policy statement that sets out how people's human rights are respected within housing. Specifically, the Housing Charter provides that a full range of available housing enables the health, economic, and social well-being of residents, and that:

- All residents should have a safe, secure, affordable and well-maintained home from which to realize their full potential
- All residents should be able to live in their neighbourhood of choice without discrimination
- All residents have the right to equal treatment in housing without discrimination as provided by the Ontario Human Rights Code, and to be protected from discriminatory practices which limit their housing opportunities . . . .

The Commission also supports the City's Housing Opportunities Toronto program, which places priority on addressing homelessness, improving the state of the City's affordable housing and building more units. The Commission is also pleased that the Housing Charter will provide guidance for the City's future planning activities. It is worth noting that the statements outlined in the Housing Charter are based on many of the Code principles of dignity, individualized support, autonomy, and full participation and integration in community life.

The Housing Charter also provides an important foundation when considering zoning practices and how these affect the availability of affordable housing and the inclusion or exclusion of people from Code-protected groups.

The City's Housing Charter provides a framework with which to ensure the equal treatment and the inclusion of affordable housing in all neighbourhoods. People living in affordable housing are often from Code-protected groups, and include families, youth, older people, people from racialized and Aboriginal communities, immigrants, women, and people with disabilities, including psychiatric disabilities. People from these groups tend to be vulnerable to discrimination in many different ways; for example, when securing housing, maintaining tenancy, and experiencing eviction. In addition, discriminatory neighbourhood opposition, more commonly known as "NIMBYism," creates a formidable barrier to establishing affordable housing projects. Negative attitudes and stereotypes about the intended residents of a housing project result in affordable housing development being unnecessarily delayed, halted or restricted . . . .

In applying these principles to the City of Toronto's proposed zoning by-law, the Commission has identified the following issues, particularly with respect to group homes, (including correctional group homes), residential care homes, seniors' community houses, rooming and lodging houses, municipal shelters, and crisis care shelters . . . .

The Commission recognizes that the proposed by-law allows group homes, municipal shelters and seniors' community houses in all of the City's residential zones. The Commission supports this same approach for other types of affordable housing where the density of the neighbourhood supports the population density of the building. The Commission encourages the City to look at other types of housing and shelters that may be excluded from various residential zones (e.g. crisis care shelters, residential care homes, etc.) and ensure that any decisions to exclude these structures are strictly based on sound urban planning rationale, and not on negative assumptions about the people living there. The City should take note, for example, that some residential zones (e.g. residential detached zones, residential semi-detached, and residential townhouse zones) are not zoned to allow crisis care shelters, but allow for municipal shelters, despite

> the fact that the definitions of these two building types are extremely similar . . . .
>
> We understand that the zoning rules around rooming houses are not yet in place, but the Commission encourages that rooming houses be allowed in all parts of the City and in all residential zones . . . .
>
> The City's zoning by-law identifies minimum separation distances that apply to some affordable housing establishments, such as group homes, residential care homes and seniors' community houses, and crisis care shelters and municipal shelters. For example, the proposed by-law indicates that group homes should be a minimum distance of 300 metres from other group homes or residential care homes.
>
> However, minimum separation distances can have a critical impact on the establishment of affordable housing by limiting the sites available for development, and forcing housing providers to turn away otherwise ideal housing opportunities. Where they are not justified on a rational planning basis and passed in good faith, minimum separation distances can be seen as placing onerous restrictions on housing serving people from Code-protected groups that are not placed on other housing types. This could be viewed as discriminatory. They are also criticized as contributing to the social isolation of group home residents, particularly people with psychiatric disabilities. The Commission encourages the City of Toronto to re-examine the issue of minimum distance requirements to allow for maximum flexibility in affordable housing development.
>
> All of these suggested changes would serve to increase the availability of affordable housing by allowing it to be developed in more areas of the City, and would remove barriers that have the potential to violate the Code.

Housing is a vexed issue. Providing housing is a prime land-use matter that has involved all levels of government. In an essay on housing, published in 1981 as part of a series examining inequality in Canada, social work professor Allan Moscovitch wrote, "Housing isn't simply some commodity like oranges or ball-point pens. It is the place in which people live and work, in which children grow up and adults grow old. It is the place for which the measures of quantity and price cannot tell the whole story."[350] Moscovitch points out that common statistics on housing, such as number of starts, draw attention away from the reality for low-income people, that they pay a greater proportion of their income for housing that is of lower quality (less space per person, older construction). Also,

350 Allan Moscovitch & Glenn Drover, eds, *Inequality: Essays on the Political Economy of Social Welfare* (Toronto: University of Toronto Press, 1981) at 321.

> Their housing is relatively less secure because . . . it is more likely to be in an inner city area, where it is subject to the continuous risk that the demands for profit will result in eviction or compulsory public purchase, making way for high-rises, town houses, and renovations of roads and airports, which are all publicly heralded as marks of progress.[351]

In the thirty-five years since these comments, not a great deal has changed.[352] David Hulchanski, the leading academic now studying housing in Canada, says,

> Canada is able to build safe and adequate housing appropriate to the needs of all its households. That is, there are no physical, institutional, or financial impediments, no shortage of building supplies, construction workers, or mortgage financing to supply adequate housing for all. After the Second World War, improvements in housing finance, residential land servicing and building techniques, materials, and regulations produced high-quality housing for the vast majority of Canadian households. So why are some Canadians still poorly housed or unhoused?
>
> The inability of a country as wealthy as Canada to adequately house all its people is usually called a *housing affordability* problem. This vague term became common about thirty years ago, when it was no longer appropriate to talk about specific problems such as the postwar housing shortage or the slum problem or the inadequate mortgage lending system—since, for the most part, these problems had been addressed. There is, however, something unsatisfactory about policy analysts' use of *housing affordability* as a problem definition. Policy experts seldom debate what it really means or ought to mean. Yet it is used in the media and everyday language as if it meant something specific. The term alludes to income levels and housing costs, so it seems to make sense. But policy experts ought to do better at naming the specific problem or group of problems—so as to better define solutions . . . .
>
> Market demand for housing is addressed; the social need for housing is not. Canada stands out as one of the few Western nations that rely almost completely on the market mechanism to supply, allocate, and maintain its housing stock. The market is the mechanism by which about 95% of Canadian households obtain their housing.

351 *Ibid* at 316.

352 For a good, though slightly dated overview of housing issues and history in Canada, see Barbara Wake Carroll, "Housing Policy in the New Millennium: The Uncompassionate Landscape" in Edmund P Fowler & David Siegel, eds, *Urban Policy Issues: Canadian Perspectives*, 2d ed (Don Mills, ON: Oxford University Press, 2002) 69.

> Canada also is one of the more inegalitarian Western nations (that is, there is a wide gap between rich and poor) and ranks near the bottom of the list in an eighteen-country comparison of net social expenditure by the OECD. The OECD defines social expenditures as "the provision by public and private institutions of benefits to, and financial contributions targeted at, households and individuals in order to provide support during circumstances which adversely affect their welfare . . . . Such benefits can be cash transfers, or can be the direct (in-kind) provision of goods and services". Given Canada's poor record on social spending, the United Nations Committee on Economic, Social and Cultural Rights, in its 1998 review of Canada's compliance with these rights, issued a highly critical and detailed report on Canada's social policies.
>
> Households living in extreme poverty with an inadequate social safety net do not contribute to market demand for housing. Markets respond to market demand. If households have too little income or wealth to stimulate market demand for a particular good, the market will ignore them.
>
> In theory, this problem can be defined as one of income inequality. Some policy analysts even claim that there is no housing problem, that there is an incomes problem—and therefore no need for housing interventions—because the problem boils down to income distribution. The housing system, they suggest, is not to blame.
>
> This oversimplification is neither logical nor policy-relevant (that is, it does not lead to useful policy). The assertion that poorly housed or unhoused people have an income problem is not analysis. It does not help us answer questions such as: Why do a substantial minority of households in a country like Canada lack enough income for housing? How and when will this problem be addressed? What do we do in the meantime?[353]

Regardless of whether the issues arise as matters of human rights, housing is an important aspect of land use. There have been two distinct uses of such terms as "affordable housing" or "affordable rent." One use is to characterize it as rents that "fall below average market rate level." This usage appears in *Toronto (City) v R & G Realty Management Inc.*[354] A similar use of the term appears in the *Halifax Regional Municipality Charter*, where it is defined as housing "that meets the needs of a variety of households in the low to moderate income range."[355]

---

353 Hulchanski, above note 344 at 1–2 [citations omitted].

354 2009 CanLII 42397 (Ont Div Ct).

355 Section 209(a).

More specific measures tend to focus on low income households and cite Canadian Mortgage and Housing Corporation (CMHC) standards that no household should spend more than 30 percent of gross income on rental shelter costs, and of a monthly occupancy cost that does not exceed 80 percent of the average market rent for that unit.[356] In *WEN Residents Society v Vancouver (City)*,[357] it was held that the governing statute did not require the municipality to create affordable housing for low-income persons, and permitted it to choose to assist in construction of for-profit housing affordable by moderate-income persons.

U. RESTRICTED NUISANCE ACTIVITIES

Several provinces have enacted *Safe Streets Acts* or equivalent.[358] And British Columia has a statute aimed at limiting behaviour that interferes with clients and staff of abortion clinics.[359]

The Alberta *Safer Communities and Neighbourhoods Act* is typical. It allows for a complaint to be lodged with a police official who may apply to a court for a "community safety order" to restrain activities that are, in essence, nuisances: illegal alcohol sales, drug houses, grow-ops, brothels, gang houses.[360]

Under British Columbia's *Access to Abortion Services Act*, "access zones" are established. While in an access zone, "a person must not . . . engage in sidewalk interference; protest; beset; physically interfere with or attempt to interfere with a service provider, a doctor who provides abortion services or a patient; intimidate or attempt to intimidate . . . ."[361] The zones are established by regulation. In *R v Watson*,[362] the court considered the statute in light of the *Charter* protection of freedom of expression. It found that the *Charter* right was violated by the statute, but was also justified under section 1.[363]

356 CMHC standards are mentioned in passing in *St Catherine's Apartments Phase Three Inc v Municipal Property Assessment Corp*, 2015 ONSC 3896.

357 2014 BCSC 965.

358 See, for example, *Safer Communities and Neighbourhoods Act*, SA 2007, c S-0.5.

359 *Access to Abortion Services Act*, RSBC 1996, c 1.

360 Above note 358, s 3(1)(e).

361 Above note 359, s 2(1).

362 2008 BCCA 340 [*Watson*].

363 The *Watson* case is also examined in Chapter 4, Section E(2).

V. RIGHT TO ROAM

In the United Kingdom, a statutory framework exists for a "right to roam." In 2000, the *Countryside and Rights of Way Act*[364] established a national framework for rambling, significantly extending to private property. It operates in conjunction with the *Marine and Coastal Access Act 2009.*[365] Special areas had already been established by legislation as available to the public for freedom to roam, just as Canada has parks or rights-of-way that have arisen through long use. There is a significant difference between public use of public lands and public use of private lands. It is for the latter that the *CRoW Act* is significant. The development of sophisticated GPS and GIS has allowed for reliable surveying of all land, especially coasts that are often of especial interest to the public. The statute includes various provisions for controls to protect wildlife habitat and for other conservation measures. One commentator says, "if the beauty of rural Britain is not preserved, access will become meaningless."[366] In essence, the *CRoW Act* changes the nature of the law of trespass. It does not offer unrestricted rights to non-owners. Cultivated land is exempt, as is a set area around a dwelling. Overnight camping is prohibited, as is straying from established paths, fires, hunting, removal of vegetation, and riding of either horses or bicycles.

The important policy question is whether similar rights ought to be established by provincial governments in Canada. To a certain extent, public access to private land, or access to facilities immediately adjacent to private land, does exist, through common law rights-of-way, hunting and fishing laws, and through the designation of public beaches. But the various rules fall far short of amounting to an organized system.

---

364 *Countryside and Rights of Way Act, 2000* (UK), c 37[*CRoW Act*], online: www.legislation.gov.uk/ukpga/2000/37/contents.

365 (UK), c 23.

366 JL Anderson, "Britain's 'Right to Roam': Redefining the Landowner's Bundle of Sticks" (2007) 19 *Georgetown International Environmental Law Review* 375 at 394. The article includes a history of public pathways in Britain.

CHAPTER 6

SOURCES OF AUTHORITY: MUNICIPAL PLANNING STATUTES

A. PRELIMINARY

Up to this point we have looked at land-use controls exercised either as a matter of the common law or by the federal or provincial governments. Here, we turn to the main aspects of land-use controls exercised by municipal governments.

Each province bestows land-use control powers on municipalities through one or two main statutes, usually termed a *Planning Act* and a *Local Government Act* or *Municipal Act*, often both together. The usual features of such statutes are as follows: the provincial role appears; public participation is featured; powers are specified, often listed in detail; sustainability objectives are often explicit or implied; the central planning mechanism is the adoption of an official plan (OP) to provide the policy context for land-use by-laws, which then set specific rules; various flexibility mechanisms are created such as minor variances or development agreements; ways to deal with common, larger scale developments are featured, especially subdivision rules; protections for certain private property interests, for example, through non-conforming use (NCU) rights, appear; often an appeal system is put in place; and various remedies for rule violation are specified.

We explore these typical features of municipal land-use planning law. In considering them, we look at cases and statutes from all provinces. The point is not so much to focus on the present state of the law in any one place, but to understand the policy issues the law is dealing with and to consider the strengths and weaknesses of the various options, plus to consider possible improvements.

To some extent, the planning law statutes offer municipalities the main power to regulate land uses, but the ultimate controlling context of provincial policies is never far from the surface. It is important to recognize this limitation, whether as Statements of Provincial Interest controlling the content of official plans, as in Schedule B of the Nova Scotia *Municipal Government Act*, or through other measures such as the power of a provincial minister to directly zone land, as in section 47 of the Ontario *Planning Act*.

Public participation is a central value of land-use planning. This is manifested in such provisions as elections, committees with citizen members, public hearings, open meetings, conflict of interest rules, freedom of information rules, appeals, and the availability of judicial review.

The existence of appeals systems recognizes that local municipal councils are subject to making decisions inappropriately, and in response to local pressures, which may divert their attention from the principles of good planning adopted through their official plan. Nine of the provinces have appellate bodies; in British Columbia, the province without such a body, there is extensive land-use litigation. The powers of the appellate bodies are not uniform, the Ontario Municipal Board (OMB) having the widest review powers.

B. MULTIPLE STATUTES AFFECTING LAND USE

Only in theory could detailed regulation of land use be implemented at the level of a provincial government. Municipal institutions have existed in Canada since well prior to Confederation in 1867. Almost as soon as European settlements appeared in what is now Canada, some form of local council came into existence. Saint John, New Brunswick, for example, has had a royal charter since 1785, thus establishing itself as the first incorporated city in Canada. The essential logic is that local government is in a position to be familiar with the physical characteristics of each neighbourhood, block, and lot and to understand how the community in some areas might best function together. As challenging as this is in large municipalities, it remains the basic rationale for the existence of municipal government. In the absence of assigned powers under the *Constitution Act, 1867*, local governments are delegated their powers and responsibilities under statute. Each province has adopted a *Municipal Act* or equivalent and/or a *Planning Act* or equivalent. Together, these main statutes set out the essence of municipal land-use regulatory powers.[1] However important these few main statutes are, land use is also regulated by a wide variety of provincial statutes, many of which confer powers on municipalities, though not always. Appendix B lists statutes affecting land use, using Alberta as a typical province. Similar sets of statutes are found throughout the country. But, as we have noted several times, land-use regulation is a complex matter involving a multitude of rules that interact.

It is common for the planning statutes to be given a status above other legislation in the event of conflict. Thus, Saskatchewan's *Planning and Development Act, 2007* says, "In the event of conflict between the provisions of this and any other Act, the provisions of this Act govern so far as they relate to urban and rural planning and development."[2] As an example of this sort of provision trumping another statute's provisions, see *Bishop-Beckwith Marsh Body v Wolfville (Town)*.[3] In *Bishop-Beckwith*, two regulation-making entities, the marsh body and the town, adopted differing rules for use of the dykes: the marsh body assigned a purely agricultural use, as did the town, but with exceptions. The situation involved no direct conflict of the statutes but of the regulations made pursuant to the statutes. In assessing which should prevail, the court considered the history of all of the relevant legislation, including the province's stated preference for the *Planning Act*, as well as "the increasing importance of land use planning in our society and the dominant role to be played by municipalities in this process."[4] In Ontario, the *Greenbelt Act, 2005*[5] provides that it prevails in the event of conflict with any other Act, as does the *Places to Grow Act, 2005*[6]; this reflects the shift towards centralization of planning in Ontario. The provision has not been tested against the same statement in section 71 of the *Planning Act*.[7]

One of the main relevant statutes is a *Building Code Act*, which establishes inspectors with powers to halt construction not in accord with

---

1 *Municipal Acts* also set out the powers and responsibilities of local governments on matters other than land use, for example, on the structure of the councils, the role of administrative officers, powers over taxation, services such as police and fire, the ability to enter into contracts, and so on.

2 SS 2007, c P-13.2, s 4.

3 (1996), 135 DLR (4th) 456 (NSCA) [*Bishop-Beckwith*].

4 *Ibid* at para 65.

5 SO 2005, c 1, s 20.

6 SO 2005, c 13, s 20.

7 Other Ontario statutes relating to land use contain provisions declaring that in the case of conflict they are to prevail, such as those establishing the municipalities of Hamilton, Ottawa, Sudbury, and Toronto; the *Far North Act, 2010*, SO 2010, c 18, s 20 prevails over the *Places to Grow Act*. Principles of statute interpretation work so as to try to avoid conflict.

applicable provisions of the code, by-laws, or other relevant law. Typically, municipalities are charged with the responsibility to administer and enforce the building code. The code is generated by the National Research Council and is amended from time to time after a consultation process. The most recent changes move to include energy efficiency standards for new construction, although some energy efficiency matters were always a part of the code. *Building Code Acts* allow for the incorporation by reference of the national code and allow for municipalities to set by-laws that are not inconsistent with the code. Some provinces have exempted small, municipally approved, home-based businesses from certain aspects that would otherwise apply to commercial establishments.

C. PROPERTY LAW INTERACTION

A major feature of land-use planning law is its effect on two important aspect of the common law bundle of rights that make up ownership—the right of alienation and the right to devise. At common law an owner was entitled to sell, or leave through a will, the whole or a part of that person's real estate. In effect, it was a common law right to create new lots or parcels of land. Under regularized land-use planning, that right is made subject to the prerequisites adopted by the planning authorities. For a lot to be sold or left by will, it first must be created as a recognized lot according to subdivision regulations. Thus, in Ontario the *Planning Act*, section 50(3) provides: "No person shall convey land by way of a deed or transfer, or grant . . . that has the effect of granting the use of or right in land directly or by entitlement to renewal for a period of twenty-one years or more unless (a) the land is described in accordance with and is within a registered plan of subdivision."[8] Section 50.1 likewise invalidates purported subdivisions by will: "No provision in a will that purports to subdivide land is of any effect to subdivide that land unless, irrespective of that provision, each part of the land divided could be conveyed without contravening section 50."[9] Both of these provisions link to the *Land Titles Act*, section 44, which disallows registration of instruments that do not comply with the *Planning Act* subdivision requirements.[10] Such provisions are a dramatic reflection of the public policy preference for organized land-use planning over traditional private rights. Such provisions are so well known among lawyers that there is now not likely to be any error, but

8 *Planning Act*, RSO 1990, c P.13, s 50(3)(a).

9 *Ibid*, s 50.1(1).

10 *Land Titles Act*, RSO 1990, c L.5, s 44(1).

as they were first being adopted, and prior to the establishment of government-guaranteed title systems, there were glitches. In *Reid v Reid*,[11] a parent had, in 1969, deeded her 25-acre property to one son, excluding her dwelling house; by will she left her property to her other son. After she died in 1973, the sons disputed who owned what. The court ruled the original conveyance void under the *Planning Act*, a formal subdivision of land not having been obtained.[12] There have also been attempts to invent schemes that bypass the *Planning Act*'s strictures, but, in general, these have been unsuccessful when discovered.[13]

Municipalities have powers of expropriation, limited to some extent. When land has been identified for future use by a municipality, as, for example, for a road or a park, there is a statutory requirement that the land be so designated in the Land Titles registry so as to alert potential purchasers, and an obligation exists to purchase the land within some set time. Thus, in Nova Scotia's *Municipal Government Act* it says: "A council may zone privately owned land for future public use other than transportation reserves if the by-law provides for an alternative zone on the land, consistent with the municipal planning strategy. Where privately owned land is zoned for future public use, the municipality shall, within one year of the effective date of the zoning, acquire the land or the alternative zoning comes into effect."[14] For transportation reserves, the municipality has five years to acquire the land. Such provisions are typical.

D. PURPOSE

The statutes often have a formal articulated purpose, either for the full statute or for that part of it most directly affecting formal planning. It is not unusual for "economic development" in some form to be cited, along with "sustainability" or "the environment." A clear power to deal with environmental matters was assigned to Quebec municipalities in 2006 in the *Municipal Powers Act*.[15] Invariably, though, two interacting ideas are set out: one to respect the autonomy of local governments, and the other for them to act in accord with provincial policies.

---

11 (1976), 22 NSR (2d) 361 (SCTD).

12 The case is not unique. The Nova Scotia court relied on an Ontario precedent, *Glen v Harvic Construction Ltd* (1958), 16 DLR (2d) 232 (CA).

13 See, for example, *Matwijow v Pelham (Town)*, 2012 ONSC 2533 and *Reference re Certain Titles to Land in Ontario*, [1973] 2 OR 613 (CA) for context.

14 *Municipal Government Act*, SNS 1998, c 18, s 222 [NS *MGA*].

15 CQLR c C-47.1, ss 4 and 19.

A statement from the legislature as to the purpose of an act is a factor affecting how a court will interpret some provision if its meaning or ambit is called into question. There are not a great many cases in which the courts have found it necessary or useful to turn to the purpose sections of land-use planning statutes as an aid to interpretation. This did occur, though, in *Funk v Alberta (Planning Board)*[16] and *MacMillan Bloedel Ltd v Galiano Island Trust Committee*,[17] both of which involved disputes over interpretation of basic planning statutes.[18] In both cases, the court found it useful to refer to the stated purposes of the statute on the basis that the powers exercised ought to be considered in the context of the legislative framework, including the stated intent of the Act.[19] Alberta's *Municipal Government Act* says,

> The purpose of this Part [Part 17] . . . is to provide a means whereby plans and related matters may be prepared and adopted (a) to achieve the orderly, economical and beneficial development, use of land and patterns of human settlement, and (b) to maintain and improve the quality of the physical environment within which patterns of human settlement are situated in Alberta, without infringing on the rights of individuals for any public interest except to the extent that is necessary for the overall greater public interest.[20]

In Nova Scotia, the *Municipal Government Act*'s purposes are to

> give broad authority to councils, including the broad authority to pass by-laws, and to respect their right to govern municipalities in whatever ways the councils consider appropriate within the jurisdiction given to them . . . (i) to provide good government, (ii) to provide services, facilities and other things that, in the opinion of the council, are necessary or desirable for all or part of the municipality and (iii) develop and maintain safe and viable communities.[21]

Often, court references to purpose sections are as part of general remarks in which the courts note a legislative intent to accord municipalities a fairly wide ambit of authority. Thus, in *Nanaimo (City) v Rascal Trucking Ltd*,[22] the Supreme Court of Canada said, "There is ample au-

---

16 (1979), 11 Alta LR (2d) 316 (CA).

17 (1995), 28 MPLR (2d) 157 (BCCA) [*MacMillan Bloedel*].

18 See Bill Bulholzer, "The Islands Trust: 30 Years of Protecting B.C.'s Gulf Islands" (2005) 10 *Digest of Municipal and Planning Law* (2d) 1.

19 *MacMillan Bloedel*, above note 17 at para 163.

20 *Municipal Government Act*, RSA 2000, c M-26, s 617. The "Part" referred to is Part 17, "Planning and Development."

21 NS *MGA*, above note 14, s 2.

22 2000 SCC 13.

thority, on the interpretation of statutes generally and of municipal statutes specifically, to support a broad and purposive approach."[23]

At the same time, there are stated limitations. In Nova Scotia, the Part of the *Municipal Government Act* (*MGA*) on "Planning and Development" is in somewhat different terms than the statute as a whole, and includes a reference to public participation, and to being consistent with the interests and regulations of the province.[24] Ontario's *Planning Act* declares that its purposes are,

(a) to provide sustainable economic development in a healthy natural environment;
(b) to provide for a land use planning system led by provincial policy;
(c) to integrate matters of provincial interest in provincial and municipal planning decisions;
(d) to provide for planning processes that are fair by making them open, accessible, timely and efficient;
(e) to encourage co-operation and co-ordination among various interests;
(f) to recognize the decision-making authority and accountability of municipal councils in planning.[25]

In Prince Edward Island, the *Planning Act*[26] says its objects are,

(a) to provide for efficient planning at the provincial and municipal level;
(b) to encourage the orderly and efficient development of public services;
(c) to protect the unique environment of the province;
(d) to provide effective means for resolving conflicts respecting land use;
(e) to provide the opportunity for public participation in the planning process.

E. PROVINCIAL ROLE

Not only is provincial-level pre-emption of local government control over land use theoretically possible, the statutes that create municipalities are replete with specified limitations on local government authority. The *Canadian Encyclopedic Digest* says, concerning Ontario but with resonance for all other provinces, "The development of Ontario planning law

23 *Ibid* at para 18.
24 Above note 14, s 190.
25 Above note 8, s 1.1.
26 RSPEI 1988, c P-8, s 2.

centres around the conflict between provincial (central) and municipal (local) control over planning and the degree of provincial control as opposed to municipal autonomy over land use decisions."[27] Elsewhere, the same author refers to "adoption of a centralized and province-led top-down planning process."[28] Whether such provincial control is appropriate is a point often debated. One book advocating for greater local autonomy does so on the basis of promotion of democratic values. Andre Carrel says,

> The anomaly of a council that is elected by citizens, yet controlled by the province, contributes in a large measure to the lack of respect many citizens have for the municipal politicians they elect. The need to serve two masters also causes many frustrations endured by municipal politicians . . . every municipal association in Canada expends enormous efforts on lobbying governments for changes in legislation, changes in regulation, and greater equity in the allocation of public funds. That the elected council of Canada's greatest cities should be treated as if they were immature juveniles in need of parental guidance is a national shame.[29]

The controlling provincial interest is manifested in several main ways in planning statutes: statements of provincial interest as guides or limits on official plans, the existence of appellate bodies, a ministerial power to zone land, provincial review of official plans, and the Crown not being bound by municipal rules.

The provincial interest is clearly manifested in Statements of Provincial Interest (SPIs). A crucial aspect of provincial-level influence is illustrated by the fact that municipalities in carrying out their responsibilities "shall be consistent with" matters of provincial interest as it appears in Ontario's *Planning Act*[30] and in provisions such as Nova Scotia's *Municipal Government Act*, where municipal planning strategies (OPs) "must be reasonably consistent with"[31] Statements of Provincial Interest. As said by Edwards J in *BM Halifax Holdings Ltd v Nova Scotia (Attorney General)*,[32]

> A[n SPI] . . . is one area of a land use planning power that the Province has reserved for itself. Specifically, it enables the Province to intervene directly in the affairs of municipalities, whether by setting the ground

27 CED (Ont 4th), vol 42A, title 117 at § 1.

28 Robert Doumani & Patricia Foran, *Ontario Planning Legislation and Commentary, 2017 Edition* (Markham, ON: LexisNexis, 2016) at 3.

29 André Carrel, *Citizens' Hall* (Toronto: Between the Lines, 2001) at 62.

30 Above note 8, s 3(5).

31 Above note 14, s 214.

32 2014 NSSC 430 [*BM Halifax*].

> rules with respect to the land uses a municipality may exclude from its borders or by setting the ground rules for development within a municipality. While true, the *MGA* was enacted as a mechanism to give municipalities more flexibility and control over their own issues, it was never intended to give *carte blanche* control over all issues.[33]

The requirement for adherence to the SPIs is much tighter in Ontario, where they are known as Provincial Policy Statements (PPSs), than in Nova Scotia. In Ontario, since 2005, municipalities and the OMB are required to make decisions that "shall be consistent with" provincial policies.[34] They also "shall conform" with provincial plans. Earlier cases, with municipalities operating under differently worded strictures, had always seen the provincial policies as having weight but not necessarily being determinative.[35] Ontario's standard has been varied over time: from 1983 to 1994, the *Planning Act* required OPs to "have regard to" any PPS, but from 1994 to 1996, the requirement was for an OP to "be consistent with" the policies; in 1996, the earlier standard was reverted to, and then in 2005, was changed again to "shall be consistent with."[36]

Even "having regard" for the PPS has been interpreted as something having real content. Krushelnicki has said,

> . . . the obligation . . . should mean that the policy, if it is relevant and applicable in the circumstances . . . should be given weight and should play some meaningful role in the decision . . . [it] should not . . . be construed to permit the policy to be disregarded or set aside where it is inconvenient or where it poses some difficulty to the applicant.[37]

The effect of the current statute is of close control of planning policy by the province.[38] The Ontario SPIs are found in PPS 2014.[39] The

---

33 *Ibid* at paras 32–33. The decision was upheld by the Court of Appeal in 2015 NSCA 89, where, at paras 34 & 35, the court said the statutes gave the province "overarching authority" to protect its interests in the use and development of land.

34 *Planning Act*, above note 8, s 3(5)(a).

35 See, for example, *Innisfill (Township) v Barrie (City)* (1977), 80 DLR (3d) 85 (Div Ct); *Supportive Housing Coalition of Metropolitan Toronto v Toronto* (1993), 30 OMBR 136.

36 *Planning Act*, above note 8, s 3(5). The changes followed changes in the political party in government. See John G Chipman, *The Planning Act in Transition* (Aurora, ON: Canada Law Book, 1996).

37 Bruce Krushelnicki, *A Practical Guide to the Ontario Municipal Board* (Toronto: LexisNexis Butterworths, 2003) at 111. He cites *Victoria Point Homes Inc v Orillia (City)*, [1998] OMBD No 684.

38 See *Toronto (City) v R&G Realty Management Inc*, 2009 CanLII 42397 (Ont Div Ct).

39 Online: www.mah.gov.on.ca/AssetFactory.aspx?did=10463 [PPS]. This replaces the earlier Comprehensive Set of Policy Statements from 1996 and 2005.

SPIs seek to promote ecosystem planning, housing, protection of prime agricultural lands, clean drinking water, energy efficiency in transportation, and sensitivity to natural hazards such as floodways. This range of provincial policies is typical.

The Ontario PPS[40] imposes minimum requirements on local authorities and directs them to adopt the policies that are relevant to their particular area through the OP. So comprehensive and important is the Ontario PPS that any appreciation of policies that will be applicable to both individual developments and general land-use plans in any community, must start with an examination of the document.[41]

In Nova Scotia, not only is the language weaker, but the policies themselves are written in terms that tend to allow for a great deal of local choice, for the most part. Thus its SPI says, "As the statements are general in nature, they provide guidance rather than rigid standards. They reflect the diversity found in the Province and do not take into account all local situations. They must be applied with common sense. Thoughtful, innovative and creative application is encouraged."[42] Still, there are some specifics; the housing policy says, "Municipal planning documents must provide for manufactured housing," thus apparently requiring a zone to allow for trailer parks. Other policies are not without some vigour: the Minister of Municipal Affairs has successfully disallowed plan amendments that he saw as conflicting with the SPIs protecting agricultural land and drinking water,[43] the Nova Scotia Utility and Review Board (NSUARB) has disallowed a rezoning that would have permitted a service station in a watershed protection area,[44] and the scope of SPIs has been ruled to extend to facilitating particular projects and not confined to preventing or prohibiting certain generalized land uses.[45]

40 It is issued pursuant to s 3 of the *Planning Act*, above note 8.

41 The PPS directs that "it is to be read in its entirety and the relevant policies are to be applied to each situation" (at 2). The PPS includes a useful, extensive set of definitions, which will be relevant at all stages of LUP in Ontario.

42 NS Reg 101/2001 as amended by NS Reg 272/2013. The SPIs are on drinking water, flood risk areas, agricultural land, infrastructure, housing, and a particular project known as the Nova Centre.

43 *Elderkin v Nova Scotia (Minister of Service Nova Scotia and Municipal Relations)*, 2013 NSCA 79. The land in question was 380 acres zoned agricultural; the municipality proposed OP and LUB changes to allow mixed uses, including residential.

44 *Re Parrsboro (Town)*, 2007 NSUARB 147.

45 *BM Halifax*, above note 32 at para 50. This is also the case in Ontario: see *St Mary's Cement Inc (Canada) v Ontario* (2013), 2 MPLR (5th) 46 (Ont Div Ct), where a declaration of provincial interest focused on one proposed quarry.

In Manitoba the SPIs are extensive and detailed. They are termed Provincial Land Use Policies (PLUPs).[46] The document is written similarly to an official plan in that it includes discussion of principles and explanations. Local development plans "must be prepared in accordance with the requirements" of Part 4,[47] which itself requires that the plans be "generally consistent" with the PLUPs.

Along with SPIs, the existence of a provincial land-use appellate body ranks as the greatest manifestation of a controlling context for local government decision-making. Bodies like the OMB are appointed by the provincial government, and their review mandate is set by provincial law. But it is simply their existence that sends a message to local municipal councils: that planning must be carried out in accordance with the process and policy framework set by the province, that planning is to be a principled and not a capricious activity, that reasonable lines of thought must support decisions, and that they are not isolated from scrutiny.

Several provinces have given to the Minister of Municipal Affairs (or equivalent) a power to zone lands directly. Ontario's *Planning Act*, section 47(1)(a), for example, provides, "The Minister may by order, in respect of any land in Ontario, exercise any of the powers conferred upon councils by section 34 [zoning], 38 [interim control] or 39 [temporary use]." The minister is not obliged to consult or give advance notice of an intention to use these powers, though notice must be given within thirty days of the making of a ministerial order.

In British Columbia, Saskatchewan, Manitoba, Ontario, Quebec, New Brunswick, Nova Scotia, PEI, and Newfoundland and Labrador, an OP or amendments are to be reviewed by the responsible provincial department as a condition of going into effect or for compliance with provincial policies. There are various exceptions and distinctions among large and small municipalities, but overall this represents a significant mechanism for provincial control in planning.

The Crown is not bound by municipal land-use rules as to Crown lands located in a municipality, unless it specifies that it is prepared to accede to this.[48] What is sometimes included in municipal legislation is a political promise not to take action that directly affects local governments

---

46 See *Provincial Planning Regulation*, Man Reg 81/2011, pursuant to the *Planning Act*, CCSM c P80.

47 *Ibid*, s 2.

48 In one Newfoundland and Labrador case, there is a statement that in St John's the Crown has so bound itself (*Friends of Ragged Beach Inc v Witless Bay (Town) Town Council*, 2011 NLTD(G) 108), but the statutes do not seem to support the statement.

without notice and consultation. Examples of such provisions are section 3(2) of British Columbia's *Local Government Act* (*LGA*)[49] and section 519 of Nova Scotia's *MGA*.[50] The British Columbia provision has been found by the courts to be aspirational and not binding. In *Greater Vancouver (Regional District) v British Columbia*,[51] the provincial government had negotiated an agreement with the Musqueam First Nation and then enacted the settlement agreement. The Greater Vancouver Regional District challenged the implementing legislation on the basis of the *LGA* promise, but the courts were not prepared to give it legal force, on the basis that laws cannot bind future legislatures except as to the manner and form of legislation, not content, unless explicit.

F. PUBLIC PARTICIPATION

Public participation has at least two main aspects. One is that land-use planning involves building a community and thus requires the members of the community to agree to what is planned. Indeed, in the participation the process of communal thought is created. The other is that useful information emerges from public discussion. So important is the need for public discussion, that the Supreme Court of Canada has recognized that a municipality may establish a formal inquiry in some circumstances. In *Consortium Developments (Clearwater) Ltd v Sarnia (City)*,[52] the city had established an inquiry into certain dubious land transactions that had taken place in a municipality later merged with the city. Various challenges were brought to the right of the city to proceed, including the scope of the city's power. The Court said,

> . . . good government depends in part on the availability of good information. A municipality . . . needs from time to time to get to the bottom of matters and events within its bailiwick. The power to authorize a judicial inquiry is an important safeguard of the public interest, and should not be diminished by a restrictive or overly technical interpretation of the legislative requirements for its exercise.[53]

The full ambit of public participation is extensive. As a principle of the appropriate process that should characterize land-use planning,

---

49 RSBC 2015, c 1.

50 Above note 14.

51 2011 BCCA 345.

52 [1998] 3 SCR 3.

53 *Ibid* at para 26. The statutory power at issue was in the Ontario *Municipal Act, 2001*, SO 2001, c 25.

public participation is an essential aspect of the enterprise. It is not an add-on or peripheral.[54] One UK text says that "planning is above all a *process* through which decisions are made, rather than anything with an absolutely definitive subject matter."[55] That process is a public one. A variety of ways exist for the public to participate.

The opportunity to vote is a starting point, though not guaranteed in the *Canadian Charter of Rights and Freedoms*,[56] as it is for Parliament or the legislatures.[57] Statutory definitions of eligibility to vote tend to mirror those of the federal and provincial governments.

There is also usually the opportunity to serve on committees. Municipal councils often are required or empowered to establish advisory committees, for example a "planning advisory committee" or "heritage advisory committee." Their composition is often required to include residents rather than or in addition to members of council. Committees perform useful screening functions, sometimes decision-making functions, and any failure to refer matters to them if required or unfairness in their processes may result in tainting of council's ultimate decision.[58]

Meetings of council are required to be open to the public, with very few exceptions.[59] This is part of the democratic accountability mechanism of government. A typical provision is British Columbia's *Community Charter*, where it is said "a meeting of a council must be open to the public, except as provided . . . ."[60] The exceptions relate to legal advice, personnel information, security, and the like. Attempts by councils to avoid the requirement of openness are carefully scrutinized by the courts. Thus in *London (City) v RSJ Holdings Inc*,[61] the Supreme Court of Canada was not prepared to exempt the city from its obligation under the *Municipal Act* to hold its meetings in public even though it was taking a decision (to adopt an interim control by-law) under the authority

54 This is discussed further in Chapter 1, Section B, and in Chapter 8.

55 Stewart Bell & Donald McGillivray, "Town and Country Planning" in *Environmental Law*, 5th ed (Vancouver: Blackstone, 2000) at 298 [emphasis in original].

56 *Constitution Act, 1982*, being Schedule B to the *Canada Act 1982* (UK), 1982, c 11 [*Charter*].

57 See *Charter, ibid*, s 3; Howard M Epstein, "Electoral Boundaries and the Problem of Vote Dilution in Municipal Elections" (2004) 48 *Municipal and Planning Law Reports* (3d) 259 at 259–60.

58 See, for example, *Sobeys Inc v Charlottetown (City)* (1966), 31 MPLR (2d) 254 (PEISCTD); *Friends of the Public Gardens v Halifax Planning Advisory Committee* (1984), 65 NSR (2d) 297 (SCTD).

59 See Jason Reynar, "Transparent Municipal Governance: When Must a Meeting Be Open?" (2011) 88 *Municipal and Planning Law Reports* (4th) 68.

60 SBC 2003, c 26, ss 89 & 90.

61 2007 SCC 29 [*RSJ Holdings*].

of the *Planning Act*; the Court did not accept claims of solicitor-client privilege or potential litigation as applicable. Meetings of committees are also usually required to be open, with the same sorts of exceptions as apply to councils. Whether a meeting is the equivalent of a council meeting is a matter of degree, measured according to whether actual decisions are made or fundamental direction is set. Thus in *Niagara-on-the-Lake Conservancy Society v Niagara-on-the-Lake (Town)*,[62] "think tank" sessions were seen as legitimate activities that might be carried out in private. Ontario also has a statutory protection for "education or training sessions," which may be closed to the public so long as there is no discussion of any matter in a way that "materially advances the business or decision-making of the council . . . ."[63]

It is not unusual for residents to be able to petition for the enactment of general by-laws. The right to petition does not, of course, determine the outcome of a consideration by the council: petition is not control or delegation of power. Where petitions are provided for, they must have sufficient particulars to allow consideration of what is being requested.[64] As in *McTaggart*, most such petitions relate to tax matters rather than to land use. Alberta's *MGA* section 233 allows for petitions over land-use matters, as does Newfoundland and Labrador's *City of St John's Act*,[65] where 10 percent of the electors may require "questions of town planning" to be put to a referendum.

Unless there are statutory restrictions, non-owner residents may apply for the rezoning of the lands of others. For an example, see *Tollefson v Gloucester*.[66] To do so, the resident petitioner must pay a fee, but the matter then goes to the council even though it may not have originated in a planning process of the municipality itself, or with the landowner.

Access to information, allied with the openness of council meetings and notice requirements, is an important aspect of democratic accountability and public participation.[67] At a minimum, public inspection of

---

62 (2001), 14 MPLR (3d) 94 (Ont SCJ).

63 *Municipal Act, 2001*, above note 53, s 239.

64 *Kindersley (Town) v McTaggart*, 2000 SKQB 130 [*McTaggart*], applying s 88 of Saskatchewan's *The Urban Municipality Act*, which requires a council to consider a petition presented by the greater of twenty-five persons or 15 percent of the electors.

65 RSNL 1990, c C-17, s 308.

66 (1976–77), 1 MPLR 11 (OMB) [*Tollefson*]. The proposal in *Tollefson* was for a downzoning and was not allowed by the OMB.

67 Though there is a "clear distinction between a citizen's right to notice and participation, and his or her right to observe municipal government in process": *RSJ Holdings*, above note 61 at para 32.

documents such as the minutes of council, is afforded.[68] Broader access to information relates ultimately to the fairness of the process of planning. Freedom of Information and Protection of Privacy (FOIPOP) statutes now exist in all provinces, dating to the 1970s.[69] Provincial governments initially bound themselves and by progressive extension have bound an array of public bodies. Municipalities are included. Despite some jurisprudence indicating that, in a challenge to a decision based on breach of fairness standards, a violation of a statutory provision will vitiate the decision, in *Heritage Trust of Nova Scotia v Halifax (Regional Municipality)*,[70] the court considered that even though the municipal planner in possession of studies done by the developer refused a request by members of the public for access, in "an erroneous interpretation of the FOIPOP provisions of the MGA,"[71] the appropriate way to treat the circumstance was as one of the "flaws in the provision of information but perfection is not the standard."[72]

Notice and mandatory hearings are discussed in more detail in Chapter 8. They are essential to effective public participation. Hearings are typically required for the adoption of an official plan, for adoption and amendment of by-laws, and for entering into zoning flexibility mechanisms such as development agreements. Indeed, for adoption of OPs, typically a municipality must go through a process that not only requires a public hearing at the time of its consideration for adoption, but that involves a public process as part of the development of the content of the OP.

Where such statutory requirements for public consultation exist, as in British Columbia's *Local Government Act*[73] consultation is an "elastic concept dependent upon the extent of the change proposed."[74] "At a minimum, 'consultation' anticipates bi-lateral conversation in which the person consulted has the opportunity to question, to receive explanation and to provide comment to the local government upon the proposal" and "includes informal communications, meetings, open houses, delegations, and correspondence."[75]

---

68 See, for example, *Municipalities Act, 1999*, SNL 1999, c M-24, s 215.

69 See, for example, Brianna J Heinrichs, *Municipal Government and Open Data* (Calgary: Manning Foundation, 2014); Michael Karanicolas, *Failing to Measure Up: An Analysis of Access to Information Legislation in Canadian Jurisdictions* (Halifax: Centre for Law and Democracy, 2012).

70 2007 NSSC 28.

71 *Ibid* at para 139.

72 *Ibid* at para 154.

73 Above note 49, s 475, formerly RSBC 1996, c 323, s 879.

74 *Gardner v Williams Lake (City)*, 2006 BCCA 307 at para 28.

75 *Ibid* at para 29.

G. POWERS LISTED

The style of drafting statutes that confer powers on municipalities is rooted in the idea that they are akin to corporations, and therefore may exercise only those powers specified or necessarily implied. This is Dillon's Rule (also referred to as "the doctrine of prescribed powers"[76]) and dates from the mid-nineteenth century. Based on this theory, such statutes have tended to be written with lists of specific powers, going on for many pages. The Rule was manifested in such Supreme Court of Canada decisions as *MacIlreith v Hart Estate*,[77] discussed in Chapter 2. Starting with Alberta in 1994, however, some provinces altered their approach to drafting. As said by Bastarache J in *United Taxi Drivers' Fellowship of Southern Alberta v Calgary (City)*:[78]

> The evolution of the modern municipality has produced a shift in the proper approach to the interpretation of statutes empowering municipalities . . . . The "benevolent" and "strict" construction dichotomy has been set aside, and a broad and purposive approach to the interpretation of municipal powers has been embraced . . . . This interpretive approach has evolved concomitantly with the modern method of drafting municipal legislation. Several provinces have moved away from the practice of granting municipalities specific powers in particular subject areas, choosing instead to confer them broad authority over generally defined matters . . . . This shift in legislative drafting reflects the true nature of modern municipalities which require greater flexibility in fulfilling their statutory purposes . . . .

The issue in *United Taxi* had to do with whether the detailed taxi regulation by-law was *ultra vires*. The authority granted to the municipality was to pass by-laws respecting "transport and transportation systems,"[79] "businesses,"[80] to "regulate or prohibit,"[81] and to "provide for a system of licenses."[82] The Act also said that "The power to pass by-laws under this Division is stated in general terms to give broad authority to councils and to respect their right to govern municipalities in whatever way the coun-

76 Ron Levi & Mariana Valverde, "Freedom of the City: Canadian Cities and the Quest for Governmental Status" (2006) 44 *Osgoode Hall Law Journal* 409 at 418.

77 *MacIlreith v Hart*, [1908] SCR 657.

78 2004 SCC 19 at para 6 [*United Taxi*].

79 *Municipal Government Act*, SA 1994, c M-26.1, s 7(d).

80 *Ibid*, s 7(e).

81 *Ibid*, s 8(a).

82 *Ibid*, s 8(c).

cils consider appropriate, within the jurisdiction given to them . . . ."[83] The Court upheld the by-law.

The case does not, however, resolve all interpretive issues associated with such statutes. First, not all provinces have moved to a "spheres of jurisdiction" mode of drafting. It predominates in the Prairie provinces and Ontario, but even in all of those provinces there remains a mix, that is, along with the broad powers there are some specifics listed. For example, Ontario's *Municipal Act, 2001* in its Part II lists "general powers" and then in Part III lists various "specific powers." In other provinces, powers remain listed in detail, inviting debate about the limits of the powers granted. Also, the issue of unauthorized distinctions is likely to remain. Since *United Taxi* in 2004, many cases have gone to the courts based on disputes over the ambit of municipal authority. For example, in *Allard Contractors Ltd v Coquitlam (District)*,[84] the municipality had adopted a fee system for permits to extract soil and other material; its basis for calculation of fees (making a distinction between commercial and non-commercial users) was challenged as not authorized by statute; the power granted was to set fees by volume; the Court found this implied a power to make distinctions between commercial and non-commercial uses and thus for the system of calculation of fees adopted. In *Keller v Big Horn (Municipal District No 8)*,[85] the municipality was seen to have the authority to create a system of transferable development credits even though no such power was specifically listed in the governing statute; the court found the power over land use and density to be sufficient. The overall result of constant disputes is, however, that drafters are still inclined to want to specify municipal powers, and any municipalities that are hesitant to move into regulation of some new topic will cite the absence of provincial authority to do so.

H. OFFICIAL PLANS AND LAND-USE BY-LAWS

1) Official Plans

Planning at the local level involves a community adopting an official plan and a set of land-use by-laws to implement that plan. This is the core, typical feature of how provinces expect municipalities to proceed with formal planning. In the classic statement, JB Milner said that an official plan is a ". . . dynamic instrument expressing the manner of

83 *Ibid*, s 9.

84 [1993] 4 SCR 371.

85 2010 ABQB 362 [*Keller v Big Horn*].

growth of the municipality and indicating the limitations the council may be expected to impose, *in the future*, on land use . . . . [An official plan is] its plans for the future, not its laws for the present."[86] While this statement was offered at the time as an analysis that suggested limitations to the efficacy of OPs, both statute and jurisprudence have evolved somewhat,[87] and in any event it seems obvious that planning is about the future. Thus, in *Denman Island v Ellis*,[88] the British Columbia Court of Appeal was explicit that the idea of "development" under the *Local Government Act* includes future development—not a surprising result.

Provinces have different names for an OP. It is the Official Community Plan in Saskatchewan,[89] a Municipal Planning Strategy in Nova Scotia.[90] In the United Kingdom, the equivalent term for an OP is a "development plan."

> The development plan is the central policy document of the British planning system. Development planning is the machinery through which decisions are made and recorded as to the policies and proposals to be pursued for the future. The plan thereafter acts as a guide for, and a constraint upon, authorities in exercising their powers of control over new development, and co-ordinates future investment and development activity in both the public and the private sector.[91]

This, along with Professor Milner's description, gets at the nature of an OP.

OPs must be developed in a process that involves public participation. Prior to preparing the OP for consideration by the council, a public participation programme is to be created. The content of the programme is for the council to determine, but "it must identify opportunities and establish ways and means of seeking the opinions of the public concerning the proposed planning documents."[92] OPs are subject to review by a provincial cabinet minister or relevant department official and require approval in order to be adopted.[93] The review will be to seek accord with provincial policies.

OPs are often written in recognizable styles and structures. To start, the municipality will be mapped to show broad categories of intended

86 JB Milner, "An Introduction to Master Plan Legislation" (1957) 35 *Canadian Bar Review* 1125 at 1170 [emphasis in original].

87 Ian MacFee Rogers & Alison Scott Butler, *Canadian Law of Planning and Zoning*, 2d ed (Toronto: Carswell, 2005) (loose-leaf revision 2013 release 6) at s 3.1.

88 *Denman Island Local Trust Committee v Ellis*, 2007 BCCA 536.

89 *Planning and Development Act, 2007*, above note 2.

90 NS *MGA*, above note 14.

91 Malcolm Grant, *Urban Planning Law* (London: Sweet & Maxwell, 1982) at 75.

92 *Halifax Regional Municipality Charter*, SNS 2008, c 39, s 219 [*HRM Charter*].

93 See, for example, Saskatchewan's *Planning and Development Act, 2007*, above note 2, ss 36, 76, and 78; Ontario's *Planning Act*, above note 8, s 17.

future use: a "generalized future land use map" (GFLUM), where the categories will often reflect the higher-level categories used in zoning, such as "agriculture," "residential," "industrial," and "commercial." In line with the idea that an OP represents plans for the future, the GFLUM will be the starting point for the evolution of actual zoning and for consideration of contract development proposals or other variants on zoning as a planning tool. OPs will often contain goals, objectives, and policies that apply both municipality-wide and in particular districts.

The idea of an OP acting as a "constraint" on municipal authorities is as accurate in Canada as the United Kingdom. The constraint derives from such provisions as that in the New Brunswick legislation: "The adoption of a regional plan shall not commit a municipality . . . to undertake any proposal therein suggested or outlined, but shall prevent the undertaking of any development in any manner inconsistent or at variance with . . . any proposal so outlined or suggested."[94] Such provisions have, however, had a chequered history in the courts. It is clear that the policies set out do not have to be implemented immediately, even though it is contemplated that a municipality will adopt an OP and an implementing LUB at the same time.[95] But the municipality is constrained from acting contrary to the OP.[96]

Courts have tended to regard OPs as statements at such a general level that they may reasonably bear a number of interpretations,[97] or as containing inconsistent statements from which the municipal council has a wide latitude of choice.[98] The courts may well look for direct collision before invalidating an LUB based on OP policies.[99] The idea of "conforming with" the OP is somewhat elusive. The British Columbia Court of Appeal in *Residents and Ratepayers Society v Central Saanich (District)*[100] said that if an OP has a specific rule that is contravened by a

---

94 *Community Planning Act*, RSNB 1973, c C-12 as amended, ss 18(7) and 27.

95 *Woodglen & Co v North York (City)* (1984), 47 OR (2d) 614 (Div Ct).

96 *Heritage Trust Inc v Fredericton (City)* (1988), 39 MPLR 64 (NBCA) [*Fredericton*]; *Sevin v Prince George (City)*, 2012 BCSC 1236; *Holmes v Halton (Regional Municipality)* (1978), 5 MPLR 158 (Ont HCJ); *Stocker v Fredericton (City)* (1978), 21 NBR (2d) 587 (QB).

97 But in *Capozzi Enterprises Ltd v Central Okanagan (Regional District)* (1978), 94 DLR (3d) 80 (BCSC), the court upheld as valid an OP that contained very specific language in its policies, even in the face of a statute that defined an OP as being "a general scheme without detail."

98 *Heritage Trust of Nova Scotia v Nova Scotia (Utility and Review Board)* (1994), 128 NSR (2d) 5 (CA) [*Heritage Trust*].

99 See, for example, *Heritage Preservation Society of New Westminster v New Westminster (City)*, 2005 BCSC 816; *Cox Construction Ltd v Puslinch (Township)* (1982), 36 OR (2d) 618 (HCJ).

100 2011 BCCA 484.

by-law, then it is likely the by-law will be struck down. At the same time, the court saw OPs as containing guidelines, and therefore questions of inconsistency were matters of interpretation. In *Cadillac Development Corp Ltd v Toronto (City)*,[101] the land in question, under both the OP and the LUB, allowed for high-density residential use; the zoning was changed to down-zone. The company argued that the change did not conform with the OP, but the court found that this was not contrary to the plan and observed that an increase in density through the LUB would have been contrary to the OP. In *Southwold (Township) v Caplice*,[102] the court went so far as to say that "[a]n official plan is not an effective instrument restricting the use of land"—a broad statement that is not reflected in the full range of cases. Non-conformity of an LUB with the OP may found an appeal to a provincial appellate body, or a court application to quash. Some court applications have been successful.[103] And appellate bodies have certainly found LUBs or specific developments to be contrary to the OP. In no instance is this easy to show. In *Queen's Square Neighbourhood Association Inc v Fredericton (City)*,[104] the association claimed that an amendment to the LUB was inconsistent with the OP. The court said that the test was whether the council's interpretation was one the OP could reasonably bear, which did not equate to the total absence of conflict; there had to be flexibility in reading the OP.

This approach is consistent with such cases as *MacNeill v Saskatoon (City)*[105] and *Old St Boniface Residents Association Inc v Winnipeg (City)*.[106] The Saskatchewan Court of Appeal in *MacNeill* says,[107]

> As might be expected, given the nature and general object of the Development Plan, it is not drawn with the precision of a statute. It employs many broad and undefined terms, elastic terms of uncertain scope befitting guidelines, rather than rules, especially policy guidelines. It is easy enough to understand what is meant generally by this provision or that, but it is often difficult to understand precisely what is meant. So applying the provisions is rather more of an art than a science, requiring good faith and a reasoned approach to the end of achieving the object of the Plan in harmony with the thrust of its provisions.

---

101 (1973), 1 OR (2d) 20 (HCJ).
102 (1978), 8 MPLR 1 (Ont Div Ct).
103 See, for example, *Fredericton*, above note 96.
104 2001 NBQB 257.
105 2001 SKCA 108 [*MacNeill*].
106 [1990] 3 SCR 1170 [*St Boniface*].
107 Above note 105 at paras 10–11.

The proposal in issue arguably fell short of meeting the whole of the terms of section 5.1.2(p) of the Development Plan, especially if, as Mr. Scherman contended, these terms fall to be construed and applied with the rigour called for in the interpretation and application of statutory provisions. But this is not what is called for, at least not in our respectful opinion. We quite agree with what is said of this matter in the current edition of Rogers, *Canadian Law of Planning and Zoning* (Toronto: Carswell 2001):

> As a rule, a [development] plan is not usually capable of exact interpretation. It is not to be subjected to the same authoritative examination as a statute. A plan is not a statute or a by-law and so it is not interpreted as such; it should be regarded as a statement of policy. A plan should be given a liberal interpretation with a view to furthering its policy objectives . . . (p. 38)[108]

To the same effect, in *St Boniface*, the Supreme Court of Canada says,[109]

> Is there non-conformity with Plan Winnipeg? As in the instant case, it may frequently be difficult to determine if a proposed rezoning does not conform with a general statement of policies and principles . . . . The question of conformity to an official plan is primarily a planning decision which is based on fact and policy. The opinion of the designated commissioner while not immune from judicial review should not be disturbed by an appellate court simply because it disagrees with the opinion in respect of policy or fact. The commissioner is in a much better position to assess whether a new development conforms to the planning policy of the municipality than is the court . . . . In light of the above, this Court would not be justified in substituting its view of fact and policy except in the most exceptional circumstances.

Professor Makuch has criticized OPs as having the potential to be "full of only pious vagaries."[110] Whether this proves actually to be the case in any particular municipality depends on the choices made by the council when developing its OP. It is entirely possible to write OPs with highly specific policies, or to indicate within them a hierarchy

---

108 This passage, quoted by the court from the first edition of Rogers is also to be found in Ian MacFee Rogers, *Canadian Law of Planning and Zoning*, 2d ed (Toronto: Carswell, 2005) at ch 3.1.

109 Above note 106 at 1201–202.

110 Stan Makuch, "Zoning: Avenues of Reform" (1973) 1 *Dalhousie Law Journal* 294 at 318.

of policies, or to manifest general policies in detailed secondary plans applicable in specific areas.

There is usually a statutory outline of what an OP is expected to include. Thus, Nova Scotia's *Municipal Government Act*[111] specifies both the purpose and range of content of policies that may be included:

> *Purpose of municipal planning strategy*
> s. 213 The purpose of a municipal planning strategy is to provide statements of policy to guide the development and management of the municipality and, to further this purpose, to establish
> (a) policies which address problems and opportunities concerning the development of land and the effects of the development;
> (b) policies to provide a framework for the environmental, social and economic development within a municipality;
> (c) policies that are reasonably consistent with the intent of statements of provincial interest; and
> (d) [specific] programs and actions necessary for implementing the municipal planning strategy.
>
> *Statements of policy in planning strategy*
> s. 214 (1) A municipal planning strategy may include statements of policy with respect to any or all of the following:
> (a) the goals and objectives of the municipality for its future;
> (b) the physical, economic and social environment of the municipality;
> (c) the protection, use and development of lands within the municipality . . . ;
> (h) the staging of developments . . . ;
> (k) non-conforming uses and structures;
> (l) the subdivision of land;
> (m) the use and conservation of energy, including the height and siting of developments;
> (n) measures for informing, or securing, the views of the public regarding contemplated planning policies and actions or by-laws arising from such policies . . . ;
> (q) any other matter relating to the physical, social or economic environment of the municipality.

This type of legislative framework is usually interpreted to set an optional range of policies that may be included in OPs, neither a minimum nor a maximum. There may be language that does require some minimum content, but even there the courts have said that such provisions do not set a maximum limit. Thus, in *Toronto (City) v Goldlist Properties*

111 Above note 14.

Inc,[112] the court said, regarding Ontario's *Planning Act*, "Section 16(1)(a) is cast in terms of the *minimum* requirements for an official plan, not the outside limits. It does not list heads of power or the subjects that may be addressed by the official plan. There are unquestionably limits to what a municipality may include within its official plan, but the wording and scope of [the section] indicate that those limits cannot be determined solely by a literal application of its terms. To determine what *may* be included in an official plan, as distinct from what *must be* included . . . reference must be had to the *Planning Act* as a whole."[113]

Goldlist said (and other cases such as *Heritage Trust*[114] have concurred) that OPs "are not statutes and should not be construed as such." What are the courts telling us when they make such a statement?

It is the case that OPs are not statutes, nor are they, as Hallet JA observed in *Heritage Trust*, statutory instruments or regulations. As he also observed, this implies that, in strictness, *Interpretation Acts* do not apply to them. Where does this leave us? In *Heritage Trust*, Hallett JA said that OPs should still be given a fair, large, and liberal interpretation: exactly the directions given by the *Interpretation Acts* for the reading of statutes. Furthermore, Driedger's modern principle[115] calls for a harmonious reading. So, if courts mean what they say, that OPs "are not statutes and should not be construed as such," that is, that technical or picky approaches should not be used, in fact modern interpretation of statutes is no longer technical or picky anyway. Can the courts mean something else?

What seems to be implied is that some approach to OPs should be taken that goes beyond the "fair, large and liberal" directive in terms of flexibility to achieve its objectives. This would explain what the courts mean by sometimes saying that OPs are a "constitutional" document for municipalities' LUP endeavours.[116] It is usually said of constitutions that they, too, are not to be interpreted as statutes, the point being that their terms are to be read very flexibly, so as to accommodate new circumstances.

There are of course serious negative aspects to an approach that allows a municipal council to interpret its OP with great flexibility. First,

---

112 (2003), 44 MPLR (3d) 1 (Ont CA) [*Goldlist*].

113 *Ibid* at para 49 [emphasis added].

114 Above note 98.

115 "Today there is only one principle or approach, namely, the words of an Act are to be read in their entire context in their grammatical and ordinary sense harmoniously with the scheme of the Act, the object of the Act and the intention of Parliament." Elmer A Driedger, *The Construction of Statutes*, 2d ed (Toronto, Butterworths, 1983) at 87.

116 Justice La Forest (dissenting) in *St Boniface*, above note 106 at para 13.

there is an economic aspect. It allows for negative impacts on investments that have been made in the purchase of land. This is readily appreciated by considering a residence nearby to land that is allowed, by a development agreement or some other zoning flexibility tool, to be built on to a height that is out of proportion to the general neighbourhood. The negative impact may be not only on the owner but on the financial institution that holds a mortgage on the property. Also, it leaves open the possible public reaction that land-use decisions are not a matter of articulated principle, but a matter of political influence. If municipal councils make what become characterized as apparently arbitrary decisions, the result could well be in calling the planning system into disrepute, and the damage will be not only to faith in democratic institutions but to faith in the relative stability of the overall real estate market.

None of this should be taken to indicate that in any focused dispute, or in all instances, OPs are always so general that any interpretation, or selection of policies, is valid. Cases do exist in which land-use appellate bodies or courts have set aside the decisions of municipal councils on the basis of an inconsistent or unreasonable application of the OP.

Goldlist also says clearly that OPs are not to be seen as being limited to the physical aspects of land use, and may extend to "broad policies to govern land use planning,"[117] even if they are to be "primarily concerned with the management and direction of physical change."[118]

Nova Scotia's Court of Appeal has pointed out that OPs may even be seen as containing inherently conflicting policies. Thus, in *Heritage Trust*, it said,

> In my opinion by-laws . . . made pursuant to the *Planning Act* would fall within the definition of a "regulation" [in the *Interpretation Act*]. It is not clear that a municipal planning strategy [the Nova Scotia term for an official plan] would . . . . [But] a municipal planning strategy should be interpreted as a remedial measure adopted by a municipality to control land use and development. Accordingly . . . the *Interpretation Act* contains provisions that are relevant . . . .
>
> I turn back to the question of what is the intent of the Plan? There is no single intent. Primarily, it is to control development of land. This is done by the establishment of policies, many of which are inherently in conflict.[119]

This last statement by the court is problematic. The statement about policies "inherently in conflict" has not been adopted by courts in any other

117 Above note 112 at para 53.

118 *Ibid* at para 50.

119 Above note 98 at 32 and 25 respectively.

province, though it has continued to be cited in Nova Scotia.[120] While in the abstract it would be possible to imagine an OP with policies inherently in conflict, such a situation would be exceedingly rare, and would probably be an error in the drafting and corrected as soon as it was noticed. The modern principle of reading such instruments harmoniously would usually call for the balancing of all policies, so as to read them together. In the case of the policy sets at issue in *Heritage Trust*—the economic development and the heritage resource policies—there is no reason to see them as inherently in conflict: preservation of heritage can be an economic development tool. What weight particular policies should be given will emerge from the wording of the OP itself, or be left to political balancing. FA Laux, author of *Planning Law and Practice in Alberta*,[121] has made the following trenchant and principled observation that explains the nature of the problem with the court's language:

> Plans are not written with the precision of legislative language that is normally found in statutes, regulations and by-laws. This imprecise syntax creates considerable ambiguity and ambivalence, and thus the standard of judicial review of interpretations given to a plan by a planning agency ought not to be too high. On the other hand, an excessively low standard of review can create problems. If judicial intervention is limited to cases where the planning body's construction is one that the plan cannot reasonably bear, a lack of uniformity of application of plans can result. Two different planning agencies considering the approval of two identical development projects could arrive at diametrically opposed conclusions after applying the same provisions of a plan. Yet each conclusion would be legally correct if the two interpretations given to the plan were both reasonable.
>
> But that does little to meet two fundamental precepts of the law: the law should give forth the same result in identical circumstances and the law should be predictable in its application. If a planning tribunal is free to follow any interpretation that a plan can reasonably bear, how can one predict with a degree of certainty what meaning will be given to an ambiguous provision of a plan? How are lawyers and other planning specialists to advise their clients at the tribunal level?[122]

---

120 The closest similar statement appears in *Schein v Saugeen Valley Conservation Authority* (1995), 29 MPLR (2d) 42 at para 34 (Ont Ct Gen Div): "There will almost invariably be inconsistencies and uncertainties when considered in light of a specific proposal." This was later cited in *3714683 Canada Inc v Parry Sound (Town)* (2004), 4 MPLR (4th) 197 at para 40 (Ont SCJ).

121 Frederick A Laux, *Planning Law and Practice in Alberta*, 3d ed (Edmonton: Juriliber, 2002).

122 *Ibid* at s 5.6(3)(a).

Probably, the decision in *Heritage Trust* should be seen within this context. *Heritage Trust* has gone further than most other cases in suggesting inherent conflict as part of OPs. Such an expressed opinion seems unique to the Nova Scotia courts. Driedger's modern principle runs counter to any serious inclination to search out conflicts. Indeed, in the *Heritage Trust* decision itself, Côté's text is extensively quoted from, including the passage stating that, "the act be read as a whole in the light of all relevant principles."[123]

What this instance illustrates is that a drafter may, in some circumstances, especially regarding OPs, choose to maintain some level of ambiguity so that political choices remain for the municipal council. OPs exist to constrain the choices available to all participants in land use: developers, residents, and also municipal councils. But such constraints do not have to be in highly precise terms. As courts and commentators have said, OPs are meant to be policy and may be set out in terms that are quite general. Conversely, some OP policies are extremely precise, not in fact much different than typical by-law provisions. A choice has to be made at the time of adoption of the OPs.

Rather than speaking in terms of conflict, analysts of OPs usually speak in terms of balancing policies. A clear example is a recent OMB decision regarding a proposal to develop a former convent property to permit two seven-storey apartment buildings with 298 units. Issues of interaction with the immediate residential neighbourhood arose. The board said,

> Based on the evidence of all witnesses, The Board finds that the subject property and the neighbourhood surrounding it, form a "wonderful" part of the City and should be protected and valued appropriately. In protecting and valuing the property and the neighbourhood, the Board must remain cognizant of the "public interest" as enunciated in public policy documents, not just "public opinion" as presented by immediate neighbours . . . . *Finally, the Board must carefully balance what may seem to be conflicting interests* in protecting stable neighbourhoods and the need for the province of Ontario to house a growing population, efficiently, without the continuing loss of irretrievable green space. The Board's role in *this balancing act* is particularly delicate when it is dealing with a well-established, stable neighbourhood . . . .[124]

123 Pierre A Côté, *The Interpretation of Legislation in Canada*, 3d ed (Scarborough, ON: Carswell, 2000).

124 *Toronto (City) Official Plan Redesignate Lands Amendment (Re)* (2006), 53 OMBR 293 at para 27 [emphasis added].

Apart from the issue of content, there is a question whether a municipality is obliged to adopt an OP at all. Not all provinces do require this. Although the idea of local planning being carried out through the combined mechanism of an OP and an LUB pervades *Planning Acts*, in New Brunswick, British Columbia, Prince Edward Island, and in Alberta for small municipalities, adoption of an OP is discretionary, unless directed to do so by the provincial level. The consequence of the absence of a local OP/LUB is not no regulation: most importantly, provincial systems will usually apply to proposals to build; thus, lots must comply with subdivision rules, environmental or health rules will control what is required for sewage systems and water, transportation rules will require and define the nature of road access, and the building code will control safe construction.[125]

Because the OP ultimately controls the content of the LUB and is the measure of whether discretionary uses of land, as through development agreements, may be entered into, it is a standard planning tactic for a municipality to change its OP so as to make it completely consistent with some specific proposal. When this occurs it becomes virtually impossible to challenge the proposal except at the initial decision-making stage. An alternative is to attempt to convince a provincial cabinet minister not to accept the OP change, but this is unlikely to occur unless the OP amendment is seen as in violation of some SPI or other identified provincial matter of concern: after all, local governments are created to relieve the provincial level of government from needing to consider lot-by-lot or neighbourhood-by-neighbourhood land uses. In Ontario, appeals of OP changes to the OMB are possible on the basis that they do not represent good planning in the public interest. OP matters are subject to limited appeal in Alberta[126] and Manitoba.[127]

A crucial point arises from whether the focus, in a court proceeding for judicial review,[128] is on the OP or on the LUB. For an OP, the courts have consistently taken the view that they "are not law," and because they contain policies that must be balanced against one another, the standard of review is one of reasonableness. However, when it comes to LUBs, which are a form of legislation, the courts' standard of review is correctness. Thus, if a case can be made that a permit has been issued contrary to the LUB in place, there is no deference to the municipality.[129]

---

125 For further detail, see the discussion of subdivisions in Section J, below in this chapter.

126 Alberta *Municipal Government Act*, above note 20, s 690.

127 Manitoba *Planning Act*, above note 46, s 49.

128 See Chapter 9, Section C.

129 See, for example, *McRae v Squamish (District)*, 2000 BCSC 1339.

A significant policy question is whether municipalities ought to be allowed to amend their OPs in the interim between formal reviews, or whether other safeguards that offer some stability and recognition of the community effort that will have gone into developing an OP ought to be in place, such as requiring a two-thirds majority vote.

2) By-laws

By-laws flow from the OP. But what is authorized by the province is for LUBs to regulate a "use of land." Thus Ontario's *Planning Act* in section 34 states, "Zoning by-laws may be passed by the councils of local municipalities: 1. For prohibiting the use of land, for or except for such purposes as may be set out in the by-law . . . ."[130] The initial power is elaborated to clarify that it extends to buildings; to dealing with marshy, contaminated, or vulnerable areas; to protecting wildlife habitat and archaeological resources; to type of construction as well as height and bulk of buildings; to loading and parking; to pits and quarries; and to density. This elaboration is useful, but does leave open some questions, as is the case in other provinces.[131]

There are two aspects of the issue of what is a use of land. The first is whether the local government is authorized to use its zoning power at all to regulate some particular activity. The second is the obverse of that, and involves whether a local government is obliged to regulate or act through its zoning power rather than through some other power.

On the former aspect, Ontario specifies that "the making, establishment or operation of a pit or quarry shall be deemed to be a use of land."[132] That the point should be an issue at all arises through the existence of a scheme of provincial regulation of pits and quarries. An earli-

130 *Planning Act*, above note 8, s 34.

131 My focus here is on the meaning of "use" of land in the provincial statutes empowering local governments, and not the co-extensive or narrower definitions of "use" subsequently adopted by those local governments. Thus in *Sanders v Langley (Township)*, 2010 BCSC 1543, parking was found not to be a use of land under the particular LUB wording. In *Whiskey Flats Investment Corp v Whitehorse (City)*, 2010 YKSC 27, the court interpreted a by-law definition of "use," the "purposes for which land . . . is arranged or intended," as extending to "good faith future intention to use land in a particular way" and not as requiring the issuance of a permit (at paras 29–30). In *Whiskey Flats*, the use at issue was a sign advertising a brand of soft drink on a site where the factory had burned down, though the owner intended to start a related business. Any by-law definition may not stray beyond what is authorized by the provincial legislation, but within that constraint, may apply the power granted as the municipality sees fit.

132 *Planning Act*, above note 8, s 34(2).

er Ontario case, *Pickering (Township) v Godfrey*,[133] had decided that pits and quarries were not a use of land, but the specific statutory provision has addressed the point. However, in other provinces, the issue has in some instances accorded with the *Godfrey* decision. Thus in *Hankinson v Annapolis County*,[134] the municipality sought an injunction to halt a gravel pit operation on land zoned agricultural and for which such an operation was not allowed; the court found pit and quarry operations not to be included in the jurisdiction granted to municipalities under provincial legislation. And in Ontario, though it is not specified, water extraction on a commercial basis has been held to be a use of land subject to municipal regulation.[135] Similar questions may arise as to a change in use; in *St Mary's Cement Inc v Clarington (Municipality)*,[136] it was held that a change in fuel from pet coke to post-composting plastic film, paper bio-solids, and the like did not change the use to a "waste disposal" category.

The requirement to use zoning powers was analyzed by the Divisional Court in *R v Donald B Allen Ltd*.[137] The defendant was charged with operating a car-wash business outside of specified hours. The regulatory by-law had been passed under the city's powers granted by the *Municipal Act*. The defendant contended that in its essence the regulation amounted to zoning and should only have been adopted under the *Planning Act*. The court said,

> It is obvious that a municipality cannot, by adopting a descriptive disguise by way of a recital to a by-law, transform it into a regulatory by-law under the Municipal Act, when in substance it is a zoning enactment as defined and described in the Planning Act. The Planning Act provides many protective measures for the benefit of the owners of property affected by planning by-laws and which give those owners rights as regards improper, unfair or arbitrary actions affecting the value and usefulness of their property. The status of a "non-conforming user", for example, is created to enable the pre-existing use of a property to survive, on certain conditions, the introduction of a zoning restriction. The regulatory by-law need include no such protective measures. The Act further describes a procedure for the passage and for the subsequent challenge of a zoning by-law. A regulatory by-law does not provide such protective procedures and rights

133 [1958] OR 429 (CA).

134 *Annapolis (County) v Hankinson*, 2002 NSSC 149.

135 *Grey Association for Better Planning v Artemisia Waters Ltd* (2002), 31 MPLR (3d) 33 (Ont SCJ).

136 2012 ONCA 884.

137 (1975), 11 OR (2d) 271 (Div Ct).

> of challenge available to the owner of property affected by the regulation . . . . It is clear that a car-wash is exposed to a restriction on hours by the presence or subsequent construction of a residential building within a certain distance. That feature or consequence, however, is not sufficient to classify this by-law as in law amounting to a zoning enactment requiring compliance with the applicable statutory procedures. In short, it does not create or prohibit a use of property and it does not carry the other attributes of a zoning enactment.[138]

In *Adams Bay Residents Assn v Muskoka Lakes (Township)*,[139] the court examined a *Municipal Act*–based change in hours of use of a public wharf and decided it did not need to be treated as a *Planning Act* matter.[140] The court's focus on whether a use has been created or prohibited is useful but not exhaustive. Other cases have indicated that use of the municipality's business powers would not be permitted to circumvent existing zoning. Thus in *Fredericton*,[141] the city granted easements over city-owned land (a former rail line) to adjacent owners; the land was zoned as park. The resolutions were challenged on the basis that they amounted to "a rezoning without a public hearing."[142] The court said,

> The city, in its appeal, submits that the resolution was not made under the *Community Planning Act* but was adopted in the exercise of its corporate business powers to deal with its lands . . . . The city says that it makes no representations in the agreements as to zoning and that even if its resolution is seen to be in conflict, the application is premature because no development of the land has taken place which is contrary to the Plan or the By-law. To accept this argument, on the facts of this case, would permit a municipality to ignore or at least circumvent the municipal plan and zoning by-law under the guise of the city's corporate business powers.[143]

We have already seen that the courts no longer tend to interpret statutes establishing municipal powers in any particular restrictive

138 *Ibid* at 277. For a parallel case on licensing as in essence zoning, see *Gulf Canada Ltd v Vancouver (City)* (1980), 118 DLR (3d) 552 (BCCA).

139 2010 ONSC 5780 [*Adams Bay*].

140 There is a puzzling discussion in *Adams Bay* about NCU, with some suggestion that an NCU could be established in favour of users of a public dock owned by the municipality, a novel proposition.

141 Above note 96.

142 *Ibid* at 65.

143 *Ibid* at 67. For other cases on contract as in essence zoning, see *Loucks v Abbotsford (City)*, 2006 BCSC 1859 and *Doherty v Southgate (Township)* (2006), 23 MPLR (4th) 12 (Ont SCJ).

way. This applies as well to by-laws. As noted by the Nova Scotia Court of Appeal in *Martell v Halifax (Regional Municipality)*,[144] owners cannot assume they may do whatever is not prohibited; a purposive approach will be used to read by-laws; strict interpretation comes into play only when there is serious doubt as to legislative intent. Some points of drafting and interpretation are basic and well-established. They may seem obvious, but some have pitfalls that are still encountered. The essential point is that some legal authority must exist for authorization of the adoption of a by-law, and the power granted must not be exceeded or abused. Consider the following:

- *Separation of Powers*: The *Constitution Act, 1867*, chiefly though not exclusively in sections 91 and 92, assigns jurisdiction over the making of laws to either the federal or provincial governments. Most municipalities are created by provincial governments, and so cannot be granted or purport to exercise any by-law–making powers that are essentially federal areas of jurisdiction.[145]
- *Charter of Rights and Freedoms*: The *Charter* protects citizens by limiting the powers of all governments. Municipal by-laws cannot violate the *Charter*; if they do violate a guaranteed right, they must then be analyzed under section 1 of the *Charter* to determine whether they are a "reasonable limit."[146]
- *Impossibility of Dual Compliance (Federal/Provincial)*: Despite the *Constitution Act, 1867*'s separation of powers, many topics have federal and provincial aspects that are both legitimate. One crucial limitation is if two sets of laws lead to a functional conflict, in which case the federal law is paramount, ousting the municipal (or provincial) rule.[147]
- *Impossibility of Dual Compliance (Provincial/Municipal)*: Likewise, many topics may be regulated by the provincial government itself directly, and if a municipal power over the same topic or some aspect of it appears to have been granted, an interpretation question

144 2015 NSCA 101.

145 The topic of federal land use powers under the Constitution is explored in Howard M Epstein, "The Living Rooms of the Nation — The *Criminal Code* and Other Federal Land Use Regulatory Powers: Comments on *R. v. Clark*" (2005) 8 *Municipal and Planning Law Reports* (4th) 234. See also Chapter 4.

146 The section 1 analysis is known as the "*Oakes* test," following the guidance of the Supreme Court of Canada *in R v Oakes*, [1986] 1 SCR 103. A leading LUB case using this analysis is *Peterborough (City) v Ramsden*, [1993] 2 SCR 1084, which deals with regulation of signage.

147 The analysis of the interaction of federal and provincial (and hence municipal) land-use regulatory powers can depend on a variety of factors and was examined by the Supreme Court of Canada in *British Columbia (Attorney General) v Lafarge Canada Inc*, 2007 SCC 23.

arises. Examples have arisen over undertakings for which there exist extensive provincial regulatory schemes, such as forestry and mining,[148] as well as a variety of other topics. The impossibility of a dual compliance test was set out in the municipal law context in *114957 Canada Ltée (Spraytech, Société d'arrosage) v Hudson (Ville)*[149] and is sometimes referred to as the "Multiple Access test."[150] "There must be an actual conflict, in the sense that compliance with one set of rules would require a breach of the other."[151]

- *Municipal Jurisdiction*:[152] It is necessary that the province grant by statute the authority for a municipality to enact the by-law contemplated. It has long been the tradition for *Municipal Acts* or *Planning Acts* to list municipal powers extensively and in detail. Some provinces have moved away from this to more general grants of powers, known as spheres of jurisdiction, as for example in British Columbia's *Community Charter*.[153] It is early to determine how effective such laws will be in broadening the approach of the courts to interpreting municipal powers. In 2001, in *Spraytech*, the Supreme Court of Canada significantly broadened its approach to municipal powers in general, and in *United Taxi Drivers' Fellowship of Southern Alberta v Calgary (City)*,[154] the Supreme Court of Canada considered Alberta's *Municipal Government Act*[155] spheres of jurisdiction provisions and was open to interpreting them broadly. This is also the case, to an extent, for "natural person" powers assigned to municipalities.[156]

---

148 See, for example, *Denman Island Local Trust Committee v 4064 Investments Ltd*, 2001 BCCA 736; *Abbotsford (City) v Jamieson's Saddlery & Feed Supplies Ltd* (1999), 6 MPLR (3d) 271 (BCSC in chambers); *Squamish (District) v Great Pacific Pumice Inc*, 2003 BCCA 404.

149 2001 SCC 40 [*Spraytech*].

150 *Multiple Access Ltd v McCutcheon*, [1982] 2 SCR 161.

151 Justice LeBel in *Spraytech*, above note 149 at para 46.

152 Municipal jurisdiction should be understood as the question whether some topic is *intra vires* the municipality or *ultra vires*. Questions of acquiring jurisdiction, abuse of jurisdiction, and losing jurisdiction are a part of administrative law matters and are highly significant for the exercise of making by-laws. Administrative law has a different focus on by-laws than is our focus here; nonetheless, there is significant overlap and it is necessary to note "jurisdiction" as a basic checklist point for drafters of by-laws. So, too, "good faith" (see below in this list) is a matter for administrative law but seems appropriate to note here because the cases tend towards a requirement for legitimate land-use planning purposes, among other indicia.

153 Above note 60.

154 Above note 78.

155 Above note 20.

156 See *St Paul (County No 19) v Belland*, 2006 ABCA 55; *Kitimat (District) v Alcan, Inc*, 2005 BCSC 44.

- *Valid Municipal Purpose*: In considering municipal powers, the Supreme Court of Canada has suggested that there is a "usual range" of municipal powers, and actions going beyond that range may be invalidated. This ruling in *Shell Canada Products Ltd v Vancouver (City)*[157] has not been abandoned but should be considered in light of the more expansive approach set out in *Spraytech*[158] and *United Taxi*.[159] To a similar effect is the more recent Ontario Court of Appeal decision in *Toronto Taxi Alliance Inc v Toronto (City)*.[160]
- *Good Faith*: A related point is that there is a general overriding requirement that powers granted by legislation be exercised in good faith. The most recent restatement of this in the municipal context was in *Grosvenor v East Luther Grand Valley (Township)*.[161] There is a presumption of good faith, but appropriate indicia can counteract this presumption.
- *Unauthorized Distinctions*: This is another example of what could be regarded as an administrative law matter and is a particular aspect of jurisdiction. It is *ultra vires* for a municipality to make distinctions in by-laws if not authorized to do so by legislation. The leading case is *Montréal (City) v Arcade Amusements Inc*.[162] This is also referred to as unauthorized "classification" or unauthorized "discrimination." How the courts will determine particular distinctions to have been unauthorized is not a matter that can be predicted with certainty. The general categories of zoning itself are not open to this allegation, nor is the mere delineation of the boundaries of a zoned area, although spot zoning may be one of the indicia of bad faith.
- *Regulation versus Discretion*: A grant of powers to a municipality to allow it to regulate cannot be converted to a power to make decisions on a discretionary basis. This general point was made by the Supreme Court of Canada in *Verdun (City) v Sun Oil Co*[163] and *Canadian Institute of Public Real Estate Cos v Toronto (City)*.[164]

---

157 (1994), 20 MPLR (2d) 1 (SCC).

158 Above note 149.

159 Above note 78.

160 (2005), 18 MPLR (4th) 89 (Ont CA).

161 2007 ONCA 55. See also *Entreprises Sibeca Inc v Frelighsburg (Municipality)*, 2004 SCC 61.

162 [1985] 1 SCR 368.

163 [1952] 1 SCR 222.

164 (1979), 25 NR 108 (SCC) [*Canadian Institute*]. Following the *Canadian Institute* decision, the Ontario Legislature retroactively validated development agreements that had been entered into under the by-law and that had been invalidated: *Planning Amendment Act*, SO 1979, c 59—see *Re Toronto College Street*

- *Regulation versus Prohibition*: A power to regulate does not imply a power to prohibit, unless so specified by the statute setting out municipal powers: *Virgo v Toronto (City)*.[165] At the same time, the Supreme Court of Canada has clearly noted that the general land-use regulatory power may be read as extending to the creation of holding zones, even though, from the perspective of the landowners, this may be tantamount to prohibition. See *Soo Mill & Lumber Co v Sault Ste-Marie (City)*[166] and *Sanbay Developments Ltd v London (City)*.[167] Such a power is not usually understood as authorized if the effect is to virtually take private land for public purposes without compensation.
- *No Fraud on Zoning*: If the essence of a by-law is zoning, it is contrary to public policy for a municipality to attempt to avoid the public process aspects required for the adoption of land-use laws by using some other approach such as licensing or by private contract, unless the statutory authorization to do so is clear.
- *Delegatus Non Potest Delegare*: Two aspects arise: delegation by a municipal council to its staff and delegation to residents in a particular neighbourhood. Unless authorized to do so by statute, a council may not delegate its decision-making power to staff, and even if authorized to do so, it must provide rules to be applied. Likewise, a council may not fetter itself to be bound by the opinions of neighbours to a proposed development.
- *Conformity with the OP*: Where there is a statutory requirement, the LUB must conform with the OP. This appears to be the case everywhere except Alberta. Non-conformity with the OP may found an appeal of an LUB to a provincial appellate body, or a court application to question the validity of the LUB. But given the general terms in which OPs are often written, along with a statutory framework that suggests OPs are to be seen as policy documents, courts are likely to look for direct collision before invalidating an LUB. Appellate tribunals, however, will apply the relevant statutory test, for example, Nova Scotia's "reasonably consistent with the intent" of the OP test. In Ontario, the OMB will consider consistency with the OP, and also has the power to make the same decisions the municipal council could have, and has developed the "good planning in the public interest" principle.

Centre Ltd and Toronto (City) (1986), 31 DLR (4th) 402 at 408 (Ont CA); see also *MacArthur v Charlottetown (City)*, 2005 PESCTD 37.

165 (1894), 22 SCR 447.

166 [1975] 2 SCR 78.

167 [1975] 1 SCR 485.

- *No Development Agreement without Statutory Authority*: No matter how "far, large and liberal" the approach of the courts to municipal powers, it is still necessary that there be some statutory basis for the exercise of a land-use regulatory power. For the most part, the basic tool is zoning, and planning statutes are usually quite clear in establishing a power to zone; if more elaborate techniques are to be used, there should be a statutory basis for them. Bonusing devices, such as development agreements, have been held to require statutory authorization, and an attempt by a council to limit zoning by a side contract was struck down. Requiring restrictive covenants has also been held to be improper without statutory authorization.

Where definitions are not included in a by-law, it is fair to resort to definitions found in related by-laws. Thus in *Central Saanich (District) v Wake*,[168] where the zoning by-law (anchored in the *Local Government Act*) did not have a definition of how "height" of a building was to be measured, it made sense to adopt the definition found in the building by-law (anchored in the *Community Charter*).

I. FLEXIBILITY MECHANISMS

Flexibility in the planning/zoning system is now an important feature. Some aspects, such as provision for accessory uses or minor variances, are of long-standing, and though important to individual owners and their immediate neighbours, tend not to be of wide public impact. Flexibility mechanisms address what is perceived as a weakness of basic zoning—that it tends to be based on old ideas of exclusive uses in specified areas, defined by broad categories such as "residential," "commercial," or "industrial." Professor Makuch points to a distinction between regulating location and regulating form. He says, "The pure zoning method emphasizes the distinctions between uses rather than any relationship that ties them together."[169] He also notes, "The criticisms of such an approach for the implementation of modern planning are not difficult to enumerate. Perhaps the most obvious is that the system is not based on realistic assumptions . . . . Its standards become minimum standards, it can impose no conditions nor positive duties . . . ."[170] Flexibility mechanisms now attempt to deal with a variety of circumstances, from accommodation of innovative development proposals to the problem of

168 2010 BCSC 1535.
169 Makuch, above note 110 at 297.
170 *Ibid* at 299.

how a municipality may respond in the face of a development that it believes might be undesirable, or when it becomes aware of changed circumstances that call for re-thinking appropriate policies. They extend to such devices as temporary zoning, holding zones, floating zones, site-plans, part-site plans, planned-unit development, and transferable development rights.

Originally, if a development proposal came forward that fit the existing by-law, there was little a municipality could do except issue a requested building permit. Thus, in *Dalhousie University v Halifax (City)*,[171] the university proposed to build a sports complex; when adjacent landowners became aware of the plan, they sought to have the zoning changed. The university applied for a building permit; the city refused it as incomplete, but was ordered to issue it by the courts. Likewise, in *Paul Esposito Holdings Ltd v Abbotsford (City)*,[172] the council had reservations about the proposed use of land for a casino; on the basis that a provincial licence had not been obtained, the municipal building permit was refused, but the court drew a distinction between use and construction, and ordered the permit to issue. The Supreme Court of Canada has said that there is a common law right to a building permit, subject to the municipality having a good faith pre-existing clear intention to change its by-laws.[173] There is thus something of an amorphous opportunity for a municipality to delay. Some provinces have legislated provisions that try to address the permit issuance question.[174]

In some provinces, the matter is addressed by the device of interim controls. In Ontario this power is assigned to municipalities. In Nova Scotia it is a power exercised by the province.

Section 38 of Ontario's *Planning Act* allows a council to adopt an interim control by-law with no advance notice or hearing,[175] to be in effect for a period of up to one year initially and up to two years by subsequent motion for continuation. The precondition for adopting such a by-law is that "the council . . . has, by by-law or resolution, directed that a review or study be undertaken in respect of the land use planning policies in the municipality or in any defined area or areas thereof . . . ." The effect is of "prohibiting the use of land, buildings or structures within the . . .

171 (1974), 9 NSR (2d) 643 (CA).

172 1997 CanLII 553 (BCSC).

173 *Ottawa (City) v Boyd Builders Ltd*, [1965] SCR 408; *HG Winton Ltd v North York (Borough)* (1978), 6 MPLR 1 (Ont Div Ct).

174 See, for example, British Columbia *Local Government Act*, above note 49, s 929; Manitoba *Planning Act*, above note 46, s 148; New Brunswick *Community Planning Act*, above note 94, s 81.

175 Notice of the decision must be given within thirty days of the by-law. The meeting at which the by-law is adopted must be public: *RSJ Holdings*, above note 61.

area . . . for, or except for, such purposes as are set out in the by-law." Established non-conforming use rights or rights that have crystallized, as through issuance of a building permit, are not affected by an interim control by-law.[176] Such by-laws

> are powerful zoning tools by which municipalities can broadly freeze the development of land . . . . The power to enact an interim control by-law has been aptly described as "an extraordinary one, typically exercised in a situation where an unforeseen issue arises . . . as a means of providing breathing space during which time the municipality may study the problem and determine the appropriate planning policy and controls for dealing with the situation."[177]

Their use is not aimed only at emergencies.[178] Bad faith in the adoption of such by-laws is difficult to show.[179] Interim control by-laws may be appealed to the OMB, which has adopted principles or criteria for their review, such as strict interpretation, the existence of a planning rationale, and a fair and expeditious planning exercise to be carried out.[180] Upon expiry of the interim controls, if no changes have been made, property reverts to its previous zoning, and no new interim control by-law may be adopted for the same area for three years.

Where interim controls exist in other provinces, they require the consent of the appropriate provincial cabinet minister, or are an instrument of the provincial government, often exercised in response to a request from a municipality. In Prince Edward Island, an interim order can be in effect for six months, as a control, while an OP is being developed.[181] In Saskatchewan, the system is very much like Ontario's, though requiring a minister's approval; the municipal council may then decide whether to approve any proposed development on a case-by-case basis during the freeze.[182] *BM Halifax Holding Ltd v Nova Scotia (Attorney General)*[183] illustrates the process in Nova Scotia, where the

---

176 *Kim v Mississauga (City)* (1996), 33 MPLR (2d) 135 (Ont Ct Gen Div); *1121472 Ontario Inc v Toronto (City)* (1995), 29 MPLR (2d) 221 (Ont Ct Gen Div), rev'd on other grounds (1998), 47 MPLR (2d) 23 (CA).

177 *RSJ Holdings*, above note 61 at para 27.

178 *Equity Waste Management of Canada v Halton Hills (Town)* (1997), 35 OR (3d) 321 (CA).

179 *Ibid.*

180 See *Nolan v McKillop (Township)* (1987), 36 MPLR 82 (OMB); *Pricewaterhouse Coopers Inc v Amherstburg (Town)*, [2008] OMBD No 1033; *Re Rosen*, 2012 ONSC 4215 (Div Ct).

181 *Planning Act*, above note 26, s 10.

182 *Planning and Development Act, 2007*, above note 2, ss 80–87.

183 2015 NSCA 89.

orders must be made by the province. The three levels of government had committed funds to a public-private partnership for a convention centre in downtown Halifax. The developer advanced in his construction faster than his processing of permit applications. In order to avoid delays, the province first declared the project to be a matter of provincial interest, and then issued an interim planning area order, allowing the project to step outside the normal municipal permit system. This was an unusual case. The legislation provides, "Within an interim planning area subdivision, development, or certain classes of subdivision or development, may be regulated or limited or prohibited in whole or in part, as necessary, to protect the provincial interest."[184] Thus, a freeze on development can be the central feature of such orders.

Statutory authority is required before a municipality may enter into a contract that commits it to control land use in a particular way. This has been stated time and again in various cases dealing with such attempts. A simple example is *Galt-Canadian Woodworking Ltd v Cambridge (City)*.[185] The city had made an agreement for the sale of land and undertook to rezone the land. Its object in doing so was to relocate an auto-wrecking yard away from a generally residential neighbourhood and into an industrial park. A business already established in the park challenged this arrangement and was successful on the basis that "it is *ultra vires* a municipality to agree in advance that it will exercise its legislative powers in a particular way."[186] This position was unaffected by the availability of a subsequent hearing at the OMB for those opposed to the rezoning. In *Harrietsfield-Grand Lake Community Association v Halifax (County)*,[187] the municipality proposed to rezone property from R-2 (low density residential) to C-1 (local commercial) but at the same time enter into a contract with the owner, to be binding on successors and registered against title, restricting the type of commercial uses. The scheme was struck down. The *Planning Act* allowed for development agreements, but only after an OP and companion LUB had been adopted, which had not occurred. The municipality was authorized to adopt by-laws, not add conditions to by-laws through a contract.[188] A subse-

184 *HRM Charter*, above note 92, s 214(4).

185 (1982), 19 MPLR 14 (Ont Div Ct).

186 *Ibid* at 19.

187 (1978), 26 NSR (2d) 198 (CA).

188 A similar case is *Fredericton*, above note 96 at 68, where the attempt was made to avoid the restrictions of the zoning through agreements granting easements. The court said, "If the city wishes to amend its by-law and plan, it may do so . . . . But it may not circumvent the Community Planning Act in a purported use of its power under another branch of its corporate body politic . . . . The provisions in

quent Nova Scotia case made it clear that even some special powers that look like development agreements are to be distinguished in that they are not binding on subsequent purchasers, and thus lapse upon sale unless registered against title.[189] In *First National Properties Ltd v Highlands (District)*,[190] the municipality denied an application to rezone property because it had requested public amenities as an adjunct to the rezoning; the refusal was set aside as being taken on the basis of an irrelevant, *ultra vires*, consideration. In *Landreville v Boucherville (Town)*,[191] the town had granted a permit to operate a quarry subject to the owner agreeing to transfer some of its land to the town; this was set aside as *ultra vires*.[192] Most recently, the Supreme Court of Canada, in *Pacific National Investments Ltd v Victoria (City)*,[193] declined to read into an agreement with a developer an implied term that the zoning of land would not change, and to pay damages in case of downzoning. The Court said, ". . . the *Municipal Act* provides for the power to zone by by-law. Inherent in this is that a municipality may change its zoning in the same way . . . . Zoning is a legislative power. On its face, the statute provides for no power to constrain the future use of this legislative power."[194] "I am satisfied that the text [of the statute] gives no support to any argument that the City could be fettered from changing its zoning."[195] The Court also cited with approval the comments from the Court of Appeal to ". . . the foundational principle that a municipal council cannot bind future councils. Previous legislation in British Columbia had made special provisions for a municipality to do just this in certain circumstances, but this legislation had been repealed."[196] Development agreements and other forms of bonusing are examined in more detail in Chapter 7, Section G.

Likewise, accessory uses and variances are flexibility mechanisms; they are looked at in Chapter 7, Sections C and D.

Temporary use categories are specified as permitted in some statutes. Thus British Columbia's *Local Government Act* allows for such designations for up to three years (subject to renewal),[197] and Ontario's

---

the agreements themselves constitute a commitment to non-enforcement of the Zoning By-law."

189 *Polycorp Properties Inc v Halifax (Regional Municipality)*, 2011 NSSC 241.

190 (1996), 32 MPLR (2d) 26 (BCSC).

191 [1978] 2 SCR 801.

192 The case also involves findings of bad faith.

193 2000 SCC 64.

194 *Ibid* at para 38.

195 *Ibid* at para 42.

196 *Ibid* at para 18.

197 *Local Government Act*, above note 49, s 492.

Planning Act allows for the same.[198] Ontario's legislation makes it clear that garden suites are contemplated as the appropriate application of this power, where the designation may be for up to twenty years. In *Kings (County) v Anderson (cob K & M Firewood)*,[199] a temporary use by-law was allowed, albeit with the court taking a somewhat restrictive view of what this might imply, pointing out that land clearing, and use of a portable sawmill to achieve that, would not amount to commercial forestry. Nonetheless, it does make sense to establish the statutory basis for the designation.

Site plans are also available to address the issue of form. Site planning focuses not on alteration of the designated use of land, but on the configuration of structures. In the Ontario *Planning Act*,[200] authority to impose detailed conditions is granted. This extends to requirements for widening highways that are adjacent to the land, lighting, landscaping, access for persons with disabilities, and various servicing easements. In Nova Scotia's statute, the emphasis is clearly on location; what may be regulated is "the location of structures on the lot"[201] as well as the location of parking, walkways, lighting, walls, driveways, easements, as well as their design.

A floating zone is a category of use that is defined in a land-use by-law but which has no area to which it attaches at the time it is created; it is said to "float" over the municipality, available for use when a decision is made to attach it to some parcel of land.

"Planned unit development" is a term primarily of American origin, though formerly used in Saskatchewan. It amounts to a development agreement for use in creation of a whole sub-community, typically a mixed-use area with residential, commercial, and perhaps light industrial uses. It is often used for creation of gated communities and/or condominium projects.[202]

Transferable development rights (TDRs) have been recognized as implied by the general zoning power.[203] In *Keller v Bighorn*, the municipality had adopted policies in its OP that allowed for the transfer of density credits and set out the conditions that would attach. The court approved the transfer from the "sending parcel" to the "receiving par-

198 *Planning Act*, above note 8, ss 39 and 39(1).

199 (1998), 172 NSR (2d) 359 (SC).

200 Above note 8, s 41.

201 Above note 14, s 231(4)(a).

202 See Daniel Mandelker, "Legislation for Planned Unit Developments and Master Planned Communities" (2008) 40(3) *Urban Lawyer* 419.

203 Above note 85.

cel," where the OP requirement for putting in place conservation easements on the sending parcel had been met.

A range of flexibility devices has been created, the result of which is that the overall picture of zoning as stifling, unimaginative, Euclidian is no longer reflective of what may be achieved. While the results of basic zoning define much of what exists in urban areas, especially in their residential neighbourhoods, new developments are more likely to be pursued through one of the flexibility devices, sometimes in those very residential neighbourhoods that do value their stability, however much it may be illusory.

J. SUBDIVISIONS

While the term "subdivision" applies to the creation of even one new lot, what we are examining here is not the bare facts of proper creation of a single lot under property or land titles acts,[204] but a larger undertaking—the creation of multiple lots. A focus in land-use planning law on the development of multiple lots by one owner is related to both the desire for rational planning and the fact that in Canada the development industry has come to be dominated by some quite large entities that desire to develop significant areas.[205] It was a feature of Ontario's first planning legislation a century ago that subdivisions in growth areas had to be submitted for review to the province. "Consideration of plans was limited to the number and width of streets, the location of the streets, and the size and form of lots. Minimum street widths were specified at one chain (66 feet, or 20 metres)."[206] It is possible to think of subdivision regulation as a form of flexibility mechanism, though its adoption preceded other similar legal tools.

One court has said, "Subdivision approval simply results in the division of property into two or more parcels. Other approvals must still be obtained before the property can be developed. These include approval by entities such as the provincial Department of Transportation and, in regard to sewer services, the Department of the Environment."[207]

---

204 This smaller undertaking may be referred to as a "severance" as in section 53 of the Ontario *Planning Act*, above note 8.

205 Gerald Hodge & David Gordon, *Planning Canadian Communities*, 5th ed (Scarborough, ON: Nelson Canada, 2008) at 97.

206 *Ibid* at 96.

207 *Oakland/Indian Point Residents Association v Seaview Properties Ltd*, 2010 NSCA 66 at para 16 [*Oakland/Indian Point*].

Crucially, initiation of the subdivision process does not lead automatically to approval. It is a way for governments to control the tempo of development and sprawl. Where organized municipalities do not exist or have not adopted their own subdivision by-laws, provincial subdivision by-laws apply.[208] There are also specified exceptions to the application of subdivision rules, such as when each lot is large (in the range of ten hectares), for cemetery plots, for registered condominiums, for lots resulting from expropriation, and for utility corridors.[209]

Usually a draft plan of subdivision is submitted. In Ontario, there are twelve mandatory pieces of information to be included, among them the proposed use, dimension, and layout of lots; natural features; water supply; nature of the soil; contours; and proposed roads.[210] Being responsive to the required pieces of information is not sufficient to gain approval. The Act sets criteria, which in effect allow the municipality as approving authority to assess a subdivision proposal according to its own overall policies. The criteria include the "welfare of the present and future inhabitants of the municipality," matters of provincial interest, "whether the proposed subdivision is premature or in the public interest," conformity with the OP, the suitability of the land, highways, conservation of natural resources and flood control, adequacy of municipal services, adequacy of school sites, conservation of energy, and restrictive covenants to be imposed.[211] Adopting the specifics of the provincially mandated criteria (such as OP policies) is the role of the elected officials. After that it becomes an administrative act, in the hands of a "development officer" to apply the criteria. While these criteria allow a municipality to set measures that may be quite restrictive, if the criteria are met, the development officer will be expected to sign off on the subdivision. Some courts refer to this as "as-of-right" subdivision,[212] although others have avoided any conclusion on this point of entitlement to subdivide.[213]

The *Oakland/Indian Point* case also indicates that it is difficult to challenge a decision made by a development officer, the standard of review being reasonableness (patent unreasonableness under pre-*Dunsmuir* classifications).[214]

---

208 See, for example, NS *MGA*, above note 14, Part IX, s 270.

209 See, for example, Ontario *Planning Act*, above note 8, ss 50(3) & (5); NS *MGA*, above note 14, s 268.

210 *Planning Act*, above note 8, s 51(17).

211 *Ibid*, s 51(24).

212 See, for example, *Oakland/Indian Point*, above note 209 at para 3.

213 See, for example, *Boisclair v Manitoba (Municipal Board)*, 2007 MBCA 6.

214 *Oakland/Indian Point*, above note 209 at para 34. *Dunsmuir v New Brunswick*, 2008 SCC 9.

As has been early noted, "One of the most important considerations in subdivision development is the servicing of the land and the allocation of the servicing costs."[215] This issue has frequently been litigated as to the reasonableness of the charges,[216] but so too have all other aspects of subdivision conditions imposed by municipalities. For example, the test of prematurity is seen as a matter of judgment on the part of the approving authority, but is nonetheless subject to challenge.[217] A part of the assessment of a subdivision proposal is consideration of its setting, that is, its potential interaction with neighbouring land,[218] which allows the OMB as the appellate body to make determinations about property ownership and easements for the purpose of exercising its supervisory function but not binding in the way a court ruling would be.[219]

The developer of a subdivision is obliged to transfer title of a set percentage of the land to the municipality or to pay cash-in-lieu. The object is to allow the municipality to develop parks or other facilities that might be needed as a result of the new units of residence. In British Columbia, the developer has the choice of option, unless there is an OP with policies and designations as to the location of future parks, in which case the municipality has the choice.[220] Whether this statutory condition had been met by a somewhat general OP was raised in *Basin Construction Ltd v Columbia Shuswap (Regional District)*.[221] The court decided that the broad OP policies satisfied the requirement of the statute. Saskatchewan's *Planning and Development Act* allows cash-in-lieu payments to be assigned to another municipality if the funds are to be used for the purpose for which they were paid.[222]

Where physical improvements are to be made prior to or at the time of subdivision, but were not, there is no obligation on the municipality to do the work that ought to have been done by the subdivider.[223]

---

215 Barbara Bence, "Thistletown: An Example of Federal-Provincial Partnership in Land Development" (1971) 9 *Osgoode Hall Law Journal* 313 at 318.

216 See, for example, *Mavis Valley Developments Inc v Mississauga (City)* (2003), 45 OMBR 1 over parkland dedications.

217 See, for example, *Re Caledon East (Town) and Lawson Subdivision* (1978), 9 OMBR 188; *McKee v Curtin (Unorganized Township)* (1997), 36 OMBR 115; *Re Schnee* (2011), 88 MPLR (4th) 317 (Alta Mun Gov Bd).

218 Ontario *Planning Act*, above note 8, ss 51(24)(c), (g), & (h).

219 *Goldlist*, above note 112, is the basic authority; the jurisdiction of the OMB to make limited rulings as to property law issues related to severance has been confirmed: see *Watt v Classic Leisure Wear Inc*, 2008 CanLII 32818 (Ont Div Ct).

220 *Local Government Act*, above note 49, s 941.

221 2011 BCSC 151.

222 Above note 2, s 197; see *Kaiser v Baildon (Rural Municipality)*, 2013 SKQB 129.

223 *Amix Salvage & Sales Ltd v Chilliwack (City)*, 2010 BCSC 1493.

Subdivisions are the typical development tool for gated communities. Gated communities are residential enclaves that restrict entry to residents and their guests; they do so by means of gates, guards, and fences. They are an emerging phenomenon in Canada.[224] The central policy issue is whether they ought to be allowed to develop. The main objection is that they manifest physically as a separation, primarily by class, from the rest of the community. The criticism is that instead of building a sense of community, gated residential areas reinforce divisions in society.[225] Other problems may have to do with interruption of traffic flow[226] and the potential privatization of other infrastructure normally publicly available, such as schools and parks. There are potential limitations on access for census and for political purposes, such as enumeration of voters or delivery of information flyers or election literature.[227] There may

---

224 Recent research estimated there are approximately 400: see Jill Grant et al, "The Planning and Policy Implications of Gated Communities" (2004) 13 *Canadian Journal of Urban Research* 70; "Open Society or Cloistered Enclaves?" (2004) 44(2) *Plan Canada* 42. In contrast, the United States has well in excess of 20,000. In the United States they are a sunbelt phenomenon, though they are not purely tied to climate, and have been classified as "lifestyle communities," "prestige communities," and "security zone communities" in the main study (see Edward J Blakely & Mary Gail Snyder, *Fortress America: Gated Communities in the United States* (Washington, DC: Brookings Institution Press, 1999)). Grand Cove and Beach O'Pines in Ontario, and Osoyoos and Parksville in British Columbia, are all communities that have gated residential areas of note.

225 Reflecting on a general polarization in society, Anthony Giddens, director of the London School of Economics and Political Science, has written,

> Two forms of exclusion are becoming marked in contemporary societies. One is the exclusion of those at the bottom, cut off from the mainstream of opportunities society has to offer. At the top is voluntary exclusion, the "revolt of the elites": a withdrawal from public institutions on the part of more affluent groups, who choose to live separately from the rest of society. Privileged groups start to live in fortress communities, and pull out from public education and public health systems.

(see Anthony Giddens, *The Third Way* (Cambridge: Polity Press, 1998) at 103). The wealthy already tend to live separated lives through their neighbourhoods, private schools, private health care, and first-class or private travel; formally gated communities just emphasize that (see Christopher Lasch, *The Revolt of the Elites* (New York: WW Norton, 1995)).

226 Andrew Curran & Jill Grant, "Private Streets: A Survey of Policy and Practice" (2006) 15 *Canadian Journal of Urban Research* 62; Andrew Curran, "Private Streets and Double Standards" (2005) 45(4) *Plan Canada* 42.

227 The *Canada Elections Act*, SC 2000, c 9, s 81 and the Alberta *Election Act*, RSA 2000, c E-1 both forbid any person in control of apartment buildings, condominiums, or a gated community from preventing a candidate or their representatives from canvassing in the daytime, but other jurisdictions do not.

be difficulties in service of court documents.[228] At the same time, apartment buildings present the same difficulties: an apartment building or apartment-building-style condominium will often have locked doors and a concierge, and it is not open to the public to walk the corridors.[229]

K. NON-CONFORMING USES: PROTECTION OF INVESTMENT

The main protection for private owners of land against political choices made by local councils is the system of non-conforming uses (NCU). The system guarantees owners the right to continue to use their land in any way it previously was used, so long as that prior use was legal, even if zoning has been changed. It is crucial that the previous existing use have been legal. Thus, in *Esquimalt (Township) v Crosson*,[230] a single-unit dwelling was lawfully entitled to convert to two units; the building inspector noted on plans that one room was "converted to kitchen," and subsequently the house was found to have three units. The court found this not to be a proper NCU since it was never legal to have three units in the building.

Although NCU rights are for the benefit of owners, the policy is not absolute in their favour. The NCU right may be lost through cessation, abandonment, or destruction of the building. The nature of what is included in the NCU is also sometimes in dispute. Every aspect of NCUs

---

228 This is referred to in *MacLeod v MacLeod*, 2003 CanLII 2328 (Ont SCJ). In Ontario, it has been decided that "lawful" for NCU purposes does not extend to a requirement to have obtained other permits such as under the *Environmental Protection Act*, RSO 1990 c E.19; it means "lawful" under a zoning by-law passed under the *Planning Act*: *1218897 Ontario Ltd (cob Castle Auto Collision and Mechanical Service) v Toronto (City) Chief Building Official*, [2005] OJ No 4607 (SCJ).

229 Condominiums are a special form of property that is purely "a creature of statute." That is, the combined effect of various provincial statutes such as a *Condominium Property Act* and a *Land Titles Act* is that what would otherwise not be a legitimate interest in land may come into existence upon registration of a condominium plan under the statutes. While condominiums are generally subject to *Planning Acts*, that is, the zoning use of the lands imposed by local governments govern, there are typically some exceptions from normal planning and development rules for subdivision processes. Thus, under Saskatchewan's *The Condominium Property Act, 1993*, SS 1993, c C-26.1, subdivision rules do not apply and the minister may exempt condominiums from other aspects of the *Planning and Development Act, 2007*, above note 2, but has generally not done so except for very minor points.

230 2010 BCSC 1490.

has been subject to testing in court. For more detail regarding NCUs, see Chapter 7, Section B.

It is central that NCU rights are limited to matters addressed under *Planning Acts* or as specified. They do not arise regarding entitlements arising under other statutes. Thus, in *Oshawa (City) v 505191 Ontario Ltd*,[231] a by-law was adopted prohibiting adult entertainment parlours except in designated areas under the specific authority of the *Municipal Act*, which allowed licensing of such businesses and defining the areas in which they may operate. An existing business asserted the right to continue, but the court ruled that NCU rights arise only under the *Planning Act* and were not applicable.

What is not offered as protection to investment is any guarantee that rules will not change, or if they do, that the owner will be compensated. An NCU right may arise, but there is no right to seek compensation if land is downzoned or if a local government refuses to change zoning. A typical statutory provision is found in the *Vancouver Charter*: "Where a zoning by-law . . . has been passed . . . or where Council . . . exercises any of the powers contained in this Part, any property thereby affected shall be deemed as against the city not to have been taken or injuriously affected . . . and no compensation shall be payable."[232]

L. APPEAL SYSTEMS

A variety of land-use decisions may be appealed, including adoption and amendment of OPs, rezoning, allowance of variances, development agreements, subdivision terms, rejections, or approvals. The range of what may be appealed is not uniform throughout the country. Rights to appeal are not inherent; they are purely statutory and must therefore be established by the governing legislation. In this regard, appeals differ from judicial review; matters that may be taken to court depend on general administrative law principles, and while some statutes do

231 (1986), 32 MPLR 158 (Ont CA). In a case in which the "adult entertainment parlour" was operating under a zoning by-law, there was a basis for a claim of an NCU, which was not successful since the previous use was of a store selling drug paraphernalia, posters, and so on, and the protected use could not be seen to extend to a strip bar: *Zanzibar Tavern Inc v Las Vegas Restaurant & Tavern Ltd*, [1995] OJ No 1605 (Gen Div). For background, see Dana M Tucker, "Preventing the Secondary Effects of Adult Entertainment Establishments: Is Zoning the Solution?" (1997) 12(2) *Journal of Land Use and Environmental Law* 383.

232 SBC 1953, c 55, s 569. See Raymond Young, "Canadian Law of Constructive Expropriation" (2005) 68 *Saskatchewan Law Review* 345.

deal with judicial review, the essential powers of the courts to examine statutory decision making are inherent and extend to such questions as legality and the fairness of the process. For a more detailed examination of appeals and judicial review, see Chapters 8 and 9.

Statutes specify what matters may be appealed, who may take an appeal, the body to which an appeal may be taken, and the criteria to be applied by the appellate body. The conformity of zoning with OPs or other defects in the by-laws may be appealed in Quebec,[233] Nova Scotia,[234] Alberta,[235] Manitoba,[236] and Ontario.[237] Saskatchewan,[238] New Brunswick,[239] Newfoundland and Labrador,[240] and Prince Edward Island[241] all have somewhat restricted appeals available. Standing to appeal is frequently an issue. Standing is "entitlement to seek judicial relief apart from questions of the substantive merits and the legal capacity of the plaintiff,"[242] a formulation often restated as "can this plaintiff take this case against this defendant?"[243] It is usually treated as a preliminary matter. Terms such as "affected," "aggrieved," "directly affected," and "interested" have all been used at various times to set out what is required to achieve standing. "Affected" is a subjective term,[244] whereas "aggrieved" requires a more objective foundation. An important problem with traditional interpretations of "aggrieved" is that it incorporates the idea of legal rights actually or potentially infringed: this tended to tie the concept to property ownership, an approach at odds with the progress of democracy generally and with the particular approach of planning systems, which look to involve all members of the public without regard for property ownership.[245]

Ontario's *Building Code Act, 1992* allows appeals by "any person who considers themselves aggrieved."[246] Despite the apparent subjectivity of

233 *Act respecting Land use Planning and Development*, CQLR c A-19.1, ss 37 and 59.3.
234 Above note 14, s 250.
235 Above note 20, ss 690, 678, & 619.
236 Above note 46, s 690.
237 Above note 8, s 34(11).
238 Above note 2, s 226.
239 Above note 94, s 86.
240 *Urban and Rural Planning Act, 2000*, SNL 2000, c U-8, s 40.
241 Above note 26, s 28.
242 Thomas Cromwell, *Locus Standi* (Toronto: Carswell, 1986) at 7.
243 See *Nova Scotia (Attorney General) v Bedford Service Commission* (1976), 1 MPLR 204 (NSCAD).
244 *Actus Management Ltd v Calgary (City)* (1975), 62 DLR (3d) 421 at 432 (Alta SCAD).
245 See, for example, *Maurice v London County Council*, [1964] 2 QB 362 for a discussion of the term "aggrieved."
246 SO 1992, c 23, s 25(1).

the provision, the courts have required some reasonable nexus of interest with the matter under appeal, though the bar is low; neighbours will virtually automatically be seen to have such a nexus of interest.[247]

M. REMEDIES

One form of a remedy is the opportunity to challenge a by-law for illegality. Ontario's *Municipal Act, 2001* provides that "Upon the application of any person, the Superior Court of Justice may quash a by-law of a municipality in whole or in part for illegality"[248]—a typical provision.[249] It also provides that if a by-law is passed in good faith, it is not open to review "because of the unreasonableness or supposed unreasonableness" of the by-law,[250] a provision that has little practical effect because of the view of courts that unreasonableness is always a valid basis for judicial review, and that the core idea of unreasonableness merges with bad faith or discrimination or taking into account irrelevant considerations so the privative clause becomes ineffective.[251]

A set of mechanisms for enforcement of by-laws is always provided. Stop-work orders, prosecutions resulting usually in fines, demolition orders, and injunctions are all typical remedies potentially available in instances of alleged violations of land-use rules. Indeed, multiple remedies may be available concurrently, such as injunctions in addition to prosecution.[252] Because the remedies represent action against private property, authority to seek a remedy may be closely scrutinized. Thus, it has been held that the general power to impose a penalty does not include the power to declare each consecutive ten-day period of maintaining prohibited conditions a separate offence.[253]

Municipal statutes will usually include provisions such as the following from Ontario's *Municipal Act*: "If any by-law of a municipality . . . is contravened, in addition to any other remedy and to any penalty

247 See, for example, *Southgate Public Interest Research Group v Southgate (Township)*, 2012 ONSC 5383.

248 Above note 53, s 273(1).

249 See, for example, *Municipal Act*, CCSM c M225, s 382.

250 Above note 53, s 272.

251 See Chapter 9, Section C(2)(c).

252 See *York (Regional Municipality) v Martin Grove Properties Ltd*, 2011 ONCA 711; *Air Ronge (Northern Village) v Werchola (cob La Family Taxi)*, 2011 SKQB 237; *Toronto (City) v Tseng*, 2011 ONSC 4594.

253 *Long Branch (Village) v Hogle*, [1948] SCR 557.

imposed by the by-law, the contravention may be restrained by application at the instance of a taxpayer or the municipality . . . ."[254]

Municipal action to enforce its rules has led to many cases. Instances extend to situations of storage of vehicles where not allowed, unsightly premises, unsafe construction, improper signage, cutting of trees without authorization, improper use of land (e.g., commercial activity in a residential area), altering the configuration of land, improper accessory use, construction or demolition without a permit, having more residential units than allowed, excessive noise, higher fences than allowed, depositing excess fill, keeping animals where not permitted, and trespass. Among the more inventive attempts at defences are that the activity is a hobby and not a commercial activity.[255]

While public participation is a core value, its manifestation varies in different circumstances, from notice, to an opportunity to participate in a decision, to a right to take an appeal, to a right to enforce by-laws. Usually, however, the last is reserved to the municipality itself. Offences or other remedies are not seen as creation of a right that may be privately enforced.

It is not generally possible to require a municipality to enforce its by-laws. Thus, in *Hanzelka v Oshawa (City)*,[256] a dispute arose over students living as groups in an area of single-family housing; mandamus was sought to force the municipality to enforce the zoning by-law. The court said mandamus was "an extraordinary and discretionary remedy . . . it will only be exercised where a legal duty exists requiring the compelled activity . . . ."[257] The court cited *Polai v Toronto (City)*[258] as authority that it is for the municipality to decide whether to enforce its by-laws. To the same effect is *Burke v Sunshine Coast (Regional District)*,[259] where the court also relied on *Polai*. It said that the decision whether to enforce by-laws is a matter of policy for a municipality and beyond the reach of court orders. Likewise, in *Myer Franks Agencies Ltd v Vancouver (City)*,[260] an attempt to force the city to prosecute individuals who gathered on corners hoping to be chosen for work as day

254 Above note 53, s 440.

255 *R v How*, 2009 SKQB 490: the owner collected and repaired farm tractors where display of commercial vehicles was prohibited; *R v Smedley*, 2008 NSSC 397: the owner had chickens as pets where keeping fowl was prohibited.

256 2011 ONSC 4435.

257 *Ibid* at para 28.

258 [1973] SCR 38 [*Polai*].

259 2011 BCSC 1636.

260 2010 BCSC 1637.

labourers, under streets and traffic by-laws or the *Safe Streets Act*, was not successful.

It is possible that a municipality could be found to have been negligent in its attempts at enforcement of its by-laws. In *Rausch v Pickering (City)*,[261] the court refused to strike out such an action where the allegation was that the municipality, in attempting to have certain animals removed from a farm, had not consulted the Farm Practices Board as to what was a "normal farm practice."

For unsightly premises, it is standard for a municipality to step in and do the cleanup itself if the owner refuses or neglects to do so, and then add the cost to the owner's property tax bill.[262] In addition, fines are imposed through a prosecution.[263]

In the worst of cases, an order may issue for demolition of a building. For demolition to be seen as an appropriate remedy rather than an order for remediation or repairs, it is necessary for a municipality or its enforcement staff and committees to have considered whether there are any other viable options.[264] Further, there must be a proper factual basis for such an order. In a case where the inspector entered the premises without permission and was therefore a trespasser, the court was not prepared to take into account unlawfully obtained evidence, and also commented critically on the inadequate efforts made to contact the owner (one phone call).[265] A demolition order has been set aside where the documentation was found to be too vague and a request for particulars was in essence refused by the municipality.[266]

An injunction is often sought. There is very limited discretion for a judge to refuse to issue a statutory injunction if the requisite facts are proven. In that regard, injunctions sought by municipalities are unlike other injunctions, where equitable principles apply, and the balance of convenience enters into the exercise of judicial discretion. See, for example, *Calgary (City) v Bullock (cob Occupy Calgary)*, where the court said that a statutory injunction would be refused only in exceptional circumstances.[267] In *Montréal (Ville) c Auberge des Glycines inc (Auberge*

---

261 2012 ONSC 4688.

262 See, for example, *Tuteckyj v Winnipeg (City)*, 2012 MBCA 100.

263 See, for example, *Portovest Inc v Prince Albert (City)*, 2012 SKQB 9, where the owner of an apartment building was fined for allowing storm windows to be in a state of disrepair, and floors to be filthy.

264 See *1251497 Alberta Inc v Edmonton (City)*, 2010 ABQB 641.

265 *Perchaluk v Roblin (Town)*, 2010 MBQB 238.

266 *Mosiuk v Kamsack (Town)*, 2010 SKQB 356.

267 2011 ABQB 764. To the same effect is *Maple Ridge (District) v Thornhill Aggregates Ltd* (1998), 109 BCAC 188 (CA).

Le Pomérol inc),[268] the court said the discretion for refusal of a statutory injunction might be exercised where there was municipal *laches*, or the landowner was unaware of a rule violation. Even selective enforcement is not a defence; it does not lead to immunity from prosecution or temporary immunity until others similarly placed are also charged,[269] and some condoning of the prohibited activity does not amount to estoppel. Some comment has suggested that, "Fact-driven and discretionary in application, the law of injunctive relief and municipalities is not so predictable."[270] But this does not seem to be the predominant view.

Even enforcement of development agreements, where failure to adhere to their terms (in one case, a failure to construct a road) has negative effects on neighbouring property owners, has been found to be within the discretion of the municipality, absent bad faith, bias, or fraud.[271]

Persistent ignoring of orders to remedy violations may even result in findings of contempt of court. In one such case, the court imposed substantial fines.[272]

N. ONTARIO SPECIAL PROVISIONS

Each province has variations on the aspects of how they empower, and limit, local governments to carry out land-use planning. There are, however, numerous special provisions in Ontario land-use legislation, and in associated rulings from the OMB and the courts, that have the effect, cumulatively, of setting the province somewhat apart from the others.[273] Not all commentators regard the full set of Ontario land-use control features as overall beneficial. Professor Makuch has suggested that continuous amendments have resulted in "a substantial reduction in procedural safeguards for individuals and those subject to the planning process and contributed to a growing sense that planning powers

268 2012 QCCA 556.

269 See *TSG Sales Ltd v Vancouver (City)*, 2012 BCSC 1177; *Burnaby (City) v Oh*, 2010 BCSC 1970.

270 Teresa Kowalishin, "Injunctive Relief and Municipalities" (2002) 28 *Municipal and Planning Law Reports* (3d) 241.

271 *Olympic International Realty Ltd v Halifax (Regional Municipality)*, 2010 NSCA 80.

272 *Neighbourhoods of Windfield Farms Limited Partnership v Death*, 2010 ONSC 1800.

273 Some of the identified features do appear in other provinces.

are arbitrary and virtually limitless."[274] He suggests that "planning values" are an amorphous concept, leading to inconsistency of result.[275]

1) Statutes

In the core land-use regulatory statutes, there are several features that stand out:

1) "H" (holding) zones are specified as allowable;[276]
2) Freezes, in the form of "interim controls," may be put in place for up to one year without advance notice or a hearing, in order to allow "a review or study to be undertaken . . . of the land use planning policies in the municipality or in any defined area";[277]
3) The minister may zone, in fact, "exercise any of the powers conferred upon councils by [various sections of the *Planning Act*]," including allowing minor variances, and such zoning supersedes existing municipal zoning;[278]
4) Height and density bonuses may be bargained for "in return for the provision of such facilities, services or matters as are set out in the by-law";[279]
5) Temporary garden suites may be allowed by agreement;[280] and
6) "Demolition control" areas may be established regarding residential property, and demolition may be allowed on conditions for new construction.[281]

The *Far North Act, 2010*[282] sets a framework for land-use planning over a significant area of the province, and emphasizes the integral role of First Nations in the process, as well as respect for ecological systems. There are also other, special areas governed by their own legislation, such as the Niagara Escarpment,[283] the Oak Ridges Moraine,[284] and

274 Stanley M Makuch, "The Disappearance of Planning Law in Ontario" in Anneke Smit & Marcia Valiente, eds, *Public Interest, Private Property* (Vancouver: UBC Press, 2016) 87 at 87.
275 *Ibid* at 89.
276 *Planning Act*, above note 8, s 36(1).
277 *Ibid*, s 38.
278 *Ibid*, s 47.
279 *Ibid*, s 37.
280 *Ibid*, s 39.1.
281 *Ibid*, s 33.
282 Above note 7.
283 *Niagara Escarpment Planning and Development Act*, RSO 1990, c N.2.
284 *Oak Ridges Moraine Protection Act, 2001*, SO 2001, c 3.

the areas covered by the Greenbelt Plan[285] and the Growth Plan for the Greater Golden Horseshoe,[286] in which the province has set policies that are to be followed by municipalities. The Provincial Policy Statement, 2014, has the status under section 3 of the *Planning Act* to require that local government and OMB decisions "shall be consistent" with the policy statements.[287] There are also detailed guidelines for agriculture (minimum distance separation: MDS I and II) as set out in Ministry of Agriculture, Food and Rural Affairs formulae, designed to reduce incompatibility of uses; they date from 1995. In addition, the Ministry of Environment has Land Use Guidelines (the six "D-Series" guidelines) to deal with potential land-use compatibility problems.[288]

2) Ontario Municipal Board

Although nine of the provinces have province-wide land-use appellate bodies, the OMB stands out as possessed of the widest set of powers. Under the *Planning Act* and the *Ontario Municipal Board Act*,[289] the OMB has extraordinary status: "the powers of a court of record,"[290] "authority to hear and determine all questions of law or of fact,"[291] "exclusive jurisdiction in all cases and in respect of all matters in which jurisdiction is conferred on it,"[292] "powers, rights and privileges as are vested in the Superior Court of Justice,"[293] to order compliance and costs.[294] The board may be asked by cabinet to inquire into "any question" relating to municipalities.[295] It is the appeal body for zoning by-laws,[296]

---

285 *Greenbelt Act, 2005*, above note 5.

286 *Places to Grow Act, 2005*, above note 6. Note that a wide review of the OMB's function in land-use matters being undertaken by the Ontario government may result in changes. For background, see "Review of the Ontario Municipal Board, Public Consultation Document" (October 2016), online: www.mah.gov.on.ca/AssetFactory.aspx?did=15814. A useful companion piece is Regional Planning Commissioners of Ontario, "Reforming the Ontario Municipal Board : Five Actions for Change" (31 August 2016), online: www.rpco.ca/files/RPCO_OMB_REFORM_Final_Report_2016_09_1.pdf.

287 Above note 8, s 3.

288 Online: www.ontario.ca/page/d-1-land-use-and-compatibility.

289 RSO 1990, c O.28.

290 *Ibid*, s 34.

291 *Ibid*, s 35.

292 *Ibid*, s 36.

293 *Ibid*, s 38.

294 *Ibid*, ss 47, 48, and 86.

295 *Ibid*, s 45.

296 *Planning Act*, above note 8, s 34(19).

OP amendments,[297] demolition permits,[298] decisions of the committee of adjustments (minor variances),[299] "H" designations,[300] interim controls,[301] site plans,[302] minister's zoning orders,[303] and demolition or removal orders for heritage properties.[304]

Although the tests to be applied by the OMB in the various appeals are specified for some of the decisions it may make, the board has adopted a general test of whether the decision represents good planning in the public interest.[305] Despite section 2.1 of the *Planning Act*, which requires the OMB to "have regard to" the decisions made by the municipal council that are under appeal, this has tended not to derogate from the board holding *de novo* hearings and exercising independent judgment.[306]

There is considerable judicial deference to the OMB.[307] As an example, in *Brampton (City) v Royalcliffe Developments Inc*,[308] leave to appeal an OMB decision was refused even though the board had approved a density twice that prevailing in the area.

The OMB in 1979 adopted what has come to be known as the "Nepean principle."[309] The board would not allow zoning that facilitated the acquiring of private property for public use without some indication that the public authority intends to expropriate the lands. Normally zoning, up or down, does not entail compensation; there is no injurious affection. But if the zoning is in aid of potential acquisition by the local government, the board saw it as contrary to public policy to allow this.

297 *Ibid*, ss 17(24) and 22(7).
298 *Ibid*, s 33(4).
299 *Ibid*, s 45(12).
300 *Ibid*, s 36(3).
301 *Ibid*, s 38(4).
302 *Ibid*, s 41(12).
303 *Ibid*, s 47(10).
304 *Ontario Heritage Act*, RSO 1990, c O.18, s 34.1.
305 See, for example, *Re 2160556 Ontario Ltd*, 2015 CanLII 22095 (OMB); *Charmchi v Toronto (City)*, 2015 CanLII 40629 (OMB).
306 *Ottawa (City) v Minto Communities Inc*, 2009 CanLII 65802 (Ont Div Ct).
307 *Ibid*.
308 2010 ONSC 5592.
309 *Re Nepean (Township) Restricted Area By-law 73-76* (1979), 9 OMBR 36; see *Brighton (Municipality) Official Plan Amendment No 20 (Re)* (2003), 46 OMBR 78 as an application of the principle.

3) Courts

There are two aspects of court rulings on land use that are particularly important in Ontario. One has to do with court deference to the OMB. The other is on recognition of a fairly wide ambit of municipal power.

As regards the OMB, appeals may be taken to the Divisional Court on questions of law, but only with leave of the court.[310] Leave is not easy to obtain[311] since it must be shown that there is reason to doubt the correctness of the board's decision on the point of law, and the point must be of significant importance to warrant the attention of the Divisional Court.[312] And although the Ontario Court of Appeal has clarified the standard of review under a section 96 appeal,[313] it has done so in a way that tends to support a wide ambit for decisions at the board,[314] including a reasonableness standard for interpretation of its own statute.[315] The courts have also seen the OMB as able to rule on administrative law issues such as bad faith,[316] the meaning and application of the *Charter*,[317] and the meaning and application of general laws if arising in relation to matters properly dealt with within its jurisdiction,[318] though the standard of review is correctness.[319]

So far as municipal powers, the Ontario courts have in general embraced the ruling of the Supreme Court of Canada in *Spraytech* so as to approve fairly wide latitude for municipalities in the exercise of their granted powers.[320]

---

310 *Ontario Municipal Board Act*, above note 289, s 96.

311 See, for example, *Lafarge Canada Inc v 1341665 Ontario Ltd*, 2004 CanLII 9072 (Ont Div Ct); *Richmond Hill Naturalists v Corsica Developments Inc*, 2013 ONSC 7894.

312 *Toronto Transit Commission v Toronto (City)* (1990), 2 MPLR (2d) 42 (Ont Div Ct).

313 See *London (City) v Ayerswood Development Corp* (2002), 34 MPLR (3d) 1 at para 7 (Ont CA).

314 *Ibid* at paras 13–17.

315 *Ibid* at para 7.

316 *Equity Waste Management of Canada v Halton Hills (City)*, above note 178.

317 *Grushman v Ottawa (City)* (2001), 20 MPLR (3d) 10 (Ont Div Ct), although the board itself has indicated that its power to consider laws as in violation of the *Charter* does not extend to declaring by-laws invalid purely on the basis of *Charter* violation alone: *Toronto (City) Zoning By-law No 138-2003 (Re)* (2004), 47 OMBR 168.

318 *Goldlist*, above note 112 at paras 44 & 45.

319 *Ibid* at para 66.

320 See, for example, *Croplife Canada v Toronto (City)* (2005), 254 DLR (4th) 40 (Ont CA); *Friends of Lansdowne Inc v Ottawa (City)*, 2012 ONCA 273.

CHAPTER 7

HOW TO GET AROUND ZONING

A. PRELIMINARY

In this chapter we have a closer look at some of the flexibility mechanisms that have evolved regarding local land use. The perspective for purposes of this chapter is primarily that of the landowner.

The main ones are non-conforming uses (NCUs), accessory uses, minor variances, pushing the limits of the land-use by-law (LUB), bonusing and its variants such as development agreements (DAs), home-based businesses, changing the rules, and ignoring the rules. All of these are extensively relied on by landowners, especially professional developers, and have occasioned a great deal of litigation. All have legal peculiarities. Because of the array of ways to treat the system of land-use rules as flexible, one of the main virtues of statutory land-use regulation in comparison to common law litigation, that is, reasonable certainty, is undermined.

The 2001 decision of the Supreme Court of Canada in *Saint-Romuald (City) v Olivier*[1] sets out guidance for assessing whether an NCU right has been pushed too far. While it is helpful to have such guidance, would a system in which NCUs were specified by agreement with the municipality (as in the United Kingdom) be a useful addition? Should NCUs be phased out over time (as is common in the United States) since by definition they represent a land use no longer considered desirable? For the

1 2001 SCC 57 [*Saint-Romuald*].

moment, NCU rights are usually considered so valuable to a landowner that, as one judge complained, the cases are "seemingly endless."

Accessory use is a device premised upon the notion that zoning by-laws are not going to be able to contemplate all possible reasonable land uses on a particular site. Allowing uses that are subordinate to the main use and normally and naturally incidental introduces some flexibility. Is this a beneficial idea? Is it too vague, or open to abuse?

Likewise, minor variance applications allow for some breakage of the rules and are usually treated as fairly routine administrative matters. Should they be? Who should be notified of variance requests? Who should decide them? Are better guidelines needed? Should there be appeals?

Bonusing, and development agreements as a form of bonusing, are a common device in major development proposals. Focused on specific development proposals, the main effect is to permit a development that would not otherwise be allowed by the land-use by-laws, and to prevent future municipal councils from cancelling the proposed development. How is the public interest best served when engaging in this type of deal? What types of public benefits are appropriate? What of cash-in-lieu?

B. NON-CONFORMING USES

Although land-use planning (LUP) as a public process could in all instances override private preferences, this is not the policy choice made in most circumstances. Respect for private property, and especially for actual investment made and manifested in developed land uses, particularly in buildings, is an important value recognized in the main governing statutes, and at the common law.[2] This is primarily manifested in provision for allowing non-conforming uses, known in Quebec as "acquired rights," to continue where they would not be permitted if coming forward for the first time. There are several variants: a non-conforming use of land, a non-conforming structure, and a non-conforming use in a structure. It is often the last that is at issue in NCU cases.

A typical provision is, "A non-conforming structure, a non-conforming use of land or non-conforming use in a structure, may continue

---

2 Prince Edward Island has no statutory protections for NCU, but official plans (OPs) may provide for them, and the provincial subdivision regulations, *Subdivision and Development Regulations*, PEI Reg EC693/00, specify that lawful NCUs may continue.

if it exists and is lawfully permitted at the date of the first publication of the notice of intention to adopt or amend a land-use by-law."[3] "Exists" includes "lawfully under construction and completed within a reasonable time" or "the permit was in force, construction commenced within twelve months, and was completed within a reasonable time."[4] NCU is not a personal right; it attaches to the land—a change in ownership does not defeat the NCU right.

The statutory policies around NCU contain two aspects: respect for a pre-existing legal use and a desire that the use be brought into conformity with the applicable laws as to use. Thus, in the case of "discontinuance" of the NCU for some specified time (usually in the range of six to twelve months) or if the structure is "destroyed or damaged" to some specified extent (usually 75 percent of the value of the structure above its foundation), then the NCU rights are extinguished. Extinguished means that only uses permitted in the zone will apply. *Toronto Roman Catholic Separate Schools v Toronto (City)*[5] has a good statement of the importance of an NCU statute.

Protecting NCUs is sensible, but not the only possible policy choice that might have been made. An alternative, easily seen as unpalatable, would be to force immediate abandonment or change of use on an owner, consequent upon a zoning change. Clearly such a policy would be onerous for many individual landowners, and could be disruptive for many others in the community (tenants, for example, if a multi-unit apartment building were required to convert to a duplex or single-family building). There might be logic to such a policy if the previous use were in the nature of a nuisance, but a requirement for immediate cessation of formerly legal activities, even in these circumstances, has not generally been allowed for in legislation.

A second alternative would be to require cessation after a set period of time, or a phasing out of the non-conforming use. This is an alternative that is or has been allowed for in some American jurisdictions (e.g., California, New York, Colorado, Pennsylvania, Ohio, Indiana, and Missouri) and is referred to as an "amortization." Periods allowed for the removal of the NCU vary quite greatly, from as short as thirty days for signage to three or five years for businesses such as junkyards or billboards, to as long as twenty or forty years for buildings that are completely non-conforming. Challenges to amortization laws have not generally been upheld, though specifics have been tested against a stan-

---

3 *Halifax Regional Municipality Charter*, SNS 2008, c 39, s 253(1) [*HRM Charter*].

4 *Ibid*, s 253(2).

5 [1924] SCR 368 at 373–74.

dard of reasonableness. See, for example, *City of Los Angeles v Gage.*[6] This possibility has been studied in Canada, but not adopted.[7]

A third alternative would be to require a municipality to treat all change of zoning as a form of expropriation calling for compensation. This would be very expensive as well as inevitably controversial in quantifying and is explicitly rejected by statute: the usual *Planning Act* provision is that zoning does not involve injurious affection.

Because compensation is generally not available in the face of zoning change, there is a strong rationale favouring restrictive reading of NCU provisions so as to protect vested or established rights. The competing rationale is, according to Professor Makuch, that NCUs are "an undesirable and inappropriate use, at least in the particular location in which [they] are found."[8] This statement is modified somewhat in the second edition of his book, where it is said that "municipalities often voice a concern that a broad interpretation of the rights of landowners with legal non-conforming properties undermines the intent of the prevailing zoning prohibition."[9]

One practical approach would be to establish a system of certificates of lawfulness, as is available in the United Kingdom. Under the *Town and Country Planning Act 1990* as amended by the *Planning and Compensation Act 1991*,[10] an application may be made to the local planning authority to obtain a certificate of lawfulness respecting an existing use of land or a building. No such system prevails here, though its usefulness is readily apparent.

The rationale for allowing an NCU to continue to exist is usually said to be that of fairness to the owner. At the same time, there is a question of the possible economic implications when it comes to commercial, industrial, or even multi-unit residential uses. American authors Haar and Wolf make this observation: "The pre-existing gas station, repair shop, or laundry surrounded by block after block of residential and recreational buildings could monopolize business within its captive market. The government officials who in their wisdom isolated the non-conforming use with a fervent prayer that it would just disappear, actually freed the

6 274 P2d 34 (Cal 1954); Osborne M Reynolds Jr, "The Reasonableness of Amortization Periods for Non-Conforming Uses" (1988) 34 *Washington University Journal of Urban and Contemporary Law* 99.

7 See Ontario, Ministry of Housing, *Amortization of Uses*, White Paper on the Planning Act, Background Paper, No 4 (Toronto: Ministry of Housing, 1979).

8 Stanley M Makuch, *Canadian Municipal and Planning Law* (Toronto: Carswell, 1983) at 262.

9 Stanley M Makuch et al, *Canadian Municipal and Planning Law*, 2d ed (Toronto: Thomson Carswell, 2004) at 239–40.

10 (UK), c 34.

owner from the burdens of competition he or she would have experienced in a zone set aside for similar pursuits."[11] Thus, Harr and Wolf regard NCUs as tending to be anticompetitive. Is this a fair comment? If a real problem has been identified, how ought it to be dealt with?

John Mascarin, editor of the *Digest of Municipal and Planning Law* (DMPL) and of the *Municipal Planning Law Reports* (MPLRs), says this about NCU:

> A non-conforming use is a use that is not permitted under the applicable zoning by-law currently in force. The general intention of planning legislation is to eventually eliminate non-conforming uses and replace them with permitted uses. A legal or lawful non-conforming use is perhaps best described as a statutorily permitted use for which a building, structure or land was put to prior to the passage of a zoning by-law which no longer provides for that use.[12]

It is probably fair to comment that the policy of planning legislation is to "eventually eliminate" any particular NCUs, although the case that Mascarin discusses[13] is to the opposite effect, recognizing as it does the strong policy of the legislation, in this instance the Ontario *Planning Act*, to "provide a limited form of protection to vested property rights in the teeth of the necessary zoning powers of local governments to control the orderly development of municipal lands in light of ongoing and constantly changing circumstances."[14] And in the unique circumstances of Nova Scotia's *Municipal Government Act*, certain non-conforming residential structures are given virtually unlimited protections.[15] Still, there are instances of statements suggesting that the eventual elimination of some particular NCU is desirable,[16] but this instance was based on a particular policy of the town's official plan (OP) and is not generally the explicitly stated policy of planning statues. In *Giannace*, the Ontario Municipal Board (OMB) did say, "The Board recognizes that the statement in the official plan to the effect that non-conforming uses should eventually cease is a principle of good planning" but this is quite a bit different

11 Charles M Harr & Michael A Wolf, *Land Use Planning*, 4th ed (Boston: Little Brown, 1989) at 505.

12 John Mascarin, "Legal Non-Conforming Use: Establishing Use, Lawfulness and Continuity" (1999) 5 *Digest of Municipal and Planning Law* 1. To the same effect, see Ian MacFee Rogers & Alison Scott Butler, *Canadian Law of Planning and Zoning*, 2d ed (Toronto: Carswell, 1988) (loose-leaf 2016 Release 4) s 5.91 at 210.23.

13 *382671 Ontario Ltd v London (City) Chief Building Official* (1996), 32 MPLR (2d) 1 (Ont Ct Gen Div) [*382671 Ontario Ltd*].

14 *Ibid* at para 19.

15 See *Tsimiklis v Halifax (Regional Municipality)*, 2003 NSCA 30.

16 See *Giannace v Town of Caledon* (1987), 21 OMBR 207 [*Giannace*].

than any recognition of cessation as a matter of statutory policy. Mascarin's point is also made by Gerald Adler in his study of the OMB, *Land Planning by Administrative Regulation*:[17] "any extension or rejuvenation of a non-conforming use is prohibited in the hope that it will eventually disappear and be replaced by a use permitted under the by-law." Another commentator, Craig MacFarlane, points out that "Non-conforming uses are not always uses which should be terminated over the long run, especially in circumstances where there has been down-zoning."[18] There is nothing special about the situation of downzoning to make an NCU either more or less protected; his statement is cited for its introductory thought, as an example expressing a different perspective than that of Mr Mascarin and the other commentators quoted.

All circumstances affecting whether an NCU has been established, what its limits are, or whether it has been lost, have been litigated.

The most recent statement from the Supreme Court of Canada is in *Saint-Romuald*,[19] which discusses intensity (size or capacity) versus type-of-use questions.

One of the most difficult problems is in characterizing the precise nature of the previously legal and allowable uses.

In *382671 Ontario Ltd*,[20] a multiple-unit apartment building had become non-conforming when the zoning by-law changed. Subsequently, the by-law was altered to deem the NCU to be a conforming use permitted by the zoning. When the owner desired to convert some internal space to an additional living unit, the municipality took the view that permission was needed, in the form of a variance. The owner challenged this and was successful. The deeming provision of the by-law, a form of subordinate legislation, was seen as inconsistent with the owner's NCU right under the *Planning Act*. The opportunity to add a living unit thus became a determination under the scope of the NCU right, not under a variance application.

This case illustrates the nature of the idea of an NCU, that it amounts to an exception or exemption (both are terms used by Killeen J) from the operation of a zoning by-law and that the exemption applies to the whole of a building. The clever device adopted by the city of "deemed conformity" to make the building accord with the zoning by making the zoning accord with the building, was invalidated as an attempt to remove a statutory right through a by-law. See also *Canadian Occidental*

---

17 (Toronto: U of T Press, 1971) at 10.

18 Craig MacFarlane, *Land Use Planning*, 2d ed (Scarborough, ON: Carswell, 1992) (loose-leaf 1993 Release 1) at s 6.2(e).

19 Above note 1.

20 Above note 13.

Petroleum Ltd v North Vancouver (District)[21] to the same effect, that is, a by-law may not undermine the statutory guarantee.

The article cited by Killeen J, Ira T Kagan's "But I Do Not Want to Be Legal,"[22] as well as focusing on the unusual ploy in this case, also discusses the approach of the courts to NCU through distinguishing between "use" and "intensity" of a use. Kagan says,

> municipalities will sometimes try to restrict the expansion of a legal non-conforming use even when this expansion is entirely within the confines of the building or structure. A position sometimes put forward by these municipalities is to define the "use" made of the premises at the time of the passage of the by-law both in terms of *type* and *intensity*. By *type* I mean such things as a restaurant, scrap yard, nursing home, school, office, etc. By *intensity*, I mean such things as a restaurant *with capacity for 200 persons*, a *40-acre* scrap yard, a nursing home *containing 15 beds*, a school *for 25 pupils*, or an office with *300 square metres of gross floor area.*[23]

As Kagan quite correctly points out, the matter of intensity of use, in the sense of an NCU implying a right to expand the use throughout the building, has been settled since the 1948 Supreme Court of Canada decision in *Central Jewish Institute v Toronto (City)*,[24] discussed below in this section. Cases to the contrary such as *R v Grant*[25] are rare and are wrong.

Nonetheless, there is room for courts to interpret the nature of the use: see *Dartmouth (City) v Ramia*,[26] where a grocery store that started to sell pizza and donairs was not found to have changed its use to a restaurant. Likewise, in *Stoneridge Properties Ltd v Bridgewater (Town)*,[27] an NCU to construct a high privacy fence on a part of the boundary line of a property was seen as a right to extend the fence the full length of the line some years later.

Although the analysis in those cases and their fundamental fairness presents no problems, there is a real difficulty in certain other cases. *Capital (Regional District) v Smith*[28] is one of the most difficult NCU cases because of the challenge to find the rationale for the distinction the court makes between the application of the by-law's density

---

21 (1983), 148 DLR (3d) 255 at 266–67 (BCSC).
22 (1993) 13 *Municipal and Planning Law Reports* (2d) 252.
23 *Ibid* at 253–54 [emphasis in original].
24 [1948] SCR 101 [*Central Jewish Institute*].
25 (1983), 23 MPLR 89 (Ont CA).
26 1991 CanLII 2549 (NSCA).
27 2012 NSSC 104.
28 (1996), 33 MPLR (2d) 15 (BCSC), aff'd (1998), 61 BCLR (3d) 217 (CA).

provisions and its floodplain setback provisions. At issue was some waterfront property in Sooke, British Columbia, that was communally owned by some nineteen persons, each having a cabin. The cabins predated any zoning. In 1977, the municipality set rules allowing for only three dwellings on a parcel the size of the one in issue. This established a protected NCU for the existing dwellings. In 1991 Smith's cabin was partially destroyed by fire. Desiring to rebuild, he arranged for the local fire department to conduct a controlled burn of the cabin as a form of demolition and as a practice for the firefighters. He rebuilt on the same site and with a similar configuration and square footage. The municipality cited the complete destruction of the property, the limit on number of units that may exist on a parcel of land, and violation of setback requirements from the shore as a flood plain setback, as violations of the NCU rules. The court observed, as Binnie J was to do several years later in *Saint-Romuald*, "it is the concept of fairness that supplies the underlying rationale for the statutory non-conforming use exemption."[29] On that basis, the court interpreted the "destroyed by fire to the extent of 75% of the value" provision to be based on the value of the whole of the structures on the property, not the one cabin; it also ruled that all of the structures on the property may continue to exist, that is, that the new density by-law did not apply: otherwise it "would result in a form of cosmic lottery where the last three structures left standing would become conforming and the remaining owners would have lost their right to meaningful use of the Property."[30] However, on the matter of setback, the court ruled that the owner "must rebuild . . . in conformity with the existing by-laws save and except for the density by-law from which they are exempted by reason of the lawful non-conforming use protection afforded to all the property owners."[31] Although not clear in the case, it appears that only Smith's cabin was in the flood plain setback area. The core point of what rules do apply to NCUs beyond bare type of use remains problematic. If the issue of rebuilding did not arise, would the municipality have been able to enforce its setback rule by requiring the existing buildings to be moved?

The real problem here is the approach to the floodplain setback bylaw. The result in the case is to recognize interests of both the owner and the municipality. The municipality's interests come into play because of the finding of destruction by fire, though this seems a very strained interpretation of the statute. But it does then allow the partial application of the municipality's by-laws so as to make the floodplain

29 *Ibid* at para 18 (BCSC).

30 *Ibid* at para 26.

31 *Ibid* at para 28.

rules applicable. It may be that the underlying value is that of public safety, as suggested by the BCCA in its review and confirmation of the original judgment,[32] but this is nowhere made explicit. The guidance to be obtained from this case as to what sort of regulatory by-laws will apply to NCUs is quite limited, but the case does sound a warning.[33]

The assumption in other NCU cases is generally that "use," however construed, may be recognized, but that regulatory rules such as building code requirements will still apply. Thus, in *R v Grant*, when the Ontario Court of Appeal suggests, in rejecting an expansion from two to four apartment units, that "if this increase were permitted, there would be no basis for restricting or controlling by means of the by-law an increase to 10 or 12 units within the exterior walls of the dwelling,"[34] either we are being told that this is a very large building or we are being told that the building code does not apply to an NCU, a very novel proposition.

If there is some doubt about what other aspects of municipal regulation apply to NCUs, the courts have been clear that business licensing may not be used to defeat an NCU right. Thus, in *Central Saanich (District) v Amaryllis Enterprises Inc*,[35] a marina and coffee shop had operated continuously since 1967 with no business licence; in 1987 the zoning by-laws changed to prohibit the uses; a subsequent attempt by the municipality to close the business on the basis of its not holding a business licence was not allowed by the court. The court recognized that requiring licensing was proper, but that any remedy would have to flow from provisions regarding licensing (involving a fine), and could not involve ending the acquired right to use.[36]

It is also important to realize that NCU rights arise (apart from common law) only under *Planning Acts*. If land-use regulation flows from

---

32 The British Columbia Court of Appeal disagreed with the trial court as to how to measure the extent of destruction, suggested the fold plain by-law be complied with "if at all possible," and, as a matter of exceptional discretion, declined to issue an injunction.

33 In a contrasting case, *Gallant v Prince Edward Island (Island Regulatory and Appeals Commission)* (1997), 42 MPLR (2d) 73 (PEISCAD) an NCU was recognized, but the shape of the lot had changed due to a partial expropriation by the province, and permission to build a driveway was denied over concerns about violation of a "safe sight" rule; the court saw the NCU as extending to allowing the driveway.

34 Above note 25.

35 (1991), 7 MPLR (2d) 264 (BCSC).

36 See John Mascarin, "Annotation" (1992) 7 *Municipal and Planning Law Reports* (2d) 265.

some other statute, such as a *Municipal Act*, NCU rights are not specified. This was made clear in *Oshawa (City) v 505191 Ontario Ltd.*[37]

NCU rights are usually considered to be so valuable to a landowner that, as one judge complained, the cases are "seemingly endless": "This is yet another in the seemingly endless and inexhaustible series of cases dealing with the zoning principle of non-conforming use."[38] The reason for the plethora of NCU cases is that this statutory protection has the greatest potential for allowing landowners the opportunity to escape zoning regulation. This is especially so when it is recognized that an established NCU may be expanded onto new land through purchase and merger of an adjoining lot.[39] It remains untested whether there is an upper limit to expansion of an NCU through this device.

Some of the issues such as expansion of an NCU throughout a building, although addressed by the Supreme Court of Canada in *Central Jewish Institute*,[40] have been addressed by statute, so as to allow a municipality to choose to relax restrictions on the NCU if policies to that effect are adopted.[41] Expansion is often also approached as an interpretation of what the original NCU amounted to; thus in *Camping Granby Inc c Granby (Ville de)*, a bid to expand a commercial campground established on part of the owner's land was not allowed to occupy the whole of the land,[42] although this is dubious in light of Supreme Court of Canada decisions.

In 2001, the Supreme Court of Canada set out a comprehensive framework for thinking about NCUs in *Saint-Romuald (City) v Olivier.*[43] A bar that was a country and western music cabaret replaced its performers with nude dancers. The issue was whether the change in use went beyond what was protected as an NCU (or, as the case arose in Quebec, its acquired right). The Court said that the range of uses allowed in the prior legal zoning category is not the test of the scope of the NCU: "The protected 'acquired right' properly relates only to the status quo. It does not protect a potential or contemplated use that has never materialized . . . . The acquired right is no more than a right to carry on using the

37 (1986), 32 MPLR 158 (Ont CA).

38 Justice Killeen in *382671 Ontario Ltd*, above note 13 at 3 [para 1].

39 *Bethany Community Church of St Catharines v St Catharines (City)*, 2012 ONSC 2359.

40 Above note 24.

41 See, for example, *HRM Charter*, above note 3, s 257.

42 2011 QCCA 819.

43 Above note 1. In the decision, Binnie J usefully cites a large number of NCU cases.

land for the purpose to which it was in fact previously being put."[44] In determining the question,

> [t]he Court's objective is to maintain a fair balance between the individual landowner's interest and the community's interest. The landowner overreaches itself if (i) the scale or intensity of the activity can be said to bring about a change in the type of use . . . or if (ii) the addition of new activities or the modification of old activities (albeit within the same general land use purpose), is seen by the court as too remote from the earlier activities to be entitled to protection, or if (iii) the new or modified activities can be shown to create undue additional or aggravated problems for the municipality, the local authorities, or the neighbours, compared with what went on before. The factors are balanced against one another.[45]

In effect, something very like the common law of nuisance has emerged as the guideline for assessing NCUs.

The Court then offered a seven-step process:

1. It is first necessary to characterize the purpose of the pre-existing use. The purpose . . . is a function of the activities actually carried on at the site prior to the new by-law restrictions.
2. Where the current use is merely an intensification of the pre-existing activity, it will rarely be open to objection. However, where the intensification is such as to go beyond a matter of degree and constitutes, in terms of community impact, a difference in kind . . . the protection may be lost.
3. To the extent a landowner expands its activities . . . the added activities may be held to be too remote from the earlier activities to be protected under the non-conforming use . . . . [They] are simply outside any fair definition of the pre-existing use and it is unnecessary to evaluate "neighbourhood effects".
4. To the extent activities are added, altered or modified *within* the scope of the original purpose (i.e., activities that are ancillary to, or closely related to, the pre-existing activities), the Court has to balance the landowner's interest against the community interest, taking into account the nature of the pre-existing use (e.g., the degree to which it clashes with surrounding land uses), the degree of remoteness (the closer to the original activity, the more unassailable the acquired right) and the new or aggravated neighbourhood effects . . . . The greater the disruption, the more

44 *Ibid* at para 5.

45 *Ibid* at para 34.

tightly drawn will be the definition of the pre-existing use or acquired right. This approach does not rob the landowner of an entitlement. By definition, the limitation applies only to added, altered or modified activities.

5. Neighbourhood effects, unless obvious, should not be assumed but should be established by evidence . . . .
6. The resulting characterization of the [NCU] should not be so general as to liberate the owner from the constraints of what he actually did, and not be so narrow as to rob him of some flexibility in the reasonable evolution of prior activities . . . .
7. While the definition of the acquired right will always have an element of subjective judgment, the criteria . . . constitute an attempt to ground the Court's decision in the objective facts. The outcome . . . should not turn on personal value judgments . . . .[46]

In two articles[47] looking at cases since *Saint-Romuald*, Professor Robert Currie has questioned whether the case offers anything substantial to aid decision-making:

> . . . the distinction between intensification and neighbourhood effects . . . is mushy at best . . . the Supreme Court's instructions to balance the three [criteria, that is, remoteness, intensification, and neighbourhood effects] together leaves open the possibility that decision-makers will simply use the criteria to ground their own "feel" on a given set of facts.[48]

Currie also correctly draws attention to the problem of burden of proof: "a party asserting a legal non-conforming use bears the burden of establishing it on the civil standard . . . . Unexpressed but implicit was the shifting of the burden to the party which asserts a change in the use . . . ."[49]

The emphasis in *Saint-Romuald* on "activities actually carried on at the site" may be intended to negate other cases in which a commitment to a use was sanctioned as a permitted part of an NCU. Thus in *Cowichan Valley (Regional District) v Yole*[50] and *Sunshine Coast (Regional*

---

46 *Ibid* at para 39.

47 Robert J Currie, "Legal Non-Conforming Uses in Ontario and Quebec: The Continuing Fallout of *Saint-Romuald*" (2003) 1 *Digest of Municipal and Planning Law* (2d) 109 at 128–30; "The Poop Factor: Acquired Rights and Legal Non-Conforming Uses after *Saint-Romuald*" (2003) 36 *Municipal and Planning Law Reports* (3d) 190.

48 Currie, "Legal Non-Conforming Uses," above note 47 at 129.

49 *Ibid* at 130.

50 (1988), 41 MPLR 78 (BCCA) [*Yole*].

District) v Bailey,[51] commitment to a use yet to be made of land was accepted as sufficient. In *Bailey*, communal owners intended to build seventeen single-family dwellings but had constructed only nine when the density rule was enacted; the full planned construction was allowed as an NCU. In *Yole*, owners had started to build a stable at the time a by-law was passed that prohibited keeping livestock in a residential area. The commitment to use was sufficient to establish the right to an NCU. This point remains unresolved.

It is not unusual for *Planning Acts* to empower municipalities to vary NCU rules. In Nova Scotia's *Municipal Government Act*, it says

> A municipal planning strategy may provide for relaxation of the restrictions contained in this Part respecting nonconforming structures, nonconforming uses of land, and nonconforming uses in a structure and, in particular, may provide for the extension, enlargement, alteration or reconstruction of a nonconforming structure; the extension of a nonconforming use of land . . . .[52]

Where adopted, such policies serve to finesse many of the difficult issues that have been brought to the courts about NCUs.

The statutes provide that there will be termination of an NCU through discontinuance or abandonment, or destruction. As with all other aspects of NCU, these circumstances have been litigated often. For example, destruction by fire or otherwise is usually expressed as measured by a percentage of the value of the structure, although some statutes are not clear whether the percentage should be measured against the total value of the property.[53] Detailed evidence is often led by builders and property assessors as to how to calculate the percentage of value lost. Abandonment for some set time has raised some clear and some clouded points. In *Dennis v East Flamboro (Township)*,[54] the pumps had been removed from a service station, leading to the conclusion that the use had been abandoned. Discontinuance for repairs has been seen not as discontinuance at all: *Taback v Rosenberg*.[55] Seasonal uses are not seen as having been discontinued through the off-season.[56] Although in British Columbia, where there are specific statutory rules governing seasonal NCUs, the specifics must be met in order to qualify for the

51 (1995), 15 BCLR (3d) 16 (SC) [*Bailey*].

52 *Municipal Government Act*, SNS 1998, c 18 as amended, s 242.

53 See *Torbay (Town) v Planchat*, 2009 NLTD 43.

54 [1956] OWN 282 (CA).

55 (1948), 56 Man R 121 (KB).

56 *Emily (Township) v Johnson* (1983), 143 DLR (3d) 576 (Ont CA).

extended period of deemed non-abandonment.[57] In *Wong v Maple Creek (Town)*,[58] the statute ended an NCU after discontinuance of the use for twelve months, but, where the discontinuance had continued for two years due to circumstances beyond the control of the owner, here flood and foreclosure, the court ruled that the NCU had not been abandoned. Whether there is a subjective (mental) element in discontinuance or cessation of use is contested. In *Stavely (Town) v Fern Brothers*,[59] the property in question was residential; *bona fide* efforts to find tenants, even if not successful, maintained the NCU. In *Saint John (City) v Killam*,[60] it was held that "discontinuance" as used in the statute did not imply "abandonment" and thus no inquiry into the intentions of the owner was necessary. In *Pontiex Properties Ltd v Victoria (City)*,[61] a restaurant had ceased to operate, apparently due to not being licensed; the court held that where cessation of use is a condition specified in the statute in terms of a specific time, intention is not relevant.

A serious policy issue is involved in the matter of destruction of an NCU. Because destruction is tied to some "acts of God" such as earthquakes, tornados, floods, or fire, there is no causal link between the actions of a landowner and the resultant damage to his property. In those circumstances, it is open to debate whether the individual ought to be, in effect, penalized for the consequences of the external act of destruction. Certainly flooding is common in locales across the country in which buildings exist,[62] and fires that can cause extensive harm to communities are likewise common.[63] There are limited opportunities for individual owners to take steps to physically protect their property, and insurance is not always available, affordable, or adequate.

---

57 See *Okanagan-Similkameen (Regional District) v Leach*, 2012 BCSC 63, relying on s 911 of the *Local Government Act*, now RSBC 2015, c 1, s 528.

58 2013 SKQB 240.

59 (1987), 56 Alta LR (2d) 359 (CA).

60 (1973), 6 NBR (2d) 642 (SCAD).

61 (1977), 75 DLR (3d) 155 (BCCA).

62 Major floods have occurred in New Brunswick along the Saint John River, in Manitoba along the Red River, in Quebec along the Saguenay River, and in Alberta along the Elk and Bow Rivers. See Natural Resources Canada, "Canada in a Changing Climate" (2014), online: www.nrcan.gc.ca/sites/www.nrcan.gc.ca/files/earthsciences/pdf/assess/2014/pdf/Full-Report_Eng.pdf.

63 In the last decade there have been major fires in British Columbia (Brittany Triangle, Binta Lake, and Chelaslie River), Alberta (Richardson Backcountry, Slave Lake, and Fort McMurray) and Quebec (widespread). See Natural Resources Canada, "Canadian National Fire Database," online: cwfis.cfs.nrcan.gc.ca/ha/nfdb, and "Canadian Wildland Fire Information System," online: cwfis.cfs.nrcan.gc.ca/interactive-map. See also Stephen J Pyne, *Fire in America : A Cultural History of Wildland and Rural Fire* (Princeton, NJ: Princeton University Press,1982).

The policy issues are complex, and this particular aspect of NCU law might need some re-thinking.

The concept of "destruction" as used in NCU provisions does not extend to the deliberate demolition by an owner.[64]

NCU claims may be challenged by objecting residents if the information given to government can be shown to be inaccurate.[65] Licences obtained on the basis of inaccurate information may be quashed, though the standard of review is correctness.

The existence of amorphous NCU rights is itself a convoluted matter, leaving huge scope for interpretation. In addition, NCU is an inducement to an owner to increase the actual uses of their property beyond those apparently allowable on the face of the zoning in the hope that, if challenged, they might be able to assert that they have acquired the right to continue the use. This is equally true for accessory uses.

C. ACCESSORY USES

It is common for LUBs to provide for accessory uses. Zoning specifies what uses are allowed in a particular zone and/or what uses are prohibited. But in addition to the basic uses, and in addition to what is also a common zoning rule providing for the number of buildings that may be erected on a lot (usually one, especially in residentially zoned areas), typically, accessory buildings are allowed so as to accommodate the accessory use.

What is implied, and is often made explicit in the LUB, is that the accessory use may not be the same as the main use. If it were the same use, then it would amount to allowing multiple buildings on the same lot dedicated to the same function. If that is intended, it is specified, and accessory use issues do not arise.

Because an accessory building is a use embedded in the as-of-right zoning definitions, no permission from the municipal council is needed, apart from obtaining a building permit, which is an administrative process. This also implies that no notice is given to owners of adjacent properties. And because an accessory use is as-of-right, just as with an NCU right,[66] it is seen as valuable to an owner. Exercise of judgment by

---

64 *Ovcharick v North Saanich (District)*, 1998 CanLII 5703 at para 26 (BCSC), aff'd 1999 BCCA 100.

65 *Paudash Shores Cottagers Association v Ontario (Ministry of Natural Resources)*, 2012 ONSC 2839 (Div Ct).

66 An NCU is a right granted by statute; an accessory use is a feature of land-use by-laws.

staff is inevitably involved in deciding whether to grant a permit on the basis of an accessory use. The scope of an accessory use is not always clear. Recall that it was the issue of what is an acceptable accessory use that resulted in a successful claim for damages based on negligent misstatement by planning staff in *Bell v Sarnia (City)*,[67] discussed in Chapter 1, Section D. Because establishing an accessory use right can be a valuable aspect of land use, each element of its definitions has been put in dispute in the collection of cases: what is "subordinate" to the main use, what is "normally incidental"?

In addition, how to understand the extent of the main use is a crucial matter. This is not always obvious, especially with activities such as "service stations" (Does the selling of gasoline extend to repair of vehicles and selling of newspapers, maps, or food?); restaurants (Does adding live music make it an entertainment facility?); nightclubs (Does offering entertainment and selling alcohol extend to a restaurant function?); or even houses of worship (Does this extend to holding classes, a residence for the staff, a daycare, a printing operation for the literature of the religion?). If the matter is put in dispute, the courts will decide how to classify the main use as well as what is allowable as an accessory use. There certainly are many cases. But it is open to a municipality to decide to write its LUB with detailed precision so as to allow all parties to understand just what is and what is not allowed, and thus minimize possible disputes.

In *Conlin v Prowse*,[68] the North York by-law in dispute provided, in an R-3 zone, for "one family detached dwellings, and accessory buildings incidental thereto." Residential use included "the erection of an accessory building which may not be used for human habitation"; an accessory building was defined as having "a use naturally and normally incidental to, subordinate to and devoted exclusively to the main use of the premises." This definition is widely used in LUBs in Canada. Sometimes "customarily incidental" is a term used rather than "naturally and normally incidental."

What is the usual and acceptable accessory use in a residential property? "It is agreed that a garage or garden shed would qualify as an accessory building . . . ."[69] But in *Conlin*, what had been built was a studio for painting, the owner's hobby. "It is acknowledged . . . that a garden shed or garage of the same dimensions and built in the same location would constitute accessory buildings in conformity with the applicable by-laws.

67 (1987), 37 DLR (4th) 438 (Ont HCJ).

68 (1993), 19 MPLR (2d) 115 (Ont Ct Gen Div), aff'd (1995), 30 MPLR (2d) 1 (Ont Div Ct).

69 *Ibid* at para 18 (Gen Div).

Is the studio used for the hobby of painting an 'accessory building' as defined by the by-law?"[70] "The studio is an attractive, cottage-like, one-storey white structure with a sloped roof. It is heated and has plumbing for a sink."[71] The court focused on the term "used for human habitation," determining that it meant something

> beyond sleeping, eating and excretory functions. It necessarily includes the types of activities of daily living which go on in a dwelling. This would include leisure activities such as sewing, reading and the pursuit of hobbies, including painting. To take a narrow restrictive approach is not consistent with the notion of a single residence on each lot. The interpretation urged upon me by the respondents would potentially allow clusters of structures for various functions, depending on the owners' areas of interest. This approach would . . . fly in the face of the overall intent of the legislation to regulate residential communities in keeping with reasonable community expectations between neighbours.[72]

The court noted that no other cottages for hobby painting existed in the neighbourhood.

This is a challenging set of facts, and the decision, nonetheless, was upheld by both the Divisional Court and the Court of Appeal. If by "clusters" the judge means several accessory buildings on each lot, that does not seem to accord with the by-law, which speaks of "an" accessory building. Does it mean that the owner may not paint in the garden shed? Or read or sew in it? Why should intention as to use or even actual use (so long as not habitation) be any part of the test? If objective facts about the structure (the presence of plumbing and heating) should be the test, would that just go contrary to the judge's expansive view of what constitutes habitation? Why should a hobby painter do so without heat or be unable to rinse brushes? Should the "normal" aspect have been tested against the immediate neighbourhood or some wider area? Is it even possible to offer evidence on something like that? Does it mean accessory uses prior to zoning prevail; that is, if the neighbourhood were a community of hobby painters, would that make it normal? Is this a question of preferring one sort of function (a garage, a gardening or tool shed) to another sort of function (sewing, painting) and if so, what sort of classification system is this? *Conlin v Prowse* is highly problematic. If the core concern is not to allow a second residence (akin to laneway houses), why not just focus on the physical infrastructure that

70 *Ibid* at para 1.

71 *Ibid* at para 17.

72 *Ibid* at para 29.

allows for an independent residence, or the actual use? What, exactly, were the objecting neighbours concerned about?

Other aspects of residential accessory use have been litigated. In *R v Badyal*,[73] the British Columbia Court of Appeal allowed the parking of a tractor unit by a tractor-trailer driver in his driveway. The court saw the parking, albeit of a commercial vehicle, as "parking of it at his residence . . . in order that he may make use of his residence as a residence and not so that he may make use of his tractor in his business."[74] "Storage" was prohibited but the court did not see this parking as storage. In *R v Bennett*,[75] the court allowed parking as an accessory use on an adjoining lot owned by the same person even though the dwelling to which the parking was accessory was on a separate lot. A hairdressing business is not an accessory use in a residential area.[76]

It is possible for a residential use to be asserted as accessory to a commercial main use. Thus in *Faro (Town) v Knapp (cob A Knapp Accounting Services)*,[77] an owner operated an outdoor tourism business on land zoned "Hinterland," which allowed only for discretionary uses. The owner had obtained permission for the business, but not for the discretionary accessory use of year-round occupancy.

Although *Knapp* is an unusual case, it is for commercial accessory uses that there has been extensive litigation. The main case is *Oriole Lumber Ltd v Markham (Township)*.[78] The company wanted to carry on a wholesale and retail lumber business on land zoned for industrial use. Industrial use, "by ordinary definition intended a use which was primarily one involving the art of production or manufacture of some item, and that it involved activity or labour whereby a saleable commodity was created or produced."[79] The by-law expanded on the basic idea so as to include warehousing or storage as permitted uses. The company claimed that wholesaling and retailing was an accessory use of the permitted warehousing use. The court rejected that:

> What is decisive, is that the wholesale and/or retail selling is not accessory to the warehousing or storage but, in fact, the warehousing or storage is incidental to the wholesale and retail selling. There can be no other purpose for the building . . . than to sell lumber therefrom

73 (1994), 24 MPLR (2d) 183 (BCCA).
74 *Ibid* at para 6.
75 (1993), 17 MPLR (2d) 320 (NSSCTD).
76 *Burns Lake (Village) v Krause*, 2007 BCSC 730. Nor was hairdressing a permitted home occupation; it was seen as a "personal services establishment."
77 2011 YKSC 43 [*Knapp*].
78 [1968] SCR 549.
79 *Ibid* at 552.

> . . . and for that purpose and that purpose only to store the lumber which is to be sold.[80]

The case in effect drew a line between industrial and commercial activity, and if a municipality were to seek to allow hybrid activity (mixed use), it would have to be clear in its zoning definitions. Indeed, since the courts have tended to read separate zoning classifications as excluding one another, unless the language of the LUB specifies otherwise,[81] any intent to nest uses or to allow overlap through accessory use rights, must be clearly set out.

Other examples of commercial disputes involving accessory use claims are *Re MM Property Management Services Inc*,[82] *T&T Mushroom Farm Ltd v Langley (Township)*,[83] *Moriarity v Sarnia (City)*,[84] *MacFarlane & Murphy v Robichaud*,[85] *Re Becker Milk Co Ltd and City of London*,[86] *Build-A-Vest Structures Inc v Red Deer (City)*,[87] and *Gabriola Island Local Trust Committee v Foley*.[88] In *Re MM*, for an RV park serving as a seasonal campsite, permanent storage sheds were not seen as an accessory use. In *T&T*, the issue was whether a composting facility qualified as either an allowable primary use or an accessory use to a mushroom farm. The zoning allowed for agricultural uses, and specified mushroom farms as part of the allowable main use. The company wanted to erect another building to process compost, which is the growing medium for the mushrooms. The court cited the Code of Agricultural Practice for Waste Management made under British Columbia's *Waste Management Act*[89] (since repealed), which contemplated on-farm production of "mushroom medium" as part of mushroom farming, and specified setback distances from watercourses and water sources. The court read the LUB as allowing "a building to store and create the medium for growing . . . mushrooms . . . as a part of the operation of a mushroom

80 *Ibid* at 553–54.

81 *Cambridge Leaseholds Ltd v Thomas C Watkins Ltd*, [1966] OJ No 65 (CA). The SCC allowed an appeal without reported reasons (see [1966] SCR v), thus affirming the dissent in the appellate court decision. See also *Berjawi v Ottawa (City)*, 2011 ONSC 236; *Moncrief v Brazeau (County)*, 2009 ABCA 329; *North Pender Island Local Trust Committee v Conconi*, 2009 BCSC 328.

82 (2012), 94 MPLR (4th) 129 (BCSC) [*Re MM*].

83 (1997), 39 MPLR (2d) 282 (BCCA) [*T&T*].

84 (1998), 48 MPLR (2d) 225 (Ont CA) [*Moriarty*].

85 (31 March 2000) New Brunswick Provincial Planning Appeal Board, unreported [*MacFarlane & Murphy*].

86 (1984), 44 OR (2d) 385 (HCJ).

87 2006 ABQB 869 [*Build-A-Vest*].

88 2007 BCSC 1294 [*Gabriola v Foley*].

89 SBC 1982, c 41.

farm."[90] Though the court did not find it necessary to go to the accessory use issue, it implied that the same result would have been found. In *Moriarty*, the zone was C-3, a general commercial-use classification that extended to various particular uses. The court found that in determining what parking requirements applied, the differing calculations applicable to the various uses should apply, according to the proportion of use each represented. In *MacFarlane & Murphy*, a lot was created in Parlee Provincial Park so that it could be leased to a private developer to build a licensed restaurant. Objection was taken to the issuance of a building permit on the basis that the land was zoned "E-Environment Conservation." A restaurant was not a listed use, and the permit had been sought as an accessory use. Evidence was led that other provincial parks in New Brunswick have licensed restaurants. Although a separate lot had been created, the province remained the owner of the lot and the rest of the park. The board focused on the lot as an entity of its own, thus sidestepping the issue of whether a restaurant was an accessory use to the park, determining that "this is not an accessory or secondary use. It is a main use being conducted by the tenant which is the company that operates the restaurant/bar."[91] In the result, the building permits were found to be invalid. In *Becker Milk*, one or two video games were found not to be an accessory use in a convenience store, a finding essentially undercut by the 1986 decision of the OMB in *Re City of Toronto Zoning By-law No 307-84*.[92] In *Build-A-Vest*, the company proposed to build a funeral home. It wanted to include a crematorium as part of the structure. The view of the municipality was that a crematorium was a distinct use of land separate from a funeral home and was also not an accessory use. Evidence was led that in Alberta, there were some thirty-five crematoriums, twenty-five of which were located in the same building as a funeral home, and had been permitted as accessory uses. Despite this evidence, the court held that a crematorium was not necessarily incidental to a funeral home and thus not an as-of-right accessory use. However, a building permit had been issued to the company, and plans submitted included a "retort room"; the city realized only when a gas hookup permit was sought that this meant a crematorium, and the permit for it was refused. The court decided that although a crematorium was not an accessory use for a funeral home,

90 Above note 83 at para 14.

91 Above note 85 at 20. But in *Toronto (City) v Canadian National Railway Co*, 1997 CanLII 4481 (Ont CA), it was held that mobile food vending carts were an acceptable accessory use in a park zone, CN Plaza adjacent to the SkyDome.

92 (1986), 18 OMBR 155, confirming the earlier OMB decision *in Re City of Toronto Restricted Area By-law 67-80* (1980), 12 OMBR 52.

a crematorium was a discretionary use that had been agreed to when the original permit was issued, and awarded damages to the company for loss of business.[93]

Accessory uses are not the same as designated home-based businesses, which are treated separately in LUBs.

A somewhat esoteric variant is how to analyze what is a permitted accessory use for non-conforming property. Should the accessory use be determined according to the NCU or according to the actual zoning? In *Prince Edward Island Museum & Heritage Foundation v Charlottetown (City)*,[94] the property was located in an R-1 zone but had an established NCU as a museum run by a non-profit society. The court, perhaps not clearly distinguishing between intensification of an NCU and accessory use, seems to have assessed the accessory use according to the NCU. In *McRae v Squamish (District)*,[95] the NCU was for a log sort facility; the owner wished to convert the use to a chip transfer facility. The court assessed what would be an allowable accessory use according to the Light Industrial zoning. In neither case was the point focused on, nor was the earlier *PEI Museum* case cited to the court in *McRae*. Since the opportunity to claim accessory use rights are purely dependent on a provision to that effect in the LUB, *McRae* seems to be the correct approach; *PEI Museum* might best be seen as a case about intensification of an NCU. However, a 2013 Ontario decision, *Kirk (cob Lakeshore Automotive) v Lambton (County)*,[96] albeit without detailed discussion or reference to any precedent, seems to adopt the view that accessory uses relate to the NCU.

There are some interesting United Kingdom cases on accessory use. Because of the differences in the legal framework, they may not be helpful as precedents here. But burial on a non-commercial basis for family members has been seen not to be a material change in use requiring formal permission.[97] Also, the landing of helicopters was seen as an acceptable incidental use for a private dwelling with extensive grounds, and for a museum focused on helicopters, though not for a department store.[98]

If anything may be concluded from review of the overall range of accessory use cases, it is that the result in any particular dispute will not be easy to predict.

---

93 The sum awarded was substantial: $279,000 for loss of profits.

94 (1998), 45 MPLR (2d) 281 (PEISCTD) [*PEI Museum*].

95 2000 BCSC 1339 [*McRae*].

96 2012 ONCJ 809 at paras 116–30.

97 See Victor Moore, *A Practical Approach to Planning Law*, 10th ed (Oxford: Oxford University Press, 2007) at paras 7.32–7.34.

98 *Ibid* at paras 7.29–7.30.

D. MINOR VARIANCES

Planning Acts generally allow for a power to permit some bending of the rules in limited circumstances. Such consents are known as "variances" or "minor variances." The Ontario Act, for example, provides:

> The committee of adjustment . . . may, despite any other Act, authorize such minor variance from the provisions of the by-law, in respect of the land, building or structure or the use thereof, as in its opinion is desirable for the appropriate development or use of the land, building or structure, if in the opinion of the committee the general intent and purpose of the by-law and of the official plan, if any, is maintained.[99]

Commenting on the provision, the OMB has said, "The board interprets that section to mean desirable not only as it relates to the subject land but also as it relates to the neighbouring land,"[100] a crucial point, and in line with the basic land-use approach of recognizing the planning enterprise as being about communal interactions.

Other provinces do not allow for such potentially wide powers of variance. For example, Nova Scotia limits the variance to such matters as percentage of land that may be built upon, yard size, lot frontage, number of parking spaces, height, area occupied by a home-based business, and signage. That statute also prohibits variances where the intent of the land-use by-law is violated, the difficulty experienced is general to properties in the area, or the difficulty results from intentional disregard for the land-use by-law.[101] The Ontario provision seems to allow applications for minor variances concerning any aspect of the use of land so long as it fits the stated criteria.

There is a difficult conceptual problem embedded in the concept of minor variance. It is especially problematic for the type of minor variance provision in the Ontario legislation. Because its scope is broader than some few specified items such as percentage of lot cover, and specifies "use," it potentially amounts to an alternative route to achieving what is in effect a rezoning. Even for more narrowly defined variance provisions, what is being permitted (e.g., greater height, smaller setback) is something that the by-law states is not allowed. Typically, an LUB will say that, in a specified zone, "[n]o person shall use any building or structure for any purpose than one of the following uses . . . ." Such prohibitions derive from the usual statutory grant of a regulatory power to a

---

99 *Planning Act*, RSO 1990, c P.13, s 45(1).

100 *Keefer v City of Toronto Committee of Adjustment* (1987), 19 OMBR 475 at 477.

101 *Municipal Government Act*, SNS 1998, c 18, s 235.

municipality that allows for zoning "for prohibiting the use of land for or except for such purposes as set out in the by-law." Allowing minor variances draws our attention to the fact that LUBs are made up of a bundle of items, some of which are perhaps more crucial to the "general intent" of the LUB than others. A continuum seems to emerge from the cases.

This point has been focused on directly in some cases. It arose as early as 1960 in *R v London Committee of Adjustment ex p Weinstein*.[102] The issue there was whether the committee's approval of a "hostel for derelict persons" would be allowed for an area zoned "light industrial." The court overturned the decision, noting that the *Planning Act* "does not give the committee any power to establish a use — it may authorize or permit a minor variance in respect of the use of the land."[103] What this meant was not clear. At one point, Ontario courts took the view set out in *Convenience Services Ltd v Barrie Committee of Adjustments*,[104] where it was said: "I cannot think of circumstances where to permit the right to a use which is not permitted under a zoning by-law can be considered a 'minor variation' of that zoning by-law." In taking this position, the court drew a line, apparently excluding changes to type of use through the minor variance power. That approach is similar to the approach generally taken in matters of accessory uses where, if what is proposed as accessory amounts to a use that exists as a separate classified use under the LUB, it is not allowable. The view set out in *Convenience Services* is not, however, the current prevailing view. This may be dated from the decision in *Fred Doucette Holdings Ltd v Waterloo (City)*.[105] The by-law in question permitted, in an industrial zone, the retail sale of foods produced on-site. The company applied for a minor variance to allow it to include in their sales foods produced elsewhere. The committee of adjustment allowed the change, and this was upheld by a majority of the Divisional Court on the basis that the industrial zoning did not prohibit retailing and allowed some complementary uses. The court commented: "With respect to a particular industrial site, the area permitted for retail purposes is relatively large — up to 50 per cent of the site. From a land use perspective, the nature of the activity of retailing is surely of considerably greater significance than what is being retailed. To the extent that the nature of what is being retailed is significant, the terms of the impugned variance cannot be said to depart significantly from the nature of what the by-law permits

102 [1960] OR 225 (CA).
103 *Ibid* at 235.
104 [1982] OJ No 925 at para 17 (HCJ) [*Convenience Services*].
105 (1997), 32 OR (3d) 502 (Div Ct) [*Fred Doucette*].

the respondents to retail."[106] The result is now an approach to minor variance applications that leaves open the possibility of achieving a different use than the basic zoning calls for, with the issue assessed on a case-by-case basis. Several cases have noted that "the definition of a minor variance has not been precisely defined."[107] Or, as said in an earlier Divisional Court decision: "The term is a relative one and should be flexibly applied . . . ."[108] As an example, in *Toronto (City) v Romlek Enterprises*,[109] approval through the minor variance process allowed, in a commercial zone, a mixed residential and commercial project with five times the permitted lot cover and seven times the permitted density. The court found the decision to be unreasonable, not a minor variance. The court responded to the city's view that this amounted to a rezoning, that it had gone too far to be a minor variance. Overall, the approach of the courts to minor variances seems to have merged with their approach to NCUs as enunciated by the Supreme Court of Canada in *Saint-Romuald*: it is a matter of judgment whether intensification has gone too far and become a complete change.

Cases exist for variances regarding height above grade, building length, size of accessory buildings, driveway width, side and front yard setbacks, percentage of lot cover, gross floor area, erection of satellite dishes, setback from waterbodies, number of residential units, signage, number of parking places, percentage of a residence that may be used as a home-based business, conversion of coach houses, and many more. Changes in the specifics of the LUB so as to allow for some variations will sometimes involve loss of privacy for neighbours. The OMB looked at this factor in a case involving a request for a variety of adjustments, saying, "As to the loss of privacy due to a new house with windows in the rear looking out on part of the rear of his yard, the board is of the view that is simply a price one must pay for choosing to live in an urban environment and in this case a congested one . . . ."[110]

Overall, the inherent flexibility of the variance provision is such that its use over time can lead to the sort of important changes in a neighbourhood that the scheme of *Planning Acts* tends to reserve for OP or LUB changes.

---

106 *Ibid* at 511–12. For comment on the *Fred Doucette* case, see Michal E Minkowski, "When Is a Change in Use 'Minor'?" (1997) 4 *Digest of Municipal and Planning Law* 111 and 121–24.

107 *Toronto (City) v 621 King Developments Ltd*, 2011 ONSC 7047 (Div Ct).

108 *McNamara Corp Ltd v Colekin Investments Ltd* (1977), 15 OR (2d) 718 at para 8 (Div Ct).

109 2008 CanLII 52618 (Ont Div Ct); 2009 CanLII 27819 at para 30 (Ont Div Ct).

110 *Keefer v City of Toronto Committee of Adjustment*, above note 100 at 476.

E. CREATIVE CONFORMITY

There are a variety of ways in which there may be construction that accords with the provisions of land-use by-laws, but that nonetheless produce surprising results. Among these are "monster homes," multiple structures on a single podium, and lot consolidations. In addition to construction that conforms to the LUB though perhaps with surprizing results, there are always issues that may arise regarding the building code. Indeed, building code issues may leave the most room for discussion with enforcement officials, leading to results perhaps not anticipated by all landowners.

Monster homes are those that are built to the full limit of the by-law rules. They raise concerns for several reasons: they stand out in some neighbourhoods and are seen as incompatible, they might raise neighbourhood land values and thus property taxes, there might be issues of privacy, and they might lend themselves to illegal internal changes to support multiple units. House construction is controlled typically through a grouping of rules: percentage of the lot that may be occupied, height, setbacks from lot lines, and total square footage of a building that may be constructed. In many established neighbourhoods, homes either were not built to the maximum allowable size, or the rules have evolved over time. The situation arises not from the absence of rules, but from builders seeking to, for example, construct a 4,000-square-foot home in an area where the neighbourhood norm has been half of that. This may be achieved through a design that goes to the full allowable height, and where two or more storeys are of equal or almost equal size. Height is often a flexible concept under by-laws, with points of interpretation arising as to how to measure the ground level (grade) on an uneven lot, and with rules that sometimes allow intrusion above the height restriction to complete a partial storey.

Lot consolidations may also lead to larger buildings than were expected. Lot consolidation is often treated as a routine administrative matter. If achieved, a larger lot than those in the immediate neighbourhood may allow for a larger building, perhaps not a higher one, but where the zoning by-law deals with what is allowable construction in terms of percentage of lot coverage, then the size of the lot becomes the important determining factor.

In what was probably not a surprising result, in *Oshawa Wholesale Ltd v Canadia Niagara Falls Ltd*,[111] an attempt was made to meet the zoning rules by presenting a shopping centre as individual stores. The

111 [1972] 1 OR 481 (CA).

zoning did not allow a shopping centre. The individual stores that were allowable under the zoning were deemed to have lost their character as individual uses when they were grouped together as a shopping centre.

In *United Gulf Developments Ltd (Re)*,[112] the landowner proposed to construct two twelve-storey towers on a single podium base, taking the view that this constituted one building. The site was part of a primarily residential subdivision, developed under a development agreement. The developer applied both for a new development agreement and for a building permit. The development agreement for the overall subdivision allowed the particular site to be used for three apartment buildings with a maximum height of four storeys each, with "the exception that one building may be permitted to be of a height of 12 storeys." The Nova Scotia Utility and Review Board agreed that the two buildings on a common podium was permissible, and the decision was upheld by the Nova Scotia Court of Appeal.[113] The board applied the National Building Code definition of a building to reach the conclusion that two towers on a common podium constitute one building.

In an example of creative conformity exercised by a municipality, in *City Sand & Gravel Ltd v Newfoundland (Minister of Municipal and Provincial Affairs)*,[114] a quarry operation was obliged under provincial rules to have a buffer setback from residential areas of 300 metres; the municipality zoned its residential area closer, thus forcing the quarrying operation to reduce its size.

F. HOME-BASED BUSINESSES

One of the main home-based businesses is the family farm. Despite evolution of farming so as to include employees, increased mechanization, large-scale operations, and sometimes corporate ownership, it remains a family-centred enterprise. For our purposes, this means the business is based in the family residence on-site and involves family members as workers. The concept of a home-based business tends to be different, however, and agricultural uses are normally regulated as a specific type of land use of its own. Home-based business refers to the use of a dwelling in a designated residential area for some commercial or minor industrial activity in addition to its use as a residence.

---

112 2008 NSUARB 167.

113 *Halifax (Regional Municipality) v United Gulf Developments Ltd*, 2009 NSCA 78.

114 2007 NLCA 51.

It is almost universal that land-use by-laws allow for certain specified traditional professions to be carried on in a home (law, medicine, accounting, engineering, dentistry, etc.). There may be some rules as to signage, but otherwise the activity has tended not to be forbidden or regulated. There were also other forms of work that were carried out in residences, such as the teaching of music. So long as these were of low impact on neighbours in terms of noise or other disruptions, such as need for on-street parking, these activities have not drawn much attention.

A new reality is that there are many types of work that may be carried out from home[115] and without much externalized impact. The trend had been identified for some decades;[116] thus it has been something of an irritant that many municipalities have not come to grips with the evolving nature of work.[117] The result is that in many communities, home-based businesses are carried on in violation of the zoning rules. Such activities as tutoring, computer repair, website design, graphics, interior design, journalism, management consultant, secretarial services, editor/indexer, freelance researcher, architect, and land-use planner may all occur with minimal external impacts. Others such as animal care, hair-cutting or beauty care, tailoring, furniture repair, catering, and some carpentry may have greater impacts, as will regular yard sales and market gardening if produce is offered for sale from the premises.

One of the advantages of working from home—no commuting—is also a services and environmental advantage for governments.[118]

With evolution of federal laws regarding prostitution and also cannabis, it is an open question whether local regulation may be needed, approaching the activities as home-based businesses.

---

115 Up-to-date statistics are not available. In 2001, Statistics Canada said that approximately 8 percent of the overall workforce worked at home between 1971 and 1991; this included the residents of the home and any employees. See Earnest B Akyeampong & Richard Nadwodny, "Evolution of the Canadian Workplace: Work from Home" (September 2001) 2:9 *Perspectives on Labour and Income*, online: www.statcan.gc.ca/pub/75-001-x/00901/4095817-eng.html. In 2008, 11.2 percent of employees worked from home, as well as 60 percent of the self-employed; between them they represent 19 percent of the total workforce. See Martin Turcotte, "Working at Home: An Update" (7 December 2010), online: www.statcan.gc.ca/pub/11-008-x/2011001/article/11366-eng.pdf.

116 Penny C Gurstein, *Planning for Telework and Home-based Employment: A Canadian Survey on Integrating Work into Residential Environments* (Ottawa: Canada Mortgage and Housing Corporation, 1995).

117 For an amusing account, see Robert Lehman, "The Case of the Erroneous Zone" (1997) 37:4 *Plan Canada* 24.

118 For a listing of the pros and cons of working from home, see Canada Business Ontario, "Home-Based Business," online: www.cbo-eco.ca/en/index.cfm/starting/choosing-a-location/home-based-business.

The rental of the whole or a part of a residence for short-term occupancy, as in Airbnb, is already a regulatory issue. Hotels, motels, resorts, cottages, cabins, inns, and other short-term residential accommodation for travellers are regulated as to a variety of matters, including minimum standards such as accessibility and fire safety,[119] though this is not the case for informal rentals. Tenants have been found to be in violation of their leases by renting their premises on Airbnb for more than their rents.[120]

In *Donnell v Joseph (cob WJ Moving & Storage)*,[121] a competing business objected to another operating its moving services out of a residence. The points raised had to do with parking the moving vans on-site, employees parking their vehicles on-site, and the presence of a "sea bin" consisting of four compartments that were used for storing packing materials. The by-law allowed home occupations as a secondary use of property if "entirely within a dwelling unit" in which the proprietor resides. In what is not an entirely convincing ruling, the court said,

> Apart from administrative aspects of the Josephs' business, which are carried out in the office in their family dwelling, the activities of the Josephs' moving business are conducted off-site—that is, off their property. That the Josephs allow vehicular parking on their property, and store materials on the property that are then sold or used off the property, does not cut against this conclusion. Further, only one employee works on the property. In these circumstances . . . the challenged aspects of the Josephs' business are, at the highest, tangential activities, carried out solely for convenience, that form no essential part of the Josephs' actual moving business. I do not think that they can be said to constitute part of the Josephs' moving business in any meaningful sense.[122]

In *Kamloops (City) v Charchuk*,[123] the by-law stated its purpose to be to "permit the establishment of small scale businesses within residential dwellings provided they have no negative impacts on other residents within the zone." It went on to permit home-based businesses but also said, "No sale of goods or provision of services is permitted on

119 See, for example, Ontario's *Fire Protection and Prevention Act, 1997*, SO 1997, c 4; *Health Protection and Promotion Act*, RSO 1990, c H.7; *Innkeepers Act*, RSO 1990, c I.7; *Hotel Registration of Guests Act*, RSO 1990, c H.17 and their regulations.

120 See *Re TSL-64867-15-AM*, 2015 CanLII 77404 (ON LTB), citing *Residential Tenancies Act, 2006*, SO 2006, c 17, ss 134(3)(a) and 234(x).

121 2012 ONCA 240.

122 *Ibid* at paras 20–21.

123 (1997), 41 BCLR (3d) 383 (CA).

the premises." Charchuk operated a meat-cutting business, particularly during hunting season. Following complaints, the city sought to shut the operation. The court found the by-law to be internally inconsistent, but in light of the overall purpose being to permit home-based businesses, it struck down the prohibition on sale of goods or services.

Although most of the focus on home-based businesses is on small commercial undertakings, Edmonton allows for "major" home-based businesses in some areas.[124]

G. BONUSING: DEVELOPMENT AGREEMENTS AND DENSITY BONUSING

In the leading cases in which either private-sector developers have asserted that a set of arrangements with a municipality has bound the municipality to change zoning,[125] or a municipality has attempted to modify as-of-right zoning through use of some contractual mechanism,[126] the courts have been clear that zoning may not be dealt with this way unless there is a clear statutory regime allowing for it. Among the legal issues is the restriction placed by provinces on municipalities not to grant bonuses to particular business enterprises. Thus, Ontario's *Municipal Act* says, "a municipality shall not assist directly or indirectly any manufacturing business or other industrial or commercial enterprise through the granting of bonuses for that purpose."[127] The underlying policy is that municipalities ought not to compete among themselves to attract business, or to favour particular businesses over others, at least not through direct financial benefits. Offering direct benefits to businesses is a power the province reserves for itself. The term bonusing is variable in its meaning, and in recognition that special land-use arrangements may confer financial benefits on landowners, cases have been brought challenging certain sets of arrangements. Writing in 1987, Professor FA Laux reviewed some cases and concluded:

> In all of the cases in which the court found there existed an illegal bonus or tax exemption, two components were present. First, the municipal council was either not purporting to exercise some sub-

124 See *Edmonton (City) v Edmonton (City) Subdivision and Development Appeal Board*, 2016 ABCA 129.

125 *Pacific National Investments Ltd v Victoria (City)*, 2000 SCC 64.

126 *Harrietsfield-Grand Lake Community Association v Halifax (County)* (1978), 26 NSR (2d) 198 (SCAD); *Fredericton Heritage Trust Inc v Fredericton (City)* (1988), 39 MPLR 64 (NBCA).

127 *Municipal Act, 2001*, SO 2001, c 25, s 106.

stantive municipal power conferred under the enabling legislation or, if it was, it was found to be a mere sham. Second, the only consideration or benefit flowing to the municipality, aside from the benefit that naturally arises out of the establishment of any business enterprise, was nominal in nature.[128]

Zoning flexibility mechanisms are, however, now common and their parameters are specified by statute. Their use tends to be directed at larger projects or those in special areas. The late Richard Matthews, a planner, writing about their use in Halifax, said, "It is economically justifiable to use development agreements for valuable, sensitive, and highly visible land, such as the [central business district], and for large tracts of new residential development, but the cost of processing and amount of time involved for small projects would not be acceptable."[129] Thus, while it is technically possible for bonusing to be used in any locale, this is not common. Matthews also says, "[i]n many regards, agreements seem like custom-tailored zoning. They are not 'spot zoning,' however, but formulated and processed in a policy environment that keeps the flexibility they provide within the bounds of consistent policy."[130] What this omits is the negotiation aspect of bonusing in which public benefits are sought in exchange for the special arrangement. Typically, the zoning flexibility mechanisms are development agreements or density bonusing. There are differences between the two, and not only as to the mechanisms. The essence of a development agreement is to allow a municipality and a developer to enter into a binding contract for a project not otherwise allowable in the LUB; density bonusing allows for more limited stepping away from the LUB.

In the Urban Land Institute text *Development Agreements: Practice, Policy, and Prospects*,[131] the Introduction says,

> Development agreements are intended to provide developers with assurances that the land use regulations in effect at the time development is approved will not change during the term of the agreement . . . . Development agreements have several purposes. The primary one is to assure the developer the rules of the game will not change, for without such assurance, the developer incurs greater risk in constructing

128 Frederick A Laux, "Municipal Bonuses and Tax Exemptions to Entice Private Developments" (1986–87) 25 *Alberta Law Review* 224 at 233.

129 Richard Matthews et al, "The Use of Development Agreements in Canada: The Halifax Experience" in Douglas R Porter & Lindell L Marsh, eds, *Development Agreements: Practice, Policy, and Prospects* (Washington, DC: Urban Land Institute, 1989) 105 at 116.

130 *Ibid* at 114.

131 Porter & Marsh, eds, above note 129.

> infrastructure and providing public benefits during a project's early stages . . . . A second purpose . . . is that they permit a more detailed and flexible means for developers and the public sector to cooperate in reconciling and addressing their concerns and interests . . . . Development agreements are based on consensus. All parties must perceive that they will benefit from the agreement and that they were not coerced into entering it. Negotiations cover a wide range of subjects: benefits, the amount and nature of the consideration from the developer, the extent to which it is appropriate to consider the project's profitability, determination and allocation of fiscal impacts to the new development and between past and future developments . . . .[132]

In this overview, development agreements are about predictability or stability, as well as project-specific flexibility for the developer, and also about benefits for the public as represented by the local government. The process for arriving at an agreement is negotiation. The concern about the "rules not changing" is difficult to assess; but even without a development agreement, changes will not affect a development that has been approved, even if not built, if a permit has been obtained. The concern seems more to be about the sequence of planning a project; that is, a developer will hope to secure binding approval as early as possible and prior to investing any significant amount of money in detailed design or even in the purchase of land. (It is possible for a developer to obtain approval for a development agreement even if the developer's status is holder of an option to purchase.[133])

The province sets the conditions for a municipality to use development agreements or other flexibility mechanisms. Thus in British Columbia, the *Local Government Act* allows density bonusing to be a part of the land-use by-law:

> 482 (1) A zoning bylaw may
>
> (a) establish different density rules for a zone, one generally applicable for the zone and the other or others to apply if the applicable conditions under paragraph (b) are met, and
>
> (b) establish conditions in accordance with subsection (2) that will entitle an owner to a higher density under paragraph (a).
>
> (2) The following are conditions that may be included under subsection (1)(b):

132 *Ibid* at 2–5.

133 See *Re Canterbury Investments Ltd* (1981), 11 PPAD 1495 (NS Mun Bd); *Heritage Trust of Nova Scotia v Halifax (City)* (1981), 50 NSR (2d) 352 at para 193 (SCTD).

(a) conditions relating to the conservation or provision of amenities, including the number, kind and extent of amenities;
(b) conditions relating to the provision of affordable and special needs housing, as such housing is defined in the bylaw, including the number, kind and extent of the housing;
(c) a condition that the owner enter into a housing agreement under section 483 before a building permit is issued in relation to property to which the condition applies.

(3) A zoning bylaw may designate an area within a zone for affordable or special needs housing . . . .[134]

The extent of the density bonus, and the conditions—clearly public benefits—are to be specified in the LUB before an "entitlement" arises. In Nova Scotia, the pre-conditions are to be set out in the official plan.[135]

A number of issues arise for bonusing schemes. The first is whether they may authorize a different use than specified in the basic zoning by-law. In *Lambert v Whistler (Resort Municipality)*,[136] it was said that "It is common ground that specific legislative authority is required for bargaining to go on between a developer and a municipal council. Section 904 of the *LGA* permits a council to zone for density in exchange for amenities; there is no similar provision that would allow the council to zone for land use in exchange for amenities."[137] In drawing this distinction between an increase in density and a change in land use, the court focused on the need for "specific legislative authority" for bargaining, the authority on point being *Pacific National Investments Ltd v Victoria (City)*.[138] In *Lambert*, it was found that it had negotiated for a large hotel, a use not permitted under the size limits for hotels prevailing in the land-use by-law. Not all provinces disallow different uses than the basic zoning provides for, as matters that may form part of such agreements. In Nova Scotia, the controlling legislation provides:

> The Council may consider development by development agreement where a municipal planning strategy identifies (a) the developments that are subject to a development agreement; (b) the area or areas where the developments may be located; and (c) the matters that the Council must consider prior to the approval of a development agreement.[139]

134 RSBC 2015, c 1, s 482. The equivalent section in the *Vancouver Charter*, SBC 1953, c 55, as amended, is s 565.1.
135 *Municipal Government Act*, above note 101, s 225.
136 2004 BCSC 342 [*Lambert*].
137 *Ibid* at para 35 [citations omitted].
138 Above note 125.
139 *HRM Charter*, above note 3, s 240.

Section 242 provides, "A development agreement may contain terms with respect to (a) matters that a land-use by-law may contain . . . ." Thus, in Nova Scotia, a development agreement may allow a type of use not allowed by the zoning for the site. Nova Scotia also provides for "incentive or bonus zoning,"[140] a variant. But for bonus zoning, there is no equivalent to the section 242 provision for extending the provisions of the agreement to all matters that a land-use by-law may contain; the implication seems to be that different uses may not be authorized. In Ontario, the *Planning Act* allows municipalities to "authorize increases in the height and density of development otherwise permitted by the by-law . . . in return for the provision of such facilities, services or matters as are set out in the by-law."[141] The municipality must have OP policies authorizing such bonuses, as well as by-laws to the same effect. Because of the words "otherwise permitted by the by-law," a change in use does not appear to be authorized.

Development agreements may be changed over time. They are registered against title and operate as a form of restrictive covenant. However, enforcement of the terms of the DA is a matter purely for the municipality and the current owner of the land; previous owners or abutting owners may not seek to enforce the terms.[142] There is usually authority for a municipality to alter a DA without a further public hearing if the matter is "not substantive" and the DA has identified what those matters are.[143]

Another issue is whether cash may be one of the "amenities" or "facilities, services or matters" to be provided to the municipality. Nova Scotia specifies, though only with respect to bonus zoning, that "the Council may accept money in lieu of a contribution" and that the money shall be used "for the purpose for which the money was accepted."[144] In neither British Columbia nor Ontario is the point addressed by the legislation. In *Lambert*, the municipality of Whistler proposed to accept various sums of cash for a variety of purposes (environmental enhancement of a creek, building trails, landscaping, purchase of youth recreation equipment), something not questioned by the plaintiffs in the case and not commented on in the judgment. It appears that in British Col-

---

140 *Ibid*, s 245A.

141 Ontario *Planning Act*, above note 99, s 37.

142 See *4067712 Manitoba Ltd v Lakeland Golf Properties Inc*, 2004 MBQB 157 at paras 30 & 31.

143 See, for example, Nova Scotia's *Municipal Government Act*, above note 101, ss 227(3) and 230(7).

144 *HRM Charter*, above note 3, s 245A. See *Can-Euro Investments Ltd (Re)*, 2007 NSUARB 100.

umbia, this is the accepted interpretation of the ambit of "amenities." Likewise, in Ontario, cash is routinely specified by municipalities as a way to achieve a bonus. The one case that focuses on this was at the OMB, *Re Copthorne Holdings*,[145] where the practice was approved.

It is not clear whether bonuses or money received in exchange for bonuses may address items for which another statutory scheme already exists. Thus, development cost charges for hard infrastructure are already a required feature of developments, and it is probably not appropriate for a municipality to include or forego contributions for such items as part of a bonusing agreement.

An associated issue is whether the OP or LUB must set out how a contribution is determined. In Nova Scotia, for bonus zoning only, the by-law must "set out the method to be used to determine the contribution."[146] This does not seem to be required by statute elsewhere. Theoretically, it then becomes an open matter how contributions are arrived at. Cases have said that there should be some rationale. This raises, however, a point not usually addressed: what is the value of the granted bonus to the developer? No meaningful negotiations can take place, and no meaningful contributions can be determined, unless there is some professional or objective estimate of the dollar value of the benefit being conferred on the developer by the public's granting of additional development rights. A 2015 "Density Bonusing Study" by the Halifax Regional Municipality[147] focused on how to calculate the "lift" in land value when a bonus is granted, and compared systems in place in various jurisdictions. Regardless of the system chosen, a clear, defensible rationale is appropriate.

Because the statutes call for policies to be in place in the OP and LUB, there is a question as to the extent to which bonusing arrangements are discretionary or amount to entitlements if the stated criteria are met. The planning literature speaks of bonusing as discretionary but within a policy context. Thus Matthews says,

> Within the bounds of policy established in the city's plan, they are given discretionary approvals by the city council . . . . The city's abilities to consider development agreements are set out specifically in the zoning by-law, but the criteria that bind the city's discretion in deciding on agreements are in its municipal plan.[148]

---

145 (1987), 36 MPLR 122 (OMB).

146 *HRM Charter*, above note 3, s 245A(2)(d).

147 Halifax Regional Municipality, "Density Bonusing Study" (8 October 2015), online: http://shapeyourcityhalifax.ca/centre-plan/documents/2547/download.

148 Matthews, above note 129 at 105 and 113.

The British Columbia legislation does speak of "entitlement." And the Nova Scotia legislation requires a municipal council that refuses a development agreement application to state reasons.[149] This point is determined by the judicial rules of deference to municipal councils: if the policies are written with precision, there may be no discretion for the municipal council, whereas if there are general words or the necessity to balance policies, there will be room for the successful exercise of discretion.

A political dimension is whether the proposed construction itself should be taken into account as a public benefit. On balance, the answer should be no. The proposed construction is what the developer seeks. There will certainly be construction work involving employment and purchases of materials, as well as the resultant building, which will be taxed. But these are inherent to the basic proposal from the developer. The idea of "amenities" or equivalent term seems to contemplate something additional, such as affordable housing or environmental benefits.[150]

An issue that has arisen is the extent to which public benefits sought must reasonably relate to the proposed development itself. Doumani and Foran note that, "The Ontario Municipal Board decisions have gone both ways as to whether the services to be provided must directly relate to the development or not."[151] The most recent of the clutch of cases have sought "a nexus between the development and the s.37 benefits . . . ."[152] In *Menkes Church Street Holdings Inc v Toronto (City)*,[153] the board said, in refusing to allow a cash contribution to be required, "The use of section 37 must be grounded in fair, clear, transparent, predictable and specific requirements that are set out in the Official Plan and that are not arbitrary in their application. The Board is adamant that the Applicant has a right to know how the figure is derived in sufficient detail."

---

149 *HRM Charter*, above note 3, s 45(6).

150 It is not clear from the studies that bonusing is effective to achieve its stated objectives, unless very carefully designed and implemented. See, for example, Marya Morris, *Incentive Zoning: Meeting Urban Design and Affordable Housing Objectives* (Chicago: American Planning Association, 2000); Robert A Johnston et al, "Selling Zoning: Do Density Bonus Incentives for Moderate Cost Housing Work?" (1989) 36 *Washington University Journal of Urban and Contemporary Law* 45; William A Buholzer, "Financing Urban Growth: Amenities and Density Bonuses" (Vancouver: Continuing Legal Education Society of British Columbia, 2008).

151 Robert Doumani & Patricia Foran, *Ontario Planning Legislation and Commentary, 2017 Edition* (Markham, ON: LexisNexis, 2016) at 88.

152 *Sterling Silver Development Corp v Toronto (City)* (2005), 16 MPLR (4th) 293 at para 81 (OMB). See also *1430 Yonge Street Inc v Toronto (City)* (2003), 46 OMBR 63 (OMB); *Irber Holdings Ltd v Toronto (City)* (2005), 14 MPLR (4th) 307 (OMB); *Dunpar Developments Inc v Toronto (City)*, [2008] OMBD No 61; *1640830 Ontario Inc v Toronto (City)*, [2007] OMBD No 914.

153 (2012), 6 MPLR (5th) 127 at para 58 (OMB).

H. CHANGING THE RULES

Because the system of land regulation is political, it is always possible to seek to change the rules.[154] Because zoning or flexibility mechanisms such as development agreements are intended to follow the policies set out in the OP, one way to insulate a decision from most forms of legal attack is to change the OP at the same time as changing the zoning or as entering into a development agreement. Thus, in *Friends of Ragged Beach Inc v Witless Bay (Town) Town Council*,[155] residents who opposed a contemplated change in zoning and the OP were rebuffed in their court challenge rather summarily. The court said,

> I am satisfied that the possible amendments to municipal plans are not limited to mere zoning changes. There is nothing in the language of the [*Urban and Rural Planning Act, 2000*] which restricts the nature or type of amendment which can be made to the Municipal Plan. Thus, I am satisfied that, as collateral to an amendment of the zoning, the Town Council can also effect changes to the Municipal Plan which are collateral to the development applications for which the zoning changes are sought . . . . Therefore, the mere fact that the development applications at present are non-compliant with the Municipal Plan does not prohibit the initiation by the Town Council of the plan amendment process to amend the zonings of the two areas in question to permit the developments and to effect any changes to collateral provisions of the Municipal Plan, which might otherwise be in conflict with approval . . . .[156]

Two examples illustrate the dynamic:

1) In Queens County, Nova Scotia, there are zoning by-laws that disallow the keeping of chickens in residential areas. An owner wishing to keep chickens could seek a site-specific amendment to the by-law. One owner, a keeper of chickens, objected, taking on the municipal council in a spate of publicity. He pointed out that he would be obliged to pay a fee of approximately $700 to have his application for rezoning processed, and of course there would be

---

154 As a way to accommodate monster homes, discussed in Section E, above in this chapter, some municipalities have considered changing their rules so as to allow larger homes. Surrey has considered increasing the allowed size for a single-family dwelling from 3,550 square feet to 4,550 square feet. See Kate Allen, "Debate Rages over Surrey 'Monster Homes'" *The Globe and Mail* (10 December 2009).

155 2011 NLTD(G) 108.

156 *Ibid* at paras 40–41.

no guarantee his application would be approved by the municipal council after the requisite advertising and public hearing.[157] He challenged the council to allow chickens as the default position, and to ban them only in problematic instances.[158]

2) In the Halifax central business district (CBD), for decades prior to 2008, land use was controlled by a blanket height restriction. As of right, an owner could build up to 40 feet (25 feet adjacent to the harbour). For anything beyond that, permission had to be sought through a development agreement, and even then there were other compatibility, height, and view planes restrictions. Because land in the CBD is valuable, proposals for new projects were almost always for buildings in excess of 40 feet. This allowed the municipality to consider building proposals on a case-by-case basis, and also required public participation through hearings and by way of a possible appeal. Developers were of the view that the process was too lengthy. Ultimately, a new legal framework was put in place that set as-of-right heights significantly different than 40 feet, and also allowed for some density bonusing and site-planning. Development agreements would not be required, thus there would be no public hearings or appeals to the provincial board.[159]

The two cases of change in the rules suggest the complexity of policy considerations that arise. Changing the rules will almost always require a public process; it is not a routine administrative step. Nonetheless, as the second example illustrates, it is possible to redesign a planning process so as to exclude or minimize public participation after the initial round of planning setting a framework.

I. IGNORING THE RULES

One possible approach to rules is to ignore them and then try to deal with the consequences if there ever are any. As some of the demolition cases show, this can be a high-risk strategy. Neighbours can be

157 Seeking to change municipal by-laws, initiated by a resident rather than through a municipal-led planning exercise, can be expensive. In another case involving urban hens, *Calgary (City) v Hughes*, 2012 ABPC 250, it was estimated that the cost would be some $6,000 in fees.

158 Yvonne Colbert, "Edward Whynot Can Keep Backyard Chickens as Council Reviews Bylaw" *CBC News* (28 July 2015), online: www.cbc.ca/1.3171069.

159 For an outline of the workings of the Halifax CBD planning system, see *Midtown Tavern & Grill Ltd v Nova Scotia (Utility and Review Board)*, 2006 NSCA 115 at paras 62–71; *Heritage Trust of Nova Scotia (Re)*, 2007 NSUARB 122 at para 537.

watchful. In *Shala v Toronto (City) Committee of Adjustment*,[160] the OMB confirmed a decision of the city's committee not to allow additional variances where the original variances authorized had been exceeded, leading to charges under the *Building Code Act*. The home, in Toronto's Parkdale area, was close to its neighbours, and the illegal construction affected the privacy of the adjacent owner as well as being out of keeping with the character of the area. The *Planning Act* contained several tests for allowing a variance:

> There is the Official Plan (OP) Test which provides that even if the variances are granted, the general intent and purpose of the OP must still be met. There is the Zoning By-law (ZB) Test which provides that even if the variances are granted, the general intent and purpose of the ZB must still be met. There is the Desirability Test by which the Board must be satisfied that the variances are desirable for the appropriate development and use of the land, building or structure concerned. There is the Minor Test by which the Board must find that there will be no unacceptable adverse impacts on the neighbours or the neighbourhood as a result of the granting of the requested variances.[161]

The Shala family were required to undo the unauthorized construction work.[162] In *Vallance v Pickering (City)*,[163] the consequence of constructing a residence that differed from the building plans submitted to obtain a permit was a substantial fine of $46,500 plus a 25 percent victim surcharge. In *So v Wyndham Street Investments Inc*,[164] the offending party ignored conditions imposed by the Committee of Adjustment and installed an improper type of window and interfered with a party wall. It was ordered to pay for repairs costing $23,000. In *Burnaby (City) v Oh*,[165] an illegal secondary suite was ordered removed. Likewise, in *R v Bhullar*,[166] an upper deck and lower patio had been enclosed to create habitable space, the result being square footage in excess of what was permitted; the changes were ordered removed.

It is also possible for a government to ignore the rules, or err in understanding or applying them. When that happens, it is a matter of built-in safeguards—open meetings, the usual requirement for a report

---

160 (1999), 4 MPLR (3d) 284 (OMB).

161 *Ibid* at para 47.

162 For another instance of ignoring the rules, resulting in prosecutions or stop-work orders, see *Bradbury v Eastern Regional Appeal Board*, 2012 NLTD(G) 31.

163 2011 ONCJ 771.

164 2004 CanLII 34380 (Ont CA).

165 2010 BCSC 1970.

166 2007 BCPC 429.

from staff as to the planning merits of a proposal, public scrutiny, and the practical ability of members of the public to challenge the decision—that will determine whether there is any restraint. *Orpen v Roberts*[167] is an example of a municipality failing to abide by its rules, for no clear reason, in that it permitted a building that violated setbacks by a significant amount. A more recent example appears in *Crawford v Torbay (Town)*,[168] where the council approved a building permit for an undersized lot in violation of its own development regulations; the town was found liable in negligence to the abutting owner and was ordered to pay damages. In *Polycorp Properties Inc v Halifax (Regional Municipality)*,[169] the city had sold land for purposes of redevelopment of a blighted area, intending a portion of the land to remain open space for use of the apartment buildings to be later constructed. The condition was not incorporated into the deed, and the city saw the restrictive term as being part of a development agreement, which was not recorded against title. A subsequent purchaser was found not to be bound by the condition.

---

167 [1925] SCR 364.
168 2008 NLTD 161.
169 2011 NSSC 241.

CHAPTER 8

PUBLIC PARTICIPATION AND FAIRNESS

A. PRELIMINARY

The materials in this chapter deal with issues associated with public participation in the planning process and form an introduction to Chapter 9, which covers appeals and judicial review. Many of the court cases on land-use issues arise from dissatisfaction with the nature of public participation that has been afforded. The legal issue is framed as one of fairness. Disputes over what are the specifics of public participation rights are the stuff of much of administrative law issues in the land-use context.

Public participation is such an important aspect of land-use planning law that it is focused on separately. Participation is a fundamental value of the process. Also, most citizens will experience land-use planning and land-use planning law through their opportunity to be involved in generalized policy decisions or in specific decisions about particular parcels of land.

Some courts have characterized citizen involvement in governance as a *Charter*-protected right, but this has not prevented disputes over land-use issues evolving into lawsuits framed in defamation. In some instances, this can be seen as anti-democratic and be characterized as a SLAPP (strategic lawsuit against public participation), discussed in Section L, below in this chapter. Should there be any special controls over SLAPPs?

So far as judicial review is concerned, questions that arise frequently have to do with entitlement to notice of a decision being made, the adequacy of the notice, and the fairness of the hearing process. The courts are asked to assess these matters on the standard of what is set out in statute, on the common law standards of due process, and in some circumstances according to *Charter* norms. What this means in any particular instance is not obvious, and a familiarity with the set of decided cases is necessary in order to judge how to structure public participation appropriately.

Whether the processes should be different is an important policy question. What efforts should be made to notify tenants, or the illiterate, or those who do not speak the local official language, or the visually impaired? Are time limits for speakers at a hearing too restrictive?

So far as appeals are concerned, what limits should apply on who can take an appeal (the issue of "standing")? What decisions should be subject to appeal? On what basis should an appellate body review the original decision?

Entirely apart from the actual mechanisms that afford public participation, there is the basic issue of political power. Analysis of participation should always be undertaken in a context that sees a full power dynamic.[1]

The political science understanding of public participation is quite broad. It extends to voting, to lobbying, to making financial donations, to organized advocacy.[2] Burt says that, "[i]ts significance is due to its centrality in democratic theory and in understandings of citizenship, or membership of a community . . . and equality. Consequently, the notion of participation allows us to differentiate among types of political regimes."[3] This is a significant claim. It suggests that we can measure how democratic a nation is by examining how freely citizens can participate in the major communal decisions that are to be made. It echoes the classic analysis of De Tocqueville in his 1835 work *Democracy in America*. Makuch et al cite De Tocqueville's observations on town meetings—the prototype of small-community direct decision-making—as representing not just something admirable in itself but as the necessary educational foundation for a free nation: "Town meetings are to liberty what primary schools are to science. They bring it within the people's reach, they teach men

---

1 For general background, see James A Draper, ed, *Citizen Participation: Canada, A Book of Readings* (Toronto: New Press, 1971); Mary Louise McAllister, *Governing Ourselves? The Politics of Canadian Communities* (Vancouver: UBC Press, 2004) chs 3 and 12.

2 See, for example, Sandra Burt, "The Concept of Political Participation" in Joanna Everitt & Brenda O'Neill, eds, *Citizen Politics: Research and Theory in Canadian Political Behaviour* (Don Mills, ON: Oxford University Press, 2002) 232.

3 *Ibid* at 232.

how to use it and how to enjoy it. A nation may establish the government but without municipal institutions it cannot be said to have the spirit of liberty." They comment: "Thus it can be argued that the purpose of local government is to foster a democratic spirit and to provide the means by which democracy can be learned. Politicians and citizens alike can gain experience at the local government level in preparation for involvement in the 'serious' matters of the federal and provincial governments."[4]

B. PLANNING LITERATURE ON PUBLIC PARTICIPATION

Politicians, planners, and the public are the main participants in land-use planning, according to most analysts. This takes a broad view of the public (and leaves aside the legal system) in that it extends to developers and their staff or consultants (architects, lawyers, planners). In general, there are expert professional participants and also the general, varied public. The professionals are often tempted to view the public and its participation as an inconvenience.

In an American Planning Association publication, *The Planner's Use of Information*, the chapter on "Public Participation" starts:

> Why Involve the Public? On the one hand, the answer to this question for planners is an easy one: "They make us do it". "They" are [agencies and local governments]. On the other hand, planners with little or negative experience may be reluctant to undertake anything more than is legally required, under the mistaken notion that public involvement is an impediment, not a help, to the planning process. To the contrary, well-designed and well-implemented citizen participation can provide tangible benefits to the entire planning process by: providing valuable insights into citizens' values and preferences; developing and nurturing an environment of goodwill and trust; helping to avoid or mitigate protracted or costly delays and conflicts; providing information about public perceptions and concerns that planners and policy makers may have overlooked; providing citizen support for a final project or strategy; engendering a meaningful, two-way dialogue between the public and the planners, leading to understandable and consensus-driven decision making; developing

4 Stan Makuch et al, *Canadian Municipal and Planning Law*, 2d ed (Toronto: Thomson Carswell, 2004) at 2.

> a reservoir of understanding and goodwill; increasing faith in the democratic system.[5]

Cogan's list no doubt represents the best wishes of the profession. Experience, however, has led some planners to wonder about their limits as facilitators of this aspect of our democracy. Professor Jill Grant has written,

> Can planners promote democracy? The appropriate role for citizens in democratic planning remains somewhat fuzzy. By and large, citizens lack the information, interest, and opportunities they need to participate effectively in community decision making. Planners lack the resources to overcome values and processes that limit the roles citizens play in community power structures.[6]

Professor Hodge sees the value of citizen participation as "enriching the substantive side of planning."[7] He praises it as giving planning "texture":

> The effectiveness of planning in a community, in the end, is more a function of the participation in planning decisions than of any other factors. Planning acts may prescribe a planning process, but it is people, individually and in groups, who make it a reality and who give it texture. A well-designed plan and a thoughtfully drafted zoning bylaw must be deliberated, communicated about, approved, and applied by members and officials of the community. The process they engage in amounts to a "flow of argumentation" . . . .[8]

But he also sees how difficult it is to effect:

> As desirable and necessary as it may be, public participation may not occur in the scope and form hoped for; in fact, it may not happen at all. Participation is a voluntary act; it can be promoted but not guaranteed. Given their experience, the poor and cultural or ethnic minorities may feel powerless to influence decisions. Middle-class citizens may choose not to participate out of cynicism or apathy. Deliberate efforts to promote participation have had only limited success, especially where the plans are for the distant future. People

---

5 Elaine Cogan, "Public Participation" in Hemalata C Dandekar, ed, *The Planner's Use of Information*, 2d ed (Chicago: American Planning Association, 2003) at 189; see also Elaine Cogan, *Successful Public Meetings*, 2d ed (Chicago: American Planning Association, 2000).

6 Jill Grant, *The Drama of Democracy* (Toronto: University of Toronto Press, 1994) at 212.

7 Gerald Hodge & David LA Gordon, *Planning Canadian Communities*, 5th ed (Toronto: Nelson Thomson, 2008) at 321.

8 *Ibid* at 299.

> respond much more readily to changes in their immediate environment than to large, remote projects or abstract plans.[9]

Professor Hodge's point about unequal participation by different classes is reinforced by various studies.[10]

Despite the frustrations suggested by both professors Grant and Hodge, they and most writers start from a perspective that citizen participation is an essential part of planning. Unfortunately, the experience of the public is that the system is open to manipulation. A vivid description of how this may occur comes from the United Kingdom, where journalist George Monbiot has described at length the experience of residents of Southampton in grappling with a proposal for regeneration of a rundown area of the city.[11] They experienced the municipality being secretive about its studies, staff or hired consultants speaking at consultation meetings to nudge views in a direction not reflective of what residents were saying, and then placing their views on record: "All this . . . was being documented as bullet points, as if this was what the community was saying. At the same time, architects from [the project proponent] who were also in the workshops, were scribbling on yellow Post-it notes which, like everyone else's were handed up to the front anonymously."[12] This account focuses only on informal public consultation meetings, not on statute-required public hearings. For those, there are other problems, such as the short amount of time allocated to each speaker, or reports being disclosed at the public hearing rather than in advance.[13]

Hodge cites sociologist Linda Christianson-Ruffman as saying, "Challenging public decisions could be viewed as a form of Kafkaesque baseball. Citizen groups are always the visiting team in their own home town."[14] Accounts exist of the disenchantment of citizens in their dealings with land-use decision-makers. John Sewell, later mayor of Toronto, wrote *Up Against City Hall*[15] in 1972, an account of his first

---

9 *Ibid* at 320.

10 See Barbara M Illsley, "Fair Participation: A Canadian Perspective" (2003) 20 *Land Use Policy* 265.

11 George Monbiot, "Breaking Point—the Smashing of Southampton" in *Captive State* (London: Macmillan, 2000) ch 3.

12 This device of placing coloured paper beside various options is sometimes referred to as "dotmocracy."

13 Delay in disclosure to the public of relevant reports can raise issues of the fundamental fairness of the process, leading to court challenges: see *Pitt Polder Preservation Society v Pitt Meadows (District)*, 2000 BCCA 415 [*Pitt Polder*] and *Heritage Trust of Nova Scotia v Halifax (Regional Municipality)*, 2007 NSSC 28 [*Heritage Trust*], discussed below in this section.

14 Hodge & Gordon, above note 7 at 299.

15 John Sewell, *Up Against City Hall* (Toronto: J Lewis & Samuel, 1972).

involvement in planning, a proposal for "slum clearance" in an area known as Trefann Court. His conclusion was that all dealings with city hall involved an overall power dynamic that was very hard for the general public to influence:

> Good intentions . . . are not enough. There must be a force strong enough to confront those with power, and take it away from them. I have found that if decision-making shifts only from one person to another, then there is little change. Would the situation in Trefann have been any better if the city had merely hired a new planner who would do a better plan? That would not have placated residents who wanted to do the planning themselves, since they felt they knew their area better than anyone else . . . . In order to get that power, they had to organize into such a strong group that they had to be taken seriously, that the city had to back down and divest itself of the right to make decisions.[16]

In Southampton, residents initiated their own consultation, and retained the Neighbourhood Initiatives Foundation, an organization that exists to conduct independent, open, and transparent public sessions, to convene it. No such organization seems to exist in Canada, though professional facilitators and mediators are available.

C. LEGAL OVERVIEW OF FAIRNESS

The courts are prepared to examine possible defects in the fundamental fairness of a variety of decisions. Land-use matters will almost always lend themselves to possible challenge in court. This can be so even where the specified legislative process for a decision is very restrictive as to issues such as participatory rights.[17] In *Mossman v Nova Scotia (Attorney General)*,[18] the designation of a beach under the *Beaches Act* was on its face entirely a decision for the Minister of Natural Resources, requiring neither advance notice to adjacent owners nor an opportunity for them to make representations. The court set the designation aside

16 *Ibid* at 169.

17 In 1863, in a UK case it was said that, "the justice of the common law will supply the omission of the legislature": *Cooper v Wandsworth Board of Works* (1863), 14 CB (NS) 180 at 194, 143 ER 414. This certainly still occurs in appropriate circumstances, even though the Supreme Court of Canada has cited this statement as "dated *hauteur*" regarding the sensitivity of law-making bodies to the rule of law need for fundamental fairness: *Dunsmuir v New Brunswick*, 2008 SCC 9 at para 129, Binnie J.

18 (1995), 140 NSR (2d) 321 (SCTD) [*Mossman*].

as having been made in breach of the general duty to act fairly on the part of a public decision-maker.[19]

It is said that "The observance of fair procedures is central to the notion of the 'just' exercise of power."[20] It affects both the quality of the decision and its acceptability.

> The underlying premise of this rationale is that the observance of appropriate procedures will increase the likelihood that decisions are more accurate, better informed and thoughtful. Moreover, it is less likely that individuals will be denied their rights or will suffer some other form of prejudice that might result if the administrative action was based on erroneous, incomplete or ill-considered findings of fact, conclusions of law, or exercises of discretion.[21]

In this, the policies of the law accord with the ideals of the planning profession. Fundamental fairness implies meaningful participation, which leads to better decision-making.

When it comes to fundamental fairness, and unlike judicial scrutiny of other issues, "no standard of review analysis governs judicial review, where the complaint is based upon a denial of natural justice or procedural fairness. Instead, a court will intervene if it finds an administrative process was unfair in light of all the circumstances."[22] This means that there is no judicial deference to the original decision-maker when it comes to fairness.[23] What is in issue is the nature of the duty of fairness as to its specifics in different circumstances. Nor will the existence of a privative clause in legislation prevent the courts from intervening if there has been a denial of procedural fairness.[24]

Assumption of jurisdiction over questions such as fairness is a major part of administrative law. Other aspects focus on legality and reason-

19 Although the judge in *Mossman* faulted the provincial government for failing to afford the affected landowners an opportunity to make representations, he declined to specify just what form that ought to take. He stated at para 81: "The nature of the process to be offered the plaintiffs, in order to meet the duty of procedural fairness, is for the Minister and Cabinet to decide. As indicated earlier, it need not include an opportunity to address or make representations directly to the Minister or Cabinet."

20 Donald JM Brown & John M Evans, *Judicial Review of Administrative Action in Canada*, 2d ed (Toronto: Canvasback, 2009) (loose-leaf release 2016-2) s 7:1210.

21 *Ibid*, s 7:1211.

22 *North End Community Health Assn v Halifax (Regional Municipality)*, 2014 NSCA 92 at paras 41–42.

23 The idea of "standard of review" is examined in Chapter 9, Section C, in the discussion of judicial review, where the Supreme Court of Canada decision in *Catalyst Paper* is cited.

24 *156621 Canada Ltd v Ottawa (City)* (2006), 27 MPLR (4th) 135 (Ont SCJ).

ableness. Public participation issues might involve questions of legality, but more often they are raised in the context of general fairness. Thus, issues of notice or participation will almost always be seen as aspects of fairness. The framework for assessing fairness has been set out by the Supreme Court of Canada in *Baker v Canada (Minister of Citizenship and Immigration)*[25] in 1999. The *Baker* factors apply wherever fairness is called for in the making of a decision. In light of *Baker*, older cases on the requirements of fairness need to be reconsidered. For example, in *Wiswell v Winnipeg (Greater)*,[26] a 1965 decision of the Supreme Court of Canada, notice of a hearing was found to have been defective in that an interested community group that had been closely monitoring a proposed development had not been notified of the hearing; once this defect was established, and the process viewed as quasi-judicial, the decision was automatically nullified.[27] *Wiswell* is still a useful case, but the analysis would now proceed differently. The *Baker* factors are considered by the court in assessing what overall standard of fairness applies to the particular decision, what that means in terms of specifics, and whether the standard has been met. Not all administrative decisions will attract the full range of procedural fairness *indicia* (e.g., full disclosure of all relevant material, a hearing, representation by legal counsel, opportunity to cross-examine, a scrupulously independent decision-maker, reasons to be given for the decision) that would be seen as necessary in a trial, for example. In *Baker* the Court said,

> The existence of a duty of fairness, however, does not determine what requirements will be applicable in a given set of circumstances . . . . "[T]he concept of procedural fairness is eminently variable and its content is to be decided in the specific context of each case". All of the circumstances must be considered in order to determine the content of the duty of procedural fairness . . . . I emphasize that underlying all these factors is the notion that the purpose of the participatory rights contained within the duty of procedural fairness is to ensure that administrative decisions are made using a fair and open procedure, appropriate to the decision being made and its statutory, institutional, and social context, with an opportunity for those affected by the decision to put forward their views and evidence fully and have them considered by the decision-maker.[28]

---

25 [1999] 2 SCR 817 [*Baker*].

26 [1965] SCR 512 [*Wiswell*].

27 For a similar case, where the absence of notice to an interested party was seen as bad faith, see *McIntyre Ranching Co v Cardston (District) No 6*, [1984] 1 WWR 36 (Alta CA).

28 *Baker*, above note 25 at 837, L'Heureux-Dubé J.

Due process may be called for, but what exact process is due is assessed according to five factors: the nature of the decision being made and the process followed in making it, the nature of the statutory scheme and the terms of the statute pursuant to which the body operates, the importance of the decision to the individual or individuals affected, the legitimate expectations of the person challenging the decision, and the choices of procedure made by the agency itself. The Court noted that "this list of factors is not exhaustive."[29] Nonetheless, most courts go through the five factors in determining how stringent the fairness requirements ought to be, whether there is a minimal duty, something higher (a moderate duty), or a moderately high or high duty. That is, the courts see a spectrum. Issues such as notice, or the opportunity for a hearing and what that hearing might extend to, are usually referred to as "participatory rights." The provision of reasons for the decision and the absence of bias on the part of the decision-maker are other aspects of the duty of fairness.

Although one of the *Baker* factors is "the choices of procedure made by the agency itself," which recognizes that there is usually some discretion to be exercised by the decision-maker as to its process, the standard of review by the courts is on the basis of correctness. That is, if the court concludes that insufficient fairness has characterized the process, there is no deference to the decision-maker as there may be for substantive issues.

All of the *Baker* factors are examined as part of the assessment of what ought to be required in the way of fundamental fairness in any specific instance. One factor that does seem to weigh with the courts is the nature of the decision being made—whether it is more "legislative" in nature or more "adjudicative" in nature. This is why cases such as *Wiswell* remain relevant. The former is characterized by being more focused on general policy, and the latter by being more focused on the rights of a particular owner or resident. Legislative processes will usually attract less in the way of procedural fairness. Ontario's *Planning Act* specifies that in hearings, "the council shall afford [persons] a fair opportunity to make representation but throughout the course of passing the by-law the council shall be deemed to be performing a legislative and not a judicial function."[30] It is not clear that this provision has any serious effect on the specifics that a court will look for.[31]

---

29 *Ibid* at 840.

30 *Planning Act*, RSO 1990, c P.13, s 61.

31 See, for example, *Spence v York (City)* (1985), 29 MPLR 85 (Ont HCJ); *Gaudaur v Etobicoke (City)* (1997), 35 OR (3d) 551 (Div Ct), in which Trainor J (dissenting) noted that the section does not address issues of notice.

Since *Baker*, the Supreme Court of Canada has examined fairness issues in the land-use context only in *Congrégation des témoins de Jéhovah de St-Jérôme-Lafontaine v Lafontaine (Village)*[32] (when reasons might be required) and *Canadian Pacific Railway Co v Vancouver (City)*[33] (adequacy of notice and disclosure of documents), both summarized in Chapter 2. Most of the other recent cases relevant to the issue have come before provincial courts of appeal or single judges. Leading cases are *Williams Lake Conservation Co v Halifax (Regional Municipality)*,[34] *Heritage Trust*,[35] *Pitt Polder*,[36] *Markwart v Prince Albert (City)*,[37] *Hubbard v West Vancouver (District)*,[38] and *PJD Holdings Inc v Regina (City)*.[39]

In *Heritage Trust of Nova Scotia*, the judge said,

> In considering the content of the notice of the public hearing, she [McLachlin CJC in *CPR v Vancouver*] said in parag. 46: ". . . what is required is fairness, not perfection." In my view, this is an accurate way to assess all elements of procedural fairness. The process must be fair but it need not be perfect.[40]

D. STANDING

The opportunity to speak to an elected official informally or take part in formal public consultations, even to serve on advisory committees, is, for the most part, not restricted in any way. Sometimes advisory committees are structured so as to require representatives from particular professions, though most participatory activity is available to "residents." But achieving access to the courts or to a supervisory tribunal by a person or organization seeking to challenge a land-use decision is a problem beset not only by the well-recognized difficulties of being able to afford the litigation or being able to marshal the resources to offer evidence, but there is also the difficulty of the restrictive rules known as the law of standing. Courts are able to decide who has entitlement to appear before them, and standing for access to tribunals will usually be specified by the controlling statute. Standing is

32 2004 SCC 48.
33 2006 SCC 5 [*CPR v Vancouver*].
34 2004 NSCA 79.
35 Above note 13.
36 Above note 13.
37 2006 SKCA 122.
38 2005 BCCA 633.
39 2010 SKQB 386.
40 Above note 13 at paras 121–22.

the question whether this particular plaintiff/appellant/petitioner may bring this particular action/appeal against this particular defendant/respondent.[41] Standing has been a besetting problem for those concerned with environmental issues[42] as well as municipal matters.[43] The category of type of action will determine the exact parameters of the test for standing.

At the moment, the tests seem to be:

- For constitutional law matters, the test is whether the matter is seen as justiciable, whether the petitioner has a genuine interest in the matter, and whether there are adequate alternative means to test the constitutionality of the impugned statute.
- For *Charter* cases, the terms of section 24(1) set out standing: "Anyone whose rights or freedoms, as guaranteed by this Charter, have been infringed or denied may apply to a court of competent jurisdiction to obtain such remedy as the court considers appropriate and just in the circumstances."[44]
- For private nuisance cases, standing is tied to some legal interest in land (ownership or tenancy). For public nuisance, some special interest beyond that of the general public must be shown.[45]
- For illegal expenditure of money, a ratepayer may bring an action.[46]
- For general challenges to municipal action, and in the absence of a statutory grant of standing, the test was akin to that for public nuisance but has generally evolved to be akin to that for constitutional law issues. The former test of special interest was tied to such commercial issues as being affected by a licensing by-law,[47] or early-closing by-

---

41 On the entire subject generally, see Thomas Cromwell, *Locus Standi* (Toronto: Carswell, 1986). Note that public interest standing has developed significantly since publication of his text.

42 See, for example, the two *Shiell* cases focused on uranium mining: *Shiell v Amok Ltd* (1987), 2 CELR (NS) 219 (Sask QB) and *Shiell v Canada (Atomic Energy Control Board)* (1995), 17 CELR (NS) 286 (FCTD).

43 For commentary on standing in the environmental law context, see, for example, Meinhard Doelle & Chris Tollefson, *Environmental Law: Cases and Materials* (Toronto: Carswell, 2009) ch 5, Parts III and IV, and Elaine Hughes et al, *Environmental Law and Policy*, 3d ed (Toronto: Emond Montgomery, 2003) ch 7.

44 *Canadian Charter of Rights and Freedoms*, Part I of the *Constitution Act, 1982*, being Schedule B to the *Canada Act 1982* (UK), 1982, c 11 [*Charter*].

45 The Ontario Law Reform Commission, in its *Report on the Law of Standing* (Toronto: Ontario Law Reform Commission, 1989), called the public nuisance rule "seriously deficient" and called for a statutory adjustment to the law.

46 *MacIlreith v Hart Estate* (1908), 39 SCR 657.

47 See, for example, *St Leonard (Town) v Fournier* (1956), 3 DLR (2d) 315 (NBCA).

laws,[48] but was more difficult to establish for zoning affecting one's neighbourhood.[49] Now the more common test applied leads to somewhat easier access to court.[50]

- For matters where standing to appeal to a supervisory tribunal is specified by statute, petitioners must fit the strictures of the statute. These can be restrictive.[51] In Nova Scotia, the requirement is to be an "aggrieved person" defined as including "an individual who *bona fide* believes the decision of council will affect the value, or reasonable enjoyment, of the person's property or the reasonable enjoyment of property occupied by the person . . . ."[52] "*Bona fide*" has been interpreted by the board to require "an objective aspect . . . in addition to the subjective aspect connoted by the sincerity with which the belief is held"[53]—something that may be difficult to establish. The board holds that the burden of showing that one is "aggrieved" is on the appellant, and being located adjacent to a site of a proposed development does not itself satisfy this burden.[54]

E. GENERAL PARTICIPATION

Opportunities for public involvement in the mechanisms of adopting policy and implementing it, particularly at the municipal level, were looked at in Chapter 6, Section F. They include the right to vote, the opportunity to participate in advisory committees, access to information, the requirement that meetings be held in public, requirements for public hearings, and the opportunity to submit petitions. They should

---

48 See, for example, *Towers Marts & Properties Ltd v St Catharines (City)* (1962), 34 DLR (2d) 547 (Ont HCJ).

49 See, for example, *Crittenden v Vancouver (City)* (1984), 14 DLR (4th) 599 (BCSC).

50 See, for example, *Dartmouth (City) v Mountain Ash Court Property Owners Association*, 1994 CanLII 3996 (NSCA). A related point is the standing of an organization, rather than individuals. Scrutiny will especially involve the point of "genuine interest": see, for example, *Yellowknife Property Owners Association v Yellowknife (City)* (1996), 40 MPLR (2d) 96 (NWTSC); *Surrey Citizens Rights Association v Surrey (City)* (1999), 1 MPLR (3d) 207 (BCSC); *Whellams Lane Residents' Assn v Winnipeg (City)*, 2010 MBQB 256; *South March Highlands-Carp River Conservation Inc v Ottawa (City)*, 2010 ONSC 6725 (Div Ct).

51 For a review of standing under various sections of the Ontario *Planning Act*, see Mark V Osbaldeston, "Challenging Planning Act Decisions: Who Has Standing to Appeal?" (1994) 23 *Municipal and Planning Law Reports* (2d) 33.

52 *Municipal Government Act*, SNS 1998, c 18, s 191(a).

53 *Re Ruffman*, [1995] NSURBD No 15.

54 *Re D & M Lightfoot Farms Ltd*, 2005 NSUARB 117.

all be understood as part of what is essential to meaningful and effective public participation, where public comments are sought.

An anomalous and interesting case is *Alberta v Beaver (County) No 9*[55] because it documents the enthusiasm of the public to see its will prevail, apparently bordering on intimidation. Various other irregularities led the court to set aside the by-law in question at the direct application of the attorney general, and the allegation of a crowd holding the council until it did what was wanted did not form the basis of the court's decision. Still, public participation has its limits.

The Supreme Court of Canada has recognized the good governance value of the availability of good information to the public. Although the observations were made in a specialized context,[56] they set a tone for general land-use law. In *Consortium*, the Court said, "good government depends in part on the availability of good information."[57]

F. ENTITLEMENT TO NOTICE

Notice is a matter taken seriously as an important threshold matter to allow the exercise of a right to be heard. Two of the leading cases are from the Supreme Court of Canada, the 1965 case of *Wiswell*[58] and the 1991 case of *Immeubles Port Louis Ltée v Lafontaine (Village)*.[59]

In *Wiswell*, a community group made up of homeowners was aware of a proposal for construction of an apartment building in its area, which it opposed. The matter had come before the municipal council for discussion and on each occasion the group had opposed the proposed development. A formal application was made for rezoning the land. Under the city's procedural rules, notice of amendment of the zoning by-law was to be published in local newspapers, and a sign was to be placed on the property. Lawyers representing the homeowners group had written the city to establish their opposition to the proposed development and to request notice of any applications in order to speak to the council. Notices were published but no sign was placed on the property; the homeowners were not specifically notified of the pending rezoning. The group was not aware of the application and did not

---

55 (1984), 8 DLR (4th) 473 (Alta CA).

56 In *Consortium Developments (Clearwater) Ltd v Sarnia (City)*, [1998] 3 SCR 3 [*Consortium*], the Court gave approval of a municipality establishing its own public inquiry regarding some land transactions.

57 *Ibid* at para 26.

58 Above note 26.

59 [1991] 1 SCR 326 [*Port Louis*].

appear at the hearing. The land was rezoned. The court found that the process before the council was not a general legislative one, but more in the nature of a dispute between particular parties (quasi-judicial); there was an obligation to act fairly and impartially, to act in good faith, and to fairly listen to both sides. The by-law was found to be void.[60]

In *Port Louis*, the municipality adopted loan by-laws to pay for some infrastructure (sewer, water, roads) with a special tax to be applicable to landowners in a part of the village. Under the *Municipal Code*, such by-laws needed to be approved by vote of the landowners affected, to be taken at a public meeting, with notice to be given to the owners at least ten clear days in advance. No notice of the meeting was given to the landowner. Although the courts recognized the failure of the village to give notice, the action was disallowed on the basis of laches (delay) in bringing the lawsuit. In discussing notice, the Court said,

> The respondent breached its obligation to inform and hear the appellant when it adopted the by-laws, thereby infringing the Act and the *audi alteram partem* rule . . . . The Council's jurisdiction is not at issue as such: what is in question is an aspect of the exercise of its powers, namely failure to comply with a legal prerequisite, that of prior notice to the owners of certain affected lots.[61]

That is, the tax by-laws were not *ultra vires* the village, but the power granted was not exercised in the appropriate manner. Further, the defect in notice, characterized as "the right to sufficient notice," was "neither a mere irregularity nor a formal defect."[62]

Although both *Wiswell* and *Port Louis* were decided prior to the Supreme Court of Canada's setting out of the *Baker* factors as a means of assessing overall fairness, they remain a good guide as to how courts will approach issues of absence of notice. Where there is a statutory requirement with regard to notice, and the statute has been breached, there will almost automatically be a finding of invalidity on the basis of unfairness. Still, the granting of the remedy to quash is discretionary,

---

60 In follow-up litigation, *Welbridge Holdings Ltd v Winnipeg (Greater)*, [1971] SCR 957, the developer attempted to sue the city for damages as a result of its failure to pass the rezoning by-law in the appropriate manner, thus depriving the owner of the opportunity to build. The suit was not allowed. The Court said that a municipality acting in its legislative capacity rather than at its operating level owed no duty of care giving rise to liability in damages for a breach.

61 Above note 59 at 340.

62 The Court identified various categories of illegality: *ultra vires* in the sense of lack of jurisdiction; abuse of power; serious illegalities that are not mere irregularities or formal defects; and, by implication, mere irregularities.

though the discretion will be exercised in accordance with established principles of law and not arbitrarily.[63] The typical statutory requirement regarding notice, such as publishing in a newspaper, if violated, will tend to mean the decisions will be set aside as nullities.[64] To the same effect is some comment in the Ontario Court of Appeal decision in *Friends of Lansdowne Inc v Ottawa (City)*,[65] though the main focus of that case was on bad faith and not notice:

> Assuming the absence of bad faith, any technical failure on the part of the municipality to adhere to its internal rules and procedures is an irregularity that does not vitiate the challenged decision. This was not a case where the City transgressed against statutorily-mandated requirements.[66]

Although notice requirements always relate to fairness for a party dealing with a decision-maker, there can be variations in how notice provisions work. Under Ontario's *Heritage Act*, an owner can apply for permission to demolish a designated structure; the municipal council must make a decision and notify the owner within ninety days, or council is deemed to have consented. That is what occurred in *St Peter's Evangelical Lutheran Church (Ottawa) v Ottawa (City)*;[67] the municipality made the decision to refuse, the Trustees knew of the decision, but the formal notice of the decision was not served on the Trustees until after the expiry of the time period. The right to demolish was confirmed by the Court on the basis of the violation of the statutory requirement.

Notice after the fact is extremely dubious, even in circumstances that might be characterized as an emergency, unless there is statutory authorization. In *E & J Murphy Ltd v Victoria (City)*,[68] the *Municipal Act* allowed councils, by a two-thirds vote, to exercise all powers necessary to deal with emergencies when other powers available were inadequate. Using this authority, the council adopted a by-law controlling demolition of buildings of historical value. The by-law was upheld. At the time, general grants of power were not usually seen as conferring much authority on a municipality, a point made in an "Annotation" of the case,[69] since it was well before the Supreme Court of Canada ruling in *114957 Canada Ltée*

---

63 *London (City) v RSJ Holdings Inc*, 2007 SCC 29 at para 39.

64 See, for example, *Hornby Island Trust Committee v Stormwell* (1988), 53 DLR (4th) 435 (BCCA).

65 2012 ONCA 273.

66 *Ibid* at para 70.

67 [1982] 2 SCR 616.

68 (1976), 1 MPLR 166 (BCSC).

69 Stan Makuch, "Annotation" (1976–77) 1 *Municipal and Planning Law Reports* 167.

(Spraytech, Société d'arrosage) v Hudson (Town).[70] Professor Makuch also notes that the decision "does not . . . seem to have given sufficient consideration to the rights of the applicants to notice and a hearing."[71] This is a good point. At the same time, the courts have given some range to the exercise of emergency powers before providing a hearing, sometimes looking to a hearing after the initial decision as adequate.[72] The problem of quick action by a municipality in order to preserve the status quo while plans are re-thought, is now usually addressed through special provisions such as declaring an "interim control area."

Where notice of a decision triggers the start of a limitation period for the taking of an appeal, and the statute provides that the notice must be to the public, and the time starts to run when the general public notice is given regardless of whether the actual appellants had earlier notice.[73]

G. ADEQUACY OF NOTICE

Attempts to abide by statutory requisites as to notice may be deficient in some ways. Whether deficiencies will lead a court to decide the process followed was so flawed as to lead to a declaration of invalidity will depend on how the court assesses the overall fairness.

In *Community Assn of New Yaletown v Vancouver (City)*,[74] a defect was alleged regarding the published notice of the public hearing for a rezoning. The title used in the newspaper advertisement was "West End Zoning Amendment," although the actual area was a different neighbourhood. The court said, "Regardless of the title, the [official plan for the correct area] was specifically identified in the notice as being affected by the proposed amendments. This was sufficient for the purposes of the Vancouver Charter."[75] The court reversed a ruling by the chambers judge, who had been of the view that the notice was insufficiently precise.[76] Certainly other cases have focused on the

70 2001 SCC 40 [*Spraytech*].

71 Above note 69 at 167.

72 See, for example, *Maidstone (Township) v Essex (County)* (1993), 15 Admin LR (2d) 228 (Ont Div Ct).

73 *Gillespie v Newfoundland & Labrador (Eastern Newfoundland Regional Appeal Board)*, 2012 NLTD(G) 59.

74 2015 BCCA 227.

75 *Ibid* at para 139.

76 2015 BCSC 117 at paras 101 and 134. The decision includes strong language regarding appropriate disclosure to allow for effective public participation.

underlying purpose of notice, which is "to inform those who might reasonably be affected by the proposed rezoning, so that those persons could make an informed decision on whether they wished to attend or make representations at a public meeting,"[77] and these cases have required appropriate and correct details in the published notice. Notice also serves to set the applicable dates for appeals or judicial review.[78]

Sometimes attempts are made to seek better or different notice processes than required by statute. These are rarely successful. Thus in *Smith v Lakeland (Regional Municipality 521)*,[79] the municipality advertised a proposed by-law change in a newspaper circulating in the area as required, but fully half of the owners of land in the municipality lived beyond the area in which the newspaper circulated, the area being one in which vacation property predominated. The court was not prepared to impose any additional notice requirements on the council.

It is not difficult to list circumstances where the traditional formal notice of publication in a newspaper and/or the posting of a notice on the property potentially affected will not be truly efficacious in notifying the public at large or some significant part of it as to matters to be decided. The illiterate are not effectively notified by written material. In communities in which the common language is other than that of the written notice, there may well be a failure to communicate the information. Visually impaired persons may well also be missed. And, where notice is to be given to landowners within some set area, if there are tenants, the tenants are omitted from such actions, although they may be numerous and may well have different views of proposed changes in their neighbourhood than do landowners.[80]

H. MEANINGFUL PARTICIPATION

In *Pitt Polder*, the British Columbia Court of Appeal set out general comments about public hearings:

---

77 Felix Hoehn, *Municipalities and Canadian Law* (Saskatoon: Purich, 1996) at 197, citing *British Columbia Rails Ltd v West Vancouver (District)* (1994), 22 MPLR (2d) 66 (BCSC); *Basic Management Ltd v Saskatoon (City)* (1983), 25 Sask R 255 (QB); and *Peterson v Whistler (Resort Municipality)* (1982), 39 BCLR 221 (SC).

78 *Miller Paving Ltd v Kawartha Lakes (City)*, 2010 ONSC 2571 at para 25, aff'd 2010 ONCA 801.

79 2009 SKQB 86.

80 And, as pointed out in an article dating from 1972, tenants may be commercial tenants, for example, a major enterprise located in a shopping centre; see David B Greenspan & Michael B Vaughan, "How the Zoning Game Is Played: A Look at Land Use Procedures" (1972) 6 *Law Society Gazette* 50 at 53.

> A public hearing on land use and zoning bylaws serves at least two important functions: it provides the opportunity for those whose interests might be affected by such a decision to make their views known to the decision-maker and it gives the decision-maker the benefit of public examination and discussion of the issues surrounding the adoption or rejection of the proposed bylaw. Procedures aimed at ensuring a minimum standard of rationality in the decision-making process are more likely to enhance the quality of the decision and the public's acceptance of it than decisions based on undisclosed information, or on incomplete or ill-considered facts. As well, participatory procedures such as public hearings on land use or zoning bylaws tend to dispel perceptions of arbitrariness, bias or other impropriety on the part of local government . . . and tend to enhance public acceptance of such decisions. Put another way, the perception, if not the fact, of arbitrariness or bias is more likely to arise if the duty to ensure procedural fairness is not observed.[81]

In a subsequent case, the British Columbia Court of Appeal said,

> procedural fairness requires [the municipality] to disclose, before a public hearing . . . the materials that [it] will consider when deciding whether to enact the rezoning by-law . . . . [S]uch disclosure will ensure citizens can make informed, thoughtful and rational comments on the by-law at the public hearing . . . .[82]

While the courts always recognize the value of public participation, including at public hearings, the specifics of what are required will be assessed in light of all of the overall circumstances. Access to appropriate information is usually seen as essential. This implies disclosure. What was said in *CPR v Vancouver* on this point is that what is required is "sufficient disclosure to allow [a party] to participate meaningfully in [the] hearing and present its case."[83] The nature of the hearing will also be part of the court's determination of what is required: in *Society for Promotion of Affordable Arts & Music v Edmonton (City Manager)*,[84] where there was an appeal before a city council committee of a decision by its licensing director, fairness was to extend to the opportunity to cross-examine the director, especially given inadequacies in information provided earlier.

---

81 Above note 13 at paras 45–47.

82 Above note 74 at para 88.

83 Above note 33 at para 56.

84 2008 ABQB 629.

Meaningful participation issues arise in a variety of ways. One frequently raised point is access to reports relevant to the decision being made. Thus in *Fisher Road Holdings Ltd v Cowichan Valley (Regional District)*,[85] the court struck down a rezoning decision where an environmental report relied on by the council had not been made part of the file available to the public even though it had been part of the record for a related municipal decision for the same lands. The court said that down-zoning that is spot-zoning attracts fairness content at the high end of the scale.[86] In *Kingfisher Inns Ltd v Nipawin (Town)*,[87] a public hearing to consider zoning by-laws was prohibited on the basis that a statutory requirement to make copies of the proposed by-law available had not been complied with in that black and white copies of coloured maps were inadequate if the colour was used to delineate between different zones.

The conduct of a hearing before a municipal council does not require the trappings of a hearing before a court. The essential point is that there be fundamental fairness, manifested as effective participation. The opportunity to ask questions is not seen as a part of that. Nor is the opportunity for discovery (examination of witnesses prior to the hearing) or to cross-examine.[88] The opportunity to seek an adjournment in order to prepare adequately is a variable point. In *Adams Bay Residents Assn v Muskoka Lakes (Township)*,[89] the court found bad faith when a council had no record that it considered or voted on a request from the public to postpone the proceedings for a few days because the hearing fell during the March school-break week, meaning that many residents would not be available to make their presentations. The case seems to be unusual, and more typical is *Botterill v Cranbrook (City)*,[90] where the court found no unfairness in a council's refusal to grant an adjournment so as to allow retained experts additional time to prepare counter-studies on the market impact of a proposed shopping centre. In *Hubbard v West Vancouver (District)*, the hearing was being held during the summer. An adjournment request was made "until September because many of the residents who indicated a desire to attend were away for the summer holidays."[91] The failure to adjourn was one factor that

85 2012 BCCA 338.

86 *Ibid* at para 33.

87 2000 SKQB 19.

88 *Mather v Gull Lake (Summer Village) (Subdivision and Development Appeal Board)*, 2011 ABCA 120, a case involving a subdivision and development appeal board.

89 2010 ONSC 5780.

90 2000 BCSC 1225.

91 2003 BCSC 1678 at para 8, rev'd 2005 BCCA 633 [*Hubbard*].

was persuasive for the judge at first instance, but was not accepted by the Court of Appeal when it reviewed the case.

I. POST-HEARING SUBMISSIONS AND THE ROLE OF STAFF

In the context of decisions requiring public hearings, there have been questions about when the council must reopen the hearing or convene additional hearings, tied to its receipt of additional information after the close of the initial hearing. The point made in challenges has been that to fail to hear further, a council would be in violation of the *audi alteram partem* principle, that is, that a decision-maker is obliged to hear fully from both sides in a dispute.

Members of the public are entitled to have that material that members of council have at the outset of the public hearing.[92] However, what of other information?

In *Williams Lake Conservation Council v Chebucto Community Council*,[93] council had a rezoning proposal to consider as a preliminary to a development agreement. The court said that, "When a municipal council considers submission by an opponent or proponent of a development after the close of a public hearing, it is generally required to hold further public hearings."[94] In *Williams Lake*, the additional information came not from an interested party, but from staff. The councillors requested clarification from staff regarding some of the points raised during the public hearing. The court saw the position of staff as different from that of a party. It cited with approval the 1978 decision of the British Columbia Court of Appeal in *Bourque v Richmond (Township)*,[95] that post-hearing, a council may hear from its staff or from an expert retained to advise it, without a new hearing. However, the court did suggest that where a post-hearing staff report contains "fresh material of an evidentiary nature,"[96] where parties might have presented additional information in rebuttal, or where the supplementary staff report contained things not mentioned in the initial reports or contained a different recommendation based on completely different factors, then the court might determine that the *audi alteram partem* principle had been breached.

---

92 *Heritage Trust*, above note 13 at para 163.

93 2004 NSCA 79 [*Williams Lake*].

94 *Ibid* at para 31.

95 (1978), 6 BCLR 130 at 135 (CA).

96 *Williams Lake*, above note 93 at para 35.

The British Columbia Court of Appeal, in *Hubbard*, examined the process at a public hearing for a rezoning. A post-hearing report was sought from staff, to comment on some issues discussed at the hearing. The court declined to set the council decision aside, agreeing with the municipality that a council may "seek advice from its own officers and employees in respect of issues that have been raised at the public hearing."[97]

The position of supplementary staff reports, as valid and not requiring further hearings, save in unusual circumstances, seems clear.

What is not so clear is the matter of post-hearing submissions from an interested party. The statement made by the court in *Williams Lake*, quoted above, was by way of *obiter*, since information from an interested party was not an issue before the court. In the 2007 NSSC decision in *Heritage Trust*,[98] the issue before council was a development agreement proposal for lands the municipality owned and would sell as part of an overall commercial arrangement. The scope of the comment from the Court of Appeal in *Williams Lake* was tested. In this case, council had, after the close of the public hearing, heard both from staff and from the proponent regarding wind and shadow impacts. These issues had been raised previously but the actual studies had not been put before council, although they were in the hands of staff. The studies had not been made public, although one persistent member of the public had been shown the studies by the proponent. The judge noted that the council's rules allowed for the proponent to "briefly respond to points raised by the speakers." Even though the wind and shadow studies took time to present and had not been given to council previously, the judge viewed this as "clarification or provision of additional information on matters already raised."[99] The court stated, "It would be procedurally unfair if the developer changed its proposal after the close of the public hearing . . . . It would be unfair to the public to have a new issue addressed after the closing of the public hearing."[100] The case raises the point of whether there is a difference between new issues and new information.[101] Overall, the specifics of how post-hearing submissions from a proponent ought to be assessed by the courts remains an open matter.

Also unclear is whether members of the public may continue to communicate with councillors post-hearing but prior to a decision

97 *Hubbard*, above note 91 at para 2 (BCCA).
98 Above note 13.
99 *Ibid* at para 202.
100 *Ibid* at para 200.
101 *Ibid* at paras 203 and 206.

having been made. In *Hubbard*, the British Columbia Court of Appeal expressed the view that letters from the public post-hearing might invalidate the process, but the issue was not directly before the court. However, in *Heritage Trust of Nova Scotia*, the court said,

> Members of Council are politicians and their constituents have every right to communicate with them. If the public hearing process were truly a judicial proceeding, such communications would be prohibited. Accordingly, since members of the public may communicate with members of Council outside the public hearing process without harming the process, the developer may do so too to a limited extent as long as what is done does not result in procedural unfairness to the public.[102]

This latter view is consistent with the approach of the Supreme Court of Canada to issues of bias for elected officials.[103] In *Roberts v Glenwood (Regional Municipality)*,[104] the municipality was considering permitting a hog operation on land in the immediate vicinity of the property of the objectors. After a public hearing, council heard from others opposed to the application, but gave no public notice of this meeting, nor was the applicant advised. Council then engaged an independent consultant and received a report, and also met with the applicant, again without public notice. It was the view of the council that, in holding such meetings, it was not continuing the formal public hearing, which was over. The court viewed the process as more a political than a judicial one, and thus not attracting a judicial-like process of natural justice. Nonetheless, there seem to be limits.

J. BIAS

Part of the concept of fundamental fairness is that a decision-maker should not be affected by bias or lack of independence. As Professor David Mullan notes, "everyone has biases in the sense of preferences, preconceptions, or predispositions . . . . What . . . is at stake is not disqualification for any form of bias but the identification of what constitute impermissible biases."[105] The concept has three aspects: actual

102 *Ibid* at para 199.

103 *Old St Boniface Residents Association Inc v Winnipeg (City)*, [1990] 3 SCR 1170 [*Old St Boniface*].

104 2000 MBQB 118.

105 David J Mullan et al, *Administrative Law*, 5th ed (Toronto: Emond Montgomery, 2003) at 571.

bias, a reasonable apprehension of bias, and institutional bias. Actual bias means a personal animosity or an interest in the outcome in the sense of the decision-maker being liable to benefit from it. Reasonable apprehension of bias refers to a situation in which a reasonable observer would believe that, given the overall situation, there is too great a risk of lack of independence.[106] Institutional bias is a characterization of the structural apparatus dealing with a decision, perhaps on the basis of adopted policies or of a pattern of decisions.

Actual bias arises infrequently as a litigated issue. There are rules about actual conflict of interest, when the personal interests of elected officials will be affected by the matters they are called upon to vote on. This extends to *Criminal Code*[107] anti-corruption provisions such as accepting benefits,[108] breach of trust,[109] or the specific municipal anti-corruption provisions.[110] It includes statutes such as British Columbia's *Community Charter*,[111] which makes municipal officials liable to lose their position if found to have engaged in conflict-of-interest voting or participation, and its *Members' Conflict of Interest Act*,[112] which governs members of the legislature. Statutes governing municipal elections also usually include prohibitions against certain corrupt practices. However, in addition to the matters these statutes are directed at, the funding of the election campaigns of elected officials is always problematic. Contributions to the campaigns of candidates for parliament and the legislatures are regulated as to total permissible spending, who may contribute, public disclosure, and how much. For municipal elections, not all provinces do regulate these matters, the result being that developers tend to predominate as contributors, and by implication as those exercising sway. This context implies that the legal rules regarding bias are somewhat beside the point.

Reasonable apprehension of bias is the most common form of challenge to the independence of a decision-maker. The concept is highly flexible, however. In the municipal context, the Supreme Court of Canada has made it clear that elected officials are expected to have opinions on matters that may come before them—that indeed they may have been elected in part on the basis of those opinions. There will be

106 The leading formulation is that of de Grandpre J in *Committee for Justice and Liberty v Canada (National Energy Board)*, [1978] 1 SCR 369 at 394–95.

107 *Criminal Code*, RSC 1985, c C-46.

108 *Ibid*, s 121.

109 *Ibid*, s 122.

110 *Ibid*, s 123.

111 SBC 2003, c 26.

112 RSBC 1996, c 287.

no reasonable apprehension of bias even if the officials have expressed strong opinions. Thus in *Old St Boniface*[113] and its companion case, *Save Richmond Farmland Society v Richmond (Township)*,[114] we see instances in which the municipal councillors were on record in strong terms regarding matters they had to decide.

In *Old St Boniface*, a municipal councillor highly favoured a development proposal. The developer needed both to purchase city land and to obtain a rezoning. The councillor attended an *in camera* meeting of the city committee that reviewed sale of city land and spoke in favour of the sale; he was not a member of the committee. The association objected to his further participation, but he did participate, including at the full council meeting, to consider rezoning. The various city decisions were challenged in court. At the Supreme Court of Canada, it was said that it is necessary to

> distinguish between a case of partiality by reason of pre-judgment on the one hand and by reason of personal interest on the other . . . . [For personal interest] both at common law and by statute, a member of Council is disqualified if the interest is so related to the exercise of public duty that a reasonably well-informed person would conclude that the interest might influence the exercise of that duty. This is commonly referred to as a conflict of interest . . . . [For partiality by reason of pre-judgment,] the test that is consistent with the functions of a municipal councillor and enables him or her to carry out the political and legislative duties entrusted to the councilor is one which requires that the objectors or supporters be heard by members of Council who are capable of being persuaded . . . . The party alleging disqualifying bias must establish that there is a prejudgment of the matter, in fact, to the extent that any representations at variance with the view, which has been adopted, would be futile. Statements by individual members of Council while they may very well give rise to an appearance of bias will not satisfy the test unless the court concludes that they are the expression of a final opinion on the matter, which cannot be dislodged. In this regard it is important to keep in mind that support in favour of a measure before a committee and a vote in favour will not constitute disqualifying bias in the absence of some indication that the position taken is incapable of change.[115]

In *Save Richmond Farmland*, a member of council who had campaigned for election favouring development for some agricultural lands

113 Above note 103.

114 [1990] 3 SCR 1213 [*Save Richmond Farmland*].

115 Above note 113 at paras 55 and 57.

voted in favour of their rezoning. At one point he said he would not change his mind regardless of what might be said at the public hearing to be held. The court did not disqualify the councillor from participating, finding that on the basis of all of the evidence, he had not closed his mind or "reached a final opinion on the matter which could not be dislodged."[116]

Although *Old St Boniface* remains the leading case setting out the test for reasonable apprehension of bias for municipal council members, the test has been held not to apply where the council member sits as a member of an adjudicative committee such as a Subdivision and Development Appeal Board. A stricter standard is required. In *Beaverford v Thorhild (County No 7)*,[117] the court contrasted the board with a municipal council, noting the board "is a body which is not exclusively devoted to polycentric issues of policy, and its decisions directly impact legal and proprietary rights of parties and the development writ large of a community, so it must exhibit 'a high degree of impartiality.'"[118]

An elaboration of bias at the municipal level appears in *McLaren v Castlegar (City)*,[119] where the council was considering whether to order demolition of buildings that had been found to be unsightly:

> In *Newfoundland Telephone Co. v. Newfoundland (Board of Commissioners of Public Utilities)*, [1992] 1. S.C.R. 623, 89 D.L.R. (4th) 289 (S.C.C.), the Supreme Court of Canada considered the application of rules against bias to administrative tribunals. Cory J., for the Court, said at 636:
>
> > Although the duty of fairness applies to all administrative bodies, the extent of that duty will depend upon the nature and the function of the particular tribunal . . . . The duty to act fairly includes the duty to provide procedural fairness to the parties. That simply cannot exist if an adjudicator is biased.
>
> Just as the extent of the duty of fairness will depend on the nature and function of the particular tribunal, so too will the degree to which members of the tribunal are entitled to have some pre-disposition toward a particular result. In *Newfoundland Telephone*, the Supreme Court said at 638–9:

116 *Save Richmond Farmland*, above note 114 at para 25.
117 2013 ABCA 6.
118 *Ibid* at para 13.
119 2011 BCCA 134 at paras 31–37.

> [T]here is a great diversity of administrative boards. *Those that are primarily adjudicative in their functions will be expected to comply with the standard applicable to courts.* That is to say that the conduct of the members of the board should be such that there could be no reasonable apprehension of bias with regard to their decision. *At the other end of the scale are boards with popularly elected members* such as those dealing with planning and development whose members are municipal councillors. *With those boards, the standard will be much more lenient.* In order to disqualify the members a challenging party must establish that there has been a pre-judgement of the matter to such an extent that any representations to the contrary would be futile. Administrative boards that deal with matters of policy will be closely comparable to the boards composed of municipal councillors. For those boards, a strict application of a reasonable apprehension of bias as a test might undermine the very role which has been entrusted to them by the legislature.

In the case before us, the nature of the tribunal—a municipal council composed of elected officials—is of considerable importance. Elected municipal officials are expected to have opinions on civic priorities and policies.

Where a matter that comes before a municipal council is a matter of policy, a member of council will not be disqualified for being pre-disposed in one direction or another.

. . .

Castlegar City Council was not, here acting as a policy-making body. Rather, it was determining whether certain buildings violated bylaws and codes, whether they were unsafe, whether they constituted a nuisance, and whether they were so dilapidated and unclean as to be offensive to the community. After making those findings, Council was also required to exercise its discretion in determining whether the appropriate remedy was demolition. These various considerations were adjudicative in nature . . . . As indicated in *Newfoundland Telephone Co.*, a tribunal exercising primarily adjudicative functions will generally be required to comply with more strict standards of fairness than a policy-making tribunal.

. . .

Unlike most adjudicative tribunals, municipal councils are not required to hear whatever disputes come before them; rather they determine their own agendas. At least some members of council, therefore, will inevitably have made some preliminary estimation as

> to the merits of a matter before it formally comes before council for resolution.
>
> . . .
>
> Because members of council were engaging in an adjudicative function, it was not sufficient that they had not irrevocably made up their minds. Rather, they had to be completely open to a fresh evaluation of the evidence and submissions presented to them. In short, they had a duty to be impartial. Keeping in mind, however, that the tribunal was made up of elected politicians who could not be expected to come to the hearing without some knowledge of the situation and without some inkling as to the appropriate disposition, it would be imposing an unrealistically high standard to expect them to come with no preconceptions or inclinations.

In the result, the court found no impermissible bias.

K. REASONS

There is a strong legal tradition indicating that municipal councils need not give reasons for their decisions. There are some statutory exceptions, such as when a development agreement is being rejected. But as a matter of administrative law, there tends to be recognition that debate, and presentations, at a council may well be somewhat amorphous, indeed may even touch on a variety of matters not strictly relevant to the decision being made. There is judicial reluctance to interfere with a decision because of an absence of reasons or a passing citation of irrelevant considerations. In *Valdun Development Ltd v Calgary (City)*,[120] the court said, "Council need not give reasons for a decision and reasons cannot be inferred from the outcome of a vote."[121] Part of the judicial reasoning on this point is that different councillors may have different reasons. In *Kirkfield Park & Arthur Oliver Residents Assoc Inc v Winnipeg (City)*,[122] the court said, "The reason why a particular councillor votes in favour of a rezoning application may be entirely different from the reasons given by a second councillor who also supports that application. The reasons for a councillor's vote may or may not be evident in the debates."[123]

Still, given the decision of the Supreme Court of Canada in *Lafontaine*, some courts have been moved to require reasons. In *Eagle's Nest*

120 [1997] AJ No 447 (CA).

121 *Ibid* at para 26.

122 [1996] 4 WWR 393 (Man CA) [*Kirkfield Park*].

123 *Ibid* at para 44.

Youth Ranch Inc v Corman Park (Rural Municipality,No 34),[124] the *Planning and Development Act* required that, where there was a discretionary power over use of land, there had to be specified procedures and criteria for the exercise of the discretion; if an application was rejected there had to be written notice of the decision based on the criteria.[125] The court read that as requiring reasons and rejected the Manitoba Court of Appeal reasoning in *Kirkfield Park*. Even where courts decide that reasons are not a requirement of the fairness aspect of the decision being made, if a council or councillor does give reasons, they may be examined. It is possible for a court to strike down a council's decision on the basis of irrelevant considerations and to examine minutes and transcripts of what was said by councillors to do so. Thus in *Pucci v North Vancouver (City)*,[126] a request to rezone property had been rejected by the council, which focused on a history of non-compliance with zoning laws by the owner; the court thought the decision was taken more on the basis of punishment than of land-use analysis. The matter was remitted to the council for reconsideration.

In the property tax case *Catalyst Paper Corp v North Cowichan (District)*,[127] the Supreme Court set out an attitude of a high degree of deference to municipal councils regarding their policy choices, and said, regarding reasons,

> It is important to remember that requirements of process, like the range of reasonable outcomes, vary with the context and nature of the decision-making process at issue. Formal reasons may be required for decisions that involve quasi-judicial adjudication by a municipality. But that does not apply to the process of passing municipal bylaws. To demand that councillors who have just emerged from a heated debate on the merits of a bylaw get together to produce a coherent set of reasons is to misconceive the nature of the democratic process that prevails in the Council Chamber. The reasons for a municipal bylaw are traditionally deduced from the debate, deliberations and the statements of policy that give rise to the bylaw.
>
> Nor, contrary to Catalyst's contention, is the municipality required to formally explain the basis of a bylaw. As discussed above, municipal councils have extensive latitude in what factors they may consider in passing a bylaw. They may consider objective factors directly relating to consumption of services. But they may also consider broader social, economic and political factors that are relevant to the electorate.

---

124 2013 SKQB 218.

125 *Planning and Development Act, 2007*, SS 2007, c P-13.2, s 54.

126 2010 BCSC 743.

127 2012 SCC 2.

> This is not to say that it is wrong for municipal councils to explain the rationale behind their bylaws. Typically, as in this case, modern municipal councils provide information in the form of long-term plans. Nor is it to say that municipalities performing decisional or adjudicative functions are exempt from giving reasons . . . .[128]

In circumstances where a council might offer reasons, but does not, the focus of a challenge will shift to the nature of the evidence before council; if there is no evidence on the record, it is possible that a court might conclude that bad faith has been shown.[129] This might be especially so if a council does not follow the advice of its professional staff. There is no obligation to follow the advice of staff, but the circumstances will raise questions about the basis of the decision made.[130]

If there is a requirement to give reasons, the reasons should be clear. In the United Kingdom case *Westminster City Council v Great Portland Estates plc*,[131] Lord Scarman said, "When a statute requires a public body to give reasons for a decision, the reasons must be proper, adequate and intelligible."

For appellate bodies, there will be a fairness requirement not only to offer reasons but reasons that are not merely conclusory but that contain an explanation of the reasoning that led to the ruling.[132]

L. STRATEGIC LAWSUITS AGAINST PUBLIC PARTICIPATION (SLAPPs)

Strategic lawsuits[133] against public participation have become a regular feature of contested land-use decisions.[134] Professor Sheldrick points out that SLAPPs "represent a very clear legalization of political life,"[135]

---

128 *Ibid* at paras 29–31.

129 See *507089 Alberta Ltd v Calgary (City)* (1996), 188 AR 384 (QB).

130 For such a case, occasioning some adverse judicial comment, but not resulting in the council's decision being set aside, see *R v Hammersmith and Fulham London Borough Council ex p People Before Profit*, [1981] JPL 869 (QB).

131 [1985] AC 661 at 673.

132 See *Young v Okotoks (Town)*, 2013 ABCA 54; *5142 NWT Ltd v Hay River (Town)*, 2008 NWTSC 2.

133 Also referred to as "strategic litigation": see Anti-SLAPP Advisory Panel, "Report to the Attorney General of Ontario" (28 October 2010) at 1, online: www.attorneygeneral.jus.gov.on.ca/english/anti_slapp/anti_slapp_final_report_en.html.

134 For a wide-ranging review, see Byron Sheldrick, *Blocking Public Participation: The Use of Strategic Litigation to Silence Political Expression* (Waterloo, ON: Wilfrid Laurier University Press, 2014).

135 *Ibid* at 148.

meaning that the courts are drawn into dealing with essentially political communication in a way that tries to exclude consideration of its real context. An Ontario advisory panel, chaired by the Dean of Law at the University of Toronto, noted,

> The Land Use Council and the Building Industry and Land Development Association (BILD) pointed out the number of opportunities that the land planning process offers for community input to development decisions. Nevertheless, when citizens' groups are sued or threatened with suits for organizing or speaking out on such occasions, it is not clear that such procedures provide a genuine opportunity for public participation.[136]

Professor Chris Tollefson has said,

> The conceptual thread that binds [SLAPPs] is that they are suits without substantial merit that are brought by private interests to stop citizens from exercising their political rights or to punish them for having done so. SLAPP suits function by forcing the target into the judicial arena where the SLAPP filer foists upon the target the expense of a defense. The longer the litigation can be stretched out . . . the greater the expense that is inflicted, the closer the SLAPP filer moves to success . . . . The ripple effect of such suits in our society is enormous. Persons who have been outspoken on issues of public importance targeted in such suits or who have witnessed such suits will often choose in the future to stay silent.[137]

Tollefson says that winning does not matter to the SLAPP filer, and winning is not enough for the SLAPP target. The fact of the lawsuit is sufficient to chill public participation.

Tollefson, the Ontario Advisory Panel,[138] and others[139] offer a number of Canadian examples of a phenomenon that had previously been more a feature of US litigation.[140] A recent example from Prince Edward Island gives something of the flavour of a SLAPP. In 2010, the Charlottetown council approved a development agreement with Pan American Proper-

---

136 Anti-SLAPP Advisory Panel, above note 133 at para 15.

137 "Strategic Lawsuits Against Public Participation: Developing a Canadian Response" (1994) 73 *Canadian Bar Review* 200.

138 Anti-SLAPP Advisory Panel, above note 133 at paras 6 and 7.

139 See, for example, Public Interest Advocacy Centre, "Corporate Retaliation against Consumers" (2004), online: www.piac.ca/our-specialities/corporate-retaliation-against-consumers.

140 See, for example, FM Rowe & Leo Romero, "Resolving Land-use Disputes by Intimidation: SLAPP Suits in New Mexico" (2002) 32 *University of New Mexico Law Review* 217.

ties Inc for a hotel in the downtown, to incorporate a heritage building and increase height from approximately 40 feet to 75 feet. The decision was appealed to the Island Regulatory and Appeals Commission (IRAC) by residents Gallant and Goulet. The developer filed a statement of claim in the Prince Edward Island Supreme Court alleging "intentional interference with economic interests" and "abuse of process" on the basis of the filing of the appeal, stating it had been taken "without any proper reason or ground."[141] A claim was made for $500,000 general damages and other amounts for special damages. The appeal was heard by IRAC and was denied. In a portion of its reasons, titled "Issue of Concern," IRAC explained that the appellants had been served with the statement of claim just as the appeal hearing was getting started. IRAC noted that there is a statutory right to appeal certain municipal decisions, and said,

> At the heart of the hearing process is the ability of all parties . . . to present evidence in an unimpeded manner, free from any threat or intimidation. The principles of natural justice and procedural fairness must prevail. In the present appeal, the Commission finds that one party, Pan American/APM, abused the hearing process by causing a Statement of Claim to be served upon the appellants shortly before they were to commence their opening submissions. This service took place on the Commission's premises and within the confines of the hearing itself and had the effect of intimidating the appellants. While Pan American/APM has the legal right to . . . initiate a legal action, the appellants have the right to have their appeals heard by the Commission. The service of the Statement of Claim could have delayed Pan American's proposed development . . . as the Commission had the authority to adjourn the hearing *sine die* [without a future date] pending the resolution of the civil action . . . . The action by Pan American/APM also showed disrespect for the legislated role and mandate of the Commission as a quasi-judicial body, [and] may have constituted contempt . . . .[142]

The defendants counterclaimed for intentional infliction of mental suffering. In the end, all parties quickly agreed to withdraw their claims.[143] Thus, there is no ruling from the Prince Edward Island Supreme Court

---

141 *Pan American Properties Inc v Lys-Ondray Goulet*, Supreme Court of PEI (General Section), No S1-GS-23777, statement of claim, para 8, filed 5 July 2010.

142 Prince Edward Island, Island Regulatory and Appeals Commission, *In the Matter of Appeals by Judy Gallant and Lys-Ondray Goulet of a Decision of the City of Charlottetown, dated April 12, 2010, Docket LA10006 and LA10007*, Reasons for Order (22 July 2010) at para 42.

143 "APM President, Residents Drop Lawsuit" *The [Charlottetown] Guardian* (4 September 2010) A6.

dealing with the nature of the legal rights that attach to citizen participation in the land-use planning process through taking advantage of a statutory scheme that allows for appeals of municipal government decisions.

Most SLAPPs are framed as defamation actions rather than intentional interference with economic interests. Whatever the form, the courts have to grapple with the value of freedom of expression along with integrity of reputation or protection of economic interests.[144] In *Fraser v Saanich (District)*,[145] Singh J said a SLAPP is an action brought "to stifle free expression by characterizing lawful conduct as a conspiracy" or as some other civil wrong. He also said,

> A SLAPP suit is a claim for monetary damages against individuals who have dealt with a governmental body on an issue of public interest or concern. It is a meritless action filed by a plaintiff whose primary goal is not to win the case but rather to silence or intimidate citizens who have participated in proceedings regarding public policy or public decision-making.[146]

Quebec has adopted legislation to make it easier for SLAPP targets to ask courts to dismiss the lawsuits.[147] British Columbia had such legislation but repealed it.[148] In 2015, Ontario passed legislation aimed at curbing SLAPPs.[149]

---

144 What is raised in some of the cases is whether freedom of expression as a *Charter*-protected right implies some special legal consequence for political communication. Defamation suits are private litigation, hence the *Charter* is not engaged directly. Interpreting the common law or civil procedure rules in line with *Charter* values has not yet led to any special alteration of burden of proof (*Maguire v Northwest Organics Limited Partnership*, 2014 BCCA 454), although it is common for a SLAPP to lead to orders for increased costs (*Scory v Krannitz*, 2011 BCSC 1344). In *Montague (Township) v Page* (2006), 24 MPLR (4th) 81 (Ont SCJ), it was the municipality that attempted to take a defamation action against a resident who had criticized the fire service over a fatal fire. The action was struck out on the basis of the *Charter*-protected right of freedom of speech.

145 [1999] BCJ No 3100 (SC).

146 *Ibid* at paras 48 & 49.

147 *An act to amend the Code of Civil procedure to prevent improper use of the courts and promote freedom of expression and citizen participation in public debate*, SQ 2009, c 12.

148 *Protection of Public Participation Act*, SBC 2001, c 19.

149 *Protection of Public Participation Act, 2015*, SO 2015, c 23.

M. NOT IN MY BACKYARD (NIMBY)

Very few cases consider the concept of NIMBYism. For the most part, the term is used not by the courts but by parties in relation to one another. The essence of the term is to suggest that objectors to development proposals are either narrowly self-interested or improperly prejudiced. The first appearance of the term in a judgment is in 1990.[150] The most significant application of the idea has been in *Pointes Protection Assn v Sault Ste Marie Region Conservation Authority*,[151] where security for costs was awarded against an incorporated society pending its application for judicial review of a decision to allow a residential subdivision in the Conservation Authority's area. The court found that the case was not public interest litigation, and that although the motives were altruistic, the association was a small group without assets and there were no general repercussions to the litigation. To a similar effect is *Galloway v Coldstream (District) (Approving Officer)*,[152] where the court commented that a NIMBY response "does not necessarily equate to public interest."[153]

Although the idea of NIMBYism may be an undercurrent in some disputes, rights to participation are either defined by statute or by judicial principles, decisions tend to be anchored in written principles or planning objectives, and the motives or size of an organization tend not to be particularly significant.

N. PUBLIC TRUST DOCTRINE

Well established in the United States, the public trust doctrine is of uncertain status in Canada.[154] Where it is recognized, it offers members of the public the opportunity to challenge government decisions that tend

150 *Tidewater Construction Co Ltd v Nova Scotia (Attorney General)*, 1990 CanLII 4180 (NSSC).

151 2013 ONSC 5323.

152 2007 BCSC 33.

153 *Ibid* at para 63.

154 See *Green v Ontario*, [1973] 2 OR 396 (HCJ); Constance Hunt, "The Public Trust Doctrine in Canada" in John Swaigen, ed, *Environmental Rights in Canada* (Toronto: Butterworths, 1981); Barbara von Tigerstrom, "The Public Trust Doctrine in Canada" (1997) 7 *Journal of Environmental Law and Practice* 379; Anna Lund, "Canadian Approaches to America's Public Trust Doctrine" (2012) 23 *Journal of Environmental Law and Practice* 105; Sarah Jackson et al, "Lessons from an Ancient Concept" (2012) 23 *Journal of Environmental Law and Practice* 175.

to privatize publicly owned resources such as Crown land through allocation of licences to harvest timber; the allegation would be that the government had breached a positive obligation to protect the resource for the benefit of the public. More than a doctrine establishing standing, it implies actual limits on any decisions to restrict or affect public use of public resources.

In the United States, the concept is that the state is "to hold ownership of certain properties and resources in trust for the people . . . the general notion is that, where agencies fail to impose restrictions on private development that threatens to destroy public access to important public resources, the courts should imply and enforce those restrictions."[155] The cases have tended to focus on alienation of trust properties and also the nature of allowable uses. In 1892, the US Supreme Court set out basic public trust law[156] followed by multiple cases achieving differing degrees of success, the prevailing judicial view being that congress and the state legislatures determine how the public trust will be manifested.[157]

The Supreme Court of Canada, in *British Columbia v Canadian Forest Products Ltd*,[158] declined to decide whether the American concept has application in Canada on the basis that the issue had not been adequately documented or canvassed in the courts below. At issue was the nature of compensation to the Crown for destruction of forest land due to a fire caused by the forestry company. The Crown sought damages as owner and "as a representative of the public to enforce the public interest in an unspoiled environment."[159] Justice Binnie said,

> It seems to me that there is no legal barrier to the Crown suing for compensation as well as injunctive relief in a proper case on account of public nuisance, or negligence causing environmental damage to public lands, and perhaps other torts such as trespass, but there are clearly important and novel policy questions raised by such actions. These include the Crown's potential liability for *inactivity* in the face of threats to the environment, the existence or non-existence of en-

---

155 Robert L Glicksman & George C Coggins, *Modern Public Land Law in a Nutshell*, 2d ed (St Paul, MN: West Group, 2001) at 93–94.

156 *Illinois Central Railroad Co v Illinois*, 146 US 387 (1892).

157 For successful use of the doctrine, see the decisions in *Sierra Club v Department of the Interior* (I), 376 F Supp 90 (ND Cal 1974), (II), 398 F Supp 284 (ND Cal 1975), (III), 424 F Supp 172 (ND Cal 1976).

158 2004 SCC 38 [*Canadian Forest Products*].

159 *Ibid* at para 64. The issue is known as "non-use values." See Anastasia M Lintner, "Trees Left Standing: A Case Comment on *British Columbia v Canadian Forest Products Ltd*" (2003) 49 *Canadian Environmental Law Reports (New Series)* 34.

> forceable fiduciary duties owed to the public by the Crown in that regard . . . . This is not a proper appeal for the Court to embark on a consideration of these difficult issues.[160]

Since then, although the issue has been raised in some cases, the matter remains unresolved. For example, in *Burns Bog Conservation Society v Canada (Attorney General)*,[161] the issue was argued regarding arrangements among the federal government, the province of British Columbia, and two municipal governments to protect a significant peat bog. Under a contribution agreement, the federal government advanced money to Delta, the Greater Vancouver Regional District, and the province to purchase more than 5,000 acres of the bog, with an obligation to put in place a management plan and to protect the bog. Shortly thereafter, the same governments agreed to construct a highway adjacent to the bog. The Conservation Society attempted to assert that the contribution agreement plus the management plan amounted to a public trust not to take any steps that might harm the bog. The court refused to see the arrangements as amounting to a public trust enforceable against the federal government.

---

160 *Canadian Forest Products*, above note 158 at paras 81–82 [emphasis in original].
161 2014 FC 1024, aff'd 2014 FCA 170.

CHAPTER 9

APPEALS AND JUDICIAL REVIEW

A. PRELIMINARY[1]

In this chapter, we examine more generally the functioning of administrative law in the land-use context. Broadly, there are two aspects: appeals, which tend to focus on the planning merits of the decision under scrutiny, and judicial review, which tends to focus on the legality of the decision, with legality being broadly understood.

Any right to an appeal must be created by statute. Appeals are usually taken to a specialized body such as the Ontario Municipal Board (OMB) or the Nova Scotia Utility and Review Board (NSUARB). Judicial review is a function of the superior courts and is an inherent court power. There is merging of the focus of appeals and judicial review, with legality being a relevant question for some appeals and the overall merits of the decision becoming a relevant question in judicial review as an aspect of the reasonableness of the decision under scrutiny.

1 This chapter and the immediately preceding one take up the focus on administrative law matters, which has been inherent in many of the other chapters. Basic texts include Gus Van Harten et al, *Administrative Law*, 7th ed (Toronto: Emond Montgomery, 2015); David P Jones & Anne S deVillars, *Principles of Administrative Law*, 6th ed (Toronto: Carswell, 2014); Colleen M Flood & Lorne Sossin, eds, *Administrative Law in Context*, 2d ed (Toronto: Emond Montgomery, 2013); Lord Woolf et al, *De Smith's Judicial Review*, 6th ed (London: Sweet & Maxwell, 2007).

Appeal and judicial review are to be regarded as part of the administrative accountability of government, especially local government.[2] Political accountability is often recognized as a prime form of accountability, tied to an idea of democracy and expressed first through periodic elections. But financial probity, administrative rationality, and legality are all other forms of accountability.

This chapter focuses first on accountability through the mechanisms for appeals, a process that grapples with the merits of the decision under consideration. It focuses next on legal accountability, that is, the accountability "of public bodies to courts in order to ensure that they keep within the limits of the jurisdictional authority conferred upon them."[3] As was said by the Supreme Court of Canada in *Dunsmuir v New Brunswick*: "The function of judicial review is therefore to ensure the legality, the reasonableness and the fairness of the administrative process and its outcomes."[4]

Fairness has been examined in Chapter 8. Here we take up cases that deal with issues such as bad faith (*HG Winton Ltd v North York (Borough)*),[5] unreasonableness (*Canadian National Railway Co v Fraser-Fort George (Regional District)*),[6] vagueness (*Canada Post Corp v Hamilton (City)*),[7] discrimination (*Scarborough (Township) v Bondi*),[8] procedural issues (*Hubbard v West Vancouver (District)*,[9] *Action Council of Reasonable Neighbours v Edmonton (City)*),[10] the exercise of discretion for an improper purpose (*Roncarelli v Duplessis*),[11] the use of irrelevant considerations/failure to consider relevant considerations (*Oakwood Development Ltd v St-François Xavier (Rural Municipality)*),[12] and illegality (*Blainville (Ville de) c Beauchemin*).[13] To some extent, the categories of attack on decisions overlap.[14]

---

2 See, generally, Martin Loughlin, *Administrative Accountability in Local Government* (York, UK: Rowntree Foundation, 1992).

3 *Ibid* at 2.

4 2008 SCC 9 at para 28 [*Dunsmuir*].

5 (1978), 20 OR (2d) 737 (Div Ct) [*HG Winton*].

6 (1994), 24 MPLR (2d) 252 (BCSC) [*CNR*].

7 2015 ONSC 3615.

8 [1959] SCR 444 [*Bondi*].

9 2005 BCCA 633.

10 2003 ABQB 895.

11 [1959] SCR 121 [*Roncarelli*].

12 [1985] 2 SCR 164 [*Oakwood Development*].

13 (2003), 44 MPLR (3d) 24 (Que CA).

14 Early articles on the topic exist, though they are, for the most part, seriously dated. See, for example, Eric L Todd, "The Quashing and Attacking of Municipal By-laws" (1960) 38 *Canadian Bar Review* 197; G Keith Allen, "Attacking By-laws" (1971) 21 *University of New Brunswick Law Journal* 1; Ann McDonald, "In

A penetrating critique has been made of both land-use planning ("the pervasive practice of *ad hocery*") and of the courts' dealings with land-use matters in administrative law. ("The courts have made it clear that law is mandatory while policy is discretionary, but they seem to have difficulty distinguishing one from the other.")[15] Professor (as he then was) Ed Morgan challenges both planning, as it is manifested in local government decision-making, and the struggles of the courts in deciding when to intervene, linking the problems as due to violation of the rule of law: "The rule of law—'open, stable, clear, and general rules, [with] even-handed enforcement of those laws'—cannot be satisfied by a discipline based on little more than ideology and taste."[16] As for the courts:

> It is simply not possible to determine whether the local authority "has taken into consideration matters which were not proper to be regarded, or has omitted to consider matters which were of direct importance," since there are no agreed upon criteria which span the potentially applicable planning approaches. The criteria are inherently subjective in every sense of the term.[17]

We have seen examples of this difficulty throughout our examination of cases and statutes. Thus in *Bondi*[18] the Supreme Court of Canada accepted that in zoning, "arbitrary" lines could be drawn such that "On one side of an arbitrary line an owner may be prevented from doing something with his property which another owner, on the other side of the line, with a property which corresponds in all respects except location, is free to do." In *Soo Mill & Lumber Co v Sault Ste-Marie (City)*,[19] it was accepted that holding zones might be put in place, with no set criteria for when or how to decide to remove them. In *Montréal (City) v Arcade Amusements Inc*,[20] it was accepted that municipalities could make some distinctions between classes of uses but not others, without a definite idea of how to identify what distinctions are legitimate. In

---

the Public Interest: Judicial Review of Local Government (1983) 9 *Queen's Law Journal* 62. For a modern account, see George Rust-D'Eye et al, *Ontario Municipal Law: A User's Manual* (Scarborough, ON: Carswell, 2010).

15 Ed Morgan, "The Sword in the Zone: Fantasies of Land-Use Planning Law" (2012) 62 *University of Toronto Law Journal* 163 at 165 and 170.

16 *Ibid* at 195, referring to planning, and citing *British Columbia v Imperial Tobacco Canada Ltd*, 2005 SCC 49 on the rule of law.

17 Morgan, above note 15 at 196, citing *R v Paddington Valuation Officer ex p Peachey Property Corp Ltd*, [1966] 1 QB 380.

18 Above note 8.

19 [1975] 2 SCR 78.

20 [1985] 1 SCR 368.

Saint-Romuald (City) v Olivier,[21] it was said that non-conforming uses could be altered but not too far. The core cases for virtually all aspects of land-use law show this problem. And yet, the conclusion is not necessarily that "the contradictory impulses found in modern land-use planning law are impossible to overcome," that it manifests "incoherence."[22] What becomes necessary is to recognize the inherently political nature of the activity and also to become familiar with the range of decided cases so as to continue to grapple with individual issues as they arise, while not being surprised that legal action is often only one stage in a long struggle over how we create and change the physical settings for our lives.

B. APPEALS

Formal provisions for the taking of an appeal are often a feature of any administrative system. Appeals seek reconsideration of the merits of the original decision. There is, however, no inherent entitlement to such opportunities. The availability of an appeal mechanism depends entirely on whether one has been established by statute. In this essential regard, appeals differ from the mechanism of judicial review, which is the inherent right of the superior courts to scrutinize government (and some other) decision-making, with the power to set the decisions aside or offer other remedies if the decisions are found to be flawed in law (taken in excess of jurisdiction or using a fundamentally unfair process). Not only must an appeal mechanism be established by statute, there will be provisions as to what decisions may be appealed, who may take an appeal (standing), what test the appellate body is to use in scrutinizing the original decision, what type of hearing the appeal will be, and what remedies are available through the appeal mechanism.

The existence of an appeal mechanism does not preclude an application for judicial review of the same decision being challenged. Because some appellate bodies do not have full power to consider all of the legal issues that may arise in relation to a challenged decision, it may be necessary to instigate both an appeal if one exists and an application to court for judicial review. Thus in a dispute over establishment of a quarry, the proponent instigated both an appeal to Nova Scotia's Utility and Review Board over the municipality's refusal of a permit, and a court challenge to the validity of the municipality's by-law on the basis that

21 2001 SCC 57.
22 Morgan, above note 15 at 163.

quarries were regulated exclusively by the province.[23] Both matters ended up at the Court of Appeal. The result was a ruling that the NSUARB validly upheld the municipality's refusal of a permit, and that the by-law was *ultra vires*, so no municipal permit was required anyway. *Northern Construction* illustrates the unnecessary proliferation of proceedings in provinces where appellate bodies, even those granted a power to rule on questions of law, are limited in how that power is applied. The Ontario Court of Appeal has taken quite a different view of the OMB's power to deal with questions of law that arise in matters properly before it.[24] It may even be that the courts in Ontario will decline to exercise their jurisdiction to rule on the illegality of municipal decisions if they see the OMB as the more appropriate choice of venue.[25] But if the issue is a direct frontal attack on the underlying validity and legality of a by-law, then the superior courts will accept jurisdiction.[26] In provinces other than Ontario, judicial review is the appropriate choice of venue if the focus is on legal issues, though both routes may be pursued simultaneously, and an appellate body may delay its hearing until the legal issues are resolved. In British Columbia, where there is no province-wide land-use appellate body, judicial review is the only available option.

In land use, a variety of appeal mechanisms have been established. For land-use regimes that are purely provincial, it is not unusual for the appeal mechanism to be internal to government. Thus, in Manitoba, under *The Provincial Parks Act*,[27] it is possible to obtain a vacation home lease in some provincial parks, with conditions to be set by department administrators;[28] if there is dissatisfaction with the conditions, they may be appealed to the minister, who may receive additional material and may refer the issues to an advisory board for advice prior to taking a decision;[29] there is no further appeal. Instead of an internal appeal

23 *Northern Construction Enterprises Inc v Halifax (Regional Municipality)*, 2013 NSUARB 28; 2015 NSCA 43 [*Northern Construction*] (appeal of NSUARB decision); 2014 NSSC 166, var'd 2015 NSCA 44.

24 *Toronto (City) v Goldlist Properties Inc* (2004), 44 MPLR (3d) 1 (Ont CA) [*Goldlist*]. But see *Toronto (City) Zoning By-law No 138-2003 (Re)* (2004), 47 OMBR 168 for a case in which the OMB took a restrictive view of its power, limiting it to not applying an unconstitutional law rather than being able to refuse to approve a by-law only on that basis.

25 See *Equity Waste Management of Canada v Halton Hills (Town)* (1997), 35 OR (3d) 321 (CA) [*Equity Waste Management*]; *Toronto (City) v 1095909 Ontario Ltd*, 2012 ONSC 1344.

26 See *London (City) v RSJ Holdings Inc*, 2007 SCC 29 at paras 36–37.

27 CCSM c P20.

28 *Park Activities Regulation*, Man Reg 141/96.

29 *Ibid*, s 62.1.

mechanism, appeals could be to a court. Thus, also in Manitoba, the cutting of timber on Crown land is controlled by a licensing system.[30] Should a licence, permit, or agreement be cancelled by the minister, there is an appeal to a Queen's Bench judge, which is a hearing *de novo*.[31] Other provinces have created appeal mechanisms for various land-use regulatory regimes such as those that deal with agricultural land reserves [32] or designation of heritage property.[33]

At the municipal level of government, some internal appeal mechanisms do exist. For example, in British Columbia, for a non-conforming use structure that has been damaged or destroyed to the extent of 75 percent or more of its value above its foundations "as determined by the building inspector," there is no right to reconstruct the non-conforming structure;[34] an appeal regarding the issue of how much of the value of the structure has been destroyed goes to the board of variance.[35] In Nova Scotia, when site-plan approval is being considered through a special mechanism in effect in Halifax Regional Municipality,[36] the application goes to a committee; appeals are to the municipal council.[37] It is not unusual for appeals to go to a municipal council when the original decision-making body is a committee or an administrative official, though appeals are sometimes specified as going to courts, as in Ontario's *Building Code Act, 1992*,[38] where an "aggrieved" person may appeal decisions of inspectors or the chief building official to the courts.

The main appeal mechanism for municipal land-use issues, however, is to a province-wide body, such as the OMB, Quebec's Commission Municipale, or Prince Edward Island's Island Regulatory Appeals Commission.[39] Nine of Canada's provinces have established appellate bodies. British Columbia has not done so.

---

30 *The Forest Act*, CCSM c F150.

31 *Ibid*, s 39(5).

32 See, for example, *Agricultural Land Commission Act*, SBC 2002, c 36: reconsideration by the Commission (s 33); a matter may be referred to a board by cabinet (ss 40–45).

33 See, for example, *The Heritage Resources Act*, CCSM c H39.1: designation may be appealed to the minister and cabinet (s 9); stop orders may be appealed to the courts (s 18).

34 *Local Government Act*, RSBC 2015, c 1, s 532.

35 *Ibid*, s 544; there is a further appeal to the Supreme Court.

36 *Halifax Regional Municipality Charter*, SNS 2008, c 39, s 246.

37 *Ibid*, s 246(6).

38 SO 1992, c 23, s 25.

39 *Ontario Municipal Board Act*, RSO 1990, c O.28; *An Act respecting the Commission Municipale*, CQLR c C-35; *Island Regulatory and Appeals Commission Act*, RSPEI 1988, c I-11. In Newfoundland and Labrador, there are regional appellate bodies.

Such appellate bodies exist mainly as an alternative to courts. Writing about the OMB, Bruce Krushelnicki refers to it as "a people's court."[40] He notes that "the formality, complexity, length and cost of court proceedings can be intimidating to ordinary citizens, especially those who are not represented by counsel."[41] The alternative, he says, "arguably is less rigid in its perspective of acceptable review, less formal in its proceedings, less complicated to the average citizen and less costly to those who come before it."[42] Much of this list of virtues is open to question. Appeals can involve procedural complexities and the expense of legal counsel and professionals as witnesses. The virtues of appellate bodies are primarily that they engage with the merits of the original decision, not just legal questions associated with it (if any), that they are likely to be more expeditious than court proceedings, and that they rarely involve an obligation to pay costs for other parties.[43]

Standing to bring an appeal varies as to its definition. In Ontario, any "person" may take an appeal. In practice, the board is prepared to assess as a preliminary matter whether the appeal is "genuine."[44] It has also determined that unincorporated entities are not "persons,"[45] which means that residents acting together need to become entities, such as societies under Part III of the *Corporations Act*,[46] rather than to attempt to come before the board as informal groups. In Nova Scotia, an appellant must be "aggrieved," the meaning of which is discussed in Chapters 6, Section L, and in Chapter 8, Section D.

In Prince Edward Island, hearings before the commission are *de novo*. In a 1997 stated case to the Prince Edward Island Court of Appeal, the court said that "the Legislature contemplated and intended

---

40 Bruce W Krushelnicki, *A Practical Guide to the Ontario Municipal Board* (Toronto: LexisNexis Butterworths, 2003) at 1.

41 *Ibid* at 3.

42 *Ibid* at 4.

43 The OMB does have the power to award costs against parties, but rarely does so. See Krushelnicki, *ibid* at 58 and 102–3, and examples of the many cases in which the OMB has considered the principles governing award of costs, such as *Wal-Mart Canada Corp v Peterborough (City)* (2004), 48 OMBR 406 and *Re City of Stratford Zoning By-law 128-2000* (2001), 42 OMBR 268. The board is alive to possible chill of an award of costs and will usually award costs only in instances of conduct that is "unreasonable, frivolous or vexatious, or . . . in bad faith," in line with the *Statutory Powers Procedure Act*, RSO 1990, c S.22, s 17(2).

44 *Planning Act*, RSO 1990, c P.13, s 34(25) allows dismissal without a hearing if the notice of appeal does not show a valid ground of appeal, or if the appeal is not made in good faith, or is frivolous or vexatious, or is made only for purposes of delay, or there is an abuse of process.

45 *Homewood Residents Association v Four Seasons Hotel Ltd* (1981), 13 OMBR 92.

46 *Corporations Act*, RSO 1990, c C.38, Part III.

that appeals under the *Planning Act* would take the form of a hearing *de novo* after which IRAC, if it so decided, could substitute its decision for the one appealed. The findings of the person or body appealed from are irrelevant. IRAC must hear and decide the matter anew as if it were the original decision-maker."[47] This is also the position of the OMB, although where new evidence that "could have materially affected the council's decision" is offered, that evidence is to be referred to the council for an opportunity to reconsider its decision.[48]

Like municipalities, the OMB must pay attention to provincial policies,[49] but it owes minimal deference to the original decision under appeal. In Nova Scotia, the test to be applied by the board is one that strongly favours the original municipal decision: appeals may only be taken "on the grounds that the decision of the council does not reasonably carry out the intent of the municipal planning strategy," and the board shall not allow an appeal unless it makes that determination.[50]

Because appeals of approvals function so as to delay construction, there is occasionally room for negotiations between the parties, just as there is in lawsuits. One instance, which has attracted adverse comment, was the appeal of approval of the Scotia Plaza development, a sixty-eight-storey cluster in downtown Toronto. The appellants agreed to withdraw their appeal in an arrangement that saw the developer donate $2 million to the Cooperative Housing Federation of Toronto to support low-income housing.[51] Professor Makuch points out that such benefits were not available for the municipality to negotiate for and were negotiated in private; though he sees "great benefit" in the financial contribution, he raises the issues of rule of law (knowing the rules and having them applied uniformly), fairness, and equity.

Legal issues will invariably arise in land-use appeals. At the most basic, the jurisdiction of the appellate body, for example as to the standing of an appellant, or how to read the official plan, are both legal issues that must be dealt with. But a broader range of legal issues may arise. The 2004 *Goldlist*[52] decision of the Ontario Court of Appeal illustrates the nature of legal questions that can be dealt with by the OMB. In *Goldlist*, Toronto had amended its official plan (OP) to limit demolition of residential property and conversion of rental units to condominiums.

---

47 *Island Regulatory and Appeals Commission (Re)* (1997), 40 MPLR (2d) 258 at para 9 (PEISCAD); confirmed in *Charlottetown (City) v Prince Edward Island (Island Regulatory and Appeals Commission)*, 2013 PECA 10.

48 Ontario *Planning Act*, above note 44, s 34(24.4).

49 *Ibid*, s 3(5)(a): "shall be consistent with . . ." See also *ibid*, s 2.1.

50 *Municipal Government Act*, SNS 1998, c 18, ss 250 & 251.

51 See Stanley Makuch, "Planning or Blackmail?" (1985) 25:1 *Plan Canada* 8.

52 Above note 24.

The OP amendments were challenged at the OMB which, in a preliminary determination, ruled it had jurisdiction to decide on the legality of the amendments. The core points raised regarding the OP amendments were that *Planning Act* matters ought to be restricted to physical changes to land rather than social issues manifesting in type of tenure, and that the amendments conflicted with the *Tenant Protection Act, 1997*.[53] The issue of the board's powers proceeded to court. The result is that the power of the OMB to rule on legal issues appears to be unrestricted, so long as dealing with the question is "necessarily incidental to carrying out its responsibilities";[54] the Court of Appeal also characterized the test as whether deciding the question of law "is incidental to its power to determine the limits of its jurisdiction"[55] and "as incidental to its administrative functions."[56] The court made it clear that such a power for the OMB is not "free-standing jurisdiction,"[57] meaning that the courts are not deprived of their jurisdiction to decide the same point,[58] and the determination by the OMB is only for the purpose of determining its jurisdiction and, unlike a court's determination, is not a ruling for all purposes.[59] Though the points were not before the court in *Goldlist*, the power of the OMB to deal with "illegality in the form of bad faith,"[60] as had been approved earlier in 1997 in *Equity Waste Management*,[61] was confirmed, as was its power to interpret and apply the *Charter*.[62]

Still, there may be outstanding questions. The issues in *Goldlist* were of pure construction of statutes. They did not involve other possible types of illegality that might be raised regarding municipal decisions, such as traditional administrative law issues of defects in fairness (e.g., adequacy of notice, the hearing process, bias, and irrelevant considerations). Though *Equity Waste Management* involved bad faith, a core administrative law issue usually litigated in the courts, and on which the courts did rule, it was noted that the *Ontario Municipal Board Act*[63] gave "exclusive" jurisdiction to the board over land-use matters, a

---

53 SO 1997, c 24 [since repealed].
54 Above note 24 at para 15.
55 *Ibid* at para 33.
56 *Ibid* at para 34.
57 *Ibid* at para 15.
58 *Ibid* at para 19.
59 *Ibid* at para 29.
60 *Ibid* at para 38.
61 Above note 25; see also *Smart Centres Inc (Toronto Film Studios Inc) v Toronto (City)* (2011), 85 MPLR (4th) 330 (OMB) in which the board disallowed the zoning on this basis.
62 Above note 24 at para 41.
63 RSO 1990, c O.28, s 36.

power to be seen as extending to considering bad faith, but this was not incompatible with the jurisdiction of the courts under the *Municipal Act, 2001*[64] to rule on "illegality." There is in the cases a strong suggestion that a full range of administrative law matters may be raised at the OMB. Certainly the board itself has been prepared to consider such issues. Thus, in *Re Port Stanley Zoning By-law 2139*,[65] the board upheld a rezoning appeal due to the absence of a planning report and no public meeting having been held; in *Somerville v Scugog (Township)*,[66] where a rezoning went through various iterations, no public notice was given nor was a public meeting held for the final version, leading the board to set it aside as in violation of the *Planning Act* and the OP; in *Landawn Shopping Centres Ltd v Bracebridge (Town)*,[67] the board considered (and approved) the adequacy of the printed notice according to statutory requirements.

In contrast to *Goldlist*, Nova Scotia's Court of Appeal has ruled that the land-use appellate body has no jurisdiction to rule on most legal issues that might be raised before it, save for very narrow points, such as standing to appeal and, anomalously, constitutional law questions. Most recently, in *Northern Construction*,[68] the court said, of the routes available to the company, "its challenge to the legality of the by-law had to be advanced by seeking a declaration in the Supreme Court of Nova Scotia, while its challenge to HRM's interpretation of the by-law had to be advanced by way of an appeal before the Respondent Board," thus confirming the generally narrow interpretation of its own powers the NSUARB has long held, based on the 1992 decision of the Court of Appeal in *Halifax (County) v Maskine*.[69]

64 SO 2001, c 25, s 136.

65 (1985), 18 OMBR 18.

66 (1989), 23 OMBR 385.

67 (1995), 32 OMBR 423.

68 Above note 23 at para 9.

69 [1992] NSJ No 292 [*Maskine*]. For an example of the board's reading of *Maskine*, see *Fryday (Re)*, 2007 NSUARB 97 at paras 84–90: "[T]he Board does not have jurisdiction to grant relief to an appellant . . . on the ground that the council acted contrary to the requirements of natural justice or procedural fairness . . . ." The position of the NSUARB regarding its power to interpret general laws in the course of appeals has recently been complicated through its ruling in *Tasty Buds Compassion Club Inc (Re)*, 2016 NSUARB 128, in which a development permit had been refused for a retail business located in a C-2 (general business) zone on the basis that it was to sell medical marijuana. The board found the nature of the business to be in violation of federal law, and sidestepped the decision in *Allard v Canada*, 2016 FC 236, since the court in *Allard* had suspended its declaration of invalidity and the suspension was still in effect at the date of the *Tasty Buds* case.

When it comes to the *Charter*, the OMB has a long history of being prepared to rule on such issues if they are pertinent to the matter before it.[70] This view of its powers has been confirmed by the Divisional Court in *Grushman v Ottawa (City)*[71] and was implicit in the Court of Appeal decision in *Goldlist*. For Nova Scotia's land-use appellate board, *Peninsula South Community Association (Re)*[72] establishes that the NSUARB can deal with constitutional law questions.[73] Other provincial boards do not appear to have decided the point. It is not entirely clear that all of the boards would be able to exercise *Charter* jurisdiction; the Manitoba and New Brunswick boards might be in the weakest position so far as the ambit of their jurisdiction to decide legal questions as part of a land-use hearing.

There are usually further appeals to the courts available after a board ruling, but limited to questions of law, including jurisdiction. Such appeals to the courts are not rehearings and do not extend to matters of fact, which are for the exclusive determination of the boards. In Ontario, the consent of the Divisional Court must be sought prior to proceeding with such an appeal. In assessing whether to grant consent, the court will determine "if the question of law is sufficiently important to warrant the attention of the Divisional Court and there is reason to doubt the correctness of the decision or the Board's interpretation of the law."[74] Even where such appeals are heard by the courts, there is some element of deference to the boards, even though the courts are then dealing with questions of law. In *London (City) v Ayerswood Development Corp*,[75] the Court of Appeal reflected on the standard of review in such appeals:

> The proper standard of review was one of either correctness or reasonableness, depending on the particular question of law. Questions of law that engage the specialized expertise of the Board, such as interpretation of its own statute, attract a standard of reasonableness. Questions of law that are of general application for which the Board has no special expertise are reviewed on a standard of correctness.[76]

---

70 See Howard Epstein, "Land Use Appellate Bodies and the *Charter*" (2002) 29 *Municipal and Planning Law Reports* (3d) 29 at 32–33.

71 (2000), 15 MPLR (3d) 167 (Ont Div Ct).

72 2002 NSUARB 7.

73 The board has ruled on a *Charter* issue, and the Court of Appeal has given tacit approval of this power of the NSUARB, exercised in its capacity as regulator of electricity matters: *Affordable Energy Coalition (Re)*, 2008 NSUARB 11 at para 130; *Boulter v Nova Scotia Power Inc*, 2009 NSCA 17.

74 See, for example, *Toronto (City) v Dunpar Developments Inc* (2008), 51 MPLR (4th) 153 at 154 (Div Ct).

75 2002 CanLII 3225 (Ont CA).

76 *Ibid* at para 7.

Despite this reference to application of the more deferential standard when the board is dealing with "its own statute" (referred to in some other administrative law litigation as a "home statute"[77]), in *Goldlist*, the Court of Appeal said,

> We have little difficulty in concluding that, even if it could be said that s. 16(1) of the *Planning Act* (which . . . loosely defines an official plan) is a provision with respect to which the Board could be said to have expertise from the standpoint of planning principles (which would lead to a deferential standard of review), on the matter of the Board interpreting this provision for the purpose of determining the scope of its jurisdiction, the relevant standard is correctness.[78]

The result appears to be that constitutional law questions, those of laws of general application, and delineation of jurisdiction between tribunals are all questions of law that would attract a correctness standard;[79] so, too would questions of the interpretation of a home statute, unless the legal question is one bound up closely with facts.

Appeals to the courts on questions of law or jurisdiction, if successful, will usually result in the matter being remitted for rehearing if there is any scope for the ultimate decision to be in question. Thus, in *Toronto (City) v R & G Realty Management Inc*,[80] the Divisional Court said,

> The Board committed fundamental and unreasonable errors . . . . The nature of these errors is such that they undermine the foundation for the decision as a whole. The decision is unreasonable and cannot stand. Accordingly, the decision of the Board is set aside. This matter is remitted for a new hearing before a Board differently constituted.[81]

But in *Mahone Bay Heritage and Cultural Society v 3012543 Nova Scotia Ltd*,[82] where the court determined that a proposed development agreement was not reasonably consistent with the municipal planning strategy (OP), it ruled to "allow the appeal and set aside the Board's Order confirming the decision of Council. I would set aside the decision of Council to enter into the proposed development agreement."[83] There was simply no point in remitting the matter to the board.[84]

---

77 See, for example, *Smith v Alliance Pipeline Ltd*, 2011 SCC 7.
78 *Goldlist*, above note 24 at para 42.
79 *Smith v Alliance Pipeline Ltd*, above note 77.
80 2009 CanLII 42397 (Ont Div Ct).
81 *Ibid* at para 44.
82 2000 NSCA 93.
83 *Ibid* at para 97.
84 To the same effect is *Kings (County) v Lutz*, 2003 NSCA 26, where the board had overturned the council's original decision; the Court of Appeal "restored" the original decision rather than ordering a rehearing at the board.

C. JUDICIAL REVIEW

Many of the cases we have considered throughout this text are examples of administrative law: they are instances of claimants seeking the assistance of the courts in challenging decisions, primarily government tribunal decisions, that are not acceptable to the objectors. The definition of a "tribunal" in the *Statutory Powers Procedure Act* of Ontario[85] is of "one or more persons, whether or not incorporated and however described, upon which a statutory power of decision is conferred by or under a statute"; this offers the basic idea of what entities and processes are subject to judicial review.

The power of the superior courts of each province to exercise judicial review authority is said to be inherent. At the same time, there has been some codification of the power. Civil procedure rules often specify time limits for commencing judicial review applications and outline what materials must be submitted to the court. In Ontario, the *Judicial Review Procedure Act*[86] addresses these issues and identifies some of the powers of the courts with respect to errors of law, absence of evidence, and procedural irregularities. The Ontario *Statutory Powers Procedure Act*[87] sets out certain requirements applicable to the original decision-makers as to form of hearings and admissible evidence. To a similar effect is British Columbia's *Administrative Tribunals Act*.[88] The codification may take the form of granting standing to members of the public, or some of them, to challenge certain decisions. Thus, Manitoba's *Municipal Act* says,

> A person may make an application to the court for a declaration that a by-law or resolution is invalid on the ground that
> (a) the council acted in excess of its jurisdiction;
> (b) the council acted in bad faith;
> (c) the by-law is discriminatory; or
> (d) the council failed to comply with a requirement of this or any other Act or the municipality's procedures by-law.[89]

It also says, "A by-law is discriminatory if it operates unfairly and unequally between different classes of persons without reasonable justification."[90] Section 384 of the Act says, "No by-law, resolution

85 Above note 43, s 1(1).
86 RSO 1990, c J.1.
87 Above note 43.
88 SBC 2004, c 45, for designated tribunals.
89 *Municipal Act*, CCSM c M225, s 382(1).
90 *Ibid*, s 382(2).

or proceeding of a council . . . may be challenged on the ground that the by-law is unreasonable or not in the public interest"—a privative clause the courts have tended to minimize, preferring to apply general administrative law standards.[91] For federal government matters, the *Federal Courts Act*[92] delineates the jurisdiction of the federal courts, which have no inherent powers, being specially created entities. In essence, the federal courts have been given jurisdiction to exercise a full range of judicial review powers when it is the federal government that is the decision-maker.

The courts have various remedies available to them. For the most part, the traditional terms such as *certiorari*, *quo warranto*, or *mandamus* are not now used, nor are their technical aspects much relevant in modern administrative law. The main powers available to the courts are to quash a decision and refer the matter back for reconsideration (*certiorari*), or to order something to be done or ceased to be done (mandamus, injunction), or to set out the legal obligations of the parties but without any order for action (a declaration).

The powers of the courts to intervene are quite strong, but are not unlimited and are also much more focused on the legality of the decision than on the decision's merits. The courts are not experts on transportation safety or on immigration and refugee issues or on licensing of professionals or on labour/management dynamics or on broadcasting or on many of the hugely varied types of decisions a modern state is called upon to make. The undoubted expertise of the courts is in assessing legality and fairness of decision-making. This is the essence of administrative law.

Citing a 1985 decision of the United Kingdom's House of Lords,[93] Professor Martin Loughlin says, "The traditional heads of review have recently been judicially reformulated by Lord Diplock into illegality, irrationality and procedural impropriety."[94] This is the same generalized classification set out by the Supreme Court of Canada in *Dunsmuir* in 2008.[95]

Illegality and procedural impropriety are concepts that are relatively easy to understand. We have already looked at procedural impropriety in Chapter 8's discussion of public participation and fairness. Illegality is a broad term and extends from violation of the separation

---

91 See, for example, *Beaulieu v Alexander (Rural Municipality)*, 2011 MBQB 213 at para 40ff.

92 RSC 1985, c F-7, especially ss 18 and 28.

93 *Council for Civil Service Unions v Minister for the Civil Service*, [1985] AC 374.

94 Loughlin, above note 2 at 121.

95 Above note 4

of powers provisions of the Constitution, to violation of the *Charter*, and to *ultra vires* decisions or actions in the sense of being beyond an assigned jurisdiction; it can also mean the exercise of powers for an improper purpose or on the basis of irrelevant considerations; it can also be co-extensive with some fairness considerations if they are seen as going beyond mere irregularities, for example, violation of a statutory requirement to give notice.[96] Irrationality is a more amorphous concept.

Finally, it is a crucial aspect of judicial review that it is to some extent discretionary. As said by the Supreme Court of Canada in *London (City) v RSJ Holdings Inc*:[97]

> The power to quash a by-law for illegality contained in s. 273(1) of the *Municipal Act, 2001* is discretionary. Of course, in exercising its discretion the court cannot act in an arbitrary manner. The discretion must be exercised judicially and in accordance with established principles of law. Hence, when there is a total absence of jurisdiction, a court acting judicially will quash the by-law. In other cases, a number of factors may inform the court's exercise of discretion including, the nature of the by-law in question, the seriousness of the illegality committed, its consequences, delay, and mootness.[98]

The Supreme Court of Canada, in 2012, in *Catalyst Paper Corp v North Cowichan (District)* offered a useful overview of judicial review in the context of municipal decision-making:

> It is a fundamental principle of the rule of law that state power must be exercised in accordance with the law. The corollary of this constitutionally protected principle is that superior courts may be called upon to review whether particular exercises of state power fall outside the law. We call this function "judicial review".
>
> Municipalities do not have direct powers under the Constitution. They possess only those powers that provincial legislatures delegate to them. This means that they must act within the legislative constraints the province has imposed on them. If they do not, their decisions or bylaws may be set aside on judicial review.
>
> A municipality's decisions and bylaws, like all administrative acts, may be reviewed in two ways. First, the requirements of procedural fairness and legislative scheme governing a municipality may require that the municipality comply with certain procedural requirements, such as notice or voting requirements. If a municipality fails to abide by these procedures, a decision or bylaw may be invalid. But in addi-

96 *Immeubles Port Louis Ltée v Lafontaine (Village)*, [1991] 1 SCR 326 at 351–56.
97 2007 SCC 29.
98 *Ibid* at para 39.

> tion to meeting these bare legal requirements, municipal acts may be set aside because they fall outside the scope of what the empowering legislative scheme contemplated. This substantive review is premised on the fundamental assumption derived from the rule of law that a legislature does not intend the power it delegates to be exercised unreasonably, or in some cases, incorrectly.
>
> A court conducting substantive review of the exercise of delegated powers must first determine the appropriate standard of review. This depends on a number of factors, including the presence of a privative clause in the enabling statute, the nature of the body to which the power is delegated, and whether the question falls within the body's area of expertise. Two standards are available: reasonableness and correctness. See, generally, *Dunsmuir v. New Brunswick*, 2008 SCC 9, [2008] 1 S.C.R. 190, at para. 55. If the applicable standard of review is correctness, the reviewing court requires, as the label suggests, that the administrative body be correct. If the applicable standard of review is reasonableness, the reviewing court requires that the decision be reasonable, having regard to the processes followed and whether the outcome falls within a reasonable range of alternatives in light of the legislative scheme and contextual factors relevant to the exercise of the power (*Dunsmuir*, at para. 47).[99]

Dunsmuir reminds us that the standard of review has become a serious aspect of judicial review. Standard of review is an instruction that a reviewing court gives to itself by way of determining, as a preliminary matter, how strict it ought to be in holding a statutory decision-maker to account.

Many decisions about land use are discretionary decisions. Discretion, improperly exercised, may be challenged in court. But it is crucial to understand the possibilities that might be available; they are limited:

> The concept of discretion in its legal context implies power to make a choice between alternative courses of action or inaction . . . . To say that somebody has a discretion presupposes that there is no unique legal answer to a problem. There may, however, be a number of answers that are wrong in law . . . . There are degrees of discretion, varying the scope for manoeuvre afforded to the decision-maker . . . . Sometimes . . . the exercise of a statutory discretion is not limited by the express provisions of the Act and in these cases the courts embark upon an interpretation of the objects and purposes of the statute in order to identify the limitations to which the discretion is subject.[100]

---

99 2012 SCC 2 at paras 10–13 [*Catalyst Paper*].

100 Lord Woolf et al, *De Smith's Judicial Review*, above note 1 at 227–28.

Whether treated as a matter of illegality or unreasonableness, abuse of discretion may found a challenge to a decision.

1) Illegality

a) *Ultra Vires*

No decision-making body may act beyond the ambit of the authority that has been granted to it. To do so is to act in a way that the courts may declare to be *ultra vires*. Justice Major said, in *Nanaimo (City) v Rascal Trucking Ltd*,[101] "[t]he process of delineating municipal jurisdiction is an exercise in statutory construction." In the 1906 decision in *Hamilton (City) v Hamilton Distillery Co*,[102] and despite its contemporary decision in *MacIlreith v Hart Estate*[103] implying a Dillon's Rule approach to interpretation of statutes granting powers to local governments, the Supreme Court of Canada first suggested a benevolent approach to interpreting municipal powers. In the present context, interpretation of statutes associated with local governments tends to be no different a process than for any other legislation. General principles apply: where there are statutory definitions, they are followed; if provisions of the *Interpretation Act* are relevant, they are followed—otherwise, the "modern principle" as enunciated by Driedger comes into play: "Today there is only one principle or approach, namely, the words of an Act are to be read in their entire context, in their grammatical and ordinary sense harmoniously with the scheme of the Act, the object of the Act, and the intentions of Parliament [or a Legislature]."[104] As Cromwell JA (as he then was) said in *Halifax (Regional Municipality) v Ed DeWolfe Trucking Ltd*,[105] "Accepting this 'broad and purposive' approach to interpretation has coincided with adoption of a new approach to drafting municipal legislation . . . . Unlike the older style of drafting that defined municipal powers narrowly and specifically [the new style] confers authority in broader and more general terms . . . ."

Justice Cromwell's statement about "a new approach to drafting" is not at all universally accurate, as we saw in Chapter 6, Section G. Statutes granting powers to local governments vary enormously as to when they are "broad" and when they are "narrow and specific." This

101 2000 SCC 13 at para 18 [*Rascal Trucking*].

102 (1906), 38 SCR 239.

103 (1908), 39 SCR 657.

104 Elmer Driedger, *The Construction of Statutes* (Toronto: Butterworths, 1974) at 67, cited in Ruth Sullivan, *Driedger on the Construction of Statutes*, 6th ed (Markham, ON: LexisNexis Canada, 2014) at 7.

105 2007 NSCA 89 at para 88.

leaves open to courts many options as to whether to view particular provisions more benevolently or less benevolently.[106]

In any event, it is the courts that decide legality issues, and with no deference to the views of the local government council's views: the council must be correct in its interpretation of statutes, even their own home statute. The 2000 decision of the Supreme Court of Canada in *Rascal Trucking*[107] sets out the basic approach of the courts to consideration of jurisdiction of municipal councils. In *Rascal Trucking*, the council responded to complaints about dust and noise associated with the company's piling of soil as a preliminary to processing it. The site was zoned for the use, and the company had a permit from the city to deposit the soil. The city declared the pile to be a nuisance and ordered its removal. The decisions were challenged as being *ultra vires* in the sense of not being authorized by the *Municipal Act*.[108] Section 932 authorized the council to "prevent, abate and prohibit nuisances," and section 936 allowed the council to declare "a building, structure or erection of any kind . . . or other matter or thing" to be a nuisance. The question was whether the power granted extended to a pile of soil. The Court found that the pile was a structure or erection: "A pile of soil does not materialize on its own. It must at least be erected presumably by piling or dumping."[109] More crucially, the Court considered the standard of review:

> Here, s. 936 requires the municipal council to apply principles of statutory interpretation in order to answer the legal question of the scope of its authority. On such questions, municipalities do not possess any greater institutional competence or expertise than the courts so as to warrant a heightened degree of deference on review. The test on jurisdiction and questions of law is correctness.[110]

The centrality of standard of review, as it is set out in *Rascal Trucking*, is a major feature of all administrative law cases.

The principles for interpretation of by-laws do not differ from the general approach to interpretation of statutes. By-laws are termed "delegated legislation." In the 1945 Supreme Court of Canada decision in *Kuchma v Tache (Rural Municipality)*,[111] the Court acknowledged that it should commence analysis of municipal by-laws with a presumption

---

106 See also *United Taxi Drivers' Fellowship of Southern Alberta v Calgary (City)*, 2004 SCC 19.

107 Above note 101.

108 RSBC 1979, c 290.

109 *Rascal Trucking*, above note 101 at para 24.

110 *Ibid* at para 29.

111 [1945] SCR 234.

they are adopted in the public interest. In a contemporary example, *Rexlington Heights Ltd v Ontario*,[112] Cumming J said, "[t]he rules formulated for the construction of statutes are also applicable to interpreting the meaning of municipal by-laws."[113]

Interpretation of official plans has been said to be a matter to be addressed by the courts on a standard of reasonableness, not correctness. This suggests that the content of official plans are not questions of law, a contested point. In *Lane v La Ronge (Town)*,[114] residents challenged a by-law permitting a multi-unit development on the basis of its location in a flood risk area. The development plan included a policy that "no development will be allowed in designated high flood risk areas . . . ." Citing jurisprudence to the effect that official plans amount to be "merely a guideline and policy rather than a rule,"[115] the court applied a standard of review of reasonableness and refused to set aside the by-law. This decision is open to doubt both as to the standard of review and as to result. Even if the standard of review is reasonableness, this is an instance in which there does not seem to be any room for the interpretation of the development plan the town relied on. A reasonableness test does not mean unreasonableness should be acceptable as an interpretation. As discussed in Chapter 6, Section H, official plans are accompanied by zoning by-laws, which are the main instruments of direct regulation of the actions of landowners, and also often contain general statements, and may contain policies that require balancing. At the same time, some policies in an official plan can be written in terms that are entirely clear, and statutes usually contain provisions that require by-laws to conform to the official plan and also forbid municipalities from acting contrary to their official plans. That is the case in Saskatchewan, where the *Planning and Development Act*[116] states that "any part of a zoning bylaw that is inconsistent with the official community plan has no effect insofar as it is inconsistent"[117] and that "no development shall be carried out that is contrary to the official community plan."[118] Such provisions give to official plans some status that in effect amounts to being law, in the sense

112 (2005), 15 MPLR (4th) 117 at para 26 (Ont SCJ).

113 For elaboration, see M Virginia MacLean & John R Tomlinson, *A User's Guide to Municipal By-laws*, 2d ed (Markham, ON: LexisNexis, 2008); Howard M Epstein, "Clarity & Legality: Drafting and Interpretation of Municipal By-laws and Official Plans in Land-Use Law: A Short Guide" (2008) 43 *Municipal and Planning Law Reports* (4th) 76.

114 2011 SKQB 160.

115 *Ibid* at para 14.

116 SS 2007, c P-13.2.

117 *Ibid*, s 34(2).

118 *Ibid*, s 40(1)(b).

that they are binding. (The provisions of the Saskatchewan *Planning and Development Act* do not appear to have been considered by the court in *Lane v La Ronge*.) This issue of standard of review of official plans arises only where challenges based upon them are taken directly to court.[119] Where appeal boards consider official plans, and further appeals are taken to the courts, the interpretation of the official plan is treated as a question of law, although due to the frequently general language of OPs, or the inherent need to balance their various policies, there is deference to local governments as to their interpretation and application.

b) Improper Motives

There are broadly two aspects to impropriety of motives, both aspects of irrelevant considerations: policy matters and personal characteristics.

In *Prince George (City) v Payne*,[120] an application had been made to the municipal council for a business licence to operate an adult boutique. The council voted not to issue the licence, apparently on the basis of its disapprobation of the nature of the business. Mandamus was sought to require the issuance of the licence. *Prince George v Payne* was discussed as a leading case in Chapter 2. The Supreme Court of Canada said that the decision, being based on moral grounds, was taken on the basis of an irrelevant consideration. In *TimberWest Forest Corp v Campbell River (City)*,[121] the council was found to have set its tax rate for the company at a high rate in order to force a change in use of the land; the decision was set aside.

In *Pucci v North Vancouver (City)*,[122] the municipal council had turned down a request to rezone land following a long history of non-compliance by the owner, with orders to abide by the by-laws. Transcripts of the council meeting showed that in effect the members made their decision as a form of "punishment" rather than on considerations of appropriate land use. The court overturned the decision and remitted the matter to the council. In *Dallinga v Calgary (City)*,[123] character evidence was seen as irrelevant. The decision before the Development Appeal Board was whether to grant a permit to operate an auto-wrecking yard. The board heard evidence that the applicant had been in contravention of the law by operating without a permit, and there were allegations from

---

119 For examples of a challenge based on an official plan, see *Fredericton Heritage Trust v Fredericton (City)* (1988), 39 MPLR 64 (NBCA) and *Re Peterborough (City) and Smith (Township)*, 1980 CanLII 1917 (Ont Div Ct).

120 [1978] 1 SCR 458 [*Prince George v Payne*].

121 2009 BCSC 1804.

122 2010 BCSC 743.

123 (1975), 62 DLR (3d) 433 (Alta SCAD).

a competitor that the applicant displayed misleading signage amounting to a "fraud." The court set aside the board's decision, saying: "[The Planning] Act as a whole makes it clear that such considerations relate solely to the use and development of land. Nowhere in the Act is there any suggestion that the character of an applicant for a permit is a relevant planning consideration."[124]

c) Violation of a Statutory Requirement

It is usually said that violation of a statutory requirement will lead automatically to a finding of invalidity of a decision. Thus in *Western Forest Products Inc v Capital (Regional District)*,[125] where the regional district was made up of thirteen municipalities but some were restricted from voting based on an erroneous view of the voting rights, the zoning by-law in question was set aside. This principle can extend to violation of a municipality's own by-laws. Thus in *Argyll Community League (1978) v Edmonton (City)*,[126] approval of a development was set aside on the basis that existing by-laws required the city to find that development in the particular, sensitive location was "essential," a step not taken. Still, there may be room for interpretation of what the statutory requirements amount to: in *Farber v Kingston (City)*,[127] a vote was improperly taken at an *in camera* meeting, but the court viewed the statute as contemplating the consequences of such votes and was not prepared to nullify the decision on that basis. *Farber* was an unusual case; normally violation of a statutory requirement is fatal.

d) Vagueness or Uncertainty

Rules, such as by-laws, which are so vague in their terms as not to set out appropriately or clearly what is allowed or forbidden may be struck down on account of vagueness. This has been a principle of the common law and has also now been seen to be an implication of section 7 of the *Charter*. Where statutes allow for the incorporation by reference of some code, as, for example, the National Building Code, it is possible that a part of the code might be found to be too vague to be enforced.[128]

There are other forms of illegality that have been identified in litigation, including converting a regulation power to a discretionary power, unauthorized delegation of a decision-making power, and making un-

---

124 *Ibid* at para 27.

125 2009 BCCA 356.

126 2009 ABQB 66.

127 2007 ONCA 173 [*Farber*].

128 See *Canadian Occidental Petroleum Ltd v North Vancouver (District)* (1983), 148 DLR (3d) 255 (BCSC).

authorized distinctions. These have been examined in Chapter 6, Sections H(2) and M.

2) Unreasonableness, Discrimination, and Bad Faith

Although a variety of terms are used in association with irrationality, unreasonableness, and bad faith, the categories tend to overlap. In *Associated Provincial Picture Houses Ltd v Wednesbury Corporation*,[129] an authoritative UK decision, Lord Greene MR said,

> What, then, is the power of the courts? . . . . [I]t must always be remembered that the court is not a court of appeal. When discretion . . . is granted the law recognizes certain principles upon which that discretion must be exercised . . . . What then are those principles? . . . They are principles which the court looks to in considering any question of discretion of this kind. The exercise of such a discretion must be a real exercise of the discretion. If, in the statute conferring the discretion, there is to be found expressly or by implication matters which the authority . . . ought to have regard to, then . . . it must have regard to those matters. Conversely, if the nature of the subject matter and the general interpretation of the Act make it clear that certain matters would not be germane . . . the authority must disregard those irrelevant collateral matters . . . . I am not sure myself whether the permissible grounds of attack cannot be defined under a single head. It has been perhaps a little bit confusing to find a series of grounds set out. Bad faith, dishonesty—those of course stand by themselves—unreasonableness, attention given to extraneous circumstances, disregard of public policy and things like that have all been referred to . . . . If they cannot all be confined under one head, they at any rate . . . overlap to a very great extent . . . . [A]ll these things run into one another.[130]

It is then not unusual for a litigant to raise several categories of challenge (discrimination, bad faith, irrelevant considerations) as in *Dong v Bowen Island Municipality*[131] a recent case in which public controversy about the length of some docks that had been constructed led to a municipal ban. The by-law was upheld.

---

129 [1948] 1 KB 223 (CA) [*Wednesbury*].

130 *Ibid* at 228–29; for a contemporary example, see *Rocky Point Metalcraft Ltd v Cowichan Valley (Regional District)*, 2012 BCSC 756.

131 2016 BCSC 553.

a) Unreasonableness

In 1898 in *Kruse v Johnson*,[132] the UK courts were considering a by-law that made it an offence to play a musical instrument or sing in a public place or on a highway within fifty yards of a dwelling house, if requested to desist by the occupant or a constable. A cheerful reveller who had emerged from a pub and was singing, refused to stop and was charged. The objection urged on the court was that the by-law was unreasonable. The by-law was upheld. Lord Russell of Killowen CJ said, in a passage that, despite evolutions in the overall language of administrative law, is still quoted and still reflects the prevailing view,

> I do not mean to say that there may not be cases in which it would be the duty of the Court to condemn by-laws . . . as invalid because unreasonable. But unreasonable in what sense? If, for instance, they were found to be partial and unequal in their operation as between different classes; if they were manifestly unjust; if they disclosed bad faith; if they involved such oppressive or gratuitous interference with the rights of those subject to them as could find no justification in the minds of reasonable men, then the Court might well say, "Parliament never intended to give authority to make such rules; they are unreasonable and *ultra vires*." But it is in this sense, and in this sense only, as I conceive, that the question of unreasonableness can properly be regarded. A by-law is not unreasonable merely because particular judges may think that it goes further than is prudent or necessary or convenient, or because it is not accompanied by some qualification or an exception which some judges may think ought to be there.[133]

Wednesbury is a companion case to *Kruse*, in the sense that it is from the United Kingdom, is older, but is still quoted.[134] It examines unreasonable exercise of a discretionary power. There is no mode of forcing a tribunal that has a discretionary power to exercise their discretion in a particular manner: "the role of the courts is limited to ensuring that discretion has been exercised according to law."[135] What has come to be referred to as the "*Wednesbury* test" is that, although there should be deference to the decisions of councils, judicial intervention would be

132 [1898] 2 QB 91 [*Kruse*].

133 *Ibid* at 99–100.

134 Above note 129. *Wednesbury* was cited by McLachlin J in her opinion in *Shell Canada Products Ltd v Vancouver (City)*, [1994] 1 SCR 231.

135 Stanley A De Smith, *Judicial Review of Administrative Action*, 2d ed (London: Stevens, 1968) at 321.

justified where there was evidence of bad faith or absurdity, although "to prove a case of that kind would require something overwhelming."[136]

The various aspects of what has been set out in *Kruse* and *Wednesbury* remain a part of the law. Recall that the Court decided in the Supreme Court of Canada decision in *Rascal Trucking* that the municipal council must be correct in its interpretation of the statute that gave it jurisdiction over nuisances, on the point of whether a pile of dirt could constitute a nuisance. The council had, however, made a second decision, that is, to apply its interpretation of a nuisance to the circumstances prevailing at the Rascal Trucking site. Such a decision was held to be *intra vires* and was reviewable by the courts on a deferential standard. The Supreme Court of Canada had previously set out a three-standard classification for judicial review: correctness, reasonableness, and patent unreasonableness.[137] In considering these classifications, the Court said the standard applicable to "a review of *intra vires* municipal actions should be one of patent unreasonableness."[138] Subsequent to *Rascal Trucking*, the Supreme Court of Canada decided that only two standards of review should be used, correctness and reasonableness (also referred to as reasonableness *simpliciter*).[139] This change in overall approach probably does not have any practical effect when it comes to judicial review of municipal decisions. The Court suggested as much in *Catalyst Paper Corp v North Cowichan (District)*,[140] a property tax case. On legal matters, the standard of review will be correctness, and for *intra vires* decisions, the standard will be reasonableness with reasonableness understood as it was applied by the Supreme Court of Canada in *Rascal Trucking*. Thus, in the post-*Dunsmuir* case *Henderson v Saskatoon (City)*,[141] a condominium conversion case,[142] reasonableness was found to be the standard of review for council's decision, and *Rascal Trucking* was relied upon extensively. Likewise, in *Craig v Bighorn (Municipal District No 8)*,[143] where the court was dealing with a refusal

---

136 *Wednesbury*, above note 129 at 230.

137 The nature of these classifications emerged beginning around 1979 in *CUPE, Local 963 v New Brunswick Liquor Corp*, [1979] 2 SCR 227, and progressing through such cases as *Bibeault v McCaffrey*, [1984] 1 SCR 176; *Canada (Attorney General) v Mossop*, [1993] 1 SCR 554; *Pezim v British Columbia (Superintendent of Brokers)*, [1994] 2 SCR 557; and *Canada (Director of Investigation and Research, Competition Act) v Southam Inc*, [1997] 1 SCR 748.

138 *Rascal Trucking*, above note 101 at para 37.

139 *Dunsmuir*, above note 4.

140 *Catalyst Paper*, above note 99 at paras 22–25.

141 2008 SKQB 135.

142 See a discussion of this case in Chapter 10, Section E.

143 2009 ABCA 119.

to amend the land-use by-law, the Alberta Court of Appeal said, "the proper standard of review for the Council's decision was reasonableness. A high degree of deference is afforded to the Council."[144]

It is not uncommon for municipal statutes to provide that "No by-law or resolution may be challenged on the ground that it is unreasonable."[145] The term for such provisions is a "privative clause." The implication of such a section was discussed in *Keller v Bighorn (Municipal District No 8)*.[146] The court did not resolve the issue, but implied that the section might not pose a barrier to court challenges:

> Prior to *Dunsmuir*, s.539 was interpreted to mean that the appropriate standard of review for *intra vires* municipal decisions should be patent unreasonableness [citing *Rascal Trucking*]. With the patent unreasonableness standard effectively collapsed into the reasonableness standard, the question raised by s.539 is whether it operates to preclude judicial review of *intra vires* by-laws or resolutions altogether, or merely evidences an intention on the part of the Legislature to provide significant but not complete privative protection, thereby weighing in favour of a high degree of deference within the reasonableness standard.[147]

Regardless of the language used as to deference, note that the courts are in fact being asked to consider whether the original tribunal made the appropriate decision. The test might be difficult to meet, but under "unreasonableness" and associated points it is, at core, the merits of the decision that is in question before the courts. Unreasonableness goes beyond what is raised when mere illegality is invoked.

The portion of the idea of unreasonableness set out in *Kruse v Johnson* that refers to action or law that involves "such oppressive or gratuitous interference" with rights that they "can find no justification in the minds of reasonable men" has survived in modern administrative law as a basis for possible attack of by-laws or decisions by municipal councils. But the scope is narrow. The very idea of "unreasonableness" has been criticized as manifesting "an attitude of suspicion and distrust . . . [and] is an arcane tool for judicial paternalism which ought to be

---

144 *Ibid* at para 6.

145 See, for example, Alberta's *Municipal Government Act*, RSA 2000, c M-26, s 539. For a case in which the court quickly accepted this stricture against judicial review on the basis of unreasonableness, see *1786889 Ontario Ltd v Toronto (City)*, 2014 ONCA 286.

146 2010 ABQB 362.

147 *Ibid* at para 18.

abandoned."[148] Some provinces offer municipalities immunity from judicial review on the basis of unreasonableness, but it is not unknown for courts to set aside by-laws on such grounds even in the face of such privative or preclusive clauses.[149] *Catalyst Paper*[150] illustrates an unsuccessful challenge to a taxation by-law based on unreasonableness. In *Catalyst Paper* the municipality imposed a high rate of tax on its one main industrial entity, a pulp and paper plant. The rate was twenty times the rate of residential taxation, although a ratio of 3.4 times had previously been a provincial regulation and the ratio imposed was one of the highest in the province. The principle of unreasonableness was used in striking down "people zoning" in *R v Bell*.[151] In *Canadian National Railway Co v Fraser-Fort George (Regional District)*,[152] the municipality imposed a special property tax to cover infrastructure, but did so by drawing the lines where the tax would apply such that the CNR lands (just its track passing through the municipality) represented 85 percent of the area to be taxed and would pay 95 percent of the cost. The court said, "The shape of the service area is so eccentric as to be an obvious gerrymander extended to include much of the C.N. rail line,"[153] and found the by-law to be unreasonable under *Wednesbury*[154] principles. *CNR* and *Catalyst Paper* are useful to read together. Both involved challenges to unusual property taxation schemes, but with different results. In *Oakwood Development Ltd v St-François Xavier (Rural Municipality)*,[155] an application for a subdivision had been denied, the land being prone to flooding; the court found that the municipality's "obstinate refusal" to consider the applicant's engineering evidence as to remediation possibilities amounted to a failure to consider relevant matters, which was just as improper as taking into account improper considerations. It is not unusual in cases of alleged unreasonableness for the courts to view with some severe scrutiny a municipal decision that goes contrary to the advice of its staff.[156] In *Fister v Willow Bunch (Town)*,[157] a case very similar to *Rascal*

148 Michelle Lawrence, "Putting an End to Unreasonableness: Judicial Review and Local Governments" (1998) 4 *Appeal* 84.

149 See *Re Vancouver (City) Licence By-law 4957* (1978), 83 DLR (3d) 236 (BCCA) as a case accepting the statutory limitation on judicial review, and *R v Bell* (1979), 98 DLR (3d) 255 (SCC) as a case that did not.

150 Above note 99.

151 Above note 149.

152 *CNR*, above note 6.

153 *Ibid* at para 9.

154 Above note 129.

155 Above note 13.

156 See, for example, *338186 BC Ltd v Vancouver (City)*, 2011 BCSC 336.

157 2015 SKQB 362.

Trucking, the court came to a different conclusion, finding that an order to remove derelict vehicles and other items as a nuisance was manifested in an order that was "too broadly cast" and therefore unreasonable. The most that can be said is that it remains extremely difficult to challenge by-laws based on unreasonableness; *Wednesbury* spoke of "something overwhelming" as being required to satisfy the test.

This standard of "a high degree of deference" to the *intra vires* decisions of municipal councils means that the doctrine of "unreasonableness" as a basis for judicial review of municipal councils is probably limited to discrimination, bad faith, or an abuse of power. As said by the Quebec Court of Appeal in *Montréal (Ville de) c Auberge des Glycines inc (Auberge Le Pomérol inc)*[158] and in consideration of the Supreme Court of Canada decision in *Catalyst*, "La seule prétention que le zonage en vigueur ne semble pas approprié aux caractéristiques physiques ou aux conditions économiques d'un terrain ou de ses environs n'est pas suffisante pour affecter la validité du règlement en l'absence d'une preuve de discrimination ou d'abus de pouvoir équivalant à fraude."

b) Discrimination

Discrimination was examined in Chapter 2 in the comments on the decisions of the Supreme Court of Canada in *Scarborough v Bondi*[159] and *Montréal (City) v Arcade Amusements Inc.*[160] The courts have said that it is inherent in the process of zoning that distinctions are made as between different properties as to what is or is not a permitted use; the drawing of lines to establish zones means that distinctions are made. At the same time, it is not desirable that such lines be arbitrary; arbitrariness may be challenged. In discussing a variant on the idea of discrimination, the courts have also said that when rules are adopted to classify persons or groups that there must be some reasonable statutory authorization for the making of the distinctions, or the by-laws may be set aside. In a contemporary example from the British Columbia Court of Appeal, it was not unauthorized discrimination for a municipality to exempt from latecomer charges for access to a sewer system, those properties that already had existing septic fields.[161]

c) Bad Faith

Bad faith is an aspect of judicial review applicable beyond local governments. Decisions of the senior levels of government are also open

---

158 2012 QCCA 556 at para 27.

159 Above note 8.

160 Above note 20.

161 *Okanagan Land Development Corp v Vernon (City)*, 2012 BCCA 332.

to challenge on this basis. The term often used is "abuse of discretion." The classic Canadian case is the 1959 Supreme Court of Canada decision in *Roncarelli v Duplessis*,[162] in which the premier of Quebec was found to have misused the licensing system of the *Liquor Control Act* so as to frustrate the economic life of a person financing Jehovah's Witnesses.[163] *Roncarelli* is foundational to the courts' understanding of proper and improper governmental use of discretion:

> [T]here is no such thing as absolute and untrammelled "discretion", that is that action can be taken on any ground or for any reason that can be suggested to the mind of the administrator; no legislative Act can, without express language, be taken to contemplate an unlimited arbitrary power exercisable for any purpose, however capricious or irrelevant, regardless of the purpose of the statute. Fraud and corruption in the Commission may not be mentioned in such statutes but they are always implied as exceptions. "Discretion" necessarily implies good faith in discharging public duty; there is always a perspective within which a statute is intended to operate; and any clear departure from its lines or objects is just as objectionable as fraud or corruption.[164]

An example in which the allegation of abuse of discretion was not accepted by the court is *Regal Goldfields Inc et al v Nova Scotia (Minister of Natural Resources)*.[165] The company held mineral exploration licences for Crown land which, though designated as a wilderness area, known as Jim Campbell's Barren, was available for surface access. The rights were withdrawn. Dealing with the portion of the challenge based on bad faith, the court said that the withdrawal of the access rights was unlawful in the sense of being "a breach of contract" but it was not motivated by "personal animosity":

> That motive has a foundation in policy, rather than personal animosity . . . . The applicants complain that the decision was "political". They use the word in a pejorative sense to say that, instead of confining himself to the commercial purpose of the legislation, the Minister responded to public pressure and served interests outside the legitimate purposes of his discretion. I am conscious that this pejorative meaning of "political" was also used [in another case] but I think it an unfortunate choice of words in judicial review of ministerial

162 Above note 11.

163 See also *Maple Lodge Farms Ltd v Canada*, [1982] 2 SCR 2 and *Comeau's Sea Foods v Canada (Minister of Fisheries and Oceans)*, [1997] 1 SCR 12.

164 *Roncarelli*, above note 11 at 140.

165 (29 July 1998), SH No 144644 (NSSC, Moir J).

> discretion, especially ministerial discretion of the broad kind that I am now reviewing, as opposed to discretion to decide an individual's issue. To be "political" in the sense of pursuing government policy is the legitimate function of the executive and an area into which judicial inquiry is seldom legitimate . . . . The hard choice was a political one, that is, between two courses of policy. That the choice was made after public debate and intensive consultation with the competing interests tends to suggest good faith, not bad faith."[166]

The court also found that the *Mineral Resources Act* has more purposes than advancing economic development.[167]

Challenging the validity of a decision on this basis is not the only possible remedy. There is a tort of abuse of public office for which money damages may be sought. A case that was unsuccessful is *Scory v Langley (Township)*,[168] noteworthy for setting out the idea of the tort: it arises where power is exercised for the specific purpose of injury and involves bad faith, improper purpose, or ulterior motive, or can arise if a decision-maker acted unlawfully with a mind of reckless indifference to the illegality and to the probable injury to the plaintiff.[169]

The courts have several times said that municipal actions should be characterized by good faith. In *Congrégation des témoins de Jéhovah de St-Jérôme-Lafontaine v Lafontaine (Village)*,[170] the Supreme Court referred to "the broad scope of the municipal power to pursue its urban planning program with fairness, in good faith and with a view to the public interest,"[171] making it clear that decisions in violation of these standards could be set aside. In *Equity Waste Management of Canada v Halton Hills (Town)*,[172] it was said that bad faith "connotes a lack of candour, frankness and impartiality" and "includes arbitrary or unfair conduct and the exercise of power to serve private purposes at the expense of the public interest."[173] The classic municipal case of bad faith is *HG Winton*.[174] The land in question was zoned R-3, which permitted churches as an institutional use. A sale to the Zoroastrian Society was being negotiated, with an intention to use the building as a temple. There was adverse public reaction, including a petition that included

166 *Ibid* at 8–19.
167 *Ibid* at 9.
168 2012 BCSC 951.
169 See also *First National Properties Ltd v Highlands (District)*, 2001 BCCA 305.
170 2004 SCC 48.
171 *Ibid* at para 32.
172 (1997), 35 OR (3d) 321 (CA).
173 *Ibid* at 340.
174 Above note 5.

the comment that "the mansion . . . has been sold to a religious order or sect, which intends to hold services of some sort on the premises." The Divisional Court said, "In light of that comment it is perhaps not inappropriate to observe that Zoroastrianism is an ancient world religion based on the teachings of the prophet Zoroaster and founded in Persia in the late seventh or early sixth century B.C. It has been kept alive by the Parsees of India who are descendants of Persian Zoroastrians who emigrated to India to escape religious persecution. About 150 to 175 families in Toronto presently practice the religion."[175] In *HG Winton*, the court pointed to several *indicia* leading it to conclude the by-law had been adopted in bad faith: the action was taken in response to pressure from residents and not as a result of a planning exercise; there were no reports from planning staff or the Planning Board; it was essentially spot-zoning; it was hurried; normal processes and formalities were not observed; and a primary concerned party, the society, was not notified or heard. The court found that the by-law "was enacted in bad faith and is discriminatory. It is not . . . a valid exercise of the legislative power of the borough . . . and cannot stand."[176]

> To say that council acted in what is characterized in law as "bad faith" is not to imply or suggest any wrongdoing or personal advantage on the part of any of its members . . . . But it is to say . . . that council acted unreasonably and arbitrarily and without the degree of fairness, openness, and impartiality required of a municipal government . . . .[177]

In a case involving planning in the city of Windsor for bridges crossing to the United States, *Payne v Windsor (City)*,[178] the judge summarized various aspects of the law of bad faith:

---

175 *Ibid* at para 6. Suspicion, intolerance, and hatred of "the other" is common; modern philosophers have focused on this: see, for example, Julia Kristeva, *Nations without Nationalism* (New York: Columbia University Press, 1993); Jean-Luc Nancy, *The Inoperative Community* (Minneapolis: University of Minnesota Press, 1991). Petitions have long been criticized by the courts as indicating little, at least to them. Thus in *Terry v Municipality of Haldimand* (1857), 15 UCQB 380 at 384, Robinson CJ said, "We could not properly, perhaps, give much weight to the circumstance of so many persons having petitioned the municipality not to license the applicant . . . because we cannot appreciate the influence which such a petition ought to have so well as the Council could, to whom the petitioners are known. We only know, generally, that it is no difficult thing to get up a petition on either side of almost any question."

176 *HG Winton*, above note 5 at para 20.

177 *Ibid* at para 21.

178 2011 ONSC 5123 [*Payne*].

At this juncture it would be useful to enumerate some of the principles surrounding the issue of good versus bad faith, which is the central objection of the applicants:

i. Pursuant to s. 272 of the *Municipal Act*, when a by-law is passed in good faith a court is prohibited from quashing it on the ground of unreasonableness provided that the council act in good faith. However, the unreasonableness of the by-law may be considered in evidence in an attempt to establish a lack of good faith when it was passed . . . .
ii. A municipal council is entitled to considerable deference, absent clear evidence that it was acting in excess of its powers . . . .
iii. To re-cap the deference test, courts must respect the mandate of elected municipal bodies and exercise caution to avoid substituting their views regarding what is best for the citizens who are governed by those municipal councils. Unless there is clear evidence that a municipality was acting in excess of its powers, the courts should not interfere.
iv. [S]o long as the measures chosen are not arbitrary and are rationally connected to a legitimate municipal objective the court is precluded from second-guessing a city council on what regulatory measures are in the public interest of that city.
v. Councils can be proactive and are therefore not limited to react only in response to complaints from constituents . . . . Furthermore, for a by-law to be set aside on the basis of bad faith, it must be proven that a majority of the council members acted in bad faith, which is a very onerous test . . . .[179]
vi. Where a municipal council is engaged in policy making as opposed to acting in an adjudicative function, a less strict standard of fairness is required.
vii. The onus of establishing bad faith rests on the person attacking the by-law . . . .

---

179 It is not always the case that a majority of the councillors must be found to have acted in bad faith. See, for example, *McLaren v Castlegar (City)*, 2011 BCCA 134, where it was the comments of the mayor that led to an examination of bias. See also *St-Cyprien-de-Napierville (Municipalité de la paroisse de) c 9110-8274 Québec inc*, 2011 QCCA 2048 [*St-Cyprien-de-Napierville*], where the focus was on two of the councillors. To the same effect is *Stewart v Lac Ste Anne (County) Subdivision and Development Appeal Board*, 2006 ABCA 264, where the bias of one member of the board was sufficient to set aside the decision. In *Kollen v Vancouver (City)*, 2007 BCCA 336, improper considerations were articulated by one of eight councillors, and though the decision is not entirely clear on the point, the court appears to consider this sufficient to set aside the decision under attack.

> viii. A municipal council's power must be exercised on a *bona fide* basis and a by-law may be quashed if, when it was passed, the council was not using its power in good faith and in the public interest. This fact is a matter to be determined by the judgement of the municipal council. Furthermore, it is not a valid objection to a by-law to say that it operates to the special benefit of some private individual if at the same time it is in the public interest.
>
> ix. Bad faith by a municipality connotes a lack of candour, frankness and impartiality and that includes the notion of arbitrary or unfair conduct . . . .
>
> x. Due consideration must always be given to the principle that a by-law is presumed to be valid and anyone attacking it bears the burden of proving the contrary. The notion of bad faith is not to suggest any wrongdoing or personal advantage on the part of members of council but rather, in the factual context of the case, it must be established that the municipal council acted unreasonably and arbitrarily without the degree of fairness, openness and impartiality required of a municipal government. The issues of bad faith and discrimination are questions which must be determined on the totality of the facts and the circumstances of each case . . . .
>
> xi. Where the *bona fide* intent that is necessary for council's decision is absent and the by-law in question is passed not for a city concern but rather, as a political measure intended to appease certain payers, it will be quashed . . . .[180]

In *Northland Material Holding Inc v Parkland (County)*,[181] a decision not to allow expansion of a private landfill was challenged as having been made in bad faith. *Northland* illustrates how the categories of challenge to decisions may overlap. Thus, although the central point urged on the court was of bad faith, the decision speaks of "illegal or improper purpose" and "inappropriate considerations." The court commented on standard of review:

> The second basis for Northland's challenge to the legality of the Council's resolution is that the Council acted in bad faith—for the purpose of harming Northland or to benefit Cholla—or acted for an improper purpose or took into account inappropriate considerations.

---

180 *Payne*, above note 178 at para 12. *Payne* also suggests that a majority of councillors citing irrelevant considerations might not be necessary for a decision to be set aside.

181 2012 ABQB 407 [*Northland*].

> In essence, Northland alleges that the Council's dealings with Cholla tainted its subsequent decision relating to Northland. Northland does not allege any benefit to any particular council member who voted in favour of the denial.
>
> Our law presumes the resolutions of municipal councils to be valid in the sense that it is presumed that a council does not intend to exceed its jurisdiction. Therefore, if a council's actions are reasonably capable of being construed as coming within jurisdiction, they are so construed. Nevertheless, if a court can conclude that the real purpose of a Council's action was a purpose unrelated to its zoning jurisdiction, then the court can declare that the Council's action is not within its jurisdiction . . . .
>
> The paradigmatic example of improper purpose is the *Roncarelli* situation where the admitted power to cancel a permit under alcohol regulation legislation was in fact used for a purpose unrelated to the legislation, which in that case was the cutting off of revenues so as to prevent Jehovah Witness owners of a liquor licence from posting bail for members of the religious group who had been charged with distribution of literature in defiance of a municipal by-law . . . .
>
> A *Roncarelli*-type situation is dealt with on a basis of correctness: no matter how justified, how reasonable, a tribunal thought its action was, where the action is taken for a purpose unrelated to the empowering statute, the action is wrong and judicial review is granted.
>
> However, unless an illegal or improper purpose is the only possible explanation for the decision of a municipal council, the council's decision must be assessed on the basis of reasonableness.
>
> Here, the material before the court establishes that there are other possible reasons for the council's decision.[182]

Bad faith was alleged in *Enterprises Sibeca Inc v Frelighsburg (Municipality)*.[183] Lands owned by the company were zoned in a restrictive way; the company proposed development that had accorded with the prior zoning, the municipality had at one point passed a resolution favouring the development in principle, and the company had obtained building permits though they had expired. The Court rejected the allegation of bad faith, noting that there is a broad discretion to change zoning, including doing so in a way that reduces the market value of land. The purpose of the new by-law was valid: "Although there is specific legislation dealing with environmental conservation,

---

182 *Ibid* at paras 61–63, 65, and 67–68.
183 2004 SCC 61.

protecting the natural environment within a municipality's jurisdiction cannot be regarded as an improper goal for a municipal council."[184] Likewise in *Friends of Lansdowne Inc v Ottawa (City)*,[185] the allegation of bad faith was not accepted. The court said there is a heavy burden to discharge to lead to such a finding. It was argued not that there was any personal advantage to the municipal councillors, but that in entering into a commercial public-private arrangement to develop a sports stadium for mixed-uses, there had been excessive favouring of one private interest, a failure in documentation to distinguish between private and public interests, or a failure to explore the pros and cons in such a way as to make the issues clear to council and to the public.

Grosvenor v East Luther Grand Valley (Township)[186] is a current example of municipal bad faith. The township had acquired an abandoned railway right-of-way and then used it as a multi-purpose trailway. Under the *Line Fences Act*,[187] it would have been obliged to repair and maintain fences around the trail, but the Act allowed an exception for a designated highway. The township designated the trail as a highway. The court found that such designation, for the purpose of saving an expenditure, was collateral to the power to designate land as a highway and amounted to bad faith. The principle of generous deference does not preclude setting aside a decision for bad faith.[188] Blair JA said, "In my view, the obligation to act in good faith continues to be an essential characteristic of the valid exercise of by-law enacting authority of municipal councils."[189] To a similar effect is *Pedwell v Pelham (Town)*,[190] where the municipality took various steps aggressively to resist issuance of building permits on one property, including increasing the required minimum size of lots. In *St-Cyprien-de-Napierville*,[191] the court was prepared to find bad faith when it examined the history of the municipality's relations with an agricultural operation, and included in its factors that the council included newly elected members who had campaigned against the landowner's proposal. This tends not to accord

---

184 *Ibid* at para 38.
185 2012 ONCA 273.
186 2007 ONCA 55 [*Grosvenor*].
187 RSO 1990, c L.17.
188 *Grosvenor*, above note 186 at para 36.
189 *Ibid* at para 37.
190 (2003), 37 MPLR (3d) 161 (Ont CA).
191 Above note 179.

with the views of the Supreme Court of Canada on the nature of bias at the municipal level of government.[192]

192 See *Old St Boniface Residents Association Inc v Winnipeg (City)*, [1990] 3 SCR 1170. For a case similar to *St-Cyprien-de-Napierville*, see *Schlenker v Torgrimson*, 2012 BCSC 41.

CHAPTER 10

ECONOMIC ASPECTS

A. PRELIMINARY[1]

The marketplace value of land is directly tied to what may legally be done with the land.[2] This is basic, though it often plays out in pointed disputes over expectations. The underlying fact is that land is a commodity in limited supply. Especially where humans have gathered in concentrations of population, the marketplace mechanism of demand interacts with the fact of limited supply so as to affect price. In places of relatively high density, one way, although not the only option available, to deal with the limited supply of land is to build upwards—in effect creating more "land equivalent." This introduces a measure of elasticity to the problem. But for the most part, inelasticity is the core fact. As said in the 1973 *Ralph Nader's Study Group Report on Land Use in California*, "Land is a unique resource. Its supply is limited. Once land has been developed, reconversion to agricultural use is costly; once a large lake has been polluted, it may remain dead for decades; once a[n] . . . airport has been constructed, it cannot be moved."[3]

---

1 A standard text on the economic aspects of law is Richard Posner, *Economic Analysis of Law*, 8th ed (New York: Aspen, 2011). There is no separate section on land use, but there is on "Property," including expropriation and nuisance.

2 Location, meaning relation to surrounding property, and suitability, meaning inherent physical characteristics, are also factors that will determine land value.

3 Robert C Fellmeth, *Politics of Land: Ralph Nader's Study Group Report on Land Use in California* (New York: Grossman, 1973) at xv.

From an economics perspective, facts such as the limited supply of land, competing demands for the use of land, and the drawbacks of traditional common law remedies such as nuisance, all lend themselves to support for effective land-use planning. UK Professor Malcolm Grant says, "The primary rationale for any land-use planning control is the perceived failure of the market to achieve socially acceptable land allocation and development."[4] At the same time, public controls may themselves introduce economic changes, such as losses or windfall gains, raising questions as to when either compensation ought to be paid to owners or taxes ought to be imposed. The Building Industry and Land Development Association, representing land developers, has tied regulation to diminished housing affordability in the Toronto area:

> The Greater Toronto Area housing market is dynamic and complicated, and while many factors contribute to increasing prices, one pivotal way to improve affordability is for governments to recognize the effect of their policies on the prices paid by consumers. These policies have a huge bearing on home prices. In the Greater Toronto Area (GTA), key contributors to the affordability challenge include land-use and land-supply rules, numerous fees and taxes charged at various levels of government, outdated municipal zoning by-laws and approval processes, and fiscal and municipal funding policies.[5]

Additional factors certainly have impact on affordability, but this focus on the interaction of government policy with private initiatives is important.

"The market" is often discussed as the central mechanism of rationality appropriate to many policy decisions by those convinced of its efficacy. It is certainly the case that a great deal of the logic of the law is

---

4 Malcolm Grant, *Urban Planning Law* (London: Sweet & Maxwell, 1982) at 16.

5 Bryan Tuckey et al, "What Will It Take to Rein In Toronto and Vancouver Housing Prices?" *The Globe and Mail Report on Business* (19 December 2015) B7. For an elaboration of this critical view of government intervention in the market, see Kenneth P Green et al, *The Impact of Land-use Regulation on Housing Supply in Canada* (Vancouver: British Columbia Fraser Institute, 2016), online: www.fraserinstitute.org/sites/default/files/impact-of-land-use-regulation-on-housing-supply-in-canada.pdf. There is an active debate among policy advocates as to the factors relevant to housing affordability, and the role of land use regulation as one of those factors: see Jennifer Keesmaat & Paul Smetanin, "'Affordable' Housing Goes Far Beyond Prices and Interest Rates" *The Globe and Mail* (10 June 2016) A11; Frank Clayton, "To Support Affordable Housing, Look at Toronto's Land-Use Planning Regime" *The Globe and Mail* (22 June 2016) B4; Mark Milke, "Some Housing Factors Are Beyond Control. Our Land Supply Is Not" *The Globe and Mail* (29 June 2016) B6.

economics. Works such as *The Transformation of American Law*[6] detail how legal subjects such as tort evolved as the nature of the economy evolved. Richard Posner, who writes extensively about law and economics,[7] emphasizes the market's virtue of efficiency, but it is, as Professor Grant suggests, market failures (inefficiencies and undesirable results) that have moved policy-makers to adopt the regulatory systems we have.

The price of land is a very basic way in which planning regimes are clearly seen to take on an economic aspect. Other aspects of the economic dimension of land-use regulation are examined in this chapter.

B. GENERAL OBSERVATIONS

The economic subtext of planning is important. Some aspects, such as the value of land being closely tied to what it is permitted to be used for, are quite clear.[8] Expropriation, serious use restrictions, or actions amounting to confiscation (see Ontario Municipal Board Nepean Rules) are ways in which land value may be affected by some level of government exercising its regulatory powers. Others, such as the importance of taxation regimes, are less obvious. But planning always has an economic dimension. Regulatory decisions affect the supply and demand dynamic: if major projects are directed to a central business district (CBD), or if only so much land is designated for residential or for commercial uses, or if greenbelts are established—all of these and other such public policy decisions will affect permitted uses and thus the marketplace. Planning will, however, strive to produce a mix of uses that, taken together, can support themselves as a community. This is true at the national and provincial levels. For municipalities, it is reflected in the purpose sections of planning statutes. Thus, in Alberta's *Municipal Government Act*, Part 17 on "Planning and Development," the purpose is stated as being to provide the means for plans to be developed "to achieve the orderly, economical and beneficial

---

6 Morton J Horwitz, *The Transformation of American Law, 1780–1860* (Cambridge, MA: Harvard University Press, 1977); *The Transformation of American Law, 1870–1960* (New York: Oxford University Press, 1992).

7 See, for example, Posner, *Economic Analysis of Law*, above note 1.

8 Restrictions on land use may combine with other forms of regulation, such as in agriculture, subsidies, or quota systems, to drive up land values beyond what only one factor would produce. See C Ford Runge et al, "Public Sector Contributions to Private Land Value: Looking at the Ledger" in Charles Geisler & Gail Daneker, eds, *Property and Values* (Washington, DC: Island Press, 2000) 41.

development" of land.[9] The statutes will not usually offer this rationale as the exclusive purpose. Alberta also lists improving "the quality of the physical environment." So what is intended as the particulars of an economic agenda is left to local governments to choose, within a context set by the province? It could be growth or it could be steady-state; it could take the form of seeking denser residential developments, or commercial/industrial uses, or low-density high-price housing, depending on the municipality's analysis of its particular circumstances and its vision for the future.[10] Official plans (OPs) will often incorporate "economic development" policies and strategies.

It is not always possible to plan for economic success. The basics (that urbanized areas offer advantages of specialization, vibrancy, innovation, and efficiency) are widely recognized, but success will also depend on factors that cannot readily be planned for (for example, the success of other places, dislocating changes in technology, wars, and environmental problems).[11] Nor are urban areas ultimately functionally separate from the rest of a province.

Taxation regimes are important because they can influence the type of construction that is undertaken or its location. Thus, federal *Income Tax Act* provisions on capital cost allowance (depreciation) can influence developers to choose to build apartment buildings or commercial buildings rather than single-family homes.[12] It is not going to be the only factor, but it will be relevant. Provincial *Assessment Acts* or equivalent often provide for differential rates of property taxation for

---

9 RSA 2000, c M-26, s 617.

10 Some economists argue that home ownership can be counter-productive for a national economy. Owning, rather than renting, can lead to a desire to stay put and thus an unwillingness to relocate, or to longer commuting times, creating costs for families as well as firms. Areas with high rates of home ownership may have high rates of resistance to new business development: having a backyard leads to NIMBY activism. See David G Blanchflower & Andrew J Oswald, "Does High Home-Ownership Impair the Labor Market?" Working Paper # 19079 (Cambridge, MA: National Bureau of Economic Research, 2013), online: www.nber.org/papers/w19079.

11 See, for example, Jane Jacobs, *The Economy of Cities* (New York: Random House, 1969); Yeong-Hyun Kim & John R Short, *Cities and Economies* (London: Routledge, 2008).

12 Douglas Clark, "Urban Renewal and Municipal Taxation" (1962) 10 *Canadian Tax Journal* 387 at 388 says: "[I]n the United States it is argued that tax law favours slum owners because of capital gains and depreciation features. These features are different from what we have in Canada and there is no reason to think that income tax has a significant bearing on urban decay in this country."

agricultural or forest lands, or for outright exemptions.[13] Municipalities may tax certain uses or locations at different rates, or may impose development charges.[14] It may even be that individuals or businesses will choose to locate so as to minimize their property tax, a factor that can lead to sprawl. As noted decades ago by Wallace Oates, choice does not enter into federal taxes the same way:

> Since all persons in the nation consume whatever units of output of the national public good the central government provides, there is obviously no range of choice for the individual consumer . . . . At the local level, in contrast, the individual has some choice among levels of consumption; he selects a community of residence that provides the public good at a level well suited to his preferences in return for which he pays local taxes.[15]

This is quite a naïve view of both how people or businesses can arrange their affairs with respect to federal tax, and of what induces or forces them to move, but the core point has some validity. Norman Williams Jr, one of the leading American planning authorities says,

> [W]e don't have one system of land use control; we have three, and they tend to work against each other. To put it briefly, the official system—zoning, subdivision control, urban renewal, and so forth—is probably the least important of the three. A more important system of public action affecting land use involves the impact of public action in planning and building public works; in particular, the location of sewers and of highway interchanges, which will clearly dominate land use decisions in most situations. Even more obvious is the impact of

---

13 In some communities, the extent of mandated property tax exemptions is significant; see Jeffrey Patterson, *An Examination of Canadian Property Tax Exemptions* (Toronto: ICURR Publications, 1999).

14 For constitutional reasons, property owned by the federal government is exempt from municipal taxation. Although not liable to local taxation, the federal government has adopted a policy that obliges it to pay local taxes under the *Payments in Lieu of Taxes Act*, RSC 1985, c M-13. Some interesting jurisprudence has recently resulted from this statute; see *Montréal (City) v Montreal Port Authority*, 2010 SCC 14; *Toronto (City) v Toronto Port Authority*, 2010 FC 687; *Halifax (Regional Municipality) v Canada (Minister of Public Works & Government Services*, 2010 FCA 196. In addition, municipalities must carefully distinguish between taxes, where they may impose only direct taxes, and fees or charges for which clear statutory authority is required and which may not be in their essence taxes; see A Neil Craik, "Case Comment: *Ontario Private Campground Association v Harvey (Township)*" (1997) 39 *Municipal and Property Law Reports* (2d) 220.

15 Wallace E Oates, *Fiscal Federalism* (New York: Harcourt Brace Jovanovich, 1972) at 127.

> local real property taxation on land use decisions. The tax system is the most important land use control we have.[16]

It is not necessary to agree completely with Williams to see that his analysis does have some merit.

Williams's point about the location of infrastructure is probably best illustrated by the well-known example of Houston, Texas, a major city that has no zoning. Development is directed through advice, private restrictive covenants, and by the placement of hard infrastructure.[17]

Whether pure economic analysis should dictate planning decisions is quite doubtful and is not often advocated, but is a potent factor. A study for the Ontario Economic Council said,

> Although we are not so naïve as to believe that economic evaluations either are or should be the only input to the political process by which policy decisions are made, we strongly believe that, for any proposal which would affect the allocation of scarce resources or the distribution of income and wealth, an explicit assessment of economic costs and benefits and their distributions is an indispensable input to the intelligent formulation of public policy.[18]

As an unfortunate example of this type of narrow approach, a recent economics study of the interaction of land-use regulation and housing supply suggested that such measures as approval timelines and the prevalence of rezoning "restricts the housing supply, encouraging the growth of prices and distorting local economies."[19] Approval timelines should be seen as accommodating public input and allowing for thoughtful planning; as the particular study admits, "we make no attempt to measure regulation's benefits . . . . [L]and use regulations are intended to correct externalities, manage infrastructure, and generally serve community interests."[20]

---

16 Norman Williams Jr, "The Future of Land Use Controls" in Robert W Burchell & David Listokin, eds, *Future Land Use*, Centre for Urban Policy Research, Rutgers, (New Brunswick, NJ: Center for Urban Policy Research at Rutgers The State University, 1975) 29. For similar points, see David M Nowlan, "Local Taxation as an Instrument of Policy" in Frances Fisken, ed, *The Changing Canadian Metropolis* (Toronto: Canadian Urban Institute, 1994) 799.

17 See the city's website, "Development Regulations," online: www.houstontx.gov/planning/DevelopRegs: "The city of Houston does not have zoning but development is governed by codes that address how property can be subdivided. The City codes do not address land use." See also Robert L Knight, "The Impact of Rail Transit on Land Use" (1980) 9 *Transportation* 3.

18 Mark W Frankena & David T Scheffman, *Economic Analysis of Provincial Land Use Policies in Ontario* (Toronto: Ontario Economic Council, 1980).

19 Green et al, above note 5 at i.

20 *Ibid* at 2.

Although general municipal politics is not our focus, there is a point relevant to land use inherent in the overall fiscal position of municipalities that affects their ability to make independent land-use decisions, especially on the construction of hard infrastructure. This is the mismatch between their revenue-generating capacity and their overall responsibilities. Municipal capacity to raise revenue is tied primarily to the property tax.[21] It, along with various special fees plus grants from the senior levels of government, supports all local activities.[22] There is no municipal income tax or sales tax. This dates to the 1941 Wartime Tax Rental Agreements.[23] Despite systems of equalization and adjustments of responsibilities between provincial and municipal levels of government,[24] the result still is the somewhat impaired fiscal position of local government, thus providing another point of entry for the senior levels of government into local decision-making.

Finally, the important point of private gains and losses through government regulation of land use has engendered extensive debate over issues of adjustments: compensation payable in the case of losses or taxes in the case of windfall gains. In Canada there is no constitutional guarantee of compensation for the taking of property as there is in the United States, where the Fifth Amendment applies.[25] Still, there is a universal adoption of public policy to pay compensation when property is taken. In its clearest form, this requires actual transfer of ownership. Issues arise when property is taken in the sense of being so seriously impaired in its practical use that it is tantamount to expropriation. In *City of Toronto v Presswood Brothers*,[26] Robertson CJO said,

---

21 The property tax is inherently problematic. For an analysis, see Roy Bahl et al, eds, *Challenging the Conventional Wisdom on the Property Tax* (Cambridge, MA: Lincoln Institute of Land Policy, 2010). Property taxes represent about 9 percent of overall government tax revenues, though as a percentage of expenditures of individuals, the rate varies widely from about 2.8 percent for higher-income earners to about 7 percent for those with lower incomes; see Neil Brooks, "The Logic, Policy and Politics of Tax Law" in Tim Edgar & Daniel Sandler, eds, *Materials on Canadian Income Tax*, 13th ed (Scarborough, ON: Thomson Carswell, 2005) 1 at 16 and 19.

22 For statistics on municipal sources of revenue, see Federation of Canadian Municipalities generally, and specifically, Don Lidstone, "Municipal Revenue: Partnerships and New Resources" (2013), online: www.fcm.ca/Documents/presentations/2013/AGM2013/Municipal_Revenue-Partnerships_and_New_Resources.pdf.

23 See Sheldon Silver, "The Feasibility of a Municipal Income Tax in Canada" (1968) 16 *Canadian Tax Journal* 398.

24 See, for example, Ontario, Ministry of Municipal Affairs and Housing, *Who Does What: Toward Implementation* (Toronto: Queen's Printer, 1997). The process is also known as "disentanglement" or "service exchange."

25 US Const amend V: "nor shall private property be taken for public use, without just compensation."

26 [1944] 1 DLR 569 (Ont CA).

in an oft-cited observation: "It is of the very essence of the exercise of the power to regulate and control the location, erection and use of buildings for designated purposes, and to prohibit the erection or use of buildings for all or any of these purposes within defined areas, that there will be interference with vested rights."[27]

Some statutes provide for compensation in these circumstances; many others do not or leave the matter ambiguous. The crucial question is whether, as a matter of policy, compensation ought to be payable. It is not, for municipal land-use regulation. Some authors suggest that there ought to be a system of compensation for downzoning, extending to losses incurred as a result of freezes during which plans are developed.[28] It is suggested by Krivel that control legislation achieves the same result as expropriation:

> the government has control over the use of the land. The only difference is that those whose lands are affected . . . retain ownership. It does not matter whether the individual retains ownership or not; because of the negative effects experienced by the owner, his land becomes virtually useless. Ownership is meaningless, and because it is meaningless there is little difference between the legislation and expropriation.[29]

As a companion to compensation, Krivel also suggests that lot levies ought to be payable "as a condition of zoning for development . . . for unspecified municipal services in addition to amounts for specified services."[30] Debate usually focuses on how specific the authorizing statute must be, as well as the extent of how reasonably related to the development the charges must be.[31] The United Kingdom has struggled with various forms of betterment charges; Malcolm Grant offers a good account of the changes made over time.[32] What has emerged in Canada is a system in which there is deemed to be no injurious affection due to local government planning, and levies for development are imposed, though there are no special taxes for increase in land value achieved through community decision-making. Michael Trebilcock, professor of law at the University of Toronto and specialist in the economic aspects

27 *Ibid* at 585.

28 Elaine Krivel, "Compensation for Downzoning; Levies for Upzoning" (1977) 25 *Chitty's Law Journal* 20. See also K Filip Palda, *Home on the Urban Range* (Vancouver: Fraser Institute, 1998).

29 Krivel, above note 28 at 23.

30 *Ibid* at 24.

31 See, for example, AJ Hudec,"Municipal Exactions and the Subdivision Approval Process" (1980) 38 *University of Toronto Faculty of Law Review* 106.

32 Grant, above note 4 at 18–35 and 501.

of law, has questioned the validity of positions that offer simple solutions. He prefers "politically optimal transition policies"[33] to an "overemphasis on purportedly universal prescriptions," including turning to the courts to claim a "regulatory taking." "Transition" is the challenge of moving from the status quo to a better alternative, a process that will "reallocate social benefits and costs in different ways."[34] He notes the availability of other "mitigation strategies such as grandfathering, exceptions, and delayed or phased implementation,"[35] though the question remains "whether and when to compensate regulatory losers or otherwise mitigate their losses."[36]

C. IMPROPER PURPOSES

In the 1937 case *Miller v Charleswood (Rural Municipality)*,[37] the council amended a by-law that prohibited fur farms so as to permit Percy James "who, in poor circumstances, desired to keep a fur farm there as a means of a livelihood." The original by-law covered an area of some 700 acres and was adopted in 1933. The amendment would have removed an area of 10 acres. James had the support of most of his neighbours. The amendment was set aside by the court:

> the by-law was passed in private and not in public interest . . . . The movement to amend the Fur by-law was initiated by Percy James . . . . Fur farming entails something of a nuisance in that it engenders very disagreeable odours . . . . Evidence of this fact was undisputed. The [original] "Fur by-law" was undoubtedly passed in the public interest to protect the residents of the restricted area and the public generally from these odours. The amendment is to permit fur farming in the very heart of a small community in the area so restricted. There can be no public need of such a change. The purpose of the amending by-law is chiefly to benefit Mr. James . . . . It seems beyond question then that the purpose of this by-law was to benefit Mr. James directly, and to benefit the municipality only indirectly. Such a by-law is invalid.[38]

33 Michael J Trebilcock, *Dealing with Losers* (New York: Oxford University Press, 2014) at 30.

34 *Ibid* at 1–2.

35 *Ibid* at 29.

36 *Ibid.*

37 [1937] 3 WWR 686 (Man KB) [*Miller*].

38 *Ibid* at paras 9–11.

NOTES

1) A modern court, even if tending toward the same result, would use a framework of analysis that would consider whether the by-law was *ultra vires* or unreasonable, though the concept of improper purpose survives. Use of the "improper purpose" or "absence of public purpose" analysis is fraught with difficulty. For example, in *Morton v Loon Lake No 561 (Rural Municipality)*,[39] land adjacent to a lake was rezoned from agricultural to recreational to allow the construction of a set of cottages. The adjacent owners of a cattle operation objected and challenged the rezoning as being for the specific economic benefit of the one owner. Because the municipality was able to show extended, careful consideration of their OP policies, including what they saw as being in the best interests of the municipality overall, the court was prepared to show deference to the council's decision.
2) The 1930s were Depression-era years. The court noted that council knew that the alternative for the James family was relying on the municipality for financial support. Avoiding public support of the James family appears to be the indirect public benefit the court refers to.
3) *Miller* is an instance of spot rezoning. If *Miller* is correct, it calls into question a great deal of municipal by-law making, which not infrequently entails special benefits. In 1959, in *Scarborough (Township) v Bondi*,[40] the Supreme Court of Canada, like the judge in *Miller*, offered as its rationale respect for general neighbourhood benefits, although it approved use of spot zoning in that case.
4) The court is not dealing with a common law nuisance action, which would still be available if James did go on to create objectionable odour. The court appears to be engaged in a planning exercise, weighing what is the appropriate way to zone the municipality. What the court appears to do is substitute its opinion about appropriate land use for that of the local council.
5) American jurisprudence has taken a dim view of spot zoning. Where there has been no real change in the neighbourhood since the original zoning ordinance, or something to distinguish the rezoned tract, then "the zoning change on its face was arbitrary, capricious and unreasonable, and the burden was on the city authorities to justify the change."[41] In *Fritts v City of Ashland*, the owners of a

39 2011 SKQB 264.
40 [1959] SCR 444.
41 *Fritts v City of Ashland*, 348 SW2d 712 (Ky Ct App 1961) [*Fritts*].

garment factory that had outgrown its locale wanted to build a new factory in a residential (R-2) zone. The company proposed to leave the city unless the tract was rezoned. As reasons, the city offered employment as a general welfare benefit. The court said,

> The argument [on employment] points up a common fallacy that seems to exist in the minds of zoning agencies. It is that the particular use that a particular owner says he intends to make of a particular tract of land is a controlling factor . . . . [T]he ordinance did not rezone the tract for use by the [company] but for any appropriate light industry use. There was no guarantee that [the company] would not change their minds, resulting in the tract being occupied by some light industry that would not have the appealing features of the proposed garment factory . . . . The point is that in establishing a light industry zone the only proper consideration is whether in the light of a comprehensive, coordinated zoning plan the particular area should be set aside for general light industry uses.[42]

6) In the UK case of *Westminster City Council v Great Portland Estates plc*,[43] "the human factor" was seen as sometimes—though only in exceptional circumstances—to be relevant to land-use planning decisions. See also *Wrexham County Borough Council v Berry; South Bucks District Council v Porter (No 2); Chichester District Council v Searle*,[44] where a Romany gypsy had purchased land in a green belt area and lived there contrary to planning control rules; an inspector had determined that she was in poor health but had a rooted fear of being moved, and allowed her to remain; the court supported the decision.

Apart from legislating for private benefit, there is also the question of whether it is proper to take into account the negative effect on land value of surrounding properties as part of a planning decision. On the face of it, this seems likely to be seen as a relevant factor. However, in a recent Ontario Municipal Board (OMB) case on whether to approve condominiums, the board, in brief reasons, said, "Ms. Guthrie has raised objections that may be distilled as being based on concern about the impact on land values and her preference for owner occupants rather than tenants. The Board finds that these are not valid land use planning grounds."[45] The personal

42 *Ibid* at 713.
43 [1985] AC 661 at 670 (HL).
44 [2003] 2 AC 558 (HL).
45 *Guthrie v Chan*, 2015 CanLII 18831 (OMB).

characteristics of prospective residents is a dubious basis for a land-use choice and may involve human rights issues, but maintenance of property values has often been assumed to be a valid planning matter, though probably not in itself. Thus in IM Rogers text, *Canadian Law of Planning and Zoning*, it is said that "The principal purpose of zoning regulations . . . is to preserve property values by prohibiting uses which are believed to be deleterious to neighbourhoods mainly residential in character. People living in an area of single family homes naturally want the same type of homes in the district."[46] The passage from Rogers is cited in *Service Corp International (Canada) Inc v Burnaby (City)*.[47]

The other side of zoning for private benefit is zoning for the fiscal benefit of the municipality. Attacks on this basis are rare. But some have been successful. In *Nordale Community Club v Prince Albert (City)*,[48] a zoning decision was set aside when it was found to have been made for an irrelevant purpose, increasing municipal tax revenues. An American parallel, with a particularly strong judicial statement, is the 1979 case of *Concerned Citizens for McHenry, Inc v City of McHenry*.[49] An application to set aside a rezoning was successful on the basis that the ordinance was unreasonable and unrelated to public health, welfare, or safety. The court said,

> the primary justification for the rezoning of this property is the anticipation of an increase of the tax base of the community. We find that such a justification is totally illusory and totally violative of all the basic principles of zoning. If the profit motive were the sole reason that zoning authorities varied their classifications, then any use whatsoever would be appropriate next to any other use so long as the maximum amount of taxes could be generated for the community's use. This is not the law. We emphatically state that an increase in the tax base is not sufficient of itself to support rezoning. In short,

---

46 Ian MacFee Rogers, *Canadian Law of Planning and Zoning* (Toronto: Carswell, 1973) at s 5.13. This passage does not seem to have been replicated in the second edition of the text, Ian MacFee Rogers & Alison Scott Butler (Toronto: Carswell, 2005) (loose-leaf release 2015/8), where the emphasis shifted to a balancing of private and public interests, for example, in the statement in s 4.2 "[z]oning is the deprivation for the public good of certain uses by owners of property to which the property may otherwise be put. Underlying planning statutes is the principle that the interest of landowners in securing the maximum value of their land must be controlled by the community."

47 (1999), 9 MPLR (3d) 242 (BCSC), rev'd in part 2001 BCCA 708.

48 2000 SKQB 142 [*Nordale*].

49 76 Ill App3d 798 (1979).

> we are convinced that this is, in fact, a case of "spot zoning." The rezoning ordinance passed by the McHenry council was arbitrary and capricious.[50]

In *Nordale*, at issue was the validity of two linked proposed by-laws, one to amend the Policy Plan (OP) and the other to change zoning for a parcel from "Restricted Residential" to "Highway Commercial." The property in question was located in a semi-rural part of the city, where the OP policies called for small residential holdings. On the particular street, several lots were zoned "Neighbourhood Commercial" (C5) for a gas bar; the owner purchased further adjacent lots, which had been rezoned from "Residential" to "Neighbourhood Commercial" to allow an auto sales business. The owner then applied for further lots to be rezoned so as to establish an auto service shop. The city planning staff opposed the application, seeing it as beyond the purpose of neighbourhood commercial uses; staff said, "any amendment to the Policy Plan should either represent a response to changing land use needs or is necessary to permit development that is expected to benefit the community as a whole." Nonetheless, city council directed that a plan and zoning changes be prepared. Planning staff suggested that all of the area's C5 lots be rezoned "Highway Commercial" (C4). After a public hearing, the proposal was defeated. The owner then again requested rezoning to C5. Staff again opposed the proposal. City council rezoned some property to C4, but consideration of the plan amendment and rezoning to C5 was held in abeyance pending court review. The Nordale Community Club, a residents' group, pointed out that no planning studies had been done in support of the plan and zoning change, cited conflicts with other parts of the OP, and pointed to likely nuisance effects from an auto repair establishment. The city said that it had been a dozen years since the last comprehensive amendment of the OP and conditions had evolved, that there was a need for more commercial zoning, and that the provincial statute did not require planning studies prior to amending the OP. The court noted that,

> The only justification offered by the respondent City for proceeding in the manner it proposes is that it will add one taxpayer to the tax rolls, if one wishes to assume [the owner] would not, nevertheless, open the same business elsewhere in the City if permission for the subject location was denied. It will also result in the sale of a parcel of City owned land. However, both of these are economic considerations devoid of any planning considerations.

---

50 *Ibid* at 806.

The court then cited the Alberta Court of Appeal decision in *Chernipeski v Lacombe (Town)*,[51] which had invalidated a rezoning based upon increasing commercial tax revenue, selling municipal property, and recouping earlier development costs; the Court of Appeal said, "the reasoning [of the town council] lay within considerations that were not keyed to the planning rationale . . . the planning power must be exercised solely for planning purposes."[52] The Saskatchewan court concluded,

> There is nothing in the evidence submitted that the proposed amendment to the Policy Plan and accompanying amendment to the Zoning Bylaw was the result of any planning. All of the evidence points to the fact that the amendment to the Plan was one of form only in an attempt to comply with . . . the *Act* which prohibited a zoning change which did not comply with the Plan. [The *Act*] requires that the municipality first plan where economic development is to take place in the municipality and thereafter pursue economic development within the parameters of the Plan. The plan may be amended upon taking into account the proper planning considerations. However, to attempt to amend the plan whenever an economic opportunity arises without taking into account the planning considerations set out in s. 51, or other provisions contained in the existing Plan, is the antithesis of planning and outside the authority granted to the municipality in the *Act*.[53]

NOTES

1) Results such as those in *Miller*, *Chernipeski*, and *Nordale* will not necessarily be avoided if the statutes granting powers to the local government are clear in extending to some forms of economic development, and if there are OPs in place to bolster this. The Saskatchewan legislation allowed OPs to identify "opportunities concerning the development of land . . . and the economic effects of that development" but the court saw the focus to be appropriately on land use and the greater community rather than on responding to individual proposals.
2) This group of cases is highly challenging for any municipality. The line between what constitutes authorized exercise of the planning function and impermissible economic motivation is not always clear at all.

---

51 1998 ABCA 344 [*Chernipeski*].

52 *Ibid* at para 2.

53 *Nordale*, above note 48 at para 36.

3) There was no discussion in *Nordale* of the standard of review. Since a provincial statute was the basis of the court's judgment, the standard may well have been correctness, and not have involved any deference.
4) The extent to which the court relied on the reports of the city's planning staff is apparent in the decision. Staff pushed for comprehensive planning.
5) For a review of the American dynamic, see Alan A Altshuler, *Regulation for Revenue: The Political Economy of Land Use Exaction.*[54]
6) Other related American cases involving improper purpose have involved restrictive zoning so as to avoid the expense associated with building schools and other services and infrastructure[55] or restrictive zoning through the device of lot size as a measure to curb growth and stabilize the tax rate.[56]
7) Could a municipality exclude places of worship (or any other use which, under provincial law, is exempt from payment of property tax) on the basis that revenues that would flow from some other use of the land would be foregone? Could a limit be placed on their number?

D. DEMOLITION AND DEMOLITION CONTROLS

A normal incident of ownership is the right to demolish a building, and to do so at the owner's discretion. This common law right has, however, been modified by statute in some circumstances. As a matter of public safety, building codes require the issuance of a demolition permit, so as to allow compliance with proper procedures. A building may be ordered to be demolished as a result of a finding that it is unsafe. There are some controls on demolition if a building has been designated as a heritage structure. Some provinces have granted municipalities the right to refuse a demolition permit for residential properties as a way to preserve rental units.

The necessity to obtain a demolition permit allows for government oversight of demolition as to legality and as to safety. Safety relates to the

---

54 (Washington, DC: Brookings Institute, 1993).

55 See *Harvard Enterprises Inc v Board of Adjustment of Madison Township*, 266 A2d 588 (NJ Sup Ct 1970).

56 See *Oakwood at Madison, Inc v Township of Madison*, 283 A2d 353 (NJ Super Ct App Div 1971); 371 A2d 1192 (NJ Sup Ct 1977).

health and safety of workers on-site as well as for surrounding premises and residents through compromising the stability of adjacent land and structures. This can extend to air quality concerns, as well as control of traffic during demolition. For the most part, the controls are exercised under a *Building Code Act*, though environmental regulations often also apply. It is possible to appeal the decisions of the building officer to a court, where the matter is treated as equivalent to a hearing *de novo*.[57]

An important financial consequence may flow for an owner who allows a building to deteriorate: a municipality may order its demolition and carry out the work. There is no compensation payable to an owner for the demolition, and the cost of the demolition may be recovered as a lien on the property. A typical case of a demolition resisted by the owner is *Mitchell v Halifax (Regional Municipality)*,[58] where the owner had allowed a commercial building to fall into such a state that the municipality saw no alternative to demolition.

For designated heritage buildings, demolition (as well as alteration) may be controlled as the essential way to preserve the heritage value that led to the designation in the first place. Depending on whether the building has been given municipal or provincial heritage designation, the nature of the controls over demolition may differ. In Ontario, the OMB has determined that it has jurisdiction over the demolition of designated heritage buildings under the *Planning Act* regardless of the procedures existing under the *Heritage Act*.[59]

Because such schemes interfere with property ownership rights, the Supreme Court of Canada has emphasized that such statutes must be strictly complied with as to specified processes.[60] At the same time, there is recognition that two sets of values are bound up in such legislation: respect for private property rights and preservation of heritage buildings.[61]

Some provinces have granted municipalities control over demolition of residential buildings.[62] The mechanism is for the municipality to declare an area to be a "demolition control district." The purpose of the legislation is to prevent undue reduction of available rental units. A

57 See *Sterling Studio Lofts Inc v Toronto (City) Chief Building Official*, 2011 ONSC 143 [*Sterling Studio*].

58 2002 NSSC 84.

59 *Rams Head Development Inc v Toronto (City)* (2010), 78 MPLR (4th) 134 (OMB).

60 *St Peter's Evangelical Lutheran Church (Ottawa) v Ottawa (City)*, [1982] 2 SCR 616.

61 See, for example, *Murphy (Estate of Dexter) v Rothesay Heritage Preservation Review Board*, 2007 NBAPAB 15.

62 See, for example, Saskatchwan's *Planning and Development Act, 2007*, SS 2007, c P-13.2, s 72 and Ontario's *Planning Act*, RSO 1990, c P.13, s 33(2).

demolition permit must be issued where a building permit has been obtained to erect a new building on the site. The courts have held that extensive renovations do not amount to demolition[63] and that the statute does not apply if the building is entirely empty of tenants.[64] Toronto, in 2007, designated the whole of its municipality as an area of demolition control, a step that has been approved in litigation.[65]

E. CONVERSION OF APARTMENTS TO CONDOMINIUMS

A striking instance of the interaction of the public interest with private maximization of value is in the control of conversion of apartments to condominiums. In addition to the usual designation and registration process, some provinces have enacted provisions that allow the local municipality to review a condominium proposal. Thus, in Saskatchewan, the *Condominium Property Act* requires that an application to establish a condominium corporation must be accompanied by

> a certificate of the clerk of the local authority stating that the proposed division . . . has been approved by the local authority . . . . On an application for a certificate . . . the local authority shall direct the issue of the certificate if it is satisfied that: . . . where the application relates to the conversion of existing premises used for apartments or flats or tenements . . . the conversion will not significantly reduce the availability of rental accommodation in the area; the conversion will not create significant hardship for any or all of the tenants of the existing premises . . . .[66]

In Ontario, the conversion is controlled through section 51(24) of the *Planning Act*, which allows approving authorities (local governments) to impose conditions that must take into account Provincial Policy Statements, one of which pertains to housing, plus OP policies that may have been adopted.[67] In Toronto, the OP policies are very detailed.

---

63 *Re Trivest Developments Ltd and City of Toronto*, 1986 CanLII 2754 (Ont HCJ), aff'd 1986 CanLII 2734 (Ont CA).

64 *Federation of Metropolitan Toronto Tenants Associations v York (City)*, 1988 CanLII 4531 (Ont Div Ct).

65 *Sterling Studio*, above note 57.

66 *The Condominium Property Act, 1993*, SS 1993, c C-26.1, s 10(1)(b)(5)(e).

67 For a summary, see *Toronto (City) v R&G Realty Management Inc*, 2009 CanLII 10683 (Ont Div Ct); 2009 CanLII 42397 (Ont Div Ct).

In *Henderson v Saskatoon (City)*,[68] tenants challenged the municipal approval of such a conversion, alleging violation of the provincial statute requirement relating to significantly reducing the availability of rental accommodation in the area. The property was located in downtown Saskatoon. The city had adopted a policy for condominium conversions that allowed ongoing occupancy by existing tenants for two years from the date of the application for conversion. Materials before the council and the court explored housing issues extensively, ranging from total number of apartment units in the city and the downtown, to size of the units, to vacancy rates to rental rates, to trends in housing construction. The court declined to find that the council had been unreasonable or erroneous in its approval.

NOTES

1) *Henderson* illustrates how difficult it is to administer such statutory provisions. Housing is a complex matter.
2) The court cited city staff's analysis that conversion "would not cause a significant reduction in the availability of rental accommodation in the area, as it would constitute a reduction of 7% of the rental stock in an area where 80% of the housing stock was rental accommodation."[69] An alternative calculation would put the change at 9 percent. Is this the measure of "no significant reduction"?
3) OMB cases suggest that many municipalities have adopted a 3 percent rental vacancy rate as the indicator that there is an affordable housing supply problem.[70]
4) The underlying purpose of the statute seems to be to protect rental accommodation in the face of significant increase in numbers of condominiums. The policy must be motivated by a view that rental is likely to be more affordable for lower-income residents than would be the purchase of a condominium. In the absence of controls on construction of new condominiums or rent controls or an effective programme of construction of affordable and/or public housing, the focus was on conversions. The policy fixes owners of rental accommodation with something of an ongoing obligation to remain in that business.
5) In terms of process, if municipal permission to convert rental property to condominium use is obtained, any tenancy still needs to be terminated. This will bring in the provisions of a *Residential Ten-*

---

68 2008 SKQB 135 [*Henderson*].

69 *Ibid* at para 70.

70 See *Haight v North Bay (City)* (1987), 20 OMBR 362; *Nenkov v Waterloo (City)* (1990), 24 OMBR 492.

ancies Act. In *Bosshard v White Fox (Village)*,[71] this situation arose: a commercial property had been taken over by the municipality for non-payment of taxes and was then to be demolished due to its dilapidated state; the municipality was obliged first to terminate the existing tenancy.[72]

F. HOLDING ZONES

Tempo and sequence of development is a central planning concern. Planning extends not only to regulation of particular uses, but to delay, including extended delay, in allowing any uses apart from the most minimal. *Canadian Pacific Railway Co v Vancouver (City)*[73] is a case illustrating this; the zoning limited the railway company to use of a virtually abandoned rail line for transportation (which was not feasible) or as pathway. *CPR*, like *Hartel Holdings Co v Calgary (City)*,[74] involved no formal holding zone, just a refusal to rezone in the face of a desire by the owner to seek their economic advantage. What motivates either putting in place seriously inhibiting zoning, or a clear overlay of a "hold" on development, may vary. The municipality may contemplate the possibility of acquisition of the land as in *Hartel*. Or it may simply take the overall view of its community that leads it to conclude that no development is appropriate until some future date, perhaps to control sprawl. Associated with this is control of the need for infrastructure expenditures. Holding zones are allowed by statute in Ontario. The *Planning Act* says "[t]he council . . . may . . . by the use of the holding symbol 'H' . . . in conjunction with any use designation, specify the use to which lands, buildings or structures may be put at such time in the future as the holding symbol is removed . . . ."[75] But even in the absence of statutory authority, the Supreme Court of Canada has said that explicit holding zones are allowable. This was established in 1973 in *Soo Mill & Lumber Co v Sault Ste-Marie (City)*[76] and *Sanbay Developments Ltd v London (City)*,[77] both discussed in Chapter 2. Instances continue to arise in which litigants attempt to establish that a freeze amounts to an

---

71 2010 SKCA 121.

72 See *Residential Tenancies Act, 2006*, SS 2006, c R-22.0001, s 60(7).

73 2006 SCC 5 [*CPR*].

74 [1984] 1 SCR 337 [*Hartel*].

75 Ontario *Planning Act*, above note 62, s 36(1).

76 [1975] 2 SCR 78.

77 [1975] 1 SCR 485.

expropriation,[78] but such attempts will not succeed if there is a legitimate planning purpose. A typical holding zone might allow R-1 uses, but only on lots in existence prior to the adoption of the tempo control by-law. Owners of land, even if not themselves ready to develop, see such restrictions as serious interference with their economic circumstances or plans. In the United States, leading cases approving similar by-laws, such as *Golden v Planning Board of the Town of Ramapo*,[79] warn that improper purposes such as exclusion (associated with race and other discriminatory bases) might invalidate by-laws that appear neutral; there are also questions of possible interference with mobility rights.

G. PROTECTION OF PARTICULAR OR ESTABLISHED BUSINESSES

The Supreme Court of Canada has said that it is up to municipalities to decide whether to concentrate or disperse certain activities, including commercial activity.[80] This may be subject to limitations associated with improper motives or discrimination. It also has potential to involve difficulties over use of land-use regulatory powers for purposes of achieving limits on competition, something which may be *ultra vires* as not contemplated by the ambit of powers granted or as dealing with a federal matter.

One of the main cases involving regulation to protect established businesses is the 1976 decision of the Alberta Court of Appeal in *Actus Management Ltd v Calgary (City)*.[81] The Development Appeal Board had granted a permit to Actus to establish retail stores on land zoned C-1 (Local Commercial District). However, the board had excluded a retail food store use from the permit. It did so in response to a request from the owners of six small owner-operated stores located in the neighbourhood, and supported by a petition signed by residents. They opposed the opening of a chain store. A part of the presentation by the representative included the following, according to the minutes:

> Many people's existence rely on your decision here today. We still feel that we are sufficiently well served by the 6 grocery stores in our area. This is a prime example of big business unjust treatment to the small

---

78 See, for example, *Rodriguez Holding Corp v Vaughan (City)* (2006), 25 MPLR (4th) 100 (Ont SCJ).

79 285 NE2d 291 (NY 1972).

80 *Montréal (City) v Arcade Amusements Inc*, [1985] 1 SCR 368 [*Arcade Amusements*].

81 (1975), 62 DLR (3d) 421 (Alta SCAD) [*Actus*].

> independent grocery store. If any chain store is opened it will destroy family businesses built up over many years . . . . This is not justice to allow this . . . . We are not opposed to development on this site, just opposed to the duplication of uses. This type of thing mushrooms and monopolizes the industry.[82]

There was apparently only oral advice given to the board by staff. The main issue brought to the court was whether on the evidence before the board, the exclusion was directed to restriction of trade and limitation of commerce, and not to planning. The objecting presentation made to the board raised two issues, competition and convenience. The court commented that

> . . . the Act does not recognize the regulation of business competition as relevant to development planning, but excessive provision for particular facilities or services would, I think, be a factor that a qualified planning consultant might properly take into account in some circumstances . . . . When such is the case, a consequential effect on competition cannot affect the relevancy of the factor . . . . The power, accorded by and under the Act, to limit to designated areas any particular uses of land carries with it as an inevitable incident of its exercise some limitation on the right that would otherwise exist to set up a competitive business. The power is given to further the orderly and economic development of the community . . . and I would think that evidence could be given as to whether or not a proposed development was excessive to reasonable need and convenience. Further . . . residents in such a district have some right to enjoy and maintain their surroundings without commercial invasion in excess of their needs or convenience.[83]

The court set aside the board's decision and referred the matter back for reconsideration.

Actus may well be seen as offering a lesson in the sort of language that a court would find acceptable when planning deals with commercial matters. At the same time, it ought not to be seen as a case that determines that matters of business competition may not be thought of as aspects of planning. The Supreme Court of Canada in *Arcade Amusements*[84] made it clear that a municipality may determine that some commercial activities may be concentrated in particular areas. Indeed, that sort of decision is of the essence of land-use planning. As early as 1961, in *Glenwood Memorial Gardens Ltd v Alberta (Planning Advisory*

82 *Ibid* at para 3.
83 *Ibid* at paras 22 & 23.
84 Above note 80.

Board),[85] a challenge to a provincial Planning Advisory Board decision that denied a permit to establish a cemetery, the court upheld the board decision, which had said, "To overprovide for a particular use does not have regard to basic planning principles . . . . It is a well-established planning principle that land, whether public or private, should not be developed or diverted from its current use in advance of actual need."[86] The art is to consider the matter within legally acceptable parameters, that is, not as a matter of economic competition, which would raise constitutional law issues, but as a matter of economy of servicing (infrastructure), or providing for synergies, or traffic, or incompatibility of size of structures with other surrounding uses, or, as *Actus* suggests, as a question of over-provision of services.[87]

The OMB has not hesitated to engage with this overall issue. To some extent it has focused on the language of "need" for a particular proposal, or considered traditional land-use planning matters such as traffic impacts or the suitability of the site for a proposed development. Yet it has also examined economic impact. Thus, in *Re Etobicoke Planning Area OP Amendment D.9.22.80*,[88] the board considered a proposal for a new shopping centre in these terms:

> The planning evidence in this hearing was generally consistent, given some variation in the terminology and extent, that impact on existing established businesses is a proper planning consideration and that impact which is "harmful" or "deleterious" to the extent that it would damage the ability of existing centres to fulfil their community planning function, would constitute valid planning grounds for rejecting a proposal which would cause such impact . . . . [M]arket evidence has some relevance to shopping centre applications such as those before the board . . . . At times the extent of the evidence of market matters and the submissions made to the board by certain witnesses and counsel, seem to indicate a suggestion that the board should regulate competition. While . . . we are of the opinion that market evidence is relevant to the planning questions of need and impact, we believe it is not within the mandate of this board to regulate market competition in a free market system nor is it the function of this board to protect a would-be developer . . . from . . . foolish investments.[89]

---

85 (1961), 34 WWR 159 (Alta SCTD).

86 *Ibid* at para 2.

87 See also *Re 757258 Ontario Ltd and Town of Orangeville* (1989), 22 OMBR 385. And for a case that tends to skirt the issue, see *1739626 Ontario Ltd v Speyside East Corp*, 2010 ONSC 4713 at para 13ff.

88 (1982), 14 OMBR 129.

89 *Ibid* at 142.

Likewise, in addressing a "big-box store" proposal, the board said in *300 John St v Markham (Town)*,[90] where the existing rules did not allow for such a use,

> the Board is careful not to be cavalier about the basic structure of the commercial designation of the Town . . . . [L]arge format warehouse retail is prohibited within the [area] . . . . The intent as to why it is the case has to do with functionality as well as impacts . . . . The Board is not impervious to the fact that de-malling might be the new state of affairs that a municipality has to countenance. It is, however, unwise to accept willy-nilly a large format "big box" in the form of a home-improvement retail centre at this locale as the latter does have a planning profile far different from a collectivity of the various retail components. A home improvement "big box" is not just a sum total of a number of retail parts . . . . There is no question it possesses a critical mass, an industrial flavour and an urban design feature markedly different from that of a supermarket or an apparel store.[91]

And in *Re Orangeville OPA 39 and Zoning By-law 22-90*,[92] the problem of central business districts vis-à-vis a Walmart was addressed:

> Impact, not regional draw, is what the town and this board are ultimately concerned about. More precisely, impact that would be so deleterious or harmful to existing facilities that it would jeopardize the planned function of existing land uses and the planned commercial structure of the town. The concern is for the health of that structure and its ability to continue adequately to serve its residents. As has been stated many times by this board, our mandate is not to regulate competition but to ensure that a proposed new retail development will not cause transfers from existing facilities in such numbers that closures will result that will cause blight or threaten the level of service offered the town's residents. It is, therefore, the effect, or impact, on the existing commercial structure that must be the focus of attention.[93]

It is clear that the OMB is finding difficulty in making any rigorous distinctions in its grappling with these matters. It claims not to be able

---

90 (2002), 43 OMBR 469.
91 *Ibid* at paras 17 & 18.
92 (1995), 33 OMBR 55.
93 *Ibid* at 117; see also *Haldimand (County) Official Plan Amendment No HC-7 (Re)* (2006), 53 OMBR 503.

to regulate competition but also to be able to protect existing businesses, statements that amount to a "first-in-time, first-in-right" approach.[94]

An interesting and unusual set of circumstances led to a finding that Statements of Provincial Interest (SPIs) could be used to advance particular projects, and not be confined to preventing or prohibiting unwanted land uses or to set general goals such as preservation of agricultural land, as is more typical of SPIs. In *BM Halifax Holdings Ltd v Nova Scotia (Attorney General)*,[95] the issue was the proposed construction of a hotel/office complex that would also include a government-funded convention centre. The developer found that complying with all existing municipal permitting rules would negatively impact the proposed construction schedule. The overall complex was in compliance with the zoning; however, other requirements would take time to meet, and construction was underway. The provincial government declared the centre to be a matter of provincial interest and then, on that basis, declared it to be an Interim Planning Area,[96] thus allowing the minister to rezone the land and do so in a way so as to avoid the need for permitting. All of this was challenged by another owner of commercial property as *ultra vires*, but without success.

H. CONFLICTS OF INTEREST WHEN GOVERNMENTS SELL LAND FOR DEVELOPMENT

Conflict of interest issues are usually addressed through such provisions as a *Municipal Conflict of Interest Act*,[97] but these statutes are focused on the interests of individual councillors. The issue here is not the personal financial interests of councillors in their private capacity, but conflicts between the revenue interests of the municipality as a whole and the council's obligation to implement its OP, which manifests land-use policies. The starting point is that a municipality may not bind itself in contract to rezone land, unless specifically authorized to do so by a provincial statute, or to bypass zoning, for example, through a development agreement. To do so without authorization is seen as con-

94 For something of a typical case so far as the language of an Official Plan that seeks to protect a central business district (CBD), see *5142 NWT Ltd v Hay River (Town)*, 2008 NWTSC 2.

95 2014 NSSC 430.

96 *Halifax Regional Municipality Charter*, SNS 2008, c 39, s 214.

97 As, for example, Ontario: RSO 1990, c M.50.

trary to public policy or a fraud on zoning.[98] *Pacific National Investments Ltd v Victoria (City)*[99] illustrates some of the perils for a purchaser when acquiring land from a municipality: in that case the peril the purchaser exposed itself to was the need for a change in the zoning after the sale and before the company had secured its right to develop phase two of the project. A variety of difficulties may arise. Typically, the core problem is the inherent conflict of interest between the municipality in its business capacity, seeking the best sale price, and the municipality in its regulatory capacity, seeking to implement appropriate land-use policies. Not everyone would see this as a situation of conflict. For those who do, challenges may be taken to decisions, though not necessarily on the basis of the alleged conflict. In *North End Community Health Assn v Halifax (Regional Municipality)*[100] the municipality owned the site of a former school and sought development proposals. Its choice of purchaser was challenged as an illegal sale below market value, raising the issue of how market value was to be determined. In *Heritage Trust of Nova Scotia v Halifax (Regional Municipality)*,[101] the municipality as approval authority considered a development proposal that involved land it had sold. This led to a challenge that the municipality took into account irrelevant considerations (the discussions at the time of the sale and an implied obligation to approve a development proposal) and had fettered its discretion by calling for proposals that included a tower. In *Friends of Lansdowne Inc v Ottawa (City)*,[102] the municipality sought development proposals for a sports stadium site. The arrangement was challenged as conferring an illegal bonus contrary to the *Municipal Act, 2001*.[103] In *Port Colborne (City) v Nyon Oil Inc*,[104] the city chose not to change its OP and land-use by-law (LUB) so as to facilitate a sale of its land even though it had recently negotiated for the sale. In *Orangeville (Town) v Dufferin (County)*,[105] the problem was the entwined interests of the upper- and lower-tier municipalities in the sale of land.

98 See, for example, *Vancouver (City) v British Columbia (Registrar Vancouver Land Registration District)*, [1955] 2 DLR 709 (BCCA) and *Harrietsfield-Grand Lake Community Association v Halifax (County)* (1978), 26 NSR (2d) 198 (SCAD). In both cases the municipality agreed to rezone land and enter into a contract with the owner to impose certain restrictions on use. The courts ruled against the municipalities.

99 2000 SCC 64.

100 2014 NSCA 92.

101 2007 NSSC 28.

102 2012 ONCA 273 [*Lansdowne*].

103 SO 2001, c 25, s 106.

104 2010 ONSC 3693 (Div Ct).

105 2010 ONCA 83.

All provinces disallow municipalities from granting bonuses to landowners. As a result of the *Lansdowne* decision, it is clear that there is a stringent test to find an illegal bonus; as John Mascarin has noted, "the courts will permit the structuring of reciprocal contractual arrangements between municipalities and private sector parties that seek to allocate mutual risk and benefits among the parties."[106] The further policy issue raised by the circumstances that have arisen in various cases is whether some particular mechanism ought to be in place to guide or govern sales of municipal lands when changes in formal use designations are involved. If so, the nature of such a mechanism is not clear.

I. EXPROPRIATION

Provinces may expropriate land. Municipalities are granted a power to expropriate land.[107] In British Columbia, universities may expropriate land.[108] In most circumstances of the exercise of the expropriation power, the purpose will be for some public undertaking. But many governments expropriate private land in order to resell it to another private owner.[109] Professor Harvey says it "sticks in the craw" to assist private developers through expropriation. The issue is the purpose for which the power may be exercised. Not all owners regard their land holdings as purely fungible and thus resist offers to purchase, or proposed ex-

106 John Mascarin, "Annotation to *Friends of Lansdowne Inc v Ottawa*" (2011) 88 *Municipal and Planning Law Reports* (4th) 133 at 136; see also John Mascarin, "Economic Development, Expropriation and the Prohibition against Municipal Bonusing" (2015) 31 *Municipal and Planning Law Reports* (5th) 7.

107 As noted several times elsewhere, regulation — even severe regulation — is not likely to be found to amount to expropriation which would thus oblige a government to compensate an owner. Some statutes allow for payments to be made on a discretionary basis. Downzoning is specified as not calling for compensation. The issue continues to be raised as a matter of policy debate and before some tribunals: see, for example, *Brighton (Municipality) Official Plan Amendment No 20 (Re)* (2003), 46 OMBR 78, where owners objecting to designation of their land as "Environmental Protection and Rural" asserted this amounted to expropriation without compensation.

108 *Universities Act*, RSBC 1996, c 468, s 51: "A university may expropriate any land that it considers necessary for its purposes." This is to be contrasted with the situation in Alberta where the board of governors of a university may request cabinet to expropriate land on its behalf "for the purposes of the public post-secondary institution": *Post-secondary Learning Act*, SA 2003, c P-19.5, s 66(2).

109 A short older article on this is Cameron Harvey, "Municipal Corporations and the Power to Expropriate Land for Private Development" (1970) 18 *Chitty's Law Journal* 118.

propriations, if they are able. Expropriation experts Stephen Waqué and Ian Mathany note: "[I]t is one thing to be dispossessed of property for a purely public or community interest, such as the need to provide clean water . . . . It is quite another thing . . . to be separated from one's property in order to advance more mixed public-private objectives."[110]

Whether there should be limits or special procedures when the land to be expropriated is being used for residential purposes, or whether any land may be expropriated in order to be sold to a third party, are lively issues, as is what should occur if, post-expropriation, the government decides it does not require the land.

Architectural historian Spiro Kostof points out that the power of expropriation originally was limited to the achievement of public works in the nature of infrastructure: roads, canals, railroads, reservoirs, and docks. But the power, which he characterizes as "Haussmannization," evolved so as to extend first to the land surrounding the public work and later to slum clearance, then to modern forms of economic development.[111] The core legal issue will be the presence of a "public" or, for local governments, a "municipal" purpose. Despite regarding interference with private property rights as a matter to be scrutinized carefully, courts have tended to see significant legitimate ambit for governments as to purpose, always subject to a challenge based in bad faith: see, for example, *Leiriao v Town of Val-Bélair (Town)*,[112] in which expropriation to create a land reserve was approved.

In most circumstances, expropriation for a public purpose, even if it involves a subsequent sale to a private entity, will be upheld as valid. In *Dales Properties Ltd v Surrey (City)*,[113] a typical case, land was expropriated for a proposed civic centre, and there was an indication that ultimately, private developers would be involved. The court found the arrangement not to be an illegal "grant, benefit, advantage, or assistance to a business" contrary to the *Community Charter*.[114] In *Piccirillo v British Columbia (Minister of Forests and Lands)*,[115] land was expropriated to build a road to facilitate access to a logging site for a forestry company. The expropriation was upheld on the basis that the road was said by the government to allow for recreational access, and for control of

110 Stephen Waqué & Ian Mathany, "Expropriation: The Raw Edge of the Conflict between Public and Private Interests" in Anneke Smit & Marcia Valiante, eds, *Public Interest, Private Property* (Vancouver: UBC Press, 2016) 261.

111 Spiro Kostof, *The City Assembled* (Boston: Little Brown, 1992) at 266–91.

112 [1991] 3 SCR 349.

113 2010 BCSC 1196.

114 *Community Charter*, SBC 2003, c 26, s 24(1).

115 *Piccirillo v British Columbia (Forests and Lands)*, 1988 CanLII 2936 (BCSC).

fire and insect pests; it was not solely for the benefit of a private entity. In *Thomas Developments Ltd v Saint John (City)*,[116] the municipality expropriated property to create a road for a proposed liquefied natural gas terminal to be built by private interests; a challenge was not successful. In fact, New Brunswick expropriation legislation makes explicit that such expropriations, at least by the province, are lawful: "Any person . . . who requires an expropriation for commercial, industrial or utility purposes may file . . . an application for an expropriation by the Lieutenant-Governor in Council."[117]

Conservation authorities, entities created by provincial statute to put in place plans to conserve, restore, or develop natural resource areas, may expropriate. However, in *LaRush v Metropolitan Authority and Region Conservation Authority*,[118] land was expropriated as a buffer around an established "Pioneer Village." The purpose was to protect the investment that had been made in the village. The court held that this was a purpose beyond what the statute authorized. In *Fouillard v Ellice (Rural Municipality)*,[119] the municipality proposed to expropriate approximately 288 acres of a 3,500-acre property in order to establish a tourist attraction based on the presence of the ruins of an 1831 trading post and fort. The owners objected and challenged the legal authority of the municipality to expropriate. The provincial statute authorized expropriation if the local council "considers [it] necessary or advisable to acquire [land] for a municipal purpose."[120] The core issue then became, what was the meaning of "municipal purpose." The court considered the general language of the purposes section of the Act and the "spheres of jurisdiction," which included power to encourage economic development, to assist heritage sites, and to engage in business itself. Taking a benevolent view of the statute and following the observation of the Supreme Court of Canada in *Spraytech* that "barring clear demonstration that a municipal decision was beyond its powers, courts should not so hold,"[121] the Manitoba Court of Appeal refused to set the expropriation aside.

An important case that slowly made its way through the courts, starting in 2007 with *Blandford Square Developments Ltd v Oxford (County)*,[122] and terminating in 2015 with the refusal of the Supreme Court of Can-

116 2006 NBQB 322.

117 *Expropriation Act*, RSNB 1973, c E-14, s 7.

118 *LaRush v Metropolitan Toronto & Region Conservation Authority*, 1967 CanLII 333 (Ont CA).

119 2007 MBCA 108 [*Fouillard*].

120 *Municipal Act*, CCSM c M225, s 254(1).

121 *114957 Canada Ltée (Spraytech, Société d'arrosage) v Hudson (Town)*, 2001 SCC 40 at para 23 [*Spraytech*].

122 2007 ONCA 298 [*Blandford Square*].

ada to hear an appeal of the Ontario Court of Appeal decision in *Vincorp Financial Ltd v Oxford (County)*,[123] raises the point of interaction of expropriation powers with the prohibition against conferring a bonus. In *Blandford Square*, the municipality expropriated land to assist with the establishment of an automobile manufacturing plant by Toyota Canada in Woodstock, Ontario. The land expropriated was a shopping mall. There was an agreement to resell the land to Toyota at the price paid to expropriate. The owner and the mortgage holder sued for a declaration of absence of statutory authority and for damages for unlawful interference with economic interests and conspiracy to unlawfully expropriate.[124] Ultimately, the ruling was that expropriation for the purpose of assisting in establishing the plant was lawful, and the owners, under expropriation legislation, were not entitled to any additional compensation due to increase in value of the land because of its new intended purpose. At the same time, the courts viewed the municipal undertaking to resell the land at the same price as paid to expropriate it as the improper conferring of a bonus. This did not, however, entitle the owner to damages; indeed, the Ontario Court of Appeal suggested the company might not have standing to challenge the conferring of a bonus.

The leading US case is *Kelo v New London*,[125] in which the Supreme Court considered the *Bill of Rights* prohibition against expropriation save for a "public use." In *Kelo*, the municipality hoped to attract a pharmaceutical company to establish a research facility. To assist the company, the city expropriated the residential properties of some nine persons unwilling to sell. The city was a "distressed municipality" that had adopted an economic development plan that looked to create a business park and associated facilities along its waterways. The Supreme Court was prepared to accept that "public use" should be seen as extending to "public purpose" and this included economic development, even where carried out by the private sector.

NOTES

1) Toyota, the company in *Bedford Square*, unlike the pharmaceutical company (Pfizer) in *Kelo*, did build its proposed facility.[126] If the contemplated project does not go ahead, should the land be offered at first instance to the original owners as no longer being needed for any public purpose?

---

123 2014 ONCA 876.

124 See *Oxford (County) v Guarantee Co of North America*, 2012 ONSC 4069.

125 545 US 469 (2005) [*Kelo*].

126 Patrick McGeehan "Pfizer to Leave City That Won Land-Use Case" *New York Times* (13 November 2009) A1.

2) *Kelo* has been criticized as unfair, but also as operating in a context of serious problems over urban renewal.[127] Many US states have since altered their expropriation statutes to impose limits on its use to benefit private owners.
3) The Supreme Court of Canada in *Toronto Area Transit Operating Authority v Dell Holdings Ltd*[128] set out some principles for interpretation of expropriation statutes. Any ambiguities were to be construed in favour of the property owner. This tends to suggest strict scrutiny of what amounts to a valid public purpose. In light of cases such as *Fouillard*, it is not at all obvious how this issue will evolve in the courts.
4) In *Fouillard*, the plaintiff also raised the issue of whether more land was being expropriated than was necessary. The court was not prepared to second-guess the municipality. In *Gray v Oshawa (City)*,[129] the same point was raised, with the court suggesting it was prepared to review the point, though it was prepared to accede to an assertion that expropriation of excess land could be justified on the basis of achieving a price advantage.
4) In *Woodburn Estate v National Capital Commission*,[130] the plaintiff's farmland had been expropriated in 1961; the plaintiff leased the land back from the National Capital Commission (NCC) and farmed it until 1994. Subsequently, the NCC determined the land to be surplus; it was rezoned and sold to a developer for a sum fifty times the original price. The plaintiff claimed a right to reacquire the land. The claim was struck out. The court said that the original expropriation had been valid, and the NCC could abandon the purpose for which the land was expropriated so long as there was no colourable scheme, for example, an intention to bank the land to gain future profits.
5) If there were to be a right for a previous owner to reacquire expropriated land on a right-of-first-refusal basis, should that apply only to personal residences or should it be a right available to all expropriated former owners? What if the dwelling has been demolished in the interim? Should there be a time limit? What price should be paid? In Manitoba, *The Expropriation Act*[131] provides a first chance to repurchase "on the terms of the best offer received" but only where the original owner retains a residual portion of the expropriated land.

---

127 See, for example, Edward J Lopez et al, "Pass a Law, Any Law, Fast! State Legislative Responses to the *Kelo* Backlash" (2009) 5 *Review of Law and Economics* 101.

128 [1997] 1 SCR 32.

129 [1971] 3 OR 112 (HCJ).

130 [2001] 1 FC 305 (TD).

131 CCSM c E190, s 51.

CHAPTER 11

SUSTAINABILITY[1]

A. PRELIMINARY

> If you're not pessimistic, you haven't read the science.
> If you're not optimistic, you haven't met the people.[2]

The need to transform our lives to a sustainable basis is widely accepted. The potential for transformation of our lives to a sustainable basis through legal mechanisms exists. All levels of government in Canada have some powers over aspects of the environment. Broadly, these powers are exercised through regulation (forbidding or setting limits on polluting emissions) and environmental assessment (EA). An EA is a process to consider a proposed undertaking in advance to decide whether it ought not to go ahead or whether it could go ahead but with safeguards. The two senior levels of government have extensive environmental law regimes in place, and they should be seen as aspects of their land-use controls. See Chapters 4 (federal) and 5 (provincial) for these discussions.

---

1 This chapter is a greatly shortened but also updated version of the author's article "Subsidiarity at Work—The Legal Context for Sustainability Initiatives at the Local Government Level" (2010) 63 *Municipal and Planning Law Reports* (4th) 56.

2 This is what has become a popular version of some lines from Paul Hawken's book, *Blessed Unrest*: "If you look at the science that describes what is happening on earth today and aren't pessimistic, you don't have the correct data. If you meet the people in this unnamed movement and aren't optimistic, you haven't got a heart." Paul Hawken, *Blessed Unrest: How the Largest Movement in the World Came into Being and Why No One Saw It Coming* (New York: Viking, 2007) at 4.

The potential for achieving significant transformation of the way we live our lives is enormous at all levels of government, including the municipal level. All too often, the barriers to change are not those presented by uncertainty as to what might be a better way of going about organizing life. Usually, in terms of the science or engineering required, we already know better ways of organizing our lives—the problem is not absence of knowledge. More usually, the barriers are political. By that I mean the barriers of lack of political will, contests over who will pay for change and how much, plus the barrier of attachment to the status quo. This last can mean simple inertia, but more often it means unwillingness to change, based on financial gain tied to how things are done now. Transformation, however, is an urgent need.[3] In the world context of global climate change, a deteriorating atmosphere, an abundance of polluted sites in need of remediation, threats to water quality and supply, loss of good agricultural land, individual and social stress (contributed to by crowding and poverty and poor living conditions), and in recognition of the interconnectedness of all life-support systems, municipalities —the governmental level usually seen as the closest to people—can have a significant role. It is this context within which I view issues of Canadian land-use planning (LUP) and LUP law.

In this chapter we consider the legal powers municipalities now have (for example, basic zoning, nuisance, and omnibus powers clauses) to advance the cause of sustainability. The suggestion to be made is that even without any alteration in municipal jurisdiction, existing powers are quite broad. The courts have recognized the environment as a legitimate municipal planning purpose.[4]

B. INTRODUCTION

Canadian municipalities have a relatively undistinguished record when it comes to sustainability initiatives.[5] No significant-sized population

3 Indeed, for some, the urgency is sometimes manifested in violence, usually directed at property rather than people. For a review, see Elżbieta Posluszna, *Environmental and Animal Rights Extremism, Terrorism, and National Security* (Amsterdam: Elsevier, 2015).

4 See *Enterprises Sibeca inc v Frelighsburg (Municipality)*, 2004 SCC 61 [*Entreprises Sibeca*] and *Montréal (City) v Arcade Amusements Inc*, [1985] 1 SCR 368.

5 For an international exploration of what municipalities have been attempting to do, see Eran Feitelson, ed, *Advancing Sustainability at the Sub-National Level, The Potential and Limitations of Planning* (Burlington, VT: Ashgate, 2004). For an American account, see John R Nolon, *Protecting the Environment through Land Use Law* (Washington, DC: Environmental Law Institute, 2014). See also

centre in Canada has a comprehensive range of programmes. The emphasis seems to be, where programmes do exist, on limiting them to municipally owned property or on voluntary compliance by the private sector.[6] The municipal record is undistinguished in comparison not only with the possibilities demonstrated in other places to be achievable, but in comparison with the global need, in comparison with Canada's notorious wastefulness, and, as I hope to demonstrate, in comparison with what the law now lends itself to.[7] To take the most pressing example, energy and the move to reduce greenhouse gas emissions,[8] the two senior levels of government have led in grappling with setting targets and adopting plans to achieve these targets.[9] I am not intending to suggest

---

Norman Christensen & Lissa Leege, *The Environment and You*, 2d ed (Hoboken, NJ: Pearson, 2016), especially Chapter 16 "Urban Ecosystems."

6 It is not the case that Canadian municipal sustainability programmes are absent. And some of the initiatives are significant: Vancouver has approved an EcoDensity Charter that includes a requirement that for any new building needing a rezoning, construction must meet Leadership in Energy and Environmental Design (LEED) standards—see online: http://former.vancouver.ca/commsvcs/ecocity/pdf/ecodensity-charter-low.pdf; other examples are Calgary's light rail system powered by wind-generated electricity, a landfill gas-to-energy project in Hamilton, and a rate structure for water that costs more per unit as consumption increases in Edmonton. In British Columbia, some 174 local governments have targeted becoming carbon-neutral, a policy pursuant to the Climate Action Charter of the provincial government, triggering eligibility for special funding, including rebate of carbon taxes.

7 For two essays reviewing what has been accomplished and what is possible in Canadian cities, see Trevor Price, "Sustainable Cities" and Edmund P Fowler & Franz Hartmann, "City Environmental Policy: Connecting the Dots," both in Edmund P Fowler & David Siegel, eds, *Urban Policy Issues: Canadian Perspectives*, 2d ed (Don Mills, ON: Oxford University Press, 2002).

8 This trend is driven by a combination of factors: global climate change, energy insecurity, fossil fuel depletion and associated increases in costs, and the development of new technologies.

9 The main federal statute is the *Kyoto Protocol Implementation Act*, SC 2007, c 30. The legal limits of the federal government's commitment to Canada's Climate Change Action Plan were recently explored in *Friends of the Earth v Canada (Governor in Council)*, 2008 FC 1183, aff'd 2009 FCA 297 in which the court concluded at para 46 (FC): "the Court has no role to play reviewing the reasonableness of the government's response to Canada's Kyoto commitments within the four corners of the KPIA." Provincial statutes include the *Climate Change and Emissions Management Act*, SA 2003, c C-16.7; *Climate Change and Emissions Reductions Act*, CCSM c C135; and the *Environmental Goals and Sustainable Prosperity Act*, SNS 2007, c 7. The various statutes set targets, not all of which are likely to be met: see, for example, Patrick White, "Saskatchewan Backs off Climate Targets" *The Globe and Mail* (23 April 2009) A7. See also Pembina Institute, "Highlights of Provincial Gas Reduction Plans" (August 2009), online: www.pembina.org/reports/highlights-of-provincial-greenhouse-gas-reduction-plans.pdf.

that the federal or provincial initiatives are adequate to address the problem; just that they are somewhat more advanced than overall Canadian municipal initiatives. Even though the Federation of Canadian Municipalities (FCM) has advocated for a 20/20 policy to be adopted by municipal councils, and many councils have passed motions, very few have adopted action plans or achieved their stated goals. FCM has said,

> With approximately 55 per cent of Canada's total greenhouse gas emissions under the direct or indirect control of municipal government, it is essential that municipal governments be fully engaged in national clean air and climate change initiatives . . . . However, municipal governments are not yet contributing to their full potential.[10]

Clearly it is legally possible for the senior levels of government to take full and exclusive responsibility for all environmental matters. But if they did so, it would bring into question the very rationale for local government at all. In their day-to-day decisions about land-use planning, municipalities make decisions that affect the establishment of residential subdivisions and thus pressure on aquifers; they also make decisions that affect transportation use and thus of necessity emissions from vehicles; a municipality that allows sprawl thereby allows more vehicle traffic and thereby allows more air pollution and greenhouse gas (GHG) emissions. Would it make sense for a province to try to direct such decisions? In some measure, Ontario has done so through the *Places to Grow Act, 2005*[11] and the *Greenbelt Act, 2005*[12] with respect to the main concentrations of population in the Greater Toronto Area (GTA). The *Places to Grow Act* especially is a major pre-emption of municipal land-use planning responsibility in which the province determines what amounts to a high-level official plan and requires municipal plans, zoning, and decisions to conform.[13] In most provinces, Crown ownership of land is an important factor, and thus the provincial gov-

---

10 The 20/20 objective is meant to set a target of a 20 percent reduction of GHG emissions below 1990 levels by 2020. FCM no longer posts its "Clean Air and Climate Change" and "Policy Statement on Environmental Issues and Sustainable Development" statements on its website. A December 2009 report, "Act Locally," online: www.fcm.ca/Documents/reports/Act_Locally_The_Municipal_Role_in_Fighting_Climate_Change_EN.pdf, and a 2011 report, "Building Canada's Green Economy, The Municipal Role," online: www.fcm.ca/Documents/reports/Building_Canadas_green_economy_the_municipal_role_EN.pdf, suggest that municipalities now have direct or indirect control over 45 percent of Canada's greenhouse gas emissions.

11 SO 2005, c 13.

12 SO 2005, c 1.

13 Above note 11, ss 3, 4, 6, 12, 13 & 14.

ernments are in a position to adopt policy or regulations that can affect large tracts. What makes sense in terms of which level of government ought to be handling what particular problem is not always obvious.

Environmental law and land-use planning are closely entwined. To the extent there is a striking difference, it may be that environmental law is somewhat grander in its scope. Land use, if left in the hands of local governments, is inevitably local in ambit, because local governments can regulate only within their geographic jurisdictions.[14] One American scholar writes of "the parochial nature of local land use control."[15] Canadian scholar Doug Macdonald has noted that "pollution was originally an urban health issue . . . . As concern over pollution has moved from immediate, local, and short-term effects to more subtle, longer-term health threats based on regional and global air and water pollution, jurisdictional authority in Canada and all other countries has necessarily moved."[16] At the same time, local governments can take account of what appears to them to be global concerns. The maxim used by environmentalists is to "think globally and act locally."

As a final preliminary point, we should remind ourselves of how serious the questions are that comprise the environmental agenda. Ultimately, what we are discussing is an array of life-support systems. Epidemiological and other studies of the health hazards associated with large-scale urbanization make it clear how fragile the overall situation is.[17]

1) Overview of Municipal Environmental Powers

For the most part, engagement with sustainability matters does not require new legislative powers to be granted. Given the typical array of

---

14 Land-use controls exist at the provincial (for example, controls over Crown land, forestry laws, mining laws) and the federal (for example, interprovincial and international infrastructure, communications, aeronautics) levels, for both of which there may be a wider geographic ambit.

15 John R Nolon, "In Praise of Parochialism: The Advent of Local Environmental Law" (2002) 26 *Harvard Environmental Law Review* 365 at 371.

16 Doug Macdonald, *The Politics of Pollution* (Toronto: McClelland & Stewart, 1991) at 87.

17 See AJ McMichael, "The Growth of Cities" in *Planetary Overload* (Cambridge, UK: Cambridge University Press, 1993); Christopher A Kennedy et al, "Energy and Material Flows of Megacities" (2015) 112(19) *Proceedings of the National Academy of Sciences* 5985. The world's largest megacities are Tokyo (38 million), Delhi (25 million), Shanghai (23 million), Mumbai, Mexico City, and Sao Paulo (each 21 million), Osaka and Beijing (each 20 million), New York and Cairo (each 19 million).

powers now granted by the provinces to their municipalities, what is required is the dedication of local government political officials to use those powers in ways that are designed to advance a sustainability objective. Little more. For no entirely clear reason, local governments have been slow to adapt their thinking.[18]

Municipalities are not all the same. The usual classification is of urban, suburban, and rural.[19] Planners and geographers debate the socio-demographic differences, and they are significant.[20] Regardless, and despite the phenomenon of major cities often having their own special statutes,[21] the general legal powers of all of the municipalities in each province, and indeed throughout Canada, tend to be quite similar.

---

18 Some writers take a relatively modest view of the powers of municipal governments. For example, in the latest edition of Elaine Hughes, Alastair Lucas, & William Tilleman's text *Environmental Law and Policy*, 3d ed (Toronto: Emond Montgomery, 2003), the chapter on municipal and land-use planning states:

> all Canadian provinces delegate to municipalities specified planning and regulatory powers over land uses. In exercising these powers, municipalities play key and critical roles in affecting environment quality—for better or worse. Through their land-use plans and policies and authority over zoning and subdivision, municipalities control and regulate many private land development and uses that affect environmental quality . . . . One land-use zone may permit intense industrial development, which could negatively affect environmental quality, while another may be structured to enhance environmental quality and maintain green spaces . . . . Also, through their land use and development powers, municipalities regulate facets of roads, sewers, and other infrastructure, all of which could affect environmental quality [at 521].

While more cautious than some of the commentary made following the Supreme Court of Canada decision in *Spraytech*, below note 30, this passage strikes me still as an excessively modest view of local government powers. Even where scholars praise municipal efforts to come to grips with sustainability issues, there tends to be a conclusion that powers are quite limited: see David Boyd, *Unnatural Law: Rethinking Canadian Environmental Law and Policy* (Vancouver: UBC Press, 2003): "Ultimately, however, municipalities are constrained by legal limits on their powers. Local governments are not explicitly assigned jurisdiction over any specific subjects under Canada's *Constitution Act, 1867*. Municipalities can take action only when explicitly authorized to do so by provincial governments" [at 221].

19 Martin Turcotte, "The City/Suburb Contrast: How Can We Measure It?" (Summer 2008) 85 *Canadian Social Trends* at 2, online: Statistics Canada www.statcan.gc.ca/pub/11-008-x/2008001/article/10459-eng.htm.

20 *Ibid*. See also Martin Turcotte, "Dependence on Cars in Urban Neighbourhoods," *ibid* at 20.

21 See, for example, *City of Toronto Act, 2006*, SO 2006, c 11, Sch A; *Vancouver Charter*, SBC 1953, c 55 as amended.

We have been told by the courts that the protection of the environment is one of the major challenges of our time.[22] We have also been told by the courts that the powers of all levels of government should be interpreted in ways that allow them to deal with the environment.[23] "Whether viewed positively as strategies for maintaining a clean environment, or negatively as measures to combat the evils of pollution, there can be no doubt that these measures relate to a public purpose of superordinate importance, and one in which all levels of government and numerous organs of the international community have been increasingly engaged."[24] Still, it is always necessary for a municipality to have a clear legislated mandate to deal with any particular topic. The issue of jurisdiction is bound to arise, especially in any novel circumstances. Perhaps the broadest endorsement for local government invocation of a sustainability purpose appears in the Supreme Court of Canada decision in *Entreprises Sibeca*,[25] a case arising in Quebec and involving allegations of bad faith. The Court said, "Although there is specific legislation dealing with environmental conservation, protecting the natural environment within a municipality's jurisdiction cannot be regarded as an improper goal for a municipal council."[26] The statement could be parsed by noting the modification "within a municipality's jurisdiction" and the choice of "natural environment" as what is to be protected. Nonetheless, it seems likely that the array of cases decided by the Supreme Court of Canada in which a sustainability agenda adopted by a local government has been approved amounts to quite a broad endorsement,[27] and would almost inevitably finesse any attack based on allegations of improper purpose such as arose in *Shell Canada Products Ltd v Vancouver (City)*[28] and ultimately originating in *Roncarelli v Duplessis*.[29]

---

22 *Friends of the Oldman River Society v Canada (Minister of Transport)*, [1992] 1 SCR 3.

23 Notably in *R v Hydro-Québec*, [1997] 3 SCR 213.

24 *Ibid* at para 85.

25 Above note 4.

26 *Ibid* at para 38.

27 See *Spraytech*, below note 30; *Croplife Canada v Toronto (City)* (2005), 10 MPLR (4th) 1 (Ont CA), leave to appeal to SCC refused, [2005] SCCA No 329 [*Croplife*]; *Nanaimo (City) v Rascal Trucking Ltd*, 2000 SCC 13 [*Rascal Trucking*]; *Montréal (City) v 2952-1366 Québec inc*, 2005 SCC 62.

28 [1994] 1 SCR 231.

29 [1959] SCR 121. As an aside, (since our focus is on municipal jurisdiction as granted by statute) there are some other aspects of judicial scrutiny of local government decision-making where sustainability may come into play. One is the fairness question. Under the *Baker v Canada (Minister of Citizenship and Immigration)*, [1999] 2 SCR 817 categorization of factors to be taken into account in determining the content of the duty of procedural fairness in a given case,

Following the Supreme Court of Canada decisions in *Spraytech*[30] and *Enterprises Sibeca*, Quebec amended its governing municipal statutes, effective in 2006, to grant local governments a clear power to deal with the environment. In the *Loi sur les compétences municipales* (*Municipal Powers Act*),[31] section 4 lists as an assigned power "l'environnement" and section 19 makes it clear that by-laws may be adopted:

---

one is "the nature of the decision being made" (at para 23) and another is "the importance of the decision" (at para 25). There is some indication that the involvement of an environmental issue may have some bearing on assessing these factors. In the British Columbia Court of Appeal decision in *Canadian Pacific Railway Co v Vancouver (City)*, 2004 BCCA 192, the contents of the requirement for procedural fairness were said to vary, and a higher requirement was to apply in decisions having "a significant and immediate effect upon the environment and the character of the community" (at para 95) as compared with by-laws tending to maintain the status quo. (The case was later affirmed by the Supreme Court of Canada, 2006 SCC 5, but nothing in the subsequent decision spoke to this point.) Given the context of various British Columbia Court of Appeal decisions about fairness in the land-use decision-making process, listed and briefly reviewed in *Wilde v Metchosin (District)*, 2005 BCCA 453, it seems likely that the court meant "environment" in the environmental law sense. See especially *Norman v Port Moody (City)* (1995), 31 MPLR (2d) 47 (BCSC), aff'd [1996] BCJ No 2642 (CA). Another aspect has to do with the character of a land user, as an issue of relevant or irrelevant consideration. In the UK case *Blake & Sons v Secretary of State for the Environment and Colchester Borough Council*, [1998] Env LR 309, the court upheld refusal of planning permission to a company with a record of convictions for pollution offences. To a similar effect is *Mocyk v East Peace No 131 (Municipal District)* (1995), 32 MPLR (2d) 77 (Alta CA). An example of a case in which the failure of the municipal council to take environmental policies into account when considering a zoning change, and thus having failed to take a relevant factor into account, is *Robertson v Edmonton (City)*, [1990] 4 WWR 232 (Alta QB). Others have noted the potential for effective local environmental action. In 1992, Larry Reynolds wrote,

> Local public authorities such as municipalities, public health boards and planning bodies in many jurisdictions presently have at their disposal a surprisingly wide array of powers which may be used for environmental regulation and management. However, to date the use of many of these powers has been limited or erratic. Factors such as low public awareness, lack of financial resources and technical expertise, and a general unfamiliarity with local environmental issues have contributed to the past failures of local public authorities . . . . This state of affairs is unlikely to continue.

See Larry Reynolds, "Environmental Regulation and Management by Local Public Authorities in Canada" (1992) 3 *Journal of Environmental Law and Practice* 41 at 43. Certainly the situation has evolved. But measured by the need, and by the potential, the change has been much too slow.

30 *114957 Canada Ltée (Spraytech, Société d'arrosage) v Hudson (Town)*, 2001 SCC 40 [*Spraytech*].

31 CQLR c C-47.1.

"Toute municipalité locale peut adopter des règlements en matière d'environnement." These powers have been used by municipalities and upheld by the courts in cases such as *Wallot v Québec (Ville de)*.[32] In being so explicit, Quebec has moved ahead of the other provinces in granting clear generalized authority over environmental matters to local governments.[33] That there is wide ambit in the term "l'environnement" is illustrated by the *Wallot* case in which the by-law required riparian owners not only to leave some borders of the shore in a natural state but to replant. Marie-Andrée Simard, in her annotated version of the *Municipal Powers Act*, says, "Le terme 'environnement' doit être compris dans son sense large et inclure notamment la protection de l'environnement, l'assainissement de l'atmosphère et des eaux, l'alimentation en eau, le rejet des eaux usées et la gestion des matières résiduelles et des matières recyclable."[34]

Even with Quebec's change in the law, the general principles enunciated in *Spraytech* still apply; so in the case of an actual conflict, the laws put in place by the province or the federal government would prevail. Neither the courts, nor I, should be taken to imply that municipal engagement with sustainability issues is, as a matter of policy, preferable to having the senior levels take charge of the various issues. Which level of government ought to take the lead, or possibly even be exclusively responsible for some environmental topic, is a complex political or public policy question, linked with but somewhat distinct from the legal constraints. What is being asserted is that municipalities as now structured should be seen to possess a wide array of legal powers that enable them to take sustainability initiatives, and that the array of powers is greater than has been previously noted. In addition, the question of the possession of legal powers is distinct from whether any particular local government council will choose to exercise the powers.

---

32 2010 QCCS 1370, aff'd 2011 QCCA 1165, leave to appeal to SCC refused, 2012 CanLII 4181.

33 For an overview of what has occurred at the municipal level in Quebec, see Jean-Francois Girard, "Dix ans de protection de l'environnement par les municipalités depuis l'arrêt *Spraytech*: constats et perspectives" in Barreau du Québec, *Développements Récents en Droit de l'Environnement*, vol 329 (Cowansville, QC: Éditions Yvon Blais, 2010) 49.

34 Marie-Andrée Simard, *Loi sur les compétences municipales annotée* (Cowansville, QC: Éditions Yvon Blais, 2011) at 36.

C. MUNICIPAL POWERS[35]

1) Purpose Sections

Not all provincial statutes include a section setting out the overall purpose of the act, though those acts that establish municipal jurisdiction do tend to include purpose sections. Not all of those specify that sustainability is a part of local government mandate. In Nova Scotia, for example, there is no such statement in the introduction to the *Municipal Government Act*[36] or in its Part VIII, which focuses on land-use planning. In Alberta, though, the *Municipal Government Act* does have such a statement:

> The purpose of this Part . . . is to provide means whereby plans and related matters may be prepared and adopted (a) to achieve the orderly, economical and beneficial development, use of land and patterns of human settlement, and (b) to maintain and improve the quality

---

35 The arrangement is primarily, though not exclusively, in terms of the legal powers, and not in terms of the identified problems or suggested policy initiatives. Statistics Canada, in its Canadian Environmental Sustainability Indicators (CESI) report, offers broad category analysis, which certainly can be used as a way to approach local government powers, accomplishments, and failings. The broad categories reported on are air quality, GHG emissions, and freshwater quality.

The health of Canadians and their social and economic well-being are highly dependent on the quality of their environment. One way to assess environmental quality is to use indicators that convey complex information in a simple form. The CESI provide an indication of the health of our environment in much the same way as the GDP and other signals provide a sense of the health of the economy. Over the long term, the intent of the CESI initiative is to supplement traditional social and economic measures with information that will allow Canadians to better understand the relationships that exist among the economy, the environment, and human health and well-being.

Other broad category approaches exist to help advance understanding of the problems, such as David Boyd's of water, air, land, and biodiversity or, from an early report generated by geographers at the University of Chicago for the US *Environmental Protection Act*, which includes air quality, water quality, solid wastes, noise, pesticides, and radiation. Another approach is to look at some of the suggested solutions. To some extent, Sierra Legal's *Municipal Powers Report* (Vancouver: Sierra Legal, 2007) takes that approach through some case studies. So, too, does one of the main American articles. The approach I have chosen here is to set out the legal tools, albeit with examples included as part of the discussion. This reflects the premise that an under-appreciation of the strength of the legal tools now available has been a significant barrier to advances, and also a belief that ingenuity will invent specific sustainability initiatives once the legal tools are better understood.

36 SNS 1998, c 18.

> of the physical environment within which patterns of human settlement are situated in Alberta, without infringing on the rights of individuals for any public interest except to the extent that is necessary for the overall greater public interest.[37]

So, too, does Ontario's *Planning Act*, where section 2 declares that municipal councils "shall have regard to . . . matters of provincial interest such as (a) the protection of ecological systems, including natural areas, features and functions . . . ."[38] Overall, though, the presence or absence of a stated purpose has not tended to be of central importance; cases in which the purpose sections of statutes are cited are relatively rare. They can arise when there is an issue over interpretation of a statutory provision: "The most direct and authoritative evidence of legislative purpose is found in formal purpose statements appearing in the body of legislation."[39]

But given the overall attitude of the courts as expressed in cases such as *R v Hydro-Québec*[40] and *Entreprises Sibeca*,[41] the courts will probably have no problem in seeing environmental matters as a legitimate goal for local government, even without a specified purpose in governing legislation.

2) General Welfare or Omnibus Powers

Since the 2001 decision of the Supreme Court of Canada in *Spraytech*,[42] there has been significant speculation about the possibility of using the "omnibus" or general powers provision that is typical of most provincial *Planning Acts* or equivalent legislation governing local governments, as a basis for sustainability initiatives. The case turned on the interpretation and application of section 410 of the Quebec *Cities and Towns Act*,[43] which granted municipalities power to make by-laws "[t]o secure peace, order, good government, health and general welfare in the . . . municipality . . . ." The Town of Hudson used this general power to enact a pesticide-control by-law. The by-law was found to be *intra vires* even

37 RSA 2000, c M-2, s 617. The "Part" referred to is Part 17, "Planning and Development."

38 *Planning Act*, RSO 1990, c P.13, as amended. Other sustainability interests are listed in the section.

39 Ruth Sullivan, *Sullivan on the Construction of Statutes*, 5th ed (Markham, ON: LexisNexis, 2008) at 270.

40 Above note 23.

41 Above note 4.

42 Above note 30.

43 CQLR c C-19.

though both the federal and provincial governments regulated some aspects of pesticides. Ontario's *Municipal Act, 2001* has the following section: "A municipality may regulate matters not specifically provided for by this Act or any other Act for purposes related to the health, safety and well-being of the inhabitants of the municipality,"[44] which, in *Croplife*,[45] was read by the Ontario Court of Appeal to have the same ambit as the similar provision in the Quebec legislation, leading to validation of the Toronto pesticide control by-law. Similar wording is to be found in municipal statutes throughout the country. *Croplife* is not the only major case subsequent to *Spraytech* in which the courts have validated environmental regulatory by-laws under the general welfare clause;[46] in Manitoba, the Court of Appeal used the equivalent statutory authority to uphold a by-law restricting the establishment of intensive livestock operations unless certain standards are met, even though a provincial regulatory scheme also existed.[47] Writers such as Dianne Saxe have suggested that "The municipalities in all provinces now have dazzling new powers, and must now decide what to do with them . . . ."[48] The FCM has explored various possibilities[49] and the Sierra Legal Defence Fund has published a commentary on *Spraytech* that includes some suggestions for possible initiatives. Following *Spraytech*, what is actually possible using municipal omnibus powers?[50]

It has to be recalled that *Spraytech* is not a complete endorsement of municipal involvement in environmental matters. The Court's judg-

44 *Municipal Act, 2001*, SO 2001, c 25, s 130.

45 *Croplife*, above note 27 (CA).

46 A pre-*Spraytech* case in which municipal jurisdiction was seen to be able to coexist with provincial jurisdiction is *Beauvais c Ste-Anne-de-Sabrevois (Paroisse)* (1986), 34 MPLR 258 (Que SC), which had to do with the preservation of agricultural lands.

47 *4500911 Manitoba Ltd v Stuartburn (Rural Municipality)*, 2003 MBCA 122.

48 Dianne Saxe, "Municipalities Can Protect the Public" *Municipal World* (September 2005); see also John Swaigen, "The *Hudson* Case: Municipal Powers to Regulate Pesticides Confirmed by Quebec Courts" (2000) 34 *Canadian Environmental Law Reports (New Series)* 162. Could a municipality, concerned with protecting organic agriculture, ban the use of genetically modified organism (GMO) seeds as an aspect of that concern?

49 See Nola-Kate Seymoar et al, "Planning for Long-term Urban Sustainability: A Guide to Frameworks and Tools" (Vancouver: International Centre for Sustainable Cities, 2004).

50 Sierra Legal, "The Municipal Powers Report," above note 35. The report contains a cautious statement: "General welfare provisions . . . can likely be used to enact a broad range of health and environmental matters, especially now that courts will accord substantial deference to local decision-makers" (at 13).

ment placed clear limits on the exercise of the power.[51] Thus, an enumerated power cannot be expanded by reference to the omnibus power. Nor will municipal regulation be effective if the by-law is in direct conflict with a regulatory measure of the federal or provincial governments. Further, it is also possible for municipal jurisdiction to be specifically negatived by some other provincial law, for example, right-to-farm laws or nutrient management laws.[52]

The idea of direct conflict is important to understand when considering stricter standards. May a municipality set stricter environmental standards than those of the federal or provincial governments, or would that amount to an impermissible inconsistency? Prior to *Spraytech*, there had been strong suggestion that municipal rules that "enhance" a provincial statutory regulatory scheme could still be valid;[53] *Spraytech* seems to endorse this view.[54]

A current example of the courts' approval of stricter standards set at the local level appears in the 2008 British Columbia Supreme Court decision in *Darvonda Nurseries Ltd v Greater Vancouver (Regional District)*,[55] in which the municipality's power to set stricter air quality standards regarding particulate matter from wood-burning boilers in its local area, than does the province, was recognized.[56] Similarly, in *Merzetti v Saint John (City)*,[57] the court approved a municipal setback from a lake providing water for the city that was greater than provided for by the provincial *Clean Water Act*.[58] In *Toronto (City) v Goldlist Properties Inc*,[59] while not an environmental law case, the Court of Appeal interpreted *Spraytech* by saying, "That decision makes it clear that, assuming the matter falls within municipal competence, a municipality is free to establish policies and standards more restrictive than those established by provincial legislation."[60] In Ontario there is an exception under the *Greenbelt*

51 See Howard M Epstein, "Case Comment: *Spraytech v Town of Hudson*" (2001) 19 *Municipal and Planning Law Reports* (3d) 56.

52 See, for example, *Hill & Hill Farms Ltd v Bluewater (Municipality)* (2006), 26 MPLR (4th) 1 (Ont CA); *Peacock v Norfolk (County)* (2006), 81 OR (3d) 530 (CA), leave to appeal to SCC refused, [2006] SCCA No 371; *Milk Act*, RSO 1990, c M.12, s 20.

53 *Ontario (Attorney General) v Mississauga (City)* (1981), 33 OR (2d) 395 (CA).

54 Above note 30 at para 37.

55 2008 BCSC 1251 [*Darvonda Nurseries*].

56 The municipal powers flow from the *Environmental Management Act*, RSBC 1996, c 118, as considered in *Darvonda Nurseries* [now SBC 2003, c 57].

57 2005 NBCA 16.

58 SNB 1989, c C-6.1.

59 (2003), 44 MPLR (3d) 1 (Ont CA).

60 *Ibid* at para 67.

Act, 2005, which provides that municipalities in the Greenbelt Plan area cannot adopt greater land-use restrictions than the Plan.[61]

Despite such decisions as *Darvonda*, if a province chooses to establish a land-use regulatory scheme that explicitly overrides municipal jurisdiction, *Spraytech* will not counteract the statute. Thus, in *Peacock v Norfolk (County)*[62] the Ontario Court of Appeal invalidated a municipal by-law's application to a hog farm where a nutrient management plan had been put in effect under a statute other than the *Planning Act*. The *Nutrient Management Act* specified that "[a] regulation supersedes a by-law of a municipality . . . if the by-law . . . addresses the same subject-matter as the regulation . . . . [Such a by-law] is inoperative while the regulation is in force."[63] As another example, the Ontario government has chosen to limit local government jurisdiction over renewable energy matters.[64] While this signals an intention to have these matters directed by the province, in effect it ousts local government jurisdiction over something that could have been particularly useful.[65]

Spraytech may have been overread to imply that only direct conflict will oust lower-level jurisdiction. Earlier cases such as two decisions of the Ontario Court of Appeal in *Ontario (Attorney General) v Mississauga (City)*,[66] regarding the burning of PCBs, and *Superior Propane Inc v York (City)*,[67] regarding the placement of commercial natural gas storage tanks, relied primarily on an understanding of "conflict" as extending to reading into a higher-level statute an intention to be a complete code for some activity; these two decisions did not apply the test of direct conflict. It would be tempting to regard the two cases as wrongly decided; subsequent to *Spraytech*, however, the Supreme Court of Canada revisited the question of incompatibility of dual regulation, this time in the context of dual federal and provincial regulation, and seems to have added to the test. In *Rothmans, Benson & Hedges Inc v Saskatch-*

---

61 *Greenbelt Act, 2005*, above note 12, s 9(2).

62 Above note 52.

63 *Nutrient Management Act, 2002*, SO 2002, c 4, s 61.

64 The *Green Energy and Green Economy Act, 2009*, SO 2009, c 12 amends the *Planning Act* by adding s 62.0.2, excluding renewable energy undertakings from the ambit of OPs and by-laws. See Dianne Saxe, "Ontario's Green Energy Act" *Municipal World* (September 2009) at 45.

65 The *Green Energy and Green Economy Act, 2009* "approach to municipalities is to support municipal ownership and proponency of green energy projects, but virtually prohibit municipal regulation of this sector": Rodney Northey, "The Role of Municipalities in Canada's Energy Strategies" (2013) 25 *Journal of Environmental Law and Practice* 135 at 150.

66 Above note 53.

67 (1995), 23 OR (3d) 161 (CA).

ewan,[68] a case involving advertising of tobacco products, the Court said that "impossibility of dual compliance is sufficient but not the only test for inconsistency."[69] The Court said, "Provincial legislation that displaces or frustrates Parliament's legislative purpose is also inconsistent for purposes of the doctrine [i.e., paramountcy].[70]" The context, and other court decisions, make it clear this approach applies in the legal assessment of municipal by-laws vis-à-vis higher-level regulation and not just to federal/provincial jurisdictional questions.[71] The result is that inconsistency will arise if a higher-level statute is seen as intending to be a complete code of conduct; in those instances, a stricter municipal rule will not apply.

It is also the case that any by-law sought to be justified by the omnibus power must actually relate to "health" or "safety" or "welfare." Certainly these are broad terms, and could be thought of as applicable to many—perhaps all—environmental matters. But that remains to be tested. *Spraytech* contains language that suggests the courts are prepared to undertake a "reasonableness" analysis of regulatory by-laws; the Town of Hudson by-law contained various exceptions to the prohibition of pesticide use, and L'Heureux-Dubé J commented,

> Without drawing distinctions, [the by-law] could not achieve its permissible goal of aiming to improve the health of the Town's inhabitants by banning non-essential pesticide use. If all pesticide use and users were treated alike, the protection of health and welfare would be sub-optimal. For example, withdrawing the special status given to farmers . . . would work at cross-purposes with its salubrious intent.[72]

Are the omnibus powers terms the equivalent of a typical statutory definition of "environmental harm," for example, as found in the Ontario *Environmental Bill of Rights:* "'harm' means any contamination or degradation and includes harm caused by the release of any solid, liquid, gas, odour, heat, sound, vibration, or radiation."[73]? How would such a question be approached by the courts, that is, what standard of review would apply? Would a municipality that sought to use the "health" power be obliged to be correct about the health effects of a substance proposed to be regulated or just show some effort to be reasonable? In order to avoid an attack on the basis of unreasonableness or bad faith, a municipality should have a written record of some investigation

68 2005 SCC 13.
69 *Ibid* at para 14.
70 *Ibid* at para 12.
71 *Spraytech*, above note 30 at para 36.
72 *Ibid* at para 29.
73 *Environmental Bill of Rights, 1993*, SO 1993, c 28, s 1.

of the factual or scientific basis for its policy choices. Thus, in *Croplife* the Ontario Court of Appeal noted that there might have been a legal challenge to the by-law that could be mounted "if there was no credible basis for enacting the by-law,"[74] but given some scientific evidence, judicial deference, including respect for the precautionary principle, as set out in *Spraytech*, will shield municipal decisions of this sort.

On the other hand, the Toronto by-law prohibition of shark fin sale and usage was struck down by the courts in *Eng v Toronto (City)*[75] as not having a valid municipal purpose, along the lines set out by the majority in *Shell Canada Products Ltd v Vancouver (City)*.[76] All attempts by the city to relate the by-law to an assigned power were rejected by the court. Commenting on the decision, municipal lawyer John Mascarin said,

> In narrow terms . . . *Eng* means that other municipal shark fin ban by-laws . . . may be susceptible to successful challenge. More broadly, however, the decision affirms that municipal powers, even the broad general powers set out in both the *City of Toronto Act, 2006* and the *Municipal Act, 2001* have limits and must be grounded in true and proper core municipal purposes.[77]

3) Enumerated Powers

Omnibus power clauses, though the focus of much discussion, have not formed the core of municipal powers as assigned by provincial statutes. The legislative drafting tradition, rooted in Dillon's Rule, which construes grants of power to localities very narrowly, has been to list in some detail the particular powers municipalities are granted. Even in provinces that have chosen to approach the granting of municipal powers as more general "spheres," there is still some attempt at definition of the ambit of powers. Enumerated municipal powers are very much oriented towards matters of public health or safety. They are a reminder of the origins of local regulatory by-laws in the common law of nuisance. Sewage, garbage, and drinking water remain central local government concerns. The core list of responsibilities has tended to expand somewhat, but viewed as a way to advance an environmental or sustainability agenda, the typical list of local government powers is highly suggestive of ways to effect change. Consider these areas of jurisdiction:

---

74 *Croplife*, above note 27 at para 71. The precautionary principle itself would not be adequate.

75 2012 ONSC 6818.

76 (1994), 20 MPLR (2d) 1 (SCC).

77 John Mascarin, "Annotation to *Eng v Toronto (City)*" (2013) 6 *Municipal and Planning Law Reports* (5th) 28 at 35.

- drinking water
- transportation
- sewage
- solid waste
- parks and recreation/trees

The simple listing of these areas of traditional municipal jurisdiction makes it obvious that effective action could be taken about serious environmental matters through use of well-recognized municipal powers.[78] Indeed, for many of the listed topics, effective actions are taken on a daily basis already. Thus, drinking water that is potable is delivered through municipal systems to millions of Canadians at low cost and at a high level of safety, every day.

a) Water

For water, the core environmental problems have to do with provision of an adequate amount of useable water. In part, this means protecting existing sources from contamination. But with global climate change, it could increasingly come to include problems of drought, so far quite localized and temporary in Canada, but with significant indication that it may become a much greater problem soon.[79] The key policy issue seems to be how to take more effective measures. It is widely recognized that "municipalities play an important role in water resource management through their responsibilities for drinking-water systems, land-use planning, and regulation of waste, storm water, and sanitary sewer discharge limits, wells, and subsurface water supplies, as well as through their provision of water directly to local citizens and businesses."[80]

---

78 In an older but important work, the role of municipalities was recognized: see Macdonald, *The Politics of Pollution*, above note 16 at 51–52:

> Constitutional authority over environmental protection is shared by the federal and provincial governments. At the same time, municipal governments, which have no constitutional authority, play a role in pollution prevention as significant as that of their federal and provincial counterparts . . . . [T]hey are . . . primarily responsible for preventing pollution in the areas of drinking water, sewage treatment, hazardous waste discharged to sewers, and solid waste disposal.

79 Witness the large fire in and around Fort McMurray, Alberta, in the spring of 2016.

80 Karen Thomas, "Instruments and Implementation Options for Water Resource Management" in Mark Sproule-Jones et al, eds, *Canadian Water Politics* (Montreal: McGill-Queen's University Press, 2008) 90 at 98–99. See also Jane M Glenn, "Planning for Potable Water" in A Smits and M Valiante, eds, *Public Interest, Private Property* (Vancouver: UBC Press, 2016) 228.

For protection of sources, the multiple-barrier system prevails and is widely endorsed by public health officials. The Walkerton Inquiry Report said, "The best way to achieve a healthy public water supply is to put in place multiple barriers that keep water contaminants from reaching people."[81] The barriers commonly used are source protection, treatment, securing the distribution system against the intrusion of contaminants, monitoring, and responses to adverse conditions.[82] In larger municipalities, it is often possible to control the land-use in areas directly around drinking water sources. Otherwise, it might be necessary to rely on controls imposed by the provincial level.[83]

Issues arise over both point source and non-point sources of pollution, and there is often municipal jurisdiction extending to both.[84] For the approximately 12 percent of Canadians taking their drinking water from wells,[85] there is a different level of risk. The standard approach is one of owner-responsibility. Landowners with well-water systems are expected to have their systems installed by licensed operators and to have the water tested on a regular basis. Municipalities could take steps to expand their service to areas not presently serviced by the local utility. Cost is a serious factor. Settlement patterns mean that areas of relatively denser concentration are more likely to have utility service, and areas of lower density none at all, and thus a higher level of risk.

It is also the case that a municipality could adopt higher standards. There are no national drinking water regulations.[86] The federal govern-

81 Honourable Dennis O'Connor, *Report of the Walkerton Inquiry* (Toronto: Ministry of the Attorney General, 2002) vol 2 at 72.

82 *Ibid.*

83 In British Columbia, there has been a difficult history involving "Land Act Reserves," watershed areas set aside for this purpose since 1904, and excluding logging, but this restriction has been regularly compromised starting in the 1970s.

84 "'Point source' water pollution refers to inputs into natural ecosystems . . . that come from easily identifiable 'end-of-pipe' sources—for example, industrial effluent . . . . 'Nonpoint source' (NPS) water pollution refers to inputs that come from multiple sources—for example, agricultural waste and pesticide runoff, urban sewage overflow, nutrient and herbicide runoff from golf courses, and runoff of heavy metals and toxic substances . . . ." per Carolyn Johns, "Non-point Source Water Pollution Institutions in Ontario before and after Walkerton" in Sproule-Jones et al, eds, *Canadian Water Politics*, above note 80, 203 at 205.

85 StatsCan, CANSIM Table 153-0062, for 2007. There is a significant range, with British Columbia and Saskatchewan having 7 percent of such households, Prince Edward Island 51 percent, New Brunswick 49 percent, and Nova Scotia 43 percent. See also Peter Clancy, "Chasing Whose Fish? Atlantic Fisheries Conflicts and Institutions" in Sproule-Jones et al, eds, above note 80, 261 at 278.

86 For a survey of the state of water policy in Canada, see various articles in (July–August 2009) 30:7 *Policy Options*, particularly Harry Swain, "Drinking Water and Waste Water: A Primer" at 26.

ment's role has been to generate "guidelines."[87] Several provinces do have legislation,[88] and several have drinking water strategies.[89]

b) Transportation

Transportation is both the topic area in which many of the high-profile and contentious problems arise[90] and for which most of the solutions have been explored. The nature of the problem is well-understood: vehicle use is an energy matter, and with the prevailing technologies this means the combustion of fossil fuels with associated air pollution and atmosphere and climate impacts. The modern city is designed around automobile traffic for passengers and use of trucks for goods. If the planning problem is limiting vehicle use, many options are known. Some are within municipal jurisdiction, though some will rely on interaction with provincial regulatory schemes set out in "highway" legislation. What is usually within municipal control will be limiting sprawl and creating public transit systems and other alternatives. Probably the most powerful municipal tool is the budget; if a municipality chooses not to assign funds to expansion of its road system, but chooses instead to maintain what exists, vehicle use will be constrained. In virtually all municipalities, significant multi-year plans exist for road building; a reassigning of these resources to alternatives would lead to major differences in local energy use. In many municipalities, public transit (buses/subways/trains/ferries) are all in place. Some municipalities

---

87 Health Canada, "Guidelines for Canadian Drinking Water Quality" (October 2014), online: www.hc-sc.gc.ca/ewh-semt/pubs/water-eau/sum_guide-res_recom/index-eng.php.

88 Ontario, Quebec, Saskatchewan, Manitoba, Alberta, and Newfoundland and Labrador.

89 Saskatchewan, British Columbia, and Nova Scotia. Bruce Pardy has argued for the setting of standards for drinking water based on the precautionary principle. He says,

> Modern water standards . . . are not based upon the precautionary principle. It is not just a question of whether standards include sufficient margins of safety. More significant is the form of the regulations themselves. They state what is prohibited, not what is allowed. All substances are allowed in water except those that are specifically identified . . . . Application of the precautionary principle would demand that regulations be developed the other way around: that all substances be deemed harmful except those that are established as benign; and that the regulations identify those substances that are permitted in specified amounts.

See Bruce Pardy, "Seven Deadly Sins of Canadian Water Law" (2004) 13 *Journal of Environmental Law and Practice* 89 at 99

90 See, for example, Frances Bula, "No-Car Days Stall on Commercial Drive" *The Globe and Mail* (3 August 2009) A3.

have experimented with fees for vehicles in the central business district (CBD), limiting parking, increased parking fees, limiting the amount of parking on-street and in buildings, creating bike paths, and express bus or high-occupancy vehicle (HOV) lanes. As electric vehicles become more common, it will be within the purview of municipalities to accommodate the placement of charging stations. Licensing other vehicles such as scooters or Segways is a policy decision usually reserved for the provincial level. The essential legal point is that most of these initiatives find authorization in the municipal authority over "transportation" both in its normal general meaning, and, in the idea of what is "fairly implied or incident to the powers expressly granted,"[91] subject to proper interaction with provincial legislation on general traffic matters.

c) Sewage

Sewage control[92] is primarily related to protecting the safety of drinking water, although avoiding pollution of fisheries waters and general nuisance are also significant factors. In most municipalities there is a collection system, but there remain many private septic systems on individual properties. Overall, for Canadian households that are not apartments, Statistics Canada reports 15 percent as having private septic systems for 2006.[93] In either case, management is the crucial focus. The federal *Fisheries Act* prohibits activities that result in serious harm to fish, extending to discharge of deleterious substances.[94] Municipalities can be prosecuted, and have been.[95] Provincial rules usually specify that permitting is required for sewage works and that works may be closed if they become a source of pollution. Many municipalities also have in place by-laws to restrict the deposition of toxic materials in the sewer system.[96]

Source controls, that is, keeping the most toxic materials out of the sewer system in the first place rather than trying to treat the flows, are

---

91 The Dillon's Rule approach.

92 On this subject generally, see Jamie Benidickson, *The Culture of Flushing: A Social and Legal History of Sewage* (Vancouver: UBC Press, 2007).

93 The range is significant, with 10 percent of such households relying on septic systems in British Columbia and 53 percent in Prince Edward Island. See Statistics Canada, "Households and the Environment Survey, 2006," Special tabulation, Catalogue no.11-526-X, online: www.statcan.gc.ca/pub/11-526-x/11-526-x2007001-eng.pdf.

94 *Fisheries Act*, RSC 1985, c F-14, ss 34–36.

95 See *R v North Vancouver (District)* (1982), 11 CELR 158 (BC Prov Ct), aff'd (1982), 12 CELR 67 (BC Co Ct), aff'd (1984), 13 CELR 60 (CA).

96 See, for example, *Environmental Management and Protection Act, 2002*, SS 2002, c E-10.21, especially s 21. See, for example, City of Calgary, *Drainage Bylaw 37M2005*, which prohibits deposition of gasoline, motor oil, solvents, paint, cooking oil, pesticides, and biomedical or hazardous waste, along with other substances.

frequently identified as an important part of the design of any system; thus, in the Environmental Assessment Report for a proposed oil-from-sludge (OFS) sewage treatment system for Halifax, the panel said, "Controls-at-source programs need to be part of the . . . [s]ystem and must begin immediately."[97] Source controls are part of an array of possible approaches. As with other parts of the land-use planning enterprise, an array of approaches is known, but not uniformly or widely applied. Thus, it is possible to require new buildings to incorporate on-site treatment prior to discharge through solar aquatics, or to require new subdivisions to build engineered wetlands. Or conventional systems could be based on separation of the waste water and sewage pipes in order to control volume of flow and avoid use of combined sewer overflows (CSOs). Or run-off controls, promoting ground absorption of higher volumes of water rather than leading it to the sewer system, could be put in place. The problem here tends not to be the absence of a municipal regulatory power but the absence of its application in a better way.

d) Solid Waste

Solid waste is an interesting and culturally significant matter, but not the most pressing environmental issue. Unfortunately, it often receives a great deal of attention as an environmental issue and to some extent serves as a distraction from more serious issues. It is certainly the case that Canada is a society built on consumption and waste associated with wealth, and thus the issue of solid waste does have to be addressed. The slogan "reduce, reuse, recycle" is often taken as expressing the appropriate agenda in matters of solid waste. But composting, especially if carried on by the property-owner on-site, is a form of reduction of the landfill load and thus an important step (the most cost-efficient tonne is the one never picked-up), a step involving a beneficial use of the product. Much composting is carried out by municipalities in centralized facilities, which has led to controversy over odour as a local nuisance as well as debate over the quality and safety of the product in its intended use to augment soil. Hazardous waste can be diverted from the waste stream. Various measures, including the use of blue or green bins, clear bags, bag limits, and the banning of toxic materials from landfills, have been implemented without serious legal impediments. Controversies certainly exist, though they manifest as political disputes more often than legal disputes. Issues have arisen around the

---

97 See Federal-Provincial Environmental Assessment Review Panel, *Report of the Federal-Provincial Environmental Assessment Review Panel for the Halifax-Dartmouth Metropolitan Wastewater Management System* (Ottawa: Canada Communications Group, 1993) at 2.

location of landfills and plans for incineration of solid waste. Incineration is probably the most controversial aspect of solid waste management. In part this focuses on whether incineration is a beneficial use of the resource, in part on whether the technology is sufficiently efficient, in part on the nature of the emissions (dioxins, furans, PCBs), and in part on the disposal of the resultant ash. There are multiple cases, but as an environmental issue, the disputes are not so crucial as those having to do with energy, unless water pollution issues are involved.

So much is known about solid waste management that it is an excellent exemplar of one of my main points, namely that barriers to change are often not the absence of knowledge.

e) Parks and Recreation/Trees

Parks and recreation are essential for physical health through activity but also present an opportunity for increased vegetation. The role of green plants in the atmospheric cycle, for soil health, as carbon sinks, and for biodiversity, is well known. There is also evidence that their presence has direct health benefits.[98] It is easy, therefore, to see the role of parks as supporting these natural functions, leading to policies favouring planting more. Formal parks are not the only way to move on these items; lot coverage is a related matter. Many municipalities have rules about lawns, but tend to categorize them as matters of aesthetics rather than ecosystem health. Community gardens as a food supply and the promotion of local farmers' markets are related issues and involve awareness of the energy used in importing food.[99] Another major contribution is for the municipality to plant trees along the streets. Although there is a maintenance cost and the possibility of damage to adjacent properties through the spread of roots,[100] the benefits are such that "urban forests" are widely supported.

Any municipality addressing the matter in terms of ecosystem health should also consider limits on pavement coverage (impermeable surfaces): this relates to sewage system capacity since water that goes into the ground does not enter the sewers. Tree planting on public property raises no legal issue. Of more significance would be forbidding the removal of trees in the subdivision development process or a

---

98 For a summary, see Patrick Barkham, "How Street Trees Can Save Our Cities" *The Guardian Weekly* (18 September 2015) 29.

99 Michael Pollan has written extensively about issues, especially environmental issues, associated with food: see, for example, *The Omnivore's Dilemma* (New York: Penguin Press, 2006).

100 See *Guinan v Ottawa (City)*, 2010 ONSC 807.

system requiring a licence to cut any tree,[101] Still, subdivision regulatory powers are considerable. Soil removal is commonly prohibited or regulated, as is the changing of contours.

An aspect of recreation now having some financial impact on municipalities is the need to phase out use of Freon in hockey rinks. Under the 1985 *Montreal Protocol* on ozone-depleting substances, the use of Freon was to be ended by 2012; conversion of rinks to a new system has been and will continue to be expensive for their owners.

In sum, local governments tend to be vested with wide traditional powers relating to the promotion of ecosystem health, should they choose to understand them in that context.

4) Zoning and Zoning Flexibility Tools

a) Traditional Zoning

Traditional zoning is a locational matter. Thus, type and intensity of use, which are relevant environmental concerns, are bound up in traditional zoning. Height, density, and parking are also usually specified as matters for land-use by-laws. The environmental aspect of this is especially evident in attempts to control sprawl. Zoning decides what is allowed on one side of a line but not on the other. So long as these decisions are not completely arbitrary, discriminatory, or made in bad faith, the core zoning power will support them.[102] Controlling sprawl[103]

---

101 For a review of the science and the policy issues, see Eran Kaplinsky, "Private Tree Protection Bylaws" in Anneke Smits and Marcia Valiante, eds, *Public Interest, Private Property* (Vancouver: UBC Press, 2016) 195.

102 *Scarborough (Township) v Bondi*, [1959] SCR 444.

103 There are various cogent statements of the environmental and other problems associated with sprawl. In one American analysis, it is said,

> The detrimental effects of sprawl are well documented. By consuming land in a manner that is poorly planned, that encourages automobile dependence, and that pushes development away from city centers on a single-use basis, sprawl imposes numerous societal costs. The costs are financial. Sprawl requires outlying local governments to expend more on services for new residences than those developments provide in tax benefits; it leads to fiscal insolvency in inner cities by eroding the tax bases; it [causes] lost time and burned fuel from increased traffic . . . . The costs are social. Sprawl creates massive inefficiencies in the delivery of government services, including public transportation; it exacerbates housing unaffordability; it facilitates architectural mediocrity and the demise of our nation's agricultural heritage; and it leads to community disintegration and the loss of sense of place. The costs are racial. Sprawl disproportionately impacts minority and low-income populations . . . in effect, re-segregating the nation. And the costs are environmental. Sprawl consumes green space and wetlands and the ecosystem services they provide; it worsens air quality; it fractionalizes plant and wildlife habitat[;] . . . it makes flood-

can be a municipal concern because of a desire to reduce the costs of infrastructure; it could be a concern because of the capacity of an area to sustain water use or absorb wastes; it could be related to a desire to preserve productive agricultural land;[104] or it could be related to a desire to reduce energy use associated with transportation and thus the generation of polluting emissions, which are a health issue as well as a climate change issue.[105] The traditional essence of zoning in itself provides municipalities with a serious power that could be used for sustainability purposes. For example, it is now quite common for land-use by-laws to include designated zones for environmentally sensitive areas.

Another example of the beneficial use of the zoning power has to do with sea-level rise or the associated issues of erosion and storm surge. Commentators suggest that there are three adaptive responses within the powers of local governments: retreat, accommodation, and protection. Retreat may take the form of establishing setback requirements for new construction, allowing wetland migration, or relocating activities. Accommodation may involve modified building codes, acceptance of development compromises, and other adjustments to reduce vulnerability. Protection requires significant capital investment in seawalls, dykes, landfill, beach nourishment, or artificial wetlands, all of which will require ongoing maintenance and upgrading.[106]

> ing more likely and more intense by disrupting flood plains; it causes water pollution and prevents groundwater recharge by increasing impermeable surfaces; and it hastens the unsustainable consumption of groundwater by encouraging private well use.

See Lincoln L Davies, "Just a Big 'Hot Fuss'? Assessing the Value of Connecting Urban Sprawl, Land Use, and Water Rights through Assured Supply Laws" (2007) 34 *Ecology Law Quarterly* 1217 at 1224–225.

Another American commentator notes that "population booms in 'bedroom communities,' where vehicle miles traveled (VTM) growth rates are highest, will substantially undermine such [i.e., technology gains regarding automobile efficiency and low carbon fuels] gains in efficiency." See Henry Stern, "A Necessary Collision: Climate Change, Land Use, and the Limits of AB 32" (2008) 35 *Ecology Law Quarterly* 611 at 613. Climate change can be linked to cancers, sea-level rise, soil productivity, and other such effects, all of which are within the ambit of recognized municipal powers, however local.

104 A classification system exists: the Agricultural Land Identification Program, which ranks soil numerically from 1 (best) to 7 (no capacity for production).

105 A basic text on urban sprawl is Robert Bruegmann, *Sprawl: A Compact History* (Chicago: University of Chicago Press, 2005).

106 DL Forbes et al, "Climate Change Impacts in the Coastal Zone of Atlantic Canada" in Jim Abraham et al, eds, *Climate Change and Climate Variability in Atlantic Canada* (Toronto: Environment Canada, 1997) at 57. This is vol VI of the Canada Country Study: Climate Impacts and Adaptation. The other volumes in the series address the other regions of Canada, and also have sectoral themes.

The 2005 damage to New Orleans as a result of its exposure to Hurricane Katrina illustrates only too well the nature of the problem. The basics of what the science is suggesting as necessary may largely be accomplished through the basic zoning power, though the necessary investment in physical infrastructure does illustrate one of the limits of local municipalities to introduce sustainability measures.

Associated with the typical zoning power expressed in use-categories are adjuncts such as home-based businesses or accessory uses. Both could be defined in by-laws to extend to such activities as urban gardens,[107] even to the small-scale keeping of livestock such as poultry. The usual by-law definition of an accessory use is of a use "normally incidental, subordinate, exclusively devoted to and located on the same lot as the principal use";[108] the amorphousness of this typical definition has led to a testing of its limits through litigation on a moderately frequent basis,[109] but any ambiguity could be removed by specifying allowed activities. Similarly, home-based businesses, which can contribute to countering sprawl, have in the past often been limited to high-end professionals (lawyers, physicians, dentists, accountants) using their homes or a part of them as offices; changing economic times have led to expansion of allowed businesses (massage therapists, hairdressers).[110] The core regulatory issue is often signage as much as traffic in residential areas. However, many businesses rely on use of the Internet, and can conveniently be carried on from home offices without any need for signage or traffic. There is no inherent barrier to zoning allowing the sale of produce grown on site. In any event, local food production has the obvious benefit of avoiding the expenditure of energy associated with transportation of so much of our food.[111]

---

107 See Lisa McLaughlin, "Inner-City Farms" *Time* (4 August 2008) 40: "urban gardeners are waging a lot of different wars—against global warming, foreign-oil dependence, processed food, obesity and neighborhood blight."

108 This wording, taken from the City of Regina, *Regina Zoning By-law No 9250*, Part 2C "Definitions."

109 See, for example, *Walton v Lincoln (Town)* (1997), 43 MPLR (2d) 291 (Ont Ct Gen Div), where the breeding of guinea pigs is an accessory use in a barn on a residentially zoned lot; *Corman Park No 344 (Rural Municipality) v Saskatoon Berry Farms Ltd* (1994), 20 MPLR (2d) 286 (Sask QB), aff'd (1995), 131 Sask R 239 (CA), where a concession selling snacks and souvenirs to berry pickers is an accessory use in an agricultural zone, but a full-scale restaurant is not.

110 Expansion of home-based businesses represents a modification of the industrial model of production and something of a return to cottage industry. On this subject, see John Kenneth Galbraith, *The Liberal Hour* (Boston: Houghton Mifflin, 1960), especially s VIII "The Nature of Social Nostalgia."

111 See Pollan, above note 99.

The land-use regulatory power can extend to "the location of disposal sites for any waste material"; "the removal of topsoil"; "methods for controlling erosion"; "floodplains"; "prohibit development within a specified distance of a watercourse"; and "prohibit development on land that is subject to subsidence, has steep slopes, is . . . marshy . . . [or] otherwise hazardous [and] is known to be contaminated . . . ."[112] Thus, there is usually built into the range of powers that are associated with traditional zoning, an expectation that at least some aspects of sustainability will be dealt with through that tool.

b) Zoning Flexibility Tools

Tempo of development controls allow municipalities to delay development. "Holding" zones, recognized in caselaw as a valid exercise of the general zoning power as early as 1975 in the cases of *Soo Mill & Lumber Co v Sault Ste-Marie (City)*[113] and *Sanbay Developments Ltd v London (City)*,[114] are now also bolstered by statutory provisions.[115] *Planning Acts* usually allow serious restrictions where land is contaminated, is subject to flooding, is marshy, contains sensitive groundwater features, or has significant natural features.[116] Treating areas as subject to council's discretion so far as development is concerned allows for stating criteria that will apply.

Bonusing is a major zoning flexibility tool. It describes a mechanism that allows landowners to build beyond the normal restrictions of the land-use by-laws in certain circumstances, and usually in exchange for some identified public benefit. Thus, section 37 of the Ontario *Planning Act*, for example, allows bonusing for height and density "in return for the provision of such facilities, services or matters as are set out in the by-law."[117] One form of bonusing is transferable development rights (TDR).[118] In TDR, the extra use in some area, typically the urban

---

112 This list is taken from the Nova Scotia *Municipal Government Act*, above note 36, s 220(5), but is similar to lists to be found in other provincial statutes granting municipal powers.

113 (1974), [1975] 2 SCR 78.

114 (1974), [1975] 1 SCR 485.

115 See, for example, *Planning Act*, above note 38, s 36.

116 *Ibid*, s 34(1), paras 3, 3.1, & 3.2.

117 *Ibid*, s 37(1). In Ontario this has routinely extended to payments to be made to the municipality tied to the provision of the facilities or services, even though some British Columbia jurisprudence has doubted whether cash payments should be read as authorized by such mechanisms. See *Lambert v Whistler (Resort Municipality)*, 2004 BCSC 342, supplementary reasons 2004 BCSC 391, supplementary reasons 2005 BCSC 1325.

118 See Arlene J Kwasniak, "The Potential for Municipal Transfer of Development Credits Programs in Canada" (2004) 15 *Journal of Environmental Law and Practice* 47.

core, is granted in exchange for a freeze on land development in some other area, typically the periphery. Thus, TDR has been used to control sprawl. In the United States (Kings County, Washington), 90,000 acres of forest land was preserved in what has been termed "the largest TDR scheme in the country."[119] A typical use of the bonusing provision has been a requirement for assisted housing or the development of a park,[120] but in *Lambert v Whistler (Resort Municipality)*, the public benefits sought included landscaping to protect a fish-bearing watercourse and enhancing public trails.[121] Official Plan policies or land-use by-laws should specify the objectives to be negotiated.

5) Subdivisions

One of the major ways in which local governments now exert some direct environmental controls is through the subdivision (s/d) mechanism. The division of one piece of property into smaller lots, which may then be conveyed and, usually, built upon, is the process of subdivision.[122] That is, there is both a land use and a land title, or direct property law, aspect to subdivision.[123] It being a commonly used device; a special set of regulations governs s/d schemes in each province, often allowing municipalities the power to adopt their own s/d by-laws, with the province-wide rules applicable in default of local regulation.[124] The matters that may be addressed in considering s/d applications are listed; an approving authority is not to approve the s/d unless the land

---

119 Harry W Richardson & Peter Gordon, "The Implications of the Breaking the Logjam Project for Smart Growth in Urban Land Use" (2008) 17 *NYU Environmental Law Journal* 529 at 533.

120 *Copthorne Holdings Ltd, Re* (1987), 36 MPLR 122 (OMB); *1430 Yonge Street Inc v Toronto (City)* (2003), 46 OMBR 63.

121 *Lambert v Whistler (Resort Municipality)*, above note 117. The attack on the by-law was successful, but not on a basis that undermines the municipality's power to focus on environmental amenities pursuant to section 904 of the *Local Government Act*, RSBC 1996, c 323. A striking aspect of various bonusing cases is that placing a dollar charge on a development, to be spent or to be transferred to the municipality as part of the bargaining for amenities, although not specified as authorized by the relevant sections of the governing legislation, has not been questioned; see also *1430 Yonge Street Inc v Toronto (City)*, above note 120, in which the decision inaccurately says that section 37 of the Ontario *Planning Act* provides "that the City can seek amenities . . . from the developer, including cash payments for public amenities . . . ." (at para 18).

122 For convenience, the Saskatchewan s/d rules will be referenced.

123 See, for example, Saskatchewan *Planning and Development Act, 2007*, SS 2007, c P-13.2, s 121(2) and cases such *as Reid v Reid* (1976), 22 NSR (2d) 361 (SCTD).

124 See, for example, Saskatchewan *Planning and Development Act, 2007*, above note 123, s 126, and *The Subdivision Regulations, 2014*, RRS c P-13.2 Reg 2.

is "suitable for the purpose for which the subdivision is intended."[125] Specific factors extend to topography; the soil characteristics; potential flooding, subsidence, landslides,[126] and erosion; the availability and adequacy of a water supply; a sewage disposal system; the existing and prospective uses of land in the vicinity; the design and orientation of the subdivision, including the size and shape of each parcel; and the need to minimize the likelihood of air, water, or soil pollution by the subdivision or the need to protect the subdivision from such pollution.[127] "Orientation" suggests that roads and general layout could be required to be in aid of maximizing passive energy, by orienting buildings to the south and west.[128]

It is obvious from the above list of conditions that the s/d process is a signal opportunity for local government to take up responsibility for review of a wide array of environmental factors prior to granting the preliminary permission for new development on larger tracts of land. More than an opportunity, it is a requirement. Many recent municipal law cases involving environmental issues have arisen in the context of disputes over s/d conditions.[129]

6) Building Codes and Energy Codes

A related municipal power is the adoption and enforcement of building codes.[130] The federal government has been the generator of the codes, provinces have set the legal context for their application, and municipalities are the usual enforcers of the codes.[131] Municipalities are generally required by provincial laws to adopt or adopt with changes, such codes.[132] Canada now has model Energy Codes for both general

125 Saskatchewan *Planning and Development Act, 2007*, above note 123, s 128

126 See James Schwab, *Landslide Hazards and Planning* (Chicago: American Planning Association, 2005).

127 *The Subdivision Regulations, 2014*, above note 124, s 14.

128 See Keith Nicol, "Building Orientation and Heating Requirements" (1987) 27(6) *Plan Canada* 154.

129 See, for example, *Wheale v Brazeau (County)*, 2006 ABCA 171; *Strathcona (County) v Allan*, 2006 ABCA 129.

130 See, generally, Ian MacFee Rogers & Alison Scott Butler, *Canadian Law of Planning and Zoning*, 2d ed (Toronto: Carswell, 2005) ch 7 "Building Construction Regulation."

131 See, for example, Ontario's *Building Code Act, 1992*, SO 1992, c 23, s 3: "The council of each municipality is responsible for the enforcement of this Act in the municipality . . . ."

132 In Ontario the code is made uniform across the province: *Building Code Act, 1992*, *ibid*, s 35. The *Municipal Act, 2001*, above note 44, also includes a power to adopt codes or standards by reference, and to require compliance: s 447.8. In

buildings and for houses.[133] The Canadian Commission on Building and Fire Codes, a division of the National Research Council of Canada, has been rewriting the two 1997 codes and has published the new code for buildings. As set out in the preamble to the draft Energy Code for Houses, the document "is essentially a code of minimum regulations for energy efficiency in small residential buildings, taking into consideration climate, fuel types and costs, and construction costs . . . ."[134] The code for "buildings" applies to other structures.

A focus on houses and buildings is significant because in Canada they can account for roughly 40 percent of overall energy use through heating and cooling and internal electricity use. Apart from the building code itself, municipalities may be empowered to "adopt by reference, in whole or in part, with changes that the council considers necessary or advisable, a code or standard and require compliance with it."[135] Clearly, a municipality could potentially require a high level of energy efficiency and have standards which manifest that. This does not have to be limited to the new federal energy codes,[136] but could extend to the LEED standard (Leadership in Energy and Environmental Design)[137] or to some other measure, and even to requiring new buildings or subdivisions to be oriented to the south and west so as to maximize passive solar gain, although this could probably be incorporated into traditional zoning and not have to be a part of the building code. "In 2005, Scottsdale, Arizona, became the first city in the United States to require that all new city buildings be certified at the LEED Gold standard level."[138] Some analysts propose that limits on height should also be seen as energy measures, pointing out that buildings over six storeys become energy inefficient.[139]

British Columbia, a Green Building Code, which includes provisions aimed at efficiencies for energy and water use, has been in place for several years.

133 National Research Council of Canada, "National Energy Code of Canada for Buildings 2015," online: www.nrc-cnrc.gc.ca/eng/solutions/advisory/codes_centre_index.html.

134 National Research Council of Canada, National Energy Code for Houses 1995, Public Review 1.0 (Ottawa: National Research Council, 1994) at 17.

135 Nova Scotia *Municipal Government Act*, above note 36, s 172(2)(d).

136 For comments on use of certain codes in the context of regulatory statutes, see Stepan Wood & Lynn Johannson "Six Principles for Integrating Non-Governmental Standards into Smart Regulation" (2008) 46 *Osgoode Hall Law Journal* 345.

137 LEED was developed by the US Green Building Council: see online: www.usgbc.org.

138 Matthew J Parlow, "Greenwashed?: Developers, Environmental Consciousness, and the Case of Playa Vista" (2008) 35 *Boston College Environmental Affairs Law Review* 513 at 519–20.

139 Larry Hughes & Tyler Wood, "Solar Energy and Multi-Storey Residential Buildings" (26 March 2007), online: http://lh.ece.dal.ca/enen/2007/ERG200702.pdf,

Despite the availability of progressive standards, the construction sector is reported by Natural Resources Canada to have increased its total energy consumption by 20 percent in the decade between 1996 and 2006.[140] One aim, not represented in the various standards that have been drafted, is of buildings being completely carbon-neutral, an aim endorsed by the World Business Council for Sustainable Development, representing some 200 of the world's largest corporations.[141] Devices such as geothermal heat pumps, rainwater collection for reuse, photovoltaics, and solar hot water systems are all available and could be mandated by local governments, though setting targets rather than particular technologies may often be a more appropriate step.

Some municipal officials are of the opinion that energy matters need to be specified in their governing statutes before municipalities may use building codes for that purpose.[142] While it is certainly the case that the traditional understanding of building codes is that they are about construction and demolition or health and safety, it is far from clear that such a modest approach to the ambit of municipal powers over energy efficiency is correct. It appears to contradict the opinion of the Supreme Court of Canada that the environment is a responsibility of all levels of government, that municipal powers should be interpreted purposefully, and that energy use is an important environmental concern. At the same time, there is a line of judicial interpretation associated with the interpretation of the term "other applicable law" as it appears in the Ontario *Building Code Act* that suggests that the building codes are not generally to be thought of as extending to environmental concerns. The point of contention is whether the official charged with issuing building permits may consider the possible negative environmental effects of the proposed project and decline to issue the permit. Jurisdiction in the Ontario

---

and "Halifax: Heritage, Height, and Heating" *The Chronicle-Herald* (19 January 2008) A11. The analysis set out by Hughes in these two articles raises a dilemma for those who see part of the answer to sprawl in construction of highrises.

140 The total increased from 50,000 terajoules to 60,000; see National Resources Canada, *Canadian Industry Program for Energy Conservation, Annual Report 2008* (Ottawa: Office for Energy Efficiency, Natural Resources Canada, 2008) at 62.

141 World Business Council for Sustainable Development, "Energy Efficiency in Buildings: Facts and Trends: Business Realities and Opportunities" (2008), online: http://wbcsdpublications.org/project/energy-efficiency-in-buildings-facts-and-trends-business-realities-and-opportunities-full-report.

142 See, for example, D Jackson, "Draft Rules for Development in HRM Released" *The Chronicle Herald* (16 September 2008) B2: "The second draft notes that the municipality doesn't have the power to require the private sector to meet the LEED environmental standard . . . . The city is still waiting on the provincial government to make legislative changes . . . ."

Act allows the official to consider "other applicable law."[143] In a number of cases, most recently in *Ottawa (City) v Ottawa (City) Chief Building Official*,[144] which contains an extensive review of the jurisprudence, the Ontario courts have said that the Act is about construction and demolition and not about use, and thus environmental considerations become an extraneous matter for the official. The test is stated as being whether there is a real and logical nexus between the other law being taken into consideration and the building code. Some clarification of the desired operation of the process might be useful. But in the absence of that, municipal adoption of an energy code would advance at least part of a local government's environmental concerns.[145]

7) Nuisance

Numerous cases exist of municipalities addressing nuisance activities such as fumes and odour[146] and noise.[147] The power to do so, specified by statute, is already in quite regular use for common forms of nuisance, but its full potential may not always be realized. In the environmental movement community, there is recognition of the utility of nuisance actions along with other aspects of the common law as a basis for challenging polluting activities.[148] In the frequently cited words of Rinfret J in *Groat v Edmonton (City)*, "Pollution is always unlawful and, in itself, constitutes a nuisance."[149] Because of the wide ambit of nuisance law, and in light of what was said in *Groat* to establish the link between nuisance and pollution, adopting nuisance regulations may prove to

---

143 Ontario *Building Code Act, 1992*, above note 131.

144 (2003), 45 MPLR (3d) 29 (Ont Div Ct).

145 In addition, and quite crucially, the existence of some specific municipal standards could assist builders in obtaining financing and insurance for buildings incorporating novel features such as green roofs.

146 See, for example, *Newmarket (Town) v Halton Recycling Ltd* (2006), 25 MPLR (4th) 249 (Ont SCJ).

147 See, for example, *Montréal (City) v 2952-1366 Québec inc*, above note 27.

148 There is also recognition of some of its problems, such as standing, expense, and uncertainty of result. See, for example, Paul Emond, "Are We There Yet? Reflections on the Success of the Environmental Law Movement in Ontario" (2008) 46 *Osgoode Hall Law Journal* 219 at 229.

149 [1928] SCR 522 at 532. On this topic, see, generally, Jamie Benidickson, *Environmental Law*, 4th ed (Toronto: Irwin Law, 2013) at 102ff; Paul Emond, above note 148 at 229–32; Richard Lindgren, "The New Toxic Torts: An Environmental Perspective" (November 2000), online: The Canadian Environmental Law Association www.cela.ca/sites/cela.ca/files/uploads/toxic_torts.pdf; Gordon Miller, "Looking Forward: The Environmental Bill of Rights. Special Report to the Legislature of Ontario" (31 March 2005).

be a major tool of local government in dealing with some aspects of environmental protection. With the reworking of some provinces' municipal statutes so as to establish local jurisdiction over only specified "spheres," even where the legislative intention is that they be broadly interpreted, there has been some suggestion in the courts that jurisdiction over the environment might be limited.[150]

The essential preliminary question is what can be considered to be a nuisance at all. In all instances, the specific statute has to be examined.

As *Rascal Trucking* illustrates, the idea of nuisance may be somewhat circumscribed in municipal legislation, though it need not be.[151] If that is the case, common law notions of what is or can be a nuisance will guide the courts when the exercise of municipal powers over nuisance is challenged. What, then, is a nuisance at common law? It is usually said that a nuisance is the use of land so as to cause an unreasonable interference with the use and enjoyment of the land of others or with some public right; hence the terms "private nuisance" and "public nuisance."[152] Nuisance must be related to substantial harm. Nuisance is a different category of land delict than trespass or strict liability. It is usually said that nuisance relates to something offensive to the senses, for example, noise, odour, dust, and vibrations, though certainly the generalized problems of air and water pollution are possible to approach as nuisances. Because the concept of reasonableness is involved, it is apparent that nuisance is to some extent an amorphous topic. Indeed, the courts have said that the categories of nuisance are not closed.[153] This should not be understood as a *pro forma* and essentially limiting statement—rather the opposite. Thus, the Canadian courts have regarded interference with the receipt of television signals through the placement of a type of building, as a nuisance, even where the building is lawfully constructed.[154] In the United States, the equivalent statement about the wide ambit of nuisance appears in the well-

---

150 See *Croplife Canada v Toronto (City)* (2003), 68 OR (3d) 520 (SCJ).

151 *Rascal Trucking*, above note 27, was a problem in statutory construction of the associated words (*noscitur a sociis*) sort.

152 For the factors that amount to public nuisance, see *Ryan v Victoria (City)*, [1999] 1 SCR 201.

153 *St Pierre v Ontario (Minister of Transportation & Communications)* (1987), 39 DLR (4th) 10 (SCC).

154 *Nor-Video Services Ltd v Ontario Hydro* (1978), 4 CCLT 244 (Ont HCJ); see also *TH Critelli Ltd v Lincoln Trust & Savings Co* (1978), 4 CCLT 217 (Ont HCJ), aff'd (1979), 111 DLR (3d) 179n (Ont CA), where the owner of a building, lawfully constructed, was found liable for the increased snow-load effect its presence caused on an adjacent lower building.

known takings case of *Lucas v South Carolina Coastal Council*,[155] where Scalia J said, "changed circumstances or new knowledge may make what was previously permissible no longer so."[156]

Given the very general notion of nuisance, such sections of *Municipal Acts* must now be seen to confer great potential for local government jurisdiction. The municipal power to regulate nuisance is akin in potential scope to that identified as inherent in the general purpose sections of statutes as interpreted by the Supreme Court of Canada in *Spraytech*.[157]

Because the remedies set out by statute tend to include both prosecution and injunctions, the position of the municipality with respect to nuisance is akin to that of the attorney general. In effect, the consent of the attorney general as a prerequisite to taking civil action to restrain a nuisance is eliminated if the complainant is a municipality enforcing

155 505 US 1003 (1992) at 1031 [*Lucas*]. In a similar case, *Palazzolo v Rhode Island*, 533 US 606 (2001), *Lucas* was applied to make it clear that the existence of a nuisance precludes allegations of any regulatory taking. This case has been interpreted to suggest that the emergence of better understanding of ecosystems, combined with a professional valuation method for natural systems, may be used to expand the scope of nuisance. Regarding this point, see JB Ruhl, "Making Nuisance Ecological" (2008) 58:3 *Case Western Reserve Law Review* 753. This volume contains a symposium on common law environmental protection. See also Jonathan Zasloff, "The Judicial Carbon Tax: Reconstructing Public Nuisance and Climate Change" (2008) 55 *UCLA Law Review* 1827.

156 The US law is worth examining in a bit more detail because of its recent elaboration of the potential environmental application of nuisance. A line of thought can be traced from the 1992 Supreme Court decision in *Lucas*, above note 155. The US Constitution protects property owners against "takings" without compensation. As early as 1922, cases had determined that excessive regulation could amount to a compensable taking. *Lucas* established that a government could defend against a regulatory takings claim by showing that the land use proposed would amount to a nuisance. Since then, in various cases, the courts have accepted that wetland destruction is a nuisance; that construction in a flood plain can be a nuisance; that saltmarsh destruction is a nuisance; and that harm to a particular watershed is a nuisance. An attempt to establish global warming as a nuisance was not successful. Although Canada does not have the same property protections in the Constitution, our focus should be on the nature of the evidence and the US court holdings on what can amount to a nuisance. Clearly, the common law is evolving, based on an appreciation of externalities, how ecosystems work, and establishing a method to value ecosystem functions.

157 As with *Spraytech*, above note 30, there may be specific limitations set out or implied in the overall provincial statutory scheme. This was found to be the case in *Ontario (Attorney General) v Mississauga (City)*, above note 53, in which the municipality purported to use its power over nuisance to regulate PCBs, whereas the *Environment Act* allowed for provincial-level regulation; the court found operative conflict.

its own by-law.[158] The court's remedial powers in such cases extend to anticipatory injunction,[159] continuing injunction, and removal or destruction of the building or structure.[160] Crucially, the standard applied by the courts when considering a request for a statutory injunction does not normally include a balancing of interests of the sort required when a private citizen seeks injunction as a civil remedy.[161]

As an alternative to the exercise of statutory regulatory powers over nuisance or taking action against a violation of their own by-laws, municipalities could act as litigators to challenge polluters under the common law, especially where the nuisance is public. It is not clear whether standing is still an issue. Some older cases have held that municipalities should not be granted standing to sue for an injunction restraining public nuisances affecting their residents.[162] This case also suggests that a municipality is unlikely to be able to bring action against a polluter on the basis of private nuisance, unless it can show that its own lands have been particularly affected. However, the law of standing has evolved significantly since those cases were decided. It may also be that the natural person powers of a municipality may assist, or, if some statutory power exists to promote the interests of residents, this may lead to a finding of standing. In the United Kingdom, there is some precedent along these lines in cases such as *Gillingham Borough Council v Medway (Chatham) Dock Co Ltd et al.*[163] In those provinces where an Environmental Bill of Rights offers citizens the right to sue in nuisance without the attorney general's consent, and local governments have been granted natural person powers, the problem may be resolved.[164] If there is municipal standing to take nuisance actions, the scope may be quite wide.

---

158 See *One Chestnut Park Road Ltd v Toronto (City)* (1964), 43 DLR (2d) 390 (SCC).

159 It is even possible that the availability of an anticipatory injunction as a remedy in nuisance cases could pre-empt an environmental assessment process being undertaken by one of the senior levels of government.

160 See, for example, Nova Scotia's *Municipal Government Act*, above note 36, ss 181(4) and 184.

161 See, for example, *Maple Ridge (District) v Thornhill Aggregates Ltd* (1998), 47 MPLR (2d) 249 (BCCA), leave to appeal to SCC refused, [1998] SCCA No 407; *Langley (Township) v Wood*, 1999 BCCA 260; Randall Balcome, "Statutory Injunctions in Municipal Legislation" (1992) 18 *Nova Scotia Law News* 145; *Metropolitan Toronto (Municipality) v NB Theatrical Agencies Inc* (1984), 44 OR (2d) 574 (HCJ); *One Chestnut Park Road Ltd v Toronto (City)*, above note 158.

162 *St Lawrence Rendering Co v Cornwall (City)*, [1951] 4 DLR 790 (Ont HCJ).

163 [1993] QB 343. In this UK case, the municipality was exercising its general power "to promote or protect the interests of the inhabitants in its area," a provision akin to the general or omnibus power.

164 See, for example, Ontario's *Environmental Bill of Rights, 1993*, above note 73, ss 84 and 103.

8) Municipal Utilities

The main reason to consider utilities is if a municipality is prepared to emphasize environmental values, especially sustainability, by use of renewables in electricity generation, through a municipal utility.

It is not uncommon for municipalities to deliver services to residents through special businesses, most typically a water utility.[165] These undertakings are often "natural monopolies," an economists' term for a situation in which it is inefficient to have more than one provider.[166] In the mixed nature of the Canadian economy, it is more usual for the public sector to deliver goods or services that are essential and also natural monopolies, and for the private sector to be involved in everything else. Publicly owned utilities operate on a not-for-profit basis; sometimes this means they operate with a deficit made up through tax revenues, and sometimes it means they operate on a full cost-recovery basis. Because the undertakings are public, their mandate can be broader than the private sector's objective of making a profit for owners; they can be charged with advancing certain policy goals; it is for that reason they are of importance to the array of means by which sustainability objectives might be advanced by local government. Whether structured as independent or quasi-independent bodies or just as a department of local government, municipalities can be involved in a variety of undertakings.[167] Water is the most common. Public transit is another example. The generation and delivery of energy in the form of gas and electricity is probably of most potential importance for our purposes.

There is no inherent right of local governments to establish public utilities; as with other municipal powers, there must be some source in provincial legislation.[168] The statutory basis for municipal utilities is often found in sections of *Municipal Acts* that set out the power to expend money. In Ontario and several other provinces, the broad "Spheres of Jurisdiction" powers are also apparently intended to support some

---

165 Municipalities may also grant rights over public property to private companies that may be classed as utilities, for example, for the placement of lines or poles. The exercise of such a power is often termed a franchise. Legislation illustrating this is the *Municipal Franchises Act*, RSO 1990, c M.55. Because it is more difficult for a municipality to influence the environmental policies of privately owned franchisees, they are not the focus of this section.

166 Jim Stanford, *Economics for Everyone* (Halifax: Fernwood, 2008) at 235. See online: www.economicsforeveryone.com for a glossary and related materials.

167 See Andrew Sancton & Robert Young, eds, *Foundations of Governance: Municipal Government in Canada's Provinces* (Toronto: University of Toronto Press, 2009) at 8.

168 *Cobalt (Town) v Temiskaming Telephone Co* (1919), 59 SCR 62.

municipal utilities.[169] In some provinces, such as Alberta, policy seems to indicate a preference to limit municipal intervention in the electricity business.[170] There is early caselaw on municipal utilities that recognizes their general legitimacy.[171]

History, as well as legislation, has led to a situation in each province in which there tends to be one province-wide electrical utility, usually publicly owned. There is some presence of municipal electric utilities in Canada, with Toronto Hydro Corporation (THC) being the most extensive.[172] Despite the established presence of THC, public policy now in Ontario appears to favour continued support of the existing province-wide utility, since it is also publicly owned.

As mentioned above, Ontario has recently limited municipal jurisdiction over renewable energy projects,[173] including severely restricting *Planning Act* controls, although the new rules do allow municipalities to engage in their own generation of electricity from renewables on a small scale (up to 10 megawatts).[174] In Nova Scotia, municipalities have been encouraged to engage in electricity generation through renewables, and several are in the process of doing so.[175]

Some legal barriers exist for a municipal electrical utility to enter into the generation and transmission business. The main one is access to a transmission and distribution grid. This is the case whether the local intention is to serve customers only within the municipal boundaries or to feed into a larger grid. Unless willingly accepted by the monopoly utility, provincial laws will have to mandate access to the grid for wheeling, and the regulator will have to establish an open

---

169 *Municipal Act, 2001*, above note 44, s 1: "public utility" means a system that is used to provide any of the following services or things for the public: water; sewage; fuel, including natural and artificial gas; energy, excluding electricity [nb]; heating and cooling; and telephone. Regarding utilities powers in Ontario, see ss 10 & 11 of the *Municipal Act, 2001*.

170 See *Electric Utilities Act*, SA 2003, c E-5.1, Parts 6 and 9 (Divisions 4 and 5). Municipalities that engaged in generating up to 1995 are permitted to continue, and special recognition is given to Medicine Hat.

171 *Hull Electric Co v Ottawa Electric Co*, [1902] AC 237 (PC); *Smith v London (City)* (1909), 20 OLR 133 (Div Ct).

172 For general information, see the corporation website, online: www.torontohydro.com.

173 See *Suncor Energy Products Inc v Plympton-Wyoming (Town)*, 2014 ONSC 2934.

174 *Green Energy and Green Economy Act, 2009*, above note 64. For analysis, see Paul Manning & Joanna Vince, "Municipalities and the Green Energy Act" *Municipal World* (January 2010) at 5ff.

175 The towns of Antigonish, Berwick, and Mahone Bay in Nova Scotia have partnered in one 9.2 megawatt wind project: "Antigonish Wind Project Ready for Big Debut" (22 September 2015), online: http://allNovaScotia.com.

access transmission tariff (OATT), setting the rate for use of the grid. It may be possible for municipalities to expropriate an existing grid, but the specifics of an array of laws, including any provisions limiting monopolies or offering protections to the monopoly or quasi-monopoly electrical utilities, will come into play. Another significant barrier is the financial one. Municipalities operate under generally strict provincial rules as to debt and capital spending, rules designed to ensure that local governments, so far as possible, do not run the risk of bankruptcy. Any expenditures involved in setting up an electrical utility would have to conform to existing financial rules. In 2007, New Brunswick made amendments to its *Municipalities Act* to make it easier for local governments to be generators of electricity, with a view to promoting wind energy, solar power, cogeneration, and biogas; the new laws included various financial oversight provisions.[176]

Associated with electrical generation by municipal utilities is the role of local government in facilitating private owners in generating their own electricity or to make it available to feed into the grid. Small-scale windmills and solar panels (which may be for hot water rather than for electricity) could be regulated as structures for safety, height, and other usual municipal purposes. California has a *Solar Rights Act* and a *Solar Trade Control Act*[177] and has, since the late 1970s, offered limited protections to structures with solar panels, the protections being from trees and not from other buildings. The *Solar Rights Act* forbids municipalities from imposing unreasonable restrictions on solar energy systems. Some form of shade protection would have to be considered in the planning process, given the absence of a common law right to light.[178] Although it was not the central reason for rejection of a proposed development, the Ontario Municipal Board (OMB) has

176 *Municipalities Act*, RSNB 1973, c M-22, as amended. Bill 59, passed 16 June 2008, added new ss 111.1–111.7 to the Act. See also Communications New Brunswick, News Release, "Electricity Generation Authority to be Provided to Municipalities and Rural Communities" (15 May 2008), online: www.gnb.ca/cnb/news/gl/2008e0732gl.htm.

177 See Scott Anders et al, "California's *Solar Shade Control Act*: A Review of the Statutes and Relevant Cases" Energy Policy Initiatives Centre, University of San Diego School of Law (January 2007), online: www.sandiego.edu/law/documents/centers/epic/100329_SSCA_Final_000.pdf. See also Craig M Kline, "Solar" in Michael B Gerrard, ed, *The Law of Clean Energy* (Chicago: American Bar Association, 2011).

178 There is at least one American case suggesting that an owner could bring a nuisance action against a neighbouring landowner to protect pre-existing solar panels: see *Prah v Moretti*, 321 NW2d 182 (Wis 1982).

considered the negative effect of shadowing on the solar panels of an adjacent building.[179]

Small-scale wind turbines also raise planning issues. A 2006 study for the Canadian Wind Energy Association reported that few municipalities had considered the issues.[180] That leaves individuals struggling with rules governing accessory structures and height.[181] For larger, commercial, "wind farms," considerations include noise and therefore separation distances as well as potential interference with aviation or electronic communications, vibrations, shadow flicker, blade throw, and aesthetics.[182]

9) Provincial Policy Statements

It is a requirement of most provincial planning laws that when municipalities adopt official plans to guide their long-term planning and the content of their land-use by-laws, they must ensure that their official plans (OPs) accord with any designated provincial policy statements (PPS) or statements of interest. The rigour of this requirement varies. Just to use the Ontario example, since its standard has been varied over time: from 1983 to 1994, the *Planning Act* required OPs to "have regard to" any PPS, but from 1994 to 1996, the requirement was for an OP to "be

179 See *Toronto (City) Zoning By-law No. 438-86 (Re)* (2004), 49 OMBR 186. The shadowing was an effect the board considered as part of its conclusion that the project was "simply too big" for its site.

180 eFormative Options LLC and Entegrity Wind Systems Inc, "Small Wind Siting and Zoning Study: Development of Siting Guidelines and a Model Zoning By-law for Small Wind Turbines" (September 2006) prepared for the Canadian Wind Energy Association, online: www.toolkit.bc.ca/sites/default/files/Small_Wind_Siting_Bylaw%20and%20Guidelines.pdf.

181 See, for example, *Re Spurr*, 2009 NSUARB 98, where a proposed turbine was seen as an accessory use, but height was limited to 15 feet under the land use by-law, thus making the turbine impractical.

182 See UK, Sustainable Development Commission, *A Guide to the Key Issues Surrounding Onshore Wind Power Development in the UK* (London: Sustainable Development Commission, 2005); Jacques Whitford, "Final Report: Model Wind Turbine By-laws and Best Practices for Nova Scotia Municipalities," online: Union of Nova Scotia Municipalities http://unsm.ca/doc_download/1569-unsm-wind-by-laws-best-practices.html. Some of these issues are regulated by the federal or provincial governments. The Whitford report says (at 25) "British Columbia, Alberta, and Ontario have opted for a sound level regulation of 40dBA." Researchers at Queen's University have started a health effects study: see Sarah Boesveld, "What's Blowing in the Wind?" *The Globe and Mail* (8 July 2009) L1. Health Canada has issued a report "Wind Turbine Noise and Health Study: Summary of Results" (10 March 2014), online: www.hc-sc.gc.ca/ewh-semt/noise-bruit/turbine-eoliennes/summary-resume-eng.php.

consistent with" the policies; in 1996, the earlier standard was reverted to, and then in 2005, was changed again to "shall be consistent with."[183]

Regardless of the province's standard of rigour, PPS tend to extend to broad environmental matters. In Ontario, the topics covered are agriculture, water, managing growth, preserving green space, air quality, and transportation. In Manitoba, the PPS under the *Planning Act* requires OPs to "ensure that development is environmentally sound and consistent with the sustainable use of Manitoba's resources including the land base, arable soils, water, minerals, oil and gas, forests, wildlife, fish, recreation areas, heritage and other resources."[184] In British Columbia, targets for reducing greenhouse gas emissions have recently been added to the requirement of providing for the needs of housing, transportation, services, parks, and economic development in official community plans and regional growth strategies.[185] The British Columbia statute says that official community plans "must include targets for the reduction of greenhouse gas emissions . . . and policies and actions of the local government proposed with respect to achieving those targets."[186] In Nova Scotia, sections 193 and 198 of the *Municipal Government Act* invokes a Schedule B series of Statements of Provincial Interest dealing with agricultural lands, drinking water, flood risk areas, and infrastructure, and requires municipal planning strategies to "be reasonably consistent"[187] with the statements.[188]

By their own terms, PPS can be effective land-use control devices, as illustrated in *Hill & Hill Farms Ltd*,[189] a case involving a hog farm. The municipality had passed a zoning by-law incorporating the minimum separation distances for intensive livestock operations (ILOs) as set out by the Ontario Ministry of Agriculture, Food and Rural Affairs, a standard known as MDSII. When the farm enterprise was refused a variance

---

183 Ontario *Planning Act*, above note 38, s 3(5). The changes in the statute followed changes in the political party in government. See John G Chipman, *The Planning Act in Transition* (Aurora, ON: Canada Law Book, 1996).

184 *Provincial Land Use Policies Regulation*, Man Reg 184/94, Policy #1, General Development, A.3. The Manitoba set of PPS is particularly oriented towards sustainability.

185 *Local Government Act*, above note 121, ss 877(3) and 850(2). The NGO Smart Growth BC has a critique of this mechanism, pointing out that compliance is voluntary in the sense that having an OP is voluntary, and the targets are not specified: see online: www.smartgrowth.bc.ca.

186 *Ibid*.

187 *Ibid*, s 198.

188 The Nova Scotia land-use appellate body has enforced the statements; see *Parrsboro (Town), Re*, 2007 NSUARB 117.

189 *Hill & Hill Farms Ltd v Bluewater (Municipality)*, above note 52.

by the municipality, it took the case to the Normal Farm Practices Protection Board, which allowed a different separation. The Court of Appeal ruled that while the board could establish normal farm practices that ignored municipal by-laws, it was not open to the board to ignore a PPS, and here one required adherence to the Ministry's MDSII.[190]

Regardless of whether the PPS is sufficiently specific to require targets, or whether a particular PPS is binding, a municipality could choose to follow the PPS set closely; close adherence could lead to higher standards than sometimes prevail. A formal planning focus on any PPS could be an occasion for a municipality to make changes to its OP. A number of municipalities have incorporated environmental sections in their OPs.[191] The British Columbia statutory requirement for greenhouse gas reduction policies and actions certainly provides a model that could be followed by any Canadian municipality, even in the absence of a statutory requirement. And once in place, OP policies can be effective in addressing environmental matters. As an example, in *Gold Mountain Springs Inc v Oro-Medonte (Township)*,[192] the OMB upheld a municipal refusal to amend its by-laws so as to allow a company already extracting water for bottling to develop a bottling plant on-site; the board cited the municipality's OP policies favouring environmental preservation, and bolstered its analysis by reference to Provincial Policy Statements.

D. CONCLUSION AND LIMITATIONS

In 1996, Felix Hoehn wrote:

> The emergence of the powers to prohibit the development of environmentally sensitive lands . . . expand[s] the purpose of land use controls from merely promoting orderly development to also limiting growth and preserving features of natural and built environments. While this reflects a growing awareness of the importance of conservation and sustainable development, a consensus on the extent that development should be limited by such concerns has not yet emerged, and it may be expected that this will be the subject of continued debate.[193]

---

190 Citing the *Farming and Food Production Protection Act, 1998*, SO 1998, c 1, ss 6(1), 6(15), and 9, and *Planning Act*, above note 38, s 3.

191 See, for example, Toronto's OP, Chapter 3; Halifax Regional Municipality's municipal planning strategy, s II-8.

192 (2002), 43 OMBR 129.

193 Felix Hoehn, *Municipalities and Canadian Law* (Saskatoon: Purich Publishers, 1996) at 210.

To a large extent such a consensus has now emerged. Our starting point was the observation that there are considerable powers available under existing legislation to enable local governments to move aggressively towards putting in place sustainability measures. I hope this has been demonstrated. At the same time, despite the wide ambit of local government powers, there are real limitations. Central to many of the cases on municipal jurisdiction is the problem of their interaction with the regulatory powers of other levels of government. It will not always be the case that local government powers can legally coexist with the regulatory powers of the province or the federal government, and in those instances they will have to give way. The main legal limitations on municipal powers over environmental/sustainability matters tend to be on account of the constitutional separation of powers, on account of direct conflicts with other valid legislation, or on account of explicit legislated exclusion of municipal jurisdiction.[194]

The existence of such limitations may be frustrating for local councils or those hoping to have those councils put in place reforming measures to advance a sustainability agenda. Nonetheless, it is just how it is. Municipalities cannot regulate everything. Other levels of government do have their own legitimate powers to use, and when the Supreme Court of Canada said in *R v Hydro-Québec*[195] that all levels of government should act to protect the environment, the implication is that the legal and political process will have to work itself out at all of those levels. Municipal governments can be powerful, but a complex system is at work in Canada.

While the focus of analysis here has been on legal powers of regulation, other approaches to transformation are of course available to local governments. Municipalities may lead by example, through control of their own buildings, fleet, and grounds; internal policies could be set that reduce energy use or forbid pesticides, as examples. Leading by example could also extend to refraining from actions that might create environmental harm; thus the building of solid waste incinerators—a highly contentious matter—might not be the method chosen to deal with garbage.[196] In addition, direct education is an option; making

---

194 We have not focused in this chapter to any great extent on constitutional questions since their ambit is generally well known. Cases such as *British Columbia (Attorney General) v Lafarge Canada Inc*, 2007 SCC 23 and *Canadian Pacific Railway Co v Vancouver (City)*, above note 29, illustrate the potential, and limitations, for provincial, and therefore municipal, regulatory action involving federal lands or federally regulated corporations.

195 Above note 23.

196 Dealing responsibly with garbage is a complex issue involving diversion from landfills by such methods as composting and recycling or reduction in packaging,

information available to residents can encourage them to make individual changes and show them how. Another aspect of leading by example could be the advancement of social norms, particularly in the development community.[197] A third additional approach would be to undertake epidemiological studies. This is particularly appropriate for environmental health risks that are suspected to exist but are not being dealt with by the senior levels of government, for whatever reason. Such studies have a long provenance, famously with contaminated wells.[198] Lead exposure for children through the pathway of paint, or asbestosis for workers or a local population, are examples where the need for epidemiological evidence was and is an important step in the development of public policy.[199] A fourth option is for municipalities to call on the two senior levels to take action. Action called for could either be regulatory in the sense of imposing standards, or could be an environmental assessment. Because EAs are a highly political process in that the relevant minister has discretion to determine the level of intensity of an EA, especially to choose whether there will be a public hearing panel, ministers are likely to be responsive to articulated requests from municipal councils. Pressure from local political leaders is a common, and often effective, way to influence the overall political agenda.[200] This could occur through resolutions passed by individual councils.[201] A fifth possibility is for municipalities to use their knowledge of appropriate local land uses to identify property that might become a part of an environmental programme offered by one of the other levels of government. For example, private land that could be set aside

197 Victor B Flatt, "Act Locally, Affect Globally" (2008) 35 *Boston College Environmental Affairs Law Review* 455. Flatt says that social norm creation is more easily accomplished at the local level; he cites US municipalities, where mayors have negotiated environmental commitments from developers without using regulation.

198 In the nineteenth century, Dr John Snow identified public water pumps as the source of cholera spreading locally in Soho, London, leading to what is known as the Chadwick Royal Commission of 1842 (*Report on the Sanitary Conditions of the Labouring Population of Great Britain*), named after Edwin Chadwick, Secretary of the Poor Law Commission. See Dorothy Porter, *The History of Public Health and the Modern State* (Amsterdam: Rodopi, 1994).

199 See David V Bates, *Environmental Health Risks and Public Policy* (Vancouver: UBC Press, 1994).

200 See materials cited in this text's Introduction at note 63.

201 In Nova Scotia, municipal councils adopted resolutions calling for a provincial [illegible] consumer society.

under conservation easement legislation could be mapped.[202] A sixth possibility is for a municipality to propose adoption of a regulatory by-law as a way of challenging the senior levels of government to assert their jurisdiction, and take regulatory action, or more expansive regulatory action than they had proposed. A good example of this is the Environmental Reporting and Disclosure Program by-law adopted by Toronto in December 2008 and aimed at tracking some twenty-five chemicals posing priority health concerns.[203] A seventh possibility is for municipalities to set up formal advisory committees, along the lines of the round tables on environment and economy that the federal government still has and many provinces once had, to generate ideas and interest.[204] In addition, staff positions could be created with a mandate dedicated to advancing sustainability.

Leading by example, public education, formal studies, round tables, and varieties of political advocacy all have their place in any government's engagement with environmental issues. The advantage of regulation is that it goes forward through a public process that inherently involves research and education, and has the potential to have wide practical effect. But it is just one of a variety of available tools.

One hard fact about urban Canada is that a lot of it is already built or built upon. The statutory protections for non-conforming uses[205] are

---

202 The federal government offers an Ecological Gifts Program that involves tax benefits, and such provincial land laws as Nova Scotia's *Conservation Easements Act*, SNS 2001, c 28; *Special Places Protection Act*, RSNS 1989, c 438; and *Wilderness Areas Protection Act*, SNS 1998, c 27, offer a framework for private land conservation. See Karen McKendry, "Turning Private Land to Public Gain" (September 2008) 2:2 *Coastlands: The Maritimes Policy Review* 18.

203 See Willms & Shier LLP, *Environment, Energy & Resources Law Report* (August 2008) at 2: "Toronto's proposed [by-law] is on hold . . . pending release of a proposed provincial toxics use reduction strategy . . . . Toronto wants assurances that the provincial strategy will encompass all the chemicals on its priority list and that threshold reporting levels will be set low enough to capture small and medium-sized businesses in the GTA." Jennifer Agnolin, "Community Right to Know: Toronto Becomes First Canadian Municipality to Require Toxic Substances Reporting" *Municipal World* (April 2009) at 21–24. The provincial Toxics Reduction Strategy is being advanced through the *Toxics Reduction Act, 2009*, SO 2009, c 19. Toronto has asserted its authority to pass the by-law under its omnibus powers, and as "complementary" to the provincial regulatory scheme, it is quite likely that a part of the political dimension of the exercise is to pressure the province.

204 Halifax had such a committee in 1992–93. Its report was titled "A Path to Sustainability" (April 1993). The committee was temporary. Toronto has a Roundtable on the Environment. Saskatoon has an Environmental Advisory Committee.

205 As set out, for example, in British Columbia's *Local Government Act*, above note 121, s 911 or Ontario's *Planning Act*, above note 38, s 34(9).

therefore an important factor in limiting the municipal use of some regulatory powers that might otherwise be available. This also implies that possessing a range of powers will not necessarily lead to useful practical applications if the residual decisions that are available to be made are themselves trifling. This is why much of the evolving municipal policy focus may well be on sprawl, transportation, and the energy aspects of new buildings.[206]

Crucially, there is no shortage of good ideas about how exactly we could transform our communities so as to achieve some degree of sustainability. In a visionary document published by the Canadian Environmental Advisory Council in 1989, Nigel Richardson wrote,

> If municipal governments and their planners tend to be preoccupied with matters other than sustainability, environmentalists and even provincial governments often show little awareness of the potential value of municipalities as allies in the sustainability cause. Municipalities have a great deal of power over the use and development of land, not only through provincial enabling legislation but also through building codes, public health legislation and other legal instruments. The legal authority is firmly established and thoroughly tested; municipal councils and officials are well versed in its use; and on the whole, the public is accustomed to and accepts the exercise of this authority. Thus municipal planning could be employed very effectively to advance the aims of sustainability.[207]

---

206 As an example of a suggested programme to engage with climate change, much of which could be undertaken at the municipal level, see Cy Gonick & Brendan Haley, "12-Step Program to Combat Climate Change" in "Toolkit for a New Canada" (May/June 2006) 40:3 *Canadian Dimension*, online: https://canadiandimension.com/articles/view/12-step-program-to-combat-climate-change-cy-gonick-and-brendan-haley. It includes the following:

> 1. Redesign our cities so that more people travel much less. Make it possible for people to live, work and shop in the same walkable neighbourhood . . . .
> 2. Upgrade our public transit system with more affordable fares and vastly improved service . . . .
> 4. Require all new single-family and multi-family housing to meet net-zero energy standards . . . .
> 5. Ban the sale of all lighting, appliances and equipment that do not meet energy star standards.
> 6. Introduce mandatory energy audits of every family home and multi-family dwelling, followed by retrofits of insulation upgrades, air sealing and the like. Oblige landlords to bring their units up to high-energy efficiency standards before they can rent them out.

207 Nigel Richardson, "Land Use Planning and Sustainable Development in Canada" Canadian Environmental Advisory Council (Ottawa: Canadian Environment Advisory Council, 1989) at 42. A similar, and even earlier recognition of munic-

In the planning of our communities, the overall situation is the same as with so many other areas of human activity, such as agriculture, the fishery, forestry, mining, and energy: in virtually all instances, we know a much better way of going about our business. Writers such as Clive Doucet,[208] Mark Roseland,[209] David Morris,[210] Guy Dauncey,[211] Jeb Brugmann,[212] and Lester Brown[213] have all focused on common sense measures that could be taken up by local governments. There are numerous other authors with good suggestions.[214] As with so many areas of human endeavour, the barriers to change are not the absence of knowledge of better ways to shape our lives; the barriers tend to be the self-imposed adherence to the status quo. It is time to let go of an outdated mode of thinking and try to manage change before it is forced upon us by disastrous external forces. The legal tools are in place.

---

ipal potential is found in a 1971 Science Council of Canada document, "Cities For Tomorrow" Report No 14 (Ottawa: Information Canada, 1971), which noted that "The city is a total system" (at 22) and that "City planning might well shift its emphasis to questions of equilibrium and continuous self-renewal, rather than stressing continuous growth" (at 24).

208 *Urban Meltdown* (Gabriola Island, BC: New Society, 2007).

209 *Toward Sustainable Communities*, 3d ed (Gabriola Island, BC: New Society, 2005).

210 *Self-Reliant Cities* (San Francisco: Sierra Club Books, 1982).

211 *Stormy Weather* (Gabriola Island, BC: New Society, 2001) especially at 96–115.

212 Primarily through the International Council for Local Environmental Initiatives, online: www.iclei.org.

213 Through the Worldwatch Institute, online: www.worldwatch.org. Worldwatch Papers, one of its publications series, has focused on municipal matters since at least 1980. See Paper 38 "City Limits: Emerging Constraints on Urban Growth"; Paper 76 "Mining Urban Wastes"; Paper 77 "The Future of Urbanization"; Paper 90 "The Bicycle: Vehicle for a Small Planet"; Paper 98 "Alternatives to the Automobile"; Paper 105 "Shaping Cities"; Paper 135 "Recycling Organic Waste"; Paper 147 "Reinventing Cities"; Paper 156 "City Limits: Putting the Brakes on Sprawl." Lester Brown is director of the Worldwatch Institute, but not the author of all of these papers.

214 On the intertwined issues of sprawl, transportation, and peak oil, see Daniel Lerch, *Post Carbon Cities* (Sebastopol, CA: Post Carbon Institute, 2007); Richard Gilbert & Anthony Perl, *Transport Revolutions: Moving People and Freight Without Oil* (London: Earthscan, 2008).

APPENDIX A

RESIDENTIAL REAL ESTATE PURCHASE—HANDOUT REGARDING LAND-USE MATTERS

The following is offered as a handout to clients who have used the legal services of a lawyer to purchase a residential property. It would be included as part of the reporting letter.

* * * * *

Notes on Land-Use for the Residential Purchaser

These notes are generalized observations about the use of your newly purchased residential property and include some associated points about surrounding uses or potential uses in your neighbourhood.

Because these notes are general, you should bring any specific questions to your legal advisor. You should especially do so well in advance of starting any construction project. Construction in violation of applicable rules may result in fines and/or an order to demolish or alter the construction in order to bring it into conformity with the rules.

One of the main points to be aware of is that the rules governing land use may change over time. No neighbourhood is immune from possible effects of land-use changes elsewhere, or from overall change in how others live their lives. For example, vehicle traffic may increase over time, and more vehicles might drive along your street than you or your immediate neighbours are comfortable with.

1. **Zoning:** Your land is zoned R-2 [amend accordingly]. Zoning is the term for the main set of municipal restrictions on land use. R-2 is defined in the municipal land-use by-law as involving prohibited,

permitted, and discretionary uses; these are listed in a table, attached. [This approach is extracted from the City of Regina zoning by-law and the table is not attached here.] Generally, residential units that are detached, duplexes, and semi-attached are permitted. While zoning rules focus mainly on type of allowable or prohibited uses, they extend also to restrictions on a wide variety of matters, such as height, percentage of lot that may be built on, setbacks from adjacent properties, signage, and so on. It is important to take note of the following:

- *Surrounding Area*: Attached is a map showing the designated zoning in your immediate neighbourhood.
- *Home-Based Businesses*: The following home-based businesses are permitted in an R-2 zone: [xxx]. Renting rooms or the whole of the property on a short-term basis, for example, through a service such as Airbnb [is or is not] currently permitted as a home-based business. Rooming houses [are or are not] currently an allowable use in an R-2 zone.
- *Accessory Uses*: You may construct [xxx] as an accessory use to your home. If your neighbours construct [xxx], you are entitled to be notified [xxx].
- *Variations*: There are rules that allow for variations, often referred to as "minor variations." Applications for these are treated as routine administrative matters, but must meet the following criteria: [xxx].
- *Non-conforming Uses*: Uses of land that do not conform to the current zoning may be permitted if they legally existed prior to the adoption of zoning rules that would otherwise prohibit them. There are complex rules about defining the nature of the allowable non-conforming use, whether it may be expanded, and whether it has been abandoned or terminated.

2. **Nuisances:** Municipal zoning is not the only applicable legal restriction on the use of land. The common law of nuisance (excessive noise is an example) may be applicable. This both restricts your use of your land to reasonable activities and restricts other owners similarly.
3. **Vegetation and Trees:** There are rules restricting the trimming or removal of trees, and growing vegetation that poses a safety factor for traffic (e.g., by interfering with sightlines). Consult the municipality if you have questions. An arborist's report may be required before removing a tree. Some trees ("border trees") are shared between adjoining landowners, thus raising other issues.

4. **Reserves and Utility Rights-of-Way:** Our title search found no recorded designations for future public use of any portion of your land for such things as the placement of utility infrastructure or use as a roadway. Should you be notified of any such pending government designation, or expropriation, please contact us.
5. **Development Applications Outstanding:** [to be included as a matter of judgment as to potential impact upon the occupation and enjoyment of the property being purchased.] You should be aware that XYZ Corporation has a proposal before city council to demolish the houses located at 1234 and 1236 Maple Street and build a four-storey, 20-unit apartment building. Information regarding this proposal may be obtained from the city's website; look for Case No. 5678.
6. **Planning Initiatives Underway:** The city operates with a general official plan as well as its zoning by-laws. The official plan sets future-oriented policies to guide decision-making about land use. The city is engaged in a process of re-thinking its official plan for the following areas: xxx. Information may be obtained at www.xxx.com.
7. **Federal Government Rules:** The federal government has its own set of land-use rules applicable to its own lands and to federally regulated enterprises. This extends to the placement of certain infrastructure, such as telecommunication towers.
8. **Provincial Government Rules:** The provincial government has its own set of land-use rules administered either separately from those of the municipality or shared with them. For example, any business serving alcohol or with video lottery terminals must be licensed by the province.
9. **Building Code:** As a matter of safety, construction of structures is governed regarding basics such as foundations, some design elements, electrical, plumbing, and so on. Normally, building permits must be obtained in advance of commencing construction.
10. **Contacts:** Information about building permits and related aspects of land use may be obtained from the [Planning and Development] offices of the municipality, for example, in the City of Toronto, information is provided, online: www1.toronto.ca/wps/portal/contentonly?vgnextoid=ae9352cc66061410VgnVCM10000071d60f89RCRD.
11. **Monitoring:** It is worthwhile to try to monitor ongoing land-use planning initiatives that might impact you, your property, or your neighbourhood. News sources often cover such stories. Formal notices will sometimes be printed or circulated regarding pending applications, or regarding decisions that have been made. These

may relate to broad area planning initiatives or be focused on particular properties. You will not have the opportunity to participate effectively in any process if you do not know it is in the works. For decisions that have been made, you may have rights to appeal: acting in a timely fashion is essential.

APPENDIX B

SAMPLE SET OF PROVINCIAL STATUTES PERTAINING TO LAND USE

While there are usually two or three main provincial statutes governing land use at the municipal level, and likewise at the provincial level, the complete set of land-use statutes in any province is extensive. Some statutes touch only partially on land use or their provisions are peripheral to the topic. It is necessary, however, to become familiar with all of the statutes that may affect land use so that a complete picture is gained.

The statutes will typically be of the following categories:

1) general planning, for example, a *Planning Act*, a *Municipal Government Act*;
2) particular municipal charters, for example, *Vancouver City Charter*;
3) property law, for example, a *Property Act*, an *Expropriation Act*;
4) special planning areas, for example, *Niagara Escarpment Act*;
5) special subjects, for example, a *Shopping Centre Development Act*;
6) governance, for example, a *Municipal Conflict of Interest Act*;
7) environmental matters, for example, an *Environment Act*, an *Endangered Species Act*;
8) natural resources and agriculture, for example, an *Agricultural Operations Protection Act*, a *Mines Act*;
9) heritage, for example, a *Heritage Property Act*; and
10) miscellaneous provincial powers, for example, a *Provincial Parks Act*.

The following list is of Alberta statutes as a sample set. The references are to the *Revised Statutes of Alberta, 2000*, unless otherwise noted. The list is alphabetical and may not be complete or entirely up to date (it is current as of October 2016). There are some 100 statutes. The list is intended to be illustrative. Each province will have a similar range of applicable statutes.

Agricultural Operation Practices A-7: offers protection from lawsuits based in nuisance if the agricultural operation is in compliance with the law. The minister may establish standards for agricultural operations.

Agricultural Pests A-8: allows the minister to declare an animal, bird, insect, plant, or disease (with some specified exceptions) to be a pest or a nuisance if it is destroying or harming land, livestock, or property, or is likely to. There is then a duty on municipalities and landowners to take active measures to prevent the harm, and inspectors may issue compliance orders.

Agricultural and Recreational Land Ownership A-9: aimed at restricting non-residents from owning land in excess of 20 acres.

Agricultural Societies Act A-11: societies may incorporate to encourage improvement in agriculture and the quality of life of persons living in an agricultural community by developing programmes, services, and facilities, including holding exhibitions. The government may guarantee borrowings.

Alberta Bill of Rights A-14: similar to the *Charter*, but includes a reference to property: ". . . the right of the individual to liberty, security of the person and enjoyment of property, and the right not to be deprived thereof except by due process of law" (section 1(a)).

Alberta Capital Finance Authority A-14.5: allows pooling of borrowing by municipalities, hospitals, and schools.

Alberta Housing A-25: establishes the Alberta Social Housing Corporation to enable the provision of a basic level of housing for persons who require assistance to obtain or maintain housing accommodation.

Alberta Sport Connection A-34: the foundation may develop and maintain parks and fish and wildlife programs, facilities, and services. It is a Crown agency.

Animal Health Act, SA 2007 A-40.2: inspectors may create quarantine areas in cases of communicable diseases, applicable to the animals, persons, and vehicles.

Animal Protection A-41: offers protections to animals from causes of distress but does not extend to "reasonable and generally accepted practices of animal management, husbandry or slaughter." There are police powers to enter land and premises.

Bee B-2: beekeeping requires registration. Apiculture inspectors may enter land or buildings at reasonable times (not dwellings) to inspect and may issue quarantine orders.

Blind Persons' Rights B-3: limits use of white canes to blind persons. It establishes rights of access to services and accommodation and provides for guide dogs to accompany a blind person.

Boundary Surveys B-5: establishes a process for determining the provincial boundaries, and confirms certain surveys with Saskatchewan (1938) and the Northwest Territories (1925 and 1954). It cross-references section 43 of the *Constitution Act, 1982*.

Burial of the Dead B-8: allows cabinet to end a lockout or strike in order to allow for burial of the dead.

Cemeteries C-3: regulates cemeteries, which are to be the only place for burial of the dead. Vaults may store bodies during the winter months. Permission must be obtained for disinterment. Plots need not be registered under the *Land Titles Act*. Provincial and municipal regulation may establish permissible location of a cemetery. There are penalties for fouling a water supply. Funds for perpetual care are to be established.

Coal Conservation C-17: establishes the Energy Resources Conservation Board with authority to prevent waste, control pollution, regulate for safe mining, and ensure the orderly, efficient, and economic development of coal resources. Reclamation schemes are mandatory. Public hearings may be held to determine if industrial development permits will issue.

Condominium Property C-22: although condominiums are a special form of property, the *Municipal Government Act* applies except for the subdivision provisions if multiple units are on one parcel of land. The condominium corporation may make by-laws dealing with nuisances and the placement of anything "esthetically unpleasing when viewed from outside the units."

Constitution of Alberta Amendment, 1990 C-24: offers protections to land assigned to the Metis Settlements General Council.

County of Westlock Water Authorization Act, SA 2007, C-29.5: authorizes a licence to transfer water between river basins as required by the *Water Act*.

Crop Payments C-33: recognizes mortgages and other hypothecations of the value of crops to be grown, up to one-third of value. The mortgagee is deemed to be the owner of the share from the sowing of the crops until sale and payment.

Dangerous Goods Transportation and Handling D-4: sets a framework for regulations to control the transportation and handling of dangerous goods, defined as explosives, gases, flammables, nuclear substances, and corrosives. The Crown is bound. Local authorities, subject to provincial approval, may establish designated routes and hours for travel for vehicles carrying dangerous goods.

Drainage Districts D-16: establishes a Drainage Council to supervise creation, by vote, of drainage districts, which may then construct works, meaning infrastructure, to convey, store, or stabilize water and extending to dams, weirs, flood-gates, drain basins, reservoirs, canals, tunnels, pipes, bridges, culverts, and ditches. Owners of land in a drainage district are liable to assessment to pay for the infrastructure.

Dunvegan Hydro Development, SA 2009, D-18: authorizes construction and operation of the Dunvegan hydro development, following an environmental assessment.

East Central Regional Water Authorization, SA 2007, E-0.2: authorizes certain inter-basin transfer of water as required by the *Water Act*.

Electric Utilities, SA 2003, E-5.1: establishes a system for the generation, transmission, and distribution of electricity, exempting certain municipal systems and private on-site generation.

Environmental Protection and Enhancement E-12: the basic environmental protection statute. The Crown is bound. Its purpose is to "promote the protection, enhancement and wise use" of the environment (section 2). It recognizes the need for economic growth, sustainable development, and polluter pay as principles. The government is empowered to develop economic instruments such as emissions trading, guidelines, and state of the environment reports. A framework is established for conservation easements. Regulations are enabled to cover designated activities and livestock operations (section 37). Part 2 of the Act establishes the environmental assessment process. Other parts deal with prohibited releases, contaminated sites, reclamation, potable water, hazardous substances and pesticides, and wastes.

Expropriation E-13: establishes the Crown right to expropriation. The Land Compensation Board is given jurisdiction to determine compensation, save that the Surface Rights Board deals with matters associated with power plants under the *Hydro-Electric Energy Act.* Mineral rights are treated as apart from land itself. An owner may challenge whether the taking is "necessary in the achievement of the objectives of the expropriating authority" (section 6). Additional amounts may be awarded if a principal residence is expropriated "to enable the owner to relocate . . . in accommodation that is at least equivalent" (section 47). Disturbance compensation is available to tenants (section 50). Re-vesting is possible if within two years of the expropriation the land is "no longer required for its purpose and the expropriating authority desires to dispose of it" (section 70); there is a right of first refusal for the former owner.

Fisheries (Alberta) F-16: regulates fisheries within provincial jurisdiction, including aquaculture ("cultured fish"). Quarantines may be imposed in cases of disease.

Forest and Prairie Protection F-19: aimed at prevention of forest fires. It allows for the appointment of "fire guardians" and for fire control agreements with commercial/industrial users of Crown lands. It makes municipalities responsible for fighting and controlling fires within their areas (section 7) and gives them power to control fire hazards (section 10). Railways are to take precautions against fires, and to fight fires within 100 metres of their right-of-way (sections 11 and 14). When aircraft are bombing fires, no-one is permitted on lakes being used or within 30 metres of the shore (section 16). Permits for outdoor fires are required during fire season, and there is a general duty of care (sections 18, 22, and 24). It allows for control of forest tree pests (section 28).

Forest Reserves F-20: allows for "land set aside as a forest reserve" and implements a federal-provincial agreement from 1948 for protection of some 8,500 square miles of forest land on the east slope of the Rocky Mountains (per SA 1948, c 20) as well as creation of other reserves; the purpose is "conservation of the forests and other vegetation in the forests and for the maintenance of conditions favourable to an optimum water supply" (section 4). The *Forests Act* and *Public Lands Act* apply. Grazing may be allowed.

Forests F-22: the basic statute for managing forestry on Crown land. A permit, licence, or quota agreement is required to "cut, damage, or destroy" any forest growth (section 10). There are wide powers to make regulations for establishing annual allowable cut and other matters. "Perpetual sustainable yield" is favoured (section 16). If quotas or permits are altered without fault of the holder, compensation may be awarded (section 27).

Freedom of Information and Protection of Privacy F-25: the FOIPOP rules are applicable to local governments (sections 1(j) and 4(1)).

Funeral Services F-29: a licensing statute for commercial operations dealing with "human remains," though the minister may make regulations "to resolve disputes about the disposition of human remains or cremated remains" (section 27(1)(aa)).

Fur Farms F-30: operations raising fur-bearing animals are to be licensed (section 4); "clean and sanitary conditions" are required (section 9). Regulations are enabled to deal with specifics.

Gaming and Liquor G-1: a licensing statute for gaming and the sale of alcohol for consumption (sections 35, 36, and 50). A vote is required for previously dry areas (section 56 ff). Advertising is controlled (section 67). Home brewing of beer, wine, and cider is permitted but not spirits (section 86).

Gas Distribution G-3: sets a framework for awarding franchises for commercial gas distribution. Easements are to be acquired and registered against title, though not in all circumstances (section 11). The *Surface Rights Act* may be used (section 12). It allows for rural gas co-ops and municipal gas utilities (Part 4).

Gas Resources Preservation G-4: allows the Energy Regulator to control export of natural gas from the province; links to *Responsible Energy Development Act.*

Gas Utilities G-5: regulates pricing and allows for creation of rights-of-way for infrastructure on municipal lands (sections 19 and 21)

Government House G-9: establishes a foundation to advise on the preservation of Government House as an historic site and building.

Highways Development and Protection, SA 2004, H-8.5: a highways code, allowing for standard controls such as designation of municipal roads as provincial highways (section 2), control of forestry roads (section 8), controlled-access roads (section 110), placement of telecommunications infrastructure (section 15), and control of commercial uses adjacent to highways (section 16), and grants certain powers to municipalities (section 26) and allows for city transit systems (section 26).

Historical Resources H-9: allows the minister to designate and protect historical resources, widely defined, and allows municipalities to do likewise subject to offering compensation for loss in value; covenants may be entered into to advance the designation.

Horse Racing Alberta H-11.3: race tracks are to be licensed

Hunting, Fishing and Trapping Heritage, SA 2008, H-15.5: declares a right to hunt, fish, and trap "in accordance with the law."

Hydro and Electric Energy H-16: electrical utilities are placed under the direction of the Utilities Commission, with a public interest in an integrated system; access is granted for infrastructure on certain public lands, and a power to expropriate may be used subject to the *Expropriation Act*, the *Surface Rights Act*, and the *Metis Settlements Act*.

Innkeepers I-2: creates an offence to cause a disturbance at an inn.

Interpretation I-8: The Crown is not bound by any enactment unless "the enactment expressly states" it is (section 14).

Irrigation Districts I-11: various irrigation districts are established to manage the delivery of water; there is a power of expropriation; there are categories of use (household, rural); boards are elected and may impose charges based on assessment rolls; there is a mechanism for dealing with disputes over seepage damage.

Land Titles L-4: establishes a Torrens system (sections 62 and 168) with a registry of instruments affecting title, including in national parks (section 30) and of restrictive covenants (section 48). It provides for unit operations for minerals (section 49), party wall agreements (section 71), encroachment agreements (section 72), and creation of lots (sections 76 and 94), including strata lots (section 86).

Law of Property L-7: partition orders are provided for subject to the *Planning Act*, although hardship may lead to variations. The surface owner is entitled to clay and marl (section 57) and sand and gravel (section 58) and may excavate for purposes of construction or to farm (section 56(3)). Minerals are defined (section 56). A life tenant may not commit waste (section 71). Injunctions may be sought against waste and trespass (section 72). Public access is allowed to private streets if they serve ten or more dwellings (section 78).

Line Fence L-13: a system of arbitration is established to settle disputes over the quality, cost, location, or repair of livestock fences.

Local Authorities Election L-21: sets limits on campaign contributions and provides for disclosure (Part 5.1).

Metis Settlements M-14: establishes general councils for governance of Metis lands on a basis equivalent to municipalities, that is, to govern land use and a range of other specified matters (Schedule 1).

Metis Settlements Land Protection M-16: provides that prospecting and mineral extraction may not proceed on Metis land without the permission of the general councils.

Mines and Minerals M-17: establishes a framework for government control of mining for minerals, coal, petroleum and gas, and oil sands in the McMurray formation. This extends to exploration as well as extraction, and allows for royalties to be paid to the Crown. It deals with carbon capture and storage (sequestration). There are definitions included of minerals (peat is excluded).

Mobile Home Sites Tenancies M-20: establishes a landlord/tenant regime for mobile home parks; it links to the *Safer Communities and Neighbourhoods Act* so that a tenancy in a mobile home may be so terminated; tenancies may also be terminated upon one year's notice if the whole of the park is to be converted to another use, including condominiums, or to a housing co-operative.

Municipal Government M-26: this is the basic statute establishing the powers of municipalities over land-use and related matters.

Natural Resources Conservation Board N-3: establishes the board to review major projects that may have environmental effects (pulp and paper plants, mines, water management, and other reviewable projects as assigned); joint reviews may be held with another body.

Northern Alberta Development Council N-4: the council is to monitor and plan for development in northern Alberta and to advise government.

North Red Deer Water Authorization, SA 2002, N-3.5: as per the *Water Act*, this is legislature confirmation of a licence for transfer of water between the South Saskatchewan River Basin and the North Saskatchewan River Basin.

Occupiers' Liability O-4: an occupier has a duty of care to every visitor to take reasonable care that the visitor will be reasonably safe (section 5); there are special provisions regarding trespassers (section 12) and child trespassers (section 13).

Oil and Gas Conservation O-6: establishes a comprehensive code for the regulation of the oil and gas industry under the supervision of the Energy Regulator. An orphan fund is created and there is assignment of costs associated with suspension, abandonment, and reclamation of works (section 30). Areas may be closed to travel in case of hazardous conditions (section 97). Waste is prohibited (section 107).

Oil Sands Conservation O-7: similar to the *Oil and Gas Conservation Act*, a code is established for the oil sands.

Parks Towns P-2: a town may be established, even if located inside a national park, subject to an agreement with the federal government.

Petty Trespass P-11: creates the offence of trespass; does not apply to Crown land that is under a grazing lease if the purpose of the trespass is recreation.

Pipeline P-15: pipelines are under the authority of the Energy Regulator (although gas utilities are regulated by the Utilities Commission); interests in land are to be acquired by negotiation or through the *Surface Rights Act* or the *Metis Settlements Act*; special authorization is required for a pipeline to interfere with an established or prospective mine.

Post-secondary Learning, SA 2003, P-19.5: the government may expropriate land for purposes of a post-secondary institution.

Property Rights Advocate, SA 2012, P-26.5: the advocate promotes private property rights and may take a role in expropriation cases.

Provincial Parks P-35: the purpose of the parks is to preserve the province's natural heritage and to facilitate the use and enjoyment of it for outdoor recreation and education. The Cabinet may classify parks and regulate a wide array of uses.

Public Highways Development P-38: this establishes a framework for regulations governing all aspects of highways; the statute abrogates common law rights such as access (section 23) and provides for removal of dangerous or unsightly buildings on adjacent land (section 26) as well as control of signage on adjacent land (section 30).

Public Lands P-40: a general framework for administration of Crown land (sections 2, 7–11, and 71.1). The Crown is declared to be owner of beds and shores of waterbodies (section 3). Crown land may be made available for homesteading (Part 3) or grazing (Part 4).

Public Utilities P-45: establishes the Utilities Commission as regulator of public utilities (electricity, water, heat, oil pipelines that are common carriers). The Commission may settle terms for use of municipal land (section 82).

Public Works P-46: land may be expropriated for public works (section 20) and there may be a designation of Public Works Development Areas (section 25) where the Crown intends to acquire land over time.

Radiation Protection R-2: regulates activities involving use of radiation, if not already regulated federally or through another Alberta statute.

Railway (Alberta) R-4: regulates industrial, heritage, and amusement railways (but not urban rail transit systems). The railway administrator may consent to expropriation of land. Railroads must trench tracks, avoid fires, and fence if necessary.

Regional Airport Authorities R-9: the authorities may manage and operate local airports.

Religious Societies Land R-15: congregations may operate through trustees for establishing houses of worship or cemeteries.

Residential Tenancies, SA 2004, R-17.1: a code to regulate use of premises for residential tenancies, including storage of goods.

Responsible Energy Development Act, SA 2012, R-17.3: replaces the Energy Resources Conservation Board by the Alberta Energy Regulator, with a mandate for "efficient, safe, orderly and environmentally responsible development of energy resources" to regulate "the disposition and management of public lands" for "the protection of the environment" and "the conservation and management of water, including the wise allocation and use of water" (section 2(1)). Its jurisdiction extends to pipelines, mines, and wells. It has jurisdiction that flows from the *Public Lands Act,* the *Environmental Protection and Enhancement Act*, the *Water Act*, and the *Mines and Minerals Act.* It supervises abandonment and closure of mines and enforces private surface agreements.

Rural Utilities R-21: recognizes these utilities and regulates removal or abandonment of their infrastructure (section 22).

Safer Communities and Neighbourhoods SA 2007, S-0.5: nuisance complaints may be made to the director of law enforcement (police) that premises are used as brothels, for drugs, for child sexual abuse, or for illegal liquour; the courts may issue a community safety order if there is a "serious and immediate threat to the health, safety and security" of a resident or the neighbourhood; the property may be closed to use. Part 2 deals with fortified buildings, which may be designated a threat to public safety; the fortifications may be removed or the building closed to use.

Service Dogs, SA 2007, S-7.5: prohibits discrimination because of use of service dogs.

Small Power Research and Development S-9: solar, wind, hydro, geothermal, biomass, and peat are all recognized as sources of small power generation, with regulation of terms of sale of the power.

Soil Conservation S-15: creates a duty for landholders to take appropriate measures to prevent or stop soil loss or deterioration (section 3); remedial measures may be ordered by agricultural officials.

Special Areas S-26: allows the designated minister, with the assistance of a board, to take direct control of land-use matters in areas designated by cabinet.

Stray Animals S-20: assigns liability for failing to close a gate (section 7) and trespassing livestock. Allows the killing of a dog worrying livestock or domestic fowl (section 25).

Surface Rights S-24: a board may determine rights of access to land for purposes of mining, oil and gas operations, pipelines, power transmission, and telephone infrastructure (section 12). This extends to injection of captured carbon dioxide (section 13.2). Compensation is set out (section 25).

Surveys S-26: the government may establish a GPS system (section 7). Surveyors have a right of entry on land to do their work, though they are liable for any damage (section 16). Part 2 establishes the sections system (1 mile square).

Tobacco and Smoking Reduction, SA 2005, T-3.8: smoking is prohibited in a public place, a workplace, a vehicle in which a minor is present, and within a prescribed distance from a doorway, window, or air intake for a public place or workplace (section 3); a home-based business is a workplace (section 4). There are certain exceptions to the application of the statute (section 5).

Traffic Safety T-6: includes regulation of off highway vehicles in Part 6.

Trespass to Premises T-7: creates the offence of trespass (section 3).

Turner Valley Unit Operations T-9: allows for creation of unit operations for oil and gas extraction in the designated area.

Water W-3: establishes a code for use and conservation of water (section 2). Water is vested in the Crown (section 3). The province is to undertake province-wide land-use planning for water, leading to management plans (section 10), including allocation and withdrawal rights as well as control of transfer and diversion (section 11). The environmental assessment process applies (Part 2, Division 2). Pre-existing agricultural rights are maintained (section 19). Riparian owners may use water for household purposes or agricultural purposes (sections 21–24). Priority rights are established (Part 3, Division 3). Water may not be exported (section 46). Transfers between major river basins must be authorized by a special act of the legislature (section 47). Flood risk areas may be designated and land use controlled (section 96).

Water, Gas, and Electrical Companies W-4: empowers municipal councils to permit the companies, by by-law, to service buildings (section 4); there is a right of entry to assess conditions (section 6); the permitting may extend to the laying of mains, pipes, and so on, and to excavation to accompany that (sections 9 & 10). Land rights may be pursued under the *Surface Rights Act* or the *Metis Settlements Act* (section 32).

Weed Control, SA 2008, W-5.1: there is a duty to control noxious weeds and to destroy them (sections 2 & 3).

Wilderness Areas, Ecological Reserves, Natural Areas and Heritage Rangelands W-9: various categories of protected areas are created or their designation is provided for. Use rules are established (section 8).

Wildlife W-10: establishes a code respecting hunting and trapping, including a system for protecting endangered species (section 6).

APPENDIX C

LAND-USE PLANNING RESOURCES

1) Canadian Institute of Planners (CIP), online: www.cip-icu.ca
The CIP publishes *Plan Canada*, a journal focused on Canadian planning issues.

2) American Planning Association (APA), online: www.planning.org
The APA publishes *Planning* and the *Journal of the APA*, both important planning serials. It also publishes books through the Planners Press and its Planning Advisory Service (PAS) Reports.

3) Provincial government departments
Provincial government departments concerned with municipal affairs such as Ontario's Ministry of Municipal Affairs and Housing offer a range of information about the land-use planning and regulatory system. So, too, do departments or special authorities that have responsibility for natural resource matters and environmental regulation.

4) Municipal governments
Municipal governments usually publish their official plans and land-use by-laws as well as some information about land-use planning initiatives underway and projects under consideration.

5) Federation of Canadian Municipalities (FCM), online: www.fcm.ca
The FCM offers the political perspective of Canadian municipalities as a collective. There are publications on planning topics.

6) *Municipal World*, online: https://municipalworld.com
   This publication includes regular columns on topical issues, including their legal aspects. Its site also offers links to a long list of associations having to do with land use.

GLOSSARY

AAC: annual allowable cut, or allowable annual cut, in forestry

Abandonment: the act and intention to relinquish certain land-use rights, for example, non-conforming use rights

Abutting: touching and sharing a common point, line, or boundary

Accessibility: the quality of affording access to a building

Accessory building: (term often used and defined in LUBs) detached subordinate building not used for human habitation and located on the same lot as the main building or use to which it is subordinate

Accessory use. *See also* **Accessory building:** use of land naturally or customarily incidental to the principal use; not the same use as the principal use, since that would just extend it into the accessory building; see *Sechelt (District) v Cutlan*, 2008 BCCA 368

Acquired rights: (Quebec term) non-conforming use; see *Land Use Planning and Development Act*, CQLR c A-19.1, s 113; see *Saint-Romuald (City) v Olivier*, 2001 SCC 57

Adaptation: changes made to respond to external circumstances, for example, climate change

Adaptive reuse: change in use of an older building, particularly to preserve buildings of heritage significance

Addition: structure physically attached, added, or connected to a building

Adjoining: abutting

Adult entertainment: goods, entertainment, or services designed to appeal to erotic or sexual appetites; see Ontario *Municipal Act, 2001*, SO 2001, c 25, s 151(2)

Adverse environmental effect: any significant adverse effect on the components of the natural environment that may reasonably be anticipated; see *Canadian Environmental Assessment Act, 2012*, SC 2012, c 19, s 52, ss 4 & 5

Aesthetics: having to do with beauty or taste; aesthetics has been recognized as a legitimate municipal concern

Affected local government: local government subject to a provincially mandated regional growth strategy; see British Columbia *Local Government Act*, RSBC 2015, c 1, Part 13

Affiliated municipality: one that is part of an agreement establishing a joint planning district; see Saskatchewan *Planning and Development Act, 2007*, SS 2007, c P-13.2, s 94

Agricultural land reserve: land (usually Class I agricultural land) set aside for agricultural purposes only; see British Columbia *Agricultural Land Commission Act*, SBC 2002, c 36

Agricultural use: one of the usual categories of zoning uses; see *Surrey (City) v Holden*, 1995 CanLII 1930 (BCSC)

Air pollution: discharge of a pollutant into the ambient air; may be from a discernible point source or non-point source; that is, discharged over a widespread area from a number of small sources

Air rights: right to use, control, or occupy the space above land; see *Windsor Family Credit Union Ltd v Barat Estate*, 2010 ONSC 4418

Allowable annual cut: harvest rate or volume of timber permitted to be taken each year from timber supply areas; see *Forest Act*, RSBC 1996, c 157, s 173

Alteration permit: permission to make changes to a designated heritage building; see *Vancouver Charter*, SBC 1953, c 55; *Heritage Conservation Act*, RSBC 1996, c 187

Amalgamation. ***See also*** **Annexation:** blending or fusion of the whole or part of two or more municipalities to become one. Although special legislation is sometimes enacted for large amalgamations, the process of adjustment to borders is not infrequent, and a standard statutory framework is usually in place to deal with applications; see *MacPump Developments Ltd v Sarnia (City)* (1994), 24 MPLR (2d) 1 (Ont CA)

Amenity: pleasant or useful feature; tangible or intangible benefits of a property, especially those that increase its attractiveness or value, or that contribute to its comfort or convenience; see *Karagic v Calgary (City)*, 2012 ABCA 309

Amortization: requiring a non-conforming use to be phased out over time; a policy choice found in the United States but not yet in Canada

Ancient light: (UK term) right to light; a common law right not to be deprived of natural daylight illumination through windows; see *Colls v Home & Colonial Stores Ltd*, [1904] AC 179 (HL)

Annexation. ***See also*** **Amalgamation:** The process of one municipality seeking to incorporate a part or the whole of an adjacent one; see *Innisfil (Township) v Barrie (City)* (1977), 80 DLR (3d) 85 (Ont Div Ct)

ANSI: area of natural and scientific interest

Antenna structure: telecommunications tower

APA: American Planners Association

Apartment building: (term often used and defined in LUBs) structure, usually of three or more self-contained rental dwelling units, but not a hotel; see *Pearson v Adams* (1914), 50 SCR 204

Appurtenant: belonging to, annexed to, or appended to; see *Edmonton (City) v LA Ventures Inc*, 1999 ABQB 649

Arcade: long arched gallery or building; series of arches with their columns or piers; passageway or avenue, for example, between shops

Architectural control district: a designated area in which a municipal council controls the architectural detail of buildings; see Saskatchewan *Planning and Development Act, 2007*, SS 2007, c P-13.2, s 73

Area redevelopment plan: municipal plan for preserving or improving land and buildings, rehabilitating buildings, removing buildings, or constructing or replacing buildings; see Alberta *Municipal Government Act*, RSA 2000, c M-26, s 634

As-of-right: entitlement of the owner of property to use or develop it, without recourse to a public hearing process or a vote of municipal council, if the proposed use accords with the zoning by-laws

ATV. ***See also*** **ORV:** all-terrain vehicle

Bad faith: corrupt or special motives, as opposed to acting in the public interest; see *MacMillan Bloedel Ltd v Galiano Island Trust Committee* (1995), 10 BCLR (3d) 121 (CA)

Beach: shore, or area between high water and low water over which the tide ebbs and flows; the term "foreshore" is also used; see *Lee v Arthurs* (1918), 46 NBR 185 (SC); designation as a beach may entail restrictions on contiguous owners; see *Mossman v Nova Scotia (Attorney General)* (1995), 140 NSR (2d) 321 (SC)

Bedrock: geologic formations not easily removed

Bedroom community: residential suburb

Bias: fundamental fairness—lack of impartiality; bias may be actual, reasonably apprehended, or structural; see *Old St Boniface Residents Association Inc v Winnipeg (City)* (1990), 75 DLR (4th) 385 (SCC)

BILD: Building Industry and Land Development Association, a group representing developers in the Greater Toronto Area

Billboard: (term often used and defined in LUBs) freestanding sign for advertising; see *Vann Niagara Ltd v Oakville (Town)*, 2003 SCC 65; any sign which directs persons to or advertises goods, products, services, or facilities situated or provided at a different location from where the sign is installed: Regina Zoning Bylaw No 9250, Part 2C

Biological diversity: variety of different species, especially genetic variability, and their ecosystems

Block: (variously used and defined in LUBs) suggests an area larger than one lot; see *Shawnnessy Enterprises v Chase (Village)*, 2006 BCSC 1455

Board of variance: committee to determine applications for minor variances; incorporates a test for relief of hardship

***Bona fide*:** (Latin) in good faith. A municipality is expected to act in good faith; see *Congrégation des témoins de Jéhovah de St-Jérôme-Lafontaine v Lafontaine (Village)*, 2004 SCC 48

Bonus: monetary or other benefit granted by a municipality; for example, a reduction in taxes or charges for services or in the price of land, or a conferral of development rights, such as density, beyond those permitted by the applicable zoning. Bonuses are usually prohibited by statute or tightly controlled; see *Ontario Municipal Act, 2001*, SO 2001, c 25, s 106; *Friends of Lansdowne Inc v Ottawa (City)*, 2012 ONCA 273

Border area: area where different land uses abut each other; see *3777783 Manitoba Ltd v West St Paul (Rural Municipality)*, 2010 MBQB 101

Buffer: zone or strip of land separating two areas, "usually to protect a sensitive area from the impacts of adjacent development activities": West Coast Environmental Law Foundation, "Guide to Forest Land Use Planning" (February 1999)

Building: something constructed on land from manufactured materials with the intention that the end product be a permanent fixture to the land: see *Columbia Shuswap (Regional District) v Giesbrecht*, 2002 BCSC 1092; a structure, erection, alteration or improvement placed on, over or under land or attached, anchored or moored to land, or mobile structures, vehicles and marine vessels adapted or constructed for residential, commercial, industrial and other similar uses: see Newfoundland *Urban and Rural Planning Act, 2000*, SNL 2000, c U-8, s 2(c); includes any well, pipeline, excavation, cut, fill, transmission line or other erection or structure or any part thereof (Manitoba *Planning Act*, CCSM c P 80, s 1(1))

Building code: regulations governing safety and related standards for structures; for example, electrical, plumbing, and heating

Building inspector: official with authority to enforce the building code

Building permit: formal municipal authorization to proceed with construction of a specific building or to undertake renovations at a particular site

Building standards: requirements for the safe construction of buildings, usually in accordance with the National Building Code

Bulk: land coverage by a building; a common form of regulation in LUBs

By-law: law passed by local government; a form of subordinate legislation

CAFO. *See also* CFO; IAO; ILO: confined (sometimes "concentrated") animal feeding operation

Carbon capture and storage: technology to remove or capture greenhouse gases before they are emitted to the atmosphere, and then to store them underground; see Alberta *Carbon Capture and Storage Development Council*

Carrying capacity: capacity of physical, chemical, and biological systems acting together to support functional ecosystems

Cash in lieu: payment made to a level of government as an alternative to a dedication of land for public purposes, for example, as part of a subdivision development

CBD: central business district; common term in land-use by-laws; usually where the main office, retail, and government uses are located and predominate over dwellings

CCME: Canadian Council of Ministers of the Environment

CCS. ***See*** **Carbon capture and storage**

***CEAA*:** *Canadian Environmental Assessment Act, 2012*, SC 2012, c 19, s 52; the statute governing environmental assessment of undertakings within federal jurisdiction

Cemetery. ***See*** **Graveyard**

***CEPA*:** *Canadian Environmental Protection Act*, 1999, SC 1999, c 33; the main federal statute setting pollution controls

CFO. ***See also*** **CAFO; IAO; ILO:** confined feeding operation

Change of use: change in the use of land, from uses permitted in one zoning category to uses permitted in another

Charter city: city having its existence and powers established by a special statute, for example, Toronto under the *City of Toronto Act, 2006*, SO 2006, c 11, Sch A

CIP: Canadian Institute of Planners; voluntary organization representing professional planners in Canada

Citizen participation: opportunities for members of the general public to have meaningful and effective involvement in important land-use planning decisions; see *Canadian Pacific Railway Co v Vancouver (City)*, 2006 SCC 5

Clear-cut: forest harvesting and silviculture method in which all trees in a stand are cut in one operation; designed to produce an even-age stand

Cluster housing: subdivision technique grouping houses close together and leaving common-use space

Clustering: land-use planning concept and tool for subdivision planning; cluster development concentrates the physical development of the area to be subdivided to minimize development impacts and to preserve desirable terrain features; see *O'Flanagan v Rossland (City)*, 2007 BCSC 1063

Coastal zone management: planning for the shore lands contiguous to the ocean

Commercial: one of the usual categories of land use specified in LUBs; commercial uses are such things as retail, services, and professional businesses

Commercial vehicle: as used in an LUB, the term means designed to be used commercially, not necessarily actually being used commercially; see *Edmonton (City) v Ungarian*, 2007 ABQB 705

Committee of adjustment: municipal committee authorized to permit minor variances to by-laws

Community plan: official plan under the *City of Winnipeg Charter*, SM 2002, c 39; related term "action area plan"

Compatible: to blend with and not threaten other uses and structures; see *Keewatin (Town) Zoning By-law 94-013 (Re)* (1996), 33 OMBR 293; official plans sometimes specify compatibility criteria such as design, height, transportation access, services, traffic generated, community benefits, and interaction with neighbours in such factors as shadow, wind, light spillover, or parking spillover; see also *Toronto (City) Official Plan Amendment No 352 (Re)* (2007), 55 OMBR 68; does not mean "the same as"; whether variations in built form are capable of coexisting in harmony: see *Jessop v Toronto (City)*, [2009] OMBD No 159; *Ladha v Markham (Town)* (2010), 66 OMBR 162

Complementary: similar in design and scale to existing structures

Comprehensive plan: official plan

Comprehensive zoning by-law: land-use by-law

Confiscation: expropriation; in the alternative, excessive restrictions on the use of land

Conservation authority: land-use decision-making body established pursuant to the *Conservation Authorities Act*, RSO 1990, c C.27, as amended

Conservation easement: voluntary agreement between a private landowner and a qualified organization whereby the landowner donates the ecological and/or natural portions of the land while still retaining title to the land: see *Alberta Land Stewardship Act*, SA 2009, c A-26.8, Part 3

Consolidation: merger of two or more lots; the merger of two or more municipalities or parts of them

Construct: to do anything in the erection, installation, extension, or material alteration or repair of a building and includes the installation of a building unit fabricated or moved from elsewhere: Ontario *Building Code Act, 1992*, SO 1992, c 23, s 1(1)) might not extend to alteration of the configuration of land: see *Vancouver (City) v Reid*, 2006 BCCA 251

Consultation: bilateral communication, including the opportunity to question, to receive explanations, and to provide comment; see *Gardner v Williams Lake (City)*, 2006 BCCA 307

Contaminated site: area of the land in which the soil or any groundwater lying beneath it, or the water or the underlying sediment, contains, (a) a hazardous waste, or (b) another prescribed substance in quantities or concentrations exceeding prescribed risk based on enumerated criteria or standards or conditions: see *Environmental Management Act*, SBC 2003, c 53, s 174

Contamination: introduction of undesirable substances into the environment

Contiguous: abutting

Contract zoning. ***See*** **Development agreement**

Conurbation: large urbanized area formed by the merger of city suburbs with nearby towns

Conversion: change in the structure of a building, as from one use to another or to a more intensive use, but not demolition and rebuilding: see *J & A Investments Ltd v Halifax (Regional Municipality)* (2000), 11 MPLR (3d) 99 (NSSC)

CORE: Commission on Resources and the Environment, established pursuant to the *Commissioner on Resources and Environment Act*, RSBC 1996, c 59 [repealed 2004]; active 1992–96

Core city: municipality whose territory corresponds to a census agglomeration defined by Statistics Canada, or is situated within a census agglomeration and whose population is the highest among those so situated; see Quebec's *Act respecting Land Use Planning and Development*, CQLR c A-19.1

Corporation: includes a municipality, hence the term "municipal corporation"; a concept tied to Dillon's Rule

Cottage: small house; building to accommodate one or more guests

Coverage. ***See*** **Footprint**

CPA: (Quebec) *Commission de protection du territoire agricole:* the provincial body administrating Quebec's statute that establishes designated agricultural zones for valued farmland under the *Act Respecting the Preservation of Agricultural Land and Agricultural Activities*, CQLR c P-41.1

CRD: construction, renovation, and demolition waste

Critical natural capital: ecological resources that provide important ecosystem services, not very amenable to substitution or replacement

Crown reserve: land that vests in the Crown but that is not dedicated to the public

***Cuius est solum eius est usque ad coelum et ad inferos*:** (Latin) maxim that the owner of land owns up to the heavens and down to the bowels of the earth; see *Abell v York (County)* (1920), 61 SCR 345

Cul-de-sac: street with a closed turning area at one end

Culvert: open drain or ditch

Cumulative effect: result of a series of successive actions or impacts; in the context of environment, a succession of impacts from the same or different sources that, taken together, result in a change to an ecosystem

Cumulative zoning. *See also* Non-cumulative zoning: early and still common feature of zoning in which less intense uses are allowed in more intense zones

Cutting permit: issued under an agreement entered into under the British Columbia *Forest Act*, RSBC 1996, c 157, s 1(1)

D-6 Guideline: guideline intended to be applied in the land-use planning process to prevent or minimize future land-use problems due to the encroachment of sensitive land uses and industrial land uses on one another; see online: www.ontario.ca/page/d-1-land-use-and-compatibility

Dark sky preserve: area in which artificial lighting is controlled so it does not interfere with opportunities for astronomy; Alberta and New Brunswick have the greatest areas so designated

Dedicated lands: lands dedicated as buffer strips, environmental reserve, public reserve, and walkways; see Saskatchewan *Planning and Development Act, 2007*, SS 2007, c P-13.2, s 2(1)(i)

Dedication: setting aside of property for the public use

Deep geological repository: site proposed for burial of nuclear waste, for example, Ontario Power Generation's proposal to do so at Kincardine, Ontario

Defensive architecture: design of buildings or associated features so as to discourage undesirable activity such as sleeping, sitting, skateboarding, climbing, graffiti, public urination; benches with separations are an example; see Ocean Howell, "The Poetics of Security" (2001), online: http://urbanpolicy.net/wp-content/uploads/2013/02/Howell_2001_Poetics-of-Security_NoPix.pdf

Demolition: destruction of a structure or alterations so extensive as to completely alter the character of the former structure; see *Re Trivest Developments Ltd and Toronto (City)* (1986), 32 MPLR 124 (Ont HCJ); *Amadon Properties Ltd v Pacific Apparel Inc* (1990), 13 RPR (2d) 186 (BCSC); Ontario *Building Code Act, 1992*, SO 1992, c 23

Demolition permit: formal municipal authorization to proceed with the demolition of a building

Density: (term commonly used and defined in LUBs) regarding the use of land, the allowable number of persons per hectare, or the allowable number of dwelling units per hectare; areas might be classed as high, medium, or low density

Density bonus. ***See*** **Bonus**

Derelict building: one in a ramshackle or rundown condition, not fit for habitation or other use; see *British Columbia v A & A Estates Ltd*, 1999 CanLII 5071 (BCSC)

Developer: one who as principal proposes to develop land; see British Columbia *Real Estate Development Marketing Act*, SBC 2004, c 41

Development: variously defined; a project or undertaking often involving construction of buildings, fences, and so on but also extending to alteration of the natural state of the land: see *Dmytruk v Lang & Sons Holdings Ltd* (1994), 19 MPLR (2d) 125 (Sask CA); *contra*: does not extend to altering the configuration of the land as the terms are used in the *Vancouver Charter*: *Vancouver (City) v Reid*, 2006 BCCA 251; includes future development under [what was s 919 but now] ss 488–91 of the British Columbia *Local Government Act*, SBC 2015, c 1: *Denman Island Local Trust Committee v Ellis*, 2007 BCCA 536.

Development agreement: contract to allow a development that would not be allowed under the land-use by-law; permissible only if the power to do this is specified by statute: see *Harrietsfield-Grand Lake Community Association v Halifax (County)* (1978), 26 NSR (2d) 198 (SCAD)

Development certificate. ***See also*** **Special planning zone:** order from a minister establishing terms and conditions for development in a set area; see Newfoundland and Labrador *Urban and Rural Planning Act, 2000*, SNL 2000, c U-8

Development cost charge. ***See also*** **Development levy:** fee imposed by a local authority to defray the cost of services to be provided by the local authority to a development; see *Cariboo College v Kamloops (City)* (1982), 18 MPLR 85 (BCSC); Ontario *Development Charges Act, 1997*, SO 1997, c 27

Development levy. ***See also*** **Development cost charge:** charge for the purpose of recovering all or part of a municipality's capital costs of providing, altering, expanding, or upgrading services and facilities associated, directly or indirectly, with a proposed development, such as sewage, water or drainage works, public highways, parks, and recreational facilities: Saskatchewan *Planning and Development Act, 2007*, SS 2007, c P-13.2, s 169(2)

Development officer: municipal official with authority to review plans and issue permits, usually for as-of-right developments

Development plan: term used in Manitoba and Quebec for an "official plan"

Development right: crystallized entitlement to the issuance of a development permit

Development works agreement: term used in British Columbia for "development cost charge"

Dillon's Rule: restrictive view of municipal powers, based on the observations in the US text by John Dillon, *Commentaries on the Law of Municipal Corporations*, 4th ed (Boston: Little, Brown, 1890) at § 89 that "municipal corporations possess only powers expressly granted, those necessarily or fairly implied, or those essential or indispensable to the declared objects and purposes of the corporation"; see *Ottawa Electric Light Co v Ottawa (City)* (1906), 12 OLR 290 (CA)

Direct control district: areas of particular development control exercised by a municipal council; see Saskatchewan *Planning and Development Act, 2007*, SS 2007, c P-13.2, s 63

Discretionary use: as authorized by section 54 of Saskatchewan *Planning and Development Act, 2007*, SS 2007, c P-13.2: use of land that may be allowed but is not as of right

Discrimination: there are two senses of the word: (1) prohibited discrimination under the *Canadian Charter of Rights and Freedoms* or a *Human Rights Code*, and (2) common law restriction on municipal decisions—a distinction made with an improper motive of favouring or hurting one individual without regard to the public interest: see *Scarborough (Township) v Bondi*, [1959] SCR 444

District: (1) zone, or (2) electoral area or ward

District heating and cooling: system for distributing heat generated in a centralized location for residential and commercial heating requirements

Ditch: sunken or low area beside roads or facilities used for the purpose of drainage. It can be either artificial or natural. Widths range from 2 to 20 metres and slopes range from gradual to sharp drops adjacent to the bank. Depths vary from less than 1 metre to several metres

DLUG. ***See also*** **SLUP:** district land use guideline (Ontario term); informal plan regarding use of Crown lands; see *Re Timber Management Class Environmental Assessment* (1994), EA-87-02 (Ont EAB)

Dormitory town: place from which many people travel in order to work in a nearby larger town or city

Downzoning: change in zoning to one seen as having a negative impact on the market value of land

Drinking water advisory: preventive measure to protect public health from waterborne contaminants that could be, or are known to be, present in drinking water; can include boil water advisories and "do not drink" advisories; see Manitoba *The Drinking Water Safety Act*, CCSM c D101

DUD: deep underground dump; site proposed for burying nuclear waste, a variant of the official term, deep geological repository

Dump: place for the generally unorganized disposal of solid waste

Duplex: house that has separate accommodations for two families; a form of attached dwelling; "triplex" and "quadruplex" are of similar design but with more units

Dwelling unit: (term often used and defined in LUBs) place designed to be used as a place of abode; any property that is used or designed for use as a domestic establishment in which one or more persons may sleep and prepare and serve meals: Ontario *Planning Act*, RSO 1990, c P.13, s 33(1); see *Neighbourhoods of Windfields Ltd Partnership v Death* (2008), 48 MPLR (4th) 183 (Ont SCJ)

EBR. See Environmental Bill of Rights

Ecological footprint: impact on natural resources implied by a given standard of living; see William Rees & Mathis Wackernagel, *Our Ecological Footprint* (Philadelphia: New Society, 1996)

EEM: environmental effects monitoring

Efficiency apartment: small apartment

Efficiency unit: dwelling unit of one room plus kitchenette and bathroom

Effluent: liquid discharge from a structure, especially sewage

Eminent domain: right of government to take private property for public purposes

Encroachment: construct that trespasses on the property of another

Endangered species: animals or plants threatened with extinction; see Nova Scotia *Endangered Species Act*, SNS 1998, c 11, s 3(d); similar or associated terms are "species at risk," "threatened species," and "vulnerable species"

Environment: "the air, land, water, plant life, animal life and ecological systems": Ontario *Environmental Bill of Rights, 1993*, SO 1993, c 28, s 1(1)

Environmental assessment (EA): assessment of the environmental effects of a project or undertaking, conducted in accordance with the governing federal or provincial laws; different levels of intensity of scrutiny exist, and most do not require public hearings; projects subject to EA are not to proceed without the EA, which is to be conducted as early in the planning stage as possible and before irrevocable decisions are made; see *Canadian Environmental Assessment Act, 2012*, SC 2012, c 19

***Environmental Bill of Rights*:** statute that provides, among other things, for effective public participation in environmental decision making: Ontario *Environmental Bill of Rights, 1993*, SO 1993, c 28

Environmental impact assessment. *See* Environmental assessment (EA)

Environmental impact statement: statement by a proponent of a project, supported by studies, as to the anticipated environmental effects of a project and possible mitigations, submitted as part of the initiation of an environmental assessment

Environmental racism: siting of obnoxious facilities or withholding of normal municipal services in communities where the predominant population is a racial or ethnic minority: see Robert Bullard, *Confronting Environmental Racism* (Boston: South End Press, 1993); Don Clairmont & Dennis Magill, *Africville*, 3d ed (Toronto: Canadian Scholars' Press, 1999)

Environmental reserve: land transferred to a municipality as part of a subdivision process where considered necessary to protect a ravine, coulee, swamp, natural drainage course or creek bed, or land subject to flooding or that is unstable, or that is abutting the bed or shore of any lake, river, stream or other body of water, to prevent pollution, preserve the bank, or protect the proposed subdivision land from flooding: Saskatchewan *Planning and Development Act, 2007*, SS 2007, c P-13.2, s 185(1)

Environmentally sensitive area: "any area in which plant or animal life or their habitats are either rare or especially valuable because of their special nature or role in an ecosystem and which could be easily disturbed or degraded by human activities and developments": California *Coastal Act*, Public Resources Code, Division 20, s 30107.5

Euclidean zoning. ***See also*** **Non-Euclidean zoning:** system of classification of permitted land uses by district; so named not for the mathematical association but for the leading US case recognizing the constitutionality of such schemes: see *Village of Euclid v Ambler Realty Co*, 272 US 365 (1926)

Exaction: (US term) concession from a landowner made to a local government as a condition of subdivision or other intensified land use (as distinguished from an "impact fee")

Excavation: removal of soil and underground material, preparatory to construction of a building

Excess or extended services: portion of a highway system that will provide access to land other than the land being subdivided or developed, and a portion of a water, sewage, or drainage system that will serve such other land: British Columbia *Local Government Act*, RSBC 2015, c 1, s 507

Exclusionary zoning: attempts to discriminate in any prohibited way under the guise of regular zoning tools

Expropriation: taking of private land by a level of government or authorized authority for public purposes

Extralateral rights: right to mine beneath the land of another, by following a vein

Exurbia: area beyond the suburbs

Facade: exterior walls of a building; often, the front wall: see *Heritage Trust of Nova Scotia v Nova Scotia (Utility & Review Board)* (1994), 128 NSR (2d) 5 (SCAD)

Fairhousing laws: (US term) statutes prohibiting discrimination on the basis of race, colour, religion, gender, or national origin, in real estate transactions or rentals

Farm retirement lot: severance of agricultural land to create a lot for a family dwelling; see *Withers v Loyalist (Township) Committee of Adjustment* (2006), 54 OMBR 454

FEARO: Federal Environmental Assessment Review Office

Fettering: (1) local government's agreeing by contract to exercise planning discretion in a particular way; held as being contrary to public policy: see *Pacific National Investments Ltd v Victoria (City)*, 2000 SCC 64, and (2) improper restriction of its powers of decision by a decision-maker, through adopting inflexible pre-existing policy; see *Bruce Farms Ltd v Alberta (Energy and Utilities Board)*, 2002 ABCA 77

Finish elevation: also "finished grade"; land surface elevation after site preparation work is complete

Fiscal zoning: zoning so as to increase municipal revenues or avoid expenditures on services or infrastructure

Floating zone. ***See*** **Paper zoning**

Flood plain: area of land subject to periodic flooding

Floor area ratio: factor applied to lot area to determine the maximum permitted habitable or usable floor area that may be constructed

FLUA: federal land-use approval; required in respect of the development, construction, demolition, or change in use of lands/buildings owned by the National Capital Commission

Footprint: (term often used and defined in LUBs) area of a lot occupied by all buildings on the lot

Form of development: any activity associated with altering the physical features of land: see Saskatchewan *Planning and Development Act, 2007*, SS 2007, c P-13.2

Free entry/Crown discretion: two approaches to mineral prospecting, the latter being a more restrictive licensing regime

Free entry system: in mining, the right to enter land to prospect for minerals; this system prevails, but a discretionary system also exists in some jurisdictions for some minerals; for a discussion, see Barry J Barton, *Canadian Law of Mining* (Calgary: Canadian Institute of Resources Law, 1993)

Front: for a building, where the main entrance is located; see *Dinnick and McCallum (Re)* (1913), 28 OLR 52 (CA)

Frontage: linear distance of a lot along a road or water body; also where the entrance to a building is located (cf rearage); see *Caponero v Brakenridge*, [1944] 1 DLR 773 (BCCA)

Funeral home: (term often used and defined in LUBs) place for the conduct of funerals; usually the term will not extend to a crematorium: see *Build-A-Vest Structures Inc v Red Deer (City)*, 2006 ABQB 869

Gabion wall: wall composed of sections made up of rock or earth encased in wire mesh; sometimes used to attempt to resist erosion of coastlands

Gated community: a residential area with access restricted to residents and their guests, as described in Edward J Blakely & Mary Gail Snyder, *Fortress America* (Washington, DC: Brookings Institution Press, 1997); see also various Canadian articles by Jill Grant

General (grants of) power. ***See also*** **Omnibus clause:** legislative authority given to municipalities, expressed in broad terms, for example, "the health, well-being, and safety" of persons and property: see *114957 Canada Ltée (Spraytech, Société d'arrosage) v Hudson (Town)*, 2001 SCC 40

Generalized future land-use map: a feature of official plans, maps showing a municipality's contemplated future land uses in various districts

General plan: term used in Northwest Territories for "official plan"

Gentrification: displacement of poor and working-class neighborhoods by the middle class; involves processes such as purchase, termination of tenancies, and conversion of rental properties to condominiums

GGH: Greater Golden Horseshoe area in Ontario; the extended region around Toronto, subject to planning under the *Places to Grow Act, 2005*, SO 2005, c 13

GHG: greenhouse gas

Ghost town: a former municipality that has been abandoned, usually because the economic activity that supported the town has failed, for example, Bradburn, Manitoba, and Val-Jalbert, Quebec

GIS: geographic information systems; the database and software for electronic mapping

Glare: light of a brightness to amount to an annoyance or nuisance

GLWQA: *Great Lakes Water Quality Agreement*, made pursuant to the *Boundary Waters Treaty* of 1906; sets principles and objectives for management of the Great Lakes and lands surrounding them; see online: binational.net

Goal. ***See also*** **Objective:** "an ideal, condition, or a quality to be sought in the community's physical development": Gerald Hodge, *Planning Canadian Communities*, 4th ed (Toronto: Nelson Thomson, 2003) at 162

Good faith: honesty of intention, and freedom from knowledge of circumstances that ought to put the holder upon inquiry; see *Congrégation des témoins de Jéhovah de St-Jérôme-Lafontaine v Lafontaine (Village)*, 2004 SCC 48

Good planning in the public interest: test used by the Ontario Municipal Board

GPS: global positioning system; a surveying technology (US-based); similar systems exist in the EU (Galileo), Russia (Glonass), and China (Beidou)

Grade: (term variously used and defined in LUBs) ground level at the foundation of a building; usually pre-existing grade, that is, pre-construction; relates to the natural elements in a residential instance and to elements the owner cannot affect, such as sidewalks, in a non-residential context; see *Lazarev v Toronto (City)* (2006), 25 MPLR (4th) 85 (Ont SCJ)

Grants-in-lieu of taxes: (also called PILTs—payments in lieu of taxes) discretionary payments made to a municipal government to compensate for services provided, even though there is no power, for constitutional reasons or otherwise, allowing the municipality to impose a tax; thus the federal government has adopted a *Payments in Lieu of Taxes Act*, RSC 1985, c M-13

Grassland: area with herbaceous plants dominated by gramineae (grasses) rather than large shrubs or trees, including hay lands, pastures, and prairies

Graveyard: cemetery; a place for the interment of dead bodies; sometimes defined in statutes as a place where a minimum number of persons (as "six or more") are buried: see *Luke v Kerr* (1891), 27 CLJ 181 (Ont Co Ct)

Green: (UK term) common open area in the centre of a community

Green building: new or retrofitted structure designed to reduce demand for energy and water

Green infrastructure: ecosystems considered as asset classes with a price attached

Greenbelt: area of parks, farmland, and so on encircling an urban area and usually subject to restrictions on new building; see Ontario *Greenbelt Act, 2005*, SO 2005, c 1

Greenbelt (Ontario): land designated by the provincial cabinet to establish a network of countryside and open space (including the Oak Ridges Moraine and Niagara Escarpment) and restricting development: Ontario *Greenbelt Act, 2005*, SO 2005, c 1

Gridiron plan: streets patterned so as to be parallel and/or at right angles to one another

Gridlock: paralysis of vehicle traffic, due to congested intersections

Grocery store: establishment, the main object of which is to sell foodstuffs; often differentiated from a supermarket; see *Minto (Village) v Corbin's Paving Ltd*, 1991 CanLII 5650 (NBQB)

Groundwater: percolating water; subsurface water that may supply wells and springs; see *Schneider v Olds (Town)* (1969), 8 DLR (3d) 680 (Alta SCTD)

Group home: (term used and defined in LUBs) building for the boarding, plus treatment, care, or supervision of persons in need of such; see *Kepron v Vogt* (1983), 24 MPLR 199 (Man QB)

Growth plan (area): area of land designated by the Lieutenant Governor in Council with limitations of population, priorities for growth, policies for the location of industry, and generally all other matters that might be found in an official plan, and requiring conformity by the official plan (Ontario *Places to Grow Act, 2005*, SO 2005, c 13)

Guideline: policy statement without force of statute, enforceable in some circumstances; see *Friends of the Oldman River Society v Canada (Minister of Transport)*, [1992] 1 SCR 3

Habitable room: (term often used and defined in LUBs) any room in a dwelling of a certain size and usually excluding bathrooms, storage spaces, and kitchens

Halfway house: residential building sponsored by an agency that seeks to help persons who have been imprisoned or otherwise institutionalized readjust to society: Regina Zoning Bylaw No 9250, Part 2C

Hamlet: village; in Saskatchewan, see *Municipalities Act*, SS 2005, c M-36.1; a category of zoning district in Northwest Territories: see *Hamlets Act*, SNWT 2003, c 22, Sch C

Hazardous conditions: land subject to flooding, mud flows, torrents of debris, erosion, land slips, rock falls, subsidence, tsunami, avalanche, wildfire, or other specified hazard (British Columbia *Local Government Act*, RSBC 2015, c 1, s 500)

HBO: home business overlay; a type of land-use designation, specifying home-based businesses as allowable uses in addition to other zoning prescriptions

Height: (term often used and defined in LUBs) for buildings, the vertical distance of the highest point of the roof above mean grade

Heritage alteration permit: authorization of an alteration of a designated heritage property, in a heritage conservation area; see British Columbia *Local Government Act*, RSBC 2015, c 1, s 617

Heritage conservation district: area of urban or rural properties (collectively) deemed to have local or community heritage values; see *Heritage Conservation Districts Regulations*, NS Reg 138/92

Heritage conservation study area: area under study as a possible heritage conservation district; see *Heritage Conservation Districts Regulations*, NS Reg 138/92

Heritage designation: historic buildings or districts may be so designated; this usually entails restrictions on alteration or demolition, and may also generate bonuses

High-rise: variously defined; generally, a building that exceeds six storeys: see *Regina (City) v Harvard Developments Ltd*, 2004 SKCA 103; some classifications suggest mid-rise as being from three to seven storeys and high-rise as eight or more: see HS Moskowitz & CG Lindbloom, *The Illustrated Book of Development Definitions* (Piscataway, NJ: Rutgers: Center for Urban Policy Research, 1981); other suggestions are of height above twelve storeys: see *Re Miller*, 2015 NSUARB 218

Highway: a place for the public passage of vehicles; may extend to bridges, etc.: *Highway Traffic Act*, CCSM c H60, s 1(1)

Holding provision by-law. *See also* Holding zone: by-law using the area designation "H" and specifying the use to which lands, buildings, or structures may be put at such time in the future as the holding symbol is removed: Ontario *Planning Act*, RSO 1990, c P.13, s 36

Holding zone. *See also* Holding provision by-law: by-law to specify when a zoning use may be allowed at some time in the future; see *Soo Mill and Lumber Co v Sault Ste-Marie (City)*, [1975] 2 SCR 78 and Ontario *Planning Act*, RSO 1990, c P.13, s 36(4); the term "freeze" is sometimes used

Holdout: owner who refuses to sell or delays selling land sought for an assemblage

Home-based business. *See* Home occupation

Home occupation: (term often used and defined in LUBs) accessory use of a dwelling unit for gainful employment, including sales; should not be such as to usurp the primary residential use; see *Murzin v Milton (Town) Committee of Adjustment* (1989), 23 OMBR 210

Hostel: (term used and defined in LUBs) accommodation consisting of rooms without culinary facilities, but not a rooming house; see *Hastings Corp v Toronto (City) Chief Building Official* (2004), 46 MPLR (3d) 87 (Ont SCJ)

Housing agreement: agreement between a local government and an owner regarding affordable and special needs housing; see British Columbia *Local Government Act*, RSBC 2015, c 1, s 483

Human scale: planning that uses the human body and its senses as fundamental units of measurement; see *Heritage Trust of Nova Scotia (Re)*, 2007 NSUARB 122

IAO. *See also* CAFO; CFO; ILO: intensive animal operation; a factory farm

ILO. *See also* CAFO; CFO; IAO: intensive livestock operation; a factory farm

Impact fee: (US term) monetary condition required for an owner to develop land in order to pay for increased demand on infrastructure

Improved land: land that is no longer "raw land" due to partial or full development for use, as through construction of buildings, clearing, excavating, landscaping, or construction of roads; see British Columbia *Builders Lien Act*, RSBC 1996, c 41

Improvement district: area exempted from normal municipal administration, by order of the minister, and under the minister's direct control, pursuant to the Alberta *Municipal Government Act*, RSA 2000, c M-26, Part 15.

***In camera*:** (Latin) in private; for example, a meeting held in private without public access; municipalities are usually limited by statute as to what subjects may be dealt with *in camera*; typically, only legal matters, including personnel issues and pending land acquisitions, are so handled; see *RSJ Holdings Inc v London (City)*, 2004 CanLII 8408 (Ont SCJ)

Industrial: typical zoning category; industrial uses include heavy or light manufacturing, factory/warehouses, research and development; "a use which was primarily one involving the art of production or manufacture of some item, and that it involved activity or labour whereby a saleable commodity was created or produced": *Oriole Lumber Ltd v Markham (Township)*, [1968] SCR 549 at 552

Industrial park: area of land set aside, usually under the development auspices of a level of government, for industrial development

Infilling: building on land between existing developments

Infrastructure. ***See also*** **Public infrastructure:** physical betterments to land, including such things as water systems, waste water facilities, storm water systems, streets, traffic signs and signals, transit bus bays; see Nova Scotia *Municipal Government Act*, SNS 1998, c 18, s 274(1)

Injurious affection: reduction in value of land due to some government action; only compensable in extreme circumstances: see *St Pierre v Ontario (Minister of Transportation and Communications)*, [1987] 1 SCR 906, and *Antrim Truck Centre Ltd v Ontario (Transportation)*, 2013 SCC 13; zoning is, by statute, not injurious affection

Inner city: usually the older, urbanized area of a city; typically, including or adjacent to the central business district and densely populated, often with low-income residents

Inside lot: lot in a subdivision having road frontage on one side

Institutional use: (term variously defined in LUBs) use of land for a public or quasi-public purpose such as for a library, school, hospital, or government office

In-stream application: those commenced prior to a change in rules, for example, for a subdivision, and therefore immunized from the new rules; see *391043 Alberta Ltd v Canal Flats (Village)*, 2008 BCSC 1043

Integrated resource management: attempt to manage two or more resources in the same area, or multiple activities associated with a resource, for example, forestry, mining, recreation, and wildlife

Intensive agriculture: use of land or buildings by a commercial enterprise for the confinement of poultry, livestock, or fur-bearing animals, or the growing of mushrooms; see British Columbia *Local Government Act*, RSBC 2015, c 1, s 555

Interested person. ***See also*** **Standing:** test of standing; see *Cal Investments Ltd v British Columbia (Capital Regional District)* (1980), 14 MPLR 94 (BCSC)

Interim control by-law: by-law prohibiting or limiting development pending a review or study of land use; not to exceed one year; after, no renewal for three years: Ontario *Planning Act*, RSO 1990, c P.13, s 38

Interim planning policy: limitations, restrictions, and prohibitions on land use pending the completion of an official plan

Inter-municipal development plan: coordinated official plan for more than one municipality

Inverse condemnation. ***See*** **Regulatory taking**

IPCC: Intergovernmental Panel on Climate Change

Island zoning: spot zoning; see *Halifax (City) v Wonnacott*, [1951] 2 DLR 488 at 494 (NSSC)

Joint land-use planning commission: (Quebec term) a commission with land-use planning authority in two regional counties

Kiosk: free-standing structure to accommodate posters and notices; see *Peterborough (City) v Ramsden* (1993), 16 MPLR (2d) 1 (SCC)

Land. ***See also*** **Real estate:** includes land, messuages, tenements, hereditaments, corporeal and incorporeal, of every kind and description, whatever the estate or interest therein, and whether legal or equitable, together with all paths, passages, ways, watercourses, liberties, privileges, and easements, appertaining thereto, and all trees and timber thereon, and all mines, minerals, and quarries, unless specially excepted: Manitoba *Planning Act*, CCSM c P80, s 1(1); surface land not enclosed in a building, land covered by water (which for greater certainty, includes wetland), and all subsoil: Ontario *Environmental Bill of Rights, 1993*, SO 1993, c 28, s 1(1)

Land assembly: purchase of various individual nearby or adjacent properties, usually with a view to undertaking a large building project

Land bank: land owned by some level of government with the intention of withholding it from development, either temporarily or permanently

Land capability classes: classification of the Canada Land Inventory, rating the suitability of land for agriculture, forestry, recreation, and so on

Landfill: place for the disposal of solid waste, hazardous waste, or medical waste

Land for public purposes: land, other than streets, for the recreational or other use or enjoyment of the general public

Land lease community home: any dwelling that is a permanent structure where the owner of the dwelling leases the land used or intended for use as the site for the dwelling, but does not include a mobile home; see Ontario *Planning Act*, RSO 1990, c P.13, s 46(1)

Landscaping: modification and enhancement of a site through the use of the following elements: (1) soft landscaping—the use of living plant materials such as trees, shrubs, hedges, grass, and other ground covers plus the modification of the landform, such as berming and terracing; or (2) hard landscaping—non-vegetative materials such as brick, stone, concrete, tile, or wood, excluding asphalt for the purpose of surface paving: Regina Zoning Bylaw No 9250, Part 2C

Land use: human use of land; involves the management and modification of natural environment or wilderness into built environment such as fields, pastures, and settlements; it has also been defined as "the arrangements, activities and inputs people undertake in a certain land cover type to produce, change or maintain it," online: www.fao.org/nr/land/use/en

Land-use planning: government process, usually resulting in an official plan and zoning by-laws, to determine appropriate land uses in light of community priorities and values

Large format retail: big box store; see *Ottawa (City) Official Plan (Re)* (2006), 54 OMBR 1

Latecomer: user of services such as water or sewage systems, who did not contribute to the original cost of their construction; see *Beaver Lake Industrial Park Inc v Kelowna (City)*, 2006 BCSC 486; *618061 BC Ltd v Anmore (Village)*, 2007 BCSC 1344; *Local Government Act*, RSBC 2015, c 1, s 508

Lateral. ***See*** **Service line (lateral)**

LCM: life-cycle management

Leachate: liquid that emanates from a site such as a landfill after having percolated through it; see *R v Kingston (City)* (2004), 240 DLR (4th) 734 (Ont CA)

LEED: leadership in energy and environmental design; a building assessment standard set by the US Green Building Council. Variations are LEED-NC (new construction), LEED-EB (existing buildings), LEED-CI (commercial interiors), and LEED-CS (core and shell)

Legibility: in architecture, the degree to which the designed features of the environment aid people in creating an effective mental image, or "cognitive map" of the spatial relationships within a building, and the subsequent ease of wayfinding within the environment: Michael J O'Neill, "Evaluation of a Conceptual Model of Architectural Legibility" (1991) 23 *Environment and Behavior* 259

Light pollution: glare from lights, for example, street lighting that interferes with observation of the sky or is otherwise unwanted; the term "light trespass" is also used; some Canadian municipalities have light pollution control by-laws, for example, Richmond Hill and Ottawa.

Littoral land: land adjoining a large body of water

LOAEL: lowest observed adverse effect level

Local government: municipal level of government

Lode claim: one based on an aggregation of minerals in place, such as a vein; distinguished from a placer claim

Lodging house. ***See*** **Rooming house**

Lot: a parcel of land to which the title may be legally conveyed; variations include "corner lot," "interior lot," "through lot," and "flag lot"; the terms relate to the shape and/or placement of the lot with respect to adjacent streets

Lot coverage limit: common zoning by-law feature, restricting the total area of a lot that may be covered by all the buildings on the lot

Lot line: boundary of a lot, usually as established by a survey

Lower-tier municipality. ***See also*** **Two-tier municipality; Upper-tier municipality:** municipality that is part of a county, region, or district municipality

Low-income housing: dwellings affordable (i.e., not exceeding 25 to 30 percent of gross family income) by families where income is 50 percent or less of the median income in a particular market area

LUB: land-use by-law, or zoning by-law

LULU: Locally Undesirable Land Use

LUST: leaking underground storage tank

LVEC: large venue entertainment centre

Manufactured home community. ***See*** **Trailer park**

Marquee: canopy or awning projecting from a building, usually over an entrance

Mass transit: shared passenger transportation service that is available for use by the general public

Massing: feature of structures usually associated with the development of three-dimensional shapes

Master plan: "official plan" has become the most common term; was in earlier use as, for example, in JB Milner, "Master Plan Legislation in Canada" (1957) 35 *Canadian Bar Review* 1125

MDS: minimum distance separation policy statement of the Ontario Ministry of Agriculture, Food and Rural Affairs; includes Formulae Implementation Guidelines; the standards may be adopted by municipalities as part of a zoning by-law; see *Hill & Hill Farms Ltd v Bluewater (Municipality)* (2005), 6 MPLR (4th) 1 (Ont Div Ct)

Megacity: a popular nickname assigned in 1996 by opponents to a provincial government initiative for a new structure unifying the City of Toronto, its surrounding suburbs, and the regional metropolitan government: James Lightbody, *City Politics, Canada* (Peterborough, ON: Broadview Press, 2006)

Mineral rights: the right of extraction of minerals or gas and oil from under land; often mineral rights are reserved to the Crown, which establishes a regime for prospecting, mining, and royalty payments; see Alberta *Mines and Minerals Act*, RSA 2000, c M-17

Minister's Zoning Order: power of the Ontario Minister of Municipal Affairs to directly zone land, pursuant to section 47(1) of the *Planning Act*, RSO 1990, c P.13

Minor variance. *See also* Variance: permission to violate some limited provision of zoning by-laws; the tests of allowable minor variances are specified by statute; see *McNamara Corp Ltd v Colekin Investments Ltd* (1977), 76 DLR (3d) 609 (Ont Div Ct); whether change-of-use restrictions may be treated as minor variances is a matter of dispute: see *Fred Doucette Holdings Ltd v Waterloo (City)* (1997), 32 OR (3d) 502 (Div Ct)

Mixed use: practice of allowing more than one type of use in a building or set of buildings, for example, some combination of residential and commercial uses

Mobile home: (term often used and defined in LUBs) dwelling usually produced in a factory, designed to be taken to a site and semi-permanently attached

Mobile home park (or court). *See also* Trailer Park; can extend to accommodation for RVs: *Sherwood (Rural Municipality No 159) v Sherwood Forest Country Club (1975) Ltd*, 2007 SKQB 11

Modal shift: in transportation planning, commuters switching their preference from one mode of transport to another

Module: cubicle

Monster home: building, especially a single-family residence, out of proportion to its neighbours, usually as a result of taking advantage of the maximum height and bulk regulations that are in conformity with zoning by-laws; see *Cole v Hamilton (City)* (2003), 39 MPLR (3d) 57 (Ont CA); synonyms include Hummer house, starter castle, McMansion, faux château

Motel: building or buildings containing housekeeping or sleeping units designed to provide temporary accommodation for the travelling public: *Muir v 403570 BC Ltd*, 2003 BCSC 575

MSD: minimum separation distance

MSW: municipal solid waste

Multiple barrier system: in the delivery of drinking water, a way to prevent contaminants reaching consumers, through physical means, operating systems, regulation, testing, and oversight: Commission on the Walkerton Inquiry, *Report of the Walkerton Inquiry* (Toronto: Ministry of the Attorney General, 2002) ch 3

Multiple dwelling: building or buildings located on a lot and containing two or more dwelling units

Municipal development plan: term used in Alberta and Saskatchewan for "official plan"

Municipal planning commission: term used in Saskatchewan for "planning advisory committee"

Municipal planning strategy: term used in Nova Scotia for "official plan"

Municipal purpose: test of the validity of municipal by-laws; the Supreme Court of Canada has suggested there is a usual range of legitimate municipal purposes: see *Shell Canada Products Ltd v Vancouver (City)* (1994), 20 MPLR (2d) 1 (SCC)

Municipal services: infrastructure relating to a subdivision and provided by local government; often referred to as "hard," that is, in which there is a direct physical correlation to the subdivision, for example, water, sewage, drainage, roads; and as "soft," for example, a public library; see *Mod-Aire Homes Ltd v Georgina (Township)* (1984), 17 OMBR 213

MURB: multi-unit residential building

National Capital Commission: an administrative and planning body established by the federal government in 1959 pursuant to the *National Capital Act*, RSC 1985, c N-4, to deal with federal lands in the Ottawa/Gatineau area

Natural heritage system: a system that identifies lands that support both natural heritage and hydrologic features and functions; see Ontario *Greenbelt Act, 2005*, SO 2005, c 1

NEF: noise exposure forecast; a measure of sound weighted to estimate its annoyance level as distinguished from its loudness; see *Sutherland v Canada (Attorney General)*, 2001 BCSC 1024

Negligent misstatement: one of the categories of tort lawsuits; municipalities have been successfully sued for the negligent misstatements of planning staff; see *Bell v Sarnia (City)* (1987), 37 DLR (4th) 438 (Ont HCJ)

Neighbour consent ordinance: requirement that consent be obtained from adjacent neighbours, or some larger group, prior to municipal consideration of permission for change in use; this has been litigated as impermissible delegation; see *Lamoureux v Beaconsfield (City)*, [1978] 1 SCR 134

Neighbourhood: some sub-area of a municipality: see *Brown v East York (Borough)* (1992), 10 MPLR (2d) 310 (OMB); *Clarke v Mississauga (City) Committee of Adjustment* (2003), 45 MPLR (3d) 301 (OMB); it implies a group that has a common interest relative to a central issue: *Manufacturers Life Insurance Co v Pitblado & Hoskin*, 2007 MBQB 72

NEP: Niagara Escarpment Plan, created under the *Niagara Escarpment Planning and Development Act*, RSO 1990, c N.2; *583753 Ontario Ltd v York (Regional Municipality)*, 2007 CanLII 40538 (Ont Div Ct)

Nepean principle: Ontario Municipal Board policy that where a municipality downzones property, it must offer to acquire it at its previous value within a reasonable time

New urbanism: urban design movement that promotes walkable neighbourhoods containing a range of housing and job types

Nibbling: taking or changing a small piece here, a small piece there, so as to effect major change over time; see *Rogers v Saanich (District)* (1983), 22 MPLR 1 (BCSC)

NILM: national interest land mass; also known as "mandate lands" and refers to land owned by the National Capital Commission and considered to be symbolically meaningful for Canadians

NIMBY: Not in my backyard

NOAEL: no observable adverse effect level

Noise: (term often used and defined in LUBs) sound of such a volume that annoys, disturbs, or is likely to disturb the peace, quiet, and comfort of neighbours; see *Reid's Heritage Homes Ltd v Guelph (City)* (2000), 14 MPLR (3d) 103 (Ont SCJ); Noise may be a nuisance and thus may be controlled by municipalities in any of three ways: by objective standards, by subjective standards, or by source: *Montréal (City) v 2952-1366 Quebec Inc*, 2005 SCC 62

Non-conforming structure: structure that violates some zoning restriction, for example, height, though not the use restrictions of the zoning by-law

Non-conforming use: use that is not permitted under the applicable zoning by-law currently in force, but which is allowed to continue if formerly legal

Non-cumulative zoning. *See also* Cumulative zoning: zoning that separates uses and does not allow less intense uses in more intense zones

Non-Euclidean zoning. *See also* Euclidean zoning: regulation of land use other than on a lot-by-lot basis, for example, site plans, planned unit developments, cluster zoning

Non-renewable resource: natural resource liable to be used up completely

Normal farm practice: a standard for agricultural activities as determined by a board acting under statute, and conferring some immunity from lawsuits based in nuisance; see *Farming and Food Production Protection Act, 1998*, SO 1998, c 1; the term does not include the fact of an agricultural operation itself: see *Oakville (Town) v Read (cob Read Farms)*, 2010 ONSC 170

Nunavut Planning Commission: body with responsibility to establish broad planning policies, objectives, and goals for Nunavut, in conjunction with government: see *Nunavut Land Claims Agreement*, SC 1993, c 29

Objective. *See also* Goal; Policy: specific or concrete target to further a goal for a community

Occupancy permit: formal municipal authorization to allow a newly constructed building to be used by its owner and/or the public

Off-grid: site that operates independent of the main electrical transmission and distribution grid

Office park: form of industrial park set aside for offices and light industry

Official community plan: term used in British Columbia for "official plan"

Official plan. *See also* Plan: document adopted by a municipality setting out policies and objectives for the development of the municipality, having regard to social, economic, and environmental matters; zoning by-laws must accord with the official plan; some provinces use other terms; historical use of the term is as a survey, usually showing original Crown grants of land: see *Canada (Attorney General) v Western Higbie and Albion Investments Ltd*, [1945] SCR 385

OMB: Ontario Municipal Board; that province's land-use appellate body

Omnibus clause. *See also* General (grants of) power: a general grant of power to a municipality, often phrased as extending to the power to make by-laws for the health, safety, and general welfare of residents; see *114957 Canada Ltée (Spraytech, Société d'arrosage) v Hudson (Town)*, 2001 SCC 40

One-family dwelling. *See* Single-family dwelling

OP: official plan

OPA: official plan amendment

Open space: park or green space

ORV. *See also* ATV: off-road vehicle; includes dirt bike, all-terrain vehicle (ATV), snowmobile

Outfall: pipe or other point at which waste water or treated effluents are discharged into a receiving environment

Overlay: technique of flexible zoning, a mapped addition that superimposes additional zoning restrictions; a device that places land in two different zones; often used to modify some of the as-of-right aspects of the primary land-use classification, for example, so as to require a development agreement for certain proposals, or to apply a special height limit

PAC: planning advisory committee

Paper zoning, *See also* Placeholder by-law: creation of a zone in an LUB for which there is no actual land so designated within the municipality: see *Dartmouth (City) v Portland Landing Beverage Room Ltd* (1989), 90 NSR (2d) 91 (SCTD); unmapped district with detailed and conditional use requirements—in effect, the zone floats over the municipality until a developer seeks to locate it: see Joseph William Singer, *Introduction to Property* (Gaithersburg, MD: Aspen Law & Business, 2001)

Parapet: that portion of the main exterior walls of a building rising above roof level

Parcel of land: a lot; a lot or block within a registered plan of subdivision; see Ontario *Planning Act*, RSO 1990, c P.13, s 46; may be defined to mean an area greater than one lot: see *Shawnnessy Enterprises Ltd v Chase (Village)*, 2006 BCSC 1455

Park: (1) Crown land established or continued as a park: see British Columbia *Park Act*, RSBC 1996, c 344, and (2) municipal park

Party wall: shared supporting wall that is in a building or between two adjoining buildings and is situated on any part of the common boundary shared by adjoining parcels

Patio: paved area adjoining a dwelling, often used for sitting or eating outdoors

People zoning: regulating the user rather than the use; for example, a zone defined as "single-family dwelling"; such zoning may be challenged as *ultra vires* or too vague or discriminatory; see *Alcoholism Foundation of Manitoba v Winnipeg (City)* (1990), 49 MPLR 1 (Man CA) and *R v Bell*, [1979] 2 SCR 212

Percolation test: measure of the ability of ground to absorb water, used in determining the suitability of soil for drainage or use as a septic system

Permit: formal municipal authorization, generally offered on a routine administrative basis, and designed to ensure conformity with zoning or safety laws, and to allow co-ordination of information with the municipality, for example, building, construction, alteration, enlargement, extension, development, occupancy, or demolition permits

Permitted use. ***See*** **As-of-right**

Person affected. ***See also*** **Standing:** test of standing; see *Pension Fund Properties Ltd v Calgary (City) Development Appeal Board*, 1981 ABCA 195

Person aggrieved. ***See also*** **Standing:** test of standing; usually more stringent than "affected" or "concerned"; having a genuine grievance because an order or decision prejudicially affects interests; see *Richard Niebuhr Enterprises (cob Niebuhr Constructions) v Vancouver (City) Board of Variance*, 2006 BCSC 1425

Person concerned. ***See also*** **Standing:** test of standing; interpreted to refer to right to notice rather than right to appeal; see *Werner v Hay River (Town) Development Officer*, 2007 NWTSC 77

Pesticide: any substance intended to destroy or prevent pests; see *Pesticides Act*, CQLR c P-9.3; similar or included terms are "rodenticide," "insecticide," "fungicide," "herbicide," "algicide."

PILT: payment in lieu of taxes; grant in lieu of taxes

Pit. ***See also*** **Quarry:** place for extraction of aggregates from the land, without the use of blasting

Placeholder by-law: zone for which there is no anticipated actual use; a device to force proponents of future projects to seek rezoning, thereby allowing a council to assess proposals site-by-site; see *Kitchener (City) Official Plan Amendment No 58* (2010), 64 OMBR 283

Place of public resort or amusement: park or playground, for example

Placer claim: one based on deposits not in place, for example, gold nuggets in a streambed; as distinguished from a lode claim

Plan. ***See also*** **Official plan:** official plan of a municipality; also termed "municipal planning strategy" (Nova Scotia), "municipal development plan" (Saskatchewan and Alberta), "development plan" (Manitoba), "official community plan" (British Columbia and Yukon), and "general plan" (Northwest Territories)

Planned unit development: land development project planned as an entity in accordance with a unitary site plan that permits flexibility in siting of building, mixture of housing types and land uses, usable open spaces, and the preservation of significant natural features; see Saskatchewan *Planning and Development Act, 2007*, SS 2007, c P-13.2, s 255

Planner: land-use planner; the profession is sometimes regulated by statute, for example, *Community Planning Professions Act*, RSS 1978, c C-21; membership in the Canadian Institute of Planners is usual as a requirement for working as a planner

Planning advisory committee: optional committee to advise a municipal council on the merits of proposed changes in zoning by-laws, or on specific developments; an opportunity for citizen involvement in the planning process; see Nova Scotia *Municipal Government Act*, SNS 1998, c 18, s 200

Planning blight: adverse effect on an owner of land (e.g., inability to sell or to develop as previously planned) due to a declared intent by a municipality as to future use

Planning board: body for providing planning advice for two or more municipalities, as designated by the Minister of Municipal Affairs and Housing under the Ontario *Planning Act*, RSO 1990, c P.13, s 9

PLUPs. ***See also*** **PPS:** provincial land-use policies

Pocket area: area zoned one way, surrounded by areas zoned differently; see *3777783 Manitoba Ltd v West St Paul (Rural Municipality)*, 2010 MBQB 101

Policy. ***See also*** **Goal; Objective:** "the preferred course of action to be followed in order to achieve an objective or goal": Gerald Hodge, *Planning*

Canadian Communities, 5th ed (Toronto: Nelson Thompson, 2008) at 181

Pollution: human damage to the environment by means of emissions, wastes, energy use, and so on

Port: place where vessels or vehicles may discharge or load cargo

Port authority: agency incorporated or continued under the *Canada Marine Act*, SC 1998, c 10

PPS. ***See also*** **PLUPs:** provincial policy statement; in Ontario, see OC 140/2005; in Nova Scotia, see *Municipal Government Act,* SNS 1998, c 18, Schedule B

Pre-emption: in Canadian law, a right of first refusal to purchase property: *Cultural Property Act*, CQLR c B-4. In US law, conflict between the law of a lower level jurisdiction such as a municipality and the law of a higher level of government such that the lower level law is rendered invalid; see *CSX Transportation, Inc v City of Plymouth*, 86 F3d 626 (6th Cir 1996)

Prescription: prescriptive easement, that is, one arising through long use, not through specific grant

Prohibition: by-law provision that regulates an activity through disallowing it; may be either objective or subjective; see *Montréal (City) v Arcade Amusements Inc*, [1985] 1 SCR 368

Proper principles of planning: good planning; a test used by the Ontario Municipal Board

Property class: classes of property used for assessment and taxation purposes; usually set out in an *Assessment Act* or regulations made under such acts

Property development: changes to property so as to secure financial returns for its owners

Property line: part of the boundary of a lot; LUBs often refer to and define side, front, and rear property lines, often in association with setbacks required from a property line

Property taxes: taxes assessed against the estimated market value of land and its associated buildings; usually the main base of municipal revenues

Protected countryside: areas designated as Protected Countryside in the Greenbelt Plan; Ontario *Greenbelt Act, 2005*, SO 2005, c 1

PSW: (Ontario term) provincially significant wetland

PTTW: permit to take water

Public hearing: formal meeting at which a statutory decision maker receives the views and concerns of the public, prior to making a decision

Public information meeting: stage in the development of a building proposed in which public views are sought; not a public hearing

Public infrastructure. *See also* Infrastructure: publicly owned infrastructure, extending to such things as roads, sewers, railways, water systems, power plants, telecommunications facilities, ports, and airports; see Tarek M Harchaoui et al, *Public Infrastructure in Canada* (Ottawa: Statistics Canada, 2003)

Public interest standing: standing granted to litigants by the court as a matter of discretion, in instances where they might not meet strict entitlement but a serious matter is raised

Public purpose. *See also* Public use: use (of land) for recreational or other use or enjoyment of the general public such as access to water, a beach, a conservation area, a community hall, a public library, open space, and so on; see New Brunswick *Community Planning Act*, RSNB 1973, c C-12, s 1; the idea does not tend to extend to private profit, although in the United States this point has become blurred

Public services: with respect to land, usually means infrastructure such as water, sewers, and roads

Public trust: doctrine that land held by a level of government may be subject to restrictions as to alienation or use; see *Prescott and Russell (United Counties) v Waugh* (2004), 15 MPLR (4th) 314 (Ont SCJ)

Public use. *See also* Public purpose: in the United States, the Fifth Amendment to the Constitution provides that property "shall not be taken for public use, without just compensation." Cases have now established that "public purpose" may amount to "public use," that is, that a level of government may expropriate private land to resell to another private owner to assist a development proposal; see *Kelo v New London*, 545 US 469 (2005)

Public utility: corporation, usually owned by a level of government, that delivers essential goods or services such as water, gas, or electricity; see Alberta *Municipal Government Act*, RSA 2000, c M-26, s 1(1)(y)

Public work: any improvement of a structural nature or other undertaking that is within the jurisdiction of the council of a municipality or a local board: see Ontario *Planning Act*, RSO 1990, c P.13

Quadruplex. ***See*** **Duplex**

Quarry. ***See also*** **Pit:** place of extraction of aggregates from land, using blasting

Range: grasslands

Raw land: undeveloped land

RD: regional district; a common category of local government designation under provincial legislation

Real estate. ***See also*** **Land:** land or an interest therein

Rearage: rear lot line of a property (cf frontage): see *Crawford v Torbay (Town)*, 2008 NLTD 161

Reeve: mayor; see, for example, Saskatchewan *Local Government Election Act, 2015*, SS 2015, c L-30.11

Referendum: vote by the public to determine the law; not effective for this purpose because of the decision in *Re Initiative and Referendum Act*, [1919] AC 935 (PC)

Regional district: form of municipal governance, sometimes involving a co-ordination of functions among municipalities

Regional growth strategy: for a regional district, a plan to guide decisions on growth, change, and development, and emphasizing avoiding urban sprawl, and protecting the environment; see British Columbia *Local Government Act*, RSBC 2015, c 1, Part 13

Regulatory taking: (US term) laws so restrictive as to the use of property as to amount to something virtually equivalent to expropriation, and calling for compensation under the Constitution's Fifth Amendment

Rehabilitation: improvement of a deteriorated building

Remote/isolated communities: settlement far removed from urban areas and their infrastructures and services; see *Provincial Planning Regulation*, Man Reg 81/2011 and *Remote Communities Regulation*, BC Reg 240/2007

Renovation: restoration to a better state, for example, by cleaning, repairing, or rebuilding; see Saskatchewan *Uniform Building and Accessibility Standards Act*, SS 1983-84, c U-1.2

Repair: includes the provision of facilities, the making of additions or alterations, or the taking of any other action that may be required to ensure that a property conforms with the standards established in a by-law; see Ontario *Building Code Act, 1992*, SO 1992, c 23

Replotting scheme: change of boundaries to redistribute ownership of land and to facilitate the development of land; see Saskatchewan *Planning and Development Act, 2007*, SS 2007, c P-13.2

Residential: one of the usual categories of use in zoning by-laws; it does not require permanence or exclusivity; see *Loyalist (Township) v Lafarge Canada Inc* (2002), 31 MPLR (3d) 109 (Ont SCJ)

Residential premises: dwellings in which people live; see Yukon *Residential Landlord and Tenant Act*, SY 2012, c 20

Residential property: building that contains one or more dwelling units but does not include subordinate or accessory buildings, the use of which is incidental to the use of the main building; see Ontario *Planning Act*, RSO 1990, c P.13

Resolution: a decision taken by a municipal council on a topic not required by statute to be dealt with by by-law

Restaurant: variously defined; generally includes every building, or part of a building, tent, or other erection used as a restaurant, café, lunch counter, ice cream parlour, or other place of refreshment where food or drink is sold to the public

Restrictive covenant: condition under which land is not to be built on or is not to be used in a particular manner, and running with the title to the land, that is, binding on future owners; see Alberta *Municipal Government Act*, RSA 2000, c M-26, s 651.1

Ribbon development: development of a row of buildings, especially housing, beside a road

Right of entry permit: permit to allow trespass for purposes of construction on an adjacent lot; see *Marks v Ottawa (City)* (2007), 40 MPLR (4th) 264 (Ont SCJ)

Right-of-way: legal right acquired by usage or grant to travel along a route through property belonging to another

Right to farm: statutory protection for normal farm practices, to shield farmers from certain lawsuits, usually those based on principles of nuisance; see *Agricultural Operation Practices Act*, RSA 2000, c A-7

Right to light: common law easement, now generally replaced by zoning by-laws regulating height and setbacks; see *Olmstead v Greenberg* (2001), 25 MPLR (3d) 61 (Ont SCJ)

Right to roam: (UK term) the *Countryside and Rights of Way Act 2000* provides for certain freedom to roam on private property

Riparian owner: owner of land through or beside which water flows

Riparian zones. *See also* Wetland: area between a defined aquatic and terrestrial area possessing characteristics of both aquatic and terrestrial habitats; includes wet meadows, marshes, swamps, fens, and bogs; the primary characteristic of these areas is water covering, at, or near the surface of the soil for part or all of the year; wetlands and riparian areas may support both aquatic and terrestrial species

Roof: upper rigid cover of a building; types include hip (pyramid style), gable (two slopes), gambrel (four or more slopes), shed (one slope), mansard (flat top with four slopes)

Rooming house: (term often used and defined in LUBs) place where rooms are rented, but where cooking is not done in the rooms and meals are not served as in a boarding house; see *Lord Nelson Hotel Ltd v Halifax (City)*, [1956] SCR 264

ROP: regional official plan

Rubbish: term related to unsightly premises: "includes all discarded, broken or useless items and without limiting the generality of the foregoing, shall include old paper or wood products no longer in use or motor vehicles that are no longer roadworthy or parts thereof": *Prince George (City) v Riemer*, 2010 BCSC 118 at para 6

Rural cluster: four or more adjacent rural residential lots, generally 1 hectare or less in size, sharing a common boundary

Rural municipality: form of municipality in Manitoba and Saskatchewan

Sanitary sewer: pipe that carries household and commercial wastes only (not stormwater)

School site acquisition charge: development charge aimed at supporting any school capital costs associated with a subdivision or development; see British Columbia *Local Government Act*, RSBC 2015, c 1

SCOOT: split cycle offset optimization technique; automated, coordinated traffic controls operating in real time to control signals and/or shift traffic

Sea level rise: rise in sea level due to the effects of climate change, for example, the melting of ice and thermal expansion of the ocean

Seasonal dwelling: cottage

Seasonal residential use. ***See*** **Seasonal dwelling**

Semi-institutional home. ***See*** **Group home**

Sensitive lands: areas vulnerable to damage through development, for example, flood plains, lake and stream shores, coastal zones, wetlands, scenic and wild rivers, areas adjacent to parks, areas of scientific interest, erosion zones; see Jon A Kusler, *Regulating Sensitive Lands* (Cambridge, MA: Ballinger, 1980)

Septic system: small-scale sewage treatment system common in areas with no connection to main sewage pipes provided by local governments or private corporations

Service line (lateral): pipe (and all appurtenances) that runs between a utility's water main and the customer's place of use, including fire lines: Atlantic Canada Water Works Association, "Atlantic Canada Guidelines for the Supply, Treatment, Storage, Distribution and Operation of Drinking Water Supply Systems" (September 2004)

Services. ***See*** **Municipal services**

Setback: common feature of zoning by-laws, requiring buildings to be some set distance away from such things as property lines, septic fields, wells, wetlands, or other buildings

SEV: statement of environmental values

Severance: dividing a property into separate lots

Sewage: refuse and foul matter, solid or liquid, carried off by sewer

Sewer system: facility consisting of a system of sewers for carrying off liquid and solid sewage

Shanty town. ***See also*** **Slum:** marginal or informal settlements; units of irregular, low-cost dwellings, usually on lands belonging to third parties, and most often located on the periphery of cities; almost always built without a licence

Shelter. ***See*** **Hostel**

Shophouse: building combining a residence and a business, usually a ground floor shop

Shopping centre: cluster of diverse commercial outlets, usually in premises planned and developed as a unit, providing parking, and under one ownership; see *Oshawa Wholesale Ltd v Canadia Niagara Falls Ltd* (1971), 23 DLR (3d) 401 (Ont CA)

Should: direction, the import of which lies somewhere between the mandatory "shall" and the permissive "may"; see *Federation of Nova Scotia Heritage v Peninsula Community Council*, 2005 NSUARB 105 for a discussion of the term in the Halifax Regional Municipality's municipal planning strategy

Sign: (term often used and defined in LUBs) advertisement, identification, illustration, or notice posted on a building or property; see *Courtenay (City) v Chris Holdings Ltd* (1989), 46 MPLR 94 (BC Co Ct); could be roof, façade, window, wall, awning, projecting, pole, ground, or portable

Signal: traffic signal

Signalized access: point of entry onto a property mediated by traffic signals; see *London (City) v Wonderland Power Centre Inc*, 2007 CanLII 19792 (Ont SCJ)

Single-family dwelling: (term often used and defined in LUBs) house occupied by not more than one family; any detached building consisting of one dwelling unit that is occupied or intended to be occupied as the home or residence of one family; see *Schembri v Scarborough (City) Committee of Adjustment* (1989), 23 OMBR 102

Single-tier municipality: municipality that is not, for administrative purposes, part of a county, region, or district

Site plan agreement: form of planning control under, for example, Ontario's *Planning Act*, RSO 1990, c P.13, s 41(13)(b) permitting designation by councils of areas in which no development shall occur unless the council has approved plans and the form of any agreement that may be required; for a history of this form of control, see *Hi-Rise Structures Inc v Scarborough (City)* (1992), 12 MPLR (2d) 1 (Ont CA)

Site profile: report on the state of a brownfield site; see British Columbia *Environmental Management Act*, SBC 2003, c 53, s 40

SLAPP: Strategic Lawsuit Against Public Participation; lawsuit usually alleging defamation, arising out of comment on a matter of public concern; see *Fraser v Saanich (District)* (1999), 5 MPLR (3d) 80 (BCSC); Chris Tollefson, "Strategic Lawsuits Against Public Participation: Developing a Canadian Response" (1994) 72 *Canadian Bar Review* 200

Slum. ***See also*** **Shanty town; Tenement:** area "characterized by overcrowding, poor or informal housing, inadequate access to safe water and sanitation, and insecurity of tenure": see Mike Davis, *Planet of Slums* (London: Verso, 2006) at 22ff

SLUP. ***See also*** **DLUG:** strategic land use plan (Ontario term); an informal plan for use of Crown lands; see *Re Timber Management Class Environmental Assessment* (1994), EA-87-02 (Ont EAB)

SMART: non-binding guidelines for agricultural operations with a focus on "separation," "magnitude," "alteration," "reduction," and "timing"; designed to minimize disputes among neighbours

Solid waste: garbage, refuse, including compostable material and recyclable material

SOV: single-occupancy vehicle

Special management zones: land-use category that emerged from British Columbia's Commission on Resources and the Environment, one intended to place temporary resource development restrictions over contested territories

Special planning area: provincially designated area of special provincial or regional significance, for reasons of environment, heritage, or industrial development; see Manitoba *Planning Act*, CCSM c P80

Special planning zone: area declared by the provincial government to be subject to special development controls set by the province, and so prompted by urgent or serious development or environmental problems; see Quebec *Land Use Planning and Development Act*, CQLR c A-19.1

Species at risk. ***See*** **Endangered species**

Sphere: field of activity or influence

Spite fence: fence erected deliberately to block the view or light amenities of a neighbour

Spot zoning: singling out of one lot for different treatment from that accorded to similar surrounding land indistinguishable from it in character, for the economic benefit of the owner of that lot; see *Lamarre v Commissioner of Public Works of Fall River*, 87 NE2d 211 (Mass 1949)

Sprawl: growth of suburban areas, usually associated with phenomena seen as problematic, such as disorganized and excessive growth, loss of agricultural land, high dependence on automobiles, low population density, and lack of diversity in land use, especially separation of residences from services

SRO. ***See also*** **Rooming house:** (term often used and defined in LUBs) single-room occupancy, that is, a rooming house

Stagnant city: settlement that formerly grew as a city, but has stopped doing so: Jane Jacobs, *The Economy of Cities* (New York: Random House, 1969)

***Standard State Zoning Enabling Act*:** (US term) prototype for statutes granting land-use regulatory powers to municipal governments, first drafted by the US Department of Commerce in 1924

Standing. *See also* **Interested person; Person affected; Person aggrieved; Person concerned:** right of a particular plaintiff to seek a particular remedy against a particular defendant; see Thomas Cromwell, *Locus Standi: The Law of Standing in Canada* (Toronto: Carswell, 1986); for a contemporary judicial discussion of standing, see *Greater Victoria Concerned Citizens Association v British Columbia (Capital Commission)* (1990), 46 Admin LR 74 (BCSC)

Statement of environmental values: required articulation by government departments of their environmental values pursuant to the Ontario *Environmental Bill of Rights, 1993*, SO 1993, c 28

Statutory Building Scheme: land development involving the placement of restrictive covenants, pursuant to the British Columbia *Land Titles Act*, RSBC 1996, c 250, s 1; see *Putt v Kunetsky*, 2010 BCSC 394

Stop order: order requiring development to stop, structures to be demolished or to be moved or replaced, or other similar actions so as to bring about conformity with the applicable land-use by-law

Storey: (term often used and defined in LUBs) that portion of a building between the upper surface of any floor and the upper surface of the floor next above, except that the topmost storey shall be that portion of a building between the upper surface of the topmost floor and the roofline: Regina Zoning Bylaw No 9250, Part 2C

STP: sewage treatment plant

Strata: term used in British Columbia for "condominium unit"

Stream: "natural watercourse including a natural glacier course, or a natural body of water, whether or not the stream channel of the stream has been modified, or a natural source of water supply, including, without limitation, a lake, pond, river, creek, spring, ravine, gulch, wetland or glacier, whether or not usually containing water, including ice, but does not include an aquifer": *Water Sustainability Act*, SBC 2014, c 15, s 1(1); see *Yellowridge Construction Ltd v Anmore (Village)*, 2005 BCSC 304

Street furniture: street fittings such as lamps, litter bins, road signs, and post boxes, installed for public use or convenience

Strip development: continuous development of a single depth on one side of a road; see *Little v Cowichan Valley (Regional District)*, 1977 CanLII 323 (BCSC)

Strip mall: open-air shopping mall where the stores are arranged in a row, with a sidewalk in front; typically developed as a unit and has large parking lot in front

Structural alteration: construction or reconstruction of supporting elements of a building; see Saskatchewan *Planning and Development Act, 2007*, SS 2007 c P-13.2

Structure: (variously defined) building; can extend to a private bridge under the British Columbia *Local Government Act*, RSBC 2015, c 1: see *Greater Vancouver (Regional District) v Stainsby*, 2007 BCSC 585; "a construction or portion thereof of any kind, whether fixed to, supported by, sunk into or located in, land, water or airspace . . . but specifically excludes paving, fences, retaining walls and landscaping": Burnaby LUB, as set out in *Burnaby (City) v Hayre*, 2008 BCCA 412

Subdivision: area of land divided into lots, especially for residential purposes

Subdivision by-law: rules specifying the process for an owner to gain approval for a proposed subdivision of land

Subsidiarity: "the proposition that law-making and implementation are often best achieved at a level of government that is not only effective, but also closest to the citizens affected and thus most responsive to their needs, to local distinctiveness, and to population diversity" *114957 Canada Ltée (Spraytech, Société d'arrosage) v Hudson (Town)*, 2001 SCC 40 at para 3, L'Heureux-Dubé J

Suburb: residential area close to a city, which provides it with employment and services

Superfund: fund established by US federal law to clean up sites contaminated by hazardous substances (polluter pays principle); see *Comprehensive Environmental Response Compensation and Liability Act*, 42 USC § 9601 et seq (1980)

Sustainability: use of resources now in a way that does not damage their potential for use by future generations; intergenerational equity

Sustainable development: development that provides for the needs of this generation without compromising the ability of future generations to provide for theirs; see Manitoba *Sustainable Development Act*, CCSM c S270

Taking: term from the Fifth Amendment of the US Constitution: an expropriation or a very severe diminution of value of property of a private owner to the benefit of the government taker; see *Lucas v South Carolina Coastal Council*, 505 US 1003 (1992); although not a part of Canadian constitutional law, the term "taking" is sometimes used in Canadian cases

TASCs: timing and sequential controls

Tax base: land and buildings viewed for their potential to generate property taxes

Telecommunications tower: structure to enable electromagnetic broadcasting; includes radio, television, and telephones

Temporary zoning approval: zoning that is limited in duration; use of the zoning can establish non-conforming use rights; see Ontario *Planning Act*, RSO 1990, c P.13, ss 34 and 39

Tenement. *See also* Slum: apartment building, especially for the poor or new immigrants

Through lot: lot in a subdivision having road frontage on at least two sides

TIF: tax increment financing; special fund for designated taxes set aside to pay for infrastructure (e.g., a stadium), remedial measures, and so on

TOADS: temporarily obsolete abandoned derelict sites

Total maximum daily load: measure of water quality: US *Clean Water Act*, 33 USC § 1251 et seq (1972)

Town: an area incorporated as a town

***Town and Country Planning Act*:** (UK Act) main planning law reform statute, dating from 1947

Town and Country Planning Association: (UK term) an NGO providing resources relating to city, regional, and environmental planning; see online: www.tcpa.org.uk

Town centre: (UK term) the central business district

Toxic tort: tort arising from pollution

Traditional mainstreet: generally pre-1945, pedestrian-oriented commercial strip street, distinguished from "arterial main streets," which are generally newer, automobile-oriented commercial roads

Traffic calming: methods to slow down vehicle speed, especially in a residential neighborhood

Tragedy of the commons: economic model suggesting that common resources will tend to be overused; see Garrett Hardin, "The Tragedy of the Commons" (1968) 162 *Science* 1243

Trail: pathway for pedestrians, sometimes for all-terrain vehicles or other off-road vehicles; see *Trails Act* for some provinces; see *Bonnyville Adjacent Landowners Group v Bonnyville (Municipal District No 87)*, 2003 ABQB 672

Trailer. ***See*** **Mobile home; Trailer park**

Trailer park: community of mobile homes; a place for recreational vehicles to stay temporarily

Transferable development rights: zoning flexibility tool whereby development rights are transferred from one lot, parcel, or area of land in a sending district to another in a receiving district

Transition: relationship between high and low buildings of different uses; a part of how to assess compatibility with existing development; see *Toronto (City) Official Plan Amendment No 352 (Re)* (2006), 55 OMBR 68

TRCA: Toronto Region Conservation Authority

Trespass: to enter onto the lands of another; actionable without proof of injury; see *Epstein v Cressey Development Corp*, 1992 CanLII 1229 (BCCA)

Triplex. ***See*** **Duplex**

Twilight zone: area of obsolete or rundown character: Royal Commission on Dominion-Provincial Relations, *Report of the Royal Commission on Dominion-Provincial Relations* (Ottawa: Queen's Printer, 1940)

Two-tier municipality. ***See also*** **Lower-tier municipality; Upper-tier municipality:** implies a "lower tier" and "upper tier"

ULURP: (US term) uniform land-use review procedure; involves public input; the formal zoning process

Unincorporated area: area with no municipal level of government

Upper-tier municipality. ***See also*** **Lower-tier municipality; Two-tier municipality:** county, region, or district municipality

Urban agriculture: food produced within a metropolitan area, often on dispersed sites and using intensive production methods

Urban fringe: transition zone where urban and rural uses mix

Urban growth boundary: defined area in a municipality within which development will be allowed but outside of which it will be prohibited or deferred; also "urban expansion area"

Urban regeneration: term used in UK for "urban renewal"

Urban renewal: redevelopment of slums and/or blighted commercial areas

Use classes: (UK term) groups of uses allowed as of right and therefore analogous to zoning; established by the Town and Country Planning (General Permitted Development) Order, SI 1995/418, and the Town and Country Planning (General Development Procedure) Order, SI 1995/419

Use of land: the limits of this term, which is basic to local government zoning authority, is a matter of difference of view: see *Vernon (City) v Okanagan Excavating (1993) Ltd* (1993), 17 MPLR (2d) 216 (BCSC)

Used or intended to be used: term to be interpreted objectively by reference to the design of the structure, not the stated intentions of the owner; see *Burnaby (City) v Hayre*, 2008 BCCA 412

Variance. ***See also*** **Minor variance:** modification of the effect of a zoning by-law on a particular lot, to take account of site conditions

Variation order: authorization for a variance; see Manitoba *Planning Act*, CCSM c P80

Venice Charter, 1964**:** international charter for the conservation and restoration of monuments and sites: the International Congress of Architects and Technicians of Historic Monuments

Vernacular architecture: buildings constructed without the benefit of professional architecture design, and local in style, materials, and tradition

Vicinity: (1) quality or state of being near, or not remote; nearness; propinquity; proximity; a region about, near or adjacent; adjoining space or country; (2) neighbourhood

View: prospect

Village: small settlement, incorporated or unincorporated; see Prince Edward Island *Municipalities Act*, RSPEI 1988, c M-13

Wall: (term variously defined) (1) upright solid structure, interior or exterior, that defines and supports a structure; (2) exposed face of an excavation in a surface mine from ground level to the working level

Ward: common name for an electoral district at the local government level

Warden: mayor of a regional county municipality under *An Act respecting Municipal territorial organization*, CQLR c O-9

Waste: (1) in the law of property, to commit waste is to reduce the capital value of land, without authorization; (2) garbage, to be understood from the perspective of the person discarding the object; see *Caledon (Town) v 541904 Ontario Ltd* (2006), 28 MPLR (4th) 316 at para 14 (Ont SCJ)

Water lot: land, some or all of which is covered by water; see *Oscar Straus III (Re)*, 2006 NSUARB 135

Watercourse: lake, river, stream, ocean, or other body of water; see Nova Scotia *Municipal Government Act*, SNS 1998, c 18, s 191(r)

Watershed: area drained by a river and its tributaries; see Ontario *Conservation Authorities Act*, RSO 1990, c C.27, s 1

Wetland. ***See also*** **Riparian zones:** land with the water table near or above the surface, resulting in saturation; includes bogs, fens, marshes, swamps; see National Wetlands Working Group, Canada Committee on Ecological Land Classification, *Wetlands of Canada* (Ottawa: Environment Canada, 1988); "lands within the coastal zone which may be covered periodically or permanently with shallow water and includes saltwater marshes, freshwater marshes, open or closed brackish water marshes, swamps, mudflats, and fens": California *Coastal Act*, Public Resources Code, Division 20, s 30121

Wharf: docking structure, including associated buildings; see *Canadian Salt Co v Irving Cedar (The)* (2000), 193 FTR 20 (TD)

Wilderness: natural areas free of industrial activity and transportation corridors

Wind farm: group of large-scale wind turbines, often owned and operated by one entity

Woodlot: wooded area smaller than 500 hectares, including Christmas tree plantations, regenerating tree stands, as well as tree areas such as parklands and private woodlots

Works: usually public construction such as of buildings, roads, bridges, dams, etc.

ZB: zoning by-law, or land-use by-law

Zoning: separation of land uses by classification according to type of use and intensity of use; see *Ingram and Scott v Lethbridge (City)* (1962), 34 DLR (2d) 490 (Alta SCAD)

Zoning confirmation: written statement from a municipality attesting to the zoning for a lot; often required as part of the documentation for business licensing, for example, under a *Liquor Licensing Act*

TABLE OF CASES

INDEX

ABOUT THE AUTHOR

Howard Epstein is a Nova Scotia lawyer who has practised, taught, and written about land use planning law for decades. His environmental and municipal interests led to his involvement in precedent-setting major Halifax land-use cases in the 1970s and 1980s. He has worked in Ottawa and in Toronto. He has long been a contributor to the Municipal and Planning Law Reports, with case comments in its first volume in 1976–77, as well as contributing contemporary articles exploring the land-use effects of some international trade treaties, Federal land-use powers, and the sustainability potential of local governments. Mr Epstein was elected to Halifax's city council in 1994 and to the council of Halifax Regional Municipality upon amalgamation in 1996. Subsequently, he was elected as a member of the Nova Scotia legislature for five terms. He taught land use and land use planning law at Dalhousie University's Schulich School of Law from 1998 through 2013 as an adjunct member of the Faculty of Law and of the School of Planning.

FSC
www.fsc.org
MIX
Papier | Fördert gute Waldnutzung
FSC® C083411

Kolibri 360 GmbH
Ferdinand-Jühlke-Straße 7
99095 Erfurt, Deutschland
produktsicherheit@kolibri360.de